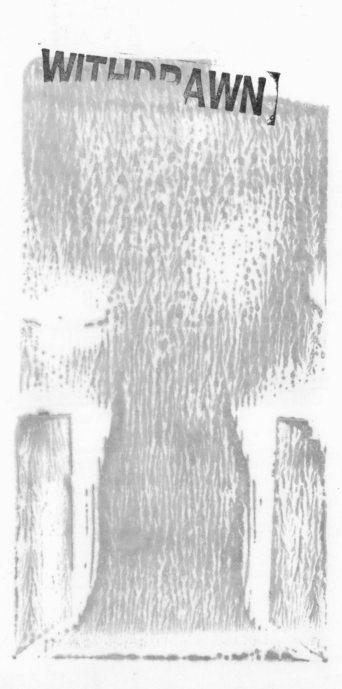

Horace Mann

Horace Mann.

HORACE MANN

A Biography

by Jonathan Messerli

New York

Alfred · A · Knopf

1972

THIS IS A BORZOI BOOK
PUBLISHED BY ALFRED A. KNOPF, INC.

ISBN: 0-394-42920-6
Library of Congress Catalog Card Number: 78-154905
Manufactured in the United States of America
FIRST EDITION

For Vi

*The struggle itself toward the heights
is enough to fill a man's heart.*

—ALBERT CAMUS, *The Myth of Sisyphus*

Contents

═══════

Contents

Preface

I N TERMS of biographers, Horace Mann has been fortunate, both in their number and good will. Grateful interpretations of his work began to emerge immediately after his death in 1859 and have abounded thereafter, reaching something of a climax in 1937, the centennial anniversary of his entrance into the common school reform movement. Six major biographies have been written, as have a score of lesser "short lives" and several book-length monographs on significant aspects of his career. In addition, a dozen doctoral students have mined his life for their special studies and more than a thousand admiring authors have published articles celebrating his contributions to the schooling of American children.

In virtually all of these, save for his stand on religious training and his belief in the power of education to overcome economic and social deprivation, his work has been set forth uncritically and in the most positive light. Thus, if the contemporary student were to limit himself mainly to these secondary sources, and were this nation to have an official pantheon with space reserved for a secular saint of our schoolchildren, he could only conclude but that the honor unquestionably belonged to Horace Mann. In a peculiar sense of the word, Mann has been quite literally canonized as the father of the American public school system.

Ironically, however, by their deliberate attempts to establish and make secure Mann's reputation as the founder of public education and a far-seeing, almost omniscient, architect of our present commitment to schooling, these numerous hagiographers have unwittingly circumscribed the true significance of his career and placed it in a sort of double historical jeopardy. First, by concentrating mainly on his work during the twelve years when he was active as the leading common school reformer of the day, they have ignored other important periods of his life, both before and after, including his work in other humanitarian reforms and his courageous efforts in Congress to stay the extension of slavery. The result has been to overlook the importance these had in their own right and to miss the powerful and pervasive influence they exerted in conditioning his efforts with a strong reformist bias as he attempted to establish a political and social basis for American public education.

Secondly, by tying his work to the fortunes of our present school system, they have also inadvertently helped yoke any future assessment of his achievements to the outcome of our contemporary Laocoön struggle to extricate the public schools from evils only recently perceived through a glass darkly. Mann's historical role has therefore been jeopardized by those who have conceived of it too narrowly in time and scope and by those who would force it to bear the burden, not of the sins of the fathers, Founding and otherwise, but, in an anachronistic *ex post facto* manner, of the sins of his educational descendants.

Living at a time when political and technological revolutions seemed to be ushering in the new dawn of an age of unprecedented human welfare, Mann hoped to accelerate "the agenda of the Almighty," as he referred to his endeavor. To accomplish this, he believed the nation needed new enabling institutions, especially public schools. Phrasing his words in the characteristically hyperbolic rhetoric of his day, he described them as "the greatest invention ever made by man." What the church had been for medieval man, the public school must now become for democratic and rational man. God would be replaced by the concept of the Public Good, sin and guilt by the more positive virtues of Victorian morality and civic conformity, and mankind would emancipate itself once and for all, not only from the relentless gnawings of a Puritan conscience but, through its own self-attained enlightenment, from the endemic evils of poverty, ignorance, violence, disease, and war.

All of this was now possible if only reasonable men and women would join together to create a well-managed *system* of schooling, where educators could manipulate and control learning as effectively as the confident new breed of engineers managed the industrial processes at work in their burgeoning textile factories and iron and steel mills. For the first time in the history of western man, it seemed possible for an intellectual and moral élite to effect mass behavioral changes and bring about a new golden age of enlightened ethics, humanism, and affluence. Indeed, so dazzling was the prospect, that Mann and his countless co-workers could not conceive of the possibility that those who would follow in their footsteps might actually build a suffocating and sometimes mind-numbing establishmentarian bureaucracy. Nor could they envision that in the hands of lesser individuals, their cherished institution, instead of functioning as a fundamental part of the social solution they sought, could become an integral part of the problem.

To study Mann's career is to learn of far more than the origins of the American public school system. We see Mann sanguinely forging his new doctrines of the perfectibility of men and institutions and testing them against the challenges of his day. Here, too, we also can identify some of the key elements in that premature sense of triumph and latent tragedy of nineteenth-century America. Projected onto a broader screen, Mann's efforts appear as a sensitive, articulate, and intense response, which embodied many of the hopes and fears of our Victorian ancestors as they optimistically pressed forward, only to fall far short of what they considered their manifest destiny in bringing about a new millennium.

*   *   *

In the research and writing of this book, I have incurred numerous and lasting scholarly debts. Professors Bernard Bailyn and Oscar Handlin of Harvard University did much to assist me in posing the kinds of questions which exposed the richness of available manuscripts dealing with Mann's life. At Teachers College, Columbia, Professor Lawrence A. Cremin provided me with a stimulating colleagueship, while Dean Robert Schaefer gave me the administrative support which helped keep the project under way. Above all, however, I am indebted to Mr. Clyde S. King, librarian of the State University of New York at Oneonta, who graciously and generously shared with me his exhaustive bibliographic notes on Mann, subsequently published as *Horace Mann, 1796–1859, A Bibliography.*

Others have commented helpfully on interpretive problems underlying the work. They include Professors Maxine Greene and Jonas Soltis of Teachers College, Columbia; Professor David Madsen of the University of Washington; Dean Jacquelyn Mattfeld of Brown University; Professor Vincent Lannie of the University of Notre Dame; and Professor Harold Schwartz of Kent State University. By their critical reading of portions of the manuscript, Mrs. Sabine Ehlers of Tallahassee, Florida, Professor Frederick Rudolph of Williams College, Mr. Paul Perry of the Harvard Graduate School of Education, and my colleague at Hofstra University, Professor Esin Z. Kaya, all have helped immeasurably in making the final version more readable.

Since the research on Mann and his immediate contemporaries

PREFACE

drew from official repositories and private collections on both sides of the Atlantic, I have benefited inestimably from the courteous and informed assistance of many individuals. My special thanks go to the dedicated and professional staff of the Massachusetts Historical Society, particularly Mr. Stephen T. Riley, Miss Winifred Collins, and Mr. Malcolm Freiberg, who provided me with a felicitous access to their holdings of Mann manuscripts, a major collection of nineteenth-century documents. At the Dedham Historical Society, Miss Marion Conant made available to me the second largest collection of Mann materials, which in turn offered many insights into Mann's early legal and political career, as well as some of the details of his domestic life. Miss Bessie L. Totten and Miss Jane Cape, at Antioch College, gave freely of their time in helping me work through the contents of the Antiochiana Collection, including the manuscripts and voluminous notes of the late Robert L. Straker, a lifelong student and admirer of Horace Mann.

Other librarians, archivists, and private individuals have responded to my appeals for assistance in the search for fugitive manuscripts relevant to Mann's life. Among the many who helped me in locating materials for this volume were: Mr. John Alden, of the Boston Public Library; Mrs. Margaret B. Andrews, of the Rush Rhees Library, University of Rochester; Mr. Howard Applegate, of Syracuse University; Mr. T. D. Seymour Bassett, of the Wilbur Library, University of Vermont; Mr. V. L. Bedsole, of the Department of Archives and Manuscripts, Louisiana State University; Miss Loretta E. Blais, of the John Hay Library, Brown University; Mr. Loriman S. Brigham, of Montpelier, Vermont; Mr. Alexander Clark, of the Firestone Library, Princeton University; Miss Doris E. Cook, of the Connecticut Historical Society; Kenneth C. Cramer, of the Dartmouth College Archives; Professor Theodore Crane, of the University of Denver; Dr. John Dahlquist, of Franklin, Massachusetts; Mrs. Howard Day of Providence, Rhode Island; Mr. Lynn de Beer, of the Cornell University Library; Miss Elizabeth S. Duvall, of the Sophia Smith Collection, Smith College; Mr. Donald B. Eddy, of Cornell University Library; Mr. William Ewing, of the William L. Clements Library, University of Michigan; Mr. Peter Farrar, of Birkenhead, Cheshire, England; Mr. Donald Gallup, of Yale University; Dr. John Gordan, of the Berg Collection, New York Public Library; Professor Gerald Grob, of Clark University; Dr. Richard Hale, of the Archives of the Commonwealth of Massachusetts; Miss Josephine L. Harper, of the State Historical Society of Wisconsin; Mr.

Preface

King V. Hostick, of Springfield, Illinois; Miss Carolyn Jakeman, of the Houghton Library, Harvard University; Mr. and Mrs. Horace Mann, of Southwest Harbor, Maine; Reverend Thomas T. McAvoy, of the University of Notre Dame Archives; Mr. Archie B. Motley, of the Chicago Historical Society; Mr. James W. Patton, of the Southern Historical Collection, University of North Carolina; Mrs. Dorothy Potter, of the Essex Institute; Miss Fiona McD. Rattray, of the National Library of Scotland; Mr. Herbert C. Schulz, of the Henry E. Huntington Library and Art Gallery; Mr. Clifford Shipton, of the American Antiquarian Society; Mr. Edwin A. Sy, of the State University of New York at Buffalo; Mr. Norman Wadham, of Teachers College, Columbia University; Mr. David B. Watkins, of Yale University; and Mrs. Manning A. Williams of Waban, Massachusetts.

Mr. Alan Gillespie, Mr. Roman Bareza, and Mr. Gerry Schur all rendered their technical and aesthetic skills in preparing the photographic materials for the book. A generous and timely grant from the Fund for the Advancement of Education through its former president, Mr. Clarence Faust, enabled me to spend a year in uninterrupted research, blissfully free of telephones and meetings, at the Massachusetts Historical Society, the Widener Library of Harvard University, and the Antioch College Library. To Jane Garrett of Alfred Knopf, Inc., my thanks for her patience and sound editorial advice; may other historians be so fortunate. Mrs. Joan Damino and Mrs. Jean Smithline prepared the final draft for the publisher with great care and never tired of the impossible task of helping me comply with editorial deadlines.

My debt to my devoted wife is reflected in the dedication of this book.

J. M.

Lanesborough, Massachusetts
April 18, 1971

Illustrations

ILLUSTRATIONS

"FRIENDS OF EDUCATION"
Above left: George B. Emerson
Above right: Cyrus Peirce
Below left: Samuel J. May
Below right: Henry Barnard

TWO GENERATIONS OF THE NEW ENGLAND CONSCIENCE
Above: John Quincy Adams
Below: Charles Sumner, ca. 1850

Horace Mann, ca. 1845

STANDING GUARD IN FRONT OF THE MASSACHUSETTS STATE HOUSE
Left: Horace Mann
Right: Daniel Webster

TWO VIEWS OF ANTIOCH COLLEGE
Above: As Planned
Below: As It Was

Horace, Jr., George Combe, Benjamin Pickman Mann, and *Mary Peabody Mann*

Horace Mann, 1859

A List of Frequent Abbreviations

AAS   *American Antiquarian Society*
ACL   *Antioch College Library*
BLYU *Beinecke Library, Yale University*
BPL   *Boston Public Library*
BUA   *Brown University Archives*
CHS   *Connecticut Historical Society*
DHS   *Dedham Historical Society*
EI   *Essex Institute*
HCL   *Houghton Library, Harvard College*
LOC   *Library of Congress*
MHS   *Massachusetts Historical Society*
MSA   *Massachusetts State Archives*
MSDE *Massachusetts State Department of Education*
NA   *National Archives*
NLS   *National Library of Scotland, Edinburgh*
NYPL *New York Public Library*
NYU   *New York University*
OHS   *Ohio Archaeological and Historical Society*
PHS   *Pennsylvania Historical Society*
SC   *Smith College*

Horace Mann

CHAPTER I

The Age of Homespun

======

HARNESSED, all together, into the producing process, young and old, male and female, from the boy that rode the plow-horse to the grandmother knitting under her spectacles, they had no conception of squandering lightly what they all had been at work, thread by thread, and grain by grain, to produce . . . . children brought up, in this way, to know things in the small—what they cost and what is their value—have, in just that fact, one of the best securities of character and most certain elements of power and success in life; because they expect to get on by small advances followed up and saved by others, not by sudden leaps of fortune that despise the slow but surer methods of industry and merit.

HORACE BUSHNELL

THE MORE intensively the family has stamped its character upon the child, the more it will tend to feel and see its earlier miniature world again in the bigger world of adult life.

CARL JUNG

———

HIS FATHER was ready to die. Thomas Mann had not enjoyed the robust health of his father and grandfather, having contracted consumption early in life. During the winter his breathing had become more labored, disrupted by coughing spasms as he struggled for air. Now as the snow left the fields and the patches of brown wet earth appeared with the coming of warm weather, it was necessary for others to step in and do his spring chores. As his coughing spells grew worse and it was evident his days were numbered, he drew up his last will and testament and signed it on June 9, 1809. Eleven days later he was dead.[1]

[1] Will of Thomas Mann, Yeoman of Franklin, County of Norfolk, Massachusetts, June 9, 1809, MS in Mann Papers, MHS; Orestes T. Doe (ed.), *The Record of Births, Marriages and Deaths in the Town of Franklin from 1778 to 1872* (Franklin, 1898), p. 148; John Livingston, "Horace Mann," *American Portrait Gallery* . . . (New York, 1852), III, Part III, 179.

3

To his wife, Rebecca, he left the title to the family pew. In addition she was also to have exclusive use of part of the house including the "east room below," "the chamber above the same," "the east bedroom below," and "equal liberty" with her oldest son, Thomas Stanley Mann, to the "back kitchen, cellar, and garret." The father also ordered Thomas Stanley, whom the family called Stanley, to bring her "ten bushels of Indian corn" annually, keep one sow for her, and have "sufficient firewood brought into the house." Perhaps it was unnecessary to spell out these duties, but Thomas Mann wanted to be certain his wife would have the security of the home and the meetinghouse. She would need little else. He provided for the others as well. To his two daughters, Rebecca and Lydia, he designated cash sums adequate for a dowry upon their coming of age. Stephen, the second son, was also given cash, together with the right to his earnings when he became seventeen. The youngest son, Horace, who had just turned thirteen, was given one-third of the remaining property. To Stanley, the eldest, Thomas gave his livestock, tools, and above all else, his land. It was the land which linked the generations and had given the Manns a sense of continuity through time. The land was Stanley's birthright and it was his duty to maintain it.[2]

More than a legal instrument for the orderly distribution of property, the last will and testament of Thomas Mann was an attempt to reaffirm a way of life followed in his family for three generations. Through it, he testified to his effective stewardship as an honest yeoman farmer. He had inherited the land from his father, and he assumed that after his death, his heirs would continue to till the soil. While less detailed, the will of his grandfather, written more than fifty years before, was similar to his own, bequeathing the land to his son and providing for the care of his widow. This will of the first Thomas Man (then spelled with one "n") proved to be an accurate prediction of the type of life his son and grandson would lead.

[2] The will effectively contradicts a widely·held belief that Horace Mann's youth was spent in abject poverty. This notion emanated from Mann himself, who furnished most of the information for the biographical sketch which appeared in the *American Portrait Gallery.* In this, Livingston accepted such statements as that Thomas Mann left his survivors only the "example of an upright life," "virtuous inculcations," and a "hereditary thirst for knowledge" without question, an error repeated by other biographers as well. On the basis of this will, Thomas Mann's estate included cash and a substantial farm. Horace's bequest was large enough to provide him with a college education, if he chose, and nine years later, Lydia's legacy was worth over $700. See the promissory note from Stanley Mann to Lydia Mann, July 30, 1818, Mann MSS:MHS.

Now as he set his hand to his own will in 1809, the second Thomas Mann believed that his instructions to his sons, Stanley, Stephen, and Horace, would be followed as well. Their success would be measured by the degree to which they succeeded their father.[3]

The Manns had descended from one of the oldest families in the Bay Colony. William Man settled in Cambridge in 1633, sharing in the distribution of the common property and farming a parcel of land near Fresh Pond. His son, Samuel Man, graduated from Harvard College in 1665 and taught school for a short time in Dedham, Massachusetts, before preaching at Wrentham. King Philip's War scattered his flock, but with peace, some of them returned and covenanted to form a congregation in 1692 with Samuel Man as their pastor. Here he preached and served the town until 1719.[4]

One of his six sons, Thomas Man, a "husbandman," established a homestead three miles west of Wrentham on the Worcester and Taunton Road where the General Court would later establish the town of Franklin. Between 1709 and 1727, he accumulated small parcels of land by purchase and through his rights to the distribution of common property in Wrentham.[5] In 1737, he donated the building site for the new meetinghouse, an act which attested to both his financial status and civic spirit.[6] As his will had directed, his son Nathan continued to farm the land which had now become known as Mann's Plain. Nathan Mann was a respected member of the community, who claimed two "Cow-Common Rights" from Wrentham, served as a deacon of the congregation, and was elected to the local Committee of Correspondence during the Revolutionary War.[7] Upon his death, the farm passed on to the second Thomas Mann, who brought his bride, Rebecca Stanley, from neighboring Attleboro and

---

[3] Will of Thomas Man, April 29, 1755, Mann MSS:MHS.
[4] Lucius Paige, *History of Cambridge, Massachusetts, 1630–1877* (Boston, 1877), pp. 33, 58–59, and 401; George S. Mann, *Genealogy of the Descendants of Richard Man* (Boston, 1884), pp. 17–18. The best accounts of Samuel Man's ministry are found in John Langdon Sibley, *Biographical Sketches of the Graduates of Harvard College . . .* (Cambridge, Mass., 1881), II, 190–192; and Joseph Bean, *A Sermon Delivered at Wrentham, October 26, 1773 . . .* (Boston, 1774).
[5] Deeds recording the sale of property to Thomas Man are dated February 8, 1709, November 8, 1714, and October 30, 1727, and are found in the Mann MSS:MHS. The three transactions amounted to about twenty-eight acres.
[6] Mortimer Blake, *A History of the Town of Franklin, Massachusetts* (Franklin, 1879), pp. 16–19.
[7] Records of the Town of Franklin, Massachusetts, 1778–1815, February 5, 1781, MS in Town Hall, Franklin, Massachusetts.

sired five children, Rebecca, Thomas Stanley, Stephen, Horace, and Lydia.[8]

More than a source of livelihood, tilling the soil of Mann's Plain was the good life for Thomas Mann. He did not exploit his land, he nourished it for himself and his posterity. His homestead was a place of residence and work, a place of healing and productivity, a place of prayer and education. What the family needed in raw materials, it produced in the field, the woodlot, the garden, and the orchard. Like their neighbors, the Manns were largely self-sufficient, processing the wool and flax for their clothing and growing and preserving the food for their table. By necessity, they were a tightly knit family maintaining an economic microcosm in which each member was required to conform to the needs of the group.

Through experience and tradition, the Manns knew the attitudes and skills necessary to survive in this independent life. On the farm, labor was divided on the basis of a hierarchy of age and need. Each person had a contribution to make. The children learned the simpler tasks by watching their elders and gradually moved on to more complex activities. Work was a way of life, and the ceaseless demands of life in rural New England made it dangerous to prolong infancy; the children were appreciated chiefly as hands to work. The young Horace was expected to shoulder adult responsibilities and learn to do what he had to do in order to be a member of the family. He started working at such an early age he could not recall when he had not worked.[9] Shortly after his seventh birthday, he was assigned to lead the horse while another steadied the plow. As soon as his hands were large enough to hold a hoe, he worked alongside of his two brothers. He also joined the family setting out rows of Indian corn and seeding the flax plots. Later in the heat of a summer day and well into the cool of the evening, he raked hay and harvested rye. The hay in and the grain threshed, there were always roofs and fences to be mended, weeds to be hoed, and brush to be cut in the yeoman's endless undeclared war to keep the forces of nature in check. Neither fall nor winter brought respite. When all else was done, there was still the care of the livestock and the need for fuel. To the young, impressionable Horace, the woodpile mounted up as

---

[8] The birth years for the children were as follows: Rebecca, 1787; Thomas Stanley, 1788; Stephen, 1792; Horace, 1796; Lydia, 1798. Mann, *Man Genealogy*, pp. 23–26.

[9] Mary Peabody Mann, *Life of Horace Mann* (Boston, 1891), pp. 10–11.

an unforgettable symbol of the interminable toil on the farm. "I believe in the rugged nursing of Toil," he later wrote of this period in his life, "but she nursed me too much." [1]

In growing flax and weaving linen, he could see the necessity of a marriage between industry and cooperation. Barely had the seed been sown when Horace, his mother, and sisters returned to weed the plot, bent over, barefooted and heading into the wind so that the trampled shoots might be lifted. The drooping blue flowers which appeared in June served notice that soon the plants would be dry, ready to be pulled up by the roots and tied in bundles for the retting process. After they had dried, the striking of the stems with a ponderous flax brake was the task for his father and brothers, who became covered with flax dirt as they pounded out the fine yellow-brown fibers. From here, his mother and sisters took over a task which lasted well into winter. At almost any time when in the house, from morning to evening, he could hear the sounds of industry, the whir of the spinning wheel, the snap of the clock reel, or the thwack of the handloom. To finish the cloth, they cleansed it with water and fuller's earth and bleached it with buttermilk. The result was the fine white homespun linen from which they fashioned their shirts and blouses. The better pieces they saved to barter for brown sugar, spices, and a few other commodities whose production defied their ingenuity and perseverance.

What was produced grain by grain and thread by thread was not likely to be squandered. The potential use of soap and candles, salt pork and fruit preserves, shoe leather and hand-wrought nails was measured in terms of their cost in raw materials and human labor. If nature gave few superfluities, poverty was also almost unknown. What material advances the Manns had made in the last hundred years were the result of a fusion of diligence, cooperation, and frugality. It was an austere existence which could not tolerate sentimentality or ornamentation. There was little room here for individual choice. Instead, it was a life of ascetic security in which the child learned to shape his interests and choose his actions in terms of their role in maintaining the family circle. The many lessons Horace learned, and the attitudes he formed, were reinforced by his sense of their concrete contribution to the well-being of the family. "Industry, or diligence," he wrote, "became my second nature. . . .

---

[1] Horace Mann to Mary Mann, May 25, 1850, Mann MSS:MHS; Mann, *Life,* p. 10.

Owing to these ingrained habits, work has always been to me what water is to fish." [2]

*   *   *

The self-sufficient households which set the pattern of life in Franklin were effectively supported by another institution, the meetinghouse. If the home welded individuals into a tightly knit unit, the meetinghouse promoted the broader social unity necessary to maintain a self-governing community. The farmers of Franklin had a reputation for independent action and strong individualism. As early as 1736, Thomas Man joined others who were unwilling to be under the direct control of Wrentham and petitioned for independent town status.[3] Franklin was not legally established for another fifty years, but while it awaited official recognition, its residents did little to prove they could become a society of God-fearing, like-minded men. A relatively high percentage of the families did not attend worship regularly, and even those who did so gave small evidence of peaceful dispositions. Since they had not clustered their homes around a town square, as had been the traditional practice, they argued at length over a site for a new meetinghouse. Thomas Man donated an acre of ground to end the dispute, but they were at odds again over the substitution of Watts's hymnal for the *Bay Psalm Book*. Word that the west precinct of Wrentham was a trouble spot spread to other communities, especially when its second minister was forced out after a stormy tenure. As a result, the congregation bided its time for five years before it was able to persuade a young graduate to become its pastor in 1773. His name was Nathanael Emmons.[4]

A casual first glance at this man could be misleading. He was small, with a tendency toward plumpness. His sallow complexion and sunken cheeks, together with a large nose and pronounced fore-

---

[2] Mann, *Life*, pp. 10–11.

[3] Blake, *History of Franklin*, pp. 23–25.

[4] Arthur Winslow Pierce, *The One Hundred and Fiftieth Anniversary of the Incorporation of the Town of Franklin, Massachusetts* (Franklin, 1928), pp. 11–13; G. E. Lovejoy, "Historical Discourse," *Our Retrospect: A Memorial Volume . . . of the First Congregational Church, Franklin, Massachusetts* (Walpole, 1888), pp. 20–21. Emmons was considered one of the brightest students in an able class at Yale which included Joseph Lyman, John Treadwell, and John Trumbull. He was given the highest oratory honor at commencement. See Thomas Williams, *The Official Character of Rev. Nathanael Emmons, D.D.* (Boston, 1840), pp. 53–54.

head, the more emphasized by the fact that his hair was pulled straight back and tightly fastened in a queue, precluded the possibility of a handsome face. Instead, his countenance gave the impression of sternness or serenity, depending upon the predilection of the observer. His dress was that of the men of the Revolution, a single-breasted coat, satin knee breeches, white stockings, and shoes with silver buckles. When traveling about the countryside in his chaise, making calls upon his parishioners, his stature seemed even more slight wrapped in a dark blue outer coat topped by a flat three-cornered hat. In the meetinghouse, the reverse was true. Standing in the high box pulpit underneath the sounding board, he was a man who commanded respect. His voice was too weak for him to qualify as an orator. At times, it was squeaky, but as he became intent upon his topic, it took on a high shrill quality, creating a tenseness which pervaded every pew in the meetinghouse. Yet it was neither his apparent stature nor his intense voice which left the most lasting impression, but his powerful and penetrating eyes, which seemed to be the key to his entire personality. At once, one sensed the man's tenacity and strength of character while experiencing the self-doubt that comes from eyes which can see into and beyond the person.

The young man's maiden voyage into the ministry was a turbulent one, but he held to his principles, refused to knuckle under to the compromising demands made upon him, and gradually exerted a harmonious influence previously unknown in the community. Probably the turning point came in 1784 when the town was swept with a revival and a tenth of its members came into his fold. Emmons, however, did not let a wave of popular repentance lull him into a false sense of security. A minister in Franklin was well advised to sleep with one eye open, ever alert for a slackening of public and private morals. On several occasions, believing his congregation inattentive, Emmons stepped down from the pulpit, and marched down the road to his parsonage. Only when the town fathers hastily gathered and pledged their undivided, more devout attention did he return.[5]

Revivals and impromptu exits from the meetinghouse were exceptional measures. For the most part, it was through his two Sunday

---

[5] See Records of the Church of Franklin, July 18 and August 3, 1790, MS in the Franklin Savings and Loan Association, Franklin, Massachusetts. After listening to Emmons's explanation for his actions, the assembly voted "that it is reasonable, the Pastor should insist upon having the proper attention of the People, in the time of public worship." A similar incident took place December 29, 1816.

sermons that the minister reached his people. As with earlier New England divines, Emmons preached in a "plain style," which emphasized logical organization and a clarity of exposition and was easily followed. He began by giving the text and explaining its context before discussing the significant doctrines which could be drawn from it. This accomplished, he laid down his small gold-rimmed spectacles and, looking directly toward his listeners, presented what the Puritans called "uses," or the application of the doctrines to the daily lives of the people. Preaching the word of God was his first responsibility. "Though men differ in their opinions what doctrines ministers ought to preach and oppose," he told his congregation one Sunday, "all are agreed, that they ought to preach all the civil, social, moral values, and oppose every custom, which tends to destroy, or even weaken, their happy influence." This he intended to do.[6]

As the result of Emmons's preaching, the Manns and many other householders of Franklin banked their fires at sundown on Saturday as the first act in preparing for the Lord's day. More than a day of rest from the toil of the previous week, Sunday became a symbol of the community's commitment to arrest any lapse into barbarism and moral degeneration. In the winter, parishioners drove their teams through snowdrifts and then sat through two doctrinal sermons in the unheated meetinghouse where the moisture from their breath congealed into ice on its frigid walls. This was not the act of a submissive people complying with an archaic "blue law," but a meaningful ritual in which scattered families came together to reaffirm their beliefs and renew their will to lead God-pleasing lives. To be a "hearer" of the word was synonymous with being a meetinghouse member. Honoring the Sabbath was the central means of maintaining a system of religious and social values, ever in danger of being eroded in an isolated community.

In Franklin, the distinction between the secular and the sacred was blurred. Between the two services on Sunday, decisions involving the welfare of the entire community were often made. Church discipline was used to punish a master for whipping his apprentice, while the civic officials attempted to enforce regulations against profanity and intemperance. Such were the means for maintaining the community, and it was totally in keeping with the spirit of the people that in one of their town meetings, they memorialized the

---

[6] *Works of Nathanael Emmons, D.D., Late Pastor of the Church in Franklin, Massachusetts,* ed. Jacob Ide (Boston, 1842), II, 81.

General Court to pass stricter laws for observing the Sabbath.[7]

Nor was the public conscience limited to local and state affairs. Fearing that "French Philosophy and Illuminatism" would soon sweep over the nation, the voters of Franklin instructed their lone representative to the General Court in 1800 to spare no effort in preventing the choice of a single state elector who was likely to support "a Man to be President or Vice President, who has . . . given his Opinion, That . . . he is quite Indifferent whether a man believes that there are Twenty Gods or no God." Then to be certain that there should be no misunderstanding, they rephrased their instructions to their representative, telling him to withdraw his support for any elector who was "likely to Vote for the Author of Jefferson's Notes on Virginia." In holding such an opinion, the yeomen of Franklin were in the national minority, and the author of "Jefferson's Notes on Virginia" was elected to the highest office in the land.[8]

Through Emmons's efforts, the meetinghouse sanctioned, supported, and directed the life of the people by institutionalizing a set of relevant values into categorical language and austere ritual. As no other man, the character of the town of Franklin bore the imprint of his presence, even as the bare plank floor of the old pulpit bore the impression made by his feet where he stood while preaching. For fifty-four years, in his uncompromising way, he rejoiced with a family at the birth of a child, married its sons and daughters, ministered to the sick, buried its dead, and comforted the survivors. A man who had known death, he could remain with the mourners, he once wrote, knowing "their heaviest burden comes upon them while they are sitting alone, and reflecting upon the nature and consequences of their bereavements." His was a ministry of authority and responsibility, and he succeeded where his two predecessors had failed. Through it, Franklin, once little more than a bickering, dissident thorn in the side of Wrentham, had taken its place among the pious and patriotic communities of the Commonwealth.[9]

*   *   *

---

[7] Confession of Jason Morse, January 22, 1786, who admitted laying forty stripes on his apprentice, MS in Congregational-Baptist Church, Franklin, Massachusetts; Town Records of Franklin, Massachusetts, 1778–1815 and 1816–1852, April 6, 1812, February 3 and May 5, 1817, and April 3, 1820, MS in Franklin, Massachusetts, Town Hall.

[8] Town Records, November 3, 1800.

[9] "Memoirs," *Works,* I, xxxii.

In such an arrangement, the indoctrination of the next generation into the ways of the adult community was largely the task of the
home and meetinghouse. Even some training in literacy was possible
here. The young Horace Mann followed his sister Rebecca about the
house, holding a Noah Webster grammar in his hand, as she listened to his lesson while attending to her chores.[1] Ostensibly he was
learning to spell, but this could not be separated from an unavoidable
concomitant. As his younger sister later described the process, he
learned "two lessons at once," one in literature and the other in the
"practical use of time or money or opportunities." Thirty-five years
later, when a biographer suggested that Mann's achievements were
largely self-attained, she curtly reminded her brother that "every
day of your life when with your parents and sister, at least, you were
at school and learning that which has been the foundation of your
present learning." [2]

For more formal instruction, the residents of Franklin established schools. From the outset, they did not create a single building
near the center of the town as had been tried earlier in other communities, but instead organized six school districts, each with its
own crude one-room edifice. In addition to contributing firewood
and labor, the Manns and their neighbors squeezed about $100 a
year out of their meager cash earnings to pay a teacher who "kept
the winter school" six or seven weeks for the older children whose
labor was needed less on the farm during this season. Hopefully,
they also had a small residue with which to hire a woman in summer
to keep the younger children out from underfoot during the harvest
time. Horace Mann's schoolhouse was an unpretentious affair at
best, its only source of heat a large, undampered fireplace. When he
was old enough to attend in the winter, Horace learned that one
traveled from the Torrid Zone to the Arctic by moving five paces
away from the hearth. As he was first assigned a bench at some
distance, his thoughts may have flowed but his ink supposedly congealed in his pen from the lack of heat. Jokingly, he later described
the numerous leaks in the roof as of small consequence and only
momentary discomfort since the floor also leaked and kept the rain
and melting snow from accumulating inside.[3]

---

[1] Among the books belonging to the Mann family still extant is Thomas
Mann's copy of Noah Webster, *English Language . . . Designed for
the Use of English Schools in America* (1784), in the Straker MSS:ACL.
[2] [Lydia Mann] to Horace Mann, August 20, 1854, Mann MSS:MHS.
[3] Livingston, "Horace Mann," *American Portrait Gallery*, pp. 178–179.

Unlike many of the lessons learned in the home, those taught in school seemed removed from the young lad's experience. And what could not be motivated by direct interest was reinforced with a liberal application of the ferule. Horace and his brothers may have found the lessons of the classroom less rewarding and relevant than those of the woodlot and meadow, but his parents considered them an important extension of household training and stood ready to back up the schoolmaster at every turn. If the young lad received a "birching" at school during the day, his thoughts as he walked east on the road towards his home centered on a similar fate inevitably awaiting him at the hands of his father.[4] Horace knew too that the classroom was also an extension of the meetinghouse. His parents provided him with a copy of the ubiquitous and venerable *New England Primer* for more than instruction in the alphabet. More directly related to religious education was the requirement to learn long sections of the *Westminster Assembly Shorter Catechism,* with its moralistic exposition of the Ten Commandments and its overriding concern that young children feel the need for salvation. To remind him of the connection between meetinghouse and school, Emmons made regular calls on the classroom, catechizing Horace and his classmates. Having announced his visit the previous Sunday in the meetinghouse, the minister would ride up to the schoolhouse at the appointed time. As he entered, the children rose from their seats and remained standing until he had been seated. Then followed questions and answers on moral and doctrinal subjects. Occasionally, Emmons discovered a pupil who did not even know the Lord's Prayer.[5] Not so, however, with Horace, who memorized both questions and answers readily. Although revealing a nervousness as he responded, intellectually he was equal to the minister's interrogation. He remembered that by the age of ten, he was "familiar with the whole creed, and knew all the arts of theological fence by which objections to it were parried." As all doctrines, tenets, creeds which did not exactly conform to a certain standard were pronounced heresies, he concluded their advocates were cast out from fellowship in this life and faced eternal perdition in the next. Learning to distinguish between what was accepted and rejected by the community

---

[4] Mann described this in one of his popular lectures on education. He did not identify the family, but from his description, it is clear that he was talking about his own childhood. See his *Lectures on Education* (Boston, 1848), pp. 336–337.

[5] N.a., *Our Retrospect: A Memorial Volume . . . of the First Congregational Church, Franklin, Massachusetts,* pp. 57–59.

in this manner, he soon expanded this to realms far beyond the classroom. As each day brought new experiences, new people, new customs, new objects, he mentally classified them, perceiving them in categories of good or evil, black or white, belonging or being outcast, saved or damned.[6]

In more secular areas also, the classroom supported the general aims of the community. While learning his penmanship, Horace practiced on such maxims as "Improve the golden moment of opportunity before it is forever too late," or "When the devil catches a man idle, he generally sets him to work." Independence and freedom were reaffirmed with "A day, an hour of virtuous Liberty is worth an eternity in Bondage." All these he executed in a generous and ornate hand, dutifully transposing them into his copybook.[7] By the end of January or early February, the best classroom work was set aside for the closing "exhibition." On this occasion, usually held on the last day of the winter session, his parents came to witness their children's progress over the past six or seven weeks. There were questions and answers, spelling bees, arithmetic drills, and memorized poetry and orations. When he was fourteen, no doubt being carried along with the patriotic fervor sweeping the nation, Horace displayed his "exhibition piece," composed of an ornate inscription of mixed biblical metaphor, "The United States of America, the Eden of the Earth and the Fatal forbidden fruit to all who Invade Them," symmetrically ringed by the sixteen states in the form of a mandala.[8]

The next year, he presented a crude satirical play entitled *The Country Justice*. In it, Mann depicted the patent ignorance of a judge dispatched to the countryside to administer the law. Attempting to impress the rural folk with legal decisions generously punctuated with malapropisms and pseudo-Latin expressions, the pettifogging justice only exposed his own ignorance. He was openly prejudiced in favor of creditors and had no faith whatsoever in a jury of twelve

---

[6] Mann, *Life*, p. 13; Horace Mann, Journal, July 2, 1837, MS in MHS.
[7] The remains of Mann's schoolwork are found in the Mann MSS:MHS and the Boston Public Library. The townspeople were rightfully proud of the library Benjamin Franklin had given them for naming their community after him and made much of its alleged salutary effect. It was more likely, however, judging from the few manuscripts Horace Mann kept from his youth, that the author of *Poor Richard* was influencing the people through his almanac more than through the collection of theological treatises and bound sermons his book agent had sent them from London. A copy of the original catalogue of Franklin's donation is printed in Blake, *History of Franklin*, pp. 70–71.
[8] Mann MSS:BPL.

men or, as the young playwright had him say, "a set of rascals and numbskulls." Finally, the judge met more than his match in the form of an honest, unsophisticated yeoman who won the litigation armed with nothing more than common sense. No doubt Mann's play was well received by his parents and friends in the audience, as it exhibited a belief, almost endemic in the rural areas of New England, that lawyers and judges were arrogant and greedy fools and the tools of creditors.[9]

In a crude and perhaps naïve way, the Manns and their neighbors had created schools to teach their children the same tenets and oral traditions as those fostered in the family and meetinghouse. What was necessary to maintain their way of life was made into a virtue and translated into simple formulas which could be internalized as enduring attitudes. The sense of exclusiveness, and the concepts of frugality, honesty, industry, self-denial, and obedience, were compressed into aphorisms to be indelibly impressed upon the minds of such as the sensitive young Horace. For a few weeks each winter, the classroom joined the chimney corner and the pew as a third place of his indoctrination.

*   *   *

As towns on the seacoast and along the inland waterways began to grow, some of the farmers, particularly those near Boston, Salem, and Providence, concentrated after 1800 on raising products which could be sold for cash in nearby markets. This shift was hastened by the establishment of mills in certain villages and the accompanying rise in the population of wage earners. None of these influenced Franklin. Lacking canals and railroads, the farmers were too far from the larger towns. The few water sites on Mine Brook were used for grinding corn, sawing lumber, and powering the fulling mill, thus helping to mitigate the more menial tasks of the local families in providing their own food and shelter. Mail reached the town once a week. The crops of flax, Indian corn, and rye which Horace Mann's father grew and the tools he used were probably similar, if not identical, to those of the first Thomas Man who farmed the land. Distant markets had little meaning to him. What he produced on the farm was mainly determined by the weather and the needs of his family.[1]

---

[9] January 18, 1811, Mann MSS:MHS.
[1] Blake, *History of Franklin,* pp. 79, 111–112.

In his will, Thomas Mann had assumed that this circumscribed world would be that of his children, and that the tenets which he held would also be theirs. Still, in a moment of retrospection, some doubt and uncertainty about the future was unavoidable. Within the last decade, he had witnessed events which seemed to undermine his ordered and stable way of life and that of his neighbors. In 1800, his son Horace was too young to have remembered the fear that the election of a Deist as President had struck in the hearts of the independent yeomen of Franklin. Of course their forebodings did not materialize.

It is also unlikely that Horace, even if he had been older, would have understood a new development decidedly more local and mundane which would begin to erode away the established pattern of life in his community. At about the same time as Jefferson's election, several of the town's women learned the secret of braiding oat straw into strands which could be used in making ladies' hats. As straw and nimble fingers were plentiful, braiding soon joined the older tasks of spinning and weaving as a central activity in the home. In this the Manns also participated.[2] Previously, the object of their spinning and weaving had been only to clothe the immediate family, but now with the manufacture of straw braid, they could produce an item sold for cash at a distant market. Surely this was a blessing promising new security in their home and enabling them to buy things formerly beyond their means.

At first the finished straw was taken to Captain Nathaniel Adams's general store and traded directly for merchandise; but by 1804, a small nearby hat manufactory bought the braid outright. Straw bonnets were fashionable and products from Franklin and Wrentham were sold in Boston, Providence, and New York. According to the local historian, one shipment even went to Maine, with "no small profit." Economic patterns in the town changed as the tempo of life seemed to quicken. As more things were now purchased and fewer were homemade, factory textiles soon replaced homespun. Now there might even be money for luxuries, a development attacked by Emmons, who repeatedly warned his congregation of the dangers of prodigality. Even more troublesome to Emmons must have been the additional money available, enabling some of his parishioners to spend more time in the village tavern away from their families and farms.[3]

---

[2] Mann, *Life*, p. 20.
[3] Blake, *History of Franklin*, pp. 112–113.

The roles of the members within the family were also changing. Little by little, the older hierarchy of authority determined by age and service to the group was being weakened by the Manns' efforts to exploit this new economic opportunity. As long as they had depended on their fields for sustenance, the judgment of Thomas Mann as head of the household was paramount; but the more their dependence shifted to the processing of straw, the more his real significance decreased. This was especially true if he were reduced to the menial task of braiding, something in which his more nimble-fingered children could excel. The older tasks about the farm continued, and although chores had a beginning and an end, there was virtually no end to braiding straw. For the young Horace Mann, self-consciously seeking manhood, braiding was doubly galling because it was also women's work. To him it seemed as if every free moment was spent in "sedentary occupations," working with his sisters. The years did little to erase his bitterness at having been deprived of a normal childhood. If he complained at the time, his parents turned a deaf ear. "My parents sinned ignorantly," he recalled, "but God affixes the same physical penalties for the violation of his laws, whether that violation be wilful or ignorant." [4]

Other changes in the family were even more significant than the possible humbling of the father and the loss of recreation for the son. Since the relation between industry, frugality, and material prosperity was not difficult to observe, the farmers in Franklin had assumed that their well-being was directly related to their diligence and thrift, factors over which they had immediate control. But now, the more the Manns specialized, the more their belief in the older mores became an act of faith less substantiated by direct experience. There had always been the unpredictability of the weather, but to this uncertainty was now added the new problem of price fluctuation. Previously, barring adverse weather, they could anticipate and meet the wants of their family with some accuracy. Now there was no way to predict, much less control, the fickle demands of thousands of distant consumers. Impersonal and complex factors influencing the Franklin farmers were beyond their control and even comprehension. In 1808 they joined the rest of New England in petitioning President Jefferson to lift his embargo on shipping, even

---

[4] Quoted in Mann, *Life*, p. 10; also see Horace Mann to Mary Mann, May 25, 1850, Mann MSS:MHS.

though his curtailment of foreign imports had assisted their new home industry.[5]

If the home, school, and meetinghouse had remained closely integrated, the young Horace Mann should have suffered little anxiety in making the transition from his family circle to the larger community. In practice, however, the actual entry of children into the elect of the congregation could be a severe personal crisis. Emmons steadfastly maintained that only through repentance and submission to God's commands could children escape the damnation which was a consequence of their innate depravity. Even though his own son died without conversion, he would not sidestep the terrible logic of this doctrine. Agonizing though it must have been, he used the incident to demonstrate both to parents and children the folly of postponing the search for God until it was too late.[6] He "who imagines he is far from the grave, may be the next to be covered with the clods of the valley," was his warning to the unconverted youth in his audience. "Week after week, death has come among us without any order," and the apathetic and unrepentant should take heed, since "this may be one of the last solemn calls that God will ever condescend to give some poor, stupid impenitent creatures, who stand upon slippery places, and whose feet will soon slide into the grave."[7]

As long as Franklin remained largely isolated and self-sufficient, this process of assimilating children into the greater society seemed effective. For many residents, the ties to the community were almost as strong as their family ties. It had probably been so for the first Thomas Man and his son Nathan. If ownership of their home and farm indicated one identity, the extension of their property to include a church pew symbolized another. Barely perceptible at first, Horace had come to recognize the steady drift of his parents and older brothers away from active participation in the affairs of the meetinghouse. Thus, by the time he himself had reached adolescence, instead of looking to it with a conditioned sense of involvement, he perceived the meetinghouse as the embodiment of a form of external coercion and an omnipresent source of irritation and rebellion. Attending the meeting on Sunday was complying with a

---

[5] A copy of their petition is in the Town Records of Franklin, August 29, 1808, MS in Town Hall, Franklin, Massachusetts.

[6] Edwards A. Park, "Reflections of a Visitor," in Emmons, *Works,* I, cxxxix–cxl.

[7] Emmons, "Death Without Order," *Works,* III, 40; see also his "A Warning to Youth," *ibid.,* 218–230.

"religious ordinance" rather than acting with purpose and devotion.[8]

Not all in Franklin were as discreet as the Manns in concealing their spiritual apathy. After 1800, membership in the meetinghouse claimed an ever smaller percentage of the total number of residents in the town. But this did not prompt Emmons to adjust his theology. "I never try to revise the statutes of the Almighty" was his typical response. Backsliding was not caused by the inadequacy of God's law. God was divine and man was sinful, and the minister never confused the two. The only concession he was willing to make in staying the drift away from religion was to welcome the occurrence of revivals. In 1808, when Horace was just twelve, he witnessed his first of these.[9] Emotional outbursts occurred during Emmons's preaching as he fed his parishioners' fears with sermons describing the eternal punishment awaiting the unconverted. Connecting passage to passage and building paragraph on paragraph, he built his case against unbelief with his searching, inescapable logic, until the interior of the meetinghouse seemed charged like the inside of a Leyden jar. Within a short time, the new converts numbered more than thirty, but the young Horace Mann was not among them.

Refusing to be swept along in the wave of popular religious enthusiasm, he nevertheless could not purge the minister's preaching from his thoughts. An evil leaven had begun to work in his mind, producing a ferment of troubled thought which he could not suppress. From the pulpit, Emmons's accusations reached him like needles probing his conscience and increasing his agony. He simply could not avoid the minister's hawklike gaze. Emmons's eyes seemed to be lenses through which the minister could see the young Mann's most secret thoughts. The more he tried, the more he failed to come to terms with the awful, unanswerable questions about God's inscrutable ways and the man who expressed them in such sharp-cut, crystalline prose. Each time he tried to conjure an image of God as a loving father, he lost control as his mind became filled with a kaleidoscope of contradictions, only to end with the same image of a vindictive judge standing before him, condemning and punishing without mercy. Repulsive though he knew it to be, he found himself imagining a physical hell and heard "the shrieks of the tormented"

---

[8] Mann, *Life*, p. 13.
[9] J. C. Gallinson, "Franklin and Wrentham," *New England Magazine*, XXI (November, 1899), 336; Thomas Williams, *Official Character of Rev. Nathanael Emmons, D.D.* (Boston, 1848), p. 58; *Our Retrospect: A Memorial Volume*, pp. 23–24.

whose fates were sealed by the "irreversible decree of Jehovah, immutable from everlasting to everlasting." [1] There were both Law and Gospel in Emmons's indictment, but he heard only the former. Seeking love, he found nothing but fear. Finally, in the grip of a paralyzing anguish and stripped of all else but a naked will power, he broke the hold the minister had upon him. In a moment of self-knowledge, he challenged Emmons's doctrines, rejected the collective security of the community of believers, and struck out on his own.

According to his own account, he experienced a trauma which was precipitous, unforgettable, and irreversible.

I remember the day, the hour, the place and the circumstances, as well as though the event had happened but yesterday, when in an agony of despair, I broke the spell that bound me. From that day, I began to construct the theory of Christian ethics and doctrine respecting virtue and vice, rewards and penalties, time and eternity, God and his providence which . . . I still retain.[2]

Attempting to deny Emmons's influence and identify himself with something more benign, he now resolved to create a personal God who was a benevolent, loving father and "the combination of all human excellences." To do this meant to adjust God to man and to turn his back on a way of life (together with a plan for salvation) which had been an article of faith in his family since one of his ancestors first preached the doctrines of John Calvin in Wrentham more than a century before.

*   *   *

A year later, his father was dead.

While the event was anticipated and Thomas Mann had opportunity to settle his affairs, his death was still a blow to the household. What was true of the family in general was especially true for Horace. Just entering adolescence and struggling to put events into their proper order, he now looked to his brothers and mother for the guidance which normally would have come from his father.

The very frequency of Emmons's entreaties to the youth of the community and his particular concern that they honor the Sabbath

[1] Mann, *Life,* p. 14.
[2] Quoted in Mann, *Life,* p. 14.

indicated that not all were heeding his admonitions. Even within the Mann household, whose members still made a practice of attending worship, Stephen, Horace's brother and the object of his admiration and affection, was not as faithful as the others. How often he missed church service is not known, but at least one Sunday, a year after his father had died, he "profaned the Sabbath" by going to a nearby pond to fish or swim. Later in the day, an urgent message reached the Manns. Stephen had drowned.[3]

Horace had come to expect his father's death, but who could have been prepared for this calamity? His immediate response was disbelief, but this only lasted until they carried Stephen's lifeless body into the house and placed it on a bed. The blue nails, the still fingers, cold hands, a last look on the lifeless face with its telltale marks of the struggle to survive, all were the silent, overpowering proof of the tragedy. Yet doubt continued to tempt him. Around the house were all the visible signs of tragedy, the covered mirrors, the turned pictures, and Stephen's empty chair at the table. Still he could not erase the thought from his mind that at any moment, his brother, full of life as ever, would come through the bedroom doorway much as he had done innumerable times before. It was all a bad dream, but each morning when he awoke, he had to remind himself that it was also real, and that Stephen was dead.

When they brought the coffin into the house for Stephen's body, he knew it was the beginning of the end. Later he joined the other mourners, following the town's black hearse as it moved west along the road towards the burying ground. Around him were stoic Yankee faces, each a tight-lipped emotionless mask from which he could read neither reproach nor comfort. Still at some distance, he began to make out the tolling of the meetinghouse bell. As the procession moved closer, the mourners' steps seemed to fall in with the slow dreadful rhythm of its cadence. Consumed in his thoughts as he moved on past the meetinghouse, he suddenly found himself in the graveyard before the open pit. Walls of dark brown earth. Here and there the white ends of severed roots protruded. Silent men carried the coffin and lowered it into the ground. "Dust to dust," fragments of Emmons's prayer hung in the air, while he fought back his tears and struggled to set the recent events in some order. There had to be a reason. The sound of shovels cutting through the recently

---

[3] Stephen Mann drowned in Uncas Pond on July 22, 1810. Orestes T. Doe, ed., *The Record of Births, Marriages, and Deaths in the Town of Franklin from 1778 to 1872* (Franklin, 1898), p. 148.

dug earth and the concussion of clods as they struck the top of the pine box forced him back to the scene before him. The dust rose from the pit and an unknown hand drew him away to join his mother and a few of the other mourners for the lonely walk back to the house on Mann's Plain.

A question remained. What would Emmons say at the funeral the following Sunday? On the basis of his remarks on other occasions, the answer should have been fore-ordained. He had said it in many ways, but it was always the same theme. Profaning the Lord's Day held terrible consequences for the evildoer. Often he had singled out the youth of the community, denouncing them as "criminally negligent in attending public worship, and far more criminal in profaning the Sabbath in every way in which it can be profaned." And that there should be no mistake about his position, he added, "Every youth who profanes the Sabbath, rejects the gospel, and despises reproof, is in danger of enduring such bitter reflections to all eternity." [4] There could be no mistake.

No expedient desire to alleviate the immediate suffering of the Manns was sufficient reason for Emmons to compromise his principles now. Nevertheless, as he entered the meetinghouse, Horace still hoped for what he called "an infusion of kindliness and sentiment." Probably, as soon as Emmons began, Horace knew that the minister had not changed. No doubt in reviewing the life of Stephen Mann, he found little or no evidence of the possibility of conversion. The inevitable conclusion was an agonizing judgment. Stephen had died unconverted and while willfully sinning. His future life would be one of eternal punishment. The only ray of comfort to be gained from the tragedy was that the incident was a sign, a special warning to the survivors of the imminence of death and the folly of placing themselves outside God's grace.

For Horace, just turned fourteen, the tragedy made an indelible scar on his memory. Previously, when thoughts of the damned filled his mind, he could depersonalize them into a faceless mass of heathen. But now he knew that God's vengeance had struck within his very family and divine condemnation rested upon one whose face seemed always before him. The family had been drifting away from the influence of the meetinghouse, but his own rejection of Emmons's God was unmitigated rebellion. He recalled that at an early age, his mind actively engaged in noting "effects in causes,

---

[4] Emmons, "A Warning to Youth," *Works*, III, 227–228.

and causes in effects." He had learned from his catechism, from sermon after sermon, and from the daily admonitions of his parents, that divine retribution followed disobedience. Now it was almost impossible for him to avoid relating the deaths of his father and brother with his own renunciation of Calvinism two years before, and once done, the connection could not be purged from his mind. The result was a burden of guilt which brought him close to the breaking point.

In an attempt to believe in a benevolent sovereign, events were pushing him towards an opposite belief. Still he resisted. It was a "fearful action upon his nerves," a close friend recalled. In place of some mediator, "He expected the foul Fiend to appear from behind every hedge and tree." Not quite sane at night, he wrestled with a personal devil he could neither let go nor subdue. In such mental chaos, it was little wonder that he felt an almost unbearable sense of desolation. One of his childhood associates noted his morbid compulsion, each time he returned to the meetinghouse, to turn to the same page in Watts's hymnal and read over a stanza depicting a solitary soul lost in eternity. The young Horace identified himself with that soul, fully understanding what it meant to be "rudderless and homeless." For him, emancipation had come at a dear price.[5]

*   *   *

Now, although he continued to hear the merits of the simple, frugal life repeated, Horace could see that rewards did not necessarily go to those who adhered to the traditional values. The more his family specialized in braiding, the more their belief in the older mores was an act of faith and less connected with their immediate experience. By the time he was sixteen, Franklin was producing over 6,000 bonnets annually. Hat making also spread to Wrentham, and when the neighboring congregation decided to make a sharp break with tradition and install an organ in their house of worship, it was money from the sale of bonnets that paid the bill. Braiding straw was not only altering the character of the local households, it was also helping change the meetinghouse into a church. Besides several hat manufactories, Franklin soon was boasting of numerous small textile mills crowded in around its water sites. By the 1820's, a

---

[5] Mann, *Life*, pp. 16–17.

traveler described it as enterprising and prosperous and trading with "almost every place in the country." He also was amazed how rapidly Unitarianism was spreading in the area.[6]

For Mann's parents, the intrusion of a new religion into the community would have been the most difficult of these changes to comprehend, and even for Horace himself, the leadership and teachings of Emmons were still something with which to reckon. To Horace Mann's niece Rebecca, however, a member of the next generation, the old minister was a museum piece and his doctrines antediluvian. Although he still walked erectly, what she noticed was his "hair powdered and in a queue, a three-cornered hat, and knee breeches." It was hard for her to believe that he had ever been a leader in the community, but must have been "some other sort of contrivance." Emmons had not changed, but Franklin and its youth had.[7]

The new opportunities in manufacturing made life on the land less attractive. Stanley Mann was certain of it. Despite the directives in his father's will, his heart was not in farming. A tall, good-looking man who met people easily and gained their confidence, Stanley spent long periods away from Mann's Plain endeavoring to use his inheritance and that of his sisters to establish himself as a manager and part owner of one of the new mills. Increasingly, Horace was left alone to work the farm, instructed occasionally by letters from his brother. At this time, nostalgic talk in the community about the virtue of farm life no doubt continued, but Horace saw it as a fixed routine of back-breaking toil. Stanley was staking his future on the expansion of the mills and a growth of the textile market. Horace, more bookish and introspective and less gregarious than his brother, looked to college and a subsequent profession as the best means to get ahead. Recently, the new wealth in the community had enabled a few Franklin boys to study away from home. Of the several schools available, most of them chose Brown University, thirty miles to the southeast in Providence. It was this avenue of escape which Horace Mann now devised for himself. Of course some Franklinites considered the events altering their community as the call of temptation. Emmons had certainly seen them this way. For others, they were the knock of opportunity; Stanley had been one of these. For

---

[6] Blake, *History of Franklin,* p. 112; Herman Mann, Journal, June 16, 1827, MS in DHS.
[7] Julian Hawthorne, *Nathaniel Hawthorne and His Wife* (Boston, 1885), I, 493.

Horace too, there could be no doubt. The long-range rewards were worth the risk and sacrifice necessary to achieve them.[8]

At first, his mother resisted his plans. With two of her sons gone, the loss of a third would place a severe burden on the household. Stephen's death had done more than widen the gap between the Manns and the meetinghouse; it had also removed the middle link within the family between the two oldest and two youngest children. Now she resisted the further erosion of her household. Horace was now eighteen, and the prospect of living with his mother and two sisters was enough to intensify his agitation to leave. Finally his mother relented. Unable to turn to Emmons for instruction as other college aspirants in the community had done, Horace was forced to resort to self-preparation. Now, unlike the winter sessions in the district school, there was a new and compelling reason to learn, and he let nothing stand in his way, seizing every opportunity for study. Others who had traveled the same route counseled that some knowledge of Latin, Greek, and mathematics would open the door to college. These were the magic three. Once in an exhibition piece he had made fun of a classically educated judge who could quote Latin and had praised a yeoman farmer whose chief virtue was common sense. But if the classics were the key to Brown and beyond, then he must take the place of the fool in his play. It took effort to change roles, but there was no other way. Beginning with *amo, amas, amat,* he worked at the tedious task of learning a foreign language. Soon he was translating line by line, memorizing the vocabulary lists and trying to understand the logic of grammar rules. Just what the intrinsic value of Latin might be remained a mystery to him. Here was another act of faith. Childhood and adolescence in Franklin had given him a set of responses, mainly conditioned or automatic, and now it was only with great personal resolution that he undertook a new program of deliberate action. He had already assumed an adult role on the farm; now his education must begin again. What he had learned previously would not do.

Unaided, he could proceed only so far. But by the time he was nineteen, unexpected help came in the form of Samuel Barrett, an itinerant schoolmaster who happened into Franklin. Barrett, an in-

---

[8] Thomas Stanley Mann to Horace Mann, March 15, 1816, Mann MSS: MHS; Clarence Sumner, *Centennial History of Montgomery Lodge, A.F. and A.M.* (Boston, 1899), pp. 92–93; see E. Smalley, *Centennial Sermon: Delivered . . . in Franklin, Massachusetts, February 25, 1838* (Boston, 1838), pp. 54–56.

dulgent and obese man, was often too drunk to teach. When sober, he was a brilliant classicist. Having committed large sections of Cicero and Vergil to memory, he rarely required a text when listening to Horace's translation. With his new tutor, Mann worked through some of the standard Latin classics and began the Greek Testament. Unfortunately, Barrett was of no help in mathematics. Rumors around town claimed he was unable to remember, much less use, the multiplication tables. Seeking help elsewhere, Horace found it far away from Emmons in the form of instruction from the Reverend William Williams, pastor of the Baptist meetinghouse in Wrentham. Williams was well recommended, having prepared dozens of local boys for his *alma mater,* Brown University.[9] Thus, in the winter of 1816, Horace walked four miles to the minister's study, a one-room building next to his parsonage, where he was introduced to the wonders of Euclidian geometry. Beginning with a fresh new copybook, he wrote down each theorem, diagrammed a problem, and outlined the steps of its solution.[1] The first problem Williams taught him to solve involved the use of a compass to locate the center of a triangle. When the young Mann prepared a figure of lines and arcs to illustrate the solution, he sketched in several buildings to add a touch of realism. At the very center of the diagram, he drew the Franklin meetinghouse.

As winter turned toward spring, he began to feel the increased pressure. Now approaching his twentieth birthday, he resolved to be ready for admission the coming autumn. Distance and the necessity of a patchwork preparation might have been hindrances, but they were not insurmountable obstacles. Self-interest and the sense of expectancy that he was about to accomplish something significant more than compensated for a lack of convenient facilities. Even the weather seemed to forbode far-reaching changes. Much of the winter snow remained on the fields in 1816, and the hills around Franklin looked as bleak in June as they had been in November. Animals died from a lack of fodder, the crop of Indian corn was

---

[9] For biographical sketches of Williams and his work in preparing boys for college, see Abial Fisher, "William Williams," *Annals of the American Pulpit; Or Commemorative Notices of Distinguished Clergymen of Various Denominations,* ed. William B. Sprague (New York, 1860), VI, 159–61; Williams, one of the first graduates of Brown, had used a small wooden building next to his parsonage for a classroom, and in this "preparatory academy," he is reported to have helped eighty local boys qualify for his *alma mater.*

[1] The copybook is dated February 3, 1816, Straker MSS:ACL.

ruined, and flowers had to push up through snow in July. By August, the few apples hardy enough to survive the cold hung from branches encased in ice. All this meant hardships to his family, but it was incidental to the young Mann, who continued to pursue his goal of preparation with a single-minded purpose. Barrett sensed the urgency of the situation and remained sober for longer periods. So intense was Horace's effort that Stanley warned him of overwork. Alexander Metcalf Fisher, a Yale student who lived three houses down the road, had studied with similar intensity and had collapsed with a mental breakdown, Stanley reminded his brother. For Horace to maintain his present pace was to invite similar consequences.[2]

In the midst of his preparations, he received a short letter from his cousin, Sylvester Bishop, commenting on the new course Mann had set for himself. "Cousin Rebecca tells me," the note read, "that you are at school studying the Latin language and I hope you will make good progress in it as a golden moment for improvement. . . ." His cousin then inserted a couplet to describe what might be gained at college:

> *There you the scientific arts may gain,*
> *And all the embellishments of life obtain. . . .*

"But for my part," the note concluded with dejection and resignation, "if I can get so as to dig and plough amongst the dirt I shall do pretty well."[3] The young Mann did not need to be reminded. He was certain that he had chosen the right way to escape from digging and plowing.

---

[2] Thomas S. Mann to Horace Mann, March 15, 1816, Mann MSS:MHS; Samuel G. Goodrich, *Recollections of a Lifetime, or Men and Things I Have Seen* (New York, 1857), II, 78–79.
[3] Sylvester Bishop to Horace Mann, January 6, 1814, Mann MSS:MHS.

CHAPTER II

Providence

===

. . . so far as I can ascertain, I have never
had so much as a peep at the genitals of
originality, . . .

JAMES HOLMES

———

HE HAD MADE a momentous decision. Determined to scrape the
mud of Mann's Plain from his boots, he was preoccupied with
thoughts about the future. To some extent he knew what to expect.
Besides Reverend Williams's advice, there was other information
about the college at hand. Since more than a dozen Franklin boys
had made it to Brown in recent years, it was hardly an unknown
institution to the townspeople. August and early September were
filled with the well-wishes of acquaintances, the expressions of envy
from his friends, and the seemingly endless gratuitous admonitions
to study, to keep a sharp eye on one's money, and to avoid the
temptations of the city. By the middle of September, a few things
remained to be decided. Repeatedly his mother measured the remaining space in his trunk against what was absolutely necessary
and what could be left behind.

His family probably took him in their chaise as far as Wrentham
to meet the stage for Providence. Here there were enquiries about
the schedule, last good-byes, and clumsy expressions to conceal the
immiscible mixture of emptiness and expectation within him. Once
seated inside the stage, he took an anxious look out the window at
what he was leaving behind. Suddenly the tension was broken by the
shout of the driver and the lurch of the coach. He was on his way.

If the countryside through which the coach traveled was new to
him, it was similar to what he knew. Only as he approached the
coast did different scenes come into view. On the outskirts of Providence, the coach hurried past the old North Burying Ground and
rolled on down the hill into the town. The hollow sounds of hoofbeats
on a wooden bridge, the jarring clatter of iron wheels on a cobble-

stone street, the barking of dogs, and the shouts of the driver as he reined in his team all served notice on the young Mann that he was entering a new world. From the Golden Bull Inn or the Montgomery Tavern where the passengers disembarked, it was but a short trip up to the high ground to the north of the town occupied by the college. Riding up Engle Street he could survey the setting he had chosen for himself for the next few years. As he approached the campus, he could see President Asa Messer's house on his left with its well-kept gardens. On his extreme right was the college well, equipped with a windlass and wooden bucket and covered with a two-pitched roof, similar to the one in the farmyard back home. Nearby the president's horse and cow kept the campus grass in check as they grazed. The center of the scene was dominated by University Hall, a large four-story Georgian building topped with eight chimneys, a captain's walk, and a cupola. Housing the students' rooms and commons, the library, chapel, and classrooms, University Hall was the college. Only by standing on its steps and looking south to the town below did he begin to appreciate how aloof the campus was from the bustle and activity of the seaport. In the far distance was the harbor with its maze of masts and riggings from a hundred vessels riding at anchor. The edge of the water was rimmed by a crescent of weathered wharves and warehouses which gradually gave way to clusters of shade trees and the rooftops of residences and shops. Here and there stately church steeples stood guard over the community like stationary sentinels. By far the most impressive of them was the tall, white-tiered tower of the First Baptist Meeting House. This was the setting the young Mann hoped to make his home for the next years.

The character of the town owed much to its Baptist ancestry, and the same could be said of the college. Over the years, many Massachusetts fathers preferred Brown to either Yale or Harvard. Yale was too orthodox while Harvard was considered a nursery of religious heresy and the last fortress of a dying Federalism. Thus they settled for a dissenting school, nominally Baptist.[1] Added to religion and politics were reasons of geography. Brown, for example, claimed all the college graduates from Franklin from 1790 to 1812, including William Emmons, Nathanael Emmons's son. In 1813, one

---

[1] Arthur Darling, *Political Changes in Massachusetts, 1824–1848* (New Haven, 1925), p. 28; Samuel Gridley Howe, *Journals and Letters of Samuel Gridley Howe,* ed. Laura E. Richards (Boston, 1906), I, 15.

Franklin man graduated from Yale, and from then until 1832, eight more graduated from college, all of them from Brown.[2]

Brown was also attractive for economic reasons. By self-sacrifice and careful economy, even less than affluent farmers could send their boys to this school. Since tuition, room, and board rarely exceeded $100 a year, it also was possible for many boys to support themselves partially by keeping school during the long winter vacation.[3] As one Brown alumnus described his classmates in this period, "they studied hard, they lived plainly. They taught school in the long vacation." [4] Brown offered a real bargain which was recognized by more than one Yankee father. Properly managed, Horace Mann's inheritance would be enough to pay for his college education.

How much it would actually cost him depended upon the results of his entrance examination. To qualify for Brown, Mann was ushered into Asa Messer's study and questioned by the president on his general knowledge. Messer was a heavy-set man with a large head and thick neck. His nose was large, almost bulbous, and his ruddy complexion suggested an outdoor life rather than one of letters. As he addressed the young Mann, his voice was gruff and his manner direct. If his critics thought him lacking in gentility and intellectual sophistication, there were others who appreciated his common sense and absolute honesty in dealing with students. A Baptist clergyman, he did not enjoy preaching and grew restless in discussions over fine points in theology. Although a college president, he was not a classicist. Instead, his interests and accomplishments were in science, especially the field of engineering in which he held several patents. A man whose talents also extended to political activity, Messer was offered a place on the State Supreme Court and was a candidate for the governorship. That he was all this and more was unimportant to the young Horace Mann, foremost in whose mind was the fact that sitting across from him was the admissions

[2] E. Smalley, *Centennial Sermon,* pp. 54–56. As far back as the catalogues go, Massachusetts men outnumbered those from Rhode Island. From 1800 to 1810, 69 per cent of the students were from Massachusetts and 20 per cent from Rhode Island. This ratio was fairly constant for the next twenty years. See Walter C. Bronson, *History of Brown University* (Providence, 1914), p. 289.

[3] Mann's first year's expenses for tuition, room rent, library fees, room and board, and admission costs were about $120. Receipts in Mann MSS:MHS.

[4] N.a.[Solomon Lincoln?], *Brown University Under the Presidency of Asa Messer, S.T.D., LL.D.* (Boston, 1867), p. 13; see also Samuel Brenton Shaw, "College and Town in 1819," *Memories of Brown,* ed. Robert Perkins Brown, *et al.* (Providence, 1907), pp. 38–39.

officer of the college and that it was imperative he make the best possible impression on him. Messer examined him on the Greek testament, attempting to be helpful, choosing sections which Mann had most recently reviewed. This completed, the two were joined by Professors Calvin Park and Jasper Adams, Park asking Mann to translate a section from Cicero and Adams a selection from Vergil. He was also asked to translate a paragraph in English into correct Latin prose. Mann then presented letters attesting to his good moral character. After this, the decision was up to President Messer. At the time, Brown was just recovering from the effects of the War of 1812 and needed an increase in its student body. This, together with the fact that Mann had given his examiners an impressive performance prompted Messer not only to admit him, but to admit him with sophomore standing.[5]

He was warned that there were deficiencies he would have to make up and that the first year would be difficult, but with effort he could keep up with those who had been at Brown for one year. His examiners, no doubt, thought he could begin work on *Cicero de Oratore* and Caesar's *Commentaries*, as well as Homer's *Iliad* and *Longinus de Sublimitate*. Classes in geography, logic, public speaking, and geometry would complete his course work.

Joining the sophomore class, Mann found that half of his new associates were over twenty years old, but there were also a few his junior, including a lad of fifteen. All of his classmates would take the same curriculum, moving *en masse* through their required courses. Pedagogically, the horse and the ox were hitched to the same plow.[6] The limitations of this lock-step curriculum were compounded by antiquated methods of instruction. With the exception of the young Tristam Burges, all the professors were past their prime. When teaching, each planted himself firmly in his armchair at the head of the class and heard recitations. Each expected his students to repeat the exact contents of the textbook, including even obvious printer's mistakes. The teaching of foreign languages was largely a

---

[5] For an eyewitness account of an entrance examination conducted by Asa Messer, see William Stanley to Horace Mann, June 24, 1822, Mann MSS:MHS; the entrance requirements for Brown at the time of Mann's application were set down in *The Laws of Brown University*, p. 1, BUA.
[6] Ira Moore Barton, "Horace Mann, 1819," in *Memories of Brown*, pp. 41–42; Bronson, *History of Brown University*, pp. 102–103; and *Historical Catalogue of Brown University, 1764–1914* (Providence, 1914), pp. 125–127.

mechanical translating and parsing. Often instruction degenerated into a guessing contest between student and professor: the former attempted to prepare for class only on those days when he thought he would be called; by going through the class list in a random manner, the latter hoped to locate the culprits who had not done their assignments. Ostensibly, the students were learning the classical languages because these strengthened their minds and sharpened their powers of reasoning. Actually, in the Latin class, the bright young men often learned to get by with minimal preparation, clever guesses, and occasional cheating.[7]

Even instruction in geography followed the same pattern. Although most of Massachusetts was *terra incognita* to him and he knew little about the geography of the United States, Mann sat in class day after day and wrote into his fresh new copybook long lists of facts about ancient and exotic places. His first lesson consisted of fifty countries, each listed with its neighbors. Subsequent assignments circled the globe with columns of distant islands, bays, and gulfs. He even prepared a lesson on the ancient and modern names of rivers as well as their sources and destinations. These he was expected to memorize for some later recitation. Anything remotely resembling economic or social geography was not presented, and at no time was he required to draw his own maps of these places. The same was true of his geometry class. Working through the first six books of Euclid, he carefully copied each theorem with its standard textbook diagram.[8]

None of this he reported to his mother. Instead, his first letter home was a model of how to communicate very little while writing what the folks back in Franklin wanted to hear. He assured his mother that he could not succeed in his difficult task without the knowledge of her confidence and esteem. She should also understand that regardless of how pleasing his new life would be, he would find it an insufficient substitute "for the guardian care of a parent" and "the enjoyments that arise from the society of kindred and the fond endearments of a parental home." His classmates were "remarkable for their steadfastness" and "deeply engaged in study." Even what leisure he had was not wasted but spent thinking about his former "friends and connexions and in recounting the happy days . . . when . . . blest with their society." In a flourish of formality he

---

[7] Alvah Hovey, *Barnas Sears* (New York, 1902), pp. 13–14.
[8] Mann's geography copybook is dated October 1, 1816, and is in the Mann MSS:MHS.

concluded, "With sentiments of unalterable affection, I remain your friend." [9]

If Mann's assurances of "recounting the happy days" were little more than propaganda for the home front, his comments about hard work were not. Once at college he found himself in a new kind of routine which made great demands upon him. He must attend classes and meals punctually. He must study at certain hours and converse only in Latin at designated times. To forget to greet a faculty member or upperclassman properly could bring uncomfortable consequences. Attendance at morning prayers was required, and each morning a few students could always be seen hurrying to make it to the chapel before the bell stopped ringing and the doors were closed from inside. The bell, the calendar, and the college rulebook were now his new taskmasters.

Every other week, he was required to write an English composition. Usually less than a thousand words, these were expected to exhibit verbal facility rather than scholarship. Anxious to satisfy his professors, the boy who until recently had been plowing his father's fields found himself expressing opinions on such diverse subjects as the national university, the love of fame, the danger of fiction, the separation of church and state, immigration, self-improvement, natural history, and God. Political topics seemed to be his favorite, but he also indicated an interest in literature and science. He avoided theology, preferring to write about toleration, morality, and patriotism.[1]

In these compositions, the incipient author was concerned with style and form rather than substance. In place of analytical discourse, his writings concentrated on eloquence and rhetoric. Regardless of the size or complexity of his topic, he always managed to deal with it within the rigid limits of two sides of a legal-sized sheet of paper. That his subject might be too large to fit into such an artificial Procrustean bed was not foremost in his mind. Filling the page, presenting it on time, and receiving the approbation of his professor were. The emergent optimistic republicanism and religious liberalism which his compositions revealed were serendipitous rather than intentional results, as he concentrated on learning to use the written word as a means of exhortation and persuasion. He

[9] Mann to Mrs. Thomas Mann, September 25, 1816, Mann MSS:MHS.
[1] More than thirty of these are in the Mann MSS:MHS; Mann came close to a genuine theological discussion in his essay dated November 20, 1818, in which he discussed differing interpretations of God.

solved thorny issues and confirmed ambiguous generalizations more by formal logic than factual research, and he used a sizable portion of his space to close each essay with a moralistic or didactic conclusion. Ethical mandates were more important than the clarification of ideas.

Both the strengths and weaknesses of instruction at Brown during this period are present in these essays. Mann's instruction emphasized a foundation of formal grammar and logic upon which he could build a superstructure of literary style amply ornamented with similes and metaphors. He was preparing to become a leader, and fundamental to the art of leading others were eloquence, polish, and inspiration. Because of his growing facility with words, Mann was soon writing with an assumed authority on a wide range of topics. He attacked English reviewers who criticized American literature, without mentioning a single critic by name nor a specific American object of criticism. He denounced fiction as dangerous to the public morals without naming a single novel he thought harmful, nor specifying any evidence of an individual or group actually having been wronged.[2] Ignoring even the meager geographical data in his copybook, he accomplished the remarkable achievement of discussing the Congress of Vienna without mentioning a single man, treaty, boundary, or economic consideration. Instead, what he put to paper was an uninformed wholesale denunciation of foreign despots who were evil by nature and therefore incapable of constructive acts. Other essays proclaimed the same themes of self-righteous republicanism and Christianity. Only the choice of topics was subject to variation. Consistently he wrote as if knowledge were static and in the safekeeping of himself and a small enlightened élite who lived in a benighted, evil world. In a sense, at Brown he was learning a secular version of the parochial superiority and exclusiveness which he had first learned from his catechism in Franklin.

Mechanical recitations and hortatory compositions his professors justified on the strength that these ordered and refined the minds of the rough-hewn farm boys who entered college each year. Unfortunately, in doing this, they subordinated the inherent values to be derived from a study of the classics to the more dubious goal of mental discipline. Rather than "liberalizing" his mind, the Brown curriculum limited Mann's perspective and channeled his mental energies to-

[2] For example, see his essay, "The Role of the Critic," November 27, 1818, and two untitled essays dated October 7 and November 22, 1817, in the Mann MSS:MHS.

wards polemical instead of intellectual ends. Avidly interested in a broad range of contemporary affairs, the young Mann was unable to appreciate, much less analyze, the complex political, religious, or social problems which they contained. Most likely his reports of hard work and almost constant study were not exaggerations, yet he only checked out a few books from the library during his entire undergraduate career.[3] The wasted effort in perfecting form and style at the expense of substance was unfortunate, but it could prove to be a far greater, perhaps even tragic, misfortune that Brown and her sister institutions were training an entire generation of future leaders who would place unwarranted faith in the power of the spoken and written word to deal with problems raised by westward expansion and the rise of the factory. Learning to write and think in this manner neither "liberated" nor "strengthened" the mind of the young Horace Mann; but it did give him a deceptive sense of competence and a false belief, endemic in the halls of the academes, that real problems could be resolved through pronouncements from the rostrum, pulpit, and printing press, rather than through the use of hard facts, tested empirically and applied systematically by process of trial and error.

The intellectual abuses in such training were patent in Mann's most spirited undergraduate writings, his political essays. With unmitigated chauvinism, he pictured European nations as hopelessly decadent, ruled by corrupt monarchs who stayed in power and kept their subjects under control only by maintaining a covert alliance with a degraded clergy and their leader in Rome, "the vice-regent of hell." By comparison, the United States was a model of virtue and innocence, soon to surpass the glories of Greece and Rome. Moreover, it was now prepared to lead so that others might follow. The people of Latin America were eager to embrace republicanism and the peoples of Europe were soon to rise and overthrow their political and religious oppressors. Reserving his warmest encomiums for the

---

[3] Brown University Library, Record of Books Borrowed by Undergraduates, 1814–1819, MS in BUA, lists the following entries under Mann's name: March 1, 1817, *Hume's History of England;* April 12 and 26, 1817, *French Revolution: Buchanan's Researches;* April 17, 1818, *Jefferson's Notes* [on Virginia?]; April 24, 1818, *Pope's Works;* August 20, 1818, *Reid's Works;* October [?], 1818, *Gray's Poems* and *Beauties of Shakespeare;* December 11, 1818, *Curray's Speeches;* December 19, 1818, *Johnson's Lives;* February 27, 1819, *Alison on Taste;* March 12, 1819, Adam Smith, *Wealth of Nations;* March 30, 1819, *Shakespeare,* Vol. V; April 9, 1819, *Johnson's Lives;* April 23, 1819, *Adventurer;* June 25, 1819, *Campbell on Miracles.*

"founding fathers," Mann insisted that the wisdom of Franklin and Washington approached omniscience. Perhaps a fear of professorial reprisal prevented him from including Jefferson, but Mann's ideas on primogeniture, a natural aristocracy, religious toleration, and the freedom of the press were all similar to those advanced by Jefferson.[4]

Understandably, the mechanical and monotonous instruction did little to narrow the generational gulf between faculty and students. Several years prior to Mann's arrival, an anonymous correspondent, "Alumnus Brunensis," had emphasized the poor relations existing between the two groups. In a series of letters to the Board of Trustees, he claimed that the faculty and students viewed each other as "hostile camps" and that anyone friendly with the "enemy" was considered a "traitor." [5]

Fortunately, most of the hostility the students had for their professors was siphoned off in the form of good-natured horseplay. Life in close quarters, uninspiring classes, and the absence of organized athletics which could release some of the students' pent-up energies were the reagents for endless pranks, some directed towards the faculty. There was always something hatching, but when Mann returned late from spring vacation to begin a new semester, he found things almost out of hand. To maintain control, the faculty severely disciplined several students and warned others.[6] Several months later Mann described a short-lived student rebellion in considerable detail. The Fourth of July was an important occasion at Brown, a sort of culminating point for all the patriotic feelings which had been expressed in various ways during the past year. This year the students felt the city fathers of Providence had not given them a sufficiently important part in the official town parade and speech-making. Therefore, they decided to hold a rump celebration. Speakers were elected from their ranks and a procession was formed. The fact that President Messer had denied their petition to use the college chapel seemed irrelevant at the moment. Ingenious hands opened the lock on the door and the triumphant band marched in to celebrate their independence. A silent observer in the affair, Mann was to be a prime instigator of a repeat performance the next year. Then, through the

---

[4] See especially his essays dated July 15 and 18, 1817, both entitled "Government," and others dated March 27 and June 19, 1818, in the Mann MSS:MHS.

[5] Alumnus Brunensis [James Burrill], *Letter to the Corporation of Brown University, Suggesting Certain Improvements in Its Academical System* (n.p., 1815), p. 9.

[6] Mann to Mrs. Thomas Mann, March 24, 1817, Mann MSS:MHS.

electioneering efforts of his friends, he was chosen the main orator of the day and therefore had a vested interest in breaking the rules. Once again the clandestine procession formed, and once again the security of the chapel door gave way to the students bent upon entry. Experiencing the glory of being cast into the role of leader by one's peers, Mann "delivered his oration amidst great applause," according to one of his classmates. He savored his moment of triumph and was ready to take the consequences, in this case a token fine imposed by President Messer. While losing no credit with the faculty, he had managed to elevate himself in the eyes of his classmates.[7]

Other pranks were more individualistic and forced the faculty and neighbors ever to be on the alert. Nearby henhouses were raided when portions became diminished at commons, and the plunder was picked, cleaned, and then roasted in the open fireplaces in the students' rooms. One cold December night, the entire student body was roused from its sleep by the smell of smoke and shouts of fire. The steward's outhouse was going up in flames, and from there the fire spread to several haystacks in the college yard. Asa Messer's letter to more than one parent the following week made it plain that he did not believe the blaze had been caused by spontaneous combustion. Samuel Gridley Howe, later to become Mann's closest co-worker in many reforms, was involved in a number of escapades. Once he filled his tutor's bed with ashes. He also performed the more remarkable feat of leading President Messer's horse up the stairs of University Hall. At the appropriate time, the bewildered animal stuck its head out a window and whinnied at its surprised master who happened by. At another time a farmer's wood sled was dismantled, carried to the roof of University Hall, and reassembled. Messer's horse also put in an impromptu appearance at a junior exhibition sporting the freshly painted letters "A.M." on its flanks. All these seasoned an otherwise monotonous fare.[8]

Asa Messer could be envied by his counterparts on other campuses during this period, however. By comparison with other col-

---

[7] Mann to Mrs. Thomas Mann, July 16, 1817; Ira Moore Barton to Mary Mann, December 4, 1863, both in Mann MSS:MHS; Barton, "Horace Mann 1819," *Memories of Brown*, pp. 41–42; the MS of Mann's speech is in the Mann MSS:MHS.

[8] Asa Messer to Amos Binney, Esq., December 18, 1817; Asa Messer to Joseph Howe, March 12, 1819, both in the Brown University—President, Letterbooks, 1811–1836, MS in BUA; *Journals and Letters of Samuel Gridley Howe*, I, 15–16; George B. Peck, "College Pranks in the Early Twenties," in *Memories of Brown*, pp. 46–48.

leges, Brown was a model of decorum. Harvard had a complete student revolt in 1807. In 1819, a Yale student rebellion rocked the New Haven community, and in 1828, while faculty members were announcing the merits of the "furniture of the mind," the sons of Eli were getting ready to put furniture of a different sort to novel uses, as the town folk activated a piece of ancient artillery and prepared to march on the campus. From 1800 to 1830, Princeton had no less than six formidable disturbances; half of the student body was sent home in 1816. Indeed, when Mann wrote to his mother that his classmates were noted for their "sobriety," relatively speaking, he was correct. Even George Fisher, a devout and orthodox Trinitarian and ever watchful of a lapse in the religious life at the college, conceded that "with respect to the general character of the college, it is comparatively speaking good. There are very few dissipated characters among us." [9]

Believing themselves perched atop a series of potential revolutions, the faculty and trustees of Brown created a blanket of rules to cover every offense. The basic fabric of their code came from the Yale College laws of 1745.[1] Upon this the professors embroidered an intricate network of special regulations pertaining to their own campus. By the time Mann was at college, there was a rule for almost everything. "All students are strictly forbidden to make indecent noises in the college at any time, either by running violently, or halloing, or rolling things in the entries, or down stairs," read one of the rules included under the general heading "Criminal Offenses." It was also illegal to speak with a roommate during study hours other than in Latin. To be in the chapel without permission was strictly forbidden. As part of their service *in loco parentis*, the faculty, especially the tutors, kept a close eye upon dormitory life. Students were constantly subjected to unscheduled inspection tours, heralded by noth-

[9] Mann to Mrs. Thomas Mann, September 25, 1816, Mann MSS:MHS; George Fisher to the alumni of Brown University Praying Society at the Andover Theological Seminary, November 11, 1817, MS in 1816–1819 folder, Brown University—Religious Society, BUA; Bernard Christian Steiner, *History of Education in Connecticut* (Washington, D.C., 1893), pp. 162–164; John Maclean, *History of the College of New Jersey* (Philadelphia, 1877), II, 72, 154, 167–168, 253, and 268; Sheldon, *Student Life*, pp. 108–112.
[1] For a selection from these laws, see Richard Hofstadter and Wilson Smith, eds., *American Higher Education, A Documentary History* (Chicago, 1961), I, 54–61.

ing more than a stamp of the tutor's foot or the tap of his white-headed cane on the door of their room.[2]

Having categorized so many offenses and believing the punishment should fit the crime, the faculty had also pieced together an all-embracing catalogue of penalties. Infractions were covered by a sliding scale, beginning with a few cents for the most picayune misdeed. Students were sconced for being away from their desks during the study period. It cost them money to turn in their assignments late. To elicit the laughter of the audience while giving a declamation cost the unlucky speaker 16 cents, while insubordination in the classroom not only drew down the wrath of Asa Messer, but also resulted in a bill for $4.[3] This imposition of fines was but part of a larger scheme in which the college authorities considered themselves to be perpetuating the close parental supervision of the home. That Asa Messer took his role as "surrogate father" seriously is evident from his correspondence with worried parents.

In dealing with Mann, however, a direct fatherly admonition was enough. With some students, even stiffer measures than fines and letters were necessary. For the chronic but not hopeless offender, the faculty resorted to rustication, a common form of discipline which was all that its name implied. After having tried other measures, President Messer would banish an obstinate culprit to a rural parsonage. Here, under the watchful and corrective eye of a country divine, the student was tutored in his courses and supposedly given the additional parental guidance necessary to help him to curb his less than constructive impulses. Messer had come to rely on several ministers for regular assistance. The Reverend Jacob Ide, son-in-law of Nathanael Emmons, took a number of "hardened offenders," including Amos Binney, one of the outhouse burners.[4]

In general, Mann himself kept out of trouble and showed little inclination to question the system of rules and penalties. After several classmates had been rusticated, his reaction was simply one of hope that the general atmosphere at college would improve and that

---

[2] *Laws of Brown University*, 1803, p. 7.
[3] Asa Messer to Simeon Daggett, May 19, 1819, Brown University—President, Letterbooks, 1811–1836, MS in BUA; see also Bronson, *History of Brown*, pp. 184–186.
[4] Asa Messer to Amos Binney, Esq., December 18, 1817, Brown University—President, Letterbooks, 1811–1836, MS in BUA; Bronson, *History of Brown*, pp. 183–184.

"with good fortune and strict adherence to 'steady old habits,' " he hoped to avoid the same treatment. With Samuel Gridley Howe, on the other hand, the fear of punishment did little to dampen his enthusiasm for one escapade after another. Finally, trying Messer's patience to the limit, he was sent out to pasture accompanied with the following note:

The bearer is Samuel Howe, a member of our Sophomore Class. We wish to put him under your instruction, and hope to keep him there until the first of next August.

And Messer added that if Howe wanted to return, he must study even during the spring vacation.[5]

The wide use of rustication as a means of discipline cannot be explained solely in terms of the reputedly salutary influence of rural seclusion. Clearly, from the faculty's point of view, whether admitted officially or not, life could be a good deal more peaceful on the campus without some of the more energetic students. From the students' point of view, also, rustication was no mean penalty. As class spirit was high at Brown, to be declared persona non grata and banished to the hills was a punishment to be avoided at all possible costs. Nevertheless, the numerous letters of rustication in the president's letterbook were impressive testimony that the problem of poor discipline was caused by factors too central to the overall scheme of education at Brown to be resolved by an occasional eviction.

How often this punishment was invoked was largely up to Asa Messer, who served as the chief disciplinary officer of the college. With the plethora of picayune rules available, it was possible to convict a student at almost every turn, and it evolved upon the president to know when it was in the interest of the college and the student to overlook a misdemeanor. Common sense dictated that he would deal one way with a boy of sixteen and another way with a young man of twenty-five. Rarely erring in his judgment of young men, Messer was quick to distinguish between transient weaknesses and incorrigibility. Yet he was not considered a great president by his colleagues or his students. Teaching in an age of elegance, they considered his language "altogether unpoetical . . . naked, plain and strong." In ad-

---

[5] Mann to Mrs. Thomas Mann, March 24, 1817, Mann MSS:MHS; Asa Messer to Reverend M. Wheaton, March 12, 1819, Brown University—President, Letterbooks, 1811–1836, MS in BUA.

dition, he was utterly lacking in charisma, and rather than inspiring awe, his physical appearance invited caricature.[6]

* * *

If discipline was one acknowledged avenue through which old-time college presidents reached their students, another was their course in moral philosophy, usually reserved for the senior class. Through their lectures, by instructing countless admiring students in the art of dealing with political and economic problems according to some overarching system of morality, more than anything else they did, presidents like Francis Wayland and Mark Hopkins created and sustained their Olympic reputations. Each man based his lectures on the premise that God, the omnipotent and omniscient creator, was the prime mover of a harmonious moral and physical universe which operated according to His fixed and immutable laws. But Asa Messer was no Mark Hopkins. Not only was his teaching limited mainly to science and mathematics, but if anything, he taught the very opposite of a closed moral system, urging his students to enquire further into the unanswered questions of religion, science, and morality. By his choice of colleges then, Mann was forced to learn his moral philosophy from the text, probably William Paley's *Principles of Moral and Political Philosophy*. At Brown, he would not be able to sit at the feet of some awe-inspiring oracle, later canonized by a generation of devoted students, who could explicate the application of the laws of God to human events. At Brown, the Olympic rostrum and one end of the log had been vacant.[7]

The other end certainly was not. Students at Brown more than made up for the lack of a Mark Hopkins and brought a vitality and variety of their own making to the college no faculty curriculum com-

[6] The quotations are from Barnas Sears, "Historical Discourse," *Celebration of the One Hundredth Anniversary of the Founding of Brown University* (Providence, 1865), pp. 44–46; *Brown University Under the Presidency of Asa Messer, S.T.D., LL.D.*; Francis Wayland, *A Memoir of the Life and Labors of the Rev. Adoniram Judson, D.D.* (Boston, 1853), I, 15; for a most abusive account of Messer, see the diary of Lincoln Fairfield, *New York Mirror,* IV, June 30, 1827, pp. 385–386.

[7] For informative discussions of the college president as moral philosopher, see George P. Schmidt, *The Old Time College President* (New York, 1930), especially pp. 79–89; Wilson Smith, *Professors and Public Ethics* (Ithaca, 1956), pp. 1–43; for descriptions of Messer as a teacher, see Alvah Hovey, *Barnas Sears,* pp. 13–14, and Sidney Williams to Caroline and Charlotte Messer, January 1, 1830, Mann-Messer MSS: BUA.

mittee would ever devise. This was most evident in the area of public speaking where Mann exploited every opportunity to learn both within and outside the classroom. A meager press, few amusements, and the high cost of books all had encouraged the development of sermons and political speeches as more indigenous and accessible forms of communication. Fortunately for him, the college had recently appointed Tristam Burges as "Professor of Oratory and Belles Lettres." Believing that the future orator learned to speak by speaking, Burges took on the exhausting task of listening patiently to dozens of declamations delivered from the chapel pulpit, his schedule building up near the end of each semester when he heard and criticized thirty student speeches in a single day.[8]

All this led up to one of the high points of the academic year, the annual class exhibitions. These were major social events as well, and one of the few times during the year when the college descended into Providence. In April and August the sophomores and juniors cooperated in two programs while the seniors demonstrated their forensic powers to the outside world each December. Held in the Old Town House, the exhibitions required elaborate preparations, often miraculously financed by a minimum of hard cash. Tickets were sold, programs printed, buntings draped, and candles lit. Borrowed curtains hung in front of the pulpit to conceal the nervous waiting performers. First they had vied with each other in class for the place on the program. Now, some of them exhibited all the symptoms of stage fright, shaking like leaves in the knowledge they were soon to stand exposed to their classmates, professors, and many blushing young maidens from the community. By ones and twos they mounted the podium as a master of ceremonies moved down the list with the methodicalness of an executioner.[9] Not that all the presentations were of a serious nature. At one exhibition, two students debated the socially significant question, "Ought those who are old bachelors by choice support those, who are old maids from necessity?" Nor was

---

[8] Brown boasted of its success in training orators. See Romeo Elton, *The Literary Remains of the Rev. Jonathan Maxcy with a Memoir of His Life* (New York, 1844), pp. 14–16; Bronson, *History of Brown*, pp. 168–169; Nicholas Brown's donation of $5,000 which earned him the right to rename the college was used to endow the professorship of oratory and belles lettres.

[9] N.a., "Exhibitions in the Old Town House," Memories of Brown, pp. 35–37; his first year at Brown, Mann gained a place on the program, reciting "A Poem" in which he labored the obvious describing the similarity between the seasons and a man's life, April 18, 1817, MS in Mann MSS:MHS.

the success of the event determined solely by the quality of the performances. In the afternoon, before the junior exhibition in 1818, a
late winter storm immobilized Providence, keeping most of the prospective audience at home. Nevertheless, Mann and his classmates
decided the show must go on. "It was but half an exhibition," he reported later to his sister in good-humored disappointment, "a whole
one consists not only of the students in the College, but the ladies in
the town, the first displaying talents, learning, & etc. and the last
their dress, beauty & etc." An exhibition it had been, but as far as he
was concerned, it was *"a feast without the trimmings."* [1]

The following August, the weather cooperated and Mann had a
full house for his first major speech at an exhibition. Choosing "The
American Navy" for his subject, he threw historical accuracy to the
winds and delivered a patriotic diatribe emblazoned with star-span-
gled prose. Other nations might misuse a powerful navy, but under
an enlightened American government, it would ever be a force for
justice and peace. American warships had traveled to the Mediter-
ranean and punished "African Pirates" there. This, however, was but
a whiff of grapeshot compared with the terrible beating the United
States had given the proud British navy in the War of 1812, an event
which surely heralded the beginning of the end for the British Empire. Virtuous republicanism was challenging European colonialism
with the outcome foreordained. The burning of the national capitol,
the routing of American militia in battle after battle, and the British
navy's stranglehold on American ports were all conveniently forgotten as Mann reached his oratorical climax. In a nationalistic gasco-
nade, the incipient orator and reformer concluded:

These achievements of the gallant living and the illustrious dead have
opened to our country another sphere of pre-eminence. Our infant
armies had before repelled the invading legions of Britain and her
hirelings; our Statesmen had before concentrated the wisdom of the
ages, in framing a government, wise harmonious, dispensing individual
happiness and securing national honor; our artists before had converted
into utility the raging fury of hostile elements; our Franklins before had
curbed the thunder of heaven; but the lightnings of our naval authority
have now light [*sic*] up the funeral pyre of British supremacy, and
America now wields the trident of Neptune.[2]

---

[1] "Exhibition in College Chapel . . . Order of Exercises," April 20,
1803, in Brown University—Programs of Junior and Senior Exhibitions,
Exercises, 1790–1881, in BUA; Mann to [Lydia Mann], April 23, [1818],
Mann MSS:MHS.
[2] August 9, 1818, Mann MSS:MHS.

In later years, the oratorical achievements of Brown alumni prompted observers to refer to this earlier period as "the golden age of forensic oratory for Rhode Island." Mann was fortunate to have had Tristam Burges, a professor willing to listen to thirty speeches in one day, and always demanding the best from his students. To have had such a training was to prepare for membership in a select group of clergymen, missionaries, lawyers, and legislators, all who would go on to lead and persuade through the spoken word.[3]

*   *   *

Important though formal training in public speaking and the exhibitions were in the life of the student, an activity more removed from the classroom and the chapel could claim even more credit for shaping the young Horace Mann. Given a modicum of freedom, Mann and his classmates made the most of it, and organized an impressive extracurricular activity known as the literary and debating society. At Brown, two organizations had sprung to life, the Philermenians and the United Brothers. The Philermenians orginated in the 1790's with an ardently Federalist membership. Their counterpart, the United Brothers, formed in 1806 for the purpose of defending Thomas Jefferson and his party. Benefitting from the rise of partisan politics with the presidency of Jefferson, these two organizations developed elaborate programs of speaking and *disputatum*.[4]

Satisfied that he met their political and social standards, the United Brothers invited Horace Mann to join their select ranks on Washington's birthday, 1817. A month later he signed their constitution, a document which began with the words: "Social intercourse is highly valuable, both, as it respects our happiness, and improvement in life." The constitution outlined the parliamentary procedures by which the Brothers conducted their bi-weekly meetings. Similar to the discipline they knew in other aspects of campus life, the members devised a scale of fines for the violation of society rules. Absences without written consent were fined 12½ cents and it cost an over-zealous member 12 cents for not heeding the president when called to order. Through its constitution, the society reinforced college dis-

---

[3] For a general description of the "golden age of oratory," see Charles Evans Hughes, "Historical Address," *Sesquicentennial of Brown University, 1764–1914* (Providence, 1915), pp. 174–177.

[4] Sheldon, *College Student Life*, pp. 126–137; for a description of the activities at Brown, see Bronson, *History of Brown*, pp. 181–182.

cipline by suspending members who were rusticated. Once suspended, a Brother remained so until President Messer recommended his reinstatement.[5]

A student at Brown joined the Brothers for two reasons. One was social. Since the barracks-like dormitories in University Hall and the regimented schedule were not conducive to fellowship, the debating society provided a welcome channel for conviviality. To be a member was to belong to the college élite, to exploit one's political and social skills, and to ascend within the student hierarchy.

The second reason was the sheer joy which came from debating. When all nonessentials were stripped away, the heart of the Brothers' activity was their deliberation on contemporary issues. At the time, Congress had no more elaborate measures for handling its business than those taken by the Brothers in carrying out their activities. An elected committee presented questions which were argued by six members, three pro and three con. Names were drawn from the club roster in alphabetical order. During the year, members were assigned equal numbers of affirmative and negative positions. The work of the committees and officers was subject to review by the entire membership, who were ready to assert the authority of the majority when they deemed it necessary. The debates were often lively affairs and the discussions which followed even more so. High points in Mann's first year included such topics as "Is the ascendancy of England more to be deprecated by the nations of Europe than of Russia?" "No"; "Is a monarchical form of Government preferable to a Republican one?" "Unanimously no"; "Have the Protestants of Europe a right to combine to destroy the Inquisition?" ". . . decided in the affirmative by a respectable majority." Once within the group, Mann did not have long to wait to take his place on the firing line. The first topic he drew was on the expedience of military schools. His team won. Four months later, he argued with effectiveness, if not total conviction, that the profession of law was not more conducive to acquiring general knowledge than the profession of divinity. Again he was on the winning side.[6]

He took satisfaction too from being elected to the post of second librarian, the lowliest position in the hierarchy of officers. The Brothers also voted "to compromise with Mr. Mann for his room as a society room during the present quarter, for two dollars and fifty

---

[5] Records of the United Brothers Society, Vol. I, MS in BUA.

[6] *Ibid.*, March 22, June 27, and October 11, 1817; April 4 and 11, May 9, June 20, July 11, and October 3, 1818, and June 18, 1819.

cents." Since cash was never in ample supply, he was "compromised" and Room 30 in University Hall became the society headquarters for the next term. He accepted his assignments on committees, including those for cataloguing books, selecting topics for debates, and proposing new members. By the end of the first year as a Brother, Mann had moved up to the position of secretary and from November 29, 1817, he kept the minutes of the United Brothers in a neat and moderately ornate hand. The following year his efforts were further rewarded when he was elected vice-president and finally president of the society.[7]

Only one post within the organization remained for him to claim. The highest honor the brethren bestowed was the designation as their official lecturer for the year. Mann won this award near the end of his junior year, and he had six months to prepare for his performance. Other responsibilities had to be met, but the need to acquit himself with honor in the eyes of his peers preoccupied his mind the first half of his senior year. Mann's preparations included a trip to Christopher Spencer's tailor shop in Providence where he ordered a suit made which cost him nearly $30. When the date for his presentation arrived, he stood up before his audience dressed in his new broadcloth coat and pantaloons, ready to deliver his grandiloquent piece. Appropriate to the occasion, Mann chose for his topic the need for eloquence in a republic, a subject which must have been dear to all those assembled. Running down a list of renowned orators, he described their contributions to civilization. With the aid of flatulent prose, vivid metaphors, and a strong sense of conviction, he was able to conceal an almost total lack of germane ideas and factual content from his audience. The actual themes treated by great orators he ignored, and only vaguely did he refer to the causal relation between their spoken word and the deeds and beliefs of the men who heard them. His audience could not have cared less.[8]

To support their extensive debating programs, both the Philermenians and the United Brothers had accumulated large collections of books. At a time when the college library was loaded down with bound sermons and theological treatises, the libraries of the societies contained more current titles. The United Brothers' holdings included novels, poetry, travelogues, history, and classical authors, besides the

---

[7] *Ibid.*, May 3 and June 21, 1817, and August 13 and November 7, 1818.
[8] "Lecture Delivered before the U. Brothers Society," March 10, 1819, Mann MSS:MHS.

ever-present works on religion. The catalogue of the society ran from *Abbess*, a novel by W. H. Ireland in three volumes, to *Zimmerman on Solitude*, a one-volume work, and listed some 1,400 volumes. At the same time, the rival Philermenians claimed an even larger collection. Thus the combined holdings of the two societies almost equaled the total college library. These collections continued to grow. By 1840, each society had more than 3,000 volumes. Yet in Mann's time, while the members were assessing themselves to increase their libraries, alumni pleaded in vain with the trustees of Brown to do the same for the college library.[9]

Strange though it seems, the professors took little interest in these extracurricular activities. Clearly the societies were achieving some of the aims of a liberal education, but the faculty remained largely indifferent to their accomplishments and at no time gave them material support. Thus the organizations worked under several handicaps. The specter of insolvency hovered over many a meeting. Moreover, the faculty did not even provide the societies with the minimal arrangements necessary for their activities. At the same meeting at which Mann was elected to membership, a committee of the Brothers studied the possibility of getting a permanent meeting room. Four months later, they were "compromising" with Mann, indicating that nothing had come of their previous efforts. During his years at Brown, the society led a nomadic existence, using one or another student's room for its headquarters. It would require another decade before the faculty finally acknowledged the contribution of the debating societies and recognized them as more than a "bootlegged" educational undertaking.[1]

Ironically, it was only after faculties began to recognize the contributions of these organizations to a liberal education that others began to point out some of their shortcomings. Learning how to think and speak on one's feet was not an unmixed blessing. To "think on one's feet" could be only the partial means to dealing with complex problems; the greater part of hard thinking should have preceded this. Sophistry and euphony pre-empted careful research and analysis

[9] *Catalogue of the Books in the Library of the United Brothers Society, Together with the Names of its Members* (Brown University, 1821); Records of the U. B. Society, Vol. I, June 14, August 8, and September 29, 1817; Bronson, *History of Brown*, p. 180; William Howe Tolman, *History of Higher Education in Rhode Island* (Washington, D.C., 1894), p. 198; Alumnus Brunensis, Letter to . . . Brown University, p. 11.
[1] Records of the U. B. Society, Vol. I, March 4, October 4 and 18, 1817, and March 28, 1819.

as the means of settling issues. To think on one's feet was to defend rather than avoid mistakes, to construct a plausible argument rather than a workable solution. To win the debate was not to resolve, much less remove the problem. The parliamentary procedures and speeches were mock democratic practice, but they lacked a crucial element, viz. responsibility for the consequences which followed the making of a decision. In debating it was more important to win than to establish truth or take effective action.[2]

In this limitation, the students were the victims of the system. In the final analyis, debating, aside from the students' strong motivation for it, was similar to writing class compositions. In both cases, the students neither appreciated the complexity of the problems with which they were dealing nor understood the methods by which they might be approached. Mann won his debate on the value of military schools, but his essay on the same subject exhibited a blissful ignorance and naïveté. Only after graduation would he perceive some of the limitations of his education and agree with a classmate who lamented that at Brown he had "never had so much as a peep at the genitals of originality," and therefore did not understand by what "instruments" ideas were conceived.[3]

No sooner had he entered Brown than the young Mann set his sights on a higher objective than mere graduation. For the next three years, many of his actions were calculated to win the distinction of being named the class valedictorian. Many students believed that in recent years the most able candidates among them had been passed over in favor of the sons of prominent and wealthy Providence families, and this made him more anxious about his own prospects. The fact that George Fisher and several other bright and eager country lads were vying for the prize also gave him little rest. Believing he "had none of those adventitious aids of wealth and powerful connections which so often . . . supply the deficiencies of merit," he compensated by making every effort to be first in his class, even though this meant, according to one of his associates, that he was severely limiting the number of friends he would make in college. Increasingly, as the competition became more intense by the senior year and always unsure of his standing with the faculty, Mann pulled himself

---

[2] *Brown Under Messer,* pp. 18–19, contains favorable comments about the debating societies. For a searching criticism of their value, see Charles Astor Bristed, *Five Years in an English University* (New York, 1873), pp. 461–475.

[3] James S. Holmes to Mann, April 7, 1821, Mann MSS:MHS.

away from his chums' whist games and returned to his desk. There, keeping his lamp burning well into the early morning hours, he rarely drew his eyes from his books, other than to rub the red marks on his forehead where his green eyeshade had dug it. More than pride spurred him on in the competition. Since his family lacked influential relatives and friends in Boston or New York City, he had no patron to launch him into business or a profession. His main assets would be his record at Brown and the fraternal help he might receive from some former member of the United Brothers. To lead his class and be its valedictorian would be the best credentials he could carry with him as he descended from the high ground of the campus to the world of business and law.[4]

In December 1818, he received the first indication that he was in the lead for the honor. The faculty designated him to give the major oration at the senior exhibition. For the occasion he chose the Congress of Vienna, a subject upon which he had previously written. The exhibition was held on New Year's Eve, and when it came to his turn on the program, Mann was ready with a scathing attack on the decadency of Europe. Once again, he claimed, European diplomats were up to their old tricks of thwarting the wishes of the common people. "Centuries of Papal despotism and civil tyranny" had caused innumerable human beings to sink into the "abyss of ignorance and turpitude," only to be followed by thousands more who were sacrificed to "the Corsican Moloch." Why then create this "perfidious coalition to restore the institutions of her calamities, her infamy, and her disgrace; to bring back the feudal vassalage; to sow again the seeds from which she reaped so plenteous a harvest of carnage and desolation and to repeople the courts of the Inquisition . . . ?" For Mann the simple answer to this was easily found in the unregenerate greed for power and wealth of rulers busy shoring up their tottering regimes. Mann, the collegiate warhawk, was too late to fight on Lake Erie or at New Orleans with fire and gunpowder. Whether the pen was mightier than the sword was an irrelevant question at the time. For him and his generation, still bent on political revolution, it was the only means available.[5]

His next laurels came from his senior oration before the United

---

[4] James S. Holmes to Mann, November 14, 1819, Mann MSS: MHS; Mann to Charlotte Messer, September 15, 1830, Mann-Messer MSS: BUA.
[5] Mann, "The Congress of Vienna," December 30, 1817, Mann MSS: MHS; a program for this exhibition is in the BUA.

Brothers where he "acquitted himself with honor." By the last Wednesday before the spring vacation, he had finished his language examinations. The holiday gave him an opportunity to speak with Josiah J. Fiske, an attorney in Wrentham and a former member of the United Brothers. Fiske agreed to accept Mann as his protégé and put him to work in his office after graduation. Back on campus in May, Mann was selected to give the oration at the banquet which came at the end of senior examination week. Since his class was soon to move out into the world, he spoke on the social responsibilities incumbent upon educated men. Unconvinced that former alumni had repaid society for the benefits of their education, he now argued that his classmates should set the account straight. Most ages achieved greatness through military conquests which left misery, not happiness, in their wake. His generation's contribution would be conquest through science. "The empire of reason has begun to be established," he claimed. And with this, the spirit of liberty would also advance. Unfortunately the pagan, the skeptic, the fanatic, and the bigot still held sway in many parts of the world, but educated men would yet annihilate these agents of suffering and servitude. Minerva would finally win over Mars for the loyalties of men. The millennium was at hand.[6]

While advancing his own cause the last semester, Mann could not forget his responsibilities for the annual anniversary program of the United Brothers which was held during the week of commencement. In costs alone this was no mean undertaking. Once the First Baptist Meeting House was reserved, the Brothers circulated invitations to former members, and negotiated with the Taunton Band if its services could be had for no more than $30. They also hired a constable, just in case of town rowdies, and a bellringer to get the program under way. Then on the last day in August, members and alumni congregated in the college chapel, formed ranks according to seniority, and marched into town, led by the Taunton Band which fortunately had been amenable to the fee of $30. While not the most objective of reporters, the society's secretary later recorded that the main orator had spoken with "eloquent elocution," "fervid imagination," and "patriotic sentiments," while the poet of the day had expressed "sentiments of exalted morality and fervent piety." By his

---

[6] Mann, "Oration Delivered at the Final Examination Dinner of the Senior Class, July 13, 1819," Mann MSS:MHS.

standards, the day was a success, and with a mixture of pride and relief, the members again formed ranks behind the band and paraded
back up to the campus.[7]

The next day was commencement. The endless hours of recitations, the poorly cooked meals, the constant financial worries, and
enforced study periods, all savored and made palatable by the fellowship of youth, were now about to end. For many a rough-edged farm
boy, commencement was the final act in the struggle from homespun
to parchment and membership in the ranks of the educated. Friends,
relatives, and alumni converged on the campus. By mid-morning, the
faculty prepared to take its place, the graduates fell in line, willing to
suppress their inclinations for mischief and play their part in the
pomp and ceremony of the day. The procession formed behind a
"select band of music," and once again wound its way towards the
First Baptist Meeting House. When all were seated within the building, President Messer opened the exercises with a long and elevated
invocation. Not known for his eloquence, upon these occasions he departed from the prosaic and pleaded that the graduates would become "most eminently useful and respectable; and having washed
their robes and made them white in the blood of the Lamb, may
they be fitted for the crown which fadeth not away. . . ." Seated
near the front of the meetinghouse, the harried tutors were probably
willing to concede that only an act of God would make these scoun-
drels take their place in society.[8]

The program finally under way, what followed was a series of
student presentations. Members of the senior class described the
search for truth in terms of a curious mixture of European rational-
ism and American evangelical Protestantism. The audience sat
through speeches on the "Decline of Infidelity," the "Value and Im-
mutability of Truth," and the "Influence of Curiosity." Taking an
earlier essay of Mann's, that eloquence was essential to freedom,
one of his classmates turned the topic on its head and spoke on "Freedom Essential to Eloquence." Ira Barton, Mann's roommate, discussed "Philosophy, the Only Permanent Basis of Political Institutions," while pious George Fisher, who had set his heart on becoming

[7] Records of the U. B. Society, Vol. I, May 14, 1818, and May 29,
August 21 and 31, 1819.
[8] Providence *Gazette,* September 4, 1819; for examples of Messer's commencement rhetoric, see Brown University—President, Letterbooks,
1811–1836, MS in BUA.

the class valedictorian, won the consolation prize and used the opportunity as salutatorian to demolish the teachings of "Modern Scepticism." The spirit of republicanism and parental pride demanded that as many students as possible have a part in the affair, and by noon the program had no more than arrived at midpoint. After adjourning for lunch, the audience returned to the meetinghouse. The afternoon brought forth more declamations, a poem, and a debate. All this finally out of the way, the moment for awarding the diplomas was at hand. One by one, the young men, proud but a little uncomfortable and self-conscious, stepped to the rostrum to receive their recognition. Only one thing now remained, the presentation of the valedictory, and Horace Mann, A.B., Brown University, Class of 1819, was ready to show why he had won the top honor of his class.[9]

Gone for the moment was his bitterness for the wasted hours braiding straw and the events which led to his break with Nathanael Emmons. Gone also was his memory of the frenetic last-minute preparations for Brown and the effort he had made to begin with the sophomore class. This was part of the remote past as all eyes centered on the young man from Franklin who stepped to the place of honor to speak on "The Gradual Advancement of the Human Species in Dignity and Happiness." In the last three years he had written and spoken of many things. Now was the time for him to present his *Weltanschauung*, a belief that man was involved in a gradual and inevitable process of perfectibility. Contrary to skeptical philosophers who argued that the pattern of civilization was cyclical, Mann insisted people would continue to rise on the scale of moral and intellectual accomplishment—war, famine, and superstition notwithstanding. Through the aid of science, his generation would surpass the accomplishments of Greece and Rome. Science, he claimed, had "amassed invention upon invention and crowned discovery with discovery, until it . . . scaled the very Olympus . . . and brought down the fire of truth from heaven." Science had gained ascendency and no corner of the globe could escape the spread of its enlightenment.

Yet is she to dart her vivifying glance into the recesses of Oriental darkness and liberate the sons of Brama, from their ancient inheritance of bondage. Yet, is she to stretch for the sceptre and smite the Mosque and the Pagoda, as she did the convent and the Vatican.

---

[9] "Program for the Commencement, 1819," in BUA; Ira Barton to Mary Mann, December 4, 1863, Mann MSS:MHS.

All that remained was for the philanthropist to make the supreme achievement and bring its benefits to all mankind.[1]

Following a benediction, the valedictorian and his classmates were dispatched officially to enter the society of men and employ the lessons they had learned in and out of the classroom. Somehow they had survived the countless recitations, compositions, and declamations, all so apparently necessary to provide a liberal education and mold Christian character. Although they were adults, they had lived under a faculty which took its responsibility to serve *in loco parentis* to the point of absurdity. Yet the experience had neither liberated them nor taught them how to seek truth systematically. Almost in self-defense, Mann and his classmates had contrived an auxiliary program—not always a complete success, but surely vital, resourceful, and capable of nurturing the beginnings of social responsibility. If the picayune restrictions and evangelical admonitions failed to effect a positive change in their values and attitudes, living among peers and creating their own standards had given them a sense of exclusiveness and *élan* which could serve as an educational rite of passage and an effective initiation into the ranks of college alumni. This was the impact Brown would have on the young Horace Mann. For him, the last three years had not been only an intellectual experience but also a socializing process. Where the classroom and the rulebook had failed, the debating society and the dormitory had, almost inadvertently, succeeded.

As the members of the Class of 1819 marched down the aisle and out of the First Baptist Meeting House, their thoughts were to the future and the opportunities it held for them. They had come to think of the world as the setting for a giant morality play and themselves as its leading actors, whose foreordained triumph over ignorance, poverty, and greed seemed just beyond their outstretched grasp. At the moment, they were unaware of possible weaknesses in their education. Only with the crucible of time would they separate the dross from true mettle.

---

[1] MS dated September 1, 1819, Mann MSS: MHS.

CHAPTER III

Rustication

═══════════

IF YOU ASK ME where the American aristocracy
is found, I have no hesitation in answering that
it is not among the rich, who have no common
link uniting them. It is at the bar or the bench
that the American aristocracy is found.
ALEXIS DE TOCQUEVILLE

────────

COMMENCEMENT WEEK involved more than oratory and celebrations; it also involved packing and final farewells. By the time of graduation, Mann's room held the accumulation of his years at Providence. Books, clothes, and a few mementos and letters made up the bulk of what he would take with him. Other things he handed down to appreciative underclassmen or simply discarded. His sorting and packing completed, he found himself in an empty room which, perhaps even more than his new diploma, presented the convincing proof that this part of his life was now at an end. The three years of college, his preparation for life, were over. Tomorrow had finally become today. After one last check of his empty desk drawers, he closed the door of Room 30 for the last time, walked down the long dormitory corridor, and passed out the entrance and down the front steps of University Hall. Outside, some of the new alumni of Brown bade each other good-bye, while teamsters and coach drivers helped load their chests and satchels on the waiting carriages and wagons. The graduates promised to write to each other, pledged eternal friendship, and exchanged optimistic predictions about their futures. Still, as they left the campus, one by one, each came away with mixed emotions. Flushed with the exhilaration of accomplishment, they also sensed a feeling of uncertainty of what actually lay before them.[1]

For Mann, who had learned to share his joys and disappointments with a small clique of classmates, severing ties with the group at University Hall was a bittersweet experience. Even prior to graduation, he had sensed the inevitable. It had been "pleasant to form connexions," he wrote to his mother, "but they must be broken." Now

──────────────

[1] James S. Holmes to Mann, October 6, 1819, Mann MSS:MHS.

54

anticipating the end of his college days, he brought himself to admit that "every moment of this pleasure is the herald of its own dissolution." Better to admit his ambivalence and then turn his thoughts toward the legal apprenticeship which awaited him in the office of Josiah J. Fiske.[2]

At first he attacked his new work with the same zeal he had exhibited on the Brown campus, but it soon became evident that the seemingly unsystematic reading of court rulings and the copying of tedious legal commentaries line by line in no way fulfilled his postgraduate expectations. To one who had thought of himself as a future leader of men, plodding through Blackstone looked like a detour to oblivion. This, however, was still more in keeping with his program of self-advancement than tending to the minor grievances and creditors' suits which were handed down to him from his busy mentor. Even to think of the discrepancy between the reality of Fiske's office and the chimerical world he described in his pre-commencement oratory must have been painful and demoralizing.[3]

Judging from the letters they now wrote, the Class of 1819 quickly became the class of disenchantment. Dismayed by the dull and seemingly crude life they found away from the campus, they soon exchanged numerous letters which offered eloquent testimony to the fact that misery loved company and self-pity required an audience. Previously, they had employed only the most elevated terms when they spoke of that grand abstraction, "the common American." Now as they confronted flesh-and-blood specimens of the genus *vulgaris americanus*, their opinions underwent a radical change. In vain did James Holmes attempt to square what he had learned at college with what he was encountering in Maine. "Everyone must feel," he wrote to Mann,

that leaving the select companions of a university for the compound and various society of the world he has a thousand inconveniences to encounter. The detractions of the environs, the insults of the vulgar, and the denounciations of a variety of sanctified opinionists are constantly disturbing that uniformity of life which he had formerly enjoyed, and require a double exertion of patience, vigilance, and discretion. Is not the independency of thought, which we learn to venerate so much in theory, and [are] accustomed to enjoy in study and retirement most seriously attacked when we come into the business of life? [4]

---

[2] Mann to Mrs. Thomas Mann, June 7, 1819, Mann MSS:MHS.
[3] Livingston, *Portrait Gallery*, III, 186.
[4] James S. Holmes to Mann, November 14, 1819, Mann MSS:MHS.

The trip from idealism to disillusionment for him had been a short one. In the brief span of two months, Holmes's Americans had changed from republicans into rabble. As Mann read the pages of one of his first letters after graduation, he could not help but recognize that Holmes, once an ardent Jeffersonian, was now looking at his world through the eyes of Hamilton. Gone was his youthful optimism and academic naïveté, and in its place he attempted to construct a worldly cynicism as he wrote to Mann that "The People, are a capricious multitude and decide their affairs with but little of the philosophy of distinction and discrimination." After searching the entire community, David Torrey, another classmate, found only four persons with whom he could discuss things intelligently. Little wonder that his thoughts continually returned "to those walls, which have so frequently resounded with the lyre of Orpheus, with the eloquence of Tully and with the thunder of Mars." [5]

At first, distance only strengthened the ties of friendship within the community of co-sufferers. "Neither lapse of time, nor distance of separation," Torrey assured Mann, "can alienate those attachments which I formed during residence in College." Increasingly, Mann's letters, and those of his classmates, dwelled upon the good times back at University Hall. The unpleasantness of the past was not mentioned. Also missing from their letters were discussions about their hopes for the future. Ironically, the much-awaited commencement had proved to be a form of permanent rustication. Commencement, as Holmes described it with his characteristic penchant for overstatement and sentimentality, meant "separating, perhaps eternally separating from any esteemed companions, 'endured by a thousand tender recollections.' " Like it or not, they had been rusticated. No longer able to rejoin their class, they depended upon letters of commiseration as one means of assuaging their growing sense of isolation. This in time proving altogether unsatisfactory, most of the Class of 1819, with the exception of Mann, contemplated a more radical solution to their loneliness, namely, matrimony.[6]

Although working but a short distance from home and many of his old friends, Mann was by no means immune to the loneliness and disillusionment which troubled his classmates. Three years at Brown

---

[5] David Torrey to Mann, January 28, 1820; Jarius Keith to Mann, March 18, 1820, all in Mann MSS:MHS.
[6] David Torrey to Mann, January 28, 1820; James S. Holmes to Mann, October 6, 1819, both in Mann MSS:MHS; for an example of matrimonial intentions, see E. S. Hamlin to Mann, March 18, 1820, Mann MSS:MHS.

had only increased his distaste for Franklin and its homely virtues. With Holmes and Keith, he also shared a sense of disgust and revulsion at the crudeness and pettiness of the world of business beyond the campus. Although he was careful to conceal his feelings in Franklin and Wrentham, he made them no secret to his former chums. Reacting to one of his complaints, George Tuft wrote to Mann, "Neither have I forgotten that a retired and undisturbed life is more congenial to your tast [sic] and feelings than the obstreperous bustle of the world and its cares." [7]

Faced with a bad situation, Mann did not wait long to consider a change. It took only three months to convince him that the rapid and sure road to legal success ran through Litchfield, Connecticut, and Judge Tapping Reeve's renowned law school rather than Wrentham and the office of Josiah J. Fiske. The replies to his enquiries all indicated that the school had prospered far beyond the expectations of the judge who had founded it many years before, having begun with a single student, his own brother-in-law, Aaron Burr. In time, young men from every state in the Union had used the little white one-room house in which Reeve lectured as the stepping stone to successful legal and political careers. By 1795, the school had outgrown its one-man faculty and needed the services of an assistant, James Gould. The word Mann received indicated that Gould was now carrying the main burden of instruction. [8]

By December, 1819, Mann had made up his mind to transfer to Litchfield the following February. Then one day during the first week in the new year, as he picked up his family's mail at the Fisher house in Wrentham, he noticed that one letter bore the heavy-handed scrawl of Asa Messer. Brown needed a tutor, the old president wrote, and Mann could have the appointment and a salary of $375 a year if he was willing to carry out the many tasks the position entailed. Since he was ready to move to Litchfield, Mann's immediate reaction was to reject the offer. He put off writing an answer for several weeks while he reconsidered the alternatives before him. Although he had missed Brown, to return to it as a chore boy for the faculty was hardly

[7] George Tuft to Mann, March 6, 1820, Mann MSS: MHS.
[8] For a general description of Tapping Reeve, see David Sherman Boardman, *Early Lights of the Litchfield Bar* (Litchfield, 1860), pp. 7–10; also see *The History of the Town of Litchfield, Connecticut, 1720–1920*, compiled by Alain C. White (Litchfield, 1920), pp. 98–101; for a general description of the early history of the school, see Samuel Fisher, *Litchfield Law School, 1774–1833, Biographical Catalogue for Students* (New Haven, 1946), pp. 1–27.

in keeping with what he considered the proper rewards befitting a college man of his talents. The remainder of January proved to be a month of indecision. Finally, by the first week in February, he had made up his mind and sent word to Asa Messer that he would return to his *alma mater*. The letter he wrote to his *praeses* was anything but candid. Concealing his misgivings about the status of a tutorship and the possibility of turning his back on a legal career, Mann explained that his delayed answer stemmed from his sense of inadequacy for such an important assignment. The letter once sent, Mann prepared to return to University Hall with a strong sense of ambivalence.[9] If he sought reassurance from his friends for this unexpected course of action, it was not forthcoming. Holmes wrote that he was glad Mann had received the appointment since less able men had been considered for the job, but he regretted that Mann would be serving on a faculty distinguished mainly by its collective senility. George Tuft, Keith, and Hamlin agreed that Brown could use Mann's abilities, but they also stated that it was a difficult, if not impossible, assignment to fill. In short, they were happy for Brown's sake and sorry for Mann.[1]

Once back in University Hall, Mann soon learned that life seemed different when viewed from the other side of the desk. Hoping to maintain a proper distance between himself and his charges and gain their respect, he was careful to dress the part of a professor and attempted to exhibit the manners of a young gentleman. Although he had spoken before many groups, he found it a new experience to stand in front of a class and keep order while holding recitations. He was struck by the naïveté and arrogance of many of the new freshmen, describing them as sitting before him with "heads erect and heart elate, thinking no doubt, that every one beholds them with awe, and envies their elevation." The self-confidence he had once admired in his own classmates now took on the appearance of a proud parochialism. "Each one thinks his own peculiar notions are standard," he wrote to his sister, and added, "probably many suppose themselves to be the smartest fellow in the company." [2]

Quickly overcoming his initial stage fright as a teacher, Mann

---

[9] Jarius Keith to Mann, December 5, 1819; Asa Messer to Mann, January, 1820; Peter Pratt to Mann, February 5, 1820; Mann to Asa Messer, February 9, 1820, all in Mann MSS:MHS.

[1] James S. Holmes to Mann, April 29, 1820; George Tuft to Mann, March 18, 1820; Jarius Keith to Mann, February 28, 1820; E. S. Hamlin to Mann, March 18, 1820, all in Mann MSS:MHS.

[2] Mann to Lydia Mann, November 25, 1820, Mann MSS:MHS.

cut the more self-centered of his charges down to size, usually with uncharitable sarcasm. Never satisfied with the bare skeleton of a translation, but insisting on a rendering which gave the elegance and full flavor of classical literature, Mann earned the reputation of a demanding teacher. Students at Brown, however, even his own, could be driven only so far. Believing he was unreasonable in what he expected of them one day, they hissed and hooted him out of class. To be driven from the classroom was a common occurrence for tutors, but in Mann's case it must have been painful and humiliating, and hardly in keeping with his self-image.[3]

If the response to his teaching was disappointing, it was exasperating to police a dormitory forever in a state of incipient anarchy. He was on call at any hour, day or night. Although living under the same roof with his charges, he was nevertheless considered an outsider. He was required to enforce study hours, see that rooms were clean, and take attendance at chapel. Making the rounds of students' rooms and announcing his presence by a tap on the door with his walking stick, Mann was soon dubbed the "Knight of the white-headed cane" by the underclassmen.[4]

If Mann could not count the students as his associates, neither was he an equal among the members of the faculty. He still looked to Asa Messer as his academic father, but the other professors whom he had saluted at graduation as men of principle he now found capable of petty jealousies and self-seeking compromises. Bridling his tongue the first semester, Mann could no longer remain silent when it became blatantly evident that the class honors for the commencement of 1820 were being awarded on the basis of political and economic considerations rather than scholastic achievement. For his attack upon the apparent miscarriage of justice, Mann received the pious contempt of several of the professors.[5] Trying to shore up Mann's spirits and bolster his ego after the defeat, Holmes wrote to him that he "would rejoice to see *one* or two of your superiors in office *ousted* of their brief authority and their names blotted from the records."[6]

Such well-intended sentiments did not keep Mann from slipping into periods of despondency. While reading law, he could at-

---

[3] Elijah L. Hamlin to Samuel Gridley Howe, August 26, 1820, Howe MSS: HCL; Lincoln Fairfield, *New York Mirror,* IV (June 30, 1827), 386.

[4] Jarius S. Keith to Mann, February 28, 1820. Mann MSS:MHS.

[5] Jarius S. Keith to Mann, September 24, 1820, Mann MSS:MHS.

[6] James S. Holmes to Mann, September 25, 1820, Mann MSS:MHS.

tribute his depression to the contrast between the idyllic life on campus and the crudity of the people in Franklin and Wrentham. Now back at Brown, he discovered a community just as petty and provincial as that of his home town. Not only did he find it impossible to recover the past, but from his new vantage point, he developed a cynicism which made it difficult for him to separate the façade from the genuine and still preserve the integrity of his college experiences. Following his disagreement over commencement honors, he fell ill and the doctor was summoned to his room. Later, back on his feet, Mann poured out his unhappiness to Holmes and Tuft. Tuft quickly responded to say he was sorry that "pale melancholy" had established "her dominion" over Mann.[7]

Nothing during the dreary New England winter served to discharge his lethargy. A short visit by Alexander Metcalf Fisher, now teaching at Yale, Mann failed to mention in his letters home. For a time he took French lessons, but nothing came of them. By spring, his spirits had sunk to an all-time low and he launched a vitriolic attack on the defenseless corpse of George III, using the columns of the local newspaper as a vicarious outlet for the hostility he could not release in a more direct way. Mann took an almost sadistic delight in the ill-fated monarch's insanity and claimed it was symbolic of an endemic corruption throughout Europe. By comparison, the United States was a political Eden. The king was dead, long live the future republics. Beating a dead king, of course, was a favorite pastime for American journalists, but the malevolence of Mann's diatribe went beyond the conventional anglophobia of the day.[8]

---

[7] James S. Holmes to Mann, September 25, 1820; George Tuft to Mann, August 17, [1820], both in Mann MSS:MHS.

[8] Mann, "Remarks on the Death of George III," Mann MSS:MHS; Providence *Patriot*, April 5, 1820. Later the same year, Mann worked for the re-election of Samuel Eddy to the U.S. House of Representatives. Eddy, a staunch Republican and previously considered unbeatable in Rhode Island because of his attack on the Federalists at the Hartford Convention, had become something of a political turncoat himself for having supported the Missouri Compromise. Coming to Eddy's support in two articles in the Providence *Patriot*, which he signed "An Enemy to the Extension of Slavery," Mann defended the Compromise as a pragmatic solution to a complex problem. Then, once more waving the yellow shirt of Hartford, Mann pronounced Eddy's challenger guilty merely by association. Again Eddy won and it would not be until several more elections that Mann's former professor, Tristam Burges, would do what earlier candidates had found impossible. See the Providence *Patriot*, August 12 and 19, 1820. A short biography of Eddy is in U.S., Congress, House, *Biographical Directory of the American Congress, 1774–1949*, 81st Cong., 2d Sess., 1950, H.R. 607, p. 1117.

Mann also took to his pen for more private consumption. One time composing a morose poem out of Gothic romance clichés, pure fantasy, and pieces of self-revelation, he pictured himself alone in his room in "sullen darkness," while from the distant horizon came the "destroying angel" whom he addressed as "MELANCHOLY." She came with "the howling of the wind . . . like a demon's yell," but as she entered his room, he found her appearance almost unbearable to behold.

> *O God! the fiend, the haggard fiend,*
> *At me that shot her glare;*
> *Her waist a braid of serpents twin'd,*
> *Of scorpions was her hair.*

Once face to face, she taunted him with a song in which she told how she tormented the student, concluding with the couplet,

> *I plunge him then in deeper hell,*
> *With this mysterious potion.*

Forced to drink from her "venom'd phial," he then saw "the choir and spirits damn'd" which danced around him. As the horde of fiends finally took leave of him, he concluded his poem with the plea:

> *My God send not that night again*
> *That demon* MELANCHOLY.[9]

Bad poetry though this was, it represented nevertheless his troubled attempt to deal with a sense of inadequacy. For the most part, he identified himself with the tortured student, but in several of the lines he also seemed to draw satisfaction from demon Melancholy's torment of her victim. Through this poem, as with his attack on the dead corpse of George III, the deep-seated anxieties which were troubling him could come to the surface, if only in the form of fantasy and hackneyed imagery.

Well into his second year, it became increasingly clear that Brown was no better for him than Josiah Fiske's law office. An increase in salary from Asa Messer was small compensation for the pains he suffered, and his appointment as school librarian offered

---

[9] Alexander M. Fisher to Caleb Fisher, November 6, 1820. BLYU: receipts for French lessons from Andrew Louis are dated September 29, 1820; the poem is dated March 1, 1821, both in the Mann MSS:MHS.

him more additional work than status. Becoming more frustrated with each day, Mann could not avoid an inevitable reassessment of his plans for self-advancement. If the tutorship at Brown was a blind alley, perhaps the other alternative, study at Tapping Reeve's Law School, was still the right move after all. A former classmate assured him this was so, and that the rewards to be reaped after graduation at Litchfield were well worth the expense of $100 for the course of lectures and $3.50 per week for board and laundry. Mann also learned that Judge Reeve had become "superannuated, and was incapable of speaking articulately," and was planning to retire. By comparison, Judge Gould, his associate, had "the reputation of possessing greater ability" to make the law "clear as light" and was a "complete lawyer and logician." If Mann still wanted to become a lawyer, this was the place.[1]

Such glowing reports helped convince him by January, 1822, that he must make a fresh start elsewhere and that Litchfield was the most likely place. For the past two years he had made little impression upon Brown, and his leaving was considered but a small loss to the faculty. A tutor was expendable and easily replaced. Perhaps the matter-of-fact comment of one of his students best expressed the lack of concern which accompanied Mann's exit from the campus. Writing to a friend, Timothy Deane simply reported that "Mann come [sic] yesterday to resign his tutorial dignities."

*　　*　　*

After a short holiday with his family in Franklin, Mann readied himself for his next move. There was an air of expectancy on the afternoon of the day before he left for Litchfield. The skies became leaden and shortly before dusk the air turned white with snowflakes. He awoke the next morning to a new universe of sky and snow, the horizon dividing them broken only by the stark outline of distant farmhouses huddled in the inadequate shelter of clusters of naked trees. It was as if the world outside his window had become a vast white tabula rasa, affording him one more opportunity for a fresh beginning. By the time he was ready to leave, the farmers with their teams of oxen and rollers had packed the snow, making the road in front of his house passable to horse-drawn sleighs. His sister

---

[1] W. Ennis to Mann, March 4, 1821, and [Welcome] Burges to Mann December 10, 1821, both in Mann MSS:MHS.

Lydia accompanied him as far as Mendon, where he was to board the stagecoach for Hartford. Riding beside her, he began to pour out his disappointments. While Stanley was making steady progress in the City Mills at Wrentham, he, at the age of twenty-six, seemed no nearer success than he had been five or six years before. In this time, he had worked, sacrificed, suffered, and endured so much, yet as he headed for Hartford, he had almost nothing to show for his efforts. Cutting himself off, first from Franklin, and then from Providence, he had no other choice but to move on. To have remained stationary or gone back was to admit defeat. "What happened during our ride to Mendon," he later wrote to Lydia, "you know as well as myself, at least as things were visible, and as to my feelings, it is of no matter for them, they are past now." [2]

Once on board the stagecoach, his loneliness grew even more intense. The scene outside, he reported, was one in which "nature in her wintry dress never made a better appearance." But to him, with each mile the coach rolled south and west, the serenity of what he saw only reminded him of the emptiness of his previous existence and the precariousness of his future. "There was an air of sadness" which he sensed and "a gloom that seemed to speak of past misfortunes or dwell on apprehensions for things to come." He wrote to his sister that he "pitied nature," as he saw her cold and serene and void of sentiment and warmth. He could "almost have wept for her," and for himself as well. [3]

As the coach approached Hartford, he gained some relief from his self-pity by recalling what he considered the political treason committed here by a group of New England Federalists in 1814. Later, as he walked about the town, he became incensed as he thought that on these very streets "the soldiers of the United States . . . by statute of this far-famed city were legally shoved off the side-walks and cast into the middle of their streets to walk with horses and cattle!" This general attitude toward Hartford was not helped by the fact that the owner of the stage line to Litchfield sent over a wagon instead of a carriage to transport him and the two other passengers. To teach the man a lesson, Mann hired a sleigh for the trip and "left the stage-owner to console himself with an account of profit and loss." In a mixture of mock and genuine indignation, Mann wrote to his sister,

---

[2] Mann to Lydia Mann, February 15, 1822, Mann MSS:MHS.
[3] *Ibid.*

O Connecticut! Connecticut! Land of bigotry! Land of superstition; Land of Intolerance. May the increasing light and intelligence of the world liberalize thy character, and may a noble posterity atone for the crimes and follies of their ancestry.[4]

Unable to understand his own plight, it helped to dwell upon the iniquities of others, particularly those of a nearly defunct political party.

* * *

West of Hartford, the storm had left a coat of ice over the trees, stone walls, and buildings which gleamed in the morning sun like polished armor. He could see Litchfield from some distance away, as the village was situated on an elevated plane which offered little shelter from the winter winds but made it an impressive sight for miles around. As he came into the center of the community, he could not help but conclude that the wide streets, large and well-built homes, and stately Congressional Church all told of prosperity and seemliness. On hand to greet him were two of his former classmates, Welcome Burges and Henry Rogers. After the initial round of greetings, they took him to Mrs. Lord, a widow who maintained a boardinghouse for some of the law students. Established in a comfortable room and among old and new friends, Mann soon felt at home.

Although not mentioned in the law school catalogue, it was no secret to young bachelors that study at Litchfield offered more than academic advantages. Miss Sally Pierce had also located her female seminary in the town. The school was patronized by some of the most prominent families in Connecticut who wished their daughters to be trained according to Miss Pierce's rules of piety, diligence, and politeness. Since the seminary was larger than the law school, the young men enjoyed a numerical advantage. "Ladies in abundance" was the enthusiastic description sent to Mann to encourage him to come, and once at Litchfield, he could agree with Ennis that the ladies were "monopolized by the students." Life in the town was more natural and less regulated than on the campus in Providence. The comfortable boardinghouses and private houses in which the students of both schools stayed were a far cry from the barracks-like dormitories at Brown. While the girls were under some supervision,

---

[4] *Ibid.*

their contacts with the law students were not infrequent. The town post office and several of the town stores were favored places for "chance" meetings, and on one romantic summer evening, three of Mann's cronies, Messrs. Loring, Burges, and Sullivan, threw discretion to the wind and serenaded some of the girls beneath their bedroom windows. Miss Pierce's rules of piety, diligence, and politeness did not permit such escapades but they did not preclude the girls' enjoying the company of young gentlemen at more carefully chaperoned affairs. Her charges gave formal balls and teas in a large classroom at the seminary, and the boys were only too happy to reciprocate with parties in the ballroom of Phelps Tavern on the village green. In addition there were sleigh rides, amateur theatricals, picnics, and numerous invitations to gatherings at private homes.[5]

On one of these social occasions, Mann met Miss Catharine Beecher, daughter of the minister of the local Congregational Church. After her mother had died when she was sixteen, Catharine spent the next two years caring for two younger sisters and five brothers before her father relieved her of this responsibility by remarrying. The unexpected domestic tasks had not prevented Miss Beecher from continuing her self-education, as Mann soon learned. Although her appearance suffered from a sallow complexion, her bright lively eyes and glossy dark corkscrew curls prevented her from being unattractive. What caught Mann's attention, however, was Catharine's remarkable breadth and depth of knowledge. Caught off guard by her quick repartee, Mann traded comments with her on Scott, but seeing she was more than his match here, he retreated to other subjects, only to hear her respond with strong opinions which prevented him from taking command of the conversation. Rarely at a loss for words, he was embarrassed to find himself parrying her incisive remarks with hastily constructed truisms. Obviously she was a woman of superior intelligence and he was unprepared for the encounter.

As he thought about it later, he comforted himself with the knowledge that there was no loss here as far as matrimonial prospects were concerned. Miss Beecher was already engaged to another young man from Franklin, Alexander Metcalf Fisher. Unlike Mann, Fisher was looking forward to an important career at his

---

[5] W. Ennis to Mann, March 4, 1821, Mann MSS:MHS; the best account of this aspect of life in Litchfield is in *Chronicles of a Pioneer School,* compiled by Emily Noyes Vanderpoel, ed. Elizabeth C. Buel (Cambridge, 1903), pp. 231–240.

alma mater, Yale, having been singled out by Benjamin Silliman as a precocious young man of great promise to further the teaching of science and mathematics. At the moment he was aboard the *Albion,* bound for Europe to study methods of teaching science in the universities there, and to procure books and laboratory apparatus in preparation for his teaching at New Haven. Telling his sister later of his meeting with Catharine, Mann summed up his impressions of her by observing that she would "make the professor a very good help-mate." [6]

In general, Mann's view of life and his own prospects took on a more sanguine perspective during his stay in Litchfield. The people were friendly and more genteel than those he knew on the Brown campus. With less demanding assignments, more freedom, and a sense that he was finally coming into his manhood, he began to regain confidence that the status and economic rewards he sought would soon be his. In a jocular mood, he reported that he was now even learning something about the business world and would soon give his brother Stanley some advice on how to turn a profit. After all, Mann commented, "here the most common thing imaginable is to rise from your knees at prayer to cheat a man out of two pence." To his friend Jessup Scott, Mann appeared buoyant and relaxed, always ready to respond with a good-natured quip or pun, but from his thin nervous lips could also come the razor-edged sarcasm capable of cutting all but the most thick-skinned. Not the least of his accomplishments in Litchfield was to gain the unofficial title of best whist player among the students. [7]

Parties were frequent, and by the end of the first year, Mann himself gave a party to celebrate the anniversary of his coming to the town. From Charles Webb, the local provisioner, his purchases for one day included "4 doz. muscatel raisins," "3 qts. walnuts," "1 doz. mor raisins," and "3 doz. best Segars." The entire affair cost him the sum of $3.45. No teetotaler, at other times his spirits were lifted by the good offices of rum and Madeira, but some of his major expenses with Webb were purchases of cloth and clothing. If one was to circulate in the best of Litchfield families as a promising young attorney, one must dress the part. [8]

---

[6] Mann to Lydia Mann, May 11, 1822, Mann MSS:MHS.
[7] Mann to Lydia Mann, April 11, 1822; Jessup Scott to Mary Mann, February 16, 1860, both in Mann MSS:MHS.
[8] Mann's receipted account with Charles Webb from June 10, 1822, to February 17, 1823, is in Mann MSS:MHS.

Rustication

Even Mann's bias against orthodox ministers was softened to some extent while at Litchfield. The leading minister in the community was Lyman Beecher, whose fame as a preacher was well established in New England. Since the Congregational parsonage was across the Common from Mrs. Lord's boardinghouse, Mann probably heard the good minister practicing his violin before he heard him preach. From his pulpit each Sunday, Beecher sought to stay the spread of intemperance and Unitarianism in the nation. Mann reported to his sister that Beecher was concerned for the "heathenist condition of the people of the U. States, six sevenths of whom according to him sitting in the region and shadow of death because, as it turned out afterwards, they had not *hopkinsian* and *liberally* educated ministers to dispense the light of the Calvinist creed. . . ." At home, Beecher also worked to keep his own congregation in good order by preventing schisms over less than doctrinal matters. Six years before Mann came, the congregation had been the scene of a major hassle over whether a heating stove should be placed in the church. The "pro-stove" faction triumphed, but Beecher found it necessary to salve the wounds of the combatants.[9]

From what he had heard, Mann expected to find Beecher a younger version of Nathanael Emmons. As he settled himself in the pew reserved for the law school students who attended worship, Mann was taken aback by the tall, square-shouldered man of forty-five who stood in the high pulpit, a man of great earnestness and obviously in the prime of life. Beecher's thin face seemed to accentuate his long nose. His hair, which stood out in all directions and might have drawn ridicule to a lesser person, somehow dramatized the restless energy and dynamism of this man whose body was a continual battleground between the contending forces of an animal violence, a powerful intelligence, and an aggressive moral probity. Beginning to listen to the sermon with a mixture of curiosity and detached superiority, Mann soon found he was by no means immune to the minister's power of persuasion as Beecher described the spiritual decline of man. With each sentence, the tension in the room heightened as the worshippers followed an account of the unsuccessful moral struggle of sinful man to keep himself from falling victim to vice and infidelity. The sermon was neither as doctrinal nor as closely reasoned as those of Emmons, but it had an arresting spontaneity and audacity which could break through Mann's crust of

[9] Mann to Lydia Mann, May 11, 1822, Mann MSS:MHS; White, *History of the Town of Litchfield*, pp. 28–30.

skepticism. Beecher emphasized many of his statements with a sweep of his arms and a finger pointed out beyond his audience, but his most telling points were made as he stood motionless, grasping both sides of the lectern and following his statement with an ironic smile which slowly spread across his face. By the time the minister had finished, Mann was ready to concede that he had never heard such a sermon and that a tragedy performed at a theater could not have produced a greater effect on his feelings. Later, regaining some of his previous composure, Mann acknowledged the power of Beecher's appeal in a letter to his sister, but hastened to qualify his reactions by adding that the minister had absolutely no effect on his "belief," since "belief belongs to the understanding and should not be biassed by hopes and fears." Beecher's emotional appeal had unexpectedly struck a responsive chord in his young listener.[1]

For a time during the summer of 1822, a pall hung over Litchfield when word reached the community that the *Albion* had run aground and sunk off the coast of Ireland. The several survivors who reached land carried with them an account of the last hours and death of Alexander Metcalf Fisher. The shock to Catharine Beecher was both acute and protracted. Fearing that her fiancé had not experienced conversion, she recognized the possibility that he was eternally lost. Shortly after the shipwreck, she moved to Franklin to live with her intended in-laws, hoping to reconstruct evidence of Fisher's regeneration. Months later she returned to Litchfield, forced to admit her mission a failure. Steeling herself against despair, she never referred again to her loss and accepted the enduring loneliness of a lifetime of spinsterhood. Her sister Harriet, however, left a fictional account of the incident in *The Minister's Wooing*, using Nathanael Emmons as her model for the minister who could not give assurance that the victim was saved. Mann was saddened and depressed by the news. He knew both Fisher and Miss Beecher and could share in the grief of the survivors. But in addition, he sensed something even more personal. The event made him aware of his recurring phobia about water and his fear that he might someday also die in a shipwreck. For weeks after the news of the *Albion*, thoughts of drowning haunted him as they had done after Stephen's death.[2]

---

[1] Mann to Lydia Mann, May 11, 1822, Mann MSS: MHS.
[2] Mann to Lydia Mann, June 13, 1822, Mann MSS:MHS; a general account of Fisher's untimely death can be found in Charles Edward Stowe, *Life of Harriet Beecher Stowe* (Boston, 1889), pp. 23–25.

Rustication

*   *   *

Breakfast at Mrs. Lord's was served between seven and eight o'clock, and lectures began at nine. Each morning Mann joined Burges and Rogers, as well as Thomas Kinnicutt from Springfield and Edward Loring and James Sullivan from Boston, and walked across the village green to the little white building next to Judge Reeve's home where classes were held. An assistant gave the first lecture of the day, and Judge Gould made his presentation at eleven. Each student took his place at a desk, notebooks were opened, pens dipped, and the class was ready for its learned mentor.[3]

James Gould had risen from humble circumstances to social and political prominence in western Connecticut by way of Yale College. Now just past forty, and at the intellectual peak of his life, he was a handsome and imposing man; but what struck one most about James Gould was the power of his mind. Known as a "philosophical lawyer," a keen reasoner, and a "most finished and competent writer," he presented lectures which did not elicit a great sense of emotion or feeling from his auditors, but instead demonstrated his almost encyclopedic knowledge of American legal cases and his ability to discuss them in the most precise language. Like his writings, they were almost perfect models of style and form, and not a few of his admirers claimed he was unable to make an ungrammatical expression or an awkward gesture.[4]

The judge sat in a large, overstuffed chair elevated on a small platform at the front of the class and read slowly from his notes. In a voice almost entirely devoid of emotion but nonetheless pleasing, he stated the principle under consideration and repeated it to be sure all had a chance to copy it completely and correctly. Then he cited cases in which the principle had been applied by the courts. Occasionally he added further explanatory remarks and illustrations concerning judicial interpretations. These too were copied down,

---

[3] Mann to Lydia Mann, February 15 and April 11, 1822, Mann MSS: MHS; Edward Deering Mansfield, *Personal Memories* (Cincinnati, 1879), pp. 126–128; Dwight C. Kilbourn, *The Bench and Bar of Litchfield County, Connecticut, 1709–1909* (Litchfield, 1909), pp. 195–212.
[4] A good description of James Gould is in Simeon E. Baldwin, "James Gould," *Great American Lawyers*, ed. William Draper Lewis, (Philadelphia, 1907), II, 453–488; other accounts are in Fisher, *Litchfield Law School*, pp. 17–22; Gideon Hiram Hollister, *History of Connecticut* (New Haven, 1855), II, 601–603; and Boardman, *Early Lights of the Litchfield Bar*, pp. 26–28.

usually set off from the rest of the notes under the heading "per J. Gould." Quills scratched hurriedly and the time passed quickly. Students were copying his concluding remarks before realizing that he had once again held their attention for an hour and a half.[5]

What they had heard were short succinct analyses of cases presented in such a lucid fashion that the essentials of each case and its dependence on certain abstract legal principles could be clearly grasped. The school catalogue explained that "Whenever the opinions upon any point are contradictory, the authorities in support of either doctrine are cited, and the arguments, advanced by either side, are presented in a clear and concise manner, together with the Lecturer's own views of the question." [6] Gould stressed that the practice of law was not an art but a system of consistent rules by which men ordered their lives. The Revolution had dealt a blow to American legal practices, and teachers like Reeve and Gould helped bridge the gap between British colonial law and the development of state and federal legal codes. Not until the publication of Swift's *Digest* and Kent's *Commentaries* was there anything equal to the lectures of these two men. In the period between 1809 and 1826, more than 800 men studied with Gould. Only Yale and Harvard graduated more students during his time. The alumni of the school included three Supreme Court justices, a Vice-President, five cabinet members, sixteen United States Senators, fifty-five Representatives, and numerous federal and state judges. Clearly, this was a time in history when education consisted essentially of the confrontation between a learned man and eager, apt students.[7]

After lunch, the students returned to take down the bound volumes from the shelves which lined the classroom and check the available authorities on the cases Gould had presented. Their afternoon was usually completed by four o'clock when they had copied ten to fifteen pages of their notes and findings into a permanent notebook. For Horace Mann, like many others who studied at Litchfield, the course under Gould amounted to the preparation of five

---

[5] Descriptions of Gould's methods of teaching are found in W. Ennis to Mann, March 4, 1821, Mann MSS:MHS; Mansfield, *Personal Memories*, pp. 127–128; Baldwin, *Great American Lawyers*, II, 461–477.
[6] Quoted in Fisher, *Litchfield Law School*, p. 8.
[7] Baldwin, *Great American Lawyers*, II, 484–486; Fisher, *Litchfield Law School*, p. 27; while Mann was at Litchfield there were nine students from Massachusetts, five from Georgia, three from New York, three from Connecticut, two each from Pennsylvania and South Carolina, and one each from Rhode Island, Maryland, and Vermont. Kilbourn, *Bench and Bar of Litchfield*, pp. 195–212.

notebooks which would be the most important part of his law library for years to come.

Each Saturday morning, Gould's assistant quizzed the class on the previous week's lectures. Mann's legal training did not end here, however. As at Brown, the law students formed two social and debating societies. One, composed of more studious members, concentrated on legal discussions; while the other organization, as one of Mann's friends euphemistically described it, undertook "miscellaneous disquisitions." In addition, Gould held moot court weekly. He proposed a question of law to be discussed and two students were assigned to argue each side the following week. When their arguments were completed, Gould presented a summation and pronounced his verdict as to which side had the better case.[8]

Mann was soon caught up in the activity of the moot court, and three months after coming to Litchfield, he argued his first case. He won, but in a forced modesty wrote to his sister that his performance was "about half-middling." His classmate, Jessup Scott, was more complimentary, recalling that Mann had a remarkable talent for identifying the pertinent aspects of each case and then presenting them with an unsurpassed clarity. In one instance, Mann grew so bold as to challenge an opinion Gould had previously written. The judge in turn attempted to sustain his position, but as he exhibited more than a little wounded self-esteem, the students felt that Mann had the better part of the argument. Not only did Mann later gain the office of "attorney general" in the moot court, but he generally excelled in his studies. Scott remembered him as the best law student and the best-read scholar in the school.[9]

The lectures, moot courts, and discussions notwithstanding, Mann found the atmosphere more friendly and relaxed than at Brown. He was out from under the hundred and one responsibilities of dormitory supervision, and since his late afternoons and evenings were often free, he had time to read according to his own interests. One of his favorite authors was the English philosopher and physician, Thomas Brown. In his writings, especially his *Sketches of a System of the Philosophy of the Human Mind* (1820), Brown had rejected both Bishop Berkeley's idealism and the empiricism of David

---

[8] W. Ennis to Mann, March 4, 1821, Mann MSS:MHS.
[9] Mann to Lydia Mann, April 11, 1822; Jessup W. Scott to Mary Mann, February 16, 1860, both in Mann MSS:MHS; a general description of these courts is in Baldwin, *Great American Lawyers*, II, 482. Some of Mann's notes on these summations are found in the Mann MSS:MHS.

Hume. In their places, he posited a more common-sense and naïve approach to the study of reality. Central to his thought was the conception of God neither as a miracle worker nor a vindictive judge, but the supreme workman. God's single and all-sufficient miracle was his creation of a universe which now ran according to fixed and harmonious laws. Nature was therefore good, and it was incumbent upon man to learn from it and direct his life accordingly. In this way, the "is" of nature would become the "ought" for man. Evil in the world did exist, but it was to be found neither in physical creation nor in man's innate nature. Instead, it manifested itself in corrupt institutions created by man as the result of his incomplete understanding of the universe. Through the power of reason, man now understood the laws governing the physical world. To Brown, and his appreciative reader Horace Mann, it was but a matter of time until reason would also expose the laws of the human mind. The result would be a mental philosophy capable of explaining the causes and effects of human behavior and thought. This new science of the mind would be not only the most recent of the sciences, but also the most exact and the most utilitarian.[1]

*   *   *

Litchfield was a long way from Franklin, and to go there had required a painful admission for Horace Mann. At the age of twenty-six his education was still incomplete and he was not ready to shoulder adult responsibilities. Nevertheless, it had been a wise decision, even though it meant additional expense and further delay in his career. He could look back on these days as happy ones, days in which he had become increasingly independent of his home and family. Litchfield was also a long way from Brown. While there had been much talk at Brown about certain principles which should direct men's activities, in his first contact with the outside world, these had proved to be ambiguous and of little help. Under James Gould, Mann came to study a different set of principles, neither absolute nor universal but still clearly defined and broadly applicable. The laws of the land seemed vague and contradictory at the time, yet in studying with a man of superior intellect such as Gould, Mann came to

---

[1] Jessup W. Scott to Mary Mann, February 16, 1860, Mann MSS:MHS; Brown's *Sketch of . . . the Philosophy of the Human Mind* was reviewed by [Samuel Gilman] in the *North American Review,* Vol. 19 (1824), 1–14; for a brief survey of Brown's ideas, see W. R. Serley, *A History of English Philosophy* (New York, 1921), pp. 209–210.

understand how reason could be used to organize a plethora of seemingly unrelated cases into valid categories and how principles could be deduced from these. Only then did men's actions, as they came under the law, become intelligible. These principles were surely more circumscribed and specific than those that had been advanced at college, but they also corresponded more closely to reality. Unlike many of his peers, Mann had gained a superior professional education and was now finally ready to capitalize on his abilities. Here was the combination of talent and training, set in motion by the catalyst of his desire to be first. These could be the reagents for fame, wealth, or both. The choice was his.

CHAPTER IV

The Republican Aristocrat

=====

THE CHIEF GLORY of the end of the year 1828, is
the situation of this Union.

We refer to the unequalled prosperity and security of the American people; their advancement
in numbers and wealth; the increase of their
reputation and influence abroad; the new and extensive conquests which they have made over the
wilderness; the diffusion of knowledge and the
means of education; the constant enlargement of
an horizon embracing the best prospects of national weal and glittering with the lights of
cultivated reason.

Boston Recorder, January 15, 1829

G RADUATION FROM LITCHFIELD was followed by another class dispersal. The students had come from almost every state in the
Union, and commencement was the time for departure in all directions. Some traveled south to practice law and begin their political
careers; others headed to the big cities of New York, Philadelphia,
and Boston, there to take advantage of family connections. A few
adventuresome ones packed up their notebooks and struck out for
the Ohio River Valley. None of these avenues seemed open to Horace
Mann, as he was still tied by obligations to his mother and sister. On
the other hand, neither Franklin nor Wrentham had been large
enough to satisfy his ambition. The town of Dedham, Massachusetts,
seat of the Court of Common Pleas and the Supreme Judicial Court
of Norfolk County, seemed to offer something of a compromise. It
was halfway between Franklin and Boston.

By the time he arrived in Dedham, however, there were indications that Mann would have to build a career in the face of obstacles which had not troubled the established lawyers already
there. In the 1820's, in most communities of New England, the legal
profession was crowded with college graduates who did not wish to
enter the ministry and had no taste for the more turbulent and
mercurial world of the merchant. Adding to the congestion in the
profession were others who had begun to practice law without a col-

lege education, it being sufficient simply to read law in the office of a practicing attorney before being admitted to the bar. Keith, who was struggling to get started in Maine, reported to Mann that his state was populated with as many lawyers as Egypt had frogs at the time of the plagues. Holmes, also in Maine, was barely surviving on the fees he received from collecting bad debts from farmers. Instead of becoming a prominent man in the community, he unwittingly found himself tagged with the derisive title of "rural solicitor." Thomas Kinnicutt, a recent Litchfield graduate, reported the situation was no better in central Massachusetts. "Business is as dull here as the sternest opposers of litigation can wish," he wrote to Mann. "I know not what will become of us poor devils," he added, "we have about two entries per man on an average through the country." Each of the Brown graduates looked with envy to Welcome Burges, who was beginning his practice in Providence and could at least enjoy the more cultured and refined atmospheres which Keith and Holmes missed. But Burges evidently did not recognize Mecca. "This is a miserable hole for lawyers," he wrote, as he enumerated the conditions which made his life anything but ideal. "Our profession is crowded thro' the country and the *pickpocketers* have become more numerous than the *pickpocketees*." Mann would have the same problem in Dedham as Burges saw it, but he did have one distinct advantage not present in Providence. Mann could use Dedham as the springboard to Boston, which Burges called the "literary emporium." [1]

Lawyers were considered leeches who, by reason of the structure of the legal system, could live off the efforts of hardworking people while producing nothing of benefit in return. Shay's rebellion had done little to endear the courts and the legal profession to the farmers, and since many attorneys were Federalists, the more recent Hartford Convention had confirmed the popular rural prejudice against them. Dedham was the county seat for an area of small landowners. In its immediate environs, one could not find as many as twenty men over thirty years of age who did not own real property. Since its lawyers traditionally had allied themselves with the Federalists and the bankers and merchants of Boston, they carried the double guilt of political treason and bad professional practice.

Mann became the sixth lawyer in a town of little more than

---

[1] Jarvis Keith to Mann, February 8, 1823; James S. Holmes to Mann, November 4, 1822; Thomas Kinnicutt to Mann, November 11, 1825; Welcome A. Burges to Mann, June 26 and November 10, 1823, all in Mann MSS:MHS.

2,500 souls. With his entry, the village had as many lawyers as clergymen and two more lawyers than doctors. Perhaps in the larger towns where social and economic relations were more complex, such a ratio was necessary, but this was not the case in the more simple life of Dedham. To make things even more competitive, these six lawyers not only vied with each other for the available local business but also had to share their slim pickings with attorneys from Boston and elsewhere. At the Norfolk Hotel, where many of the out-of-town lawyers stayed while on business, one could find such prominent men as Lemuel Shaw, Daniel Webster, Joseph Story, and Robert Rantoul. When the Norfolk County Court was in session, Dedham was crowded with lawyers, and to a hard-pressed debtor facing litigation and possible foreclosure, it would indeed look as if the "pickpocketers" outnumbered the "pickpocketees." In the winter session of 1824, more than 30 attorneys tried 120 cases in the Court of Common Pleas. Competition for the more lucrative cases with the lawyers of reputation from Boston was especially keen. Certainly the doctors and ministers in the community did not experience such rivalry. Faced with a problem of survival, the Dedham attorneys had divided their time between law and business endeavors, a development which was judged detrimental to the profession.

Once situated in Dedham, Mann was expected to undergo still more training before he was permitted to practice law. Even his study with James Gould was not accepted as adequate for admission to the bar. Gould's lectures were theoretical, the older lawyers rationalized, and before Mann was to gain the right to try cases, he must first have practical experience by reading in the law office of a practicing attorney. Mann convinced James Richardson to accept him, and for almost another year he repeated many of the tasks he had learned from Josiah Fiske. Finally, on December 21, 1823, he took the oath required by law and was granted the privilege of practicing law in the Norfolk Court of Common Pleas.[2]

It should have been a moment of triumph for him. "I am, at least, admitted into the great fraternity of lawyers," he reported to

[2] Blake, *History of the Town of Franklin*, p. 166; see also Samuel Gridley Howe to John A. Andrews, 1865, Andrews MSS:MHS; Bar Book of Norfolk County, MS in Clerk's Office, Norfolk County, Dedham, Massachusetts. Mann was recommended for admission to practice on December 21, 1823, "It being understood that he will not commence practice untill [sic] the first of January next." Also see the Records of the Court of Common Pleas, 1823–1824, MS in Norfolk County Court House, Dedham, Massachusetts.

Burges with a combination of fatigue and delight. He also had decided "to *settle* (damn the occult significance of the word) to settle,
then, I say, in this far-famed town." Having been received into the
"Great Temple of Justice," he asked if this were not grounds for a
certain amount of pride, since he had joined the ranks of such lawyers as Cicero, Confucius, and Demosthenes. With a self-conscious
irreverence he added that even Saint Paul should have been included
in this illustrious group since the apostle "read law in Dr. Gamaliel's
office." Two years later, when the Norfolk Bar Association recommended Mann's admission to practice before the Supreme Judicial
Court, "He being duly qualified and sustaining a good moral character," as the secretary of the Bar recorded, his legal apprenticeship
was finally completed. He was almost thirty years old.[3]

If he suffered the twin handicaps of a late start in the profession and a lack of influential acquaintances, Mann was prepared to
compensate for these. He set up his office within the shadow of the
Court House at the corner of Court and Church Streets and lost no
time in building up a clientele. Soon the tall, wiry figure of the young
man with a hurried step, bent slightly forward as if he were leaning
into the wind, became a familiar sight to the residents of the village.
Checking records and making notes, Mann wore a path between his
office and the Court House. And when he was neither at his office nor
at the Court House, he was usually traveling about the countryside.
Too impatient and realistic to believe that business would come in
through his front door, Mann rented a chaise in summer and a
sleigh in winter from Moses Gregg and Francis Alden, the town
livery men, and criss-crossed the county, seeking cases and listening
to grievances wherever they might be found.[4]

Before the winter session of the court had adjourned, he defended Oliver Pierce in *Whitney* v. *Pierce*. Mann's client defaulted
and the plaintiff was awarded $96.60 plus costs. In the same ses-
sion he had five other minor cases. It was an inauspicious but typical
beginning for a neophyte lawyer. The following session brought
eight more cases, and the number continued to grow. Within three
years, he was averaging more than fifteen cases each session. Numbers of court appearances did not tell the whole story. Much of his
work never went before the bench. Like Holmes, he too was becom-

[3] Mann to Welcome Burges, January 10, 1824, Straker MSS:ACL; Bar
Book of Norfolk County, December 21, 1825.
[4] N.a., "Horace Mann," *Dedham Historical Register*, VI (1895), 17;
Samuel Gridley Howe to John A. Andrews, 1865, Andrews MSS:MHS.

ing something of a "rural solicitor." Frequently, Boston and Dedham merchants engaged him to apply pressure and collect bad debts from local farmers and laborers. When a debtor still resisted, he could be taken to court. Under such circumstances, it was not difficult for Mann's friends to maintain later that he won four-fifths of all the cases committed to him. Neither the heroic defense of exploited widows and orphans nor the well-paid counsel to growing corporations, this was rather tough, debilitating legal work of the most pedestrian sort. Although time-consuming and uninspiring, it was a beginning.[5]

Free to give his ambition full sway, Mann invested much of his energy towards becoming a success. Long hours, attention to detail, and a self-interest in winning his clients' cases caused his reputation to spread and his practice to grow. Now finally on his own, he began to recognize the validity of some of the maxims of his childhood which taught that material rewards came only to the ambitious and industrious. As his bank account increased and he was invited to the better homes in Dedham, he had the most convincing kind of proof that sacrifice and effort would bring him social status and a modest wealth. Nevertheless, his childhood belief in the virtue of work needed accommodation. Instead of grain and cloth, he was now producing services, and by a remarkable alchemy, he was converting these less tangible things into money. As he wrote to a correspondent, he was actively engaged in changing "wind into material." [6]

*   *   *

His first winter session of the court completed, Mann devoted his free time to preparing for an event which might further his fortunes. As the most recent college graduate to arrive in the community, he was asked to make the annual Fourth of July address in 1823. Organizing his time so that he would be ready for the affair, Mann held himself to a demanding schedule, writing and rewriting

[5] Livingston, *Portrait Gallery*, III, 187–188; Court Docket, 1824, Court of Common Pleas, Norfolk County; the increase in Mann's cases can be noted in the court dockets for 1825, 1826, and 1827; a typical receipt from Mann's legal papers: "Sept. 15, 1830, received of Horace Mann twenty six dollars, in full for money collected of Joe Richards. Two dollars for costs deducted from the debt, leaving the above sum of $26. [signed] Daniel Baster," Mann MSS:DHS.
[6] Mann to Charlotte Messer, February 28, 1830, Mann-Messer MSS: BUA.

his speech, memorizing parts of it, and ordering a black speaker's robe. Two weeks before the Fourth, all was proceeding according to plan when disaster struck. As Mann described it to his sister,

That long Quixotic visage of mine has suddenly received such accretions on both sides, that Jupiter himself, if he should blow out his cheeks on a wager, could scarely hope to equal them in size and rotundity. In plain English, I have got the cursed MUMPS.[7]

Well aware of the high stakes involved, Mann applied warm flannel pads to his swollen jaws and counted the days. The fact that the local paper announced that this was to be a celebration for all the people and stated that "Citizens of this and neighboring towns are again invited to join a celebration *where no distinction of party* will be recognized," did not make him feel any better. Fortunately, the swelling receded in time, and when the festive day arrived, Mann was ready to make the most of his opportunity.[8]

Communities such as Dedham did not make light of their obligation to commemorate the young nation's independence. At eleven o'clock in the morning on the Fourth, a large group of people gathered at the Norfolk Hotel and formed a procession. In the lead was an "Escort of Light Infantry," followed by the parade marshals and the committee on arrangements. Next came the "President of the Day," James Richardson, followed by the "Orator of the Day," and the "Chaplain of the Day." Still farther back was the "Vice-President of the Day," and the "Reverend Clergy." Bringing up the rear were "Military Officers in Uniform" and "Citizens generally." The procession, once under way, passed by the swinging wooden sign of the local tavern with its bust of George Washington, and moved along the main street. A noisy happy affair, with more enthusiasm than precision, the parade came to a halt in front of "Rev. Lamson's Meeting House," the Unitarian Church. Honored guests took their places on the rostrum, the soldiers leaned on their firearms, and the crowd gradually became quiet. After the invocation, it was time for the young speaker, draped in a mock Roman toga, to lift and inspire the patriotic and nationalistic sentiments of those assembled.[9]

---

[7] Mann to Lydia Mann, June 14, 1823, Mann MSS:MHS; Mann's official invitation to speak is in the Mann MSS:MHS, and is dated June 4, 1823.

[8] Dedham *Village Register,* July 4, 1823.

[9] The complete plans for the procession were announced in the Dedham *Village Register,* July 4, 1823; see also Mann to Lydia Mann, June 14, 1823, Mann MSS:MHS.

He began by contrasting the governments of the Old World with the United States. After fashioning European kings and clerics into straw men, he depicted the American patriots as men of unsullied virtue and selfless dedication. Surely they had accomplished "one of the most transcendently important and glorious events in history." Mann described the nation as a vast cathedral of liberty from coast to coast, in which a free people praised their heavenly father and venerated their republican saints. Monarchs, tyrants, and priests were all irredeemably corrupt. There was almost no end to the catalogue of human miseries they had caused. Working up to a climax, Mann concluded that American liberty and freedom were in harmony with the laws of the universe. And to this synthesis of republicanism, nationalism, and Protestantism, his audience gave an enthusiastic assent.

That evening, before retiring, the town printer, Herman Mann, probably expressed the opinion of many as he recorded the events of the day. In his private journal, he wrote: "The oration was pronounced by Horace Mann, Esq.; it was a masterly production, and was worthy the head and heart of an American freeman." [1]

Perhaps believing he was entitled to a short holiday after such an effort, Mann took a trip to Boston. While there, he spent the afternoon walking alone along Nahant Beach, his solitude interrupted only by the gulls which glided near him and then out over the water. Mann was entranced by the sweeping beauty of the expanse of sea and sand, stretching out before him as far as his eye could see. Writing his impressions to his sister, he composed descriptions approaching the poetic, but as in so many cases, the muses failed him and nature simply provided the stimulus for moralizing. As a contrast to Nahant, he also visited the Charlestown Navy Yard. There set up in stocks were two vessels under repair. As he walked the decks and went below, he marveled at the complexity of the rigging, the superb mahogany cabinet work, the massive oak ribs, the innumerable brass fittings, each serving a specific purpose, and the giant chains wound around the capstan which hauled up the anchor. But what struck him most was the number of guns on the larger of the two vessels, 120 according to his count. All this he observed with the wide-eyed wonderment of one discovering yet another new world.[2]

---

[1] Mann, *An Oration, Delivered at Dedham, July 4, 1823, on the Forty-Seventh Anniversary of American Independence* (Dedham, 1823); Herman Mann, Journal, No. 2, July 4, 1823, MS in DHS.

[2] Mann to Lydia Mann, July 26, 1823, Mann MSS:MHS.

After the Fourth of July address, other opportunities came his way. Mann turned down several requests from the United Brothers to speak at their celebrations, but he did so in such a way as to encourage still another invitation. In the summer of 1824, when the Brothers failed to make their intentions official until a month before the celebration, Mann peevishly declined, informing the society that he was "indispensably engaged every day of the present week; & . . . should regard an attempt to prepare myself after its expiration as criminally presumptuous." Not satisfied with this, he lectured the ill-fated Brothers that "no celebration is infinitely preferable to a poor one." Still, considering his ability to prepare a speech even at short notice, time was not his real reason for turning down the Brothers. No doubt, Joseph Jenekes was closer to the cause when he apologized to Mann that "So far from intending to slight you, we have all been so much elated with the bare idea of having you for our champion, as to neglect the etiquette, which the occasion required." But from his vantage point, Jenekes could not know the intensity of Mann's previous disappointments at Brown and his desire to gain some measure of revenge and return triumphantly for all to see.[3]

The following year, the United Brothers observed the "etiquette, which the occasion required." Letters were exchanged in good time and Mann prepared for what he hoped would be a stunning success.[4] Those who remembered his predilection for embellished and aureate prose, and had expected more of the same, did not go away from the celebration disappointed. In an introductory statement he needed more than a hundred words to say that different forms of education produced different kinds of knowledge and happiness. Education could be "verdunless, an inbound zone, desolate in eternal sterility," but ideally, it should "elevate and purify the affections." Unappreciative of the aesthetic values to be derived from literature and painting, Mann stressed that learning must always be directed to improving the morality of man. It was therefore necessary to be vigilant and screen the reading of those of a "susceptible age." But after his critique of a broader use of literature, he acknowledged, perhaps a little too late, that some grain also grew among the tares. Correctly managed, learning would raise the standards of morality

---

[3] The episode is pieced together from Joseph Jenekes to Mann, July 28 and August 6, 1824, Mann MSS:MHS; Mann to the United Brothers Society, August 9, 1824, United Brothers Letterbook, Vol. I, BUA.
[4] Mann to the United Brothers Society, August 6, 1825, BUA.

as well as achieve freedom for all men. To argue both for liberty and censorship of learning involved Mann in a possible dilemma. At the moment, however, he was unaware of the possible contradiction between making men free and controlling their environment to make them virtuous.[5]

Dealing in superlatives of similar magnitude, the Providence *Gazette* stated that "It is sufficient to observe, that Mr. Mann equalled the expectations of his friends, and was heard with much satisfaction by a numerous and attentive auditory." [6] Mann had given the missionary zeal, ever present at Brown, an idealistic focus, urging that republicanism, like Christianity, had to be planted from Greenland's icy mountains to India's coral strands, and he promised that its success was inevitable.

The following year, while heavily involved in his legal work, an unexpected historical coincidence gave him a second opportunity to reach a large audience in Dedham. Fifty years to the day after they had signed the Declaration of Independence, two of the surviving patriarchs of the Union, Thomas Jefferson and John Adams, both died on July 4, 1826. As church bells tolled and flags flew at half-mast across the nation, community after community organized memorial services to honor the dead. In Dedham, a committee of leading citizens cast about for a speaker equal to the demands of the occasion, before deciding upon Dedham's youngest attorney. Mann had less than two weeks to prepare.[7]

When the day arrived, about 200 people gathered at the Norfolk Hotel. At two o'clock in the afternoon, mourning badges were distributed, last-minute arrangements were made by the Reverends Lamson and Boyle, the officiating clergymen, and the procession finally got under way with the dependable Dedham Light Infantry in the lead. As he marched among the mourners moving around the square towards the Unitarian Church, Mann could not help but be struck by the differences between this occasion and the affair two years before when this same route of march had been the scene of a noisy, carefree celebration. Now all was quiet, save the muffled beat of the drums of the infantry and the shuffle of the marchers' feet in the gravel and dust of Court Street. A feeling of uncertainty seemed

---

[5] Mann, "Oration before the United Brothers Society," Mann MSS:MHS.
[6] September 7, 1825.
[7] A notation on the MS copy of Mann's "Eulogy of Jefferson and Adams," in the Mann MSS:MHS, states he had to prepare with such short notice that he refused a copy to the press.

to intensify the sense of loss of the mourners. As the last of the Founding Fathers were passing, they knew a new age was at hand. They, the living, must complete the unfinished business, and as they walked in silence toward the church, there was cause to reflect on the dimensions of the task.[8]

The white interior of the meetinghouse made the black cloth draped about the windows all the more stark. At the front of the hall stood two large portraits, one of Adams and one of Jefferson, also draped in black. When all the pews were filled, the ceremony began. The Dedham choir sang an anthem, one of the clergymen gave the invocation, and a second read from Scripture. After another hymn, it was time for the eulogy. As Mann looked across the audience, he could see that his listeners included the leading citizens of Dedham and nearby towns. Their presence made him more aware of his hurried preparation and the unfinished condition of the manuscript before him. But neither the presence of community leaders nor the limited time he had had to ready himself was the chief source of his momentary anxiety. Sitting before him was the President of the United States, John Quincy Adams.[9]

In a calm and solemn voice, Mann explained that they had gathered to contemplate "in the wonderful economy of Providence, what unbounded rewards result from the labors of a lofty mind and the sacrifice of a generous soul." Mann singled out Jefferson for his authorship of the Declaration of Independence. "There is not in the moral history of man a sublimer scene," he claimed, "than that of the youthful Jefferson, preparing the Declaration of Independence of his country." Neither sculptor nor painter could capture the true greatness of the event. Years of martyrdom, sacrifice, and struggle for human freedom, all had come to an ultimate triumph in this one supreme achievement.

Turning then to John Adams, Mann pointed out that he too had been a fearless defender of true freedom since he as few of his

---

[8] Dedham *Village Register*, August 3, 1826.
[9] John Quincy Adams had dutifully gone to a number of such observances. Obviously, he could not go to all of those held even in the immediate vicinity, but he considered the one in Dedham important enough to attend. Charles Francis Adams, ed., *Memoirs of John Quincy Adams* (Philadelphia, 1875), VII, 138. Adams recorded that one of the hymns sung at the ceremony was written by Horace Mann. This was incorrect. The composer was "H. Mann," probably Herman Mann, the town printer and a composer of sorts. See Dedham *Village Register*, August 3, 1826; Herman Mann, Journal, No. 3, September, 1824 to August, 1828, July 24, 1826, MS in DHS.

contemporaries understood how the desire for liberty had been perverted in the French Revolution. He knew that the overthrow of the French monarchy was not an unfolding of the laws of nature, as the American Revolution had been, but rather the last act in the tragedy of "fourteen centuries of corruption and misgovernment." In France, reason had been so annihilated among the people that, like maniacs, they had finally broken the chains "that would have bound sane men." At great personal and political sacrifice, Adams had kept the young nation free from foreign entanglements and maintained an island of sanity in a world of chaos.[1]

The young attorney had spoken to the people, but he had also spoken for them. Another anthem was followed by a benediction. The audience rose, emptied the pews one by one, and formed the procession back to the Norfolk Hotel. There, before returning to his home in Quincy, the President of the United States met the young man from Franklin and thanked him for his inspiring address. Later he wrote that Mann's eulogy was "of splendid composition and lofty eloquence." The correspondent for the *Village Register* went further. "The Eulogy . . . by Horace Mann, Esq. was replete with pathetic eloquence, descriptive metaphor, imagery, and characteristic trait. An attempt in this small space, at panegyric on this classical production would be futile." The press elsewhere carried accounts of the affair, and probably for the first time in his life, the name of Horace Mann appeared in a Boston newspaper.[2]

*   *   *

Mann's star was rising in Dedham, and his selection as speaker for the memorial service was evidence of this for all to see. Other men had been available, both among the lawyers and clergymen. Instead, the committee had chosen a young man in their midst but three years and still an outsider in the community by staid New England standards. With the building blocks of ambition, hard work, and a reputation as a public speaker, Mann began to shape his legal career, and after several lean years at the outset, his files grew thick with the papers of his clients.

Talent, training, and perseverance aside, there was another

---

[1] Mann, "Eulogy of Adams and Jefferson," MS, Mann MSS:MHS; Dedham *Village Register*, August 3, 1826.
[2] John Quincy Adams, *Memoirs*, VII, 138; Dedham *Village Register*, August 3, 1826; Boston *Daily Advertiser*, July 28, 1826; *New England Palladium*, July 28 and August 8, 1826; Boston *Patriot and Mercantile Advertiser*, August 7, 1826.

reason for his success for which he could claim little credit. The town of Dedham itself was growing and changing its character. By 1826, it could boast of two woolen mills, two cotton mills, and fourteen other small manufactories, as well as five taverns, eleven retail stores, two apothecaries, one bank with a capital of $100,000, and one mutual fire insurance company. Several entrepreneurs were getting a start in shoe manufacturing, and in less than ten years, the community would be producing over 18,000 pairs annually. With commercial growth had come several problems. Worthington, the town historian, had noted the increase in the number of debtors within recent years, while Herman Mann recorded a growing concern over the prevalence of intemperance. The character of Dedham was shifting from a town of self-sufficient landowners to a place of employers and wage earners. Drawn into the economic orbit of Boston, the old Dedham, with its role as a small marketplace for agricultural goods and legal decisions, was becoming a part of the past.[3]

To note this shift to more commercial activities, one had only to scan Mann's files. The fees he collected between 1827 and 1830 grew, and the court docket recorded his name more frequently as counsel for both plaintiffs and defendants. Furthermore, he was allowed increasing latitude by his clients in pressing their claims. "You will please use your own discretition [sic] to the manner of collecting these demands," was typical in spirit, if not in spelling, of the carte blanche given him by anxious creditors. His effectiveness as a solicitor was expedited through the formation of a loosely organized network of lawyers in other parts of New England. Through friendships made at Brown and Litchfield, young lawyers like Burges in Providence, Thomas Kinnicutt in Worcester, and Sydney Williams in Taunton maintained reciprocal relations in collecting debts. Mann even helped Holmes, who was still up in Maine, to collect money from a person in Pawtucket.[4]

A more significant change was the growing complexity and importance of the cases brought to Mann. In 1826 he was named counsel for the Boston and Providence Commercial Stage Company.[5]

---

[3] Herman Mann, *Annals of Dedham* (Dedham, 1847), pp. 46–49; Erastus Worthington, *History of Dedham from the Beginning of Its Settlement* . . . (Boston, 1827), pp. 90–91.
[4] E. Copeland, Jr., to Mann, December 5, 1828; Welcome Burges to Mann, July 19, 1828, both in Mann MSS:DHS; James S. Holmes to Mann, June, 1826, Mann MSS:MHS.
[5] Mann's legal papers for this company are in the Mann MSS:DHS, 1826 ff.

To his office also came business involving domestic relations, corporation lawsuits, boundary disputes, and the defense of criminals. Within a remarkably short time, he had made himself familiar with complex legal questions, including the labyrinth of laws surrounding corporate financing and water rights at mill sites. The notes for some of the cases ran as high as twenty pages, ranging from heavily documented histories of legal interpretations in agreement with a client's position to a shrewd and compelling emotional presentation, designed to have maximum imprint on a jury's sense of fairness and desire for simple justice.[6]

The most far-reaching development in his career in this period, however, was the beginning of legal work for merchants and legal firms in Boston. A Boston broker appointed Mann his solicitor for Norfolk County, and Charles G. Loring, prominent Boston attorney and cousin of Edward G. Loring, Mann's classmate at Litchfield, sent Mann his Dedham accounts. New work now sought him out and it was no longer necessary to travel about the country and seek out new cases. In a few years, Horace Mann, despite the obstacles indigenous to Dedham, had built a successful legal practice which extended clear to Boston. In the future, there would always be some lawyers from the big city competing for the more lucrative local cases, but there were others who found it convenient to place their Norfolk County affairs in the hands of this promising young man who was tallying up an impressive record of legal victories. It was a proud young man who rented a chaise from Moses Gregg, owner of the Norfolk Hotel, and returned to Franklin on July 4, 1826, there to participate in the fiftieth anniversary celebration of Independence Day. It was an even prouder young man who was asked to offer the first toast at a banquet held there. His glass raised, Horace Mann, Esq., saluted "Washington, Jefferson, Madison, Monroe, and the two Adamses—Six conclusive arguments against the doctrine of legitimacy."[7]

By 1829 he also had surplus money to loan. At first he probably viewed this as a device by which his clients could postpone the payment of their bills, but he soon learned that it could also mean additional income. In order that his clients understood he meant

---

[6] Mann MSS, 1826–32:DHS, *passim*.
[7] Charles G. Loring to Mann, December 3, 1829, Mann MSS:DHS; and C. G. Loring and L. Stanwood to Mann, April 13, 1830, Mann MSS: MHS; the receipt for the chaise is in the Mann MSS:DHS; Dedham *Village Register*, July 6, 1826.

business rather than philanthropy, he clearly specified the going rate of interest on the promissory notes he accepted.[8]

Personal loans were catchpenny, however, when compared to the larger financial plans in the mind of the young attorney. Most of these centered upon a business partnership he was developing with his brother Stanley. There had been times when Stanley's earlier dealings had put the entire Mann family's assets in jeopardy. To the conservative farmers around Franklin, his manipulations appeared all the more irresponsible since, from their point of view, he had neither the desire to farm nor an inclination to learn a trade. But such opinions were of little concern to Stanley Mann. A schemer and incurable optimist, he was ready to take a risk and stake his future on getting a foothold in textile manufacturing. What he lacked in hard cash, Stanley made up in personal appeal. One of his nieces remembered him as a "tall, large, fine-looking, handsome man, with very generous impulses," and with such personal assets and connections from his membership in the Masonic order, Stanley was obtaining credit and attracting new associates.[9]

For some time, he had had an eye on the Eagle Manufacturing Company, a small woolen mill in Wrentham which had been organized in 1818 and steadily lost money until its capital was exhausted. Through his friends, Stanley borrowed enough money to gain control of the factory, and as he did so, he was probably the first person in six generations of Manns to be called a "businessman." Under his direction, the Eagle mill soon turned a profit. With financial success came a rise in status. A "valuable and active member," whose services in Masonry were in "frequent demand" according to the lodge historian, Stanley, in 1824, was elected the "Worshipful Master" of the Wrentham Lodge and soon moved up to become the "District Deputy Grand Master" of the Fourth Masonic District. Finally making money, he also shared it, gaining a small amount of notoriety by presenting the volunteer firemen of Franklin with a new hand pumper.[1]

---

[8] For example, see the promissory note given to him by John Gouldring for $40, dated April 10, 1830, Mann MSS:DHS. By 1832, Mann was even loaning money in other towns such as Taunton, through Sydney Williams, another attorney.

[9] Eliza Scott Wilbur Mann to Benjamin P. Mann, MS notes of Benjamin P. Mann, Straker MSS:ACL; Clarence Sumner, *Centennial History of Montgomery Lodge, A.F. and A.M.* (Boston, 1899), pp. 92–93.

[1] *United States Documents* 221, 22d Congress, 1st Sess., 1831–32, House Executive Documents, Vol. I, Document 3, No. 164.

Flushed with his first success, Stanley, in 1826, cast about for a second opportunity. He did not have far to look. In Franklin, the City Manufacturing Company was about to capitulate to its creditors. For ten years, it had never paid a dividend and was now on the brink of bankruptcy. Stanley took over its dubious assets at a large discount; but despite the apparent bargain, he could not procure enough credit to negotiate the transaction. He turned to Horace, who was able to raise $2,000 and purchase nine shares of Eagle stock. Then, using the Eagle Manufacturing Company for collateral, the two brothers borrowed enough money to purchase fifty shares of the City Manufacturing Company from Otis Everett for $22,500 and twenty-five shares from John French for $12,500. The difference between the value of the nine shares of Eagle and the seventy-five of City was covered by mortgaging all the City shares as well. It was a tenuous arrangement, but the two brothers were willing to take the risk. Through such a maneuver, Horace and Stanley had expanded their limited capital and were now in control of two companies. According to the terms of the mortgages, they expected to be debt-free in five years. Like most of the other lawyers in Dedham, Horace Mann was now very much involved in other money-making activities.[2]

By 1831 the Eagle Manufacturing Company was employing eight men, four boys, and fourteen women, converting raw wool into sheeting with a yearly production of 175,000 yards. City Manufacturing Company was a larger operation, consuming 187,000 pounds of raw cotton, and producing 563,000 yards of sheeting annually with a work force of sixty. Its real estate, buildings, and machinery were valued at $47,000, and the value of its average stock on hand was about $29,500.[3] But Stanley, unwilling to rest on this achievement, dreamed of building a new factory from the ground up and already had purchased a mill site by 1829.[4]

In five years, Horace Mann had become an entrepreneur as well as a successful lawyer, but for a young man of his ability and ambition, there was still the third avenue of politics available for ad-

---

[2] *United States Documents 221, ibid.;* papers for these transactions are dated February 21 and February 25, 1826, Mann MSS:DHS. According to the records, Horace was the sole owner of the City stock. That Horace Mann was no mere silent partner in all this can be seen from Stanley Mann to Mann, September 1826, Mann MSS:MHS.

[3] *U.S. Documents, 1831–32, ibid.* The men were paid $1:25 per day, the boys 25 cents, and the women and girls 50 cents.

[4] Contract of sale dated September 15, 1829, MSS:MHS.

vancement. In Dedham, it was easier to begin than to climb. Like other towns, the fundamental form of government was the Town Meeting. Mann soon was active in these as a matter of course and his participation became the second phase of his political education. In the United Brothers Society, the students had practiced with mock government. Here he became involved in the genuine thing. Dedham Town Meetings were often spirited affairs, in which opposing factions displayed some of the finer techniques of parliamentary procedure and political maneuvering, all of which Mann occasionally observed from the vantage point of the moderator's chair. Later he was also elected to the School Committee and appointed a Justice of the Peace for Norfolk County on January 22, 1828.[5]

For the serious politician, the real goal, however, was election to the General Court. This was not an easy matter, but it helped if one had party support. Clearly not in agreement with the few diehard Federalists in town, Mann was unmistakably Republican, supporting the election of John Quincy Adams in 1824 and keeping abreast of state and federal affairs through his subscription to the *National Gazette*. As a Republican, he was in an enviable position in Dedham as the Republicans easily outnumbered both Federalists and the supporters of Andrew Jackson. In the election of 1828, Mann's political loyalties might have been out of step with the nation, but he was certainly in agreement with the voter sentiment in his town, as the citizens of Dedham cast 214 votes for Adams and 34 votes for Jackson.[6]

The preponderance of Republican voters meant that in order to be elected, a candidate had to contend with other members of his own party. Often the outcome was determined by one's personal popularity. Worthington's caustic observation was that the successful candidate was the one who evaded issues and never took a definitive stand. One issue, however, was difficult to avoid. Dedham, like other towns in New England, was concerned with the growing membership of the Masons and the abduction and murder of Captain William Morgan, reputed to have been a Masonic turncoat.

---

[5] Herman Mann, Journal, No. 3, November 3, 1828, MS in DHS; Records, Town of Dedham, 1819–34, MS in Town Hall, Dedham, Massachusetts. Mann was chosen moderator on October 31, 1825; May 1, 1826; March 5, September 24, and October 15, 1827; and May 5, 1828.
[6] Livingston, *Portrait Gallery*, III, 188–189; receipts for his *National Gazette* subscription, from 1823 on, are in the Mann MSS:DHS; Herman Mann, Journal, No. 3, November 3, 1828, MS in DHS.

The tension came to local climax in 1829 when the town was host to a large anti-Masonic convention. Somehow, Mann steered clear of the controversy. Generally aloof from local squabbles, he worked to elevate himself within the state party organization. By 1827 he was secretary of the Republican Party of Norfolk County, and campaigned for the election of Governor Levi Lincoln. Already, the year before, a group of voters had supported him for the General Court, and Mann obtained enough votes to be elected as the second representative from Dedham. The town, however, wishing to conserve its funds, decided this time, as it had in the past, to send only one person to the legislature. The office fell to Richard Ellis, who polled twice as many votes as Mann.[7]

The following year, Mann's supporters organized a discreet campaign for him and managed to get a letter urging his election published in the *Village Register*. In the typical political hyperbole of the day, Mann was described as

qualified by talents and acquirements to enter into the discussion of important subjects,—so that the principles, for the constant support of which the town has been distinguished, may be maintained by the powers of an *advocate* as well as by the unaffected good sense and respectable character of her representatives. In looking around for such an one, among many deserving of the honor, few possess such qualifications as HORACE MANN, Esq.

The letter also called attention to Mann's rise in the community by his own boot straps, never having been "borne on the shoulders of patronage." Instead, "by diligence and perseverance he has conquered, thus far, his own fortunes."[8]

Just what Mann's attitude was on the controversial Warren Bridge Bill, the correspondent neglected to mention. Not that the good men of Dedham were uninterested in the dispute over the construction of a free bridge over the Charles River connecting Charlestown to Boston, then before the General Court. Rebuffed during the previous legislative session, Charlestown and Cambridge

---

[7] Worthington, *History of Dedham*, p. 91: Dedham *Village Register*, March 22, 1827; Herman Mann, Journal, No. 3, January, 1829, MS in DHS; strong anti-Masonic feeling continued as late as 1831, as can be seen from articles in the *Independent Politician and Working Men's Advocate* (Dedham, Mass.), Vol. I; Records, Town of Dedham, 1819–34, MS in Town Hall, Dedham, Massachusetts. On May 1, 1826, Mann received 51 votes to Ellis's 123.

[8] Dedham *Village Register*, May 3, 1827.

planned to send their complete legal representation to the next session. Other towns, sensing the need to protect their own interests, also planned full delegations. Such was the case in Dedham this year. On May 8, 1827, the villagers and farmers came into the center of Dedham to cast their votes. When the ballots had been counted, they had elected Horace Mann as their second representative to the Massachusetts General Court and had started him on his political career.[9]

Twelve years after leaving Mann's Plain, he had become a promising young lawyer and legislator. Twelve years of education, effort, and luck had transformed the son of a yeoman from Franklin into a republican aristrocrat. As Mann began his new life, another man's career was drawing to a close. Two days before Mann took his seat in the General Court, Nathanael Emmons, back in Franklin, retired from the ministry.[1] His resignation marked the end of more than a half century of service to his people and the passing of a way of life. Although much of the old life would remain with him, Horace did not wish to dwell upon his legacy from Emmons and the other people from Franklin. For the moment he was more concerned with the remarkable incidents of the last five years in Dedham which had brought him to the threshold of a new life. His success had been accompanied by an increase in his ties with the city. Dedham had indeed proved to be halfway between Franklin and Boston.

---

[9] Dedham *Village Register*, April 26 and May 10, 1827.
[1] *Manual of the First Congregational Church, Franklin, Massachusetts,* p. 23.

CHAPTER V

Bridges, Railroads, and Religious Freedom

========

PERHAPS at no period since the settlement of Boston has its prosperity been so flattering as at the present time. . . . We now rely on our own resources—agriculture and manufactures, and commerce with all nations with whom we can exchange our commodities at fair prices. So long as we are blessed with union, good institutions and good laws, our city, under Providence, will continue on in the forward path to prosperity and happiness.

JOHN HAYWARD

————

THREE WEEKS AFTER his election, Horace Mann was on his way to Boston for the opening of the General Court on Election Day. The stagecoach left Dedham on its summer schedule at seven o'clock in the morning. This fifteen-mile trip, the last leg of a long journey begun years before when he first had left Franklin, took an hour and a half and cost him 50 cents. As he approached Boston, his coach rolled along a strip of land which connected the city to the mainland like a wrist to a large hand. The thumb of the hand was the Mill Dam and the many wharves reaching into the harbor to receive the wealth of seven seas were its fingers. Here was the India Wharf designed by Bulfinch and the pride of the town fathers. Nearby was the Central Wharf, jutting a quarter mile into the bay, and the Commercial Wharf, with its thirty-four granite warehouses, reputed to be the finest accommodations in the world. The port received more than 600 foreign arrivals each year as well as 3,000 coastal vessels, and through its facilities passed more than 300,000 barrels of flour and 45,000 bales of cotton annually.

Back away from the waterfront was Faneuil Hall, with its golden grasshopper weather vane high above the cupola. A sacred shrine to American liberty, the building continued to be an active forum and public conscience where the voices of the spiritual descendants of Sam Adams and Paul Revere still were raised to air divergent views and agitate unpopular causes within its historic walls. On one side of the hall was Merchants Row, a street lined with busy countinghouses. Radiating away in another direction were Cornhill, Brattle, and Elm Streets, with their bookstores and shops filled with imports from every known place on the globe.

Boston had changed from a town into a city, a transformation guided by its able mayor, Josiah Quincy, and belatedly acknowledged in the state statutes. A few cows still grazed on the Common beneath its ancient elms and mottled sycamores, but of late, it had mainly become a park for children's play and a place for handsomely dressed women to stroll and display their fine brocades and crinolines. With the help of cobblestones in its busy streets and stone slabs and wooden planking for its sidewalks, the city had finally conquered its old enemy, mud, and in a few years Mayor Quincy would banish cows from the Common altogether as a gallant gesture to Boston's ladies and as a sign of his commitment to Boston's urban future.

On a hill above the Common and commanding the city was Bulfinch's State House, a massive building of tall Corinthian columns and walls of warm, salmon-colored brick trimmed with stone. To cap his edifice, the architect had designed a golden dome, visible for miles in the bright sunshine and crowned with a square lantern which could serve as a beacon at night. It was said that he chose the dome shape to soften and add variety to the skyline of a city rendered both monotonous with its hundreds of flat-roofed residences and commercial houses and harsh by the sharp slender steeples of its many churches. Arriving at the State House, Mann learned that other towns besides Dedham had sent complete delegations to the General Court, and as a result, the number of representatives present exceeded the available seats on the first floor of the Representatives' Chamber. When the official tally sheets were prepared, it was apparent that the membership of the House exceeded 300 men and that it would be necessary to place the overflow at desks installed up in the visitors' gallery. In the lottery for place assignments, Mann drew number two and thus had a front-row seat for his first session in the legislature.[1]

After whitening every sea with their canvas, the men of Massachusetts were now turning inland in search of other wealth and challenges equal to their ingenuity and acquisitive temper. No doubt

---

[1] *Journal of the House,* Vol. 48, May 30, 1827, p. 5, MS in MSA; the designation of seats is on the vote tally sheets attached to the back of this volume; *Columbian Centinel,* May 30, 1827.

it was an unintended sign of the times, but when the workmen replaced the "sacred cod" above the Speaker's desk after having re-
modeled the House of Representatives, they pointed this symbol of
New England's well-being inland, rather than out to sea as it had
always hung before. If Horace Mann imputed any significance to
this, he did not mention it in his letters to his sister. What did impress him was the large number of men who milled about in the
chamber and nearby halls. Topics of conversations ranged from the
spring weather and bad conditions of roads in the state to the need
for higher tariffs and the chances of making a fortune in railroad
construction and textile manufacturing. Inevitably, however, talk
in the State House corridors and nearby taverns centered upon the
much more immediate legislative task of authorizing the construction of a toll-free bridge across the Charles River.

For years, the people of Charlestown had pressed for a free
bridge linking them to Boston. To them, the tolls they paid on the old
Charles River Bridge amounted to a tribute extracted by its owners
who, by reason of an ancient charter, held a monopoly on what
should have been the property of all. From the point of view of the
stockholders of the Charles River Bridge, a free bridge would make
their holdings valueless, and they did everything in their power to
prevent what they considered a confiscation of their property. Influential merchants and politicians were among the owners; so were
a few widows. Even Harvard College owned shares in the bridge.
The agitation from Charlestown and neighboring Cambridge finally
took the form of lengthy petitions to the legislature to incorporate a
second company which would build another span across the river.
These proposed that tolls would be charged upon it until the project
was debt-free and the original backers had received a small return on
their investment. Then the bridge would revert to the Commonwealth. In a stormy session in 1827, the Charlestown delegation in
the General Court finally forced through a free bridge bill over a determined and bitter opposition. With victory now just beyond their
outstretched grasp, they suffered a temporary setback when Governor Levi Lincoln refused to sign the bill. Undaunted, they regrouped
their forces and resubmitted it to the House where they were sustained by a two to one majority. From here the bill moved on to the
Senate. When the clerk tallied the votes, sixteen Senators supported
the bill while twelve stood with the Governor. The Charlestown faction had come within two votes of its goal. Lincoln's veto had held,

and the proposed "free bridge" would wait until the General Court reconvened in May, 1827.[2]

Now as Horace Mann took his seat in front of the Speaker's desk, he knew that a showdown was imminent and that the balance of power rested with the large number of new Representatives sitting in the chamber for the first time. If he had managed to conceal his own opinions on the Warren Bridge Bill in Dedham, he could tell by the pressures put upon him by men from both factions that soon he would have to take a public stand. One of the first orders of business was the announcement of the powerful standing committees. Veterans of many past sessions such as Francis Baylies, William B. Calhoun, and James Savage were given key appointments. Richard Ellis of Dedham was named to the Committee on Education, a minor post; long before the Committee on Appointments had worked its way to Horace Mann's name, far down on the seniority list, it had filled all its vacancies. If he was denied for the moment, the situation called for patience. The next day the name of Horace Mann was read before the assembly. Together with two others, he had been given the responsibility of studying existing legislation concerning "Hawkers, Pedlars and Petty Chapmen." A pedestrian assignment when compared with the weighty problems he had fielded in his oratory, it nevertheless received his full attention as, once again, the young lawmaker began yet another form of apprenticeship.[3]

The next few days were occupied with additional procedural matters while the opposing camps lined up support for the coming show of strength. Mann witnessed a minor skirmish over the appointment of a special joint committee on bridges, but probably did not understand its implications fully. Then a temporary halt in the hostilities was declared to enable both chambers to hear the annual address of Governor Levi Lincoln. Lincoln had scuttled the last bridge bill, and now all attention was centered upon his words in the expectation that he might set forth a possible compromise.[4] Only as he finished was it apparent that His Excellency had chosen to remain

---

[2] Dedham *Village Register,* March 15, 1827.

[3] Journal of the House, Vol. 48, June 1, 2, and 11, 1827, pp. 8–10, 17, and 73, MS in MSA; *Columbian Centinel,* June 6, 1827.

[4] Journal of the House, Vol. 48, June 6, 1827, pp. 42–43, MS in MSA; "Speech of His Excellency Levi Lincoln Before the Two Branches of the Legislature in Convention June 6, 1827." *Massachusetts House Documents, 1827–1828, passim.*

silent on the matter of bridges, but there was to be no denying the Charlestown delegation. For them it was now or never. Barely had the Governor disappeared from the room and the Senators filed back to the upper chamber when the Representatives turned to processing the petition of John Skinner, *et al.,* that is, the Warren Bridge Bill. Negotiations ground on, but before either chamber could take action, the Governor prorogued the session. Some lawmakers breathed a sigh of relief as they left for their homes; others were angry and disappointed. Neither of these reactions was shared by Horace Mann.[5]

For him the month had been an intensive period consisting of almost an endless series of introductions to men whose lives orbited around the State House. Every day brought new names, each to be matched with a new face and an evaluation of the individual's political influence. Edward Loring, Mann's classmate from Litchfield, served as his social and political mentor. Loring, just beginning his law practice in Boston, was a member of one of the town's first families. By marriage and business relationships he was allied with the family of Mayor Josiah Quincy, and with the family of Edmund Dwight, which was amassing a fortune from its textile mills along the Connecticut River. If it was a heady experience meeting some of the first social and economic families of Boston, this did not prevent Mann from doing yeoman's work in the legislature and he applied himself to whatever tasks came along in the General Court. Quite possibly, working on the licensing of pedlars and hucksters could be the first rung in the political ladder he wanted to climb. Actually, so rapid had been the passage of events that he had little time to reflect on all this. Returning to Dedham, he found a month's work piled up on his desk. Legal briefs had to be prepared for the September and December sessions of the Court of Common Pleas, and there were always innumerable documents to process which never reached the courts. The next six months passed quickly, and by January, 1828, Mann again left for Boston to continue to build his political fortunes.

New assignments to ad hoc committees stimulated his interest during this apprenticeship, as did the contents of a few of the many bills under consideration. Partly due to his efforts in committees, the Chelsea Beach and Meadows moved one step closer to their preservation. At the time, he had little interest in the petition to

---

[5] *Journal of the House,* Vol. 48, June 6 and 18, 1827, pp. 44 and 127–128, MS in MSA; *Columbian Centinel,* June 13, 1827.

incorporate the India Rubber Company or bills for the inspection of hops and pickled fish, but he did examine a proposal to provide better care for "lunatics and people furiously mad." Here his interest was short-lived as action on this was deferred until the next session.[6] The approaching national election also drew his attention. After a certain amount of hair splitting, Mann together with 224 other Representatives went on public record as endorsing the re-election of John Quincy Adams. Not that Mann was unalterably for the Adams and Clay party. When one of his legal colleagues, and something of a political opportunist, John Barton Derby, worked for the election of Jackson, he quickly drew the wrath of the "Adams' Press" in Boston. Rallying to Derby's support were a number of lawyers, including Horace Mann. Years later, Derby would remember that the several resolutions passed by the members of the Norfolk County Bar in his behalf were "sustained by Horace Mann of Dedham." But aside from this, there was little in January and the first part of February which enabled Mann to gain more than the outer edges of the political limelight.[7]

*   *   *

When the chance finally presented itself to move to the center of the stage, it came from an unexpected set of circumstances. The previous June, an apparently innocuous petition had been filed by the First Religious Society of Blandford, Massachusetts, asking that the legislature incorporate a group as the "Trustees of the Ministerial Fund of Blandford." Four years before, several benefactors had bequeathed money to the Society to serve as an endowment, with the intent that the income accruing to it be used for the religious work of their organization. The initial request of the Society in 1824 had simply asked that the General Court incorporate a board of trustees and "confer on them and their successors in office forever, the powers and privileges usually granted to similar corporations." [8]

---

[6] Journal of the House, Vol. 48, June 11 and 13, 1827, and February 27, 1828, pp. 72, 93, and 378, MS in MSA.

[7] Journal of the House, Vol. 48, February 27, 1828, pp. 343–344, MS in MSA; John Derby, *Political Reminiscences, Including a Sketch of the Origin and History of the "Statesman Party" of Boston* (Boston, 1835), pp. 30–31.

[8] Senate Document 8109, Petition of the First Religious Society of Blandford, May 22, 1824, MS in MSA; Journal of the House, Vol. 48, June 2, 1827, p. 20, MS in MSA.

Just why the General Court did not act upon the 1824 petition is something of a mystery, but in the ensuing four years, events in Massachusetts's ecclesiastical history caused the petitioners to question the adequacy of the "powers and privileges usually granted similar corporations." Since 1820, Unitarianism had been making major inroads into what had once been the stronghold of orthodox Congregationalism. Following the bitterly contested "Dedham Case," it became painfully evident to more than a few that as parish after parish called Unitarian ministers to replace Congregational men, church properties and endowed funds, once bequeathed by devout Trinitarians, were now falling into the hands of apostate Unitarian trustees who were dispensing them to support ministers of their own liberal persuasion. No endowment seemed completely secure from this, and it now was considered mandatory to the believers in Blandford, still thoroughly orthodox and untainted by the heresy of Unitarianism, to seek legal protection against such a development.[9]

On January 30, 1828, the Blandford petition was sent to the House Committee on Parishes. From here it was reported out and apparently on its way to a perfunctory passage when Reuben Boies, a Representative from Blandford, proposed an amendment to the bill. That there be absolutely no doubt about the future disposition of its income, Boies introduced the further proviso "that the income of

---

[9] Frank Smith, *A History of Dedham, Massachusetts* (Dedham, 1936), pp. 80–89; Leonard W. Levy, *The Law of the Commonwealth and Chief Justice Shaw* (Cambridge, 1957), pp. 32–38. Actually the Blandford petitioners were extending the precautions taken by other orthodox societies in recent years. Following the "Dedham Case" (*Baker v. Fales*, 1820), several of these groups, in requesting incorporation, asked that their funds be used only to support a "Congregational minister." Others, more evasive but seeking the same end, asked that "The income of the property thus held shall be appropriated according to the original design of the donor or donors," or that the funds support a minister "in the way and manner which may be prescribed by such future subscriptions, donations, grants, bequests, devices, and appropriations." Still uneasy about the security of their funds, petitioners from a Congregational society in Amherst submitted the additional proviso that "No alterations or revision, in the act to which this is in addition shall ever be made, so as to alter the appropriation of said fund, or any parts thereof, made by the donor, grantors, or devisors respectively; but such appropriations shall remain permanent and unalienable."

Thus by the slow process of legislative accommodation, many orthodox religious societies were attempting to make their endowments secure from Unitarian encroachments. It was such an ironclad protection that the Blandford Society now wished to obtain. For examples of this legal metamorphosis, see *Laws of Massachusetts*, Vol. IX, Ch. CXVI, pp. 582–585, Ch. CXLI, pp. 626–628; Vol. X, Ch. XI, p. 607, Ch. LXXI, pp. 433–434, Ch. CXV, pp. 503–507, and Ch. CXXIII, pp. 515–520.

said fund shall be forever applied to the support of a learned, pious, Trinitarian Congregational minister." Here, to date, was the most overt attempt to prevent the Unitarian expropriation of Congregational funds, and it proved to be the unanticipated catalyst which precipitated an impassioned debate. For the next two days, at least on the floor of the House, the Free Bridge Bill was all but forgotten.[1]

One group argued that Christianity and republicanism were inseparable and interdependent components of a free society. To support the Christian ministry through legislation was in the self-interest of the state, since the ministry served to prevent a deterioration of public and private morals. In addition, they insisted that citizens had an inalienable right to dispose of their property as they desired. The liberal opposition countered with a more complex argument. The Blandford petition amounted to an appeal to establish a perpetual support for a particular "opinion." If its requests were granted, so must those from other denominations seeking similar protection. The result would be sectarian strife, which was "inconsistent with . . . republican institutions and the discovery of truth." In words reminiscent of the Dedham Case, they argued that it was the majority of the parish which should decide the doctrines fostered by endowed funds, rather than the dead hand of a donor.[2]

From every corner of the chamber, men motioned for the chance to speak. Party lines were crossed with impunity as William B. Calhoun, Theodore Sedgwick, Francis Baylies, Leverett Saltonstall, and Thomas Savage entered the debate. All this Horace Mann watched with an aroused interest. Tolerant although he was in many areas, even in politics, Mann had little sympathy for orthodox clergymen.[3] Although he had matured immeasurably since his youth in

---

[1] Journal of the House, Vol. 48, January 30 and February 20, 1828, pp. 251 and 352, MS in MSA.

[2] *Christian Register*, March 22, 1828; *Columbian Centinel*, February 23, 1828.

[3] Two years before, Mann's old president, Asa Messer, had been hounded by conservative Baptists who were certain they had uncovered the taint of Unitarianism in his writings. After holding his attackers at bay for a time, Messer finally quit the field and resigned. Actually, the accusations brought against him did little but establish him as a selfless defender of religious freedom. Mann became more directly involved in religious controversy at the time when he was hired as counsel to defend the town of Walpole in a suit brought against it by the local Congregational Society. Impatient with the claims of the plaintiffs, Mann dismissed them as a "lot of old women," an indiscretion he was later to regret. See Walter C. Bronson, *The History of Brown University* (Providence, 1914), pp. 186–191; Willard De Lue, *Story of Walpole* (Norwood, Mass., 1925), pp. 177–178.

Franklin, when dealing with the orthodox in general and their clergy in particular, Mann could not free himself of a childish devil theory which impugned their motives and saw them as variations all cast from the mold which had formed the unyielding Nathanael Emmons. The orthodox, he had come to believe, had a compulsion to persecute and coerce all those who did not share their beliefs, and Mann still nursed the wounds which he thought had been inflicted upon him by their oppressive doctrines.

Now, here in the House of Representatives, he had the chance to even accounts. After hastily scribbling some notes on the back of a letter, he was recognized by the Speaker and rose to deliver his first speech in the Massachusetts General Court. Mann pointed out that it was patently wrong for the Commonwealth to grant something it could not rescind at a later date. He opposed the Blandford petition, furthermore, because it would result in assisting one group at the expense of another and would bias an individual's judgment in adopting a personal creed. This, he argued, was an "invasion of Heaven's prerogatives." Finally, to those who feared a deterioration of morality in the absence of legislative support, Mann lectured that degeneration took place only when the individual had "abandoned his reason as no further use and forgone his inquiries after truth." Such a person was then "degraded into hopeless and remedyless servitude." As reasonable men, the members of the House in good conscience could not support the Blandford petition.[4]

---

[4] Mann to Nahum Capen, June 3, 1850, BUA. Mann wrote: "My first speech in the House of Representatives was for *Liberty of Conscience.*" The account in Livingston, *Portrait,* III, 189–190, says Mann's first speech was in favor of "religious liberty," and briefly describes the circumstances surrounding the Blandford petition. This entire incident has largely been ignored by Mann's biographers since his manuscript for the speech has been overlooked and political and religious historians have passed over the defeat of the petition in preference to the Dedham Case. That Mann's speech on "Liberty of Conscience" was connected with the Blandford petition can be deduced from several facts. The petition was the only one which aroused such a controversy during the sessions of 1827 and 1828. Mann recorded that his second speech in the House was in support of railroads. This can be dated about March, 1828, shortly after the Blandford debate. The *Christian Register,* March 22, 1828, reported that Mann was one of the leaders in the opposition to the bill. The above quotations are taken from manuscript notes on the back of an undated letter from Silas Holbrook to Mann, Mann MSS: MHS. It is evident that the arguments Mann presented here were tailor-made for the Blandford controversy. Two years later, Mann felt called upon to defend the position he took in the Blandford dispute. He reminded his audience in the House that individuals wished to be incorporated to manage endowed funds which were to be perpetually

It had been a dramatic and challenging speech. The "freshman" Representative from Dedham had delivered a trenchant plea for religious liberty in the spirit and tradition of Roger Williams and Thomas Jefferson. By the end of the day, when the Speaker called for a vote, the Boies amendment was handed a stunning setback, and the bill minus the special proviso was ordered to a third reading. The opposition, which had begun by straining at legal gnats, had slowly come to recognize during the heat of the debate that they were in fact defending the greater cause of religious liberty, as Mann had argued. Then when it seemed that the House would go on to pass a bill purged of all limiting clauses, Boies asked that action on it be postponed indefinitely.[5] Mann and his ad hoc allies had won what amounted to an unconditional surrender. More important, without realizing the full significance of their victory, they had brought about a turning point in religious legislation in Massachusetts. Never again were petitions of the Blandford type presented. Even more important, subsequent acts of incorporation included the proviso that they could be "altered or repealed at the discretion of the Legislature." Perhaps, at the Exchange Coffee House, Mann's friends toasted their new hero and his successful baptism of fire in political debate. The General Court had taken a stand. No longer would it invade "Heaven's prerogatives."

*   *   *

At the time, few anticipated the significance of the Blandford incident. For most of the harried lawmakers, it was simply a momentary and welcome diversion from the troublesome free bridge issue. During the first two months in 1828, the backers of the bill had survived four days of continuous debate and every conceivable parliamentary delaying action. On February 29, they gained its third reading by the narrow margin of six votes. By this time, Mann joined those opposed to the bill. With the major roadblocks removed,

---

devoted to a predetermined object. Thus there was a strong possibility of a new generation being forced to appropriate these funds against their wishes and conscience. Mann continued, "Sir, no one living has a right to give his property a perpetual destination. . . . I approve the generosity which makes a charitable bequest; but if it is avowed that it is to bind posterity, though it were abundant as Potosi, I would say it basely given." See Boston *Recorder*, March 24, 1830.

[5] *Columbian Centinel*, February 23 and March 8, 1828; Journal of the House, Vol. 48, March 6, 1828, p. 413, MS in MSA.

the bill authorizing the construction of a toll-free bridge linking Boston to Charlestown passed both chambers and was ready for Governor Levi Lincoln's signature. Before he signed it into law, however, the opposition took an extraordinary step in a last-ditch effort to block its enactment.[6]

In a virtually unprecedented move, they submitted a public protest containing their reasons why the bill should not have been passed. The document was based upon four propositions, all challenging the wisdom of the enactment: (1) neither public convenience nor necessity required another bridge, (2) Charlestown did not require relief from paying tolls, (3) the bridge would injure the property rights of the Charles River Bridge Proprietors and the law was actually a violation of their charter if no indemnity were given them, and (4) a legislature had no right to obstruct a navigable river by an unnecessary bridge. The protest contained more than sixty-five signatures. Among them was the name of Horace Mann. Fifty-four signers endorsed all the reasons, but a few qualified their positions. Mann asked that the words "for reasons 1 & 4" be placed after his name. Evidently, he had formed his opinion somewhat independently of the rest. In agreement with his earlier arguments in the Blandford debate, Mann was unwilling for the Commonwealth to relinquish its right to repeal what it once had granted, even if this involved property. Thus he could not agree with the third argument in the protest. In any case, the last-minute remonstrance proved futile. The very next day, believing the people had expressed their will through their representatives, Governor Lincoln signed "An act to Establish the Warren Bridge Corporation." It was now part of the law of the Commonwealth.[7]

John Skinner, *et al.*, had won the right to form a corporation and build their bridge. When it became debt-free and its backers had earned a 5 per-cent return on their investment, the structure was to become the property of the Commonwealth. In their desire to obtain the law, the free bridge faction failed to prescribe procedures for operating the bridge structure once the state took title, but at the time this seemed to be a trivial omission. It was now more important

---

[6] Journal of the House, Vol. 48, February 17, 28, and 29, and March 1, 1828, p. 393, MS in MSA; Boston *Commercial Gazette*, March 3, 1828, and *Columbian Centinel*, March 1, 1828.

[7] Journal of the House, Vol. 48, March 11, 1828, pp. 432–436, MS in MSA. See also *Columbian Centinel*, March 15, 1828; *Laws of Massachusetts*, Vol. X, Ch. CXXVII, pp. 851–855.

that the lawmakers move on to some neglected matters. If this episode shook Mann's faith in his own judgment or the wisdom of the majority, he didn't record the fact. Instead he turned his interest toward other projects which he could support wholeheartedly.

*   *   *

The decade of the twenties witnessed a growing concern about the future of the commerce of Boston as transportation developments in neighboring states were beginning to draw on territories which the Hub had always assumed were its rightful hinterland. The port of Providence, Rhode Island, was using the newly constructed Blackstone Canal to siphon off heavy freight from the rich Worcester County, while Albany, New York, at the juncture of the Hudson River and the Erie Canal, had begun to draw off goods produced in western Massachusetts. Most recently a new threat to Boston's commercial life had come in the form of a canal being projected from New Haven, north to Northampton, Massachusetts, to tap the productive Connecticut River Valley. These threats to Boston's commercial supremacy called for positive action and more than a few people looked to the legislature for help. Most considered better transportation as the best means to help the Hub retain her position as the leading port in New England.[8]

Once the lawmakers had acknowledged the superiority of railroads over canals, Mann joined those who advocated a survey to determine the best route from Boston to the Hudson River. The following year a bill to create a Board of Internal Improvements was up for consideration. It is not clear whether this was ever in danger of defeat, but during its deliberation, Mann asked for the floor and publicly cast his lot with Edmund Dwight, Josiah Quincy, and others who were pressing for state-supported railroad construction.[9]

Boston, like other great cities, he maintained, had thrived because of its accessibility to the sea and the transportation it afforded.

---

[8] For a description of this concern for Boston's future, see Edward Chase Kirkland, *Men, Cities, and Transportation* (Cambridge, 1948), I, 93–97.

[9] Journal of the House, Vol. 48, June 13, 1827, vote tally sheet, MS in MSA. In a letter to Nahum Capen, June 3, 1850, BUA, Mann stated that his second speech in the House was in support of railroads. "This was a time when everybody was laughing at them." About this same time, a writer credited Mann with having given one of the first speeches in favor of railroad construction ever made to a legislature. See James Spear Loring, *The Hundred Boston Orators* (Boston, 1854), p. 599.

Now if the city was to stave off its competitors, it must develop a superior system of inland transportation as well. On land, the great obstacle was friction. Canal transportation had overcome this, but it was too slow and cumbersome. Actually, it represented no progress since first attempted by the ancient Egyptians. Mann urged his colleagues to consider the immense advantage New York had gained with its "big ditch," and how this project was "ministering to the power and happiness of the people." A railroad from Boston to the Hudson would enable the Bay State to obtain some of the benefits New York had expected to keep for herself. The challenge from other states made it imperative that the lawmakers consider the welfare of the entire Commonwealth. Instead of each community selfishly lobbying for a rail line to stop in their hamlet, Mann argued that such local loyalties were shortsighted and urged all to join in supporting a road between two really significant communities. Only then would rail transportation have a fair chance to demonstrate its merits.[1]

Such sentiments could bring applause from his new associates in Boston, but their acceptance elsewhere in the state was not a foregone conclusion. If a strong sense of localism had hamstrung previous statewide legislative action, the issue of railroads could further expose the depth of the roots of local interests and loyalties. Small towns like Salem and Newburyport, within the shadow of Boston, were unwilling to see the Hub gain additional economic advantage over them, and farmers in this area, never very enthusiastic for additional taxes, were unwilling to vote tax funds which would enable more distant farmers to compete with them for city markets. Others took the broader view that the Commonwealth was an economic unit and must resolve its problems accordingly.

Understandably then, the reaction to Mann's speech back in Dedham was mixed. A few in the community were out for Mann's scalp. Old Edward Dowse, one of the patriarchs of the town, was outraged at the unmitigated gall of this parvenu and attacked him in a series of articles carried in several local papers. To Dowse, Mann's stand was motivated neither by a concern for the prosperity of the Commonwealth nor by some nebulous national purpose, but rather by an undisguised desire to gain important financial and political connections in Boston. He denounced Mann, saying that if the young politician's talent was equal to his insatiable ambition, he

---

[1] Dedham *Village Register*, March 20, 1828.

would someday occupy a seat in Congress. Mann survived the attack. Not only was the bill to encourage railroad construction passed, but Mann was returned to the General Court for a second term by a majority of satisfied townsmen.[2]

The next two terms found him back at work on additional railroad legislation. Repeatedly the Governor urged the legislators to forget their local vested interests and work for the good of the state. Mann, in wholehearted agreement with this, voted consistently for bills that encouraged and facilitated construction. For this, he was rewarded in June, 1828, with a seat on a joint committee on railways and canals. Two years later when a bill to incorporate a company for a railroad from Boston to Albany, New York, was being debated in the House, Mann was in the thick of the fight. Not only did he furnish estimates of costs and income; he also led the fight to strip the bill of its crippling amendments. Attempts to kill the bill outright failed, as Mann doggedly pushed for quick, positive action. By the end of the 1830 session, the legislature had chartered three railroad corporations.

Not satisfied that the state simply act as a referee between competing railroad promoters, Mann also urged that it help bear part of the cost of construction. Thus when the city of Boston requested permission to invest $1 million in stock for a rail line running from its limits to the west, Mann supported its petition. Although he had strong personal reasons for supporting the petition, since his new friends, the Quincys, were heavily involved in promoting the scheme, Mann also found the proposal completely compatible with his general political philosophy of positive republicanism. Speaking before a committee of which he was a member, Mann argued that the people of the Commonwealth would gain immediate benefits if the state used tax monies for internal improvements. In a republic, the people held the right to provide for their own protection, help the poor, educate the youth, and elevate the general morality. All these were essential to the well-being of a society. Assuming agreement on this, Mann claimed the same was true of opening channels of communication. If all private property could be taxed to support militia, schools, and asylums for the poor, it could also support internal improvements. In the final analysis, he argued, "it is owned that a

---

[2] *Ibid.;* Livingston, *Portrait,* III, 190; Loring, *Hundred Boston Orators,* p. 598; *Laws of Massachusetts,* X, Ch. CXVI, pp. 815–818, "An Act to Provide for Internal Improvements by Railroads."

majority of the legal voters can lawfully and rightfully control it" for the common good.[3]

No advocate of *laissez faire,* Mann believed the role of republican government was broad in scope and positive in action. Progress was inevitable, but it could be expedited if the legislature played an active role in furthering those things which held the most promise for social progress and human happiness. But although many in the General Court may have agreed with such a political philosophy in general, they were as yet unwilling to apply it to state aid for railroad construction. Mann's arguments notwithstanding, a majority of his committee submitted a report opposing the use of municipal funds in Boston to finance part of the road. Allocating public monies in such a manner, this said, was to use them for "purposes foreign from their character, and the ends for which they were not instituted." [4]

Even though state financial aid was not immediately forthcoming, by the early 1830's Mann and his co-workers had obtained half their loaf. They had gained the passage of charters for several roads running from Boston, including one as far west as Worcester. This accomplished, their major unfinished task was the acquisition of a franchise to build a road across the state clear to the Hudson River. In 1833, a bill incorporating a group to construct a line from Worcester to Albany, New York, came under debate. Mann, by this time recognized as one of the most articulate advocates of rail transportation, presented a carefully reasoned speech, marshalling an array of facts to substantiate his argument for action and positive involvement by the state in such a venture.[5]

He built his case on three major premises. Citing figures from the 1830 census to corroborate what he had already learned as a boy in Franklin, he first argued that "the agricultural resources of this state *are altogether* inadequate to furnish sustenance to its present population." Regardless of the investment in human toil, the rocky soil and severe climate were immovable stumbling blocks, ready to

---

[3] Undated MS of Mann's speech, in Mann MSS:MHS; *Independent Chronicle and Boston Patriot,* January 26, 1831; in Journal of the House, Vol. 51, January 15, 1831, p. 150, MS, MSA.

[4] "Report of a Committee on the Petition of the City Council for Permission to Subscribe to a Railroad from Boston to the Western States," *Massachusetts House Documents,* 1830–1831, No. 54.

[5] *Laws of the Commonwealth of Massachusetts, 1831–1833* (Boston, 1833), Vol. XII, Ch. LXXLL, pp. 152–162, "An Act to establish the Boston and Worcester Rail Road Corporation."

frustrate every attempt to make Massachusetts self-sustaining in the production of foodstuffs. "My Second position is," he continued, "that it is to commerce and to manufacturing and mechanic arts that we owe those supplies for the body and for the mind, which we so abundantly enjoy." In the past, men had not been able to provide for some of their most elemental physical wants. Now in some areas, one person and a machine could supply the needs of a hundred people. His final premise was that "a railroad would advance to a degree almost beyond our ability to comprehend, the interests of agricultural, of commerce, manufacturing and the mechanic arts," and therefore would promote the welfare of all classes of citizens in the Commonwealth.[6]

Shortly after Mann's speech, both chambers approved a bill to continue a railroad to the Hudson River, and on March 15, 1833, Governor Levi Lincoln signed it into law. For the railroad promoters, the act represented a major step towards a new prosperity they expected would come on rails and wheels. The future belonged to the enterprising, the bold and daring, and to the unsqueamish.[7]

*   *   *

Mann's railroad expansion speech revealed certain changes taking place in his outlook. For one thing, while retaining his penchant for polemics and hyperbole in public speaking, he now recognized the necessity of basing his arguments on a foundation of statistics. The result was a tough-minded argument, especially convincing to a Yankee audience. Facts, he recognized, could undercut myths. Surely figures proved that Massachusetts's agriculture no longer enjoyed its traditional hegemony over the economic life of the state that many still claimed. Looking to the future, Mann placed himself squarely in favor of industrial development, improved transportation, and the growth of towns and cities. In concrete actions, this meant that his voting record was almost identical with the solid block of votes from Suffolk County, i.e., Boston. To do this was to invite political repercussions from the hinterland, since at the time, more than 40 per cent of the lawmakers registered themselves as "farmers," by far the largest single-interest group in the General Court. But coming to

---

[6] Mann, "Argument for a Western Rail Road" [1833], MS, Mann MSS: MHS.
[7] *Laws of Massachusetts, 1831–1833*, Vol. XII, Ch. CXVI, pp. 660–670, "An Act to establish the Western Rail Road Corporation."

Boston and moving among the Lorings, Quincys, and their ambitious associates, Mann quickly grasped the potential for economic gain. No novice at taking calculated risks, he found in Boston that the rewards to be won by the venturesome were well worth the risks involved.[8]

In criticizing what he considered a lack of foresight in viewing the industrial potential of the state, Mann did not intend to lay bare any essential antagonism between rural and urban interests in Massachusetts. His advocacy of state support for manufacturing was but one aspect of his general faith in science and technology and his belief that it was the responsibility of republican government to make their benefits available to all the people of the Commonwealth. Far from fearing the results of industrial development, he viewed it optimistically as the long-awaited touchstone for greater human happiness. If technical progress had not been accompanied by desirable social and ethical changes in Boston and some of the burgeoning mill towns, this he considered a temporary setback which would soon be solved with the additional application of scientific knowledge.

He was not alone in holding such a view. A respectable core of lawmakers in the General Court agreed that the government should play an active role in both the economic and cultural development of the state. They made no sharp distinction between charters for philanthropic and educational institutions and those concerned with banking, insurance, manufacturing, and transportation. From the Governor on down, men spoke of railroad promotion and the establishment of a school for the blind with the same rhetoric and justified both as scientific means for alleviating suffering and furthering the happiness of the people and the good of the Commonwealth. In his annual messages, Levi Lincoln in one breath could speak of the benefits accruing to the people of New York from the Erie Canal, and in the next, laud the blessings Connecticut was bringing to its citizens by supporting the work of Thomas Gallaudet with the deaf and dumb.

The accomplishments of Gallaudet with the deaf and dumb and

---

[8] *Columbian Centinel*, February 3, 1830; the *Independent Chronicle and Boston Patriot*, February 17, 1830, published a breakdown which indicated that more than 40 per cent were farmers and less than 5 per cent were manufacturers. For a more sophisticated analysis, see Horace B. Davis, "Occupations of Massachusetts Legislators, 1790–1950," *New England Quarterly*, XXIV (1951), 89–100.

Eli Todd with the insane indicated what enlightened men might accomplish to alleviate suffering and improve the conditions of the unfortunate. Reports on prison reform were equally sanguine. Even men normally conservative and slow to adopt new measures were included among those who thought that problems long considered an inevitable part of human existence—poverty, disease, hunger, and ignorance—could now be eradicated. The optimism overran class lines, cut across political loyalties, and was shared by members of every religious denomination. Lincoln even thought that education could be reformed radically by systematizing teaching into a scientific pedagogy and had called upon the legislature to build a state teachers seminary for this purpose. Others looked to the fusion of philanthropy, science, and government to abolish imprisonment for debt, vice, and intemperance once and for all.

For Mann, whose agreement with such sentiments was unreserved, the opportunity to bring about concrete action came through his appointment to an increasing number of House committees. In his second term, he was awarded a seat on the Committee on Matters of Probate and Chancery. A year later he won a seat on the powerful Committee on the Judiciary, a position he held for several terms. In addition to annual appointments, Mann served on an average of five special and joint committees each session. In 1830, these included such diverse responsibilities as lumber inspection, claims for Massachusetts's service in the War of 1812, and debtor law revision. About the only things which did not come before him as a committee member were educational matters. Some appointments were important because of the influence wielded by the committee; all were important to Mann, as they put him in touch with the most influential men in the General Court.[9]

Thus, while he was defending religious freedom and promoting railroads, he also served on a committee seeking ways to suppress lotteries. "Legislation which is confined to pecuniary considerations, [is] narrow and disastrous," he insisted. The real objects of legislation were to promote industry and morality, and both of these were bound "indissolubly to the prosperity of the individual." His early legislative work also focused on the prevention of intemperance and the improvement of care for the insane. None of these social evils

[9] Journal of the House, Vol. 49, June 2, 1828, p. 25, and Vol. 50, May 27, 1829, pp. 2–19, MS in MSA; *Columbian Centinel*, June 3, 1828.

were compatible with a society of industrious, thrifty, and enlightened people.[1]

For a time, much of his attention was drawn to the revision of laws governing capital punishment. Under the leadership of William Sullivan and Robert Rantoul, a group had urged the abolition of the death sentence. Mann disagreed, still believing that the fear of the hangman's noose helped preserve the peace and check violence. Yet he did work to ensure that all executions were done as privately as the existing laws permitted. No doubt he considered the public hanging in Dedham in the summer of 1829 of John Boies, a convicted murderer—which was attended by more than 1,500 people, many of whom came with their picnic baskets for the outing—a barbaric practice which turned his stomach.[2]

During his maiden voyage into political life, Mann gave convincing evidences of an ambitious and dedicated young lawmaker who had allied himself with powerful commercial and manufacturing interests in Boston. His speeches, committee work, and parliamentary maneuvers presented a broad cross section of the problems confronting the Commonwealth. Optimistic, enterprising, and conscientious, he was a confirmed convert to the doctrine of the perfectibility of individuals and institutions.

In no time at all, he also became enamored with the style of life of the city. For him it was a marvelous experience just to stroll down Summer Street and admire the magnificent chestnut trees which lined it on either side creating an arbor that filtered the warm spring sunlight into every shade of green. Not that he ignored the fair maidens he passed, dressed as if they had stepped out of their grandmother's picture album, or the smart carriages which rolled past him carrying members of the first families of the city to social and business affairs. Nearby he could walk through Franklin Square, the citadel of Boston's merchant princes, which boasted of sixteen mansions, all designed by Bulfinch, and admire their classic entrances of white paneled doors, carved cornices, and wrought-iron balustrades. Occasionally as he walked past them on a spring eve-

---

[1] Journal of the House, Vol. 49, February 2, 1829, p. 221, MS in MSA; *Columbian Centinel*, February 4, 1829; Mann's undated notes for this remark on lotteries are from several sheets among his legal papers, Mann MSS, 1830 Folder: DHS.

[2] "Report on Punishment by Death," *Massachusetts House Documents, 1831–1832*, No. 2, pp. 5–19; *Columbian Centinel*, March 7, 1832; Journal of the House, Vol. 61, January 20, 1831, p. 173, MS in MSA; Herman Mann, Journal, July 7, 1829, MS in DHS.

ning, the voice of a woman singing at the pianoforte could be heard from an open window.

If the city lacked places of public amusement for him, Edward Loring and James K. Mills provided him with ample introductions to private society and Mann soon was a guest in some of Boston's first homes, being invited to dinner parties where he was served at tables set with the finest imported linens, china, and silver. In return, he gave parties for his friends at the Exchange Coffee House and the new Tremont House. As host he ordered the best food and made certain his table was always well supplied with sauterne and Madeira. One of his affairs in the dining room of the Tremont House cost him almost $30, or more than his board for an entire semester back at Brown, ten years before. But at college there had been neither well-paying clients nor a growing coterie of affluent friends who were accustomed to the best.[3]

Through the Loring family, Mann met several eligible ladies from Boston society, obviously intent upon finding a suitable match. Although always careful to be courteous, he gave no indication of any special interest in them. Still his social life was an active one. The Lorings introduced him to the theater and Mann was delighted with a performance of the play *Master Burke*. But for home consumption, he was careful to distinguish between *Burke* and any "low dramatic presentation where the grossness and loathesomeness of vice is made almost beautiful." [4]

All of this was new and exhilarating. In Boston he found a variety of people, sparkling conversation, and a quickened pace of events, and after a few sessions of the General Court, considered himself a zealous convert to this way of life.[5] Mann had caught something of the tempo and dynamism which existed in large concentrations of persons. Every individual had become of interest to him, both in terms of what he could observe and what was still a mystery about their present and future.

These years of experience had taught him to deal with complex situations. Nothing in his youth at Franklin or at Brown had ever

---

[3] James K. Mills to Mann, May 5, 1828, Mann MSS:DHS; Mann's receipts from the Tremont House are in the Mann MSS:DHS.
[4] Mann to Charlotte Messer Mann, March 5 and 8, 1831, Mann-Messer MSS:BUA; "Master Burke" was a satire on the current belief held by many that anything could be taught. See Edward Everett Hale, *A New England Boyhood* (New York, 1893), pp. 25–26.
[5] Mann to Charlotte Messer, June 9, 1830, Mann-Messer MSS:BUA.

suggested the intricacy of social problems he faced in the legislature. The older clear-cut absolutes and the bombastic and righteous exhortations of the debating society now seemed archaic and a little embarrassing. This was increasingly evident with each return to the General Court. Since his first election he had grappled with difficult problems, made crucial motions, guided important committees, and authorized influential reports. He was a man with a promising political future, an effective ally or formidable antagonist, but in either case, a man to be watched and reckoned with. Perhaps in a moment of anger old Edward Dowse had spoken the truth. Horace Mann's ambition might well carry him on to greater political heights.

CHAPTER VI

The Shoulders of Atlas

===

THE POWER which is at once spring and regu-
lator in all efforts of reform is the conclusion that
there is an infinite worthiness in man, which will
appear at the call of worth, and that all particular
reforms are the removing of some impediment.
RALPH WALDO EMERSON

THERE ARE a thousand hacking at the branches
of evil to one who is striking at the root.
HENRY DAVID THOREAU

AT TIMES, Mann found it almost impossible to keep pace with the
rapid tattoo of events which pressed upon him in Boston. All
about him was activity, much of it centered upon the making of
money. It was true that some people he met exhibited the early
symptoms of a genteel poverty soon to overtake them. Others, far
more visible, were well established in the mercantile world, benefit-
ing from the rewards which came from several generations of prudence, effort, and good fortune. Some of Boston's most wealthy and
prominent families were now shifting their resources inland, to manufacturing and transportation, in anticipation of a magnitude of
wealth their ambitious and diligent progenitors never dreamed possible. Yet the prosperity at the time was so general and expansive
that the well-established could no more keep it to themselves than
they could monopolize the fresh air and sunshine. In fact, the economic expansion was so broad that there were not only open channels for new blood and new talent, but an absolute need for them.
In law, politics, real estate, banking, merchandising, and above all,
manufacturing, young men could rise, backed by little more than
the assets of a quick mind and a willingness to sacrifice immediate
gratification for the long-range goal. They came from farms, towns,
and cities. Some traveled via college, others via the countinghouse
or the quarter-deck; yet all were driven by an unbounded optimism
which knew few reservations, and they rarely let themselves be di-

verted from the task of laying a foundation from which they might then erect the twin pillars of status and wealth for all to see.

Surely, Horace Mann included himself among this group of incipient parvenus and entrepreneurs. Nevertheless, his system of values would not let him divorce self-interest from social responsibility. If his was a world of individual opportunity, it was also a world of fixed laws in which self-gain could be compatible with community interest. This he had learned in his moral philosophy at Brown. After one stripped away the flatulent prose of his valedictory in 1819, what remained was a dogmatic belief in an ordered universe where a rational republicanism demonstrated that the interest of the community was true self-interest writ large. Now and then, in moments of retrospect, he could not avoid pangs of self-reproach from the fact that his own decision to leave home and enter college had forced additional sacrifice upon his mother and sister. With time, Mann gradually accommodated his values and justified his removal from Franklin, but he never shed his belief that individual and social responsibility were as bound together as the warp and woof of a homespun fabric.

Although he witnessed a number of struggles between vested interests, Mann found the environment of the General Court conducive for further development of his sense of stewardship and social responsibility. Not only did he frame his arguments for manufacturing and railroads in terms of the indirect benefits these corporate undertakings would bring to all citizens in the Commonwealth, but he also recognized a growing number of poor, insane, and intemperate who needed more direct assistance. Thus he also worked in the legislature for laws to protect and assist these people. Thinking about the constructive legislation passed at the end of the General Court session in 1830, he wrote that "after such reflections, I feel my desire for human and benevolent effort invigorated." [1]

The General Court was soon to gratify his desire for "benevolent effort," even beyond his youthful dreams. In the process, Mann would cast himself in the role of a humanitarian reformer and be instrumental in defining the right of the state to intervene in curbing the appetites of the intemperate and treating the insane, a definition which would endure for more than half a century and, by transfer, would shape the beginnings of the American public school system.

---

[1] Mann to Charlotte Messer, June 9, 1830, Mann-Messer MSS:BUA.

By the 1820's, the presence of intemperate men was perceived by many as a direct threat to the social and economic harmony of the village. Furthermore, it had national implications since many feared that intemperance would corrupt the electorate and therefore erode away the very foundations of a republican society. As early as 1813, a group of ministers, lawyers, and merchants had organized the Massachusetts Society for the Suppression of Intemperance and had made it their task to "discountenance and suppress the too free use of ardent spirits, and its kindred vices, profanity and gaming." Despite their fears that these had become serious problems, they also optimistically predicted that through the establishment of their voluntary societies and the "simple and reasonable expedient" of disseminating information, they would apply "a grand healing measure . . . to the disease of the country." If men were beings who determined their self-interest through rational means, then upon learning of the consequences of intemperance, they would reform themselves.[2]

In the years which followed, the "grand healing measure" produced little change in the drinking habits of the people, and by 1820 the Society placed less credence upon moral suasion and began to consider legal restrictions.[3] Still a residue of older beliefs that the individual was an intelligent being who would alter his habits on the basis of a reasonable appeal, especially if it was reinforced by religious sanctions, remained as an article of faith with some. For the moment, however, time seemed against them.[4] By 1825 the *Annual Report* of the Society candidly admitted that the "ravages of intemperance have been often stated . . . and its ruinous tendencies explained and enforced by the most eloquent appeals. . . . Still the evil prevails, is apparently increasing, and the victory over it seems to many, not only unobtained, but even hopeless." Furthermore, as the evil persisted, it had become less one of the "kindred vices" and more the "cause of causes." "Banish intemperance from among us,"

[2] *Constitution of the Massachusetts Society for the Suppression of Intemperance* (Boston, 1813), pp. 3–6; Samuel Dexter, *Circular Address to the Members of Massachusetts Society for Suppressing Intemperance* (Boston, 1814), pp. 3–15, and *passim*.
[3] *Report of the Board of Counsel to the Massachusetts Society for the Suppression of Intemperance, Presented at their Eighth Anniversary, June 2, 1820* (Boston, 1820), pp. 1–17.
[4] William Jenks, *Sermon Delivered before the Massachusetts Society for the Suppression of Intemperance at their Annual Meeting, June 1, 1821* (Boston, 1821), pp. 3–18.

one reformer claimed, "and our almshouses would fall to the ground —our jails would become empty." [5]

At about the same time, the Reverend Lyman Beecher, having moved from Litchfield and now preaching from the pulpit of the Hanover Church in Boston, began to attack intemperance on different grounds. In a series of six sermons, Beecher brushed aside both legal and economic considerations with characteristic impetuousness and pressed on to what he considered the central issue. The use of ardent spirits "in any form, in any degree" was neither an act of ignorance nor a statutory misdemeanor, but an unmitigated sin. To be intemperate was to be on the road to Hell. Beecher's sermons were read, quoted, and discussed in Boston and its hinterland, and they proved to be the inspiration for a group of orthodox clergy and laity to bolt the old Massachusetts Society and form the more radical American Society for Promotion of Temperance, which soon had hundreds of voluntary temperance societies organized within the churches. Despairing of legal restraints, they believed that for the Christian there was but one right way, total voluntary abstinence.[6] Challenged by these new dissidents with their single-purpose societies, the parent Massachusetts Society clung to the notion that the "influential portion of society" should set an example for the "poorer and the labouring classes" to emulate, insisting that "Reformation must begin at the top of society, and not at the bottom." [7]

The two organizations then differed substantially on their *modus operandi*. One urged legal restrictions and an exemplary role for the upper classes; the other was a vigorous evangelical campaign

---

[5] *Report of the Massachusetts Society for the Suppression of Intemperance* (Boston, 1825), pp. 1–25; John Ware, *An Address Delivered before the Massachusetts Society for the Suppression of Intemperance at their Annual Meeting, May 1825* (Boston, 1826), pp. 1–15.

[6] Lyman Beecher, *Six Sermons, on the Nature, Occasions, Signs, Evils and Remedy of Intemperance* (Boston, 1827), *passim;* George Faber Clark, *History of the Temperance Reform in Massachusetts, 1813–1883* (Boston, 1888), p. 19; for a description of the beginning of this organization, see Clark, *History of Temperance Reform,* pp. 19–22, John Allen Krout, *The Origins of Prohibition* (New York, 1925), pp. 111–126, and Ernest Hurst Cherington, *The Evolution of Prohibition* (Westerville, Ohio, 1920), pp. 95–96.

[7] *Annual Report of the Board of Counsel of the Massachusetts Society for the Suppression of Intemperance* (Boston, 1826), pp. 1–24; Gamaliel Bradford, *Address Delivered before the Massachusetts Society for the Suppression of Intemperance, June 1826* (Boston, 1826), pp. 1–15; *Fourteenth Annual Report of the Massachusetts Society for the Suppression of Intemperance with Resolutions Passed at the Public Meeting Held November 5, 1827* (Boston, 1827), p. 7.

to win the minds of men through religious persuasion. Any use of ardent spirits was immoral, defiling the soul and corrupting the body. Both, however, agreed on the goal of a society of sober and industrious individuals, pious families, and an enlightened electorate. Thus by a slow and irritating process of attrition, the earlier optimistic assumption of the reformers that intemperance was but one of several vices troubling society had been reduced to a hard-core article of faith that it was the fundamental cause for the alarming spread of poverty and crime. Drunkards there had always been, but to the keepers of public and private morals in Massachusetts of the 1820's, their presence was more visible, and they were seen as a threat to the peace and order of the Commonwealth.

Troubled by the specter of unprecedented numbers of paupers and criminals in Massachusetts, Horace Mann made a motion early in the 1829 session of the General Court for the House to study whether there was, as he phrased it, any "practicable mode of ascertaining the amount of crime and pauperism arising from the intemperate use of ardent spirits." For his trouble, Mann was given the chairmanship of a study committee which asked, among other things, "The number of persons whose offences resulted from or were occasioned by the intemperate use of ardent spirits" and the number of pauper cases which "have resulted from, or been occasioned by, the intemperate use of ardent spirits." In the very wording of this and other questions, intemperance was predetermined the root evil. The fact that Mann believed that his respondents, selectmen, jailers, and overseers of the poor could determine what something as complex as human behavior was "occasioned by," was an indication of a compulsion on his part, and one shared by many of his contemporaries, to make intemperance the scapegoat for social maladies whose complex causes were beyond their understanding and control. This he and thousands of other true believers did not recognize as they tried to label drunkenness as the only impediment holding men back on the path of human progress.[8]

Nevertheless, they were aware of a thorny question which their reformist intentions posed. If the excessive drinker lowered the quality of life for others in the community, he was disturbing the harmony of society. Moreover, since society had reserved the right to step in and manage the affairs of those who were unable to care for

---

[8] Journal of the House, Vol. 49, February 16, 1829, p. 287, MS in MSA; *Columbian Centinel*, February 21, 1829; the report was printed as *Massachusetts House Documents*, 1829, No. 36.

themselves, the intemperate person was subject to collective restraints. But this easily infringed upon his rights as an individual
and raised the possibility of a cure far worse than the sickness. Thus
for the time being, Mann believed that "moral persuasion, the power
of argument and truth, addressed to the understanding and conscience," were the most rational means of dealing with the problem.
With a group of close friends, he formed the Dedham Temperance
Society, a voluntary association which would "discountenance the
improper use of ardent spirits." Although the group gave no indication whether they expected to affiliate with either of the two statewide
organizations, the fact that they viewed themselves as an élite, did
not insist upon total abstinence, and assumed that the dissemination
of facts had the power to change men's habits, suggested an approach similar to that of the Massachusetts Society. To lead their endeavor they elected Horace Mann as president.[9]

By 1829 the Dedham group was but one of hundreds of temperance societies which had sprung up all over New England. While
Mann was caught up in the groundswell of enthusiasm for organized
action, he had taken the stance of a moderate reformer. On the local
level, he thought it was most reasonable to "discountenance" intemperance and present truths about its effects to the "understanding
and conscience" of the individual. Personally, he saw no reason to
change his own style of life, which included social drinking, for the
austere regimen of total abstinence. Truth and moderation, not radical prohibition, would change the ways of men.

Having grown by the end of the decade to a size where it wished
to be incorporated by the state, the American Society for the Promotion of Temperance petitioned for such a recognition. In the House,
Mann's Judiciary Committee studied its application for a charter and
stunned the petitioners with an adverse report. Then, much like the
Blandford petition, what had begun as a simple request suddenly
blew up into a *cause célèbre*. While agreeing with the aims of the organization, Mann questioned its structure and membership, noting
that both offices and membership in the Society were limited largely
to Congregationalists. Why, he asked, should an association dedicated to furthering broad ethical goals limit its voting membership to
a "single sect or genus"? The work of temperance was based on universal, not sectarian, principles. In return for his effort, he drew an
attack from the Boston *Recorder*, organ for orthodox Congregational-

---

[9] Dedham *Village Register and County Advertiser*, August 27, 1829.

ism in New England.[1] Exclusiveness did not hinder effective reform, its editor declared. To take Mann's position that reform must be based upon universal assent was the same as saying that

. . . no individual must attempt to convince his neighbor of any evil way, until he has gone through the town, inquired what others think of the matter, and invited them to unite in bringing down at once a torrent of public sentiment upon the head of the man in danger.[2]

The debate provided copy for the local newspapers for several weeks before the petition went down to defeat. While those closely identified with either side were quick to accuse their opponents of motives stemming from sectarian and partisan jealousies, the actual arguments pointed to a cleavage of ideas for reforming society. Aside from their desire for the advantages of incorporation, those in the American Society were hesitant about appealing to the state for assistance in achieving temperance reform. Moral suasion in the form of Christian admonition and not legal coercion was their answer. Their cause had no place in the legislature, where it could easily become the battleground for a partisan struggle. Temperance was not an issue to divide Whigs from Democrats. Using the same type of reasoning, Mann and others arrived at an opposite conclusion. This reform was based upon universal truths and could only be hindered by denominational rivalries. If it was nonpartisan, it was also nonsectarian. As he emerged from the debate, Mann's model for the best means of dealing with any social problem was a voluntary association of principled men who would rise above sectarian and political biases and influence both the legislature and their immediate communities.

Consistent with this stand, he worked for a clarification of the existing laws which would facilitate stricter enforcement. The main problem as he saw it lay in the antiquated laws of the state. Victualers and innkeepers were fined $20 for selling liquor without a license, but this penalty was so excessive that it was impossible to collect. Enforcement, therefore, had become lax, permitting unlicensed dispensers of ardent spirits to spring up like weeds in an unattended garden. Lowering the fines would make stricter enforcement possible and help stamp out unauthorized retailers.[3] He also thought the Com-

---

[1] *Columbian Centinel*, March 10, 1830; Boston *Recorder*, March 10, 17, and 24, 1830; *Christian Register*, February 13 and 20, 1830.

[2] Boston *Recorder*, March 31, 1830.

[3] *Independent Chronicle and Boston Patriot*, May 29, 1830, and February 9, 1831; Journal of the House, Vol. 51, June 3, 1830, pp. 56–57, MS in MSA.

monwealth would benefit from a reduction in the number of licensed vendors. A recent census indicated there was one licensed person selling ardent spirits for every fifty male adults in the city. Assuming that a lawyer, a doctor, and a minister could care for the needs of 1,000 persons, Mann found it difficult to understand the need for such a large number of liquor dispensers. And finally, he believed that selectmen should take an oath that they would recommend no person for a license whose business would not be in the public good.[4]

All these remedies Mann wrote into a bill which he had before the House in 1830 and 1831. In the meantime, the liquor retailers and the members of the American Society became the strangest of bedfellows in forming a coalition against his measure. But Mann, quickly learning the art of parliamentary maneuver and vote-getting, urged his supporters to hold the line, and after an animated debate which lasted well into the afternoon of one of the sessions, he moved for the question and had the satisfaction of listening to the roll call and knowing he had won. That evening he shared his elation with a correspondent. "I have had hard work in the Legislature today," he wrote, "having stood upon the defensive with what has been commonly called here, this winter, *Mann's License Bill,* and after six hours hard fighting we have carried it by a large majority." He had withstood attacks from reformers who thought he was licensing a sin and from retailers who feared his law would put them out of business. For him the outcome was a moral victory.[5]

The chief purpose of the law was to board up the Boston grog shops. Through its licensing structure, those vendors who sold for consumption on their premises were also required to provide food and lodging for their customers. Those who did not were classified as retailers and could only sell liquor to be consumed elsewhere. This put the grog shops in a third and illegal category, since they neither sold spirits to be drunk off the premises nor furnished the services of an inn or tavern. According to Mann's bill, they had no legal claim to a license and if they continued to operate, they were subject to a $30 fine. Hopefully, several such penalties for the few who continued to violate the new law would put them out of business, once and for all. The law also required all selectmen to take an oath "to discharge the duties of their office respecting all licenses." In summary, the law set

---

[4] *Independent Chronicle and Boston Patriot,* February 16, 1831.
[5] Journal of the House, Vol. 51, February 12, 1831, p. 279-¾, MS in MSA; Mann to Charlotte Messer Mann, March, 1831, Mann-Messer MSS:BUA.

out to regulate certain types of vendors, close up others, and put teeth into the means of enforcing its provisions.[6]

If he was staking his political future on the issue of temperance, for the moment, the immediate events augured well for him. His close friend, Edward Loring, wrote that he thought Mann's stand was "a steady and unflinching and able defense of the *principles* of the License Law" against "a ferocious and reckless opposition." To him and others, Mann had become "the champion of sobriety and public virtue—and god-father to the statute." Accordingly, Loring reported that "the best men in society" had noted his work in the House and "desire to trust their cause to you, so Atlas must spread his shoulders." [7]

The matter, however, was not settled with the Governor's signature on the bill, and Mann was in for a rude awakening when he returned to the General Court for the next session. In the interim, the opposition had gathered its forces in the House for a repeal of the new license law. Mann had no other course but to defend his work, and he did so with a detailed and carefully reasoned exposition of his views on why licensing was the best means of controlling intemperance in a republican society.[8]

The issue of licenses, however, was only incidental to the broader problem of the responsibility of the state to control intemperance. His opponents had questioned the constitutionality of restraining a man from drinking. Mann's answer was that the power of restraint was necessary "to maintain order, and morality and secure the safety of the people." Admittedly, there was no constitutional right to interfere with the activities of "the domestic circle," but when a person's behavior was injurious to the general community, the government was obliged to act. This was society's means of self-preservation.

Understandably, Mann was soon under fire from several directions. One lawmaker urged nothing less than "free-traffic universal"; another argued that laws only dealt with superficial acts and failed to root out the cause; a third criticized the 1831 law because of its requirement for selectmen to take an "obnoxious oath" to enforce the

---

[6] *Laws of the Commonwealth of Massachusetts, 1828–1831* (Boston, 1831), XI, 700–704, "An Act in Addition to the Several Acts for the due regulation of licensed Houses," Ch. CXXXVI.

[7] Loring to Horace Mann, n.d. [November or December, 1831], Mann MSS: MHS.

[8] *Columbian Centinel,* February 4 and 8, 1832.

law. A revised version was approved, which again classified vendors as innholders, common victualers, or retailers, and specified that retailers could not sell for consumption on the premises; but the "obnoxious oath" was repealed. Thus the classification of the former law stood, and while the Commonwealth was to be the recipient of increased license fees, the means for stricter enforcement were removed.[9]

As Mann worked for a revision of the laws, he gradually embraced one of the two diverging ideologies. From the vague and alarmist opinions of the Dedham Temperance Society, he had emerged by 1832 as an active spokesman for reform through legal means. Although he had come to believe that intemperance was the unitary cause for crime and poverty, rather than just one of several symptoms pointing to more deep-seated social changes, he refused to endorse the radical doctrine of total abstinence and prohibition. Instead, he subscribed to the more moderate reforms of the Massachusetts Society for the Suppression of Intemperance. Consistent with this was his more general belief that social maladies could be eradicated by reforming rather than destroying existing institutions. Since the task of reformation was beyond the scope of sectarian and partisan groups and had gone beyond the control of public opinion and local law enforcement, it was therefore necessary to exert the superior authority of the Commonwealth.

*   *   *

"I would not suffer my hogs to be confined in it," was the best way the Sheriff of Norfolk County could describe his disgust when he inspected the House of Correction at Dedham in 1828. Early that year, an insane inmate had died, unattended and in an unheated cell. The incident and conditions surrounding the incident might have been quietly forgotten had not the situation in the house deteriorated to such a point that the cries and groans of the surviving inmates would "frequently disturb the neighborhood." Reading the account in the local paper, the citizens of Dedham could 'no longer ignore the problem. Clearly, something had to be done.[1]

---

[9] *Independent Chronicle and Boston Patriot*, March 7, 1832; *Laws of the Commonwealth of Massachusetts, 1831–1833* (Boston, 1833), Vol. XII, Ch. CLXVI, pp. 473–482, "An Act for the due regulation of Licensed Houses."

[1] Dedham *Village Register*, January 31, 1828.

According to a report filed by a House committee the year before, other Massachusetts towns were equally derelict in their care of the insane. In their inspection of "the state of several Gaols," the lawmakers found six classes of inmates. Five were various types of criminals and debtors; the sixth was a category labeled "Lunatics and persons furiously mad." The former received satisfactory treatment; but as for the latter, their report read, "The situation of these poor wretched beings calls for some redress . . . they seem to have been considered as out of the protection of the laws." In general the committee thought the jailers to be humane people, but it was evident that they were unqualified to care for the insane. In moving from one jail to the next in gathering data for their report, the lawmakers first suffered an initial sense of shock, which gave way to a feeling of nausea welling up inside them; and upon their return to Boston, nausea in turn gave way to righteous indignation. Summing up their observations, they could only conclude that less attention was given to the cleanliness and comfort of lunatics than to farm animals at a county fair. Some of the inmates had literally wallowed in their own filth for more than twenty years. It was evident that "something must be done." [2]

Barely had the members of the General Court time to recover from the revelations of the committee when the Prison Discipline Society, a voluntary association, issued an even more shocking report. That truth could be more grim than fiction was given credence by the fact that their description of the inmates in one of the county jails was worse than anything in Dickens:

. . . one was found in an apartment in which he had been nine years. He had a wreath of rags round his body, and another around his neck. This was all his clothing. He had no bed, chair, or bench. Two or three rough planks were strowed around the room: a heap of filthy straw like the nest of swine, was in the corner. He had built a bird's nest of mud in the iron grate of his den. . . . The wretched lunatic was indulging some delusive expectations of being released from this wretched abode.

In another prison five lunatics were confined in separate cells,

. . . which were almost dark dungeons. It was difficult, after the door was open, to see them distinctly. The ventilation was so incomplete,

---

[2] *Massachusetts House Documents, 1827–1828*, No. 50, "Report," February 16, 1827.

that more than one person entering them has found the air so fetid, as to produce nauseousness, and almost vomiting. The old straw on which they were laid, and their filthy garments were such as to make their insanity more hopeless.

In some cases, the insane were the sources of perverted entertainment for the convicts. The most pathetic cases were found in one prison containing ten lunatics, including a man and woman each about seventy years old.

The female was lying on a heap of straw, under a broken window. The snow, in a severe storm, was beating through the window, and lay upon the straw around her withered body, which was partly covered with a few filthy and tattered garments. The man was lying in a corner of the room in a similar situation, except he was less exposed to the storm. The former had been in this apartment six, and the latter twenty-one years.

Another inmate at the same place had only been out of his unheated cell twice in the last eight years. His door had not been opened for eighteen months and his food was passed to him through a small orifice. Peering through this opening into the semi-darkness of the cell, the examiners asked, "Is that a human being?" Five other lunatics were kept in the cellar. As there was no heat here either, the woman in charge reported, "We have a sight to do to keep them from freezing." The report concluded with an argument that the loss of reason should not be compounded by imprisonment and made an optimistic prediction of what might be accomplished by more humane treatment:

If this shall be done, the Prison doors will be thrown open for another large class of prisoners, and hundreds, who now remain in Prison, till they become incurably insane, will be placed in Asylums, where three fourths of the whole number may be restored to reason.

It was an eloquent plea on behalf of a group of forgotten men and women.[3]

Earlier, in many of the more self-contained villages such as Franklin and Dedham, where the outer edge of the family blended almost indistinguishably into the greater community, the responsibility for an occasional lunatic or village idiot had been the concern of both

---

[3] *Second Annual Report of the Board of Managers of the Prison Discipline Society, June 1, 1827* (Boston, 1827).

family and community. Now it had become the concern of neither. Perhaps in an economy of subsistence or self-sufficiency, the lunatic had some place, or at least could be tolerated. But by the 1820's he was seen as a nuisance and in the way of persons who wanted more system and order in their communities. If the desire for more efficiency and safety placed the lunatic in jails, a growing humanitarianism would not let him remain there. Realizing that the towns were unwilling or unable to give the insane proper attention, humanitarian reformers used the two reports of 1827 to press the General Court into action and take measures to provide a new form of institutional care.

Unlike railroad construction, the towns seemed willing to relinquish their authority to the state when it came to caring for the insane. A bill for the "Safe Keeping of Lunatics and persons furiously mad," was filed in the General Court the year following the two reports. It received no decisive action at the time, but on February 3, 1829, Horace Mann moved that it be taken from the files and referred to a committee of which he was chairman. Through his efforts, the House ordered a state survey to determine the number of lunatics in the Commonwealth, where they were kept, and their length of confinement. Then while the study was under way, Mann found time to travel to Hartford and observe the treatment being given the insane by Eli Todd at the Connecticut Retreat.[4]

With the convening of the January session in 1830, Mann's committee studied the returns as they came in. While they were preparing their report, the public interest in the care of the insane was kept alive by an article in the *Christian Register*. In an open letter to Mayor Harrison G. Otis of Boston, Reverend Joseph Tuckerman drew an alarming picture of the conditions in the House of Correction and the Common Jail in Boston. One of the sensational disclosures made was the fact that among the women inmates, Tuckerman found more than fifty female lunatics.[5]

Now armed with figures from the state survey, Mann filed a report which gave the first general description of the care of lunatics in the Commonwealth. Actually, his statistics covered only half the population since many selectmen and overseers of the poor, either be-

---

[4] Journal of the House, Vol. 49, February 3, 1829, pp. 229 and 357, MS in MSA.
[5] "A Letter addressed to the Hon. Harrison G. Otis, Mayor of Boston, respecting the House of Correction, and the Common Jail in Boston," *Christian Register*, January 16, 1830.

cause of apathy or fear of criticism, had failed to return their questionnaires. Of the communities reporting, 289 "lunatics or people furiously mad" were reported. Most were confined in jails or poorhouses and only a few were receiving any hospital care. Mann's report also dealt with the length of confinement of these people. Many had been imprisoned for less than five years, but he also found pitiful cases where lunatics had been locked up in jails for more than twenty years. The survey even uncovered one hopeless wretch who had been behind bars for forty-five years. These people, Mann argued, required special care, and he called upon the state to purchase a site and erect a hospital capable of accommodating 120 patients. Subsequently, he submitted a bill to transform these recommendations into law.[6]

Pleading his cause before the House, Mann broke new ground as he gave the first speech ever made in the General Court advocating state care for the insane. His speech, one of the most moving he ever made as a lawmaker, was an eloquent and compelling plea for a group of persons by-passed by society in its quest for affluence and well-being. Beginning with a recent history of the treatment of the insane, he noted that until 1798, a person could be jailed as a lunatic by the simple action of two Justices of the Peace. Here he would remain until a friend or relative would vouch for his actions. Mann thought the human mind would be hard-pressed to devise a method less conducive to helping a sick person back to health. Jailers were not qualified attendants, nor were prisons, where the insane were "cut off from the kind regards of society and friends," as Mann described it, a place for healing. In such a practice, there was little from which the humanitarian could take satisfaction. For those still blissfully ignorant of the recent reports, he described the suffering of the lunatics; how many could not be trusted with fire and therefore had not experienced heat in the winter for twenty years; how some had not seen the light of day for this length of time; how most were clothed in rags and slept in nests of dirty straw on the floor. The exact number in the Commonwealth who were actually in such lamentable conditions was difficult to say, but on the basis of the partial returns of the questionnaires, Mann estimated at least 500. The aggregate of their confinement came to a millennium of human suffering; or, as he phrased it, giving his words an intensity which drew his auditors to the edge of their seats: "A thousand years during which the mind had been sequestered from the ways of knowledge and use-

---

[6] *Massachusetts House Documents, 1830–1831*, No. 39, "Report," pp. 1–4.

fulness, and the heart in all its sufferings, inaccessible to the consolations of religion." [7]

This still left open the question of whether lunatics could actually be cured. But Mann had something to say about this also. Until 1800, it was generally believed that insanity was the result of divine visitation and therefore beyond human help. Now he could report "the most welcome fact, that with the appropriate treatment, there is a larger proportion of recoveries from insanity, than from most other diseases." It was a startling claim, but Mann thought he had the proof to back it up. Quoting statistics from an *Inquiry into Certain Errors Relative to Insanity* by the English doctor, George Man Burrows, he maintained that 40 per cent of all mental patients in a group of European hospitals had recovered. Mann also cited the work of Dr. Francis Willis, again of England, who had claimed that nine out of ten patients could recover if they received treatment within three months after their first attack.[8] Reports from the Connecticut Retreat of Eli Todd which he had visited were equally hopeful.[9] Here was what Mann called "irrefutable proof" from both sides of the Atlantic that at least half of the insane people might have been cured, had they received prompt and humane treatment.

Mann then gave a brief explanation of the type of building needed. It should be "commodious but economical," he said, "for whatever was devoted to munificence must be abstracted from charity." The plight of these outcasts of society called for prompt action. Mann clinched his appeal with the words, "*We* delay, *they* suffer." In conclusion, he apologized for the directness of his appeal. But there was no alternative. They could not plead their own case. Then as an afterthought, he added that this might be a mistake. Letting his voice drop almost to a whisper, he explained that in their muted silence,

---

[7] *Independent Chronicle and Boston Patriot*, February 17, 1830.

[8] Willis, who had treated George III, maintained a private asylum in England. In the course of the parliamentary investigation of the King's illness, he claimed to have cured nine out of ten patients. While reputable physicians considered him a charlatan, his claim was believed by many. In the pamphlet by Burrows that Mann cited, one of the main theses was that mental illness was far more amenable to therapy than was supposed at the time. While other hospitals were reporting up to 40 per cent recoveries, Burrows was insisting he had cured 80 per cent of all mental patients referred to him and an average of 90 per cent of those cases which were less than one year in duration. See Albert Deutsch, *Mentally Ill in America* (New York, 1949), pp. 133–134.

[9] *Third Report of the Directors of the Connecticut Retreat for the Insane, Presented to the Society, May 11, 1827* (Hartford, 1827), p. 5; this document claimed that out of 23 recent cases, "91³⁄₁₀%" were cured.

they spoke more eloquently of their needs than through his words. It was an eloquent appeal and it did not fall on deaf ears. By using humanitarian arguments as well as the claim of curability, Mann made it clear to the legislature that they could no longer ignore the needs of the insane. By the default of local communities and families, the insane had become wards of the state. Whereas the General Court had formerly exercised an exhortatory and supervisory role, it must now function in an initiatory and sustaining capacity. And it would.

Mann's bill passed the House and Senate, and on March 10, 1830, Governor Levi Lincoln signed a "Resolve for Erecting a Lunatic Hospital" into law.[1] It authorized the purchase of a site in the name of the Commonwealth, "regard being had, in the selection of such site, to the centre of population, and to the cheapness of labor and materials for construction," and the appointment of three commissioners who "shall cause to be erected, on said site, a Hospital, suitable for the accommodation of a Superintendent, and one hundred and twenty lunatics or persons furiously mad." Aside from the fact that the commissioners were to devise "a system of discipline and government" for the hospital and to do all this within a budget of $30,000, there was little else in the bill! The types of patients, their support, and the procedures for admitting and releasing them could be decided later. Since much of the success of the undertaking depended on the commissioners, Governor Levi Lincoln gave the appointments careful attention. From his executive council he chose Bezaleel Taft, Jr., and from the General Court he named William B. Calhoun, Speaker of the House. For chairman of the commission he chose the individual who, more than anyone else, was responsible for securing passage of the law, Horace Mann. When Mann at first declined the appointment, Lincoln replied, according to Mann's later account, "You got us into this scrape, and you must get us out." Thus, at the age of thirty-four, after several false starts, the young man from Franklin was about to direct the establishment of the first state mental hospital in the United States.[2]

*   *   *

It was remarkable that the legislators voted the funds with little real understanding of the difficulties involved in establishing such an

---

[1] *Resolves of the General Court of the Commonwealth of Massachusetts, 1828–1831* (Boston, 1831), Ch. LXXXIII, March 10, 1830, pp. 296–297.
[2] The certificate of appointment, dated March 10, 1830, is in the Mann MSS:MHS; Mann to Austin Craig, February 26, 1853, Mann MSS:MHS.

institution. It was even more remarkable that Mann, Taft, and Calhoun, none of whom were trained either in architecture or in the treating of the insane, never doubted their ability to build, equip, and staff the hospital and devise the procedures for its operation. No one else seems to have had misgivings about their ability either. At a time when Eli Todd and Thomas Gallaudet, both "amateurs," were achieving impressive results in their work, such a project as the lunatic hospital was expected to be one more demonstration of what could be accomplished through humane and enlightened methods.

In keeping with his own high hopes for the institution, Governor Lincoln informed the legislators that while price was one consideration in choosing a site, he also wanted the hospital located where there would be "pleasant scenery, clear and salubrious air, a market for supplies, opportunity for medical counsel and for constant visitorial inspection, and facilities of access and communication from all parts of the State." After an inspection of more than thirty places, a location on the outskirts of Worcester, Lincoln's home town, was finally selected.[3]

In carrying out their assignment, the commissioners demonstrated an interesting combination of idealism, energy, and Yankee resourcefulness. By serving as their own general contractor, they assumed they would save money. Once plans were drawn up, they let out contracts only after the closest scrutiny as to quality, price, and reputation. The mails were heavy with letters between Mann, Taft, and Calhoun as they compared notes on such things as the qualifications of competing brick contractors or the relative merits of Welsh and Vermont slate. If economy was one of their chief concerns, good workmanship was another. Taft, who had more building experience than the other two, made regular inspection tours as construction progressed. Fearing shoddy millwork might be sent out from a shop in Boston, at added expense he hired housewrights on the job where their work could be kept under closer supervision.[4]

---

[3] *Massachusetts House Documents, 1830–1831*, "Speech of His Excellency Levi Lincoln, Delivered to the Two Branches of the Legislature, in Convention, May 29, 1830" (Boston, 1830), pp. 13–15; *Independent Chronicle and Boston Patriot*, June 12, 1830.

[4] For a general description of their preliminary plans, see *Massachusetts House Documents, 1830–1831*, No. 19. An account of the numerous details that claimed their attention is related in the correspondence of the commissioners in the Mann MSS:MHS, covering the period of construction between August 21, 1830, and October 29, 1832. These letters are ample evidence of the commissioners' humanitarian ideals and their

Gathering information from other hospitals, Mann learned that while no two agreed on basic architecture, all seemed to have three basic problems in their operations.[5] These were noise, sanitation, and security. Unable to locate a satisfactory model, he and his co-workers devised their own plan, always keeping in mind the nature and function of the building they were creating. They laid out halls so as to minimize the amount of noise transmitted. To facilitate sanitation, they designed an aqueduct running from a nearby spring that rose above the highest part of the building. Water flowed into cisterns in the garret by a gravity system, and from there to other parts of the building. In addition, they planned an elaborate conventional ventilating and heating system, furniture that could be secured in each room, and ward arrangements which permitted segregation of inmates according to the nature of their sickness. Even the brick construction did not miss their attention. By insisting that a continuous dead air space be left between the outer and inner courses, condensation on the inside walls was minimized. The technique, relatively new at the time in Massachusetts, was widely adopted by builders soon thereafter.

Their basic plan was a central building with two wings which could be expanded later.[6] The main external architectural feature was the symmetrical placement of the windows which were necessary for lighting the interior. If this suggested Georgian style, the similarity was slight since the commissioners had decided against any form of ornamentation. As the building neared completion and its plain appearance became more patent, Bezaleel Taft began to have second thoughts about its austere exterior. Would it not be possible, he wrote to Mann, to place a dome on the center section of the building? Although Taft insisted it would cost no more than $600, Mann, backed up by Calhoun, refused to give in and the roof of the hospital went

concern for the quality of construction. See, for example, Bezaleel Taft to Mann, November 2, 1830, April 4, June 6, and November 30, 1831.

[5] The best general account of the planning of the hospital and its early treatment of patients is in Gerald Grob, *The State and the Mentally Ill* (Chapel Hill, 1966).

[6] The dimensions of the building, its general floor arrangement, and the novel features incorporated into their plans are given in *Reports and other Documents Relating to the State Lunatic Hospital at Worcester, Massachusetts* (Boston, 1837), pp. 5–16. While Mann reported that the commissioners used no hospital as a model, the exterior style and the idea of a central building with two wings was the same as used in the Connecticut Retreat.

unadorned. There were others, also, who expected a more ornate edifice as a public building, but Mann, who made no great claims to a sense of aesthetics, lectured his would-be critics that the purpose of the hospital was not to "gratify the eye of the tasteful, but to alleviate the distress of the afflicted." Refusing to go along with the beginnings of a trend which would culminate in the garish and gaudy monstrosities of the Gilded Age, whose forms had little relation to the functions they were to perform, Mann, by his lack of aesthetic appreciation and adamant insistence upon simplicity and utility, had inadvertently produced a public building with the tasteful and uncluttered lines that had been a tradition of better New England architecture.[7] With good reason, after the project neared completion, Governor Lincoln called public attention to the commissioners' "intelligence, energy, discretion, and deep interest."[8]

* * *

The directive from the General Court had also ordered the commissioners to devise "a system of discipline and government" for the hospital. On the basis of Mann's speech and his report of 1830, he apparently assumed that all lunatics then in confinement would be transferred to the new hospital. Upon closer examination, he discovered that this was not possible under existing laws. According to the statutes of the Commonwealth, he found three classes of lunatics and subsequently filed a report which clarified the categories and explained which mentally ill had a legal right to treatment financed by

---

[7] Bezaleel Taft to Mann, September 16, 1831, Mann MSS:MHS; *Massachusetts House Documents, 1830–1831*, No. 19, pp. 3–4. More than twenty years later, Dr. Isaac Ray, a pioneer in treating the mentally ill, criticized the design and quality of construction of the Worcester Hospital. Ray stated that since the building was intended for the poorer classes, it was decided that every other consideration be subordinate to economy. See Isaac Ray, "American Hospitals for the Insane," *The North American Review*, LXXIX (1854), 60–90. This accusation is repeated in Deutsch, *The Mentally Ill in America*, pp. 138–143. The correspondence between the three commissioners indicates this is incorrect. A later generation of philanthropists would build "pauper palaces" with copious amounts of "gingerbread" and every conceivable shape of nonfunctional tower that had little to do with the healing of the sick. By comparison, the original and practical thinking that went into the design of the Worcester Hospital seems to have been more to the point.

[8] *Massachusetts House Documents, 1830–1831*, No. 1, "Message of His Excellency Levi Lincoln, Communicated to the Two Branches of the Legislature, January 5, 1831" (Boston, 1831), pp. 15–16.

the state. The first category included those lunatics whose continued freedom threatened the public welfare. As it was the duty of the Commonwealth to maintain the general safety of its citizens, these people had been committed to jails by state magistrates. By such action they became wards of the state. The more Mann studied the lot of this particular group of mentally ill, the more it seemed that the law treated them as if they were "rather the objects of vengeance than of commiseration." Now it was evident that society had been long in arrears to "all those lunatics, whom the *Commonwealth,* by virtue of its sovereignty and for the security of its citizens, sentences to imprisonment." Therefore he recommended that all of these people be transferred to the Worcester Hospital and placed in the custody of its superintendent.[9]

A second group could be classified as town pauper lunatics. These were people who had established residency in a town and while not threatening the peace of the community, were still unable to support themselves as a result of their mental illness and therefore were declared public charges. Upon examining the laws of the Commonwealth, Mann uncovered an archaic legal and social development nearly two centuries in the making. From the outset of settlement, the General Court of the Massachusetts Bay Colony considered the dependent poor as the responsibility of the various towns. Yet as the result of disasters such as Indian massacres which destroyed entire communities, there were displaced people whom the Commonwealth at large was required to support. While it was assumed this would be only a temporary expedient, the reluctance of towns to accept new arrivals produced a growing number of nonresident paupers.

Since the care of the poor was a heavy financial burden, often exceeding the costs of keeping the schools, the towns enforced stringent residency regulations, thus disclaiming responsibility for many who lived within the town limits but could not meet their requirements. These then became de facto state paupers. Those paupers who were town residents were frequently auctioned off to the lowest bidder at the annual Town Meeting in March or April, usually to farmers who would feed and clothe them in return for a weekly fee from the

---

[9] *Resolves of the General Court of the Commonwealth of Massachusetts, 1828–1831,* Ch. LXXXIII, pp. 296–297; *Report of Commissioners Appointed under a Resolve of the Legislature of Massachusetts, to Superintend the Erection of a Lunatic Hospital at Worcester and to Report a System of Discipline and Government for the Same* (Boston, 1832), p. 11.

town and all the labor they could get from their charges.[1] Thus by the 1820's, what had once been a form of stewardship in which the community worked together to care for its weaker members had degenerated in many places into a cruel practice of neglecting or exploiting paupers and lunatics. Towns were anxious to farm out their charges at the lowest possible cost to the public treasury and inhumane treatment often resulted when farmers tried to make this their chief source of income. At the same time, in some towns, unscrupulous selectmen hired local ruffians to kidnap local lunatics and have them deposited in towns sufficiently distant and strange to prevent an easy return. Town officials also spent much time trying to persuade other towns to pay for the support of paupers living within their boundaries but who allegedly had legal residence elsewhere. Even death did not let the pauper rest, as indicated from the following copy of a letter recorded in the Book of Minutes of the Selectmen of Dedham, dated June 30, 1824.[2]

This is to inform you that George Adams, Junr. had lately deceas'd in our Town, and we have charged the Expense of his Burial to your town, which Expense you are requested to pay as soon as convenient.

By order of the Overseers of the Poor,
Richard Ellis, Chn.

After a study of existing laws, Mann reluctantly concluded that town pauper lunatics were not the responsibility of the state and therefore not entitled to free care at the Worcester Hospital. The best he could salvage from what he considered an unfair situation was that once the state had shown the way, towns would provide similar care for their own charges. Hopefully, he said, the "courses pursued by the towns under past circumstances will prove no indication of their future practices." As a preliminary measure to make this possible, he proposed that towns be allowed to send their pauper lunatics to the hospital for a fee below the actual cost of the care. Such sanguine hopes did not materialize. Many lunatics in this category remained in local jails for another twelve years until their cause was

---

[1] Robert W. Kelso, *The History of Poor Relief in Massachusetts, 1620–1920* (Boston, 1922), pp. 35–61; Franklin B. Sanborn, *The Public Charities of Massachusetts* (Boston, 1876), pp. 110–127; "Report of the Commissioners . . . on the Subject of the Pauper System," *Massachusetts House Documents, 1833*, No. 3.
[2] Book of Minutes, 1817–1855, MS in Town Hall of Dedham, Massachusetts.

taken up by a second reformer, Dorothea Lynde Dix, who publicized their plight in her dramatic *Memorial to the Legislature* of Massachusetts in 1843.[3]

The third class of lunatics were those who were neither a threat to public security nor charges of the towns. These, too, while not under the direct control of the legislature, were encouraged to come to the hospital for treatment, providing their expenses could be paid by their family or friends.

Summing up his views on how the Commonwealth was to serve its citizens through the hospital, Mann presented a broad outline of the responsibilities of a republican government:

It [the hospital] was a necessary part of the great circle of duties to be fulfilled by a government, constituted for the benefit of the people. Gratuitous education, universally diffused; laws repressing licentiousness, and encouraging industry by securing to every man his honest gains, may be the primary duties in order of performance. But, though secondary in time, it is a duty no less sacred in obligation, to furnish all needful succor to those, whose position has been assigned them in the great machine of the Universe, that they suffer without fault or offense of their own.

The legislature agreed. Not only did it pass a law for the safekeeping of lunatics based on Mann's classification, but with little hesitation it also appropriated an additional $20,000 to cover the cost of furnishing the building and operating it for the first year, even though at the time the Commonwealth faced what some considered the enormous deficit of $150,000.[4]

Aside from the countless details of getting the building completed and furnished during 1832, the commissioners' major task remaining was the selection of a superintendent. Mann did not think the position called for a clergyman, but he insisted that it should be filled with "a humane man" and "a man of science," not only a physician, but also "a mental philosopher." After several enquiries and interviews, they decided that Dr. Samuel B. Woodward, Eli Todd's assistant at the Connecticut Retreat, was their man, and he accepted the post as the first superintendent of the hospital.[5]

---

[3] *Report of the Commissioners . . . Lunatic Hospital,* 1832, pp. 25–27.

[4] *Laws of the Commonwealth of Massachusetts, 1831–1833* (Boston, 1833), Vol. XII, Ch. CLXIII, pp. 466–470, "An Act concerning the State Lunatic Hospital"; *Massachusetts House Documents,* 1832, No. 14, "Report of the Committee on Finance," February 1, 1832.

[5] *Independent Chronicle and Boston Patriot,* February 17, 1830; F. C. Gray to Mann, October 5, 1832; Mann MSS:MHS.

With most arrangements completed near the end of the year, on December 6, 1832, the commissioners reported to the Governor that the facilities would be ready to receive patients on January 10, 1833. A schedule for receiving them from the county jails was prepared, jailers were notified that inmates to be transferred were to be bathed and given a new change of clothing, and early in January, His Excellency, Levi Lincoln, chief executive of the Commonwealth of Massachusetts, issued a proclamation which stated that "the State Lunatic Hospital, at Worcester, *is prepared for the reception of the insane."* [6]

Across the state from the jails and houses of correction of every county, the lunatics were prepared for transfer. Amidst oaths, obscene language, and a general chorus of demented cacophony, the products of years of neglect were led or forced from their stench-laden cellars, cages, and closets. Coming into the daylight, they could be seen in all their disfigured hideousness—the fierce testimony of the ravages of filth, anguish, and barbarism. As the jailers cut off their garments stinking with sweat and urine, scrubbed their bodies with strong soap, and dressed them in new clothes, they could not be expected to comprehend that they, who had been forgotten by one generation, had now been singled out as the objects of intense hope by the next. Within their new home, they were to become the living demonstration of what could be accomplished through humane and enlightened methods. In place of restraint, exposure, and cruelty were to be substituted sanitation, love, and understanding, as the aspirations of humanitarian reform were to be put to a test on the outcome. It was a time when men believed the deaf could be taught to "hear," the dumb to "talk," and the blind to "see." To an age that expressed a faith in science, progress, and the perfectibility of men, the insane were an ultimate challenge.

Through it all, Horace Mann sensed the deep satisfaction which came from public service and philanthropy. Three months after the opening of the hospital, he wrote to his sister of his feeling of achievement and hopes for the future.

I hear from Worcester very frequently, and the accounts are most flattering. Everything seems to have commenced under very favorable auspices, and so far the success has very far transcended my most

---

[6] *Reports and Other Documents . . . State Lunatic Hospital,* "Communication from the Commissioners and Trustees," pp. 30–36; *Massachusetts Spy,* January 1, 1833.

sanguine expectations. Individuals who had for years while subjected to the severe rigors of confinement in jails and Houses of Correction, been so frantic and ferocious, that their keepers had not ventured to go into their cells, had not been at Worcester a week before the powerful and reviving influences of good air and suitable diet and cleanliness and warmth with the expression of kindness on the part of their attendants, had so far transformed them into men, that they became quiet and manageable, and declared themselves happy in their new condition. We have an excellent Superintendent and everything now promises well. I most ardently hope the promise may be fulfilled.[7]

If he was proud, those close to the project knew Mann's was a just pride. His fact-finding survey, his eloquent plea in the House, and his careful planning of the hospital all earned him a rightful sense of accomplishment he had not known before. At the beginning of a decade that soon was to grow white hot with fervor for every conceivable reform and panacea, Mann had marshaled the resources and authority of the state, to reclaim the lives of men and women "whose position has been assigned them in the great machine of the Universe, that they suffer without fault or offence of their own," as he put it. Moreover, he believed that through this, the Commonwealth would "by the exhibition of an example worthy of imitation of other communities, aid, still more extensively, the general cause of philanthropy." [8]

The hospital was referred to as "Horace Mann's Monument," and when the first major treatise was published on the medical jurisprudence of the insane in 1838, it carried the following citation:

TO THE
HON. HORACE MANN
TO WHOSE PERSEVERING EXERTIONS
OUR COUNTRY IS MAINLY INDEBTED
FOR ONE OF ITS NOBLEST INSTITUTIONS FOR AMELIORATING
THE CONDITION OF THE INSANE
THIS WORK IS RESPECTFULLY INSCRIBED
AS A HUMBLE ACKNOWLEDGEMENT OF ESTEEM [9]

Through his work for the suppression of intemperance and the building of the Worcester Hospital, he had taken his place with those

---

[7] Mann to Lydia Mann, March 18, 1833, Mann MSS: MHS.
[8] *Report of the Hospital Commissioners . . . Lunatic Hospital*, 1832, p. 27.
[9] Isaac Ray, *A Treatise on the Medical Jurisprudence of Insanity* (Boston, 1838).

who also believed that part of their destiny was inextricably tied to promoting the happiness of mankind. With the aid of science and the sheer force of human energy, they would accomplish what men in former ages had conceded beyond the reach of human endeavor. Coming from static and homogeneous Franklin and Brown, Mann was sensitive to the rapid social and economic changes he found in Dedham and Boston. These he had interpreted as the knock of opportunity and the call to duty. Within the General Court, he used his power of persuasion to convince the state to take a larger hand in dealing with those developments he thought were beyond the scope of individual town action. Whether his beliefs that intemperance was the cause of causes, that most mental diseases were curable, or that the increased use of machines in industry and transportation would improve the lives of men were actually valid would require more time. But he asked for nothing more. Surely time was on his side.

CHAPTER VII

The Lonely, Empty Life

———————
———————

To everything there is a season . . . A time to
plant . . . a time to pluck . . .
A time to heal. . . .
                    Ecclesiastes

———————

F ROM THE VIEW of his associates, fortune was surely smiling upon
this young man. Yet in Dedham there would always be mothers
with unmarried daughters who considered his accomplishments incomplete as long as he remained one of the town's most eligible bachelors. Foremost among these was Mrs. Samuel Haven, wife of a local
judge, and mother of two daughters, Catherine and Elizabeth. Mann
obviously exceeded her minimal social criteria. Finding him good-
looking, an immaculate dresser, a witty conversationalist, and the
possessor of the proper social graces, Mrs. Haven insisted he become
a regular caller at her home. She even invited him to join a reading
circle drawn from the local social register which met at her house
weekly. By this means, Mann was introduced to the most influential
families in Dedham.[1]

Soon his name appeared on numerous invitation lists and he attended many of the formal and informal affairs of the young people.
In the summer they invited him along on their boating and walking
parties and their all-day excursions and picnics to Cow Island on the
outskirts of the town. In 1828, Moses Gregg added a ballroom to
Alden's Tavern and it soon became the focal point for much of the
winter social life. The hotel itself, always a busy place, was especially crowded with lawyers and litigants during the court sessions.
Inevitably, when the happy parties and conversations around the
large fireplace came to an end as the logs became embers and his
friends departed for their homes, Mann found the distance between
gaiety and depression a short one. He could return to nothing better
than his room on the second floor of the building, his residence dur-

———————

[1] Catherine Haven Hilliard to Mary Peabody Mann, February 13, 1860,
Mann MSS: MHS.

ing these years. As a place to stay, the hotel was a convenient base of operations and provided him with a degree of freedom not possible in a boardinghouse, but it lacked the warmth and security of family life. Even though he had lived in Dedham for several years, he found it difficult to avoid the feeling of transience. Desiring to be mobile, he also sought a sense of stability, and there were times, when he reflected upon his personal affairs, that he found it a lonely and empty life.[2]

The misgivings he suffered for having left his mother and sister in Franklin were compounded by a series of deaths within his immediate family. Besides the loss of his brother-in-law, Calvin Pennell, in 1824, death struck the Manns again the next year when Stanley lost three children in a matter of days. It was a terrible blow and one not easily forgotten even for someone as active and buoyant as Stanley. For a time, Mann too could not shake himself free of what seemed to be a chronic illness. The town physician, Dr. Jeremy Stimson, called upon him several times in 1823 and 1824. In 1825, Stimson came to Mann's room frequently, and it even became necessary to summon him once during the night. To be sick in a new town and without the attention of his family only made Mann's recurring sense of isolation more acute.

Although women fed his ego at social gatherings, he could never bring himself to be completely at ease with the opposite sex. Not really confident of himself, not certain of who he was and what he would become, despite all the outward appearances of success, he could not dispel fears that someone might penetrate his outer defenses, see through his façade, and understand him even better than he knew himself, perhaps even finding him to be an impostor. In public he played the role of the handsome young bachelor, gay, witty, and the epitome of politeness. As a conversationalist, his skill in wielding the clever pun and sharp quip, as well as evoking a noble sentiment, enabled him to dominate the circle of admiring persons who inevitably clustered about him at social gatherings. Yet in all this, he could never relax his guard and let them know who he really was. Only when he could separate one from the group and converse on a more intimate basis could he share his more personal thoughts about himself. Even in this, he was careful to let a confidant enter his innermost thoughts only on his own terms, seeking admiration and sym-

---

[2] Frank Smith, *A History of Dedham*, p. 173; Austin, *Tale of Dedham Tavern*, pp. 68–69.

pathy more than understanding and love, much as he did with his mother and younger sister.

In periods of despondency, Mann gradually found Catherine Haven a sensitive person in whom he could confide some of his more personal misgivings. Since Dedham was a small community, which maintained its social mores through an unstructured but highly efficient system of surveillance by gossip, Mann found it difficult to make their relation appear purely platonic. Apparently Catherine understood the limits of his intentions, but her father did not. After the friendship had gone on for some time, Judge Haven, goaded on by his son, Samuel, Junior, summoned Mann into his parlor, and having noted that the young man's interest in his daughter was sufficiently public to ward off other suitors, he bluntly asked Mann to declare his intentions. Piqued and embarrassed because his motives were questioned, Mann withdrew from the Haven household. He thought he had offended no one, but some wags in the village spoke of his conduct as reprehensible.[3]

Labor as he did, the success this brought in no way dispelled his despondency. By 1828, his legal work prospered; in the General Court he was marked as a man on the rise; and there were no adverse reports from his joint financial ventures with Stanley. As the farm boy who went to Brown a decade before, such an array of accomplishments would have seemed the culmination of his most sanguine aspirations and more. Yet, now having come so far, he could not extract from his achievements the sense of satisfaction and well-being which he sought. Although too busy for sound sleep and a good digestion, his pace of activity in no way suppressed the dissatisfaction which gnawed at his mind and permitted him only partial peace. Each month found him devoting more time to building his legal and political career, relaxing when he could among his new friends in Dedham and Boston. None of this, however, brought him the contentment and enduring serenity which he craved. Drawn though he was to his career and his friends, at the end of each day he found himself returning to nothing more than an empty hotel room.[4]

There were of course advantages to his lonely existence. Aside from occasional concerns for his mother and sisters, he was unim-

---

[3] Catherine Haven Hilliard to Mary Peabody Mann, February 13, 1860, Mann MSS:MHS; Elizabeth Peabody to Mary Peabody, June 2 to 5, 1834, Cuba Journal (hereafter, CJ), in the Berg MSS:NYPL.
[4] Mann to Charlotte Messer, September 1, 1830 [?], Mann-Messer MSS:BUA.

peded by the familial and social responsibilities which might have hobbled a more secure person. A free agent, he could devote long hours to personal advancement without considering the needs of those who might be dependent on him. During his first years in Dedham, the local social levees and the dinners in Boston with Edward Loring and the other members of the "Club" did help to fill a void in his life. He thought he found something more enduring, however, in his visits to Providence, where he was the guest of the Messer family. Here within the white clapboard house with its pretentious Greek revival columns guarding the front doors, Mann, perhaps for the first time in his life, sensed how much one could gain from the reciprocal devotion within a closely knit family. Here in the household of his former *praeses* there was something more lasting and satisfying than ambition and wealth, and with each return to Dedham, Mann's loneliness impressed him more than his freedom.[5]

*   *   *

The fact that he had also become a secret admirer of Charlotte Messer, youngest of the three Messer daughters, intensified his loneliness. By the time the General Court had adjourned in the summer of 1829, he decided to take a radical step towards alleviating this problem. Although able to talk down a hostile opposition in the House of Representatives, when it came to making his intentions known to this young and attractive woman, thirteen years his junior, Mann could not speak directly to his purpose. Instead, on July 8, 1829, the post carried a letter to the Messer home. After a number of drafts, Mann had finally managed to come to the point with his very first sentence:

Miss Charlotte Messer,
In obedience to feelings whose utterance I can no longer repress, I take the liberty of this mode to request permission to visit you hereafter in the character of an *avowed*, as I have hitherto done, in that of a *secret* admirer.

In his letter he also promised,

---

[5] Mann to Elizabeth Peabody, November 6, 1836, and Catherine Haven Hilliard to Mary Peabody Mann, February 13, 1860, both in Mann MSS:MHS.

With sentiments of regard . . . which will survive even the wreck of hope, and flourish in my heart, though all else there should be desolate, I shall always remain, as I have been, ever since I knew the beauties and excellence of your nature, your *more than friend*.

A postscript stated that any answer she might have would find him at "the hotel opposite the market." He waited for an answer. But none came.[6]

At the time, Mann was on his way to Connecticut to learn about Eli Todd's methods of treating the insane at the Hartford Retreat. Charlotte may have been waiting until he returned to Dedham before she answered such an important request, but travel did not prevent the anxious suitor from writing. In Hartford he took time to dispatch a second missive in which he complained that because of her silence, his heart was "torn by the conflict of desire and fear." Returning to Dedham, he learned that his fear was unfounded. Charlotte had consented for him to call on her as "an *avowed*" and he was ecstatic.[7]

The courtship which followed was conducted mainly via the mails. In August his letters began with "My *Dearest* Miss Charlotte." By September it was first "My Dearest & Loveliest Charlotte" and then "My most Dearest and Lovely Charlotte." In October it was "My own Dearest Charlotte" and by November he addressed her as "My ever dearest Charlotte." One can only imagine his let-down when he broke the seals on her first answers to his passionate appeals and read "My friend" and "My Dear Friend." Occasionally impatient with such exchanges, Mann would dress in his finest, rent a chaise, and urge his horse south to Providence. On one of these visits he brought Charlotte a fine gold ring he had purchased in Boston. When he left the Messer house on this trip, he had made the engagement official.[8]

Memories of his despondency made the anticipation of a future happiness all the more exhilarating. "Does the darkness of fear in which I am somehow enveloped, come from a cloud, that extends along the whole path of my future life, or is it the darkness that precedes and presages the dawn?" he asked. He needed Charlotte's continual reassurance, and when she withheld this from him, his spirits collapsed. After several unanswered letters, he complained, "you cannot conceive my regret and disappointment in not hearing from

---

[6] Mann to Charlotte Messer, July 8, 1829, Mann-Messer MSS:BUA.
[7] Mann to Charlotte Messer, July 14 and 24, 1829, Mann-Messer MSS:BUA.
[8] On September 3, 1829, Mann purchased a gold ring from John B. Jones of Boston. Receipt in Mann MSS:DHS.

you." That he was capable of all the irrational action usually attrib-
uted to those in love was evident by the fact that when Charlotte *did*
write, he now feared her answer was prompted by pity or had been
coerced from her! One thing only slowly he came to realize. In such
matters, one did not court a single person, but negotiated with an entire family. Back in Providence, Charlotte's two sisters insisted that
Mann's letters were entirely too passionate for the initial stages of a
proper courtship. Not until the end of October would Mann let himself be convinced that he was receiving unsolicited reassurances of
Charlotte's love. "Now I am at the *Zenith* of elation," he boasted. Only
one thing marred his happiness. Charlotte had been troubled by a
persistent cough.[9]

On Thanksgiving Day, the roads to Providence were impossible,
but at Christmas, Mann was able to spend several happy, albeit
closely chaperoned, days with his betrothed. On his return to Dedham, he stopped off at Franklin to tell his mother and Lydia about
the woman he planned to marry. Fully aware of the new turn his life
was about to take, he forced himself to revisit the pain and pleasure
of his youth in Franklin. Early Sunday morning he left the old farm-
house alone and walked about his "paternal fields." The air was cold
and clear, and the beauty and peace of the New England countryside
made it difficult to recall that these same fields and lanes had been
the scene of "those catastrophes that were not forgotten." The meetinghouse bell heard from a distance only spoke of the past; it held no
meaning for the present. Little by little as he walked along, familiar
objects stirred his memory, a leaning gatepost, the surviving apple
trees in the orchard, a stone fence which contained more than a few
stones of his own placing. Finally with almost each step there was yet
another memory and another boyhood dream which fell to the test
of time. Climbing to the top of a small hill he looked about, recalling
that it was here where he first experienced a sense of the eternal.
Here was the same tree he had lain under in summer, looking upward
and imagining analogies suggested by its gnarled branches. Gradually his attention shifted to the shafts of light which came through a
thousand vistas in its foliage, tracing them upward to the firmament
and the limits of his imagination. All of this he wrote to Charlotte,
describing an episode from his past when the ecstasy of youth was
evolving into the reverence and awe of manhood. The lantern he now

---

[9] Mann to Charlotte Messer, August 1, September 17 and 28, and October
12 and 22, 1829, Mann-Messer MSS:BUA.

carried in his life cast but a small circle of light before and behind him. On this morning as he walked about on his "paternal fields," it was as if in contemplating its backward rays, he was able to see further forward as well.[1]

With the opening of the General Court in January, 1830, Mann again moved to Boston, this time taking his quarters in the new Tremont House, the most fashionable hotel in town. Compared with what he had known in the past, this building with its more than 150 rooms and suites was nothing less than a republican palace. The fact that the building was a rather plain stone box with ornamentation tacked on here and there was noted only by uncharitable European observers. For Mann and most Bostonians, the Tremont House—from its façade of fluted Doric pillars to its interior rooms and halls furnished with thick carpeting, lavish crystalline chandeliers, imported furniture, and oversized paintings and mirrors—was proof of a new luxury and magnificence possible in their country. To become one of its tenants was to serve notice that one must be counted among the successful men of New England.

His room was on the south side and overlooked the Old Granary Burying Ground, but he was not depressed, or so he told himself during the day. It also faced the "sweet South," which made him feel closer to Charlotte. Friends in Boston sensed a new sparkle in his speech, and upon learning the cause, spent many of their dinner conversations at the Exchange Coffee House toasting Charlotte with glasses of dark red claret and jesting about the incipient bridegroom's waning freedom. Still when the friends had parted and Mann returned alone to his room, the exhilaration of the evening wore off. Even writing to Charlotte and planning their future did not buoy up his spirits. As he sat at his small writing desk and looked out over the gravestones which now caught the flickering light from the hotel windows, thoughts of her health gnawed at his composure. And the later at night, the more ominous the things he imagined. "Why is it," he wrote to her, gradually sinking into a mood of depression, "that I am doomed to suffer this misfortune! I entreat you to be well. These repeated colds may lead to ——— but I cannot write it or think it." [2]

But the daylight and his many responsibilities would not permit moping. Up at the State House, he was busy studying the returns of the latest survey on lunatics. Later he issued a report calling for the

[1] Mann to Charlotte Messer, January 6, 1830, Mann-Messer MSS:BUA.
[2] Mann to Charlotte Messer, January 18 and February 4, 1830, Mann-Messer MSS:BUA.

erection of a hospital for the insane. Other reports followed. In March, he was chairman of a committee for the revision of laws on debtors and creditors and the month of May found him at the head of a group advocating stricter temperance legislation. When the Speaker of the House, William S. Calhoun, gaveled the last session to a close in June, Horace Mann could look back on his work with a sense of relief and accomplishment. It had been a grueling schedule, but this he expected and more if his political star were to rise.[3]

Strangely enough, Mann considered none of his activities at the State House as the proper topics for his letters to Charlotte. Accounts of the turbulent, sometimes cynical, sessions in the legislature and the courts he considered inappropriate for their unsullied correspondence. Instead, he filled pages with vows of undying love, while Charlotte responded with pious sentiments, references to her health, and occasional coquettish teasing.[4]

Sometime during May, Charlotte and her family decided on a September wedding, and Mann arranged to rent Herman Fisher's house, the best available in Dedham, beginning on the first of October. Health remained the one disturbing element in their plans. During the summer, Mann had been called in to draw up a will for a young minister who was dying of consumption. In robust health the year before, the doomed man had contracted a cold which became chronic. He was now given but a short time to live. Mann prepared the will and hurried away from the tragic scene, troubled by thoughts of the frailty of life and by fears that his future happiness was equally vulnerable. That evening his letter to Charlotte expressed an increased sense of urgency as he pleaded that she take care of herself.[5]

By early September a number of wedding details were still pending, and Mann made a hurried trip to Providence which clarified things sufficiently to permit him to post his "intention of marriage" in the Dedham newspaper. The Messers had insisted that the bride and groom remain in Providence for a few days after the ceremony to pay calls on friends of the family. Mann wished to leave with

[3] Journal of the House, Vol. 50, January 7 and 25, and February 13 and 27, 1830, pp. 120, 206, 302, and 364, MS in MSA; *Columbian Centinel,* March 10 and June 2, 1830; *Independent Chronicle and Boston Patriot,* May 29, 1830.
[4] Mann to Charlotte Messer, March 23, 1830, and September 19, [1831], Mann-Messer MSS:BUA.
[5] Mann to Charlotte Messer, May 16, and 25, 1830, Mann-Messer MSS: BUA.

Charlotte immediately after the reception, and finally made his point, but only after learning that in gaining a wife, he was also becoming more deeply involved with the collective will of his new in-laws.[6] Then on the appointed day, September 29, friends and family gathered at the Messer home to witness the service. Looking at his beloved Charlotte as he repeated the minister's words, Horace Mann promised to "love, honor and cherish, in sickness and in health, until death do us part." [7]

*   *   *

Arriving in Dedham, Mann removed his belongings from his bachelor quarters, paid what he assumed was his last bill at Alden's Tavern, and moved with Charlotte into their rented house at the corner of Church Street and Franklin Square across from the Court House. As the bridegroom had neither time nor inclination, he hired Joel Richards, the local handyman, to make alterations Charlotte thought the house needed. In the meantime, the newlyweds made frequent excursions into Boston, purchasing the necessary items to make their house a home. On one trip they bought carpeting, on another furniture, and on a third they purchased dishes and a silver ladle which caught Charlotte's fancy. For all his anticipation of the future, he could not have imagined the happiness he experienced showing his wife the many shops and public buildings in the city.[8]

Now the creation of a comfortable home became almost an obsession with Mann. His mother and father had worked side by side for years to create the Franklin homestead, but the wife of Horace

---

[6] Charlotte Messer to Mann, September 17, 1830, Mann-Messer MSS:BUA; *The Record of Births, Marriages, and Deaths . . . Town of Dedham*, ed. Don Gleason Hill (Dedham, 1886), p. 185.

[7] Charlotte Messer to Mann, September 17, 1830, and Mann to Charlotte Messer, September 20, 1830, Mann-Messer MSS:BUA; James N. Arnold, *Vital Records of Rhode Island, 1636–1850*, first series (Providence, 1908), XVII, 487.

[8] The annual rent was $175. The purchases of house furnishings included the following:

Moses Pond	Oct. 15	$ 17.64	(dishes)
John Doggett & Co.	Oct. 18	134.36	(included 56¾ yds. of carpeting)
Alfred Welles	Oct. 18	7.50	(mantle lamps)
William Willis	Oct. 29	2.00	(silver ladle)
D.H. Hunnewell	Oct. 29	17.24	(knives and forks)
Samuel Beall	n.d.	211.42	(furniture)

All receipts are in the Mann MSS:DHS.

Mann was to possess a fine home from the outset. The sight of the Fisher house as he came down Court Street, the fire in the hearth, and Charlotte's cheerful voice to greet him when he returned at the end of the day, at last provided the physical manifestation of the security and contentment which had eluded him from his youth. One more piece had been fitted into the superstructure of achievement and happiness he was erecting for himself.

Because of her frail constitution and her parents' ideas on the proper rearing of a daughter, Charlotte had led a sheltered existence in Providence. Conducting oneself in a genteel manner was stressed more than the domestic skills of cooking and sewing. In agreement with this attitude, Mann viewed his wife as an object of his affection, someone to pamper, protect, and idolize, rather than someone who would play a more active and integral part in his future conquests. Because of his recent affluence, Charlotte would never have calloused hands, the trademark imposed upon his mother and sisters by the grueling monotonous tasks of rural life in Franklin.[9]

There would be another difference in this marriage as well. Both Mann and Charlotte were now separated from their families. Charlotte was moving away for the first time. Having experienced it before, Mann, shortly before the wedding, had attempted to prepare her for the separation which was to come. "I shall never forget while I remember anything, the rupture of those tendrils of affection which had clasped and turned around the objects of home and family, when I first left my mother's door. . . . Now it is your turn to be separated," he wrote to her and then added, "The knife must pass between the parent-stock and the scion before it can be transplanted to flourish in another soil." Charlotte was moving to a strange town and would need to make new friends. Still there were also advantages to this arrangement. At home in Dedham, the couple found a joy in their conjugal isolation, unhampered by the superintendence of their elders. They experienced at once a stimulating sense of independence and a feeling of exposure to a strange and exciting world.[1]

Charlotte was sick in December, and Jeremy Stimson, who earlier had cared for Mann, was now called to the house on Church Street. The week before Christmas she showed signs of improve-

---

[9] Catherine Haven Hilliard to Mary Peabody Mann, February 13, 1860, Mann MSS:MHS; Charlotte knew little about cooking; see Charlotte Messer Mann to Mann, [March 17, 1832], Mann-Messer MSS:BUA.
[1] Mann to Charlotte Messer, September 15, 1830, Mann-Messer MSS:BUA.

ment, but the doctor was again needed on Christmas Day and during the first week in January. As Mann had to be in Boston for the opening of the General Court at this time, he was forced to leave Charlotte in Dedham. A week later she was able to rejoin him, hoping to get more exercise walking on the sidewalks of Boston.[2]

She found Boston much less friendly than Dedham. Mann, faced with a mountain of legislative work to be moved by the end of March, frequently was forced to leave her to her own resources. The bill for the lunatic hospital had reached the floor for debate, and Speaker Calhoun expected the Representative from Dedham to lead the fight to procure its passage. In a previous session the House had rejected a move to abolish all capital punishment. Now Mann was working for a measure which would require executions to be conducted in maximum privacy. The lawmakers were also considering a bill for stricter regulation of the sale of liquor in taverns and hotels. All these kept Mann away from Charlotte, and despite social calls on some of her husband's friends and the efforts of the Lorings to introduce her to Boston society, her loneliness increased. By February, Mann acknowledged that he had a homesick wife on his hands and reluctantly conceded it was best for her to return to her parents for the remainder of the General Court. They had been together less than five months.[3]

In the correspondence which followed, the flowery rhetoric of courtship gave way to expressions of love and devotion between husband and wife. Sitting at his desk in the House gallery above the main floor, Mann easily lost interest in the tedious reports and prolonged debates. Below him it looked as if 400 men were making "more clamor than so many bees." "Mr. Speaker Calhoun is putting motions, Messrs. Every body are debating the question pro and con, hands fly up in the affirmative and in the negative and the current of business sweeps along below me without drawing my attention from you," he wrote to Charlotte. Others were busily engaged, but he found little interest in bank examinations, the mandatory mowing of Canadian thistles, the prohibition of narrow-rimmed wheels on town streets, or the protection of sepulchers. She in turn could not understand why the "collected intelligence of the honorable House

---

[2] Charlotte Messer Mann to Lydia Mann, January 23, 1831, Mann-Messer MSS:BUA.
[3] *Journal of the House*, Vol. 51, January 7, 1831, p. 112, MS in MSA; *Independent Chronicle and Boston Patriot*, February 16, 1831; *Columbian Centinel*, January 22, 1831.

of Representatives" could not devise a more expeditious means of transacting their business. If other wives wanted to see their husbands as much as she wanted to see hers, they would get their work completed in much less time.[4]

By this time, it was evident that Charlotte would be unable to do their housework when she returned, and Mann asked his sister Lydia and Mary Messer for help. Unfortunately neither of them could leave their homes and come to Dedham. Charlotte looked in Providence for someone she might hire while Mann enquired in Boston and Dedham. The two had enjoyed their short independence, but now in time of stress, it was necessary to hire someone where the family members had always served before.[5]

Finally the session was prorogued. Mann hurried to Dedham, cleared up his legal work, and looked for an improvement in the weather which would permit Charlotte to make the trip from Providence. When the General Court reconvened on May 25, 1831, he did not answer the roll call. Once again he had been re-elected, but this time he declined to serve. Instead, he readied their house and purchased a special surprise for Charlotte, a rocking chair he thought particularly suited to her convalescence. She returned in July, and the next two months on Church Street were idyllic save for the occasional need to call Dr. Stimson. During this time, Governor Levi Lincoln offered Mann the position of Judge Advocate with the rank of major in the First Division of the Massachusetts State Militia. It was his first military duty other than the annual Muster Day celebration back in Franklin. Mainly an honorary appointment, if any work did arise, it would be the conducting of courts-martial rather than the wielding of weapons and commanding of troops, so Mann, smiling at the thought that even his military talents were being tapped, accepted his call to arms.[6]

By the end of August, Dr. Stimson's calls were more frequent, and it was again decided that Charlotte should return to the Messers until Mann could find someone to take care of her. The rocking chair would be empty on their first wedding anniversary. Upon her arrival

---

[4] Mann to Charlotte Messer Mann, March 5, 1831; Charlotte Messer Mann to Mann, March 13, 1831; both in Mann-Messer MSS:BUA.

[5] After trying several places without success, Mann prepared to swallow his prejudice and hire "Mrs. Darkie," if he had it in his "power to whiten the complexion" and "sharpen up the noses." Mann to Charlotte Messer Mann, March 24, 1831, Mann-Messer MSS:BUA.

[6] Journal of the House, Vol. 52, p. 1, MS in MSA. *The Independent Politician and Working Men's Advocate*, May 12, 1831.

in Providence, Charlotte stayed to her room, experimenting with a diet of oyster and chicken broths and powdered chamemilo flowers to build up her strength. Mann continued to look for a housekeeper. By the end of September, he was ready to hire just about anyone, "black, white or grey," if it meant having his wife back with him. Meanwhile, Charlotte had abandoned her special diet and, on the advice of a friend, was taking port wine as a tonic. Since she now occasionally coughed up blood, her worried husband pleaded with her by mail to abandon her home remedies and seek the advice of a local physician. He even went so far as to ask Dr. Stimson to send her a prescription.[7]

In October, there was a trace of desperation and resentment in Mann's letters.

If you stay away much longer, I shall have to marry you over again. . . . Sometimes, my love, I can hardly help repining at your protracted illness, at the privations of enjoyment to which it subjects us all—at the sufferings which it inflicts upon you. That, I *hope*, is the only cause that shuts you out from what is attainable of human happiness.

Since the wedding they had been brought to the very brink of human happiness, but it had always eluded their grasp. The separation forced Mann to swallow his prejudices, and he arranged to have a "black lady" come and do the housework. But the "sovereign two," Mary Messer and her mother, insisted that Charlotte was now too weak to travel. At one time Mann got them to agree to let Charlotte return, but before she could leave, the "sovereign trio," now including Asa Messer, reversed the decision, and she was kept in Providence. Such reasoning was simply beyond Mann's comprehension. He assured her parents that a cook had been hired, and although he had not seen her, she was coming with good references. With a mixture of humor and sarcasm, he added that when she did appear,

---

[7] Charlotte Messer Mann to Mann, [September 16 and 19, 1831] and September 28, 1831; Mann to Charlotte Messer Mann, September 24 and October 14, 1831, all in Mann-Messer MSS:BUA; Stimson prescribed one grain of sugar of lead, half a grain of ipecac, and one-fourth grain of opium. The inadequacy of Charlotte's medical treatment is suggested by the fact that while she was continually coughing up blood and losing her strength, she was taking port wine or Stimson's prescription, a diet of oyster and chicken broths, and using a mustard plaster to draw out poisons, all supposedly to build up her strength. The assumption seems to have been that all she needed was confinement and the right kind of tonic.

she would probably turn out to be "white, or perhaps a little inclined to the gingerbread complexion,—probably between four and six feet in height, and equiped [sic] with all the needful means of annoyance, offensive and defensive." Two more weeks dragged on before the "sovereign trio" would give their consent, and it was not until the middle of November that husband and wife were finally reunited in the house on Church Street. In the future it would take more than the call of the General Court to separate Mann from his beloved Charlotte.[8]

*   *   *

In 1832, much unfinished business remained from the last session, and Mann faced another heavy schedule. Somehow he had to keep the bills for better care of the insane moving through the House and Senate. Edward Loring urged him to give priority to the beleaguered license law. Assuming that Charlotte was feeling better, Loring suggested that the Manns come to Boston and stay at a boardinghouse. They took his advice and Dr. Stimson made a final call on Charlotte the third of January.[9] The next day as she rode beside Mann on the trip to Boston, Charlotte had a special reason to be proud. Her husband had been honored by appointment to a "select committee" to inform His Excellency, Levi Lincoln, that both chambers had completed their preliminary business and were ready for the traditional Election Day sermon which signaled the official opening of the legislature. According to custom, the Independent Corps of Cadets of the Massachusetts Militia, this year under the command of Lieutenant Colonel Grenville Temple Winthrop, were to escort the Governor, his council, and members of both houses to the Old South Meeting House. Bothersome Indians and Redcoats no longer threatened the peace, but the formality of "protecting" the chief executive was still observed. By 1832 only a ritual, it nevertheless set in motion a train of events which would place an almost intolerable strain on the marriage of Charlotte and Horace Mann.[1]

[8] Mann to Charlotte Messer Mann, October 5, 14, and 29, 1831; Charlotte Messer Mann to Mann, October 15, 1831, all in Mann-Messer MSS:BUA.
[9] Edward Loring to Mann, November 12, [1831], Mann MSS:DHS.
[1] Journal of the House, Vol. 53, January 4, 1832, p. 6, MS in MSA; Records of Courts Martial &c., Vol. 19, March, 1832, "General Court Martial of Lieutenant Colonel Grenville Temple Winthrop of the Independent Cadet Company, 1st Division." MS in Adjutant General's Office, Military Archives, War Records Section, Commonwealth of

Until 1832, the legislature convened in May or June for its opening session and completed the political year with an additional session the following January. Then, to simplify matters, the two meetings were condensed to a single session which began the first week in January. Accordingly, with the convening of the General Court on January 4, 1832, after opening ceremonies in the House and Senate, a "select committee" was sent to inform the Governor and his council that they were ready to proceed to the Old South Meeting House.

Although the commanding officer had furnished some of his men with winter uniforms at his own expense, the frigid weather became unbearable to the "citizen soldiers," who in civilian life were mainly clerks and students and usually paraded only during the summer. At the start of the procession, their band of four musicians struck up a cheerful march, but soon a sub-zero wind howling up Park Street began to take its toll. The valves of the trumpet and the slide of the trombone froze, and the fife player found his instrument filling up with ice. Only the drummer beating a vigorous cadence seemed able to cope with the cold. Finally, the church was reached and the lawmakers gratefully filed inside to be out of the wind. Unfortunately, no seats had been saved for the military. Rather than invite pneumonia and frostbite, an order was given for the cadets to retire to the warm interior of the Exchange Coffee House. Thirty minutes later, when an orderly failed to return with intelligence about the progress of the sermon, Winthrop marched his corps back to the church. Faced by his grumbling men and learning that the preacher "had progressed but a little way" and needed at least another thirty minutes to exhaust his text, Winthrop ordered a second retreat to the shelter of the coffeehouse. As luck would have it, his information proved incorrect. The sermon was unusually brief and the ceremony concluded far ahead of schedule.[2]

As soon as the benediction was pronounced, Governor Lincoln dispatched his aide-de-camp to alert the honor guard, but they were

---

Massachusetts. See "Item no. 14." The corps was composed of four commissioned officers, nine noncommissioned officers, eleven privates, fifteen volunteers, and four musicians. Thirteen men were absent. See "Item no. 15."

[2] *Trial by a Court Martial of Lieut. Col. Grenville Temple Winthrop* (Boston, 1832), pp. 152, 160–164, 187, and 207–208. This is a printed record of the trial, together with a commentary by Winthrop in which he attempted to vindicate himself.

nowhere to be seen. After an uncomfortable moment of indecision on the church steps, His Excellency decided it was less embarrassing to return without an escort than to wait for the derelict cadets, and struck out on his own for the State House, accompanied only by his council and a few lawmakers. When word reached the cadets, they rushed from the coffeehouse hoping to outflank the Governor before he reached the corner of Park and Tremont Streets. The cold was forgotten. Officers who could, organized their men to march double time. The rest simply ran along whatever avenue seemed the shortest negotiable distance between two points. For a moment, it looked as though Winthrop would rally his forces and snatch victory from the jaws of humiliation by presenting arms to the Governor as he passed the Park Street Church. But luck was not with him. Two blocks short of his objective, his forces became entangled in a funeral procession and lost valuable time. The race ended in a tie, with both parties meeting head-on at the fateful corner. Spectators who had gathered to watch the procession return could never have anticipated the scene which followed. While cadets attempted to form ranks, Winthrop breathlessly ran to Lincoln asking if he had further orders. The Governor refused to recognize him, and with as much dignity as his rising temper would permit, made his way up Beacon Hill. As the streets were now filling with curious by-standers, confused lawmakers, barking dogs, and puffing cadets unable to find room to line up and present arms, Lincoln had to pick his way along the sidewalk and in the street as best he could. After a quick conference in the State House, the chief executive, who was dubbed the "prince of punctilio" for good reason, ordered Winthrop's arrest for "Disobedience of Orders," "Neglect of Duty," and "Unmilitary and Unofficerlike conduct." [3]

While the citizens of Boston enjoyed accounts of the military faux pas and exchanged descriptions of the Governor making his way back to his chambers unescorted through snowdrifts and milling people, Horace Mann addressed himself to more serious things. Besides his regular duties, he was now chairman of several important House committees. Moreover, his docket of cases before the

[3] The account of Winthrop's attempt to rally his men can be found in the voluminous testimony recorded in *Trial by a Court Martial, passim.* Other accounts can be found in the *Independent Chronical and Boston Patriot,* January 7, 1832, and Edward Everett Hale, *A New England Boyhood,* pp. 107–108.

Court of Common Pleas in Dedham for the February session was heavier than usual. For the moment, the Election Day incident seemed of tertiary importance compared to his work and his concern for Charlotte. Then on February 6, Lincoln's military aide announced a general court-martial to convene on March 5. His proclamation included detailed specifications against Winthrop and listed the officers who were to conduct the trial. The president was drawn from the Fifth Division of the Militia, the marshal of the court from the Third. The First Division would provide the services of its judge advocate. Major Horace Mann was about to begin his "military career." [4]

At first Mann assured Charlotte that the contending parties would be satisfied with a two- or three-day hearing, but when he learned that Winthrop had retained two of the best attorneys in the area, William H. Gardiner and Franklin Dexter, it was apparent to him that the trial might last for weeks. Now with the work of the court-martial added to his unusually heavy schedule, and with the Messers again insisting that Charlotte should stay with them for a short time, he sadly resigned himself to the inevitability of another separation from his wife. Holding off on his decision for as long as possible, he finally agreed to send her once more to the "sweet South." [5]

The correspondence which followed indicated how mature Charlotte had become and how deeply she had come to love her hus-

---

[4] General Orders Nos. 6, 1826–1833, Headquarters, Boston, February 6, 1832, pp. 277–278. MS in Adjutant General's Office Military Archives, War Records Section, Commonwealth of Massachusetts. Lincoln's insistence on the prosecution of Winthrop was motivated by more than his momentary embarrassment and anger. The entire system of the Massachusetts Militia, especially the requirement that all able-bodied men within certain ages regularly appear for training sessions, was under attack at the time. In a previous session, Lincoln had acknowledged this as well as the fact that the Commonwealth was less in danger of war each year. Still he insisted that the state militia was essential to the Union and rather than discontinue it, he urged the General Court to "increase the penalties for neglect of duty. . . ." He also wanted a more severe penalty authorized against those officers who "treat [their men] with ardent spirits, on days of military duty. . . ." Having taken this position, he was forced to prosecute Winthrop for disobedience. Levi Lincoln, "Message of His Excellency Levi Lincoln, Communicated to the Two Branches of the Legislature, January 6, 1830," *Massachusetts Senate Documents, 1829–1830*, No. 1, pp. 12–16.
[5] Mann to Charlotte Messer Mann, March 18 [?], 1832, Mann-Messer MSS:BUA; Grenville T. Winthrop to Mann, February 10, 1832, Mann MSS:DHS. Both of these men were prominent attorneys.

band. Gone was the coquetry and superficiality of her earlier letters and in their place she wrote of her loneliness, her sense of desolation when she awoke in the morning only to realize she would not hear her Horace's voice before she slept again. Of course there were old friendships to renew, "But you my love," she assured her husband, "are what my heart clings to and will not be satisfied to be withdrawn." If Mann's work necessitated the separation, it also provided a certain balm for the pain which accompanied it. He applied himself to his tasks with a new intensity, attempting to forget his personal distress. From the House floor he called for a state redistricting convention. In order to break the deadlock over a bill regulating the sale of liquor, he agreed to join five others and restudy the controversial measure. One day he argued three cases before the Court of Common Pleas and on the next four more. At one time the next five cases on the docket were all his.[6]

Then on the first week of March he was cast in a new role with a costume fitting the occasion. On the eve of the court-martial he wrote to Charlotte asking her to picture him in his "regimentals" as he entered the court room. On his head was a *"chapeau bras,"* such as once crowned the head of Napoleon, as "lofty and widespread as the banyan tree." When he put on the officer's coat, his breast swelled "with emotion and padding" and from his side hung the reinforcement of a "thirsty sword" that had tasted neither flesh nor blood, but was long enough "to scare away the millennium."[7]

The opening day of the trial, Mann administered the oath of office to members of the tribunal. He read the charges and asked Winthrop how he pleaded. "Not guilty," was the answer, and the trial was under way. Mann took painstaking notes of the proceedings, as it was one of his responsibilities to begin each session by reading a résumé of the previous day. Soon the judge advocate was required to render an opinion whether the Governor actually had the legal right to order out the militia. Not daring to fumble his first real assignment, he responded in the affirmative, supporting his opinion with an exhaustive analysis, starting with Coke, then working through Massachusetts and federal laws, *The Federalist*, Montes-

---

[6] Charlotte Messer Mann to Mann, February 21, 1832; Mann to Charlotte Messer Mann, February 26, 1832, both in Mann-Messer MSS:BUA; *Columbian Centinel*, February 18, 1832; Journal of the House, Vol. 53, February 7, 1832, p. 227, MS in MSA.

[7] Mann to Charlotte Messer Mann, March 4, 1832, Mann-Messer MSS:BUA.

quieu's *Spirit of the Laws,* and even resurrecting a general order issued by Governor Shirley in 1741. His ruling went unchallenged,
and Mann felt he had put on a convincing performance.[8]

Session after session, through interrogation and cross examination, a parade of witnesses—thirty-seven in all—furnished corrobo-
rating and conflicting testimony. Not even the most trivial details
were overlooked concerning escort duty, military discipline, and the
sequence of events of Election Day. Witnesses were questioned as
to whether church pews had been reserved for the cadets, how cold
it was, the condition of the men's uniforms, and the amount and
exact nature of refreshments imbibed in the Exchange Coffee House.

The court-martial dragged on through all of March. As each witness added his own contribution of picayune detail, Mann could
agree with Charlotte who wrote that it was "all nonsense." What began as a comedy and public show had quickly evolved into an exasperating sifting of legal and military minutiae. The General Court
was prepared to dissolve after the middle of March, and were it not
for the court-martial, Mann would have been free to return to Charlotte. His patience wore thin as the trial became less an administering
of justice and more a ludicrous attempt to restore several persons'
wounded dignity. Adding to his frustration at the moment was the
suspicion that things were not going well for his and Stanley's commercial ventures. He had heard unconfirmed reports that their mills
were in financial trouble, and when Charlotte asked him for information, he did not answer this part of her letters. In return, she did
not respond to his question about her health.[9]

Mann found some relief during this ordeal by leaving his room
at the Tremont House and walking to North Square near the waterfront to hear "Mr. Taylor" preach. On several Sundays he sat in a
crowded pew, rubbing shoulders with seamen just from their ships,
still wearing their red flannel shirts and reefer jackets. Captains,
sailors, whalemen, and fishermen, once in port, were drawn to the
magnetic preaching of this unsophisticated and rough-hewn man. At

---

[8] Records of Courts Martial, Vol. 19, pp. 1–2. The records are in Mann's
handwriting, running to more than 325 pages. For his services, Mann
was paid $132 according to the *Massachusetts Acts and Resolves, 1833,*
"Military Accounts," pp. 523–524; *Trial by Court Martial,* pp. 16–77;
Mann to Charlotte Messer Mann, March 12, 1832, Mann-Messer MSS:
BUA.
[9] Mann to Charlotte Messer Mann, March 12 and 18, 1832, and
Charlotte Messer Mann to Mann, n.d. (postmarked March 5, 17, and 28,
1832), Mann-Messer MSS:BUA.

a time when Calvinists and Unitarians were deadlocked over whether Reverend Howard Malcom or Reverend Ralph W. Emerson should be the next chaplain in the House of Representatives, Edward Taylor could not be bothered by such sectarian squabbles. Instead, he preached a simplistic evangelical message of man's sinfulness and God's forgiveness. Mann was fascinated by the preacher's "impassioned and glowing earnestness" as he would pray "Oh Lord, deliver us from bad rum and bigotry." And he reported to Charlotte that Taylor preached a genuine Christianity, without "a chinkle of metaphysical nonsense." [1]

On March 26, Mann dismally reported that the General Court had risen but "the miserable court martial has by no means." Realizing that it would now run into April and that he would have to wait until after he had argued his cases in the Probate Court before returning to his wife, Mann lashed out at what was the both ludicrous and impossible task of restoring the wounded dignities of Lincoln and Winthrop. "I would that there had been no 'Winthrop,'" he wrote, no longer making any pretense at concealing his mounting frustration,

and if that must be, that there had been no "Grenville Temple Winthrop," or if that must be that there have been no "Company of Cadets" nor any

---

[1] Mann to Charlotte Messer Mann, March 18, 1832, Mann-Messer MSS: BUA. During this period, Mann does not appear to have been a regular church member. Neither his nor Charlotte's name appears on the membership roster of the First Church in Dedham (Unitarian) where Mann's friend, Reverend Alvan Lamson, was the minister. See *Articles of Faith and Covenant—Adopted by The First Church in Dedham, 1821, with a List of the Members* (Boston, 1836). Reverend Edward T. Taylor had been something of an itinerant preacher since 1819. In 1828 he was invited to preach to a gathering of seamen in Boston. As he had been to sea, Taylor knew how to reach such an audience. His sense of conviction and ability to present vivid illustrations of man's need for God made him an immediate success with the sailors. As the Methodists had decided to abandon their "Methodist-alley Chapel," Taylor begged for funds to keep it open. Not only did he save the existing church, but he was able to enlist support for the construction of "Seamen's Bethel," a mission and boardinghouse for sailors which was completed in 1833, at a cost of $24,000. It was from here that Taylor's reputation spread among sailors, philanthropists, and preachers throughout the world. Mann heard Taylor at the culmination of the drive for money for Seamen's Bethel. See Gilbert Haven and Thomas Russell, *Father Taylor, The Sailor Preacher* (Boston, 1872), pp. 104–110; also Robert Collyer, *Father Taylor* (Boston, 1906), *passim*, and R. E. Walters, "Boston's Salt-Water Preacher," *South Atlantic Monthly* (July, 1946), XLV, 350–361. The dispute over the House chaplaincy is recorded in the Journal of the House, Vol. 53, January 6, 1832, p. 19, MS in MSA.

"Lieutenant Colonel" of the same, nor any Militia to be ordered out, nor any escort service ever invented, nor any Election Day, nor any Governor, nor any Court Martial, nor any *anything*, nor that either to keep me away from you another week.

So exasperated was Mann at having become involved in this imbroglio that he was ready to eat his "thirsty" sword for dinner.[2]

Several days later, he realized that even when the court-martial was over, he still would not be free to return to her. Instead he had commitments in "the Great and General Court, the Little and particular Court and the Probate and the Common Pleas Court and all the Justices Courts and . . . particularly the Supreme Judicial Court at Taunton." The reports of Charlotte's health made things seem even worse. Since going to Providence, her eyes had grown weaker. Now almost desperate with loneliness for his wife, yet entrapped in a web of responsibilities which were largely due to his inordinate ambition, he began to question some of his goals. Things which he had once considered so important now prevented him from gaining what he really wanted from life.[3]

Learning of Mann's dejection, Charlotte's first impulse was to return to him immediately, but in Providence there were always more than one's own inclinations to consider, and, as usual, caution prevailed. But now time hung heavy on her hands, and she only looked forward to the day when she could return to her home in Dedham. It was an unhappy and forlorn wife who wrote to her husband, "If we ever do meet again I hope most sincerely we shall not soon part." Three days after this her loneliness was so unbearable that for once she made a decision independent of anyone else and informed Mann that she was returning to Dedham even though the court-martial was unfinished and she would have to remain alone until he had completed his work. Weather permitting, she would come within the week. "I want to see you, good bye my dear," she wrote. The spring weather cooperated, the sun dried out the roads, and the young couple were finally reunited in their home. Mann still traveled to Boston for the court-martial, but when he remained overnight, one of the neighbor women stayed with his wife. Dr. Stimson paid several calls on Charlotte and satisfied himself that his further immedi-

---

[2] Mann to Charlotte Messer Mann, March 26, 1832, Mann-Messer MSS: BUA.
[3] Mann to Charlotte Messer Mann, March 28, 1832; Charlotte Messer Mann to Mann, [March 5 and 28, 1832], all in Mann-Messer MSS:BUA.

ate attention was not required. In the future Mann promised to let neither political nor military commitments cause another separation.[4]

By the middle of April both sides had concluded their cases. Mann followed with a summary of the entire proceedings, and a day later the tribunal handed down its long-awaited verdict. Winthrop was found guilty on eight of the nine specifications and, for his "military crimes," the slow but exacting hand of justice sentenced him to be "reprimanded in orders." Justice had been meted out, the dignity of the Commonwealth and Governor Lincoln saved, and the public entertained, but all of this had been at the expense of one more painful separation for Charlotte and Horace Mann.[5]

*   *   *

They now believed heartaches were part of the past and could quickly be forgotten as they settled down to experience the elusive happiness which finally seemed within their grasp. May and most of June were filled with many sunny days on Church Street. Charlotte felt stronger, her spirits improved, and color again returned to her face. All expectations were now for her rapid and complete recovery. Then one night she unexpectedly grew weaker and Mann again summoned Jeremy Stimson. The doctor confined her to her bed for two weeks and Mann confided to his sister Lydia that he did not "anticipate, at the best, a very speedy recovery." For a few days Charlotte rallied, but by the middle of July, Dr. Stimson resumed his daily calls and continued them to the end of the month.[6]

What was to have been a center for idyllic bliss had now become a place of lonesome vigil and waning hope. The same sun that had brought light and warmth in June now blanketed the village with oppressive heat. Revelers gathered in the streets to celebrate the Fourth of July and hear another speech on independence, but Mann sealed himself inside the house, attempting to keep the noise and excitement outside. Finally, when Charlotte became too

---

[4] Charlotte Messer Mann to Mann, [March 28, 1832], March 31 [1832], and April 3, [1832], all in Mann-Messer MSS:BUA.

[5] *Trial by a Court Martial,* pp. 248–442; Records of Courts Martial, Vol. 19, pp. 327–329, and "Item No. 16" and "Item No. 17"; General Orders No. 6, 1826–1833, Headquarters Boston, May 23, 1832, pp. 296–311. MS in Adjutant General's Office, Military Archives, War Records Section, Commonwealth of Massachusetts.

[6] Mann to Lydia Mann, July 2, 1832, Mann MSS:MHS.

weak to walk, he gently lifted her frail body from the bed each morning and placed her in the rocking chair. Now he gave her almost constant attention, adjusting her pillow, wiping the beads of perspiration from her brow, helping her take water, and entertaining her with cheerful and reassuring conversation. Through all this, he managed a stiff upper lip, but he could not conceal the deepening lines of worry which marked his face. Bezaleel Taft, one of the trustees of the lunatic hospital, urged him to attend a crucial meeting at Worcester. "Summer is passing away," he wrote, "and much must be done." Mann knew this too. It was the very reason he would let nothing now draw him away from Church Street.[7]

On Tuesday afternoon, July 31, there were signs of an imminent crisis. Dr. Stimson rushed over to join Mann in his grim vigil at the bedside. As afternoon shadows blended into evening, Charlotte began to lose consciousness. Aside from her labored breathing, the ominous silence was broken only by moments of fevered delirium as she struggled to survive, aided only by a will to live and a husband's love. Mann remained by her side as the delirium increased. It was "a scene of anxiety, of dismay, of struggling, of death," he later recalled. By two o'clock, the pain subsided and Charlotte breathed her last. It was the morning of Wednesday, August 1, 1832, a date indelibly stamped into Horace Mann's memory. She was just twenty-three.[8]

Later, as the sun came up, Mann left the room and summoned all his strength to write the tragic news to Asa Messer, his tears dropping on the letter as he wrote,

It has been the will of Heaven to bereave you of the most filial, affectionate, and excellent of daughters and me of the most fond, devoted and excellent of wives. She breathed her last about two o'clock this morning apparently without much pain, after having endured all the distress of her illness with a resignation that might have made an angel covet humanity. Instead of being the broad and signal mark for consolation, I could wish it were in my power to impart it to yourself and your afflicted family, we must both find it in the wisdom of that being, who

---

[7] Bezaleel Taft to Mann, July 23, 1832; Mann to Lydia Mann, July 2, 1832, Mann MSS:MHS; Mann to Mary Messer, August 25, 1832, and October 19, 1839, Mann-Messer MSS:BUA.

[8] Mann to Mary Messer, August 25, 1832, and October 19, 1831, Mann-Messer MSS:BUA; Mann, Journal, July 31, 1837, MS in Mann MSS: MHS. *The Record of Baptism, Marriages and Deaths . . . Town of Dedham, 1638–1845,* p. 134, contains the following entry: "Augt. 1, Mrs. Charlotte, wife of Horace Mann, Esq., aged 23."

orders our destinies far differently, and I hope, we can both of us say
with sincerity, far better than we could do ourselves. . . .

He added that he preferred to have Charlotte buried in Franklin by
the side of his father and "by the spot where, in all probability, my
mother will erelong lie," but he had no wishes independent of the
Messers.[9]

The next day, Mann purchased a mahogany coffin from Joel
Richards, the same man who, less than two years before, had come
to make alterations in the Fisher house for the newlyweds. As the
Messers once again preferred to have their daughter with them,
Charlotte was buried in the family plot in Providence. She would
go to the "sweet South" for the last time.

Mann also went south, beginning what he called "the sad circuit of sorrow." After the burial in Providence, he traveled to Franklin, there to gain comfort and sympathy from his mother and Lydia,
who were "ready and willing auditors." Unable at first to bring himself to leave, he stayed longer than he planned, dreading to go back
to the scene of the tragedy. Upon his return to Dedham after the
burial, Mann moved back to Alden's Tavern as it was impossible to
live in the Fisher house with its bitter-sweet memories. As the furnishings of the house had been a symbol of his future domestic bliss,
now dismantling the household became a manifestation of the total-
ity of the tragedy. He wanted no remembrance of his ill-fated attempt
to create a hearth and home other than a lock of Charlotte's hair
which he asked his sister to braid for him. Everything else, Charlotte's clothes, the furniture, and other household items they had
purchased on those carefree trips to Boston, even the rocker, all had
to go. They were no solace, only a reminder of his shattered hopes.
Since Dr. Messer offered to dispose of most of the items, Mann engaged "Mr. Gay . . . a careful and trustworthy man" to carry the
last material evidences of his married life to Providence.[1]

But what emotion had begun, the mind could not check. When
the flood tide of anguish had finally receded, not only physical reminders had been swept away. Gone also were many of his earlier
aspirations. His law practice, his career in politics, his future in

[9] Mann to Asa Messer, August 1, 1832, Mann-Messer MSS:BUA.
[1] Mann to Lydia Mann, August [11] and 22, and November 13, 1832;
Asa Messer to Mann, August 16 and 23, September 9, 1823, all in the
Mann MSS:MHS; Mann to Mary Messer, August 9 and 17, 1832, and
Mann to Asa Messer, August 25, 1832, all in the Mann-Messer
MSS:BUA.

manufacturing, all were without purpose in a world which lacked his beloved Charlotte. For all his efforts, he had but a handful of ashes, the bitter residue of memories and disillusionment that followed such a tragedy. A week after the funeral, a few friends gathered to help him remove the last of the furniture. When all had been carried out of the house and his helpers had left, Horace Mann remained, looking about the rooms, compelled by some unexplainable power to stay. Some strange unseen force seemed to bind him there. As he moved from one empty room to another, the hollow sound of his steps on the bare floor reinforced his feelings of utter desolation. Finally, he found himself standing before the cold hearth. Now came the full realization of the finality of death. Now he knew he would have to "drain the chalice alone." How long he stood there gazing into it, beyond it, he did not remember, but gradually the spell was broken. He turned his back and left the house, walking across the village green in the cool evening air, back towards the garrulous noise and bright lights of Alden's Tavern.[2]

---

[2] Mann to Mary Messer, August 17, 1833, Mann-Messer MSS:BUA.

CHAPTER VIII

To the Brink

═══════

IF I JUSTIFY myself, mine own mouth shall
 condemn me: . . .
I am afraid of all my sorrows, I know that thou
 wilt not hold me innocent.
     JOB

───────

SEVERAL WEEKS AFTER Charlotte's death, Horace Mann sat in his room at Alden's Tavern and read through their correspondence of courtship and marriage. The same eagerly awaited letters which had once radiated such buoyant hopes for happiness, now were a reminder of unfulfilled dreams and terrible disappointment. In reading them again, the expressions of hope and optimism turned into cruel jests. Only those passages which spoke of the pain of separation contained enduring truths. "How hard separation is," Charlotte had once written to him, "I feel it more everytime I have it to endure. To feel when I awake in the morning that I shall not hear the sound of your voice before I sleep again. —but I will not repine. I must not." Each separation had been faced as a painful prelude to a future association which promised to be all the more happy by contrast. Now it was clear to Horace Mann as he read these lines that his former isolation was to be the prelude to further pain and suffering. Moving from one letter to the next, he began to apprehend the finality and intensity of the separation which he was now to bear alone. After he had read all the letters, he placed them in a small black cardbox and never looked at them again. Time in no way erased his fear that to reread them in the future would reopen wounds he could not survive. Loneliness would now be a permanent condition of his existence.[1]

As he began to comprehend his loss, the same objectives in which he had invested so much of himself now became symbols of the half-life he was condemned to live. "That gentle spirit is gone,"

───────

[1] Mann to Asa Messer, August 25, 1832; Mann to Mary Peabody Mann, February 25, 1849, both in Mann MSS:MHS.

he wrote to a friend. "I trust she now lives in a more congenial realm." But for his own future he added, "the world is changed . . . I seem to stand in a world of shadows. That which gave light and beauty and reality to all is gone. But it is within, that desolation has done its perfect work." A year later there was little change. No doubt the Havens and Stimsons in Dedham who were close to Mann assumed that the date of August 1, 1832, had marked the end of a tragedy. They could not have been more mistaken. After this date, Horace Mann moved in a "world of shadows" and "gloomy images," as he described it, and began a slow and tortuous task of re-establishing his values and surviving a despondency which threatened to erode away his will to live.[2]

Recognizing that an iron had been driven into his soul, Mann's friends rallied to his support as best they could. Both Loring and Silas Holbrook came to see him in Dedham, Loring dragging himself out of his sickbed to shore up Mann's sinking spirits and Holbrook staying with him "A number of nights to beguile my thoughts from the sad theme to which they cling," as Mann later wrote. Sydney Williams also made several trips from Taunton for the same purpose, and others who could not come wrote letters. All stressed the same point. In his present state of mind, it was useless and even dangerous to dwell upon the past. Loring even went so far as to say it could be suicidal. Mann's only resource was to look to the future and take up the tasks where he had left off. Regardless of how painful it was to be, he had no other safe alternative than to return to his legal, political, and humanitarian endeavors. And even if the heart denied this, his mind told him it was so. "The great, I may almost say, the only object for which I have lived is no more," he wrote, "if my feelings do not fasten on something else, I shall be without a motive in life." [3]

Sydney Williams had asked Mann to live with his family in Taunton, where he hoped the two might form a legal partnership. At first Mann was inclined to accept, but he kept putting off the final decision. As the weeks passed, Sydney pressed his offer. At the same time, Holbrook and Loring had been urging him to come to Boston. Holbrook insisted Mann's future was in the city. Loring concurred and proceeded to organize what amounted to a full-blown

---

[2] Mann to Mary Peabody, August 26, 1833, and March 26, 1834, Mann MSS:MHS.
[3] Mann to Mary Messer, November 18, 1832, Mann-Messer MSS:BUA; Mann to Lydia Mann, November 13, 1832, Mann MSS:MHS.

legal brief urging Mann's move to the Hub. For good measure, Loring added that his cousin, Charles G. Loring, would help the two start a legal partnership. With this he was willing to rest his case.[4]

The proposal contained several points Mann clearly understood. He had been attracted to the city, and if he was to continue his work in the legislature, particularly his promotion of humanitarian reforms, it was best to live in Boston. Added to this was a hard argument from economics. The demand for textiles had collapsed, and the market was nearly glutted. As a result, for the last year neither the Eagle Mills nor the City Manufacturing Company was turning as much profit as anticipated. Stanley's loans had to be paid, and since Horace was his co-signer, he was liable as well. To make matters worse, Stanley had not kept accurate records, and Horace shuddered at the thought of unraveling Stanley's skein of mortgages and promissory notes. This much he knew. He was in debt and needed the kind of income which would come from legal fees in the city. By November he had decided on Boston. If he and Stanley were to save their mills, he had no other choice. "My first object," he wrote to his sister, "is to get out of debt. That with every exertion and privation will take several years. I know not how many, even if I should be so fortunate as to have my health." [5]

Six years before, he had left Dedham to enter the General Court and begin his political career. Now he was again being drawn to Boston, but the circumstances and the man were radically changed. Earlier, time had been on his side. Now, in 1832, it was evident that the future was not to witness the fruition of his hopes. The city was to be his escape. More important, it was to provide the setting for a personal ordeal. Now little else was left but his many unfinished tasks of reform. Loring suggested that his philanthropic work could become a memorial to Charlotte, yet in his state of mind, it was pos-

---

[4] Sydney Williams's first proposal was on August 22, 1832. Others are dated September 4, October 4, and December 15, 1832; Silas Holbrook to Mann, August 16, 1832; Edward G. Loring to Mann, [November], 1832, all in Mann MSS:MHS.
[5] Mann to Mary Messer, November 18, 1832, Mann-Messer MSS:BUA; Mann to Lydia Mann, November 13, 1832, Mann MSS:MHS; Stanley had mortgaged seven-fifteenths of the City Manufacturing Company to Chloe Richardson for $3,560:66 on November 23, 1830. The conditions of the contract provided that Mrs. Richardson could take possession of the mill if Stanley defaulted on his payment. The mortgage is in the Mann MSS:DHS. Horace Mann was a co-signer of the note, although he did not realize that Mrs. Richardson could demand compound interest.

sible that each accomplishment would also be a reminder that he was living but half a life which could never be complete. Probably for the first time, Horace Mann began to see that time was his enemy, a creator of cruel delusions and an unyielding tyrant offering little mercy or understanding.

Mann did not move in with the Lorings but took a room in the genteel boardinghouse of Mrs. Rebecca Clarke at 3 Somerset Court near the State House. The group which gathered at her table each evening was hardly the congenial and reassuring company he needed. There was George Hillard, destined to become one of Boston's most prominent attorneys, but at this time a sickly young man subject to periods of depression. Across from him was Jared Sparks, the biographer of Washington and future president of Harvard, a brusque man who gave the impression of being both ill-tempered and devoid of empathy. Mrs. Sparks rarely put in an appearance, preferring for some unknown reason to take her meals in her room. When young Sarah Clarke ate with the group, she blushed at the slightest cause and exhibited a self-consciousness which made everyone uncomfortable. Her mother labored to keep the dinner conversation at a polite and cheerful level, while hoping in some way to pry into Mann's past. And then there were the Peabody sisters who kept school in the morning and busied themselves with editing work in the afternoon. Mary tended to be quiet and reserved and was difficult to draw into a conversation, while Elizabeth chattered like a magpie, attempting to dominate the conversation which roamed from metaphysics to gossip and seemed to touch on every point in between. Such a menagerie Mary Peabody could only describe as a "hodgepodge." [6]

As these people turned their attention to Mann, they had little reason to suspect anything of the ordeal through which he was passing. Although his hair had turned almost completely gray by this time, they did not know until later that his friends in Dedham only thought of him as having dark hair. At the table he attempted a gay and witty façade, always careful to let no chink develop which would expose his true feelings. As Mary Peabody reported to her sister, he was "intolerably witty," a raconteur who had "an anecdote,

---

[6] Mary Peabody to Sophia Peabody, February 17, 1833, Berg MSS: NYPL; Elizabeth Peabody to Mary Peabody, December 16, 1834, CJ in NYPL; Mann to Elizabeth Peabody, [September, 1834], Mann MSS: MHS; James Freeman Clarke, *Autobiography, Diary, and Correspondence* (Boston, 1899), p. 10.

a story or a saying for every emergency." What she was only to understand later was that his public euphoria was always followed by periods of private depression.[7]

As their suspicions that Mann had recently gone through a terrible tragedy were confirmed, the Peabody sisters became the self-appointed custodians of his welfare. Pleased with their attention, Mann gradually let them into his more personal thoughts. What he did not tell them was that his torment was increasing as the date of the first anniversary of Charlotte's death approached. In fact, he was so overpowered with a feeling of depression that he packed his belongings, fled from the boardinghouse without saying good-bye, and took a room elsewhere. At first in a quandary, the sisters concluded that his actions were the result of some unintentional blunder on their part. Considering it improper to call on him, they sent him an apologetic note and begged for an explanation. Feeling obligated to reply, Mann gave a detailed explanation of his retreat. "Let me assure you, which I do upon my honor," he began,

that the whole body and substance of the apprehensions, which formed the subject of your letter, are without foundation. . . .

The change I contemplate has had no connection with the causes you suggest. To part with my friends, (if I may call them so) at the house, was long an insuperable obstacle to the adoption of another mode of living. When I first went to the house where we are, I had hopes, that the intellectual and refined society of its inmates would do something towards filling up the void in my life. But . . . I only found so much of that which I mourned, as to be a perpetual remembrance of it. Often I have retired from the gratifications of . . . society to weep over the blessedness of that I had lost. . . . At this time, too, the anniversary of that fatal day, when all the foundations of earthly happiness sunk beneath me, was approaching and drawing me into its vortex, I will not attempt to describe to you the power of imagination where memory supplied it with such materials, I saw the necessity of effort; and in the hope of being able to break the spell that bound me, I resolved upon the proposed change. I need to reverse this fatal current of tho't. The ties of association must be broken. If it is possible I must rectify the

---

[7] Writing to her sister, Elizabeth Peabody described a meeting between Catherine Haven and Mann in 1834. Catherine, who had probably seen Mann only occasionally until Charlotte's death, was amazed in 1834 to find that his hair was white. Elizabeth Peabody, who first met him five months after Charlotte's death, commented that she had never seen it any other way. See Elizabeth Peabody to Mary Peabody, August 24–25, 1834, CJ in NYPL.

ruins of my mind. . . . I hope, tho' I can never again be happy, as I have been happy, yet, that I may be less sorrowing myself and less the occasion of sorrow to others.[8]

It was an obvious rationalization, but the Peabody sisters accepted it at face value, grateful that Mann had not cut himself off from them completely. Mann wished to convey the impression that his suffering was so great that it was cruel to share it with others. Actually it was the opposite. He had become so demoralized that he believed he could not survive this ordeal unless given an inordinate amount of pity from those nearest him. Pity, his retreat from Mrs. Clarke's boardinghouse achieved, but it also gave rise to a despair among his friends that he was a broken man and would never recover. When Edward Loring heard that Mann was living alone, he could only conclude that he was wrapping himself in a cloak of "despair and courting death." James Mills agreed. In fact, if one were to believe Elizabeth Peabody, his *"gentlemen friends* universally" thought there was *"no hope"* for improvement. Miss Peabody also understood that August 1 would return as regularly as the seasons to trouble his memories. As she attempted to understand and help Mann, she would refer repeatedly to Mann's explanation of why he left Mrs. Clarke's boardinghouse.[9]

Mann's self-imposed solitary confinement was prompted by another factor which he preferred to keep secret beyond his immediate family. As he studied Stanley's casual records and calculated the money necessary to redeem the promissory notes he had co-signed with his brother, he realized he had no alternative but to restrict his living expenses. Moving his personal belongings to his office on the third floor of the building at 4 Court Street in Boston, he took up quarters where he was to live for the next three years, sleeping on a horsehair couch and taking his meals outside. Even practicing further economies, he asked Lydia to mend his clothes and frequently skipped his dinner.[1]

The building was a center for many of Boston's legal and financial transactions, and such prominent lawyers as Rufus Choate, Theophilus Parsons, and John A. Andrews had their offices there. On

---

[8] Mary Peabody to Sophia Peabody, [August, 1833], Berg MSS:NYPL; Mann to Elizabeth Peabody, [1833], Mann MSS:MHS.
[9] Elizabeth Peabody to Mann, September, [1834?], Straker MSS:ACL.
[1] Mann to Lydia Mann, June, 1835, Mann MSS:MHS; Mann, Journal, November 28, 1837, MS in MHS.

the same floor with Mann were Edward Loring and Luther S. Cushing. The activity here during the day made one feel the emptiness of the place at night all the more. Mann frequently was the sole inhabitant of the building, a place which Robert S. Rantoul remembered as "a dismal, blue granite pile." It was here, alone at night, that Mann would relive the elemental night of chaos of August 1, 1832, and endure the solitary vigil which only the sleepless know. Seated at his desk on one of these anniversaries, he poured out his innermost feelings in his private journal:

I have felt unable to give my feelings even this private utterance. But tonight, this fated night—has come—and again are visibly present before men, that scene of anxiety, of dismay, of struggling, of death and of the agony of surviving, worse than a thousand deaths. . . . Who can then know the entirety, the completeness, the universality of that loss? My nature has felt it thru' all its capacities of suffering. A clock strikes *eleven*. It was about this hour, as I watched over her and sought to relieve her distress, but signs of mental alienation became visible and sunk as dismaying omens upon my heart. Two hours which followed, until the struggle was over; and the hours, that followed the close of that struggle, until morning—yes and the days and the hours that have since passed so slowly away have been full of a history of suffering such as no mortal can ever record. But they *must* terminate.[2]

The year 1833 was a period of isolation from many of his friends, both by circumstance and intent. He withdrew himself from the Lorings' social circle and traveled to Dedham only when forced to by his legal work. Holbrook was on his way to Europe and Mary Peabody left for Cuba, where she would help her sister Sophia back to health. Mann's isolation would have been nearly complete had it not been for Elizabeth Peabody's growing interest in his future. For the next two years, Horace Mann became her personal object of philanthropy. As the result of frequent invitations, he was soon her regular caller on Sunday evenings. At times she and Mann talked about his childhood, his disappointments, and his work at the Worcester Hospital, as she attempted to help him reconstruct some religious faith in place of a cynicism which permitted a "passive endurance" and nothing more. At other times as he stretched out on

---

[2] Joseph A. Willard, *Half a Century with Judges and Lawyers* (Boston, 1895), p. 285; Edward L. Pierce, *Memoirs and Letters of Charles Sumner* (Boston, 1877), I, 147; Robert S. Rantoul, *Personal Recollections* (Cambridge, 1916), p. 22; Mann, Journal, July 31, 1837, MS in MHS.

a sofa in her parlor, he talked about whatever came into his mind.[3]

Regardless of how many diversions were made into other topics, inevitably Mann returned to the imponderable question of why a God of love had permitted Charlotte to die. Gradually, Elizabeth Peabody realized that the recent events had resurrected many of the "horrible associations" he had had in childhood and that Mann's faith in a beneficent God which he had so carefully reconstructed since rejecting Emmons's doctrines was completely shattered. Moreover, he was void of any will to refashion the fragments, and repeatedly slipped into a slough of self-pity and defeat. For him the present was an "eternity of woe" and he could only view the death of another "with a pang of envy." Even this death wish was muddled in his mind. While desiring it for himself, he remained perplexed as to Charlotte's possible existence after death. Elizabeth Peabody attempted to speak metaphorically of the nearness of the deceased as well as the impenetrable "wall of separation" between the living and the dead. But such an explanation only compounded Mann's confusion. "Do you think," he blurted out, "I could sleep tonight if I thought my wife was in the room?" Elizabeth could not answer, and after a tense period of silence, Mann continued in words barely audible, "This thought of nearness *overwhelms* me." Later, in thinking back to this strange conversation, Elizabeth concluded that in order to weather this crisis, Mann "required as *a frame*—the more general truth of the absolute presence of God in love—which he had not." [4]

Recalling that Mann had once told her he considered the entire meaning of the universe to have been compressed into Pope's "Essay on Man," Elizabeth pointed out the implications of such a belief for his own life and that he must accept that "whatever is, is right." To this she added, "My friend . . . *you are not living*—you are dying, and this suffering is the dissolution of body and mind." When the Lord said, "Turn unto Me," Elizabeth concluded, this was the voice of "reason" as well as the "poetry of Revelation." Only as the conversations continued with no apparent change in his outlook did Elizabeth begin to recognize the magnitude of the psychological

---

[3] To support Sophia and herself, Mary had accepted a position as governess in a wealthy Cuban family. She and Sophia sailed on the *Newcastle*, December 6, 1833; Boston *Daily Advertiser and Patriot*, December 6, 1833. The numerous notes between Mann and Elizabeth Peabody in the Mann MSS:MHS, indicate both the frequency and importance of these visits.

[4] The account of this conversation is given in Elizabeth Peabody to Mary Peabody, December 21, 1833, CJ in NYPL.

block which stood in the way of Mann's recovery. Metaphors, logic, and her transcendental philosophy did not contain the key to the mystery with which he wrestled and perhaps for the first time in her life, Elizabeth Peabody found herself at a loss for words. She simply did not have the answers to Mann's anguished questions.[5]

Unwilling to admit defeat, she enlisted the help of her religious mentor and friend, William Ellery Channing. With Mann in tow, she made regular calls at the Channing home on Beacon Hill. In the course of his conversations with Channing, Mann pieced together the events of his childhood and dredged up memories long forgotten. He described his early recollections of God as a vengeful ruler. He also recalled that when he later suggested the power of God to elicit love, his mother rejected the idea and insisted that true virtue could only come from a fear of the Almighty. Channing found it hard to believe that throughout Mann's childhood, Christ had never been presented as the great moral teacher. Mann insisted this was so, and that it was only with great effort that he had been able to reject the stern doctrines of his youth. In their place, he had come to believe that it was the love of God and their fellow men, rather than a fear of retribution for sin, which motivated men to ethical lives. With his rejection of divine retribution for sin, Mann discarded a belief in anything supernatural or miraculous. If laws were broken, God did not step from the clouds to mete out punishment. Rather, in the harmonious order of the universe, punishment was the natural result of a violation of either physical or moral laws. But if this were so, how was Charlotte's death to be explained? As long as he had assumed that the universe was governed by a beneficent sovereign and was a friendly habitation for men, he could also assume that good would eventually triumph. Now he was unable or unwilling to admit that his personal loss was part of a harmonious and reasonable creation. Beneath the sereneness of a natural world, he had experienced an elemental cruelty. Charlotte's death was an undeniable fact which challenged all his sentimental beliefs in a moral universe.[6]

In Franklin, years before, Nathanael Emmons, whose first wife

---

[5] Elizabeth Peabody to Mann, December 18, 1833, Mann MSS:MHS; Elizabeth Peabody to Mary Peabody, July 31 to August 3, 1834, CJ in NYPL.
[6] The discussions with Channing and Mann's religious ideas are described in Elizabeth Peabody to Mary Peabody, March 22–24 and April 10–13, 1834, CJ in NYPL; Mary Peabody to Elizabeth Peabody [ca. 1834], Mann MSS:MHS.

had died under similar circumstances, had accepted his loss and acquiesced in a belief that the ways of God were inscrutable to human reason.[7] Unable to fit Charlotte's death into his present beliefs, and unwilling to return to Emmons's position, Mann realized he had really never emancipated himself from the religious beliefs of his forefathers. He had placed God in a closed system of rational explanation, only finding himself unwilling to accept the recent events. Then, for a time, he vacillated between a belief in a vindictive or capricious God and the more radical doctrine that his world was not ruled by any spiritual being, but was rather the result of blind forces; that there were no ideals, moral or otherwise; and that the universe was an immense spiritual void, completely indifferent to mankind.

Both Elizabeth Peabody and Nathanael Emmons, while poles apart theologically, still maintained that man must acquiesce in either the love or the commands of God. Yet compliance and humility were components of character strikingly absent in Mann, a fact not missed by Miss Peabody. "But as the plainest truth in mathematics," she wrote to him, "cannot be put into a mind which will not put itself into the attitude of inquiry, so the vastest and noblest and sweetest object of affection cannot find entrance into the *heart,* that will not put itself into the attitude of loving toward it." Emmons simply would have said, "Be ye reconciled to God." [8]

The more Mann was convinced that God had failed him, the more he apotheosized his departed wife. In his writings, he described her as "the loveliest of beings," "a light upon the earth," a "blessed being whose heart was touched so quickly at others' sorrow," who "never said an unkind word." [9] Probably Mann's most eloquent apotheosis of Charlotte was written to Mary Peabody shortly after the first

---

[7] See his sermon, "God Incomprehensible by His Creatures," *Works,* I, 76–91. In this and in other sermons, Emmons stressed the perfection and excellency of God, which could only be known in part by sinful men.

[8] Elizabeth Peabody to Mary Peabody, November 7, 1834, CJ in NYPL. In this letter, Elizabeth reported that James Mills was amazed to learn of the hold that Calvinism still had over Mann. See also Elizabeth Peabody to Mary Peabody, March 22–24, 1834, CJ in NYPL, and Elizabeth Peabody to Mann, December 18, 1833, Mann MSS:MHS.

[9] Mann to Lydia Mann, August 11, 1832, and January 6, [1833]; Mann to Mary Messer, August 5, 1833, all in Mann MSS:MHS; Elizabeth Peabody to Mary Peabody, June 2–5, 1834, CJ in NYPL; Mann Journal, July 31 and August 1, 1837, MS in MHS.

anniversary of the tragedy. After describing "the melancholy texture of his own life," he depicted Charlotte's angelic nature:

Within her influence there could be no contest with sordid passions or degrading appetites, for she sent a divine and overmastering strength into every generous sentiment, which I cannot describe. She purified my conceptions of purity and beautified the ideal of every excellence. I never knew her to express a selfish or an envious thought, nor do I believe that the type of one was ever admitted to disturb the peacefulness of her bosom. Yet in the passionate love she inspired, there was nothing of oblivion of the rest of mankind. Her teachings did not make one love others less, but differently and more aboundingly. Her sympathy with othes [sic] pain seemed to be quicker and stronger than the sensation of her own; and with a sensibility that would sigh at a crushed flower, there was a spirit of endurance, that would uphold a martyr. There was in her breast no scorn of vice, but a wonder and amazement that it could exist.

When Channing first met Mann, he had been unable to comprehend the origins of Mann's religious doubts. Elizabeth's explanation was that in his confusion, Mann had supplanted the image of an unreal Charlotte as the embodiment of love for the love of God that had failed him. To show Channing how sacred Charlotte's memory had become, she had him read the eulogy sent to Mary Peabody. As he read it, the minister was visibly moved and asked to keep it in order to read it again. Considering Mann's occasional misgivings about Charlotte's actions during their courtship and marriage, the contrast between his intense eulogy and the actual person was marked. His wife had not been even a little lower than the angels.[1]

Grief fed panegyric, and panegyric made his loss all the more inconsolable. The more he elevated Charlotte's memory, the more he questioned his former belief in God. This cynical rejection of divine providence was accompanied by a recognition of the futility of his previous goals. Happiness, he had told himself when he left Franklin, would come when he made the most of the "golden moment of opportunity." Through intelligence, industry, and a willingness to take a risk, he had left Franklin and its provincial concerns far behind. Now, even if those about him did not realize it, his suc-

[1] Mann to Mary Peabody, August 26, 1833, Mann MSS:MHS; Elizabeth Peabody to Mary Peabody, March 22–24 and April 5–7, 1834, CJ in NYPL.

cess was a hollow victory. If his public record of achievements still evinced admiration and envy, privately he believed it was all a lie. His actual activities after his marriage indicated an intensification of his personal ambitions. Nevertheless, it was not only a self-serving ambition, as his efforts were motivated by a humanitarian desire to serve others almost as much as they were attempts at personal aggrandizement. But if Charlotte's memory was to be preserved, he found it necessary to polarize his life into two periods. Before she had come into his life, he had been self-seeking and callous to the needs of others. Then, "one after another," he claimed,

the feelings, which before had fastened on other subjects, loosened their strong grasp, and went to dwell in the sanctuary of her holy and beautiful nature. Ambition forgot the applause of the world for the more precious gratulation of that approving voice.

A change did take place in the way Mann perceived the world, but this did not come until after 1832, and it was the result of Charlotte's death, rather than her life. But in his mind, her life had to be exemplary, and the only way he could explain her death was by a self-imposed sense of guilt, accusing himself of false objectives and a spurious belief in a benevolent God.[2]

This change of attitude he now attempted to convey to those about him. When Mills, Loring, Holbrook, and the others gathered at the Exchange Coffee House for dinner, Mann's chair was vacant. From a punctilious concern for his appearance and a desire to wear the best cut of clothes, he degenerated into a slovenly dress, his waistcoats and pantaloons in need of pressing and mending. Anything bright and showy in his wardrobe he discarded. To his nieces and nephews, he passed on advice which repudiated his former ways. In place of property and ornamentation, he urged them to "adorn themselves with higher beauties of simplicity and propriety of manners." And they should understand that while "wealth would perhaps make them acceptable in some circles, modesty and gentleness of demeanor will attract notice and command the admiration of everyone." In view of Mann's penchant for polished prose at college and during the early years at Dedham, his remarks to Elizabeth Peabody on the topic of style also illustrated this shift.

. . . the idea perpetually recurs to me, how much vain, frivolous and even pernicious matter is every day devoured by the public merely be-

---

[2] Mann to Mary Peabody, August 26, 1833, Mann MSS:MHS.

cause it is recommended by some prettiness of style while truth eternal, world-regenerating truth is liable to be cast aside, because it lacks an attractive exterior.

His niece later described the impact of this tragedy on his life as a stroke which "paralyzed everything of him but—his moral nature. Glee was hushed. Ambition for what the world covets killed." Now in his despair, Mann was grasping for the pristine and uncorrupted tenets of modesty, simplicity, sobriety, and kindness, all familiar teachings of his youth.[3]

*   *   *

He was reordering his values, and in the process, Stanley inadvertently became a hapless victim. By 1834, City Mills was bankrupt, and Stanley's creditors were pressing for payment. Unable to meet their demands, he took the easy way out and left New England, abandoning his wife and children in Wrentham and placing his meager assets in the hands of Josiah J. Fiske. In a parting note to Horace, he wrote, "I can say no more but leave the rest for you and those who have been my friends in fair times of prosperity." He was heading for the West and a new start.[4]

The future of their joint undertakings only reinforced Horace Mann's disillusionment about material goals. Stanley, even more than he, had broken with the family traditions at Franklin. Now the result was financial disaster, both for himself and the Mann family. But if Horace had lost hope in the future, Stanley had not. Soon he was in Louisville, Kentucky, establishing the partnership of Hanna and Mann Grocers and hoping for a financial comeback by shipping pork and beef to Boston. To Horace this was just one more scheme to get rich. Coming at a time when Horace would have sacrificed everything for the companionship of a devoted wife and children, Stanley's desertion of his family seemed all the more irresponsible. His unbridled ambition had brought more than misery and embarrassment to the Manns. It had all but destroyed the family.

In Louisville, Stanley issued a sight draft on Horace which he

---

[3] Mann to Lydia Mann, June 5, 1834; Mann to Elizabeth Peabody [ca. September, 1834]; Rebecca Pennell Dean to Mary Peabody Mann [ca. 1861], all in Mann MSS:MHS.
[4] Josiah J. Fiske to Mann, June 28, 1834; Thomas Stanley Mann to Mann, June 18, 1834, both in Mann MSS:MHS.

thought could be covered by the sale of some of his assets back in Wrentham. If the check was to be honored, Horace would have to use his personal funds. Probably for the first time in his life, Horace Mann refused to go along with his brother's ventures. He reported to Lydia, "I have written to S.—I have declined accepting his draft, but sent a small sum of money to soften his disappointment." Charity he still would give, but an investment in a commercial venture was a thing of the past. The draft had been written in favor of Amos Lovering, a former neighbor from Wrentham, now also in Louisville. Lovering wrote to Mann, urging him to support Stanley in his new effort. Mann refused, saying that he had no funds for Stanley's newest scheme of speculation. Two months later, Lovering sent an urgent plea for Horace to come to his brother's assistance, denying that the money was wanted for speculation. He described Stanley's "prostrating sickness among strangers," his desire "to go to work for his children," his "entire destitution," and his professed anxiety to do "something to soothe and save the remnant of his days from a premature grave where none cared to throw a clod on him." He added that Stanley had not been drinking lately, but that he was badly in need of clothes. Horace Mann now turned a deaf ear to all these pleas. He could not or would not help his brother again. Within a year, Stanley was dead. He was buried in an unmarked grave in Louisville, a long way from the churchyard and Mann farm in Franklin.[5]

*   *   *

In an attempt to explain recent events by seeking a sense of guilt for following false idols, one flaw in Mann's rationalization gradually became apparent. Life after death had been an integral part of his former faith. Now in his shift towards skepticism, he was troubled by a recurring fear that this was also a delusion. And if this were so, then what was Charlotte's present state? As late as one year after Charlotte's death, he had expressed his hope that she was in a better world; but by this time Mann was vacillating between faith and doubt, at once believing that Charlotte was near him in spirit and yet fearing that she had no existence beyond the grave. If God's providence and a moral universe could be a delusion, then too life

---

[5] Mann to Lydia Mann, June 5, 1834; Amos Lovering to Mann, June 18, August 15, and October 15, 1834, all in Mann MSS:MHS; Mann, *Mann Geneology*, p. 26.

beyond the grave; and it could be argued that all that remained of Charlotte now rested in the North Burying Ground. But Horace Mann was in no condition to accept the conclusions of such a cruel logic.[6]

Early in 1834, William Ellery Channing's sister-in-law died. On Easter Sunday the Unitarian minister chose to preach on the death "of an Excellent and Very Dear Friend," and express his own belief in the Resurrection.[7] As usual, Elizabeth Peabody was on hand to hear her "great high priest." Looking towards the front of the congregation and watching Channing enter the pulpit, she also recognized the back of a familiar head. Horace Mann was there to hear the Easter sermon. Physically, the man to whom all eyes were now drawn had a slight and fragile frame which appeared to have weathered the ravages of illness with only partial success. No doubt those who came to hear him for the first time were disappointed at the appearance of this wisp of a human being. With his first words, however, Channing often transformed their disappointment into rapt attention and respect. The quality of his sentences bore witness to a man of almost totally pure mind and conscience. To New England audiences wearied of the thundering jeremiads of a Jedediah Morse or a Lyman Beecher, Channing offered sweet relief. In place of moving his listeners to repentance and a submission to God's will, the Unitarian minister spoke of God's love and human perfection. But more than this, his appeal as a preacher came through the quality of his voice. Soft, yet audible, clear and pure, yet penetrating, he achieved a quality of intensity and sincerity through a rising inflection as he spoke. Emerson claimed his voice was one of the three most eloquent he had ever heard. And it was said by others that if Henry Clay's voice was like an organ and Webster's that of a trumpet, Channing's voice was truly a harp.

On this Easter Sunday he spoke on Ephesians 1:20, "He raised him from the dead, and set him on his own right hand in the heavenly places." Noting that many teachings have been drawn from Christ's Resurrection, Channing thought this historical event was particularly fitted to confirm the Christian doctrine of life after death. He realized this was a difficult teaching. As rational men watched a body lowered into the grave, their senses almost com-

---

[6] Elizabeth Peabody to Mary Peabody, December 21, 1833, and November 29–30, 1834, CJ in NYPL.
[7] William Ellery Channing, "The Future Life," *Complete Works of William Ellery Channing, D.D.* (London, 1884), pp. 273–278.

pelled them to admit that the victory of death was complete, an experience Horace Mann knew well. To counteract such despair, Channing proposed to draw a clearer picture of man's future life through the means of "reason" and "Scripture."

He first depicted how the virtuous die and join Christ to experience unutterable happiness. Their survivors should remember that the departed also retained their deepest interests in the world and that ties were not dissolved, but only refined. Death then actually opened a new channel of love to the survivors. Moreover, Channing added, in joining Christ, the departed also joined in the labors of those who had gone before. According to him,

In that world, as in this, there are diversities of intellect, and the highest minds have their happiness and progress in elevating the less improved. There the work of education which began here, goes on without end; and the diviner philosophy than is taught on earth reveals the spirit to itself and awakens it to earnest joyful effort for its own protection.

Channing concluded by assuring his listeners that the greatest joy of all came from the fact that the departed not only went to Jesus, but to God himself, "to be gathered together safe from every storm, triumphant over evil;—and they say to us, come join us in everlasting blessedness."

The past events had conditioned Mann's receptivity to such a message. He wanted to believe that Charlotte existed in a state of bliss and he was ready to accept Channing's presentation as a valid description of the resurrection of the virtuous. Channing had spoken directly to Mann's suffering with a conviction and understanding that came only from personal experience. He too had lost a wife, gone through a valley of despair, and ascended to a new faith in the Resurrection. As she listened to the sermon, all of Elizabeth Peabody's thoughts were on Mann and his possible reactions. Hesitant to ask him directly at their next meeting, she attempted to draw him out by casually mentioning that she was copying the sermon for a friend. To this Mann responded, "Did you ever hear such a sermon?" and without waiting for an answer, continued, "It gave laws to the imagination and landmarks to the affections, what I have never known before." Later he repeated his words, insisting the sermon had taken full possession of him and that he was "lost in exaltation—or *found* rather." Never had he heard such a compelling appeal. To Elizabeth anxiously awaiting any sign of change for the better in Mann, this had to be a turning point. "The veil is lifted," she reported to her sister with relief and hope, "he does not feel any longer as if fettered to the grave—but has risen." Mann further confirmed her hope when he wrote her a short note, asking her to convey his appreciation to Channing, hoping she might give the minister some idea of the influence the sermon had had on him. He thought this might be the best form "in which *gratitude* could make itself known to a heart like his," and he assured Elizabeth that she "need not fear exaggeration." [8]

In reading the printed text of the sermon, one finds it difficult to share in Mann's reaction. The fact that the imagery was sentimental and the exegesis more imaginative than reasoned suggests that Channing had not helped Mann analyze his difficulties by presenting any religious insights, but rather had scored a solid emotional impact. Addressed to the heart instead of the mind, his appeal to Mann's sentiments and affections had succeeded where Elizabeth's appeal to reason had not. Of the three, Channing understood this most clearly. When Elizabeth asked him for his permission to copy the sermon for Mann, Channing replied that it was better for him to have only the experience of hearing it, rather than "diluting" the effect by reading it. Well aware of the type of response he had elicited, Channing did not want Mann's present comfort disturbed by additional intellectual analysis. [9]

Mann traveled to Providence during the week following Easter. For the first time since her death, he mustered up enough fortitude to visit Charlotte's burial place. As he stood by the grave, he was now ready to believe that " 'What he loved was not there.' " On the almost bare surface of the mound, a lone violet was blooming near the headstone. He stooped down, picked it, and took it back to Boston, and he carried it with him for the next two years. [1]

As the year of 1834 wore on and the second anniversary of Charlotte's death approached, Elizabeth Peabody's optimism gradually waned. Mann's masochistic brooding was far more deeply entrenched than she had realized. While the recent emotional release had soothed his spirits, it was soon evident that it had produced only a transient effect. Mann was not satisfied about Charlotte's

---

[8] Elizabeth Peabody to Mary Peabody, April 4 and 5, 1834, CJ in NYPL; Mann to Elizabeth Peabody, Aprill 11, [1834], Mann MSS:MHS.
[9] Elizabeth Peabody to Mary Peabody, April 6–19, 1834, CJ in NYPL.
[1] Elizabeth Peabody to Mary Peabody, April 13–17, 1834, CJ in NYPL; Mann to Mary Messer, October 2, 1836, Mann MSS:MHS.

state in the hereafter, yet this was but one part of the larger problem of understanding his own place in the present. By summer, he was again referring to his suffering, as his insomnia ate its way ever deeper into his nights. Within four months after Channing's sermon, he complained to Elizabeth that he was "tightly swathed in cold bands," and that his nerves were "at so great a tension as to engender their cohesion." Clearly, the mortal coil remained. Tempering her earlier optimistic reports at first, Elizabeth finally admitted his future looked as dim as ever. "It is heavy to see him suffer so," was part of her disappointing report to Mary, as she resigned herself to the long task ahead. Once again, August would be a "terrible month." [2]

In the past two years, Horace Mann had only seen through a glass darkly, as he struggled to construct an acceptable meaning to the events of his life. In coming to grips with them, he had cut himself off from many of his former friends and activities. Living on an austere budget, he had permitted himself a bare minimum of necessities and no luxuries whatsoever. In addition, he had worked himself almost to the point of collapse. As painful as this routine was, it did not compare with the agonizing introspection and pitiless self-accusation he had forced upon himself. Five years after Charlotte's death, he would still write in his Journal,

Oh! Dearest! Dearest! How far removed from everything upon earth, how unutterably alone, I dwell in this world. Its beauty is perished. Its music is discord. Its pleasures have become pain, but none of its pains have become pleasures. And will this always be . . . yes. I had rather it would, than that I should ever forget thee, my beloved wife!

When asked to justify the severity of his actions, he simply insisted they were necessary for his "self-preservation." Despite all the attempts of a few close friends to ease his suffering and restore him to some sort of inner peace, he felt compelled to continue on a course of self-flagellation. In his search for deliverance, he had willingly grasped a crown of thorns.[3]

---

[2] Mann to Elizabeth Peabody, July 18, 1834, Mann MSS:MHS; Elizabeth Peabody to Mary Peabody, August 1, 1834, CJ in NYPL.
[3] Mann to Mary Messer, December 10, 1836, Mann MSS:MHS; Mann, Journal, November 4, 1837, MS in MHS.

CHAPTER IX

The Reluctant Crusader

========

REFORM, that you may preserve.
THOMAS BABINGTON
MACAULAY

————————

MANN HAD THOUGHT that his repudiation of Emmons's God was final, but Charlotte's death served notice that the last two decades had only been a moratorium and the struggle must now be renewed. The many discussions in Channing's parlor had not gotten to the root of his problem. Realizing that he could not live down the past in order to cope with the future, Elizabeth Peabody turned to restoring Mann's interest in politics in the hope that this might succeed where her quest for a religious explanation of his tragedy had failed. In her effort, she was helped inadvertently by less personal forces also drawing Mann back to greater activity. At the time of Charlotte's death he was heavily committed to several humanitarian causes, and even though he now would have preferred to withdraw from these, his former associates would not permit him this indulgence. Unlike his social life, he soon learned that retreat from the insane, the intemperate, and the impoverished was impossible. If anything, the enthusiasm for reform was gaining momentum, and Mann, as a reluctant participant, was now forced along against his will by a relentless avalanche he had helped set in motion.

At Worcester the hospital was just under way and despite his best-laid plans and the able administration of Samuel Woodward, a number of unexpected problems demanded his attention. The distinction between the criminal and the insane proved to be a vague one, and the state magistrates needed guidance on whom should be committed for treatment. One "patient" dispatched to the hospital was described by a trustee as "a plane [sic] and ugly jailbird who had manifested no symptoms of insanity." Another arrived with a full complement of tools to facilitate his escape. Later he made good in this and while he was at large, the citizens of Worcester, who had previously begged the Governor to select their town as the site for the hospital, entertained some second thoughts about the benefits of having the hospital nearby. Other patients proved to be more violent than anticipated and numerous changes in the security of the wards were necessary. Moreover, the hospital had been in operation less than six months when it became evident that its 120 beds were insufficient to care for all the persons sent to it for treatment. Barely was the paint dry on some of the walls before the trustees began plans for expansion. By June, still another problem had developed. Massachusetts was suffering from a drought and the springs which were the source of the gravity flow water system for the institution had dried up. It was now necessary to lay an emergency pipeline from a distant pond.[1]

Even in his depressed state, however, Mann admitted to some satisfaction when the first patients were released to lead sane and productive lives. He spoke of being unable to "bear the burden of life" had he not been "sustained by the conviction of having done something for the alleviation of others." From this he all too easily moralized that "nature sends us no solace for our own sufferings, as when she inspires us with the desire to relieve the sufferings of others."[2] If this were true, then Mann had ample opportunities to save himself by helping others. While busy at establishing the operations at the Worcester hospital, Governor Lincoln appointed him as a trustee for the New England Institution for the Education of the Blind. This school, which would some day gain international renown, was just beginning under the energetic and resourceful direction of Dr. Samuel Gridley Howe. Mann served on the visiting committee and was the legal counsel for the school. Shortly after his appointment, he took the Peabody sisters to an exhibition of the work being done under Howe's guidance.[3]

At the school he met Howe, still full of the same restless energy which had kept him ever on the verge of rustication back at Brown.

[1] A. D. Foster to Mann, March 30 and 31, April 27, and August 23, 1833; Bezaleel Taft to Mann, March 6, 1833; William B. Calhoun to Mann, June 28, 1833, all in Mann MSS:MHS; William B. Woodward to Mann, March 11 and 22, and April 1 and 16, 1833, Woodward MSS: AAS.
[2] Mann, Journal, May 9 and June 27, 1837, MS in MHS.
[3] Quarterly Report to the Trustees, 1832–1837, MS in Perkins School for the Blind, Watertown, Massachusetts; Samuel Gridley Howe to Mann, October 4, 1833, Mann MSS:MHS; *By-Laws, Rules and Regulations of the New England Institution for the Education of the Blind* (Boston, 1833).

After graduation, Howe had traveled abroad to fight for the Greeks and had become one of the heroes of their revolution against the Turks. Upon his return to Boston, he could have chosen any one of several avenues open to him for self-advancement, but he had turned his back on all the obvious ones and elected to work with blind, deaf, and mute children. At his institution, he now had six charges. It was evident to Mann and the Peabody sisters that even though Howe was presenting an exhibition, his progress had been painfully slow at first. He showed them pages of raised letters made of string glued to cardboard. In this manner he also had produced maps and raised geometric designs. Thus through the means of touch, Howe was groping hopefully and desperately for a way to communicate with these children whose imperfect bodies had cut them off from the world and sealed them in cells impervious to a ray of light or a particle of sound. Admittedly, Howe had accomplished little to date, but Mann found the prospect of what might be done almost overpowering. Here too was yet another test of whether human will and enlightenment could triumph over obstacles deemed insurmountable for centuries. In fact, Mann was so moved by what he witnessed that he prepared a memorial to the House of Representatives requesting the opportunity to show the legislature what was being done at the school. Convinced that the blind, like the insane, were "susceptible of great progress in intellectual and moral improvement," Mann hoped the General Court would appropriate additional funds to Howe.[4]

*   *   *

Although the visits with Channing failed to restore Mann's total peace of mind, they did give him a sympathetic listener to his ideas for reforming society. The two men found themselves in essential agreement on slavery. Both considered it a sectional problem, but admitted that some in the North were accessories to the evil of human servitude by profiting on the cheap raw cotton from the South. They also agreed that the North would inevitably pay a price for these ill-gotten gains. Both held high hopes that once emancipated, the Negro could be recolonized in Africa through the

---

[4] Elizabeth Peabody to Julia Ward Howe, February 9, 1876, Howe MSS: HCL; *Letters and Journals of Samuel Gridley Howe*, Lawra Richards, ed., II, 16; *Commonwealth of Massachusetts, House Documents*, No. 22 January 15, 1833, "Memorial."

efforts of the American Colonization Society. The development of superior agricultural lands in Africa, Mann reasoned, would produce cheaper sources of cotton and make the operation of plantations in the South unprofitable. Channing tempered Mann's optimism for colonization by pointing to Garrison's argument that emancipation and colonization would cause a shortage of slave labor and encourage slave breeding by unscrupulous men in the South.[5]

Although envisioning an all-white America in the distant future, Mann still held that his ideas on human progress were also valid for Negroes. Upon hearing that black applicants had been refused admission to the school for the blind, he sent Howe a note, asking for an explanation. Howe equivocated, fearing the attendance of a Negro pupil would frighten away support from Boston's upper classes and prevent the school from becoming a model for others throughout the country. Mann, on the other hand, being more removed from the problem, thought the issue could be decided "on general principles." He fully recognized that the presence of Negro students might prevent white parents from making the school available to their children, but he did not consider this objection a formidable one. Benevolence and justice presented a stronger mandate than expediency. "I should still contend," he wrote, "that as the blacks had been so long and so universally sacrificed to the whites, it would be no departure from even-handed justice for one to adjust the balance between. . . . I would found their claim to relief upon a very simple principle—*the necessity of one party and the ability of the other*. If they are capable of being taught, it is our duty to instruct." White and black alike could sink to "the depths of moral polution and wretchedness," or could rise to "glory by the path of virtue." And he added,

. . . to be alike and to know and feel that we are alike in all these things—is it not enough to blast and annihilate the *entire organ* in which pride dwells, that forbids our seeing, notwithstanding a diversity of color or form or circumstances, this great community of our nature and destination![6]

---

[5] Elizabeth Peabody to Mary Peabody, March 22–24, 1834, CJ in NYPL; Elizabeth Palmer Peabody, *Reminiscences of Rev. William Ellery Channing* (Boston, 1800), pp. 383–384. For a discussion of the strong interest and optimism many persons at this time held for Negro colonization, see Early Lee Fox, *The American Colonization Society, 1817–1840* (Baltimore, 1919). Channing's published views are in his *Slavery* (Boston, 1835).

[6] Mann to Elizabeth Peabody, August 23, 1833, Mann MSS:MHS.

Frequently Mann and Channing also discussed the problem of intemperance. Here too, they were in essential agreement, both believing that the chief agent for reform was moral suasion. Anything less compelling dealt only with symptoms rather than causes. It was the reformer's role to convince men that ardent spirits were not simple stimulants, but actual poisons. Moreover, by this time, Mann was ready to concede that it was logical to reinforce moral suasion with a rigorous regulation of the sale of liquor on the same principle that the state regulated the sale of more widely recognized poisons. This seemed to be its reasonable service in helping reinforce the voluntary efforts of reformers to rescue men and restore their human dignity.[7] Not all reformers agreed with this approach, and from within the ranks of the movement, increasingly militant groups placed their hopes solely upon legal prohibition as they came to share the common ground of disappointment and frustration with their previous measures. In their attempts to persuade individuals of the evils of intemperance, reformers had collected a mass of genuine and fictitious evidence against the use of ardent spirits. Now unable to ignore what they had amassed and finding human nature far more intransigent than anticipated, they were forced on by an iron law of logic to employ the superior power of the state to check the further spread of intemperance. To them it was painfully obvious that preaching and pledges were not enough.[8]

For the moment, however, Mann could not bring himself to embrace complete legal prohibition. Instead, he concentrated upon the economic consequences of intemperance. Invited to speak to a convention of the Massachusetts Society for the Suppression of Intemperance late in 1833, he worked up an extended analysis of the debilitating effects intemperance had upon the economy. His presentation was not only novel, but probably sparked the most tough-minded and unsentimental discussion of the convention. In his speech, no doubt to the surprise of his listeners, he discarded the shopworn arguments about sobriety and took a new tack with the following announcement:

---

[7] Elizabeth Peabody, *Reminiscences of Channing*, p. 383.
[8] Mark Doolittle, "Examination of the Massachusetts License Laws," *American Quarterly Temperance Magazine*, II (1834), 46–49; *Sixth Report of the American Temperance Society, May 18, 1833* (Boston, 1833), pp. 44–69; *Massachusetts Spy*, March 27, 1833; Clark, *History of Temperance Reform*, pp. 26–27; Krout, *Origins of Prohibition*, p. 138; *Massachusetts Acts and Resolves, 1833*, p. 265, January 8, 1833.

Resolved, That the pecuniary interests of Grocers and Retailers throughout the Commonwealth, and especially in the city of Boston, would be
greatly promoted by the entire disuse of ardent spirits; because of the
increased ability of the community to purchase other kinds of commodities in which they traffic.

What followed was described by the secretary of the Society, admittedly not the most impartial reporter, as a speech "of much
interest and originality on a hacknied subject." He added that it was
"a compact and ingenious argument addressing itself irresistibly to
the reason, and in a manner calculated to force conviction upon all
who are not blind intellectually as well as morally." [9]

Having tried out his ideas, Mann sent them forth in the form of
a pamphlet under the cumbersome title of *Remarks upon the Comparative Profits of Grocers and Retailers as Derived from Temperate
and Intemperate Customers*. In this, he argued that the grocer's
profits did not depend on his ability to sell, but on his customers'
ability to purchase. In New England, where there were neither
mineral resources nor the automatic harvests of warmer climates,
this ability to buy came from three sources of wealth—the health,
strength, and skills of the people, their industry and perseverance in
applying their talents, and their "frugality, economy and sound
judgement in preserving, investing and managing what has been
acquired." It naturally followed that "whatever, then, wastes health,
consumes strength, deadens skill, or substitutes indolent for industrious habits must necessarily diminish the wealth of the community
and in that way, must as necessarily, subtract from the amount of
the Grocer's business." It was then in their own self-interest that
retailers and grocers should labor for a temperate society.[1]

Admittedly, there was a general validity in what Mann said
about the buying power of sober customers, but his assumption that
through industry and frugality almost anyone could succeed sounded
more like a humorless paraphrasing of *Poor Richard's Almanac*. If
this was true at all, it was true only within a society of farmers and
artisans and not one including a growing number of wage earners
and unemployed. In less than six months, *Comparative Profits* was
on the "best seller" list of the Massachusetts Temperance Society,

---

[9] Walter Channing and J. G. Stevenson, *Doings of the Council of the
Massachusetts Society* (Boston, 1834), pp. 3–16.
[1] *Comparative Profits of Grocers* . . . (Boston, 1834), pp. 4–5.

being surpassed only by its *Temperance Journal* and one other tract. By May, 1834, more than 5,000 copies had been distributed.[2]

With the publication of the speech, Mann assumed a prominent role in the statewide endeavors of the Society. In the summer of 1834, a convention was called for the formation of a Young Men's Temperance Society. At the meeting, Mann was elected chairman and presided over several lively sessions as two factions began to form. One claimed that the existing license laws were archaic and needed a thorough revision. A second eschewed legislation and in its place urged the members of temperance societies throughout the state to pledge themselves to "abstinence to all alcoholic drinks." Earlier reformers had limited their attacks to the *excessive* use of "ardent spirits," that is, rum, whisky, and brandy. Then, as drunkenness persisted, they came to claim that any use of ardent spirits was an evil. Now when Mann listened to some of the more vehement speakers, he recognized that they were going even further and were attacking "all alcoholic beverages." Alcohol and not rum was the demon, and since it was present in all fermented drinks, he could predict that wine and ale would soon join the ranks of the banned.[3]

Thus by the middle of the 1830's, in their incessant search for "principles as fixed and certain in their operation as those which regulate the rising sun or the return of the seasons," the more radical reformers had convinced themselves that all alcoholic beverages rather than just ardent spirits were sinful and the means of self-destruction. What had once begun as a program of moral exhortation had, in less than two decades, become an organized and concerted effort by militant groups to achieve total abstinence either by mass emotional appeals and pledges or by using the superior power of the state to enforce prohibition.

Still Mann held to a more moderate course. Earlier in the legislature, he had urged state action to deal with both old and new problems which were beyond the scope of families and towns. Since he had also worked for a revision and stricter enforcement of licensing laws, one could expect him to consider further state action as desirable. But where others now led, he was reluctant to follow. He still enjoyed drinking wine and did not want to abstain from this

---

[2] *Twenty-first Annual Report of the Massachusetts Society* (Boston, 1834), p. 9.
[3] *Massachusetts Spy*, July 2 and 9, 1834; Mann to Sydney Williams, June 25, 1834, Mann MSS:MHS.

pleasure. Then too, he had begun to question the limits of political means to achieve social ends.[4]

*   *   *

The importance of the shift towards extreme measures in temperance, as well as Mann's waning faith in legislative action, would only become apparent in the succeeding years. During the summer of 1834, the people in and around Boston, including Mann, had other things to hold their interest. Charles Durant, American balloonist, had promised to make an ascent from the Boston Common. Early in August, a crowd of more than 20,000 persons gathered to see this daring aerialist travel through the air. Among them was Horace Mann. With all preparations completed and Durant in his gondola, a hush came over the people as one by one the moorings of the vessel were released. Slowly the balloon rose until it was above the tree tops. For a moment, it yawed to the side, caught in an eddy of air, and then moved up and away. As Durant became more distant, Mann expected the crowd to cheer. Instead, a spontaneous silence prevailed, as if it were fearful to see this man cut off from the earth and drifting into space.[5]

Several blocks away on Beacon Hill, two of Mann's friends stood on a roof top, watching the same event. During the preparations for the ascent, their conversation, as it often did, turned to Mann's plight and their hope that a return to politics might be his salvation. One of these persons was James K. Mills. The other was Elizabeth Peabody. For the past year, Elizabeth had made the rounds among her influential friends assessing Mann's chances of being elected to the General Court. Henry Lee, a man of both wealth and political stature, had heartily agreed with her that Mann should run for a seat in the state Senate. If Mann would just let his friends know he was a willing candidate, Lee stood ready to support him. But even aside from personal reasons, Mann was out of touch with politics. After the defeat of John Quincy Adams in 1828, he had considered the remnants of the National Republican Party in Massachusetts to

---

[4] Receipts as late as 1837 in the Mann MSS:DHS indicate that Mann continued to drink wine while abstaining from distilled liquors.
[5] Elizabeth Peabody to Mary Peabody, August 4, 1834, CJ in NYPL.

be acting and speaking increasingly like unregenerate Federalists. Henry Lee, an outspoken advocate of free trade, conceded that Mann's observations were generally correct.[6]

Internal dissensions among the legatees of national republicanism were gradually set aside after 1830, as they formed a new Whig Party to oppose "King" Andrew Jackson. While George Bancroft and David Henshaw were trying to build a Democratic Party in Massachusetts with the help of presidential spoils, the Whigs were organizing to prevent a takeover of the General Court. The political scene was further confused by the emergence of two other factions, the Anti-Masons and the Workingmen's Party. All groups made a concerted effort for the vote of the common man. In an attempt to demonstrate their egalitarianism, the Whigs in May, 1834, welcomed Davy Crockett to Boston, heralding him as a unique combination of the noble savage and true aristocrat while denouncing Andrew Jackson as an unscrupulous barbarian and tyrant. On the Fourth of July, each party staged a public spectacle to rally its members and gain new converts. The Workingmen organized a flamboyant parade, with members from each of the unions carrying an array of banners and marching alongside elaborate floats depicting their stock in trade. The most impressive of these was an actual ship constructed by the shipwrights and drawn by twenty-four horses. The Whigs put up a large pavilion on the east side of the Common and sponsored a banquet where speaker after speaker urged them to close ranks and wage a vigorous campaign against the Jacksonians in the upcoming elections. In 1823, a much younger Horace Mann had been the center of attraction at a nonpartisan Independence Day celebration in Dedham. In a flood of roseate prose, he had pledged to do his part to help fulfill the nation's destiny. Now a decade later, he recoiled from these partisan celebrations with a strong distaste. Society was coming apart at its seams and such irrational appeals to mob psychology only hastened a total rupture. The commemoration of the nation's independence, he felt, "ought to be celebrated otherwise, than it generally is." It had become "a custom 'more honored in the breach, than in the observance.' " While Mann watched the trade unions' parade with a mixture of apprehension and alienation, he absented himself from the Whig

---

[6] Elizabeth Peabody to Mary Peabody, December 11, 1833, and July 31 to August 3, 1834, CJ in NYPL.

affair completely, retreating to the seclusion and solitude of his
office and implying a plague on both their houses.[7]

As late as the summer of 1834, Mann was not only loath to have
certain social problems become the fodder for partisan debate in the
General Court, but he was also reluctant to return to the political
arena. At the time, the sensitive and reassuring discussions in the
peace and security of Channing's parlor were more to his liking than
the struggle for power in the House or Senate. With the election
several months away, however, Elizabeth Peabody still hoped that
she could draw him back into politics. James Mills and Henry Lee
both agreed with her that Mann could be a selfless, unsullied candidate, who would take a strong moral stand at a time when so many
were shifting their positions on the basis of expediency. Elizabeth
reported to her sister that Mills's enthusiasm for Mann made *"ours*
look pale. There was no measure of his admiration and respect."
Mills also was confident that if Mann was nominated for the Senate,
his election was assured. By the time Elizabeth recounted her interview to Mary, she embroidered it until she had Mills saying that
Mann "was profoundly respected on all sides—he was single minded,
clear headed and beyond suspicion of selfish aims—by those who
ever knew him in public." If Mann could only be convinced of this.
The task remained Elizabeth's main object during the summer and
autumn of 1834. Some of those from whom she sought help considered her effort a lost cause. Publicly, Elizabeth spoke of Mann's
prospects only in the most sanguine terms. Privately, she found
herself admitting to her sister Mary that "his gentlemen friends
think his case even more desperate than we." [8]

There was much in Elizabeth's aggressive approach which was
self-defeating. She would exhort and argue and Mann would half-
heartedly respond or offer a silent resistance, then retreat further
into his shell of self-pity. Her sister Mary, no less interested in his
future, operated upon him in a much more subtle, albeit more effective way. Living in the shadow of her illustrious and loquacious
sister, she gave the impression of leading a life of self-denial and
service to others. Friends and acquaintances who only saw this

---

[7] Mann to Mary Peabody, July 4, 1834, Mann MSS:MHS; Boston *Evening
Gazette*, July 4, 1834; Darling, *Political Changes in Massachusetts*,
pp. 85–129; C. Grant Loomis, "Davy Crockett Visits Boston," *New England Quarterly*, XXI (1947), 396–400.
[8] Elizabeth Peabody to Mary Peabody, July 3 to August 3, and August 7
to 10, 1834, CJ in NYPL.

missed another part of her character. Concealed behind her mild and humble appearance were intense moral convictions which at times bordered upon fanaticism. Elizabeth often publicly convinced others as a means of privately convincing herself. By comparison, Mary was so certain of her beliefs that she could devote her full energies to persuading others by more indirect means. The more vocal and active people about her frequently thought the ideas they expressed were their own, yet in fact it was often Mary who first planted and then nurtured them. Capable of working towards her ends through others and confident of the outcome, she did not depend upon the kind of frontal attack employed by Elizabeth.

This was particularly true in her relations with Mann. While patiently enduring his self-pity and brooding, she fed his self-image of an individual capable of striking one more blow for a righteous cause. Carefully she placed the seed of an idea in his mind, then helped it grow until he thought he had originated it and went to her for reassurance. Thus without directly urging his return to politics as Elizabeth had done, she made no secret of her contempt for what she considered to be a calculated destruction of republican government under President Jackson. By comparison, she considered the recent Whig victories in New York "the triumph of the right cause," and it was only surprising to her it had not happened before. "Can there be any doubt," she asked, if "it will be followed up everywhere?" Of course, "everywhere" included Massachusetts, and Mary wanted Mann to think that the "right cause" would triumph only when individuals rose above self-interests and acted upon principles instead of expediency. She did not lecture Mann on his duty. Mary knew it was more effective to write of an impending evil and describe what others were doing.[9]

*   *   *

Having exhausted every avenue at her disposal to draw Mann back into public life with little apparent success, Elizabeth received unsolicited assistance from an unexpected event which shocked the moral sensitivities of many Bostonians. What appeals for Mann's personal welfare and for the welfare of the Commonwealth could not bring about, a plea for justice and retribution for the helpless and persecuted did. For six years, the Ursuline Nuns had operated a

---

[9] Mary Peabody to Mann, May 12, 1834, Mann MSS:MHS.

convent in Charlestown, across the river from Boston. Here they had maintained a private school for girls patronized by both Roman Catholic and Protestant families. On the night of August 11, 1834, a mob gathered before the school and its leaders ordered the sisters out of the building. After the women had fled, the rioters battered down the doors and entered the school, desecrating its chapel, pillaging the rest of the premises, and finally putting the torch to the entire establishment. The following morning, Boston awoke to the ugly fact that a lawless mob had attacked a group of defenseless women and that the authorities had done little to prevent it. Property had been destroyed, lives endangered, and violence had supplanted public law and order.[1]

At a public meeting the next day, the mayor agreed to appoint an ad hoc committee of citizens "to investigate the proceedings of the last night and to adopt every suitable mode of bringing the authors and abettors of this outrage to justice." The first task of the committee was to select an attorney to organize and conduct the investigation, and both Loring and Charles Lee, a member of the group, thought Mann the most likely choice. He was a lawyer and had a reputation for public service. Perhaps even more important, the investigation might be the means of drawing him back into political life. One member of the committee challenged Mann's nomination on the grounds that he might be too orthodox and therefore prejudiced against Roman Catholics. Lee offered quick assurance that Mann held strong liberal religious sentiments and had little sympathy for militant orthodoxy. Satisfied with this explanation, the committee asked Mann to conduct their investigation.[2]

Privately, Mann considered the burning of the convent a "horrible outrage" and for ten days worked on the investigation "almost without intermission." Both Henry Lee and Elizabeth Peabody hoped this would prove to be Mann's first step back into public life. Optimistically, Elizabeth wrote to Mary, "The Committee consists of fifty of the first gentlemen in the town—and Mr. Lee says nothing can be better for Mr. M.—— than to be thus displayed." The conspirators,

<hr/>

[1] *Independent Chronicle and Boston Patriot*, August 16 and 20, 1834; *Report of the Committee, Relating to the Destruction of the Ursuline Convent, August 11, 1834* (Boston, 1834), pp. 2–16; the standard historical treatment of the event is Ray Allen Billington, "The Burning of the Charlestown Convent," *New England Quarterly*, X (1937), pp. 3–24.
[2] Elizabeth Peabody to Mary Peabody, August 18, 1834, CJ in NYPL. Elizabeth found it humorous that Mann had been accused of being too orthodox; Mann to Elizabeth Peabody [August, 1834], Mann MSS:MHS.

however, had not taken Mann's health into their plans. Just when he was making headway in his investigation and it seemed that their hopes for him would be realized, he became so ill that he was put to bed and could not complete his assignment. Although he was among those who signed the final report of the committee, he in no way gained the prominence from it that they had expected.[3]

It was as if Mann even through his sickness were telling Elizabeth that his reinstatement was a lost cause. Now fearful of what might happen to him in his condition if left unattended in his office, yet realizing that Victorian convention prevented her from taking personal care of him, Elizabeth sent him a train of notes as well as flowers and fruit by way of her cousin William, a discreet personal messenger. In addition, she sent a close friend to check on his condition, only to learn the disturbing news that Mann could not rid himself of a low fever and chills, even though Dr. John Ware was bleeding him and restricting his diet. So close and yet so far from Mann, she could stroll past the dark gray stone building which housed his office but was held back from entering by social sanctions as well as if the front door had been chained and padlocked. Up in his room, Mann was almost completely cut off from the world, and this was as he wanted it. Nevertheless, he assured Elizabeth of his gratitude for her concern. Finding it difficult to write with a quill while lying in bed and too weak to sit up, he scribbled a note to her in pencil:

Your flowers do me good for I can look at them and think of you— your fruit does me *indirect* good for I hang it up, and let the birds that come to see me peck at it,—your billets do me good for I can read them all to myself—and you would do me more good than all, if I could have a good long visit from you.[4]

During the last year, Elizabeth had invested her time and energies in more than Mann's welfare and that of the Commonwealth. She was a single woman who at the age of thirty had not acquiesced in the likely prospect of spinsterhood. On the basis of her actions

---

[3] Mann to Sydney Williams, August 24, [1834]; Mann to Elizabeth Peabody [August, 1834], both in Mann MSS:MHS; Elizabeth Peabody to Mary Peabody, August 19, and September 8–13, 1834, CJ in NYPL; *Report of the Committee . . .* , p. 16.
[4] Mann to Elizabeth Peabody [September, 1834], Mann MSS:MHS; Elizabeth Peabody to Mary Peabody, September 2–7 and 8–13, 1834, CJ in NYPL.

alone, it was difficult to determine her full interest in befriending Mann, but her correspondence with her sister suggested that she was agreeable to having her relationship with him go beyond mere friendship. Mann in turn gave her little hope for this, other than his reassurance of his need for her sympathy and assistance. "I go to see your sister as often as possible," he reported to Mary Peabody. "She has a mansion in her heart for everybody who suffers, and truths in her mind enough to heal them all." He was also careful not to give any public indication of more than a platonic relationship. Even so, people were inclined to extrapolate where the evidence was insufficient. At least one of Mann's associates, writing to a correspondent, described Elizabeth Peabody as "a maiden lady" and Mann as a "widower" who were "in the habit of 'taking sweet counsel together,' at least upon literary subjects." Apparently during his illness Mann came to recognize Elizabeth's intentions. As soon as he recovered enough to travel, he returned to his mother at Franklin to complete his convalescence. While there he clarified his own thoughts about their relationship. When he returned to Boston, he sought her out and in a manner Elizabeth found "unembarrassing," he explained that his love for her could never be more than that of a brother to a sister. Although disappointed, Elizabeth now knew it could not be otherwise. "Not that it would not be impossible for Mr. M.—— to make me love him exclusively," she rationalized to her sister,

But I could not do it unless he had or did try for it. And his situation —his greying hairs and his sorrowfulness ever precluded from my imagination that possibility—I know what the feeling of *love* is—for I have been sought and all but won . . . strong as my friendship is— deep as my interest in Mr. M.—— is [it is] a total different feeling.

At this time, Mann did not wish to reach a similar understanding with Mary.[5]

*　　*　　*

With the election less than two months away, the Whigs, not knowing what coalitions the Workingmen, Democrats, and Anti-

---

[5] Mann to Mary Peabody, March 26, 1834, Mann MSS:MHS; Julius Rockwell to Lucy Walker, January 23, 1836, Rockwell MSS: Lenox Library; Elizabeth Peabody to Mary Peabody, December 21, 1833, April 13–17, and September 10–October 6, 1834, CJ in NYPL; Elizabeth Peabody to Mann, [September, 1834], Straker MSS:ACL.

Masons had forged against them, but fearing the worst, were casting about frantically for popular candidates who could add strength to their ticket. When Elizabeth informed Mann that James Mills wanted him to move in with his family and was also prepared to back him for a seat in the Senate, Mann refused to believe her. Later, he acknowledged that he had received "an admirable note [from Mills] . . . having a stronger tendency to accomplish your wishes than I had supposed." Not wishing to impose upon Mills, Mann was also concerned that he did not refuse his overtures ungraciously.[6]

A month before the election, the editor of the *Evening Mercantile Journal*, a spokesman for the Whig Party, was in a pessimistic mood. As he surveyed the political scene, he feared the results which might come from a possible amalgamation of several political factions. A second Whig editor was more candid, denouncing what he claimed was "a coalition, consisting of Jackson men, Anti-Masons, workeys, Fanny Wright men and infidels of all descriptions." If the Commonwealth was to be saved from mobocracy, the *Journal* thought it was imperative for "the Whigs to be up and doing." As the Whig slate for Senators from Suffolk County was one of the last to be prepared, Mann's friends had a reprieve after his sickness in which to urge him once more to be one of their candidates. Even though he had not completely recovered, they would not leave him alone. They appealed to his sense of duty; they appealed to his pride; they described what might happen at the State House if they lost the election; and they held up the rosy prospect of what they could accomplish if they won. In short, they brought up every argument they could muster, and when the list of Senators was finally added to the general Whig ticket on October 24, Horace Mann's name was among the nominees.[7]

Campaigning now began in dead earnest. Whig leaders at hundreds of meetings throughout the state urged their members "to

---

[6] Elizabeth Peabody to Mann, [September, 1834], Straker MSS:ACL; Elizabeth Peabody to Mary Peabody, September 20–October 6, 1834, CJ in NYPL; Mann to Elizabeth Peabody, September 24, 1834, Mann MSS:MHS. For a description of the problems confronting the Whigs in their state campaigns of 1834, see E. Malcolm Carroll, *Origins of the Whig Party* (Durham, 1925), *passim*.

[7] *Evening Mercantile Journal*, October 15, 1834; Boston *Commercial Gazette*, November 17, 1834; Boston *Daily Advocate*, October 24, 1834; *Columbian Centinel*, October 27, 1834; Mann to Theron Metcalf, October 9, 1834, PHS.

be up and doing." Young men in the party, such as Edward Loring, neglected their work and their families as they spoke at one rally after another. In the meantime, the Jackson Party was not standing still. Through its mouthpiece, the Boston *Morning Post,* it attacked the Whigs as men of wealth and privilege who exploited the common man. The *Post* found the opposition's candidates for the Senate particularly odious and reserved some of its choicest political invective for them. In the course of the campaign, each Whig candidate took his turn at being vilified, but when the *Post* came to Mann, sensing he was the weakest person on the ticket, it unloosed a double measure of abuse.

The *Post* ridiculed Mann on three counts. It depicted him as a visionary "projector of lunatic hospitals," a "total abstinence man," and a political mercenary brought in from Norfolk County by the moneyed interests on State Street. It also claimed that Mann was ready "to brand 'criminal' upon every man's forehead in this free state, who will not join him in his temperance crusade." The diatribe concluded with the parting shot, "This man . . . is more of a hypocrite than a fool. He means to *use* the people." In subsequent issues, the *Post* continued its attack, deriding Mann as the "great reformer." [8]

Of the three accusations, Mann was most vulnerable to that on his temperance record. Two days after the first article in the *Post,* the "Grocers, Distillers, and Inn-Holders" of Boston held a meeting in which they resolved to support five of the Whig hopefuls for the Senate but refused to endorse a sixth, Horace Mann. Yet it was the partisan abuse which came because of his stand upon the moral issue of intemperance which gave Mann his greatest satisfaction. The more the attack upon him intensified, the more he seemed to recover some of his former zeal for political controversy. As the day of reckoning approached, Mann, quite understandably, came to

---

[8] Boston *Morning Post,* November 4, 7, and 10, 1834; it is unlikely that Mann by this time had made any public statements supporting legal prohibition of all sales of ardent spirits, but in its frantic attempt to demoralize the opposition, the *Post* had come very close to expressing Mann's personal opinion on this question. Writing to his sister about the campaign, he boasted, "They held public meetings at which I was denounced and one of the morning newspapers, (for the rum-party have a paper) opposed my election most strenuously, calling upon all rum sellers to vote against me, and doing me the distinguished honor to say, that if I were in the Senate, I should cause all the license laws to be repealed, and should enact others, making the sale of ardent spirits a crime." Mann to Lydia Mann, [November, 1834], Mann MSS:MHS.

identify his opponents with everything he detested in politics, including logrolling, expedient bargains, and appeals to class interests. "What pleases me especially," he reported to his sister in the heat of the campaign, "is that as soon as my nomination appeared in the papers, all the taverners, distillers, and grocers, or as we call them retailers, entered into a league to defeat my election. . . ." No doubt he spoke in the same vein to William Ellery Channing. Theoretically, Channing could agree with him; but in actuality, the minister thought that the split ticket which had resulted from Mann's temperance stand did not augur well for his political future.[9]

The *Evening Mercantile Journal* met the attack of the *Post,* article for article. It decried the fact that there were a few prejudiced people in Boston who thought a man was unfit for the Senate because he was a philanthropist. The *Journal* was glad that Mann was "a friend of temperance," but it categorically denied that he had ever made a public statement in favor of total abstinence. To those who wanted to learn Mann's opinion on the issue, it recommended his speech on the "Comparative Profits of Grocers." The *Journal* also assured its readers that Mann had been nominated for far more important reasons than his stand on temperance reform. If he were elected, he would go to the Senate *"untrammelled* and *unpledged"* and act "with a view to promote the general interest of his fellow citizens." Clearly he was a man of principles who would remain uncorrupted by the political opportunism of the day.[1]

On November 6, the Saturday before Election Day, the citizens of Boston turned out for what one newspaper described as a GREAT WHIG MEETING AT FANEUIL HALL in order "to secure the TRIUMPH OF LIBERTY and the CONSTITUTION over TORYISM and TYRANNY." One of the speakers, Charles Curtis, singled out Mann and gave a panegyric on his role in the erection of the lunatic hospital and temperance reform. According to Elizabeth Peabody, Curtis's remarks were greeted with "an uproar of approval." [2]

From the confines of his study, Channing could not appreciate the intensity of the emotional appeal the Whigs had produced in

[9] Mann to Lydia Mann, November, 1834, Mann MSS:MHS; Elizabeth Peabody to Mary Peabody, November 9–12, 1834, CJ in NYPL; *Columbian Centinel,* November 10, 1834; *Daily Evening Transcript,* November 6, 1834.
[1] *Evening Mercantile Journal,* November 4, 7, and 8, 1834; Elizabeth Peabody to Mary Peabody, November 7, 1834, CJ in NYPL.
[2] *Daily Evening Transcript,* November 6, 1834; Elizabeth Peabody to Mary Peabody, November 9–12, CJ in NYPL.

their effort to retain control of the State House. When the votes were tallied, the most optimistic among them stared at the returns in disbelief. Whigs of every description and ability were swept into office upon the crest of a groundswell of antagonism towards Andrew Jackson's recent withdrawal of federal deposits from the banks. Despite all the affirmations about principles and principled men, the Whig success hinged upon a financial issue. Mann's particular assets and liabilities had little impact upon the outcome, the *Post* and the *Journal* notwithstanding. All six Whig Senators from Suffolk County were elected by large majorities. A Whig was elected to every seat in the Senate and the party held 348 seats in the House, compared with 62 for the Democrats and 61 for the Anti-Masons. They had increased their hold on the General Court by 192 seats. Once again, the sons of the Patriots had risen and formed a solid phalanx against "Toryism and Tyranny." [3]

Mann could now reassure Mary Peabody that Massachusetts had been saved. In victory his party now looked much more like the National Republicans of old. "Whiggism," he wrote, "has at least one place in the states left to rest his foot." In the Bay State it had triumphed over "the united forces of anti-masonry, Jacksonianism, and workeyism." Mann jubilantly reported that "every representative to Congress is Whig, the state Senate is entirely Whig. The House of Reps. is 5/6 Whig. Every department of the state government is Whig! Whig! Whig!" The enthusiasm was his, but Mary Peabody knew she had been at least in part a progenitor of his pro-Whig sentiments; and the sense of achievement belonged to both of them. [4]

On the Sunday following the election, Mann sat down with Elizabeth Peabody and took inventory of the recent events. It was true that the Whigs had won an impressive victory, but since he had been singled out for a special attack by their opponents, he considered his election a personal triumph as well, and a demonstration that virtue would succeed even when pitted against self-seeking ends. His election was a clear mandate from the people, and he was "encouraged to push all his projects." It was in the General Court that he had initiated some of his earliest ideas on reform, and now he would return there to his unfinished tasks. [5]

---

[3] *Daily Evening Transcript*, November 13, 1834; Boston *Commercial Gazette*, November 17, 1834; Darling, *Political Changes in Massachusetts*, pp. 127–129.
[4] Mann to Mary Peabody, November 15, 1834, Berg MSS:NYPL.
[5] Elizabeth Peabody to Mary Peabody, November 18, 1834, CJ in NYPL.

The first week in January, 1835, the duly elected Representatives of the voters of Massachusetts gathered at the State House. It was a more serious and less self-assured Mann who now took his seat in the Senate. The world had lost much of its rosy promise. Neither his private nor his public hopes had been realized. At best he considered his life but a shadow of its former self. For the past two years, Channing, Loring, Mills, and Lee had helped him regain a new interest in his career. Probably more important than their combined assistance was the sympathy and understanding he had received from the Peabody sisters. While all his friends rejoiced in his return to the legislature, their sense of accomplishment, although resting upon a precarious base, was especially reassuring. After watching the lawmakers on Beacon Hill take the oath of office for the next term, Elizabeth returned to her room on Bulfinch Place. Later that afternoon she wrote her sister, Mary, "The Senate sat today and our friend Mr. M—— [is] an Honourable!" [6]

---

[6] Elizabeth Peabody to Mary Peabody, January 6–7, 1835, CJ in NYPL.

CHAPTER X

Moralist in an Immoral Society

═══════

OUR COUNTRY is swept along by mighty impulses. The causes which act on character are extensive and exceedingly strong. There is so much in our condition to stir up restlessness, wild schemes, extravagant speculation, a grasping spirit, ambition, and fanaticism in a thousand infectious forms, that there is not much chance for reflection, for moral self determination. . . . That a worldly, national, mercenary, reckless spirit should spring up in these circumstances we must expect. . . . The commercial system, which is the strongest feature of our times, is for the most part my abhorrence; and yet I do see that it is breaking down the feudal system, the military system, old distinctions and old alienations, and establishing new ties among men. I therefore hope.

WILLIAM ELLERY CHANNING

─────

THE POOR, Massachusetts would always have, and as soon as Mann had taken his desk in the Senate, he was faced with the necessity of dealing with their problems, which seemed to have more than the fabled nine lives of an unwanted cat. Benjamin Pickman, president of the Senate, appointed him chairman of the Committee on Matters of Chancery and Probate, and in this capacity Mann began a study of the debtors laws of Massachusetts. Under existing legislation, it still was *legally* possible for a creditor to jail a man who could not pay a $10 debt. Thus the dead hand of the past held a grim warning for the prodigal and the unlucky. Unwilling to countenance a radical revision of its debtor laws, the legislature in recent years had moved towards leniency, if not justice, by extending the limits of the jail "as to comprehend all places within the actual boundaries of the city or town in which gaols are instituted." Even with this modification, the creditor still held all the trump cards. He retained the unchallengeable right to his payment, and for the "paltry sum of ten dollars," as one reformer called it, he could force the state to deprive a free-born American citizen of his personal liberty. Understandably, some reformers considered imprisonment for debt for any reason a vestigial remnant from the Dark Ages, or as one group succinctly described it, "one of those abuses, which should have long shared the fate of other relics of ruder times." In an age of optimistic humanitarianism, the persistence of such an injustice was both incredible and intolerable.[1]

Braced with the sense of recent political victory, many younger Whigs considered the moment opportune to rid the state of this "relic of ruder times." Surely the sentiment behind the remarks about the improved treatment of lunatics at the Worcester Hospital made by John Davis, newly elected Whig Governor, was also applicable to debtors. Addressing the opening joint session of the General Court, Davis argued that a person should never be deprived of his personal liberty for petty causes. Personal liberty, he insisted, was "of higher importance than the title of property." Davis's immediate objective was the passage of a law prohibiting the consignment of persons to Worcester without the decision of a jury, but it took neither great sensitivity nor intelligence on the part of reformers to recognize that the same humanitarian arguments he had fashioned on behalf of lunatics made imprisonment for a debt a patent anachronism in an age of republicanism and reform. But not all agreed. Some lawmakers considered the recent extension of jailyards to the town limits an indirect attack upon the right of property and were ready to submit legislation to rescind the more lenient penalty. Thus Mann's committee had a choice.[2]

Mann combed through both ancient and modern laws on the subject and then filed a report he hoped would clear out the legal impedimenta accumulated through the centuries and be the first step in Massachusetts toward removing what he considered a medieval malpractice. Since the beginnings of liberty in England, Mann noted that the Crown never had had the right to imprison a subject without "primary presumption and ultimate proof of guilt." But in Massachusetts, a private citizen wielded the power to imprison another, even when the question of guilt had never been raised. "It seems

---

[1] Journal of the Senate, Vol. 51, January 12, 1835, p. 25, MS in MSA; *Laws of the Commonwealth of Massachusetts, 1834–1836*, XIII, *Massachusetts State Documents, 1835*, No. 59, pp. 6–7.

[2] "Address of His Excellency John Davis, Delivered before the Two Branches of the Legislature, January 13, 1835," *Massachusetts House Documents, 1835*, No. 3, p. 13; *Massachusetts Senate Documents, 1835*, No. 59.

scarcely credible," Mann continued, "that the champions of freedom should have continued so long and so strenuously against the odious prerogative of suspending the habeus corpus act, and yet should have suffered a prerogative no less odious to be exercised by thousands at pleasure." An honest man could be snatched away from his work-bench or fields on a simple warrant, prevented from restoring his estate, and lose his "birth right of liberty." Admittedly the creditor's use of arbitrary power in recent years had been tempered by public opinion and humane sentiments, but this was small gain. "The right of one citizen," he shrewdly argued, "should never depend on the spontaneous lenity [sic] of another." So much for Mann's legal argument. But there was also a greater moral issue at stake. While the state had the lawful authority to jail any man who did not pay his debts, it was immoral to punish the honest debtor for events beyond his intent or control. What was needed was a distinction between the victim of misfortune and the swindler or confidence man. Through his report then, Mann refused to stay within his committee's mandate and simply recommend better and more humane modes for enforcing the collection of debts. The time was at hand for the lawmakers to make "the *legal* coincident with the *moral* code." [3]

In dealing with debtors, Mann had reasoned that the right of property was subservient to moral imperatives of a higher order. As he moved on to other problems before the General Court which were the concomitant of industrial growth in Massachusetts, the assumption of higher moral laws, self-evident in a more simple agrarian society, now was being put to a new test. Each day he sat in the Senate brought additional petitions for the incorporation of banks, mills, mercantile houses, and private academies. While still justifying their appeals for corporate privileges on the basis of promised benefits to the Commonwealth, it was evident that the profit motive and not a desire to render public service drove the petitioners to make their requests. Although unable to appreciate it at the time, Mann and his associates were enacting legislation which was to become a great watershed in Massachusetts legal history. Slowly and painfully they were delineating the private and public sectors of

---

[3] Elizabeth Peabody to Mary Peabody, February 28 to March 13, 1835, CJ in NYPL; *Massachusetts Senate Documents, 1835*, No. 61, pp. 3–5, 18, and 21–23. Commenting on Mann's report, one European observer reported that it was "replete with admirable views eloquently expressed." He also stated that certain of its sections should be adopted by the legislature of every civilized state. See George Combe, *Notes on the United States of America* (Philadelphia, 1841), II, 207–208.

society; slowly because they found their traditional concepts of good and evil as applied to these two separate categories restrictive and outmoded; painfully because it was difficult to depart from the security of the past. Wrestling with the Warren Bridge question, they could not find a moral solution which would make the bridge free to the public while still upholding the property rights of its owners. Mann may have satisfied himself that in dealing with debtors he had made the legal coincident with the moral, but the same could not be said of efforts to codify the rights and responsibilities of the new corporations.

Nevertheless, there were many other areas where this was still possible. In 1831, he and Ira Barton, his former classmate, had instigated a movement to revise the state laws. Both houses complied and resolved to appoint three commissioners "whose duty it shall be to faithfully revise, collate and arrange, as well the colonial and provincial statutes, as all other general statutes of the Commonwealth." The Governor appointed Charles Jackson, Asahel Stearns, and John Pickering to the task, and after three years of work, their first efforts were ready for legislative review in 1835.[4]

While adopting a few of the more radical reforms recently incorporated into the new legal code of New York, the commissioners considered their responsibility as one of clarification and simplication rather than legislation. In their opinion, the advantages of having the new laws be a code in which the "numerous principles of the common law" were sharply defined were "not sufficient to outweigh the advantages of leaving them to be applied, by the courts, as principles of common law." Clearly, it was impossible to construct a series of a priori laws to cover every specific case. Instead, they had concluded that the flexibility of the common law was more suited to a rapidly expanding and changing society.[5]

Early in 1835, a joint committee of the House and Senate began the tedious process of reviewing the commissioners' proposed revisions. Believing the committee should not adjourn when the regu-

---

[4] Mann to Lydia Mann, June 2, 1835, Mann MSS:MHS; *Journal of the House*, Vol. 53, January 19, 1832, p. 119, MS in MSA; *Resolves of the Commonwealth of Massachusetts, 1832–1834* (Boston, 1834), Ch. XXX, "Resolve providing for a revision of the General Statutes of the Commonwealth," February 24, 1832; *Journals of the Committees on the Revised Statutes* (Boston, 1835), p. 11. Reports of the commissioners' work are found in *Massachusetts Senate Documents, 1834*, Nos. 12 and 51, and *Massachusetts Senate Documents, 1835*, No. 7.

[5] *American Jurist and Law Magazine*, XIII (1835), pp. 344–378.

lar term of the General Court had ended, Mann made a motion which kept it in session during the summer. Then when Franklin Dexter, a committee member, was unable to attend in June, Mann filled his vacancy, and also served as chairman *pro tempore* when the committee chairman could not be present. Since the group met in the Senate chamber where the high ceilings kept the air relatively cool, Mann sat in the chair of the president of the Senate, a new vantage point for him.[6]

Whether in the chair or not, Mann played a leading role as the work progressed. Occasionally he argued for substantial changes in the statutes. Building upon his previous success in defeating the Blandford petition, he convinced the committee to restrict the donor's control over funds given for charitable and religious purposes. Usually effective, he was particularly so when he argued for revisions based upon some moral imperative. After getting parts of his report on insolvent debtors incorporated into the new document, he proposed a more stringent statute limiting Sunday activities, including the outlawing of all travel by commuters, wagoners, and teamsters from sunrise to sunset, the prohibition of all forms of public entertainment, and the closing of all stores and workshops. According to him, the law was to embrace all persons except those who "conscientiously observe the whole or any part of Saturday, as Sunday, in which case such person shall not be prohibited from such work or amusement on the corresponding parts of Sunday." Justifying his position to Elizabeth Peabody, he wrote,

I do not believe the Sabbath is any more *holy time*, than any other day of the week, but I believe that *as a social and political institution*, it is invaluable. My neighbor believes it is set apart, sanctified, hallowed, by heaven itself. It is wrong for me to unite with him, or for him to unite with me in the adoption of civil regulations for its proper observation. Such a notion appears to me to stand on the very lowest ground of partisan and sectarian prejudice,—That I will not cooperate with a man in anything, because I differ from him in something.

Stripped of its religious sanctions, the "Lord's Day" was still an important social observance to be enforced by the state.[7]

---

[6] Journal of the Senate, Vol. 56, March 17, 1835, p. 295, MS in MSA; *Journals of the Committees*, pp. 1 and 118.

[7] *Journals of the Committees*, pp. 15–68, 317, and *passim;* Mann to Elizabeth Peabody, July 5, 1835, Mann MSS:MHS.

Mann also convinced the committee to adopt a stronger law controlling the importation, printing, and distribution of material containing "obscene language or obscene prints, pictures, figures, or descriptions, manifestly tending to the corruption of the morals of the youth." Still later, partly due to his maneuvering, the words "wine or" were inserted before "spiritous" in one of the license laws. By August, much of the work was finished and the committee voted itself a three-week recess. Before adjourning, however, it extended its thanks to Mann for his "faithful, laborious, and dignified discharge of . . . duties." [8]

The next month, the two houses met in special session to review the revised statutes and enact them into law. Occasionally, it took as much time and effort to obtain affirmative action on "Lost Goods and Stray Beasts" as it did to demarcate the jurisdictions of the various courts of the Commonwealth. Session by session and chapter by chapter, the work moved steadily on, until the people of Massachusetts had a new set of laws by which to govern themselves. At the last moment Mann helped iron out procedural differences between the House and Senate for repealing existing statutes, and by November 4, the Commonwealth had completely revised its laws. [9]

Mann was mistaken if he expected his work would be finished with the end of the special session. Just before adjournment the two chambers appointed him and Theron Metcalf to oversee the publication of the new laws. In addition, he and Metcalf were directed to prepare "an exact and copious index" and marginal notes for each section, an assignment which gave evidence of Mann's legal reputation among the legislators and paid him $900 for services rendered. For Mann the intensive labor of the last months had been accompanied by good health. At the end of the session he reported to his sister that "Hard work suits me, it diverts my mind from contemplation of subjects, more exhausting than the severest toil." And he added, "I think I shall always look back upon this year's labor with satisfaction; and with consciousness of having performed a service, which will live after me." He also took no small satisfaction from the fact that these laws bore the stamp of his own version of public and private morality, a development certainly outside the original

---

[8] *Journals of the Committees*, pp. 219–229, 436, and 459.
[9] Robert Rantoul, *Memoirs, Speeches, and Writings of Robert Rantoul, Jr.*, ed. Luther Hamilton (Boston, 1854), p. 46; Journal of the Senate, Vol. 56, Pt. 2, p. 39, September 16, 1835, MS in MSA.

intent of the commissioners, but perhaps an inevitable outcome
from the deliberations of fallible men.[1]

*   *   *

Still viewed as a new arrival from the hinterland by Whig
political leaders in Boston, Mann considered his re-election to the
Senate the next year as a significant step in the right direction.
Actually, he was lucky. No longer saddled with Andrew Jackson's
unpopular bank policy, the Massachusetts Democrats had scored a
major political comeback. In the Senate, always considered an im-
pregnable Whig stronghold, Mann's party was reduced to twenty-one
seats, while the opposition parties almost matched it with eighteen.
In the swing away from the Whigs, George Bliss, heir apparent to
the presidency of the Senate, was defeated in his county, and the
position was open for a second time within the year. The *Evening
Mercantile Journal* reported that the Democrats had decided to support Abel Cushing for the post, while the Anti-Masons were backing
Seth Whitmarsh. It was also rumored, according to the *Journal,* that
in the wake of their setbacks at the polls, the Whigs were in a state
of confusion and split down the middle between William Sturgis and
Horace Mann. Attempting to squelch further rumors, the Boston
Evening Transcript simply predicted that Sturgis would be the next
head of the Senate.[2]

When the first ballot was tallied, it was evident that the two
Whig factions were still at odds. With the support of several dissident
Democrats, Whitmarsh led with thirteen votes. Mann had eight and
Sturgis seven. Twenty votes were needed for election. On the next
four ballots, Mann gained strength at Sturgis's expense, but could
muster no more than fifteen votes, while Whitmarsh's count fluctu-
ated between twelve and fourteen. Then from the sixth to the thirteenth ballot, a number of Whigs shifted their support back to
Sturgis, until Mann was down to four die-hard supporters. Refusing
to give in, they gradually picked up strength after the fourteenth

---

[1] Mann to Lydia Mann, November 20, 1835, Mann MSS:MHS; *Massachusetts Senate Documents, 1836,* No. 3, "Report Respecting the Printing and Publishing of the Revised Statutes," p. 5; *Resolves of the
Commonwealth of Massachusetts, 1835,* Ch. CIII, pp. 422–423, April 16,
1836.
[2] Mann to Lydia Mann, November 20, 1835, Mann MSS:MHS; *Evening
Mercantile Journal,* January 5, 1836; Boston *Evening Transcript,* January 5, 1836.

vote. Wearying of the ordeal, Sturgis then withdrew his name from contention and his backers looked for a compromise candidate that all the Whigs could support. In the meantime, the opposition was stuck with Whitmarsh, who consistently received a block of fourteen votes. Mann was up to seventeen votes on the sixteenth round and gained one more supporter in the seventeenth. Finally after eighteen ballots, the junior Senator from Suffolk County received the necessary twenty votes and was declared the new president. The short but relatively peaceful reign of old Benjamin Pickman over the Massachusetts Senate had come to a close.[3]

No sooner had Mann taken the chair than he found himself embroiled in a controversy over contested elections. Although vigorously opposed, the Whig maneuvers to have certain Democratic majorities disqualified were generally successful. On eight town elections, they prevailed only because Mann cast a tie-breaking vote in favor of his party. Thus with the help of their new president, the Whigs had weathered their first turbulence, but it was soon evident that this was only a squall preceding the storm to come. Mann, a reluctant partisan at best, an obvious political debtor, and the nominal leader of a party in severe straits, would soon learn if he could enjoy the command from the bridge.

As in the year before, the Senate calendar was swamped with petitions for corporate charters, ranging all the way from incipient would-be enterprises hoping to erect a private wharf, manufacture India Rubber, establish the United States Exploring Company, or found the Belchertown Classical Academy. By a standing vote of seventeen to fifteen, after a heated debate, the Senate decided to limit the charters of all new banks to ten years before going on to authorize a total of thirty-four new institutions. From everywhere it seemed as if groups large and small had money to invest and wanted to make their fortunes under the protective wing of the Commonwealth.[4]

Not only was Mann increasingly identified in the legislature as a loyal Whig, but also a staunch ally of the railroad promoters. Since the cost of establishing such roads as the Boston and Lowell exceeded the estimates of the planners, additional financing was

---

[3] The account of the eighteen ballots is given in the Boston *Daily Advertiser and Patriot*, January 7, 1836, and in the Journal of the Senate, Vol. 57, pp. 2–3, January 6, 1836, MS in MSA.

[4] Journal of the Senate, Vol. 57, pp. 68–164 *passim*, and pp. 195–196, 320–325, MS in MSA; *Massachusetts Senate Documents, 1836*, No. 53, pp. 1–4.

needed, and previous legislatures had been reluctant to commit public monies to meet this demand. The result was that the original promoters such as the Dwights and the Quincys had gone to private investors with the promise of generous profits. This placed them in a dilemma. Only by convincing the legislature that the Boston and Lowell would serve a public purpose could its directors receive the right to raise additional capital; but only by making profit an incentive could they attract private investors. Thus their problem offered an illustration of the slow evolution by which a public function was transformed into private enterprise, even though at the moment, many lawmakers thought it only necessary to make a temporary legal accommodation until the state would finally take title to the roads. In time, profit would supersede public interest, but Mann still believed that railroads would provide the best of both possible worlds and he saw no reason to alter his optimism at this point.[5]

The difficulty of clarifying the distinction between the public and private interest was even more clearly demonstrated in resolving the conflict over the Warren and Charles River Bridges. Since the Warren Bridge became public property in 1832, the Commonwealth had continued to charge tolls on it, thus depriving Charlestown residents of a free access to Boston. Several bills introduced to pay the proprietors of the Charles River Bridge for their property were particularly repugnant to the citizens of Charlestown, since the money was to come from "legal" tolls on the Warren Bridge. According to their view, what the legislature did about the Charles River Bridge was an independent issue. They had built and paid for the bridge and had subsequently passed on their title to the Commonwealth in good faith with the understanding it was to be free. Most of the lawmakers refused to separate the issues, however. In 1835, a frustrated Senate committee reported, "Seldom has any subject, apparently so local and private in its character, excited so much legislative debate, so much legal discussion, and perhaps, so much popular feeling." After depicting some of the history of the controversy, the report concluded,

This controversy presents one of those extreme cases, so near the middle line which divides the law of private rights from the law of sovereign

[5] For a general discussion of the factors causing the general shift from the corporation's public to private function, see Oscar and Mary Flug Handlin, *Commonwealth: A Study of the Role of Government in the American Economy: Massachusetts. 1774–1861* (New York, 1947), pp. 115–149 and 172–173.

power, that it would be better never to receive a judicial determination, hereafter to be quoted as an established precedent of constitutional law and legal authority.

By implication, the committee was conceding that the older maxims of individual honesty, honor, and justice were inapplicable to such an involved problem. Conflicting types of property rights were in competition, and it fell to the state somehow to guarantee both the right of private property and its own sovereignty. No single compromise brought forth was able to satisfy a majority of the lawmakers, and contrary to the recommendations in the 1835 report, the issue was ultimately settled in the United States Supreme Court. Here Chief Justice Roger Taney cut the Gordian knot and drew a necessary but painful distinction between "the law of private rights" and "the law of sovereign power." [6]

Mann would gladly have entered a debate on behalf of the insane or the intemperate, but disputes over property rights were no longer to his liking. Although he was not completely aware of it, his older patriotic rhetoric and moral absolutes were now less relevant in directing and controlling political and economic developments. As a lawyer, he should have been one of the first to recognize the implications of this change, but he had become more interested in moral than legal issues and more involved in saving individuals than in understanding the complexities of broad social changes. Writing to Mary Peabody, Mann lamented that he must apply himself "to the code of Judge Jackson instead of the story of Miss Sedgwick. Our examination for tomorrow is 'the actions relating to real property.' " As he had come to believe that men were acting to protect and further their own vested interests rather than the good of the Commonwealth, he found more certitude in the simplistic moral imperatives which Catherine Sedgwick wove into her popular sentimental stories than in the tough-minded amoral legal briefs on real property prepared by Charles Jackson, one of the commissioners who had helped revise the state laws.[7]

*   *   *

---

[6] For an example of the debate on the issue, see the Boston *Morning Post*, February 27, 1836; *Massachusetts Senate Documents, 1835,* No. 58, pp. 5 and 24.
[7] Mann to Mary Peabody, n.d. [ca. 1836], Mann MSS:MHS.

Even within the field of reform the older conservative doctrines were being challenged by more radical ideologies which threatened to divide rather than unify the ranks of the virtuous. For several years, a group of vociferous abolitionists in Boston under the leadership of William Lloyd Garrison had made themselves obnoxious to the establishment with their anti-slavery agitation. Southern legislatures had risen to their bait and demanded that the Massachusetts authorities suppress them, thus giving the Garrisonian cause the cloak of respectability as a crusade for free speech. Soon the General Court was besieged by petitions from militants in every part of the state who insisted that it take an unequivocal stand for the immediate emancipation of southern slaves. Although most of the legislators detested the institution of slavery, their racism and sense of nationalism made them loath to support emancipation if this would either put the Union in jeopardy or encourage the migration of free blacks into Massachusetts. Mann generally concurred in this. He had no liking for the institution of slavery, nor for its apologists, who falsely pictured the happy tranquility of the southern Negro. These amounted to "portraying the happiness of the dancing and singing *animals* and rejoicing in their attachment of their masters and mistresses, which could only exist with ignorance of themselves," according to him. Generally supporting those in the American Colonization Society who espoused gradual emancipation and the return of blacks to Africa, he viewed the abolitionists as troublemakers who would do more harm than good.[8]

Upon hearing an account of Prudence Crandall's ill-fated attempt to establish a school for free black girls in Connecticut, Mann blamed the mounting antagonism not so much on racism as upon the agitations of the abolitionists. For him while the harassment of Miss Crandall was reprehensible and a patent violation of human rights, it was also proof that the abolitionists were up against "an insuperable obstacle in the accomplishment of their plans." Slavery had grown out of a complex of interrelated economic and social elements and therefore could not be destroyed in one fell swoop. "All the movements of the abolitionists, so far as I am concerned," he argued with remarkable foresight and common sense, "tend not to weaken but to strengthen the cohesion of these elements." The Garrisonians, unlike those of the Colonization Society, irresponsibly proposed "to leap to

---

[8] *Massachusetts Senate Documents, 1836*, No. 56, pp. 7–18; Mann to Elizabeth Peabody, July 5, 1835; Mann to Mary Peabody, June 25, 1837, Mann MSS:MHS.

the accomplishment of ends, without the intervention of means." No captive of a doctrine of "immediatism," Mann continued to fall back on his older faith in human perfectibility, even though the experiences of the last few years had tempered his optimism and forced him to extend the time table for his humanitarian celestial railroad.[9]

Along with this change, he also abandoned his hope for a quick political solution to slavery. If a debate on the issue forced its way into the General Court, it would most likely polarize the body and degenerate into a name-calling contest. One faction could be expected to label the abolitionists as incendiaries, ready to destroy law and order as well as the institution of private property. In reply, the abolitionists could be expected to repay in kind, describing their opponents as mercenaries serving the interests of textile manufacturers and merchants who readily bargained away the birthrights of countless Negroes for the pottage of quick profits. Obviously there was little consensus here on which to base political action. The emancipation of slaves, Mann thought, would come about through voluntary, charitable, and educational efforts and only be made official by legislative action. Far too simplistic were the abolitionists, mistakenly believing that they could change human behavior by legal fiat. "Centuries have been employed in complicating the evil," he wrote to Elizabeth Peabody, and then added prophetically, "I fear centuries may be required for its removal." Thus when his sister Lydia considered a school for black girls in Massachusetts similar to Prudence Crandall's undertaking, he assured her that it might be "one of the most Christian works in which anyone can engage." Believing himself free "of what is called the 'prejudice of color,'" he also believed that charity and education rather than abolition eventually would solve the "Negro problem."[1]

*   *   *

At the moment, abolitionism was a single *enfant terrible* in what appeared to the public view as a generally harmonious family of humanitarian reforms. By 1835, there was almost complete unanimity in support of Mann's efforts to heal the insane. With a small expenditure of money, he had procured an appropriation from an

[9] Mann to Elizabeth Peabody, July 5, 1835; Mann to Mary Peabody, July 25, 1837, Mann MSS:MHS.
[1] Mann to Lydia Mann, n.d. [ca. 1835]; Mann to Elizabeth Peabody, July 5, 1835, Mann MSS:MHS.

otherwise parsimonious General Court to add new wings to the Worcester Hospital. Actually, the expansion was an absolute necessity. While the public press lauded Mann for laying the ax to the belief that insanity was a direct visitation from God and not subject to "scientific treatment," those working in the hospital were becoming painfully aware that many of their patients were incurable. As their number grew, the space for remedial cases was diminished until the trustees feared that the hospital might become a monument to the incurability of the insane rather than the opposite.[2]

Similar to the treatment of the insane, a handful of leaders in the temperance movement also were worried about their slow progress and stood ready to move on a new tack. By 1835, a group of dissident activists, no longer satisfied with a moderate approach, were ready to steer the movement towards the goal of total abstinence. Instead of harmony, a giant rally sponsored by the Massachusetts Society for Temperance had spawned a pamphlet war in which one orthodox clergyman went so far as to quote the "prophet of Mecca" to prove that drinking was a carnal sin. As late as 1836, the moderates still were able to beat back all efforts to have the words "all intoxicating liquors" inserted into the organizational pledge, but they must have realized that their opponents would eventually prevail.[3]

By this time Mann, ever ready to mount a speakers platform and expound the virtues of total abstinence, had come to side with the radicals, his forced vehemence on the subject indicative of a weakening confidence. The early Massachusetts temperance men had depended on their ability to persuade the common man to a life of sobriety once they explained the dangers of intemperance. In the

---

[2] William B. Calhoun to Mann, January 1, 1835, Mann MSS:MHS; in their first proposals for the hospital, repeated statements were made that large percentages of the insane could be cured. As the result of this unexpected trend, however, the trustees used a different form of statistics and stressed individual cases in which there had been dramatic recoveries. See *Massachusetts Senate Documents, 1836*, No. 7, "Third Annual Report of the State Lunatic Hospital at Worcester, December 1835." Here the cases of twelve violently insane people who had previously been in chains for years—some even having committed homicides—were described. Now, at the hospital, all were leading a docile existence.

[3] *Proceedings of the Temperance Convention held in Boston on the Twenty-third of September, 1835* (Boston, 1836); Lucius M. Sargent, *Letter on the State of the Temperance Reform to the Reverend Caleb Stetson of Medford, Massachusetts* (Boston, 1836), p. 18; *Evening Mercantile Journal*, January 26 and 30, 1836; Mann to Mary Peabody, October 4, 1836, Mann MSS:MHS; Elizabeth Peabody to Mary Peabody, January 31, 1835, CJ in NYPL.

disappointing years which followed, they blamed wrong principles for their lack of success and spent interminable sessions debating the validity of voluntary total abstinence versus the necessity of legal prohibition as if these were their two vital and exclusive alternatives. What they did not understand was that both positions were but symptomatic of a gradual erosion of their faith in human reason and free will.

This change of faith only became evident as they began to shift their tactics. If calm intelligent appeals to reason would not work, then something both more evangelical and legal should be tried. In time, the Washingtonians and the abolitionists would mount an anti-intellectual and emotional attack to reshape human behavior, as would the more aristocratic Whigs in the political realm in electing the hero of Tippecanoe as President in 1840. Mann understood the limitations of persuasion and appeal to reason from firsthand experience. His carefully reasoned reports on comparative profits had saved no drunkards but had earned him the enmity of Boston grocers for his efforts. Now by 1836, he too was prepared to forge his message into the rhetoric of "a good old orthodox divine," as he described it, in order to achieve his ends.[4]

Revealing his loss of faith in the reasonableness of the common man, he criticized Elizabeth Peabody for including a "disrobing scene . . . such as usually have curtains drawn between them and the public eye," in a commentary on the *Iliad* she was writing. While not imputing Miss Peabody's purity of intent in using such illustrations, Mann priggishly doubted if there was "purity enough in the public mind for such an account." Similarly, he could now refer to the Federal Theater, where he once had enjoyed performances, as a "rallying point of dissipation" and give his hearty approval to plans for its alteration into a place of worship.[5] Mann's lack of confidence in the unguided intelligence of the public mind pointed to a more fundamental philosophical difference developing between himself and Elizabeth Peabody. In their discussions on the future of reform movements, she had expressed her belief in the power of an innate and independent moral faculty or free will by which each individual could overcome physical obstacles and moral temptations. Mann dis-

---

[4] Mann to Mary Peabody, October 4, 1836, Mann MSS: MHS.
[5] Mann to Elizabeth Peabody, September 6, [1836?], Mann MSS: MHS; [Elizabeth Palmer Peabody], *Record of a School Exemplifying the General Principles of Spiritual Culture* (Boston, 1835), pp. 9–10; Mann to Mary Peabody, March 6, 1837, Mann MSS: MHS.

agreed. Admittedly a man's action was the result of some "innate propensity," but he wanted Elizabeth to realize that it was also the result of "education, association, external condition, and a thousand other things, all which if we could see and measure, we should know their result, with just as much certainty as we know that a warm sun and genial rains will waken the earth to vegetation." Later, in a more jovial mood, he compared their two positions with considerable clarity.

You *will* have it, that there is a *will*, and I am under a *necessity* of maintaining *necessity;* and tho' you may associate, that I exhibit a most ungovernable will in maintaining necessity, yet I am certain that nothing but inexorable necessity could make you so stickle for the will.[6]

But beneath this humor lay two antagonistic positions. Miss Peabody was prepared to defend the omnipotence of free will, and the more she pressed her case, the greater was Mann's insistence upon the necessity of a controlled and supervised environment which would coerce men to lead virtuous lives. Halfway between an uncorrupted child of nature and a brutish beast, the common man needed guidance and directives from an ethical élite. "We all know," he wrote to his sister, "*that as a matter of fact,* men have some and even many righteous impulses and they are capable of having more, just as they do many wise and rational deeds and are capable of doing more." [7]

This qualified cynicism expressed itself in Mann's attitude towards abolition. As the movement gained public attention, it was embarrassing to note that some of the assumptions and goals of the abolitionists were not unlike those of other reforms. By attacking slavery as a violation of moral law, advocating the dignity of the individual, and appealing to humanitarian compassion, its spokesmen were claiming to rescue a class of persons that had been by-passed by other reformers. Noble as their singular intent was, they had gained only abuse for their efforts, and now seemed ready to pay any price, even that of civil war, to gain immediate manumission. Mann could only believe that their singlemindedness would jeopardize other humanitarian causes. While other reformers were attempting to unify and strengthen society, the Garrisonians in Massachusetts threatened to split it asunder.

---

[6] The quotations are from two undated letters from Mann to Elizabeth Peabody, 1836 file, Mann MSS:MHS.
[7] Mann to Lydia Mann, October 30, 1836, Mann MSS:MHS.

Even though he rationalized that human behavior stemmed from extremely complex origins and therefore concluded that the simplistic moral *modus operandi* of the abolitionists would not work, Mann was unable to apply the same critique to his own efforts. Early in his career he had enthusiastically identified the development of factories and railroads as embodiments of a long-awaited progress and prosperity. But opening the Pandoran box of "progress" had not produced a procession of unmixed blessings. It was easier to support industrial expansion in general than to make the numerous legal and social adjustments necessary with the rise of milltowns and the appearance of a propertyless proletariat of wage earners. Mann was at his eloquent best when he lauded the virtues of republican government, and he sincerely believed that within it resided the power ultimately to redeem all oppressed peoples in the world; but he was singularly inept in learning the art of compromise within the two-party system upon which his own government rested. Clearly "progress" had brought new problems and these were not amenable to the older moral absolutes of his childhood. The time had come for men to reformulate their values and walk upon the uncharted and untried ground of pragmatism and accommodation.

In some endeavors, such as his work with the insane, Mann was relatively successful. He also succeeded in his efforts to revise the state statutes, but here he made his best contributions in those areas in which an incisive sense of morality could actually simplify the issues. When he worked for a clearer definition of public and private property or proposed means for assisting insolvent debtors, his contributions were limited by his compulsion to conceive of the issues in terms of moral absolutes rather than working for an understanding of the indigenous forces which were creating them. Since he believed that private property provided the foundation for the existence of the family and also gave men the essential incentive to labor, he was unprepared to cope with developments in which property was taking new forms and serving less individual and moral purposes. When controlled by an impersonal corporation, property could become the means for concentrating economic power and procuring wealth for a few at the expense of the general community. And now most recently, he could not miss the fact that the right of property was being used to justify the institution of slavery. Rather than creating a social unity and a sense of Commonwealth, it seemed to be bolstering an even more rigid class society.

With such developments, Mann's belief that the state must serve

the people was being put to a demanding test. In rescuing the insolvent and the insane, he had assumed that neither the family nor the
village were fulfilling their duty towards their less fortunate members. Therefore, it had become necessary for the state to act as "the
parent of the people" and fill the void left behind as other agencies
abandoned their traditional responsibilities. But in the last two years
in the Senate, he had also seen the power of the state prostituted by
ambitious men to further their own selfish ends. Rather than restoring individual lives and protecting natural rights, the power of the
state was becoming a prize sought by opposing vested interests.

As issues in the Senate became more complex, the more the
older absolutes sounded like platitudes and less like viable principles.
How was one to determine what was true, honest, and just, when
dealing with contested elections, bridge charters, or the private and
public nature of the railroads? Moreover, how could one who had
learned to think in categories of right and wrong, or good and evil,
adjust himself to negotiations and compromises which were inevitable when political parties attempted to serve diverse and often conflicting groups in the Commonwealth? It was equally disturbing to
note that even when the state seemingly did act wisely, the action at
times was too late. Men, while theoretically amenable to intelligent
political and social efforts, often responded too slowly, hesitantly,
and with less than desirable results.

* * *

Mann did not miss the implications of all this for what remained
of his own family. Fully aware of the importance of "the malleability
of the metal as well as the strength of the blow," he increasingly
turned his attention to the education of his young nieces and nephews. Especially concerned about their reading matter, he sent them
didactic and moralistic volumes which emphasized the virtues of piety, obedience, frugality, and patriotism.[8] In his search for peace and

---

[8] Mann to Lydia Mann, November 20, 1835 and [1835?], Mann MSS:
MHS; Catherine Maria Sedgwick, *Home* (Boston, 1850), and *The Linwoods, or "Sixty Years Since" in America* (New York, 1835). The writings of Catherine Sedgwick found special favor with Mann and he
dispatched a copy of *Home* to his sister, hoping the children would not
only read it, but "imbibe its very substance and spirit." He also sent his
sister a copy of Miss Sedgwick's *The Linwoods* with a similar commenda-
tion.

security, Mann spoke increasingly of the family as the one remaining reliable and uncorrupted social institution. That which was unattainable to him became all the more idyllic and precious. "I suppose," he wrote to Mary Messer in mixed tones of envy and depression, ". . . you are returned from your visit and are once more in that most sacred of all places upon earth—*home;* and a member of that most divine institution in the worl *family.*" Such a joy, he hastened to add with self-pity and finality, could never be his. "I am shut out from society, for its common conversation inflicts wounds upon me perpetually, and when alone, I hear no cheering voice, I can see no affectionate looks, I have none of the endearments of home or family, and the heart famishes for want of its natural aliment." During his youth in Franklin, the family was taken for granted, and its outer edge blended almost indistinguishably with that of the community. Now in the Boston of his maturity, he frequently eulogized it and drew a sharp demarcation between the domestic circle and the more general society.[9]

After Charlotte's death, Mann had come to view the Messer family as the epitome of domestic bliss. Within their ranks, he had observed "a common consciousness and a desire for each other's welfare . . . [possessing] all the energy of self-love with the self-sacrifice of disinterested affection." Gone were his memories of their selfish overprotection of Charlotte which had robbed him of her companionship during their brief marriage. Instead, he only acknowledged their "inter-community of thought and feeling" and *"absolute unity,"* which now seemed so pure and benign, in comparison with the greed and self-seeking he had experienced in the world.[1]

The tenuous link he maintained with this little society of mutual help and respect was further weakened by the death of Asa Messer in 1836. Mann attended the funeral out of a sense of duty and devotion to this man whose help had meant so much to him. Yet as the group of mourners approached the North Burying Ground, the anguish which had gripped Mann at another burial there again came over him. Standing by the open grave as Messer's remains were lowered next to those of Charlotte, he experienced such a sense of desolation

---

[9] Mann to Mary Messer, October 2, 1836, Mann-Messer MSS:BUA.
[1] Mann to Elizabeth Peabody, November 6, 1836, Straker MSS:ACL; Mann to Lydia Mann, October 30, 1836, Mann MSS:MHS. After Charlotte's death, Mann continued to correspond with Mary Messer and sent Asa Messer copies of Boston newspapers. See Sydney Williams to Mann, January 28, 1835, Mann MSS:DHS.

that he could hardly keep from breaking down. Describing the intense agony of the incident, he recalled,

I looked upon the whole with the outward indifference of a statue. I felt my own heart compress and congeal and turn into stone and refuse communion with their outpouring sorrow. I looked upon the dead with envy and pitied the living, because they still lived. I escaped into insensibility—for had I wept like a true mourner one minute, I should have laughed like a maniac the next, and with the deepest hypocrisy, I administered consolation which I did not feel.

Only by forcing himself to play the role of a detached observer, apart from the group of mourners and refusing to identify himself with their grief, could he endure his misery.[2]

Messer's death was actually the second of two tragedies for Mann during this period. The year before, Silas Holbrook, a close associate, had died. Expressing his sense of irreparable loss, Mann wrote, "There is no man left in the world who loved me half as well, or would have done so much for me. . . . I do not expect to ever find another such friend to travel with me the residue of this wearying journey of life." With the demise of these two, he had lost the friendship of a man to whom he looked as a father, and another he had learned to love as a brother.[3]

One by one, death with an unrelenting and impersonal finality was methodically picking off the remaining members of his circle of family and friends. On one of his visits to the North Burying Ground in the autumn after Asa Messer's death, Mann stood in the cemetery, watching the western sky as a magnificent sunset reached a crescendo of light and color. Overwhelmed by its beauty and serenity, he momentarily lost all sense of the passage of time until he suddenly realized the color had turned to black and gray and he was standing alone in the twilight beside Charlotte's grave. To Mann, who was al-

---

[2] Mann to Elizabeth Peabody, November 6, 1836, Straker MSS: ACL.
[3] Mann to Lydia Mann, n.d. [1835], and Mann to Elizabeth Peabody, June 1, 1836, Mann MSS: MHS. Silas Holbrook died May 25, 1835. He had been a member of the Class of 1815 at Brown. During his friendship with Mann, he wrote the European section of Peter Parley's *Pictorial Geography* and was a popular contributor to the *New England Galaxy*, writing under the name of Jonathan Farbrik. Of him Mann stated, "I have never known a man who formed so correct a graduation of things according to their intrinsic and permanent values"; Mann to Mary Peabody, June 1, [1835], Mann MSS: MHS; *Appleton's Cyclopaedia of American Biography* (New York, 1887), III, 231.

ways seeking a moral from nature, the incident was disconcerting. Was this a demonstration of the universal peace and harmony in the world, he asked, or was it a mockery of the ever-present chaos, and a mockery of him? Even the signs from nature were no longer clear and explicit.[4]

Contrary to Elizabeth's hopes, Horace Mann's return to the General Court had not provided the means for his personal rehabilitation. While placing him in a position of political leadership, it had compounded his uncertainty about himself and his world by forcing him to deal with issues for which he was unprepared, both by education and temperament. During these two years in the Senate, the lawmakers had been confronted with problems less amenable to older modes of political action. Group loyalties were coalescing around new vocational, monetary, and religious centers of concern. Mann neither understood nor appreciated this, and usually viewed the new forms of collective action as thinly disguised attempts by special groups to utilize the power of the state for their selfish ends rather than furthering the interests of the entire Commonwealth. By habit and instinct, he continued to appeal to an individualistic sense of duty, honesty, and responsibility, even though at times it must have been clearly evident, even to him, that his efforts were inconsistent with the general trend of events.

*   *   *

By April, 1836, after having produced some of the most acrimonious and confused debates in its history, the Senate neared adjournment. In the course of the last three months, Mann had been accused of every highhanded method and form of duplicity in furthering the interests of his own party. Now, when the appropriate time came, the same Seth Whitmarsh who had bitterly opposed him for the president's chair rose and offered a resolution. Unanimously approved by the group, it thanked Mann "for the faithful, impartial, and satisfactory manner in which he . . . had discharged the duties of the chair. . . ." For the moment, it appeared as if the chamber was a forum of principled gentlemen, devoting themselves unselfishly to the service of the Commonwealth. Mann responded according to custom, thanking them for their sincerity and acknowledging that there was "no higher ambition than the performance of duty" and that

---

[4] Mann to Mary Messer, October 2, 1836, Mann-Messer MSS:BUA.

"among the noblest . . . rewards" was the "approbation of intelligent and virtuous men." He promised to retain the fondest recollection of their "generous and confiding conduct" towards him and wished them the best of "individual prosperity and happiness." The ritual completed, the Senators returned to debate a remaining bank charter bill still on their agenda. Once again factions formed and accusations flew. And it took six standing votes before Mann could gavel the final adjournment.[5]

---

[5] Journal of the Senate, Vol. 57, April 16, 1836, pp. 535–536, MS in MSA.

CHAPTER XI

The Transient and the Intrinsic

The greatest obstacle to being heroic is the doubt
whether one may not be going to prove one's self
a fool; the truest heroism is, to resist the doubt;
and the profoundest wisdom, to know when it ought
to be resisted, and when to be obeyed.
NATHANIEL HAWTHORNE

IF 1837 WAS TO BE a year of decision for Mann, the events of January and February gave him few clues to this possibility. The first sessions of the Senate began much as they had before, with one exception; he was re-elected president on the first ballot. Otherwise, it seemed as if he had lived through all this once before and was beginning the second cycle of a tedious legislative treadmill with troublesome issues at every step. Once again the Democrats claimed "foul play" in the local election returns, only to be silenced by the Whig majority. Next, the backers of the still uncompleted Boston and Lowell Railroad returned, this time asking permission to go hat in hand to private investors for an additional $150,000. Mann appointed a committee to study the request, and the result was a comprehensive report which went far beyond the subject of railroads and laid a basis for distinguishing between private and public corporations.[1]

Every mailbag also brought petitions for new bank charters. From the same bags came other requests from existing banks for the right to increase their capital and thus maintain their lead over the new entrepreneurs. Abandoning any guise of impartiality, Mann repeatedly stepped down from the chair and opposed the would-be *nouveaux riches* in favor of established institutions. Those banks al-

---

[1] *Journal of the Senate*, Vol. 58, January 6, 1837, MS in MSA; accounts of the opening of the General Court and Mann's re-election are in the *Daily Advertiser and Patriot*, January 4 and 5, 1837; the Boston *Evening Transcript*, January 4, 5, and 7, 1837; *Journal of the Senate*, Vol. 58, January 4–11, 1837, pp. 1–40; and *Massachusetts Senate Documents*, *1837*, No. 83.

ready under the control of the Commonwealth could be given additional power, he reasoned, while chartering a menagerie of new lending agencies only made the supervisory work of the state more difficult.[2]

Then, too, the abolitionists refused to leave the General Court in peace. Just when it seemed these agitators had exhausted their arsenal of causes and everyone's patience, southern Congressmen imposed the "Pinkney gag rule" on all anti-slavery petitions sent to the House of Representatives. In so doing, they unwittingly handed the Garrisonians a new issue on which to regroup. Now bombarding the General Court with petitions containing thousands of signatures, they insisted that theirs was not only the cause of the enslaved, but of all freemen as well, since the southern "slavocracy" had begun to undermine the rights of petition and free speech. When it was no longer possible to ignore their clamor, Mann appointed a committee to study the recent actions at the Capitol. Later the Senate issued a surprisingly sharp attack on any attempt to suppress the right of petition. Then going beyond this, the Senators also deplored the existence of slavery in the District of Columbia and called for its prohibition in any new states admitted to the Union. Reluctantly agreeing with the abolitionists, the Senate labeled any attempt "to abridge the free expression of opinions through the medium of public mail" an attack on the Constitution and an "infringement of the dearest rights of freemen." [3]

It was something of a relief to deal with such an issue. The shift from abolition and the rights of corporate property to the rights of free speech and petition enabled the lawmakers to take an unequivocal stand. Here compromise was unnecessary. The "Pinkney gag rule" was a clear-cut violation of human rights, and in a rare show of unanimity, the Senate rose, almost as a man, and approved a resolve

---

[2] For Mann's stand on a number of these proposals, see Journal of the Senate, Vol. 58, March 9, 16, and 28, and April 4 and 11, 1837, pp. 312, 338–340, 399, 437, and 486, MS in MSA.

[3] For a discussion of the petition strategy of the abolitionists, the gag rules, and John Quincy Adams's attempts in the House of Representatives to vindicate the right of petition, see Gerald P. Nye, *Fettered Freedom: Civil Liberties and the Slavery Controversy, 1830–1860* (East Lansing, 1949), pp. 32–54; Gilbert H. Barnes, *The Antislavery Impulse, 1830–1844* (New York, 1933), pp. 109–145; *Massachusetts Senate Documents, 1837*, Nos. 65 and 84; *Acts and Resolves of the Commonwealth of Massachusetts, 1837* (Boston, 1837), Ch. LXXV, "Resolve on the Sundry petitions relative to Slavery in the District of Columbia, and the right of Petition."

condemning the recent action of the House of Representatives. With expressions reminiscent of earlier struggles in Boston, the sons of the Revolution now had their chance to rise and defend their inalienable rights as freemen. In this, Mann joined wholeheartedly.[4]

Similar unanimity could not be found on any other question. When it came to the education of children, the issue was the cost of schools rather than the right to a free education. By the early 1830's the federal government was finally prepared to compensate 'Massachusetts for the services of its militia in the War of 1812. Anticipating a windfall, a few men in the General Court urged that the money received be used to form a fund whose income would be spent to improve public education throughout the state. An early plan for this failed in the legislature, but in 1834, a law was passed which provided that part of the money received was to be deposited in an interest-bearing common school fund.[5]

How these funds were to be distributed was specified in the revised statutes which Mann had helped create. These required that each town raise "one dollar for each person belonging to said town" in order to share in the income from the fund. Clearly the intent was to use state money to stimulate local efforts. Good intentions, however, were a poor safeguard against the very opposite happening. According to Governor Edward Everett, so distributed, the income from the fund encouraged towns to raise only the very minimum required by the laws and then look to the state for the rest. Noting that New York had apportioned its funds to communities in a direct ratio to the amount they raised by taxing themselves, Everett thought this arrangement might be used to reinforce local initiative.[6]

Until 1837, the educational problems confronting school committees and parents had consumed a very small portion of Mann's time. In both the House and Senate, he had passed up appointments on the Committee on Education to take posts on the more influential Judiciary Committee. Nor had he been as active outside the General Court in working for better schools as he had been in the temperance

---

[4] Journal of the Senate, Vol. 58, March 30, 1837, p. 413, MS in MSA.
[5] *Massachusetts House Documents, 1831*, No. 22; *Laws of the Commonwealth of Massachusetts, 1834* (Boston, 1834), Ch. CLXIX, "An Act to Establish the Massachusetts School Fund"; Charles Bullock, *Historical Sketch of the Finances and Financial Policy of Massachusetts, from 1780–1905* (New York, 1907), p. 37.
[6] Edward Everett, "Address of his Excellency Edward Everett to the Two Branches of the Legislature . . . January 4, 1837," *Massachusetts Senate Documents, 1837*, No. 1, p. 18.

cause. Some of his closest friends, including Samuel Gridley Howe and William B. Calhoun, had helped organize the American Institute of Instruction, which hoped to spearhead the reform of the common schools; but Mann considered other humanitarian causes more promising.[7]

Once established, the school fund became a plum which the legislators simply could not leave alone. A few visionaries thought it could be the means by which the state would assume control of all the public or "common" schools, as they were called. Mann went along with a handful of others who wanted the income to support a public high school in each county. Meanwhile, a petition from the American Institute of Instruction called for the establishment of several state teachers' seminaries. This latter proposal received the backing of James G. Carter, chairman of the House Committee on Education and staunch advocate of the public education. Speaking in support of the petition, Carter pointed to recent "riots . . . by infuriated mobs." In part, these had happened because a large class of citizens had not been educated to respect the law. As suffrage was extended to all men, so must the opportunity for free public schooling. Instead of this, however, Carter claimed that those who should have known better, the propertied classes, had responded by establishing private academies so that their children could be segregated from those of the common man. If this continued, he feared the nation would become irreparably divided. The solution was to improve the common schools so that children from all classes would attend them.

---

[7] Mann was not listed as a member, officer, nor participant in any of the years from 1830 to 1836. See the *Lectures Delivered before the American Institute of Instruction, Including the Journal of Proceedings* (Boston, 1830–36). Mann did give one lecture on education in 1832 before the local teachers organization in Dedham. The speech was general, filled with a mixture of common sense and exhortations, Mann spending a good portion of his time elaborating on the invaluable service teachers rendered in educating the future electorate. His summary of the educational process included the following definition:

Hence a general idea of education, we perceive, involves a consideration of all those processes by which one portion of the human race can rescue another portion from all the degradations and sufferings of ignorance, of oppression, and can confer upon them both the pleasures and the utilities of knowledge and the peace, the happiness and the security of freedom.

It was clear that he conceived of education as one more endeavor through which a group of men could save others and restore them to some sort of individual dignity. He paid lip service to education as an important reform, but at the moment, and in the immediate future, he would confine his interests to the Norfolk Association of Teachers at Dedham, Feb. [25], 1832, MS in Mann MSS:MHS; Records of the Norfolk Association of Teachers, February 25, 1832, MS in DHS.

To accomplish this, the first step would be to improve the quality of teaching and this could best be done by using the income from the school fund to establish teachers' seminaries as the American Institute of Instruction had requested.[8]

While the House debated the desirability of special schools for training teachers, the Senate considered a plan for the direct support of the common schools. Realizing that the payment from the federal government might be as much as $2 million, Mann reported to Elizabeth Peabody that "A few of us have set our hearts upon it being restricted to purposes of education. We mean if possible to turn it all into ideas." In previous sessions he had successfully advocated the cause of religious freedom, the building of the lunatic asylum, and the passage of stricter licensing laws. In each of these he had triumphed by persuading a majority to his side. It was now time that he threw his weight in support of education. Recognizing far more latent opposition then he thought existed, Mann took special pains to prepare a speech in behalf of more aid to the schools. At a crucial moment in the debate, he stepped from the chair and took the familiar role of advocate for an unpopular cause.[9]

The people had a choice. Either they could invest the money in "some great, permanent, public object, where its benefits will be universal, enduring and progressive," or it would be wasted for "objects of a transient nature that at the end of a year neither the money nor the object will remain." [1] Mann therefore proposed that the money be distributed as a bounty to those towns which taxed themselves $3 for every student between the ages of four and fourteen within their boundaries.[2] Then professing his own brand of egalitarianism, Mann continued,

---

[8] Journal of the Senate, Vol. 58, February 16, 1837, pp. 214–215, MS in MSA; Henry Barnard, *Normal Schools and other Institutions, Agencies, and Means Designed for the Professional Education of Teachers* (Hartford, 1851), p. 84; James G. Carter, *Speech of Mr. Carter, of Lancaster, Delivered in House of Representatives of Massachusetts, February, 1837* (Boston, 1837), pp. 5–18, *passim.*

[9] Mann to Elizabeth Peabody, February 7, 1837, Mann MSS:MHS.

[1] This and the succeeding quotations are taken from [Horace Mann], "Speech on the Disposal of the State Fund of 2 Million Dollars," [February, 1837], MS in Mann MSS:MHS.

[2] The figure was about the average spent per pupil at the time. In 1836, the school committees spent $439,590:40 on 166,912 pupils, or a little less than $3 per pupil, as reported in the *American Annals of Education*, VII (1837), pp. 93–94. Mann's proposal would have encouraged those communities spending less than the average to increase their expenditures.

My creed is that God made of one blood all children of men, and that circumstances have caused the diversities among them. Those orders and conditions of life amongst us, now stamped with inferiority are capable of rising to the common level, and of ascending if that level ascends. Any other faith is arrogant towards men and impious towards heaven.

In a republic, diversity was unwelcome and even detrimental. The schools had the responsibility to protect the equality of its children.

Yet something was wrong with the general public intelligence, Mann thought. How else could one explain the fact that the people had paid the unprecedented amount of $50,000, or as much as the combined salaries they paid all their teachers, to be titillated by the French dancer Fanny Ellsler, whose chief attraction he claimed "consisted in the scantiness of her wardrobe"? Such twisted values must be laid at the doorsteps of the schools. The nation was in trouble, and in a spirited climax, Mann vividly described the urgency of the situation. "Sir, the folly of sitting still, while houses adjoining mine, on either side, are on fire, is not to be compared with the folly, in a government like ours, of neglecting the education of the young."

Having been disappointed by the intelligence of the people, Mann was soon to be disappointed by the intelligence of their representatives as well. Actually, none of the proposals for public high schools, teachers' seminaries, or more direct state aid to the common schools had a chance. A majority of both Whigs and Democrats had agreed from the first weeks of the session that the money from the federal government should be spent otherwise. After giving everyone a chance to speak in behalf of the schools, they unceremoniously pushed through a law which allocated but half of the sum to the school fund and then removed the minimum tax requirement of $1 per person in order for a town to qualify for income from it. The other half of the money, they distributed directly to the towns for roads, bridges, almshouses, jails, and "other public objects of expenditure." When the smoke had cleared, it was evident that the crucial vote had nothing to do with the future of republican government or the need for higher moral standards. Instead, it dealt with whether the 1830 or the 1837 census was to be used in distributing the funds. For these hardheaded and sometimes cynical lawmakers, it was more important to serve their grassroots constituency by lowering local taxes than to worry about the amount of money Bostonians were paying to ogle at a shameless French dancer.[3]

Understanding their motives made it all the more difficult for Mann to endure the defeat. He could even understand their reluctance to finance a new scheme for teacher training, but how was one to explain their rejection of his arguments for more aid to the time-honored common schools which he based upon the good old-fashioned virtues of patriotism and public duty? If he had done his homework in preparing his speech back at his law office, however, he had not done his footwork in the corridors of the State House to garner the votes. He could no more prevent the dispersal of public money for transient purposes with rhetoric and moral fervor than he could hold back the tide with his hands. To be defeated on a specific measure was a common happening in the life of a politician, but Mann was unaccustomed to losing a debate and found the rejection of his arguments particularly humiliating. In a mood of disappointment and dejection, he reported to the Peabody sisters that "My ideas produced no effect." Such an experience could only reinforce Mann's belief that the public needed guidance in seeking its true interests and determining the good of the Commonwealth.[4]

*   *   *

One of the decisive roll calls which signaled the complete rout of the school proponents took place on February 28. On this same day the Massachusetts Temperance Society joined with hundreds of sister organizations throughout the world in observing an International Temperance Day. If on Beacon Hill Mann was unable to prevent the legislature from cheating children out of their educational birthrights, at the Odeon, where temperance reformers from all over the state were gathering, he saw to it that the children received their due.

---

[3] The *Daily Centinel and Gazette* on January 18, 1837, reported both parties agreeing that the federal surplus should go to the towns. As a pro-Whig paper, it wanted to spike any Democratic attempt to claim all the credit for obtaining the money for the local committees. Also see the *Centinel* for February 2, 1837.

For a record of the Senate, see Vol. 58, February 16, 21, and 28, 1837, pp. 213–215, 240, and 398, MS in MSA; the final law passed is in *Laws of the Commonwealth of Massachusetts, 1837* (Boston, 1837), Ch. LXXXV; *Massachusetts Senate Documents, 1837*, No. 42.

[4] Mann to Mary and Elizabeth Peabody, n.d. [February, 1837], Mann MSS:MHS.

In addition to the general evening meeting for adults, Mann arranged to have the teachers bring their charges for a special afternoon rally, believing that the children would benefit from "early impressions in favor of temperance," and that by appropriating one afternoon in the year to the subject, the community was contributing to "the welfare of their whole lives." On the appointed day, the children filed out of their classrooms throughout the city and marched to the Odeon where they sang "America," and were addressed on the evils of intemperance by no less than eight speakers. Then probably welcoming the slight relief, they rose and sang a hymn which included the following stanza:

> " 'Tis but a drop,—I need it now"—
> The staggering drunkard said:
> "It was my food in infancy—
> My meat, my drink, my bread.
> A drop—a drop—Oh let me have,
> 'Twill so refresh my soul!"
> He took it, trembled, drank and died,
> Grasping the fatal bowl.

Program organizers distributed tracts and medals. From all of this, the correspondent for the society ecstatically reported that it was always delightful "to see the Odeon filled with human beings, congregated for some holy purpose," but the present occasion "was one of thrilling interest, and caused tears of joy to roll down the cheeks of the spectators; for instead of parents were to be seen the *children*." Naïve, and even ludicrous, perhaps. Yet it was also a sign of the urgency sensed by the temperance reformers, who felt compelled to save the pure in heart before they were corrupted by society.[5]

All this did not imply any slackening in their efforts to convert adults. Mann had written numerous invitations for speakers in order to assure an impressive array of talent at the evening meeting. While the young Charles Sumner brusquely turned aside his request, no less a personage than William Ellery Channing had consented to be on hand. That night the Odeon was filled with a standing room only crowd of old-time supporters and recent converts, everyone expecting a boost for his morale and a reaffirmation of his convictions. As one

---

[5] A description of the event is found in N.a., "Juvenile Temperance Celebration," *Twenty-fifth Report of the Council of the Massachusetts Temperance Society, Presented at the Annual Meeting, May 26, 1837* . . . (Boston, 1837).

speaker relinquished the rostrum to the next, the audience sensed that the high point of the evening was at hand when Channing, the leader of New England Unitarianism and genteel philosopher of social reform, stepped to the podium. They were not disappointed, but they were surprised.[6]

After giving perfunctory attention to the cause of temperance, Channing urged his listeners to think about improving the common schools. On every hand men were ready with solutions to social problems, ranging from simple-minded panaceas to far-reaching political and economic reforms. Channing reminded his listeners, however, that nothing was more necessary than "men of superior gifts, and of benevolent spirit," who would "devote themselves to the instruction of the less enlightened classes." He encouraged reluctant philanthropists to support such men. Summing up the benefits which might result, he concluded:

One gifted man, with his heart in his work, who should live among the uneducated, to spread useful knowledge and quickening truth, by conversation and books, by frank and friendly intercourse, by encouraging meetings for improvement, by forming the more teachable into classes, and giving to these the animation of his presence and guidance . . . one gifted man, so devoted, might impart a new tone and spirit to a considerable society.[7]

For all of his efforts, Mann could not attend the celebration at the Odeon. After two years of the most grueling schedule of legal cases, he was approaching the point where he would soon be out from under his and Stanley's debts. The last week in February found him back in Dedham, representing his clients before the Court of Common Pleas. At the very time when Channing was speaking, Mann himself was giving an address on temperance at Reverend Lamson's meetinghouse. This was not to say that he had missed the general content of Channing's remarks since he had heard them earlier when given to a smaller audience. Mann heartily approved of the speech and probably urged Channing to repeat it at the Odeon. "One gifted man" with an active and generous mind was all that the

---

[6] Mann to Charles Sumner, February, 1837; Mann to Mary and Elizabeth Peabody, n.d. [March, 1837]; Mann to Mary Peabody, March 6, 1837, all in Mann MSS:MHS.
[7] William E. Channing, *Address on Temperance Delivered by Request of the Council of the Massachusetts Temperance Society at the Odeon, February 28, 1837* (Boston, n.d.), pp. 2–25.

preacher requested, and yet from such leaven, he hoped to improve the "tone and spirit" of a considerable portion of the community. It was an optimistic and possibly unrealistic proposal, but the reform impulse was made of such stuff.[8]

At a time when so many others were bent on making money, Channing's words rang true and clear to Mann. Within the temperance movement he had gained a sense of identity, purpose, and permanence, which had eluded him in both the General Court and his law practice, and he gave every indication that he received more satisfaction from being elected vice-president of the Massachusetts Temperance Society than president of the state Senate. "I begin to believe," he wrote to Mary Peabody, "that the triumph of this cause will be one of my compensations, if doomed to live much longer. . . ." And when he failed to observe a single "staggerer" on the Boston Common on Independence Day, he jubilantly recorded in his Journal, " *Laus Deo et societatibus temperantiae!* " Since the will power and moral resolution of the common man at times was inadequate and it was therefore necessary to remove temptations along his path, Mann thought that there were literally "thousands and tens of thousands of inebriates who never would have been so, had the tavern and the dram shop been five miles from their homes." Somehow he would not allow himself to think that the temperance reform, and all other efforts to perfect men and women, might be doomed because excessive and irrational behavior was an inextricable part of human nature.[9]

*　　*　　*

If a juxtaposition of his recent experiences in the General Court with those of the temperance movement helped Mann to distinguish between the transient and the intrinsic, other events in 1837 etched the distinction even more sharply in his mind. During this period, death again visited his diminishing circle of family and friends, and with each tragedy, Mann let himself sink more deeply into a miasma of morbid self-pity which far outlasted any conventional period of mourning. His mother died early this year and as he attempted to record the salutary influence she had had upon his life, he soon fell

[8] Mann to Lydia Mann, January 25, 1836; Mann to Mary Peabody, March 6, 1837, all in Mann MSS:MHS.
[9] Mann to Mary Peabody, March 6, 1837, Mann MSS:MHS; Mann, *Life*, 56, April 29, 1837; Mann, Journal, July 4, 1837, MS in MHS.

back to his own plight as he had with the deaths of Asa Messer and Silas Holbrook. "My first feeling is," he lamented, "not that bad, but that good fortune had overtaken the departed." He thought of himself "on the isthmus, between time and eternity," having "long ago left the earth," but not yet having "entered the world beyond it." And with the loss of his mother, once again the memory of Charlotte's death overflowed the mental restraints in which he attempted to confine it.

Little now remained of his immediate family. His father, a proud yeoman of Franklin, had sired three sons and two daughters, who were to have been the fourth generation to live on Mann's Plain. Now both parents had died and both his brothers' lives had ended in tragedy. All that remained was a sister, Rebecca, widowed a few years after her marriage; Lydia, well on her way to spinsterhood; and himself, a widower. Even the farm, which through the years had remained a symbol of independence and continuity for the Manns, was now in jeopardy.[1] Within a year, it too would be lost to Lydia's creditors, a last bitter reminder of Stanley's excessive ambition. When she was finally forced to leave the house on Mann's Plain, Mann offered his sister the grim consolation that "the line of human beings, that preceded us into the world, have now almost all left it . . . and in all probability [we] shall be the next to leave it." If the family line was to continue, the responsibility rested with the next generation, the children of Stanley and Rebecca.[2]

Acting on this belief, Mann invited his nephew, Calvin Pennell, now in his late teens, to come to Boston during "anniversary week" when the many reform societies held their annual meetings. Lest Calvin expect a week of carnival and sightseeing, Mann was specific in what his nephew could anticipate.

Three or four public societies will hold their meetings each day, when the general condition of the Society, the prosperity of the cause in which they have embarked etc., etc., will be the subjects for reports, speeches etc. Among them will be the Education Society, the Abolition Society, etc., etc. It is a most interesting week, full of instruction and of stimulus to a young mind. I wish you to witness it.

[1] Mann to Mary Peabody, March 6, 1837; Mann to Elizabeth Peabody, March 20, 1837; Mann to Lydia Mann, n.d. [February, 1837], all in Mann MSS:MHS.
[2] Mann to Lydia Mann, n.d. [ca. 1837], and November 27, 1837, Mann MSS:MHS; Journal, March 28, 1838, MS in MHS.

When he arrived in the city, Calvin found the Boston Common virtually covered with large tents. Some societies met here while other less prosperous ones congregated in nearby churches. Each day brought more meetings. Minutes were read, reports given, and spirited speeches delivered to goad the backsliders and strengthen the less than zealous. Occasionally it was not the outside world which was the enemy, but a dissident member who expressed some heresy to the true believers. The meetings came to life as new policies on manumission, the licensing of taverns, and the right of women to vote were hammered out. All this could be downright tedious, even for a country lad on his first trip to Boston, but for Mann, it had become the central purpose and saving grace of his life. Calvin dutifully followed his uncle from one meeting to another, being introduced to the leading reformers of the day and forced to listen to Mann's running commentary as the sessions progressed. Even when they took relief from this and visited the Charlestown Navy Yard, there was no respite from Mann's moralizing. While the teen-ager could be fascinated by the complex network of the rigging, the gleaming brass fittings, the polished rosewood railings, the somber cannons, and the sheer size of the ships in drydock, as his uncle had once been, the older man now could only decry the huge sums being expended on "mighty engines" of destruction, which should have been "devoted to the development of reason and the diffusion of Christian principles."[3]

Clearly, Mann's commitment to what he considered the highest interests of humanity was almost becoming an obsession with him. Four days after his forty-first birthday, he wrote to Lydia claiming that his desire for "worldly distinction" had died away. In its place was his hope that "such parts of the social system" as were within his influence would be left "a little better than when he found them." In his remaining days, he would concentrate on those things which would directly help mankind. In these there was at least some semblance of permanence.[4]

Nor did he limit such sentiments to his immediate family. The last few months had witnessed particularly stormy sessions in the General Court. Repeatedly, Mann's rulings were challenged by an angry opposition which had demanded more than ninety roll-call votes. On one occasion his opponents had brought all proceedings to a halt by boycotting a session and preventing a quorum. Then just before

---

[3] Mann to Calvin Pennell, May 23, 1837, Mann MSS:MHS; Mann Journal, June 1 and 2, 1837, MS in MHS.
[4] Mann to Lydia Mann, April 8, 1837, Mann MSS:MHS.

final adjournment, ceremonial equanimity returned to the chamber as one of the Senators rose and thanked Mann for the "faithful and impartial manner" in which he had "discharged the duties of the presiding officer." The words had a familiar ring in his ears, and for good reason. They were a carbon copy of those spoken in a similar ceremony the year before. Mann, however, was thoroughly nettled by this time and refused to be a partner to such a hollow ritual. Instead of glossing over the partisan disputes, he responded by lecturing his contentious colleagues on their duties as representatives of the people. It was their task to put personal interests aside and work so that those "social institutions" which they had been called to administer were "both wiser and better" because of their service. Only in so doing would they earn "the highest of all human eulogies." If the admonition did not resemble his remarks on a similar occasion the year before, it did bear a striking resemblance to his recent correspondence with Lydia. Much of what he wrote at this time was a variation on the single theme of fulfilling one's duty.[5]

* * *

If Mann needed additional proof to convince himself of the virtue of helping others, he thought he found it in the efforts of two of his friends, Dr. Samuel Gridley Howe and Reverend Edward Taylor. By 1837, after a slow and tedious beginning which would have stopped a man of lesser mettle and optimism, Samuel Gridley Howe was finally making headway with his charges at the New England Institution for the Education of the Blind. Here Mann observed students "reading" maps, designs, and raised letters through their finger tips and writing their names on slates especially devised by Howe. In fact he was so impressed with what he saw, that he urged the trustees

---

[5] Journal of the Senate, Vol. 58, April 7, 1837 (unnumbered page inserted between pp. 452 and 453); April 19, 1837, pp. 549–550, MS in MSA; *Daily Centinel and Gazette*, April 20, 1837; what Mann did not say is perhaps even more revealing of his attitude toward politics at the time. In a preliminary draft for this speech in the Mann MSS:MHS, he wrote the following paragraph which he later deleted:

The opportunity to compare and interchange opinions with wise and honorable men, upon great question[s] of public and individual welfare, thereby to select and adopt whatever is right and to repudiate or rectify whatever is wrong, I have always regarded one of the choicest privileges of a human being. It is, therefore, with a proportionate regret, that I see the present opportunity, hastening to its close. I feel, too, that it is not as Senators only, that we have assembled in the chamber and met around this board, but that we have associated together in the higher character of citizens and men.

of the school to send copies of the New Testament to each state governor and to schools for the blind in Europe. Typically, he also drew a moral for himself and others from Howe's work, claiming that "If the powers of the human mind and the resources of wealth were directed to ameliorate the condition of the unfortunate and afflicted instead of being devoted to selfish and sensual gratifications, what a different world this would be." Men could speak in general terms about the "recuperative powers of the race," but Howe was actually proving what this meant in a demonstrably concrete way. If the blind could make progress toward perfectibility, how much more was possible for those who labored under far less imposing handicaps. The remarkable joining of Thomas Perkins's money and Howe's selfless and resourceful teaching gave an aura of plausibility to Channing's idealistic proposal that a similar combination of philanthropy and dedicated effort would work wonders in the common schools.[6]

Mann also had unbounded admiration for the efforts of "Father" Taylor. Often finding the clientele of Channing's Federal Street Church too rich and exclusive for his tastes, Mann walked down to the waterfront and listened to the preaching of the rough-hewn, outspoken preacher at Seamen's Bethel. What a remarkable man Edward Taylor must have been to have captured the imagination and admiration of both the tough-minded and the sentimental of the time. Emerson described him as a second Jeremy Taylor; Whitman claimed he was an "essentially perfect orator"; Melville was moved to use him as the prototype for Father Mapple in *Moby Dick;* but to Mann, he was even more. He was "the noblest *man*" he had ever known. At times Father Taylor could be embarrassingly candid when he described the temptations which abounded in the seaport of Boston. Violating virtually every rule of grammar, he called up nautical metaphors not always perfectly spliced to the real event he was describing. Mann excused all these faults in Taylor as he would in no other. Here was a minister who spoke as "soul speaks to soul." [7]

At the time it was probably difficult to explain how Mann and other sophisticated Bostonians could be attracted to both Channing

---

[6] N. Adams to Mann, January 28, 1837, Mann MSS:MHS; Mann, Journal, May 4 and 12, 1837, MS in MHS; *Letters and Journals of Samuel Gridley Howe,* II, 96–97.

[7] Mann Journal, May 21, 26, and 29, 1837, MS in MHS; Ralph Waldo Emerson, *Journals* (Boston, 1910), IV, 155–157; Harriet Martineau, *Retrospect of Western Travel* (London, 1838), III, 240–250; Walt Whitman, *Complete Prose Works of Walt Whitman* (New York, 1902), VII, 110–111.

and Taylor. Superficially the men were poles apart; the one phleg-
matic, sensitive, and nervous, a genteel and highly articulate soft-
spoken minister, who in the course of his thoughts had attempted to
reduce the practice of religion to pure reason. The other a robust and
impulsive man, a fire-and-brimstone evangelist, preaching to the human flotsam of the seven seas, to whom, as Mann recognized, words
and sentences were subordinate instruments to the vivid images and
moral lessons he drew. Yet both the philosopher and the revivalist addressed themselves to social evils, agreeing that these were neither
the result of any innate depravity in man nor simply caused by de-
fective social and economic institutions which could be corrected.
Rather, they were the result of increased temptations, and a weakening of men's moral resolution. One man expressed a rational, humanitarian optimism, while the other used an evangelical vocabulary
which included universal atonement, quick conversion, and an imminent millennium; but both agreed on the possibility of human perfection and emphasized the importance of individual free will and
the need for society to elevate all its members as intelligent moral beings. Their settings and their audiences were different, but to Mann
each of the ministers was an embodiment of the ideals which he himself was seeking. As an expression of his special appreciation for Father Taylor, Mann took up a collection from "a few gentlemen" and
sent him $70 with which to take a vacation, reasoning that through
the "alchemy of exercise," inanimate money could be transmuted
into health. Charity still seemed the most effective way to change
wealth and effort into good results.[8]

How different Channing, Howe, and Taylor were also from the
men who spent most of their working hours on State Street. As he
spoke with his colleagues and solicited their support for one or another humanitarian cause, Mann was pained to see how much their
interests lay elsewhere, in new sources of water power, discount rates
on out-of-town bank drafts, cheap Irish labor, and prospects for markets yet undeveloped. All these were the means to no better and more
lasting purpose than personal aggrandizement and the accumulation
of wealth. Although Mann always pressed the causes of temperance,
education, and charity with them, invariably they turned the conversation to ways of reducing costs and enlarging their profits. Missing was any older sense of paternalism or responsibility to their em-

[8] Mann to Mary Peabody, June 25, 1837, Mann MSS:MHS; Mann,
Journal, May 26 and June 4, 1837, MS in MHS.

ployees and customers. Mann may have deplored the fact that the new impersonal corporations they were founding were not subject to moral law since they had neither a soul to damn nor a body to kick, but it was this very impersonality which made the corporation a more effective instrument for amassing wealth. Apparently, these were a new breed of Yankee enterprisers whose quest for economic power outweighed every other consideration. "When," Mann asked in a moment of utter dejection, "will the human mind be instructed to arrange things upon a scale according [to] their intrinsic value, so as to refuse for the future, the precedence to trivial and transitory objects over universal and immortal interests?" [9]

That economic success could indeed be a transitory object was bitterly acknowledged by many others than Horace Mann during April and May of 1837. Unprepared for the consequences of Andrew Jackson's war on the United States Bank, and therefore caught in the financial panic which followed in its wake, hundreds of Boston merchants were pushed to the wall. With every edition of the newspaper came announcements of additional business failures, including some of the most respected names in the city. By May 12, seventy-eight major mercantile houses had gone under and many others were on the verge of bankruptcy. Even the apparently sound and well-established firm of Henry Lee, Mann's friend and benefactor, had collapsed, setting off a chain reaction of failures among Lee's creditors. No one considered himself safe as the effects of the panic reached an ever wider circle of victims; and to make matters worse, its causes seemed beyond the control and understanding of those involved. Mann himself made no attempt to analyze the economic processes at work. Instead, he could only conclude that recent events offered the most convincing proof of the futility of an inordinate quest for money and the power it could wield, at the expense of every other value.[1]

That the entire community was beginning to reap the fruits of its ill-gotten gains was also evident from other events during this period. One night while he was asleep in his office, a gang of incendiaries attempted to set fire to the roof and attic of the building. Although it did not come close enough to singe Mann's hair, just the threat of a fire, the smell of smoke, and the shouts from men on the

---

[9] Mann, Journal, May 13 and 15, 1837, MS in MHS.
[1] Mary Peabody to Mann, May 7, 1837, Mann MSS:MHS; Mann, Journal, May 11 and 16, 1837, MS in MHS; *Evening Mercantile Journal*, May 12, 1837.

pumpers to flee the building was a terrifying experience. "Would such things happen," he asked himself, "if moral instruction were not infinitely below what it ought to be?" These atrocities were not motivated by a spirit of revenge, but "from the wantonness of malignity." And in his Journal that night, he wrote, "When will society like a mother, take care of *all* her children?" [2]

Less than two weeks later, Boston witnessed an ugly riot which was too large to hide from the public view. While on their way to answer a fire alarm, a group of hot-headed engine men collided with an Irish funeral procession on Broad Street. In the violence which erupted, stores and houses were pillaged and dozens of persons injured. When the smoke had cleared and the debris been carted away, Mann brooded over the episode. No doubt, still remembering the destruction of the Ursuline Convent, he assumed that the Irish would bear the brunt of the blame. "Antipathies will pursue the foreigner . . . sympathies will protect the natives, punishment will be administered with an unequal hand," was his gloomy threefold prediction. Nevertheless, he did what he could by meeting with some of the leading citizens of Boston at the office of the Visitors of the Poor and forming a committee to organize a collection for the relief of the riot victims. [3]

Beyond his inclination to sympathize with the less fortunate, in this case, the "foreigner," the event gave him cause to analyze the reason for a growing disrespect for order in Boston. It seemed to him that men thought force rather than due process was the way to redress their grievances, and when they violated the rights of others through overt acts, they were "*almost* applauded" by the public. For this Mann blamed neither ethnic differences nor economic factors, but what he called the "condition of the common mind," in which "an occasion was only waiting for thoughts to become actions, for ideas to find arms, for impulse to take the weapon." The "real culprits," he thought, were "those who formed this opinion" and those "who enhanced their private fortune and ease upon the sufferings of the ignorant, the malicious and the depraved." Such violence stemmed from "licentious impulses" and "selfish enjoyments," which could be

---

[2] Mann, Journal, May 30, 1837, MS in MHS.

[3] Mann, Journal, June 11 and 12, 1837, MS in MHS. For a contemporary account of the Broad Street Riot, see the *Massachusetts Spy*, June 14 and 27, 1837. The Irish losses from looting were considerable since many of them had withdrawn their life savings from the banks to avoid losing them in the panic.

shaped by "the vicious" and "the depraved" into an "uncontrollable power." But the key to all of this was the common man's motives. If the "educated, the wealthy, the intelligent" abandoned their responsibility to shape these, then by default, other less enlightened, less ethical persons would move into the vacuum. For Mann, the Broad Street Riot had implications which could shake the very foundations of the nation.[4]

When he compared the general suffering in society with his personal suffering, Mann always returned to the same conclusion. The only "predominant motive" left in his life was commitment to duty. Hope of future happiness no longer remained. Confiding his intimate feelings in his Journal, he wrote,

Had I a wife and children, the pleasure of providing for their wants would cheer my hours of industry, would multiply the motives to generous and praiseworthy conduct and enhance beyond measure, that honest pride, which I think a man may lawfully indulge, in the possession of the respect for the honour of his fellow citizens. . . . Of all these aids and helps to virtue, and sources of contentment and joy, I am bereft. Nothing but the stern mandate of duty urges me forward. . . .[5]

The "stern mandate of duty" he still had, and this was driving him relentlessly on. To what ends he did not know, but he did know that sensual pleasures and material benefits were no part of them. As a legatee of Puritanism, he was prepared and conditioned for an ascetic life devoted to duty, but having discarded the aggressive sanctions of its theology, he assumed more of the stance of a martyr than a conqueror. For him the experiences of 1837 were a clarion call for men of his kind to stay the flood of vice and corruption which threatened to envelop the land. In a letter to the young Charles Sumner, Mann described his compulsion to eradicate evil wherever it existed and his hopes to enlist others in the same crusade.

My attention, having been now for many years drawn to all that variety and enormity of evils which make up the hell of Intemperance —I have acquired what the artists call a *quick eye,* in discovering them—the consequence of which is, that wherever I go, some *species* of that *generii* honor afflicts me, and who can see it, to a ten thousandth part of it unmoved.

---

[4] Mann, Journal, June 11 and 12, 1837, MS in MHS.
[5] Mann, Journal, June 10, 1837, MS in MHS.

Knowing too, as I do that if the talented, respected and influential young men of the city—even to the number of *one hundred*—would stand in the pass of this Thermopylae, that host of evils might be excluded forever. I have sometimes felt, as tho' I had a right—in the sacred name of humanity to call upon everyone to contribute his assistance in so beneficent a work, and I am aware that I sometimes speak to my friends, as tho' they must yield obedience to the highest law of their nature and perform their duty.

Fearing an impending chaos, both for himself and for society, Mann saw duty as the one remaining and unfailing certitude upon which he could rely.[6]

*   *   *

Actually, Mann could not count the recent legislative session a total loss to the humanitarian cause. True, his associates had rebuffed him in his attempt to channel funds to the common schools. Nevertheless, he and others had pushed through a proposal to establish a State Board of Education which would collect and distribute information about the schools. To Mann, the Board's power must have appeared as a feeble force for good, a small cloud on the horizon no larger than a man's hand; little did he understand at the time, despite his unqualified optimism for reform causes, that it would someday bring an end to the educational drouth in the Commonwealth. Little did he also suspect that this legislation would change the course of his life as nothing had done since Charlotte's death.

Early in the session, Governor Edward Everett had urged the legislature to establish just such a board. Having observed the efficient Prussian school system while a student at the University of Göttingen, Everett considered the establishment of a State Board of Education the first step in bringing some order and system into the common schools of Massachusetts. No solitary voice crying in the wilderness, the Governor was soon supported by memorials sent to the General Court. One appeal from the Bristol County Education Convention conceded that "The pulpit, the press, the Sunday-school, the healthful discipline of the family" all were helpful for "intellectual and moral well-being and progress"; but it went on to argue that the people had singled out the agency of the public school "in preference to all others as the instrument best calculated to be used by

---

[6] Mann to Charles Sumner, February, 1837, Mann MSS:MHS.

them . . . to carry on the great and important work of qualifying every individual to add strength and beauty to the temple of republicanism in which they dwell." Going beyond Everett's modest proposal, the Bristol memorialists urged the establishment of a state board of control for the direct supervision of the common schools.[7]

A committee in the House under the chairmanship of James G. Carter gave the idea a warm reception. The same was true in the Senate, where Josiah Quincy, Jr., one of Mann's closest associates, added the blessing of his Committee on Education. But when the bill came to the floor of the House, it encountered unexpected opposition and was refused a third reading by a two to one margin. A motion for reconsideration met a similar fate. Meanwhile in the Senate, Quincy had gained approval of the measure. Then with the added support of the upper chamber, Carter called for the House to reconsider its actions. A sufficient number of Representatives switched sides and by the end of April, Everett took special satisfaction in signing into law this act which embodied his earlier proposal.[8]

The statute authorized the Governor to appoint eight persons, who with himself and the Lieutenant-Governor, were to serve without compensation as the Massachusetts State Board of Education. Each year the Board was to prepare an abstract on the common schools for the legislature and make recommendations how public education might be improved. To facilitate efforts at collecting data the Board was empowered to hire a salaried secretary. It was a modest law. At the time, even its supporters were not clear as to what it might accomplish, but they did understand that the Board was to function in an advisory capacity rather than as "a board of

---

[7] Edward Everett, "Address of His Excellency . . . to the Two Branches of the Legislature . . . January 4, 1837," *Massachusetts Senate Documents, 1837*, No. 1; "Memorial of the Bristol Co. Education Convention," *Massachusetts Senate Documents, 1837*, No. 44.

[8] *Massachusetts House Documents, 1837*, No. 50, and *Massachusetts Senate Documents, 1837*, No. 81; Journal of the House, Vol. 59, April 12 and 14, 1837, pp. 485–486, 489, and 502, MS in MSA; *Laws of the Commonwealth of Massachusetts, 1837*, Ch. CCXLI, "An Act Relating to Common Schools." During the session, education had been an issue in which the Senators bolted their usual partisan loyalty. Repeatedly they voted almost as a block on bank charters, railroads, and the tariff increases. But when the schools were considered, neither county nor party loyalties held. The solid Whig delegation from Boston found itself voting on the same side as their opponents from Middlesex County. See Journal of the Senate, Vol. 58, February 16, 22, and March 28, 1837, pp. 213–215, 240, and 398, MS in MSA.

control" as recommended by the Bristol County Convention. To those hoping for a radical and immediate change in the schools, this was even less than half a loaf, but it would remain to be seen whether it would whet or deaden the people's appetites for further reform. Determined to make the most of the new law, Governor Everett appointed men to the Board who would give it the power of prestige and a wide representation. His list included Reverend Jared Sparks, historian, president of Harvard, and Unitarian; Edmund Dwight, manufacturer, philanthropist, and Whig; Reverend Emerson Davis, Congregational minister from Westfield; Edward A. Newton, banker and prominent Episcopalian from Pittsfield; Reverend Thomas Robbins, a leader in Congregational circles from Rochester; Robert Rantoul, Jr., lawyer, Democratic politician and Unitarian from Gloucester; James G. Carter, Whig representative from Lancaster; and Horace Mann.[9]

Given only advisory power, the Board's operation would be similar to the numerous voluntary organizations which promoted other reforms, and because of its similarity to private groups, it was recognized that its most important act would be to choose an effective secretary. The achievements of Justin Edwards in the American Temperance Society and Frederick Packard in the American Sunday School Union pointed to the importance of the right man. Front runners for the position were James G. Carter, George B. Emerson, and Reverend Charles Brooks. Each had been prominent in organizations urging school reforms, and Carter had the added distinction of having carried the effort into the legislature. Those advising Everett, however, "a little volunteer council" as they were called, and led by Edmund Dwight, had decided that the reform of the common schools was too important and difficult an undertaking to be placed in the hands of a mere educator. What the group wanted instead was a man prominent in public life, with strong political connections. In addition, he needed to be dedicated and unselfish, driven by an inexhaustible reservoir of energy and a man who, by the sheer force of his determination and will power, could both overcome a small hostile minority opposed to public schools and stir up a large apathetic majority which simply did not care. In other

---

[9] An official document dated May 27, 1837, appointing these men is in the Mann MSS:MHS. For a biographical background of each member, see Raymond B. Culver, *Horace Mann and Religion in the Massachusetts Public Schools* (New Haven, 1929), pp. 31–32; Mann, Journal, May 27, 1837, MS in MHS.

reform movements, men were rescuing the slave, the drunkard, the pauper, and the lunatic. Now with the help of the state, surely the same could be done for children. Clearly the job called for a man of prominence, but also a person who had proven in other reforms that he could fire the imagination of people, prick their consciences, and forge a coalition of support for humanitarian causes. A rare find, Dwight and his cohorts openly admitted. Yet in their opinion just such a person was Horace Mann.[1]

The task of convincing Governor Everett of this was a relatively easy matter, but to convince Mann of the same was an undertaking of a different magnitude. It amounted to convincing him to exchange his position of leadership in the Senate and the Whig Party, and a certain chance at the governorship, for an obscure advisory post with few guidelines and no established salary. This, at least, was what the public believed. But Dwight, who knew Mann intimately, also knew of his disillusionment with politics. Therefore, a week prior to the official announcement of the Board appointments, he drew Mann aside at a social gathering and suggested that few persons as he were qualified for such a challenge. Dwight understood his quarry and knew that once the idea was presented, Mann himself was the best person to test its validity.

Privately Mann had spoken repeatedly of seeking some chance within the reform movements to work for objectives of permanent value, but now when actually confronting an opportunity, he shied away, uncertain of himself and his true intentions. The size of the task, however, and the potential of altering thousands of human lives were ideas which refused to leave him. The day after Dwight's suggestion, he was unable to concentrate on his affairs. That evening in complete frustration, when he came to record his

---

[1] The fact that Carter was not appointed secretary has never been satisfactorily explained by historians. Generally overlooked has been the fact that Dwight and others might have felt Carter's former controversy with his church council five years before would limit his effectiveness in a program which needed the support of Congregational clergymen throughout the state. For a description of the dispute, see [Nathaniel Thayer], *Records of the Church* [of Lancaster, Massachusetts, Congregational] *in the Case of Deacon James G. Carter and a Reply to the Communication Made by Him to the Brethren on the Day of His Removal from the Office of Deacon* (Lancaster, 1832), pp. 5–136. For an appraisal of Carter's contribution to common school reforms, see [Henry Barnard], "James G. Carter," *American Journal of Education*, V (September, 1858), 407–416. For Dwight's attitude towards Carter, see Francis Bowen, "Memoir of Edmund Dwight," *American Journal of Education*, IV (September, 1857), 5–18.

activities in his Journal, he had nothing to report and simply entered the couplet,

Count that day lost, whose low, declining sun,
Views from thy hand, no worthy action done.

Subsequent entries in the days which followed amounted to a searching soliloquy in which Mann once more examined his hopes for the future. Concerned that he was inadequate to the task, he asked, "Will my greater zeal in the cause than others supply the deficiency in point of talent and information?" If he was ignorant of specific problems the secretary would encounter, Mann did know from experience some of the general difficulties of reform:

Whoever shall undertake that task must encounter privation, labor, and infinite annoyance from an infinite number of schemers. He must condense the steam of enthusiasts—and soften the rock of [the] incredulous. . . . How many dead minds to resuscitate, how many prurient ones to soothe, how much of mingled truth and error to decompound and analyze.

Yet there were also compensations.

But should he succeed, should he bring forth those germs of greatness and happiness, which nature has scattered abroad, and expand them into maturity and enrich them with fruit, should he be able to teach even a few of this generation, how mind is god over matter, how, in arranging objects of desire, a subordination of the less valuable, to the more, is the great secret of individual happiness, how the whole life depends upon the scale which we form of its relative values;—could he do this, what diffusion, what intensity, what perpetuity of blessings he could confer.

He wanted to believe that there was an immutable law of the universe, that altruistic endeavors promoted the most personal satisfaction as well as the most permanent social effects, even though he was surrounded by evidence to the contrary.[2]

By this time, Mann had become a devotee of natural theology, even over the persistent protests of Elizabeth Peabody who still hoped to convert him to her own brand of transcendentalism. Especially influenced by the urbane writings of Henry Lord Brougham, he

---

[2] Mann, Journal, May 6, 7, and 18, 1837, MS in MHS.

could agree with a review in the *Edinburgh Review* of Brougham's *Discourse of Natural Theology,* which claimed that revelation and miracles had no place in true religion. The validity of religious teachings was better determined by scientific proof. Although Mann suspected most professing Christians would consider this a "fatal heresy," he was prepared to go even further than Brougham and claim that "Natural Religion stands as preeminent over Revealed Religion as the deepest experience over the slightest hearsay," and he added that "the time is coming when the light of Natural Religion will be to that of Revealed, as the rising sun is to the star that preceded it."

According to Brougham and others, the human mind was nothing metaphysical but part of the natural and scientific world, subject to laws which could be discovered through inductive reasoning and investigation. Once these laws were learned, the clergyman, the educator, and the statesman could guide people to more virtuous lives. Mann could not have agreed more.[3]

The official announcement of the Board appointments was made late in May, but Mann still had come to no firm decision. With each ensuing day, the possibility of what he might accomplish continued to expand in his mind like a heady vapor until it filled all his thoughts. No state, he reasoned, was properly organized, if it lacked a "minister or secretary of instruction." Perhaps in a simple society the family could still educate its children, but such an arrangement was no longer possible in Massachusetts. Considering the need to diffuse knowledge throughout the republic, he came to the conclusion that "every child should be educated," and "if not educated by its own father, then the State should appoint a father to it." The law establishing the Board was the "first great movement toward an organized system of common education, which shall at once be thorough and universal."[4]

But when he added his own possible involvement with the work of the Board, he was far less certain. "I cannot think of that station, as regards myself," he wrote, "without feeling both hopes and fears, desires and apprehension, multiplying in my mind." On the one hand, he expected "so glorious a sphere, should it be crowned with success." Still there was always the possibility of "disappointment and humiliation, should it fail through any avoidable misfortune."

[3] *Edinburgh Review or Critical Journal,* LXIV (1836–37), 263–302; Mann, Journal, May 8, 1837, MS in MHS.
[4] Mann, Journal, May 27, 1837, MS in MHS.

Each time Mann rehearsed the dialectic in his mind, he seemed to dwell longer with the former. To the reformer, it was a chance to shift one's efforts from hardened and unamenable adults to impressionable children not yet corrupted by society. "What a thought," he wrote in his Journal, "to have the future minds of such multitudes dependent in any perceptible degree upon one's own exertions!" This was a radiant vision which continued to shine through foreboding clouds of failure.[5]

He was approaching another turning point in his life, and it did not help that he was approaching it alone. The Peabody sisters were ignorant of his deliberations and few of his friends had any idea of what he was contemplating. While pondering Dwight's offer, he skipped Channing's sermon and visited the Mount Auburn Cemetery, probably to go once more to the grave of Silas Holbrook. On his return to Boston in the afternoon, he stopped in to hear Father Taylor preach, and in the evening, he listened to George Briggs deliver the annual address before the Massachusetts Temperance Society. Returning to his room late that night, thoughts of death still preoccupied his mind. In his Journal he recorded his sense of desolation and his compulsion to retain Charlotte's memory, whatever the pain. "I never see a grave," he wrote,

nor hear ought mentioned concerning a resting place for the dead, but that spot where all my earthly treasures were laid, is present like a reality before my mind. These days of sorrow, these nights of tears and mourning for the purest loveliest being, whose brightness was ever shrouded in mortality, when, when will they cease!

> *Oh! Charlotte! "Dear departed shade,*
> *Look from thy place of heavenly rest;*
> *Seest thou, thy lover laid,*
> *Hearest thou the groans, that rend his rest?"*

And a short time later, almost in desperation, he exclaimed, "When, oh when, will it cease." [6]

* * *

Each day he wrestled in vain with the accumulation of imponderables upon which he tried to fashion a decision. But if his

[5] Mann, Journal, May 27, 1837, MS in MHS.
[6] Mann, Journal, May 28, and June 9 and 15, 1837, MS in MHS.

troubled mind could not accomplish the task unaided, the calendar with its total disregard for the complexity of mental dialectics inevitably drove him on to a choice. Governor Everett had called the first meeting of the Board for the end of the month and its first order of business was to elect a secretary. Mann pressed Dwight for a clearer idea of what the office might entail, but his benefactor remained disturbingly evasive when called on for specifics. What he did promise Mann was an additional annual stipend of $500 from his own funds to augment what was likely to be an all too meager salary established by a parsimonious General Court.[7]

Finally, on the very last day before the meeting, he made his decision. His present legal and political tasks now brought him both money and status, but somehow, he had convinced himself that he had no right to them, and therefore could not enjoy them. Thus if asked by the Board, he stood ready to cut himself off from this part of his past and set a course for almost totally uncharted waters. To do so, he admitted, was to expose himself to "hardships and privations," but he preferred such a hair shirt and he welcomed "the jealousies, the misrepresentation, and the prejudice almost certain to arise" from his new crusade. Later the same evening, as he contemplated his future adversaries and the obstacles they would cast in his way, he took refuge in an almost overpowering desire for self-denial as he recorded in his Journal that he was

. . . ready to meet them in the spirit of a martyr. Tomorrow will probably prescribe for me a course of life. Let it come! I know one thing; if I stand by the principles of truth and duty, nothing can inflict upon me any permanent harm.

Upon the self-imposed ascetism of the last five years, he now hoped to superimpose a new altruistic purpose. Taking the classical stance of a martyr and envisioning himself clad in an armor of "truth and duty," which shielded him against the slings and arrows of his adversaries, he stood ready to face the imminent challenge.[8]

The next morning, the Board met behind closed doors. As soon as its members turned to the selection of a secretary, Mann with-

---

[7] Mann, Journal, June 28, 1837, MS in MHS.
[8] Mann, Journal, June 28, 29, and 30, 1837, MS in MHS. The strength of his sense of martyrdom at this time is clearly evident from his Journal entries where one finds such expressions as "the spirit of self-abandonment, the spirit of martyrdom," and statements that he was embarking on a crusade "with a right spirit,—with a self-sacrificing spirit."

drew to an adjoining room in order to permit them a more frank discussion of his candidacy. While awaiting their decision, Mann need not have been anxious about their deliberations. Everett, Dwight, and several others had canvassed the group before the meeting, and Mann's actual election to the secretaryship was little more than a formality. Soon Lieutenant-Governor George Hull and Reverend Emerson Davis came into the room and handed him a note. It read:

Dear Sir,
The undersigned have great pleasure in communicating the result of the recent balloting for a Secretary of the Board of Education,—You were elected to that office and it will gratify us to announce to the board your acceptance of their adjourned meeting at 9 o'clock tomorrow morning.

[signed]
George Hull ⎱
Emerson Davis ⎰ Committee

This simple note, the epitome of plain language, brevity, and directness, was Mann's summons to shape the destiny of American education. As he read it, however, he saw it more as an immediate opportunity to mold the children of his generation in his own image.[9] Recounting these events to his sister and describing his hopes for the future, Mann promised to "collect and diffuse as much information as possible on the subject of common school education." Since his new duties were prescribed by law in "the most general and comprehensive manner possible," he intended to examine and improve every facet of public education. Exhibiting an ignorance of the complexity of processes at work in education, he confidently spoke of the immediate objective of "ascertaining what is the best construction of houses, what are the best books, what is the best arrangement of studies, what are the best modes of instruction." Beyond this, he expected to discover "by what application of means a non-thinking, non-reflecting, non-speaking child can most surely be trained into a noble citizen, ready to contend for all the *right* and die for the *right*." When he sent similar statements to Mary Peabody, his dispatch brought back her conditioned refrain—an adulation of his

[9] June 29, 1837, Mann MSS:MHS; an account of the first session of the Board is found in Records of the [Massachusetts State] Board of Education, June 29, 1837, pp. 5–9, MS in the Massachusetts State Department of Education (hereafter MSDE).

efforts and the new title of "high priest of education." Naïve though he was about the intricacies and complexity of the processes of teaching and learning, Mann did understand the difficulties of awakening an interest in the Commonwealth for any humanitarian reform. Thus he wrote back to her that he was more likely to become an evangelist or a "post-rider from county to county," looking after the welfare of children.[1]

Why did he do it? This was the question most of his friends asked. Only someone such as Channing who had been close to Mann during the last five years and had witnessed his suffering could see through the apparent enigma. One day when it seemed he could bear no more urging from self-appointed advisers to reconsider his decision, Mann opened a letter from the Unitarian minister which dispelled all doubt from his mind. How close the two men had come in their view of society could be seen by a careful reading of Channing's words:

I understand that you have given yourself to the cause of education in our Commonwealth. I rejoice in it. Nothing could give me greater pleasure. I think I have long desired someone uniting all your qualifications should devote himself to this work. You could not find a nobler station. . . . When will the low, degrading party quarrels of the country cease, and the better minds come to think what can become toward a substantial, generous improvement of the community? "My ear is pained, my very soul sick," with the monotonous, yet furious clamors about currency, banks, and etc., when the special interests of the community seem hardly to be recognized as having any reality.

If we can but turn the wonderful energy of this people into a right channel, what a new heaven and earth must be realized among us! . . . There must be many to be touched by the same truths which are stirring you.[2]

In these halcyon days of unprecedented opportunities for the able and the venturesome, both men were attempting to distinguish the transient from the intrinsic. With the coming of factories, railroads, and ever larger numbers of immigrants swelling the crowd of unpropertied, wage-earning natives already collecting in the cities, Mann's world was changing and would continue to change. He un-

[1] Mann to Lydia Mann, July 16, 1837; Mary Peabody to Mann, August 26, 1837, Mann MSS:MHS.
[2] *Memoir of William Ellery Channing with Extracts from his Correspondence and Manuscripts* (Boston, 1848), III, 89.

derstood this. He also knew that the old tightly knit families and clans, the rural congregations with their selective membership, and the self-sufficient villages whose sense of community provided a security which was suffocating, would not survive unchanged. In his youth, these agencies still provided a centripetal function, giving individuals a sense of identity within the community and binding them together into larger collective endeavors. Now they were less effective in maintaining their sanctions and the mores they preached were as often flaunted as followed. If this deterioration went unchecked, Mann was certain of a crumbling of his social world and the emergence of anarchy.

In casting about for a remedy, he thought that education provided the best means to maintain a set of common values and re-establish the older community of consensus on a newer urban and industrial foundation. He could agree with Channing that there was still time to turn this new robust energy of a rising people "into a right channel." Using a different illustration, but speaking in the same spirit, Mann wrote that he had "abandoned jurisprudence" for "the larger sphere of mind and morals." And he continued,

Having found the present generation composed of materials almost unmalleable, I am about transferring my efforts to the next. Men are cast-iron; but children are wax. Strength expended upon the latter may be effectual, which would make no impression upon the former.

Too late for his own generation, there was still the chance to shape the next.[3]

Such was the holy and patriotic crusade which Mann envisioned for himself. A person seeking martyrdom could not have found a more seductive cause. He explained his motivations to his sister, "if I had power to make a world and to prepare a station of duty for myself in it, I could not devise one more desirable than this." And for his own edification, he wrote in his Journal, "henceforth, so long as I hold this office, I devote myself to the supermost welfare of mankind upon the earth." Without acknowledging the biblical parallel, Horace Mann had maneuvered himself into a position where he must lose his life in order to save it. This paradox of human existence he did not understand, but he willingly accepted it nevertheless. During July and August he closed most of his legal accounts. With his final fees and personal loan from James K. Mills, he retired the

---

[3] Mann, *Life*, I, 83.

remainder of Stanley's debts. Now it would no longer be necessary for him to live in the loneliness and austerity of his office and he could seek more comfortable lodgings. He had found a new form of sacrifice and asceticism.[4]

---

[4] Mann to Lydia Mann, January 25, 1836, and July 16, 1837, Mann MSS:MHS; Mann, Journal, June 30, August 28, and November 29, 1837, MS in MHS.

CHAPTER XII

Circuit Rider to the
Next Generation

===

. . . in a Republic ignorance is a Crime.
HORACE MANN

O
NE MONTH BEFORE his first public appearance as the new secretary, Mann's second thoughts about leaving the Senate told
him that his recent decision must have been prompted by equal parts
of ignorance and arrogance. Ignorance, because aside from the
common folklore about education, Elizabeth Peabody's transcendental theories about child development, and his own childhood recollections, he knew virtually nothing about education in the common
schools of Massachusetts. And to assume that of all people, he
could reform the schools when he could not even straighten out his
personal affairs, approached some sort of summit of arrogance.
Even more disconcerting was the question of how his efforts would
be received by the people. By the end of his first circuit through the
state, he would know the answer to this, but a thorough knowledge
of conditions in the schools would take much longer. Even if there
were to be no new schools and he visited one school each day for
the next decade, he still would not have set foot in every one.

What he could do was read, and this occupied the majority of
his time in July. Considering the legion of intellectually lightweight
rubbish later to appear, the books on education available in 1837
were mercifully few. Mann studied a work by James Simpson, an
English crusader for popular education. He also read an English
translation of Victor Cousin's celebrated report on the superiority
of Prussian schools and *Lectures on the Philosophy of the Human
Mind* by his favorite Scottish common-sense philosopher, Thomas
Brown. Then, too, he worked through the back issues of the *Journal
of Education* with its potpourri of information ranging from a pedan-
tic description of the curriculum of the mechanics institutes in London to an account of the "progress of Education" among the Hotten-

251

tots. In paging through the numerous newspapers of the state, he noted that editors often sandwiched in the topic of education as filler between the national and local news on the first and second of their four-page dailies. Even the brahmin editors of the prestigious *North American Review* occasionally adulterated their esoteric fare with a review of recent domestic and foreign works on the topic. All of these he consumed as one desperately starved, but to devour them in so brief a time was to invite a bad case of intellectual indigestion.[1]

The writings all confirmed his own conviction that where other reforms had proven disappointing, common school education now loomed large as the reform to end the need for further reform. Nevertheless, faced with the very real task of bringing this about, he found little upon which he might build. According to the town reports available to him, most of the school buildings were small and shabby. In Westport, a teacher held class for fifteen children in a room fourteen by sixteen. Tyringham boasted of its "good" school, where seventeen pupils were closeted in a fourteen by eighteen space. Great Barrington reported sixteen students in a building sixteen by twenty-four whose condition was described as "bad . . . stands in road." Other towns complained of equally depressing conditions. Out of seven schoolhouses in Ashburnham, the Town Committee declared five as "bad," one "decent," and one "good." And little more could be said for the furnishings inside these. To the question, "What is the furniture of the School House, and the apparatus including maps?" the Lanesborough Committee responded with a sense of hard-won accomplishment, "All the schools are provided with stoves, tables, pails and dippers." Wilmington simply answered, "None," while the Taunton officials gave the more descriptive response, "Inconvenient benches, a clumsy desk, chair for the master, —bare walls,—no maps,—nor other apparatus, save school books, and the switch or ferule." Many town and country folk even tolerated the absence of that all-important convenience, the outhouse; but when a school in Kingston even lacked its substitute, "the shades of the surrounding forest," one school board member finally erupted in righteous indignation, "What sort of a place is this, to send your sons and daughters to learn that most desirable of all virtues, Mod-

---

[1] Mann, Journal, July 9, 1837, MS in MHS. For examples of writings on education available to him, see *Journal of Education,* I, 632, 690, 691, and 694, and Orville Dewey, "Popular Education," *North American Review,* XXXVI (January, 1833), 73–99.

esty?" In terms of comforts and conveniences, much less the simple amenities, the rural and townsfolk of Massachusetts provided better shelter for their livestock than for their children.[2]

But this was not to say that most parents were unconcerned about the future of their sons and daughters. Far from it. Assured by the folklore surrounding the self-made man, they assumed their children learned morality in the home and church. Citizenship came by a process of patriotic osmosis always at work in the village. Pluck, ingenuity, ambition, and "horse-sense," all present in the successful man of the day, were learned in the field, the shop, the marketplace, and on the quarter-deck. Admittedly, literacy was a necessary tool for the successful man, but many parents thought this was the result of a variety of experiences, one small part of which came from a few winters spent in the local district school.

Dilapidated buildings and barren interiors were one sufficient testimony to an overt lack of commitment to formal schooling; the town reports were another. To an enquiry about parental interest, Sheffield's committee answered "Not much," while a similar group at Wilmington stated: "[T]hey do, tho' not so generally as could be wished." A Raynham report claimed that "Some feel and manifest much interest, but a majority are very deficient in their duty." It would be Mann's task then to begin with the few who would "manifest much interest" in the schools and use them as a nucleus around which he could build a broadly based coalition.[3] Parents, citizens, taxpayers, all must be converted to a new religion, which taught that the older informal modes of learning were no longer adequate and that there must be far greater reliance on formal systematic schooling. Just four years before, the voters of Massachusetts had officially disestablished the old Congregational Church. Now Mann was about to preach a new religion and convince his constituency of the need for a new establishment, a nondenominational institution, the public school, with schoolmasters as a new priestly class, patriotic exercises as quasi-religious rituals, and a nonsectarian doctrine stressing morality, literacy, and citizenship as a republican creed for all to confess.

But Mann had no priestly class upon which he could build.

---

[2] The conditions and statistics on schools are taken from the School Returns of Massachusetts, 1835–1839, *passim*, Archives of the State of Massachusetts, State House, Boston, Massachusetts. The outhouse complaint is recorded in Joseph S. Beal *et al., Report of the School Committee of Kingston* [Massachusetts] (Plymouth, 1839), p. 5.
[3] School Returns of Massachusetts, 1835–1839, *passim*, MS in MSA.

Communities seemed all too ready to hire some pedagogical transient who happened by, or a local girl unskilled in any *really* useful activity. Evidently those who kept school were paid no more than they were worth. Women received from $5 to $8 per month and their male counterparts about twice the sum. In addition, they also "boarded round," staying a week with a family and then moving on to another, all the time receiving free meals and lodging. In the early 1800's, the coming of the teacher was a special event and families spared no effort to make him comfortable and serve him the best from their larder. But not in 1837. Boarding the teacher was simply an economy measure which reduced their individual taxes. They put out the most meager fare with little embarrassment and many teachers complained that obtaining good room and board in Massachusetts was as difficult as plucking quills from a live barnyard fowl.

At the very time when Mann was poring over pedagogical writings in Boston, twenty miles to the west in Concord, the young Henry Thoreau, fresh from Harvard, was finding that conditions in his classroom made it impossible to try out his educational ideas. After a two-week trial, he gave up. Believing that "cowhide was a non-conductor," he refused to whip his charges even though parents expected him to lay it on. Meanwhile at the other end of the state in a country school outside Pittsfield, Herman Melville stuck it out for the winter session, then left, thoroughly disgusted. Clearly, the few able persons who did teach often left the schools, impelled like pawns by an educational version of Gresham's Law in which the good were replaced by the bad.[4] Those who had failed to establish themselves in the countinghouse, the parlor, or the pulpit reluctantly accepted the classroom as a poor consolation prize and a place to give vent to their disappointment and frustration. True, the American Institute of Instruction was a going concern by 1837, attempting to raise the level of instruction in the schools. Apparently believing it was a matter of publish or perish, the Institute had printed and distributed seven bound volumes of collected lectures given at its yearly meetings as evidence at least of a verbal vitality.[5] But if the seven years had been fat in words, they had been lean in actual

[4] Herman Melville to Peter Gansevoort, December 31, 1837, Gansevoort-Lansing MSS:NYPL; William H. Gilman, *Melville's Early Life and Redburn* (New York, 1951), pp. 84–86; Lawrence Willson, "Thoreau on Education," *History of Education Quarterly*, II (March, 1962), 19–29.
[5] *Journal of the Proceedings of the American Institute of Instruction*, I–VII (1831–38).

accomplishments. Each of its annual conventions had brought forth more speeches, more breast-beating, and more resolutions; but by 1837, any objective witness would have conceded that the Institute had accomplished virtually nothing in improving teaching. In his accolade of the Prussian Schools, Victor Cousin had written "as the teacher, so the school." Had he looked for negative evidence for his dictum on this side of the Atlantic, he would have found an abundance among the descendants of Ezekiel Cheever and Cotton Mather.[6]

*   *   *

His new education barely under way, Mann was forced to set aside his books for the annual Independence Day celebration in Boston. Once again as if guided by some ancestral homing instinct, persons from far and near had come to the place where liberty was born. As a boy, Mann had eagerly awaited the coming of the local celebration with its mustering of the Franklin militia; at Brown it had been the happiest of reprieves from classes during the year; and as a young lawyer in Dedham, the day had furnished him with the occasion to stand before the town fathers and depict a rosy prospect for the nation. Although all this was now past and his desire to participate in a simplistic patriotism would never be rekindled, time could not erode the rudimentary habit of at least witnessing the activities of others. The streets of Boston were choked with wagons and carriages. All rooms in its inns and hotels were filled with overnight guests, and the townsfolk had done their best to bed down countless visiting country cousins in their own homes. In taverns and coffeehouses, farmers and city dwellers renewed friendships, caught up on local news, and more than a few declared a temporary moratorium on their temperance pledges. For the more select, Mayor Eliot was holding open house in his handsome mansion, while at the Marlboro Hotel, the temperance reformers were hurrying the com-

---

[6] Victor Cousin, *Rapport sur l'état de l'instruction publique dans quelques pays d'Allemagne, et particulièrement en Prusse* (Paris, 1835). Newspapers and school reports were filled with complaints about poor teachers. For a general synthesis of these, see my "Horace Mann and Teacher Education," *Yearbook of Education*, ed. George Z. F. Bereday and Joseph Lauwerys (London, 1963), pp. 70–84, and "Consensus and Controversy in the Reform of the Common Schools," *Teachers College Record*, LXVI (May, 1965), 749–759.

pletion of last-minute details in preparation for their annual dinner. Judging by the noise, the decorations, the press of people, and the general sense of expectation, the morning of this Fourth gave indication of being the biggest and most colorful the city had ever seen.

It was a day when all the streets and sidewalks led to the Common. Here a dozen societies and associations had pitched their tents and pavilions on the green. In addition, a number of speakers' platforms had been assembled from rough-sawn planks hurriedly nailed together, the makeshift carpentry concealed with bright semicircles of red, white, and blue bunting, Hucksters worked through the crowds, hawking balloons, flags, and sweets for the children. Everywhere an atmosphere prevailed of religious revival, agricultural fair, and town meeting all wrapped up in one.

As he entered the north end of the Common, Mann noticed that the Friends of Bunker Hill were meeting in still one more effort to raise funds and complete the obelisk rising on a knoll across the Charles River. Nearby, the Baptist Sabbath School Union and the Mechanics and Apprentices Association had arranged benches for their sessions later in the day. Moving across the Common past one organization after another, Mann had the impression that an increasing number of booths and tents were set up for entertainment rather than public service. On one side, a traveling showman stood in front of his tent selling admissions to a panorama of the burning of Jerusalem. Another had brought a menagerie of wild animals, including a live elephant. And at the very bottom of the Common, one could buy a ticket to see a forty-foot model of Niagara Falls complete with running water.

By noon, activities were well under way with the annual parade, this year led by the Fuselier and Washington High Infantries and supported by bands, floats, and other marchers, including the "orator of the day," state legislators, foreign consuls, the "Observers of the Poor," and just plain "citizens." One event followed another, all pointing to a climactic evening display of fireworks prepared by a certain "Mr. Hall," who had traveled north all the way from Hackensack, New Jersey, to put on his show. According to the edition of the *Daily Advertiser* which came off the press that morning, Bostonians were most fortunate. The gentleman was an artist of "high reputation" and had brought a program of thirty different items, culminating in a spectacular extravaganza. Billed as "the largest piece of fireworks ever exhibited in America," it extended two hundred feet in length and thirty in height, and came to a fiery climax with a discharge of "golden rockets." [7]

As he looked out of the window from his office in the State House, Governor Edward Everett thought the mass of humanity bursting the seams of the Common was a "dreadful crowd." Mann more picturesquely described the situation as "a quart of spectators put into a pint of commons." [8] Picking his way in the crowd, Mann appeared tall, thin, and slightly stooped. His white hair was all the more pronounced in the sunlight. Although among the celebrants, he was not of them, having no zest for entering into the spirit of the day. To have studied him carefully was to note a man who remained aloof, a dignified and detached observer with traces of cynicism detectable from the lines about his lips. Now and then, from the press of people, a friendly face appeared. After the initial greetings, the same question was raised. Surely he was not really giving up the Senate for the Board of Education as the papers had stated, and if so, in God's name, why? [9]

Was there not "more dignity or honor or something" in being the president of the Senate and possibly the next Whig governor of the state? Patiently, Mann listened to their queries, knowing all too well that no answer he could give would satisfy them and they would walk away more puzzled than before. Perhaps, during the course of the day, the steady stream of inquiries began to shake his convictions; but later in his room, after all the public festivities including the "golden rockets" were over, he looked at his growing library of books on education and his stacks of notes, convinced he was doing the right thing. Although the incredulity of his friends still rang in his ears, his self-doubt had vanished and he could assure himself that given just ten years to mount a campaign for the common schools, he "would show them which way the balance of honor lies." [1]

When doubts recurred later in July and August, he could always turn to his letters from Mary Peabody for reassurance. "I like the

---

[7] For details of the celebration, see the *Columbian Centinel*, July 4 and 5, 1837, and the Boston *Daily Advertiser*, July 7, 1837.

[8] Mann, Journal, July 4, 1837, MS in MHS; Edward Everett, Diary, July 7, 1837, MS in MHS.

[9] By the Fourth of July, accounts of Mann's decision had appeared in many of the Boston newspapers, including the *Independent Chronicle*, the *Mercantile Journal*, the Boston *Evening Transcript*, and the Boston *Patriot*.

[1] Mann, Journal, July 4, 1837, MS in MHS.

change of occupations for you very much," she wrote during a lull in her teaching duties in Salem. "That fatiguing round of law business seemed to wear upon you, and the moving life will be of great service to you. . . ." Later she added, "How could there be a more beautiful transition of office than yours? After being the breaking up plough of temperance, you are now to tell the people what to do with their soberness. . . . Our country can only prosper by the worth of individuals that compose it and therefore your's is a holy office indeed." As usual, Mary could be depended upon to write what he wanted to hear.[2]

* * *

Try as he would to compose his first address to the people, Mann found this impossible as long as he stayed in Boston. He must resign his presidency of the Suffolk County Temperance Society and help his fellow travelers find a replacement; almost daily Josiah Quincy pressed him to come for an overnight stay and he finally consented. Having decided to buy a horse, there were last-minute arrangements to be made with David Homer, the livery man; and there seemed no end to the stream of friends and clients who passed through his office. At length conceding that his efforts in Boston had accomplished little and well aware that September 1 and his first public presentation were ever closer, Mann retreated to Franklin, hoping to accomplish what still remained to be done. With each return to Mann's Plain, the first day or so was a period of morbid introspection, reverie, and melancholy. The Mann homestead, the meetinghouse, the town graveyard, all presented scenes from his childhood, and with them came the question of who he really was and what he might yet become. "How many times," he asked himself, "has my identity changed. Who ever left the house of his parent, with hopes of happiness, more eager and inspiring, than mine;—though I have known happiness, yet how little of it has come in the way, that I then looked forward to?" He did little the first two days, slept poorly, and got up each morning "trying to think and trying to write." By the middle of the week he had convinced himself that he could put off the preparation of his inaugural lecture no longer. The first pages came slowly, very slowly for one as facile with words as he. Every sentence was an ordeal. The subject was large and so much of his reputation

---

[2] Mary Peabody to Mann, July 15 and August 26, 1837, Mann MSS: MHS.

was at stake. It was as if he were attempting to grasp the world with arms too short. Nevertheless, near the end of July, he was ready to "get hold of a few handfuls." [3]

Actually, it was impossible to separate himself from Boston even in his Franklin retreat. The papers had published the Board's "Address to the People of Massachusetts," explaining its function and announcing forthcoming county conventions. This brought new enquiries. Letters came asking for information about the Board. G. T. Thayer invited Mann to address the American Institute of Instruction meeting in Worcester and Mann asked James G. Carter if it would be possible to combine the meeting of the Institute with his own Worcester County Convention. Politely, but with a trace of superiority, Carter advised Mann to speak to the Institute on the general goals of the Board and schedule a separate convention of his own. The incident warned Mann to be more careful in the future about exposing his ignorance of the schools and educational associations. Besides embarrassment, the communication with Carter meant that he now had an additional speech to prepare.[4]

With the end of July came another anniversary of Charlotte's death. As the dreaded days drew closer, it was evident that his new work had in no way tempered his painful memories. A week before the tragic date, he could not concentrate on his writing. Each evening, as he sat down to make an entry in his Journal, his hand and mind refused to record the intensity of his remorse. Then on the actual anniversary day, he could contain his anguish no longer. So intense had his memory of the ill-fated night become with visions "of anxiety, of dismay, of struggling, of death, and of the agony of surviving worse than a thousand deaths," that he finally gave words to his emotions. Sitting at his desk he began to fill the blank pages of his Journal book with sentences describing his anguish. "I had been rapt away by demons—was then, to the centre, as it seemed to me of universal darkness. Oh what months and years of gloom, of solitude I have passed through." Then followed the agonizing introspection:

---

[3] Boston *Mercantile Journal,* July 22, 1837; Mann, Journal, July 19 and September 21, 1837, MS in MHS.

[4] Boston *Weekly Messenger,* July 20, 1847; *Independent Chronicle* and *Boston Patriot,* July 15 and 17, 1837; *Evening Mercantile Journal,* July 17, 1837; Boston *Morning Post,* July 19, 1837; G. T. Thayer to Mann, July 20, 1837; James G. Carter to Mann, July 21, 1837, Mann MSS:MHS; Mann, Journal, July 24, 1837, MS in MHS.

I loved success, but it was always because it increased my means of adding to her enjoyment. If I had done aught of good, my reward did not consist in the gratitude, it awakened, but the pleasure it gave to her. Thus no plan, no scheme, no purpose, was resolved on, until the thought of her had been at the council, and my heart grew fastidious, and refused [any] enjoyment, that did not come to it, refined, purified and heightened through her enjoyment. Who then can know the entirety, the completeness, the universality of that loss.

Even with the next morning, after such an emotional catharsis, there came only a partial recovery. Thoughts of the awful tragedy stubbornly hung in his mind like bats in the roof of a cave, apparently taking flight when he slept, but always back at their roost by morning. Ready to accept a temporary armistice with his doubting, accusing self, he wrote, "So if the bond *must* be broken—if the unity *must* be divided, —then has it happened rightly." But still the question persisted, "*Why must* it have been so? Is not that an inscrutable mystery?" [5]

Personal suffering notwithstanding, there was no postponing his appearances at the Worcester Convention of the American Institute of Instruction. By the first week in August the *Columbian Centinel* and the Boston *Weekly Messenger* carried announcements on the forthcoming meetings and the Boston *Daily Advertiser and Patriot* editorialized that Mann's presence would "greatly increase the interest of the meetings." [6] Mann returned to Boston for several days and dispatched copies of the "Address of the Board" and the "Circular to the School Committees" to school committee members in every town, informing them of the time and place for the convention he was to hold in their county. In addition, he wrote letters to individuals throughout the state, asking for their help. Among them was Reverend Thomas Robbins, a staunchly orthodox and respected Congregational minister and member of the Massachusetts State Board of Education. Mann asked Robbins to publicize the meeting and do whatever he could to ensure a good turnout. Since he had also scheduled meetings in Nantucket, Barnstable, and Plymouth, Mann hoped Robbins would accompany him to these places and lend the support of his presence. "My purpose," he wrote to Robbins, "is to prepare an address explanatory of the objects of the Board and noticing some particulars, in which our means and methods of education may be

---

[5] Mann, Journal, August 1, 1837, MS in MHS.
[6] August 5, 1837. See also the *Massachusetts Spy*, August 16, 1837.

improved." To Jared Sparks he wrote for similar help. He also purchased a saddle for $26 and a dark bay mare "warranted sound and
seven years" for $150.[7]

Everything apparently in order and his speech put to paper,
Mann shipped a small trunk from Attleboro and left Wrentham for
Worcester a few days later. Although a newcomer to the Institute,
upon his arrival he was hardly among total strangers. The evening
before the first session, he visited far into the night with his old friend
and associate, William B. Calhoun, the most level-headed of the
three trustees who had directed the building of the lunatic asylum.
Mann considered Calhoun "of good sense, if not of genius," and as
others shared this opinion, Calhoun found himself the next day
chairman of the first session as the delegates filed into Bromley Hall
and organized their agenda. Partly as a courtesy and partly to take
his measure, the members asked Mann to serve on a panel with Cyrus
Peirce of Nantucket, A. Bronson Alcott of Boston, and James G. Carter of Lancaster, to discuss school libraries and teaching apparatus.
Sensing the audience was mainly interested in his views, Mann kept
his statements general and noncontroversial. If he had any misgivings of how well his words were received when he left the meeting
hall that night, they were quickly dispelled the next morning when
it was decided by acclamation to add his name to the list of Institute
vice-presidents, there to join such illustrious men as Carter, Lyman
Beecher, Theodore Dwight, and Jacob Abbott.

The next days were taken up with additional discussions and
impromptu speeches sandwiched in between some ten prepared addresses later to be published and distributed by the Institute. Much
of what he heard impressed Mann and he took special note of the
remarks made by Reverend Charles Brooks of Hingham. Upon his
return from Europe two years before, Brooks had met a certain Dr.
H. Julius, and during their forty-one-day passage from Liverpool to
New York, Julius had completely convinced Brooks of the superiority
of the Prussian system of education, especially its network of state-
controlled teachers' seminaries. By the time he returned to the Old
Bay State, Brooks was an unquestioning convert, fired with a zeal for
his new cause which approached fanaticism. He begged newspaper
space when he could, paid for it when he must, and launched a statewide campaign for the establishment of public teacher training in-

---

[7] Mann to Thomas Robbins, August 10, 1837, Robbins MSS:CHS; Mann
to Jared Sparks, August 10, 1837, Sparks MSS:HCL; receipts for both
saddle and horse are in the Mann MSS:DHS.

stitutions. Often forsaking the needs of his local parish in order to meet a larger and more distant one, this Unitarian clergyman took to his carriage and for two years, backed up by his printed and spoken word, exhorted men to his cause in any hamlet where two or more were gathered to receive him. Both Carter and George B. Emerson had also advanced the cause of special teacher training, but they were mere armchair philosophers compared to this one-man crusade. Already from what he had read and observed, Mann could see that Brooks had stumbled onto something which might be a key element in reforming the schools.[8]

But his purpose in coming to the convention was more political than intellectual. Here the only major organization in the state which he might use to improve the schools had gathered in the meeting hall. Its membership included many of the leading citizens in the towns of Massachusetts who held the reins of local political power, and it was in the towns where the real reform of the schools must be effected. Carefully choosing his words in his conversations with them, Mann explained that the Board would assume no more than an advisory function. Occasionally, eyebrows were raised and distrust crept into the faces of those to whom he spoke, but for the most part, he was communing with the converted. Session by session, by talking, listening, and resolving, the convention ground its way along, until it was ready to adjourn. Before dispersing, however, the delegate from Worcester rose and resolved that the Institute congratulate the friends of education on the establishment of a Board of Education in Massachusetts "whose co-operation in the cause in which this Institute is engaged, is a strong guaranty of its ultimate success and triumph." It was adopted unanimously.[9]

*   *   *

He had survived his first skirmish but the real battle for the public mind was still to come. Mann had scheduled his own Wor-

---

[8] Ellwood P. Cubberley, *Public Education in the United States* (Boston, 1934), p. 361; Charles Brooks, "School Reform or Teachers' Seminaries," *Introductory Discourse and the Lectures Delivered before the American Institute of Instruction . . . Including the Journal of Proceedings and a list of the Officers*, VII (Boston, 1838), 159–179.

[9] The details of the meeting are found in *The Introductory Discourse and the Lectures Delivered before the American Institute of Instruction at Worcester, Mass., August, 1837. Including the Journal of Proceedings and a List of the Officers* (Boston, 1838); Mann Journal, August 23 and 31, 1837, MS in MHS.

cester County Convention on the heels of the Institute and while the reassuring words of the resolutions were yet echoing in his ears, he had to move on to his own meeting. His convention was decidedly more local and its specific form untried. He knew he could count on such Worcester residents as Thomas Kinnicutt, Samuel B. Woodward, and Calhoun to be present and lend their support, but would citizens from Shrewsbury, Sturbridge, and Oxford also appear and would they join his crusade? The answer to the first part of his question he soon had. Word of mouth, posted circulars, announcements from the pulpit, and gratis newspaper advertisements drew the concerned and the curious from all over the county, and by the time the convention was to start, Bromley Hall was filled again.

Live bodies were important, but they alone were no guarantee of a favorable response to his message. The reserve of a Yankee audience could be frigid to a less than convincing speaker. Appropriately, the convention named James G. Carter as its president and by eleven o'clock the group voted to hear the man from Boston. As he took the rostrum, Mann began rather defensively, compared with his usual style of speaking, and attempted to probe the temper of his audience. He assured them that he had come neither to demand nor coerce. The reform of the schools was a voluntary endeavor, and the real effort must come from persons such as themselves, the responsible citizens in each community. As he would later write, "the maintenance of free schools rests wholly upon the social principle. It is emphatically a case where men, individually powerless, are collectively strong." [1]

Signs of his nervousness gradually gave place to an earnestness which compelled his audience to listen. Effectively appealing to their prejudices, Mann made his case much as he would fashion his plea to reach every member of his jury. To those citizens concerned about the future of the nation, he depicted the common schools as the necessary foundation of republican government; to worried parents, he described the schoolteacher as their partner in accomplishing what neither could do alone; to the anxious workingman, he spoke of education as the great equalizer and the "creator of wealth undreamed of"; to the religious, he held up the common school as the only agency capable of moral education in an age of endemic sectarianism; and he assured the wealthy, whose property taxes were to bear

---

[1] Mann, *First Annual Report of the Board of Education Together With the First Annual Report of the Secretary of the Board* (Boston, 1838), p. 49.

most of the burden in financing the schools, that only educated children would grow up to respect their property. In an emerging industrial society where the older paths to economic success could no longer be traveled, the public school was the best means for maintaining an equality of opportunity. Furthermore, as the ballot was increasingly extended to the rank-and-file citizen, education was the only means for providing a literate electorate essential to representative government. And finally, as other agencies seemed unable to fulfill their traditional responsibilities, the public school must come to their aid. Basically, however, its function was neither economical nor political, but moral. As Mann summed up his points, he insisted that the ultimate object and end of public education was "to form character." Here then were the embryonic themes he was later to develop into a common-sense rationale for public education which was to endure for more than a century.

Skillfully he drove home his points with aphorisms which could both prick sensibilities and remove doubts. His audience sensed a historic moment as they listened to this man on a mission whose message was intended for an entire nation. Carefully, Mann emancipated them from their own immediate concerns and enlarged their perspective, until he had drawn them into his vision of a land of free men where, for the first time in the history of mankind, the opportunity to learn would become the birthright of every American child. When he had finished, the metamorphosis was complete. The aggregate of passive listeners had become a unified group, eager to do their part to usher in a golden age of justice, enlightenment, and unlimited opportunity. To have heard this man was to agree with him that the common school was "the greatest discovery ever made by man." [2]

For an hour and a half they listened, and when the applause subsided at the end of his remarks, men from all corners of the room rose to their feet to make resolutions in support of Mann's presentation. They resolved to form the Worcester County Association for the Improvement of the Common Schools. They also reaffirmed the "high importance of Common Schools" and the need for "school apparatus and libraries." They elected James Carter president of their association and from all over the hall ministers, lawyers, and merchants volunteered to restate Mann's message throughout the county

[2] Accounts of the Worcester meeting were printed in "Lecture on Common Schools," *American Annals of Education*, VII (1837), 463–470; *Massachusetts Spy*, September 6, 1837.

until it had been carried virtually within listening range of every citizen. Clearly to all present, Mann had achieved his goal. Without exaggeration the local newspaper described Mann's presentation as "a performance of a superior order, and listened to with an intensity of attention." Mann's own evaluation was far more modest. In his private Journal he recorded that the meeting was "generally satisfactory" and offered evidence that there was in this part of the State "a good degree of interest in the subject . . . which only wants a right direction." And direction he was prepared to give.[3]

Returning to Boston, he read through an accumulation of letters, paying special attention to responses to his requests for help in making arrangements for other conventions. Many had answered, but he was troubled by the absence of any word from Edward A. Newton, a banker in Pittsfield and a member of the Board. Mann suffered premonitions that his Berkshire meeting would be his most difficult and now Newton's silence increased his anxiety. In the afternoon, he rode out to Cambridge to hear Ralph Waldo Emerson deliver an oration before the Phi Beta Kappa Society assembled at fair Harvard. Mann had heard Emerson before, largely at the prompting of Elizabeth Peabody. He could subscribe to the philosopher's individual statements, but found Emerson's total transcendental framework much too ethereal and abstract. Admitting to too hasty a judgment, Mann now listened with growing fascination to this small man with the hawk nose and a serene countenance delivering one caveat after another to the smug and self-satisfied élite who had gathered once again for their annual ritual of self-aggrandizement in Harvard Yard. Like Emerson, Mann considered himself outside the establishment. Thus he understood what this man, part sage and part gadfly, meant when he looked straight at his audience and said, "I ask not for the great, the remote, the romantic; what is doing in Italy or Arabia; what is Greek art or Provençal minstrelsy; I embrace the common, I explore and sit at the feet of the familiar, the low." Mann thought such ideas were long overdue on a campus he considered produced useless and self-centered gentlemen rather than selfless men of strong moral fiber. As the oration continued, Mann sensed that Emerson was deflating more than an occasional ego among those present. Surely the literary and social élite would punish the speaker with an even more complete ostracism for his outspoken and radical

---

[3] *Massachusetts Spy*, August 30, 1837, and Boston *Daily Advertiser*, August 31, 1837; Mann, Journal, August 31, 1837, MS in MHS.

thoughts. It "was very good—for anybody else," Mann later observed back at his room in Boston, "but hardly so for him." [4]

He stayed but a few days in Boston. The newspapers carried the terse announcement that the "Hon. Horace Mann" had declined to be a candidate for the Senate; from this his Whig and Democratic associates were to understand that Mann considered the reform of the schools a full-time activity. He was now convinced more than ever that the children of the state had as much claim to the humanitarian concerns of their elders as did the slave, the drunkard, and the convict. In one of the responses he had received, a correspondent reported upon a survey he had made of the lighting, ventilation, seating, and heating of some 500 schoolhouses in Essex County. On the basis of his finding he had come to the painful and disconcerting conclusion "that in most of these particulars which contribute to the common comforts and conveniences of life . . . the convicts are better provided for than the children." [5] Mann spent most of his time at his desk, sending out a steady flow of letters to community leaders and other "friends of education" in Springfield, Pittsfield, Northampton, and other towns where he planned his conventions. He also placed announcements in the Salem *Gazette,* the *Columbian Centinel,* and the *Massachusetts Spy.* In the time remaining, benefitting from his experiences in Worcester, he made a few modifications in his speech or "preachment," as he called it, which he planned to repeat at each of his forthcoming meetings.[6]

Correspondence could be accomplished from his office in Boston, but the crucial acts in the reform would be consummated elsewhere, in the local communities themselves. Uncertainty lurked behind each letter he wrote, and it often emerged in the form of a brittle and transparent facetiousness. To Elizabeth Peabody he reported that he would visit all the counties in the state and "aim at a very narrow mark, lest in speaking to the learned, I should get above the unlearned, or vice versa as Finn says." To another correspondent he wrote that his words might "*diffuse* more *hearers* than *knowledge.*" [7] Nervous humor aside, the question still remained,

---

[4] Ralph Waldo Emerson, "American Scholar," *Nature, Addresses and Lectures* (Boston, 1830), pp. 105–111; Mann, Journal, August 31, 1837, MS in MHS.

[5] Boston *Daily Transcript,* September 1, 1837; Boston *Daily Courier,* September 4, 1837; Gardner B. Perry to Mann, August 29, 1837, Mann MSS:MHS.

[6] September 26, September 30, and October 11, 1837.

[7] Mann to Elizabeth Peabody, August 4, 1837, and Mann to William Gray, August 14, 1837, Mann MSS:MHS.

would the people actually turn out to hear *him* in the same numbers they did to hear politicians and temperance reformers? And if they did, could he convince them to join the cause of public education? Carter had written, Brooks had lectured, and the entire American Institute of Instruction with a membership of the most prominent names in New England had deliberated and passed pious resolutions; yet all of their ideas remained largely in quarantine. True, during his brief stay in Boston, he was heartened by an offer from Jonathan Phillips, a wealthy bachelor merchant and member of one of the first families in the city, to give $500 to help get school libraries under way. But this was Boston, the place where citizens had always prided themselves on their support of schools; whether the same would be true of the townspeople in the Connecticut River Valley, the Berkshires, and Nantucket was an unanswered question which continued to bedevil his sleep.[8]

*　　*　　*

Having dispatched a chest with his clothes and books the day before, Mann rose early before sunup and walked to David Homer's livery stable. After slipping a few personal belongings and the precious manuscript of his speech in his saddlebags, he mounted his bay mare and headed out of Boston. The early morning September air was warm and dry, still giving the impression of summer. As he rode past rows of shops and residences, once strange when he first came to this city but now familiar to him, he approached the limits of Boston and the entrance to the long causeway which linked it to the mainland. Along its one side, a row of lamps still burned, having guided travelers during the night. Here too were a few young lads fishing, their backs to him, intent on catching a flounder on the incoming tide. Turning in his saddle, as he neared mid-point on the causeway, Mann looked back on the city slowly rising from its sleep. Deceptively peaceful, only here and there was smoke beginning to curl from a few of its myriad of chimneys. The golden dome of Bulfinch's State House had just caught the first rays of the morning sun. This building which commanded the skyline of the city had provided the setting for his rise to prominence and, perhaps for a fleeting moment, one last lingering doubt rose to the surface of his consciousness to question the wisdom of leaving all this behind. But he could

---

[8] Mann, Journal, August 31, 1837, MS in MHS.

not turn back without reliving all the pain and uncertainty of the past.

In an hour or so, the city would come alive with the movement and noise of money changing, trade, and manufacturing; with it would re-emerge another day and the forces which must be controlled and redirected for the good of the Commonwealth. His future and that of the state and nation lay not in strengthening the power and increasing the wealth of the merchant princes and incipient captains of industry, but in improving the schools and enlightening the children of all the people so that everyone might benefit from the promised wealth.

An all-day ride brought him to Worcester where he stayed for the night. The next morning again found him on the road at daybreak, heading for Chicopee Village and the home of Edmund Dwight. By evening he had covered more than twenty miles and reached his destination, bone-weary and all too happy to enjoy the hospitality of his wealthy benefactor. Unpacking his saddlebags, he was upset to learn that the two-day trip had caused more than just wear and tear on his body. The constant jogging up and down had worn the covering pages of his manuscript to tatters, and after dinner he retired to his room and recopied the damaged pages, wanting to have it ready for the meeting on the morrow. The repairs completed by eleven o'clock, he brought his Journal up to date before retiring, concluding a long entry with

Tomorrow it is to be delivered in the Village of Springfield. Ah, me! my fate will be determined for life by tomorrow night at this time, in the minds of hundreds, who now know nothing of me. But I can do nothing to avert this impending judgment. It is of no use to say, let it come, for it will.[9]

The next morning Mann left the Dwight home and turned his horse south towards Springfield. As he rode along the post road which followed the Connecticut River in a long arc around Mount Tom, he was amazed at the changes which had taken place in the last few years. Dwight and other entrepreneurs had gathered together enough capital to dam the Chicopee River just before it entered the larger Connecticut. Now company houses and red brick factories had arisen where sunny meadows had been once before and the mechanical chatter of spindles and the hum of belts and shafts which drove

---

[9] Mann, Journal, September 6, 1837, MS in MHS.

them had replaced the lowing of cattle and the occasional barking of a dog in the distance. A thousand new families had come to the valley, some Irish immigrants, some French Canadians, and a few Yankee farmers who had abandoned lands owned by their families for generations, all now lured to this burgeoning industrial area by the prospect of steady wages. Here there were new occupations as the energy of falling water, hitherto largely unused, was now finally replacing the muscle power of men and beasts.[1]

Once in the center of Springfield in front of the town hall where he planned to hold his meetings, Mann quickly saw that at least in numbers, things augured well. Both "ladies and gentlemen" had come, and every town in the county was represented. By the time of the meeting all seats were taken and many were forced to stand outside. After a hurried conference, it was decided to hold the sessions in a nearby church and by three o'clock all was ready. After brief formalities, in which the group voted to hear the secretary from Boston, Mann spoke for an hour and a half. As in Worcester, they also passed resolutions in support of public education, the new State Board, and its secretary. Here too they formed an Association for the Improvement of the Common Schools. Even more significant in Mann's eyes was the formation of a team of speakers from the leading men in the community who promised to carry Mann's message to adjoining towns. From all points, Mann considered the encounter in Springfield a success. And the morrow, he turned towards the Berkshires with renewed optimism.[2]

With the Coffee House at Lenox as his next base of operation, Mann rested his mount and hired a gig and horse for a preliminary trip to Pittsfield. Calling upon Edward Newton, he soon found his most serious premonitions fulfilled. While Edmund Dwight had everything ready for the meeting in Springfield, his colleague on the Board had done absolutely nothing in Pittsfield. Adding to Mann's chagrin was the fact that during their tense conversation Mann found it difficult to conceal his growing irritation as Newton spent most of the time giving him gratuitous advice. To make a bad situation even worse, Newton had not thought it necessary to fore-

---

[1] Dwight had laid the groundwork for amassing a considerable fortune in textiles. Within a decade, he would be listed in a Massachusetts directory as worth more than $600,000; *Our First Men: A Calendar of Wealth, Fashion and Gentility Containing a List of Those Persons Reported to be Worth One Hundred Thousand Dollars* (Boston, 1846), p. 20.

[2] Mann, Journal, September 10, 1837, MS in MHS; a receipt dated October [sic]14, 1837, from the Coffee House, Mann MSS:DHS.

warn Mann that the local anti-slavery people had scheduled a rally at the very time Mann expected to hold his own meeting. Believing their anti-slavery cause in the ascendency and soon to draw to it all the humanitarian fervor now flowing to other reforms, they saw no reason to adjust their meeting to the convenience of a rival from out of town. Driving about in the little time remaining, Mann called on persons in Lanesborough and North Adams one day and others in Great Barrington and Stockbridge the next. Fortunately two former legislative friends, Julius Rockwell and Charles Sedgwick, came to his aid, each promising to bring a delegation. As a result, Mann was able to enlist some last-minute interest in the surrounding towns, but on the eve of his meeting he still considered his prospects "pretty flat." [3]

Postponing his meeting until evening in the hope that some of the more curious of the anti-slavery people would stay over for his session as well, Mann commandeered the grand jury room in the courthouse for his rostrum. The crowd was small, but so was the room and Mann was spared the embarrassment of speaking to rows of empty benches. Here too he persuaded his listeners to organize an association, but whatever spark of optimism this kindled for him was almost immediately smothered when the group elected Edward Newton as its president. Since the reform required tireless and dedicated workers, this action sealed the fate of any effort in the Berkshires for the present. Sarcastically, Mann commented on Newton's vitality in his Journal that night, "If there be no more life in the body than in the head, it will decompose very soon." [4]

Considering Pittsfield a loss for the time being, Mann shook the dust from his boots, mounted his horse, and headed east. He made it to Worthington the first night and although he stopped wherever he could to visit schoolhouses along the way, he arrived in Northampton by the second night and took a room at the Mansion

---

[3] Mann, Journal, September 11, 1837, MS in MHS.

[4] Mann, Journal, September 13, 1837, MS in MHS. What Mann did not know was that Newton's lack of support stemmed from deep-seated religious convictions rather than apathy or ennui. A leading Episcopalian in the area, Newton was one of those vanishing Americans with monarchical rather than republican loyalties who privately lamented the fact that the Church of England had never become the established church in the New World. Thus Mann's claim that non-sectarian common schools and republican government were interdependent may have been close to anathema to Newton. Nevertheless, Newton was a close friend of Governor Everett and Mann was in no position to make public record of his inactivity.

House. That evening he called on Franklin Dexter, a prominent attorney and one of the leading men of Massachusetts. If Mann was upset by Newton's apparent foot-dragging, he was in for a real shock in his encounter with Dexter. No sooner had Mann broached the subject of enlightening and elevating the common people than Dexter cut him off and gave his opinion of the undertaking in clear and unambiguous terms. To him it was plain for anyone to see who would not let himself be misled by all the nonsense about democracy and the wisdom of the majority. Society had been, was, and always would be sharply divided into two classes, commoners who were destined by nature to work and support themselves by the sweat of their brow and an aristocracy of birth and position who were obligated to guide and govern the less fortunate. Not only did Dexter invoke the spirit of a dead Federalist past, but he had the effrontery even to claim that the "British Government of Kings, Lords and Commons" was superior to American constitutional government and that it was the duty of the American wealthy and well-born to prevent ingress into their ranks by those below. Only in such a way could a society maintain standards of morality, justice, and good taste. By implication, Dexter was placing a slur on Mann's own common origins and indirectly suggesting that he was a parvenu attempting to exploit a situation for his own advancement. No doubt Dexter couched his arguments in the best of Burkean terms, but for Mann they boiled down to the simple reactionary premise that "one portion of mankind are to be refined and cultivated, the other to suffer, toil, and live and die in vulgarity." Later back in his room at the Mansion House as he attempted to reconstruct the interview, Mann felt helpless to deal rationally with such antediluvian propositions. At best he could denounce Dexter and others of the same ilk as reactionaries and "a powerless, conceited, haughty race, who have little or nothing beside adventitious merit." [5]

Committed to common school education as he was, Mann had no choice in the matter. Once one granted Dexter's division of society, then the entire scheme of a comprehensive public system of education, which furnished avenues of upward mobility for all children, regardless of race, creed, or financial position, emerged as a foolish and even dangerous experiment. Perhaps Dexter would concede that even the lowliest needed a modicum of literacy if they were to know their place, remain law-abiding and docile, and show proper

---

[5] Charles Sedgwick to Mann, September 27, 1837, Mann MSS:MHS; Mann, Journal, September 15, 1837, MS in MHS.

deference to those above them, but schooling which was the vehicle for a mobility that crossed class lines and challenged the established order was an American form of Jacobinism. Yet just coming from Pittsfield with the first sense of public apathy for his cause lingering in his mind, Mann was in part vulnerable to Dexter's caveats. In his first tour of the state he was attempting to reach the influential people in each community. He knew, however, that the time would soon come when he must also persuade the less articulate but far more numerous group of common people who harbored many suspicions about the merits of formal schooling and book learning. If the more élite were inclined to see public education for all as an impossibility or even a dangerous adventure in egalitarianism, those less elevated perceived it as an unnecessary nuisance to keep their children subservient to the established order rather than opening for them a free and early access to the "real" education and rewards of the farm, the factory, and the frontier. Both groups differed in the reasons for their opposition, but they could agree that extended schooling was largely a wasted effort. True, in almost every town he found individuals whose commitment to public education for all was an article of faith. Starting with these "friends of education" as a nucleus, he would have to bring various factions together until he had fashioned a community of consent and a broad coalition of support for his cause.

But at the moment, such long-range strategy had to be pushed into the background in favor of tasks immediately at hand. His Northampton convention still several days away, Mann took time to visit some of its schools. This lovely New England community was sometimes boosted as the "Athens of the Connecticut Valley," and according to the *Hampshire Gazette*, its schools were not excelled by any town in the United States. "By this provision of the town," the *Gazette* boasted, "every family, however numerous, or whatever may be its circumstances, can give its children a good education. Is not this a wise provision? It renders taxes rather high, but it is money well spent." [6] And Mann heartily agreed. The girls' school he visited had been recently built according to a floor plan published by A. Bronson Alcott in the *Proceedings of the American Institute of Instruction*. The school offered instruction from reading and spelling to chemistry, French, and algebra. It was a pleasant sight to see these girls, neatly dressed in freshly ironed pinafores and blouses, apply-

---

[6] February 15, 1837; see also the *Report of the School Committee of Northampton* (Northampton, 1838), pp. 1–5.

ing themselves to studies usually available only to boys. The three teachers, Misses Smith, Strong, and Warner, were in charge of some 160 girls and were proud that every girl in town received "a finished and thorough education, rich or poor, at public expense," provided that parents availed themselves of the opportunity. Equally impressive to Mann was the boys' high school. He observed a physiology lesson in which the students named the principal bones of the body and explained in a rudimentary fashion the processes of circulation and digestion, which included the "putrefactive action of ardent spirits upon the delicate tissues of the stomach." [7]

He also spent a reassuring evening with Samuel Lyman, who not only told him of the many arrangements made for Mann's Northampton meeting, but introduced him to his house guest, Baron de Boene, the Prussian Minister to the United States. Attempting to maintain a discreet distance which foreign visitors normally found all too absent in their encounters with Americans, Mann did not press the Baron at the time, but hoped to see him again in order to learn more about the celebrated "Prussian system" of education. For most of the evening, Mann's mind again was focused on the imminent. The next afternoon was his convention, where he was "to be led out . . . for execution, or for triumph." And it turned out splendidly. Lyman had done his work well and the townsfolk from near and far turned out in quantity and quality. Mann considered it a "capital convention" and thought his audience responded to his challenge "like heroes." [8]

It was then on to Greenfield, his spirits never better as he rode up the scenic Connecticut River Valley under a warm benign sun. Now in late September he could see that the dry summer had brought an early autumn. Along the banks of the river all was still lush and green, but in the distant hills, individual birches and maples had turned golden yellow and flaming scarlet, dazzling solitary prophecies of what soon would come to the entire landscape. Wherever the valley widened, he passed gardens and orchards where orange pumpkins and red McIntosh apples glowed in the sun, the timeless symbols of the season upon him. In the fields entire families were shucking corn and gathering the last of the grain and hay into their barns with that organic sense of well-being and feeling of security which only belongs to the men and women of the soil who

---

[7] *Hampshire Gazette*, July 5, 1837; Mann, Journal, September 18, 1837, MS in MHS.
[8] Mann, Journal, September 17, 18, and 19, 1837, MS in MHS.

lay in store what they have grown and harvested. To complete this most idyllic day, upon arriving in Greenfield, Mann was welcomed by Reverend Emerson Davis, orthodox Congregational minister and a person quickly identified as a future leader in the cause. Like Dwight and Lyman, Davis too had done his work well, and the following afternoon, Mann inadvertently demonstrated that the spoken word could be as appealing as the sword. He talked to a full house, even though he was in direct competition with a local muster day celebration.

The Greenfield convention buoyed up the momentary loss of confidence he had suffered with Newton and Dexter. "Some obstacles will stand in my path always. Some untoward events will occur. Some accidents will thrust aside well aimed blows," he conceded. "But can anything overcome perseverance? We will see." He could expect empty halls and knew there would be other Newtons and Dexters to endure, but as he took inventory of his efforts of the last few weeks, Greenfield, Northampton, Springfield, and Worcester demonstrated that he had a core of influential and responsible persons on his side, that he could anticipate the slings and arrows of a small but by no means impotent minority, but that by perseverance he could capture and inspire the apathetic and generally inarticulate majority to his side.[9]

Yet it was not merely public approval which enabled him to continue. In fact, had everyone agreed with him, Mann would have lost interest in his cause. What he needed was a strong and determined opposition. Only in a "selfless" struggle with opponents could he draw upon the wellsprings of duty, an act which was essential to what self-composure and certainty he could maintain. Without physical and human obstacles, how could one persevere? For some men, the great battles to be fought were internal; within themselves were to be found highly individual dialectical struggles between good and evil as they attempted to achieve meaning and personal worth in their lives. Mann too had his struggles, but through the reform causes he advanced, he gradually was able to externalize the conflicts which had been within, by identifying a visible external opposition which he labeled as evil, self-seeking, and irresponsible, and placing himself, now purged of self-doubts, uncompromisingly on the side of the angels.

The following morning, a Saturday, he left the town and headed

---

[9] Mann, Journal, September·19 and 21, 1837, MS in MHS.

east for Boston, staying on his mount until he had covered forty miles, attempting to accomplish two days' ride in one since he could not travel on the Sabbath. On Monday he again saddled up and rode as far as Lancaster, where he spent the afternoon and evening reporting his experiences to James Carter. Another day's ride and he was back in Boston. If his view of the city as he approached had not changed markedly since his departure, the beholder of the sight had. He had left as a lonely individual, uncertain if he could garner enthusiasm and support for the cause. Now it was a wiser, more confident man riding across the causeway and back into the city, who knew a good deal more of the prospects and pitfalls which beset him as he prepared for a circuit of conventions in another part of the state.

*   *   *

Once back in his quarters, Mann received a reassuring letter "full of spirit" from Channing; descended into a spell of melancholy during the seventh anniversary of his marriage; listened to a sermon by Father Taylor at Seamen's Bethel; accepted Iona Worcester's invitation to speak to "the more intelligent portion of our citizens" by delivering the first lecture of the winter season of the Salem Lyceum; dined with Mills; and was then off again on another circuit, this time to the southeast, to the "Old Colony" and the offshore islands of Nantucket and Martha's Vineyard.[1] His first meeting was at Taunton where half a crowd listened in a *"half-spiritless"* fashion. Fortunately, Channing had journeyed up from his summer home in Newport and also gave an address. That Channing had lent his tremendous prestige to the cause was newsworthy and at least two Boston newspapers used up the better part of two columns in printing long extracts from his speech. Mann then boarded a packet for Edgartown on Martha's Vineyard, where he spoke to "a very goodly number" including a delegation which had sailed across the sound from the neighboring Chilmark Islands for the specific purpose of hearing him.[2]

It was next on to Nantucket, but barely had Mann cleared the

---

[1] Iona F. Worcester to Mann, September 6, 1837, Mann MSS:MHS; Mann, Journal, September 27 and 28, and October 1 and 2, 1837, MS in MHS; Boston *Weekly Messenger*.

[2] Mann, Journal, October 4 and 6, 1837, MS in MHS; *Independent Chronicle and Boston Patriot*, October 14, 1837, and Boston *Weekly Messenger*, October 19, 1837.

Edgartown jetty before he heard that his visit had caused ill-will among the local clergy. Since all three meetinghouses were orthodox, he chose not to attend the services of any of them and spent the Sabbath visiting a nearby Indian village inhabited by a remnant of what he could only describe as "a failing and white-man stricken race!" In preferring to commune with these Samaritans rather than sit in a temple with Pharisees, he had offended at least one local clergyman who thought that if Mann did not wish to show a preference, he "might have gone to . . . each during the day." For Mann, the ordeal of hearing three orthodox sermons in tandem was worse than "being burned—at least a little." [3]

In no way did he let the incident detract from his enjoyment of the sail to Nantucket. Standing at the railing of the quarter-deck, he scanned the horizon where, save for a distant sail, the ocean was bounded by an infinite sky. The early morning fog had burned off and high overhead the blue sky was flecked with a roof of mackerel clouds. Ever attempting to raise his sensual experiences to a more elevated metaphysical plane, Mann realized that the short voyage had forced a humble serenity upon him as the words "I do not comprehend it yet" moved through his mind in a steady refrain. A stiff offshore breeze pushed up a cross swell and filled the sails as they popped and chattered in their irons. Soon his vessel was entering Nantucket Harbor, with its white stately mansions and dignified meetinghouses on the high ground overlooking the fleet of whaling vessels and coastal schooners tied up at the busy wharves. The island was enjoying an unprecedented prosperity, yet somehow it still maintained such pristine virtues as honesty, hard work, and respect for authority which Mann thought were rapidly diminishing on the mainland. As the crew hauled in the sails, the vessel slowly eased into its mooring until the sudden lurch as it came up against the dock piling and the cry of those mendicant sentinels at every waterfront, the seagulls, brought Mann's thoughts to the immediate present. Walking down the gangplank, he spotted a local drifter to carry his bag to the inn. He followed the man on foot, walking on the smooth cobblestones to the main thoroughfare of the town. [4]

For several days, he visited schools on the island. The best one he found to be taught by Reverend Cyrus Peirce. At the time, Mann was simply impressed with the rare teaching ability of this Unitarian clergyman and his sound views toward maintaining a strong system

---

[3] Mann, Journal, October 10, 1837, MS in MHS.
[4] Mann, Journal, October 10 and 11, 1837, MS in MHS.

of common schools. So new was Mann to his mission that he did not envision the central role Peirce would soon play in establishing normal schools in Massachusetts. Instead, his thoughts focused on the morrow and his meeting with the community. The next day, the small group in attendance were so impressed with his ideas that they promised him a larger audience if he would make the same presentation the following evening. Well aware that it would be difficult to serve up "cabbage twice boiled," Mann agreed and found "a bumper" of an audience "rammed, crammed, jammed" into every part of the meetinghouse.[5]

Returning to the mainland he spoke to a meeting at Barnstable with delegates attending from every town in the county save four. Then he and Thomas Robbins rode to Plymouth where they inspected several schools and visited the graves of the Pilgrims. Sensing that he stood on hallowed ground and attempting to place his own endeavors in some historic perspective, Mann remarked, "How little they saw two centuries ago of the present! Who can fathom future time?" In terms of the most immediate future, the next day brought out a good convention in Plymouth. Robbins thought Mann's address "was received, as at other places, with the highest approbation." Reverend Charles Brooks spoke in the evening and the convention concluded with a doxology of resolutions supporting the common schools. The next morning Mann was back on his horse by eight o'clock and was entering the outskirts of Boston as the sun was setting. After a warm meal, he returned to his rooms with little else on his mind but the need for sleep.[6]

In Boston there was a round of social calls with the Mills, Quincy, and the Lorings, all of whom wanted a report on his recent circuit. Finding his clothes the worse for wear, Mann also ordered a black coat and pants from his tailor. Charles Sumner, who was about to leave for Europe, asked Mann to dine with him. Mann found something attractive about this troubled young lawyer who was struggling to find his niche in Boston society. At the moment, neither

[5] Mann, Journal, October 13, 14, and 15, MS in MHS. This was the beginning of one of Mann's most enduring friendships. For some strange reason, never explained in their correspondence, Mann insisted on spelling Peirce's name, "Pierce." For an example of Peirce's ideas on the importance of public schools, see Cyrus Peirce, *et al.*, *Address to the Inhabitants of Nantucket on Education and Free Schools* (Providence, 1838), pp. 3–24.
[6] Thomas Robbins, *Diary*, II, p. 471; Mann, Journal, October 20, 22, 23, and 25, 1837, MS in MHS.

man had much sense of how their careers would later converge, but even at this early date, Mann sensed the dimensions of greatness in Sumner. "When he goes," he recorded in his Journal, "there will be one good fellow on that side and one less on this." There were also arrangements to be made for still other conventions. Mann wrote to Robert Rantoul, Jr., asking him to have things ready in Salem and to "induce the towns to send full delegations, and to awaken the regards of citizens generally. . . ." He asked Jared Sparks to join him at Concord and lend "the weight of his presence" and the "value of his counsel," and he accepted Ralph Waldo Emerson's invitation to stay at the Old Manse during the convention. Since the local newspapers had reported that Mann had resigned as secretary of the Board, confusing this with his resignation as a regular member of the Board, he also found it necessary to have them print a correction.[7]

During the week in Boston, Mann slipped in a short convention in Dedham. If he in any way hoped or feared that his new cause was sufficiently strong to divert all of his emotions to the present, he was mistaken. Once again in Dedham the past came out of the shadows. Almost fleeing back to Boston, he found the image of the house where Charlotte had died lodged in his mind, creating a paralyzing despair from which he had no will to escape. "When I go back to that place," he wrote, "my mind, my eyes, involuntarily turn to the consecrated spot. . . . I cannot walk near it,—when I look at it I feel as though I must look from it,—for the sight becomes almost intolerable and yet I am compelled to gaze at it again.

Oh! dearest! dearest! how far removed from everything upon earth, how unutterably alone I dwell in this world. Its beauty is perished. Its music is discord. Its pleasures have become pain, but none of its pains have become pleasures. And will this all always be so. Yes. I had rather it would, than that I should ever forget thee, my beloved wife!"

He also shared his thoughts with Mary Peabody. Wishing to sympathize with him, yet saddened by the death of her younger brother Wellington the week before, she could only offer him a muffled ex-

---

[7] Mann, Journal, November 5 and 6, 1837, MS in MHS; the receipt for Mann's new suit is dated October 26, 1837, MS in DHS; Mann to Robert Rantoul, Jr., October 30, 1837, EHI; Mann to Jared Sparks, October 31, 1837, Sparks MSS:HCL. Mann to Mary Peabody, November 5, 1837 and Mann to Ralph Waldo Emerson, November 7, 1837, Mann MSS:MHS; Boston *Daily Advertiser,* October 27, 1837; *Independent Chronicle and Boston Patriot,* October 28, 1837.

pression of her own bitterness. "I am disposed to murmur against heaven," she wrote, "that time and the exercise of noble duty brings you no solace." The trip to Dedham once again brought to the surface a fundamental contradiction in his life which would not succumb to an easy resolution. Only by gratifying his self-imposed mandate to respond to "the hard forcings of duty" could he repress the contending drives and self-doubts which taunted him. Considering himself "driven and scourged away from pleasures," he could "thank the creator for a sphere of duty" from which he could fashion his own tenuous version of happiness. But like the intemperate man whom he despised, Mann craved an ever greater gratification, even though this could only come from a heightened sense of sacrifice which in turn fed on an acute awareness of his own suffering. Thus to travel back to Dedham or Providence was to slip back into a slough of despond which he both loathed and sought.[8]

As this first circuit through the state was the beginning of a new career for Mann, so it also marked the end of that period in his life which had begun with the rise in Massachusetts politics. A summer interval of uncertainty had been followed by an autumn of new purpose and conviction. Almost with a sense of guilt and fear he wrote of his new-found satisfaction. To his sister, he explained, "I confess I feel, now, more as though life had a value, and as though I had a specific work to do, than I have done before for these last sad five years. Yet, if I am to be used through life, and not enjoy its highest blessings, so be it. In one thing however, I have faith, that it is the highest happiness, which is born of duty." Thus as he closed his law books for what he thought would be the last time, he could make his pledge to his own future as well as that of others with the words, "Let the next generation, then, be my client."[9]

[8] Mann, Journal, November 4, 1837, MS in MHS; Mary Peabody to Mann, November 18, 1837, Mann MSS:MHS; Mary Peabody to George Peabody, November 16, 1837, Berg MSS:NYPL.
[9] Thomas Robbins to Mann, November 14, 1837; Mary Peabody to Mann, November 27, 1837; Mann to Elizabeth Peabody, December 2–16, 1837; Mann to Lydia Mann, November 27, 1837, Mann MSS:MHS; Mann Journal, November 3, 11, 15, and 27, MS in MHS.

CHAPTER XIII

A New Shay:
The Deacon's Masterpiece

> . . . this government never of itself furthered any
> enterprise, but by the alacrity with which it got out
> of its way. *It* does not keep the country free.
> . . . *It* does not educate. The character inherent in
> the American people has done all that has been ac-
> complished; and it would be somewhat more, if
> the government had not sometimes got in its way.
> HENRY DAVID THOREAU

> OUR ENORMOUS BURDENS, instead of being car-
> ried on shoulders as had been the custom of old,
> were all snugly deposited in the baggage car, . . .
> NATHANIEL HAWTHORNE

MANN WAS BOTH EXHAUSTED and worried by the time he had
completed his first circuit and returned to Boston. The ex-
haustion was understandable. Since September he had ridden more
than 500 miles on horseback and would soon need a new saddle and
riding breeches. The source of his worry was more elusive. Since the
public response to his conventions added up to a series of successes
other reformers might well have envied, he should have been ex-
hilarated; and perhaps he was for a brief moment. Yet exhilaration
quickly deteriorated into doubt when he admitted to himself that in
these first sorties he had brought the reform little beyond the verbal
threshold. Between the real present and the ideal future he sought lay
a journey with innumerable obstacles, many of which had humbled
and defeated lesser men. Thus for all the immediate support he had
gained, he knew that monumental efforts were necessary in the next
few years, if he was to make any headway at all.

Disparate elements of his reform kept circling through his mind;
teachers' seminaries, improved buildings, more taxation, and better
books. In addition, it took considerable mental effort to separate the
real solution to educational problems from what might prove to be
the passing fads of the day: music in the schools, monitorial instruc-

tion, health education, the teaching of reading by the phonetic method, permissive behavior, and the abolition of corporal punishment. For all the momentary confusion these caused as he attempted to place them within some framework of priorities, he was reasonably clear from the outset on his more general goal. His task as he conceived it was to fashion a coalition of diverse interests in support of the schools and to create a unified community of consensus which would back his cause. He would avoid those things which would divide men: class interest, sectarian religion, local pride, partisan issues, and familial loyalties. The past particularism of churches, villages, and clans represented outmoded cultural forms and was increasingly divisive and dangerous in the age of the factory, the railroad, republican government, and science. Rather than stressing apparent differences, his task was to seek out those social norms to which a majority of men agreed—if not in terms of a creed, then at least in terms of their behavior. Men might disagree verbally on immersion or sprinkling as the correct form of baptism, Jackson or Adams as the most desirable President, or the farm or the factory as the best place of labor. But if they practiced the same desirable social amenities, observed the laws of the land, and lived according to the golden rule, the future of the Commonwealth and the nation was secure. To accomplish this required a public school which would be civilized, republican, and Christian. If what he espoused would someday be unmasked as a scrimping set of middle-class rather than a body of universal values, the revelation would not take place in his own time.

Yet the school was not to be a parasite of the social body on which it grew. Mann conceived of a symbiotic relationship in which neither the republic nor the school could exist without the other. This would only be so if the public treasury would support the schools, but the schools would promulgate a set of values or basic natural laws which all reasonable Americans could support. That there was no automatic agreement between the collective social will and individual self-interest, he understood all too well. Adam Smith's "invisible hand" might still be guiding the transactions of the free marketplace, but Mann did not believe in the existence of a similar hand at work harmoniously guiding the affairs of men. There were always shortsighted, selfish men who manipulated situations for personal gain and all too easily misled the multitudes. The common man, at least for the present then, required guidance by enlightened men of good will and needed to be educated by an institution which taught him to live within existing legal restraints while paradoxically finding an expanding personal freedom. Mann considered himself just such a leader and the public school which he advanced just such an institution.

Holding fast to such a vision and determined to see it triumph regardless of what this required in personal sacrifice, Mann forged himself into a total reformer whose cause had the purity, brilliance, and irresistible cutting edge of a diamond. Never did he question the validity of his ideology. Nor would he tolerate less than total allegiance from others. Those who did not agree with him were against him and his cause. Severe, dogmatic, and scathing in his rebuke, he had no room for those who did not see the light as he did. Thus, he welcomed public controversy, demanding though it was on his energies, as a righteous opportunity to smoke out the heretic and brand the evil doer. Compromise, dissent, and alternative actions had little place in his world. The answers to all social, political, and economic questions were found ultimately in the realm of morality. Mann believed that a knowledge of good and evil could be distilled into moral principles formulated with almost mathematical precision and acted upon with scientific exactitude. In essence, he worshipped truth as revealed by reason and had come to believe that he and the common school were its sacred vessels.

*   *   *

Unfortunately, there were enough unscrupulous men at the time to confirm Mann in at least one part of his views on the workings of society. Early in December he witnessed a most blatant attempt to betray the public interest for personal gain. On November 7, 1837, a mob had murdered the Reverend Elijah Lovejoy at Alton, Illinois. As the news of the atrocity spread across the nation, a wave of indignation followed in its wake. In Boston a group of its first men gathered to condemn the action. Even the mild-mannered Channing was so outraged that his name headed a petition for the use of Faneuil Hall for a mass meeting. After first being denied on the grounds that the meeting might degenerate into "a scene of confusion which would be . . . injurious to the glory of that consecrated Hall," Channing appealed the decision in an open letter to the people of Boston and the hall was opened to him. At ten o'clock on the morning of December 8, Mann was one of the multitude who packed the hall. Since all in the auditorium stood, many more were inside than had there been seats. Even so, the crowd overflowed the building onto the streets outside. Jonathan Phillips, who had offered Mann $500 for school books, took the chair. Channing made a brief but moving address. Resolutions denouncing the mob action followed, when James Austin, Massachusetts Attorney General and a leading member of Channing's Federal Street Church, elbowed his way through the crowd and gained the rostrum. Obviously not on the planned program, the popular politician began what Mann quickly recognized as an harangue to subvert the intent of the meeting. Almost incapable of believing what he heard, Mann listened to Austin appeal to the base emotions of the audience, claiming that the Alton rioters were the modern counterparts of the Boston patriots who had emptied British tea chests into the harbor in 1776 and that Lovejoy had received his due reward. The roar of approval which followed broke in on Mann's ears like a torrent. To him the speech was "so flagrantly wicked as to be imbecile." How could a public servant, he asked himself, "either pervert himself so or be so perverted"?

But before the resolutions went down to defeat, Mann saw the young Wendell Phillips also force his way to the rostrum amidst cries of "question!", "hear him!", and "no gagging!" Phillips leveled a devastating counterattack on Austin. Reaching a climax, he pointed to the portraits of James Otis, John Hancock, and John Adams hanging on the walls and exclaimed that to compare these men with the Alton mob was a libel to their memory and a slander of the glorious dead. The hall now in an uproar, Phillips held the lectern to the end, closing with:

I am glad, sir, to see this crowded house. It is good for us to be here. When liberty is in danger, Faneuil has the right, it is her duty, to strike the keynote for these United States. . . . The passage of these resolutions, in spite of this opposition, led by the Attorney General of the Commonwealth, will show more clearly, more decisively, the deep indignation with which Boston regards this outrage.

Channing's resolutions were carried by an overwhelming majority; and once more, according to the Boston *Times*, Faneuil Hall had spoken for freedom in "thunder tones." Good had triumphed over evil; but for Mann, the event was filled with foreboding. Both Austin and Phillips were extremists playing to the emotions of the audience to seek their ends. Admittedly, as far as his humanitarianism was concerned, Phillips was on the side of the angels, but Mann could not approve his methods and those of other abolitionists.[1]

There was a better way to obtain justice, and later the same week he joined a group meeting at Jonathan Phillips's apartment to review the recent events at Faneuil Hall. After a discussion they decided that the abolitionist's right to free speech must be protected, but then equivocated by insisting that the views of this particular group of anti-slavery agitators should not emanate from Faneuil Hall, lest people in other parts of the country conclude that Boston now favored a new form of radicalism. Mann's reasoning was contrived and less than heroic; but his position indicated his concern for public peace, his desire to build his own reform movement on a more solid middle ground, and his intent to bring men together under his own ideology. His motto for the next year would be "sow the seed—keep sowing. . . . Agitate, agitate, agitate—but nevertheless, in a proper way and for a good cause only." [2]

Building a reform required work and Mann plunged into his task of summarizing his experiences, preparing abstracts from several hundred school committees, and writing what was to become his first *Annual Report*.[3] Slowly he worked through the stack of papers before him, attempting to bring the raw data into some systematic form. A few towns had sent in answers to all the questions in his circular; many had sent in very little and a few did not bother to reply at all. But if the sheer size of the pile of documents was impressive, the story in its contents was even more revealing. By thumbing through the top few, he could see the widest variation in school practices. Although for decades the politicians never seemed to tire of bragging about the "Massachusetts system" of free schools, Mann now had before him the crude statistical proof that in fact, there was no "system." Furthermore, instead of documenting a conscientious support of education, the reports told a story of neglect, parsimony, apathy, and sometimes even chaos. How else was one to describe the fact that in the previous school term more than ninety

---

[1] The account of the Faneuil Hall meeting is drawn from Mann, Journal, December 10, 1837, MS in MHS; *Liberator*, December 15, 1837; Wendell Phillips, "The Murder of Lovejoy," *Speeches, Lectures, and Letters*, first series (Boston, 1894), pp. 1–10; and Oscar Sherwin, *Prophet of Liberty* (New York, 1958), pp. 58–72.

[2] Mann, Journal, December 15, 1837, and January 26, 1838, MS in MHS.

[3] Most of the information for the discussion which follows was drawn from the school returns for the year 1837, which are on file in the Archives of the State of Massachusetts. Other sources will be cited specifically.

schools were closed prematurely or "broken up" by rowdy students, a term used by the school committees which was as true literally as it was figuratively.[4]

Chaos was also the appropriate word to describe the ways in which the communities paid for their schools. As he read the returns, Mann noted that some towns raised less than $1 per child to keep a schoolmaster while some spent six times as much. Most of the support came from taxes, but even here there was little system or order. Some taxpayers paid a cash assessment; others furnished room and board for the teacher; and some furnished cordwood to satisfy the insatiable appetites of the school stoves and fireplaces. Some communities still nursed the delusion that someday, through the interest which would come from a large school fund, annual taxation would be unnecessary. A false dream from colonial times, the school returns before him bore potent evidence of the futility of self-perpetuating school funds. The village of Southwick with its nest egg of $15,000 producing an income equal to half of its school expenses was clearly the exception. By comparison, Boston's fund of $8,000 produced a mere $500 toward an annual budget of $185,000; Sudbury received $26 from its fund and Marlborough's school levy of nearly $2,000 was reduced by $22. Some communities resorted to even more ingenious if archaic practices to avoid taxes. The town of Weymouth anticipated $400 each year from the proceeds of the town fishery. Thus in this community, there was a direct correlation between the length of the school term and the duration of the herring run.

Even direct taxation proved to be an inadequate support for the schools. As expenses mounted, rather than raise assessments, the more general practice was to shorten the school session. A few parents rebelled at this when the term was reduced to as little as four weeks in the winter, and voluntarily kept the schoolmaster on for another month. In Williamstown, the community raised $1,600 for its teachers; but when this money ran out in eight weeks, a small number of parents paid an additional $800 to keep the teacher just for their own children. Thus, for all of the rhetoric about generous public support for education, some communities were resorting to an unofficial rate-bill system—a controversial practice in neighboring New York.[5]

---

[4] Mann, *Ninth Annual Report* (Boston, 1845), p. 40.
[5] The rate-bill system was a practice in which the school costs exceeding the tax income were billed to those parents having children in school.

Compounding the problem of support was the competition of academies. Mann believed that since the common school should be both controlled and supported by the public, it had prior claim to tax monies. The relationship between the semi-private academies and public authority was more complex. Some who argued for public support of all forms of education including academies and colleges stated their case much as Mann had argued earlier for state support of canals, bridges, railroads, and factories. Not only was it believed that transportation and industry would add to the Commonwealth but there were even a few who argued that their presence would raise the level of morality in the state, even as schools and churches did. Thus with utter sincerity, William Savage, who would soon lead some of Mann's legislative battles for better schools, would also serve as chairman of the Committee of Correspondence for the Western Rail-Road Corporation and circularize the following request among the clergymen in Massachusetts:

. . . we take leave, most respectfully, but earnestly, to ask you to take an early opportunity to deliver a Discourse before your Congregation, on the Moral effect of Rail-Roads in our wide extended Country.

One could substitute "schools" for "Rail-Roads" without in any way changing the meaning of the appeal.[6]

Actually railroads were mixed enterprises and the pawns of a threeway struggle between state and local politicians and private investors whose concerns were also threefold—profit, promotion, and control. The same could be said for the academies. In Massachusetts, the state had contributed land to found them; local communities wanted such institutions within their boundaries as a matter of local pride and boosterism; individuals wanted the private benefits of education for their children. As Mann increasingly conceived of railroads and factories as nonpublic corporations producing private profits, he saw the common schools as a public venture supported by the public taxes and producing a form of public profit.

Academies then were transitional institutions soon to be replaced by public schools, but their very presence hindered the transition since they continued to attract children from the more wealthy families Mann thought belonged in the public schools. Where some

---

The net result of this was that the poor people, not able to afford the additional expense, kept their children at home. It was not totally abolished in New York until 1867.

[6] A copy dated December 19, 1838, is in the Robbins MSS:CHS.

communities, such as Lowell, had strong public school systems, less than 10 per cent of the children were in academies. South Reading had nothing but public instruction. On the other hand, the town of Sandwich had more private schools than public and in Salem about 40 per cent of the students took private instruction. And in Cambridge, where more than 20 per cent of its children were in private institutions, their tuition almost equaled the cost of publicly educating the remaining 80 per cent.

Also bordering on chaos was the Babel of books used in the schools. Legally, school committees were empowered to determine which texts should be used, but in reality, children studied from whatever their parents could provide. Mann noted that a few books appeared more frequently than others on the town lists. Besides the ubiquitous Bible, Frederick Emerson's speller, Warren Colburn's text on mental arithmetic, and Samuel Goodrich's United States history were all popular, but their competitors were legion. From what he could make out of the confusing titles on the returns, Mann concluded there was a minimum of fourteen spelling books, fifteen geographies, and eight grammars all of comparable difficulty in a single school. This variety did not mean a broad curriculum. A town like Cambridge offered an impressive list, including the following:

Colburn's First Lessons in Arithmetic; Colburn's First Second and Third Reading Books; New National Spelling Book with the Introduction; Emerson's North American Arithmetic, First Part; Hall's Childbook of Geography; Mount Vernon Reader; American Popular Lessons; Emerson's Third Class Reader; Colburn's Fourth Lessons; Colburn's Introduction to Arithmetic; Olney's Geography; Alger's Murray [sic]; American First Class Book; Pierpont's National Reader; Introduction to the National Reader; Second Class Reader; Colburn's Sequel; Goodrich's History of the U. States, with Emerson's Questions; Worcester's Elements of General History, with Charts; Colburn's Algebra; Park's Natural Philosophy; Geometry; the Abridgment of Wayland's Moral Science; Paley's Natural Theology. The Bible or Testament to be used in all the schools at the discretion of the instructor.

But more typical was the offering in the town of Shrewsbury, which included:

Cumming's Spelling Book; New Testament; National Reader; Leavitt's Easy Lessons; American First Class Book; Adams' and Colburn's Arithmetics; Murray's grammar, Parley's and Olney's Geographies, Goodrich's History.

Portions of these texts were memorized or "mastered" by the students. Between the ages of four and sixteen, the pupil was expected to have worked through a speller or two, Colburn's arithmetic to the "fourth rule," and a United States history. Occasionally, a teacher also held recitations in geography, science, and surveying. Mann noted too a few who were teaching Mrs. Lincoln's *Botany,* Francis Wayland's *Elements of Moral Science,* and something listed as *Abercrombie on the Intellectual Powers.*

*   *   *

Organizing a school abstract with its masses of statistics proved a tedious and time-consuming job; but this was largely a clerical task requiring more patience than insight. His *Annual Report* to the Board, which he was to present on January 1, 1838, was a far more intellectually demanding task. As November passed into December, nothing Mann put to paper satisfied him. Still searching for a form in which to present his ideas, he spent a disappointing afternoon at Edmund Dwight's visiting with Joseph Cogswell, one of the founders of the Roundhill School at Northampton. Unimpressed with Cogswell's Pestalozzian approach to education, Mann returned to his office complaining, "My cavern has not been so much lighted by this luminous body. This may be *part* guess-work, part inference and *all* wrong; but it is at present the state of my mind." [7] Even Emerson's third lecture in his Boston winter series was not up to Mann's expectations. "Not so lucid—pelucid—as the others!" he thought. By a most circuitous and cluttered route, Emerson had finally arrived at the point where he could offer two imperatives: "know thyself" and "improve thyself." [8]

As in the previous September, an immovable deadline forced Mann finally to put his ideas to paper. Once under way he let nothing interfere, neither friends nor the Christmas holidays. Statistics and school descriptions were inserted, later to be deleted; arguments were rephrased; here and there he softened or veiled an admonition for public action; at other places he became more bold, sharpening an aphorism to drive home a point which would create a twinge in the public conscience that could be felt even in the inner reaches of the Berkshires. By New Year's Eve he had finished, not because he

---

[7] Mann, Journal, Decemer 18, 1837, MS in MHS.
[8] Mann, Journal, December 20, 1837, MS in MHS.

was satisfied with the end result, but because he had neither time nor energy to do more.

The next morning the Board assembled to hear his report in the council chamber just off from Governor Everett's office. Thomas Robbins had traveled north from Braintree, Robert Rantoul had taken the coach up from Gloucester, and several others had come from Worcester, Springfield, and Pittsfield. Of all those who sat expectantly around the polished mahogany table, Mann was beholden to no one as much as Edmund Dwight. The report he was about to give would be the first sign of the wisdom or the folly of Dwight's support of a State Board of Education and Mann's role in it.[9]

He began by restating the responsibilities of his office, ". . . to collect information of the actual condition of the common schools. . . ." and explaining his method of gathering it: "I have traveled between five and six hundred miles . . . to inspect the conditions of many school houses." Actually, he had obtained specific information on at least 1,000. Lest any should take offense at what was to come, he cushioned his next statements about the Massachusetts "system" by insisting that he had found a "vast preponderance of its excellences over its defects." [1]

Nevertheless, defects needing immediate action there were, and Mann organized these under four headings. He began with school buildings. So much had to be said here that he proposed to present a more detailed discussion in a separate report. He then spoke about the duties of school committees. The committeemen, he claimed, were "the administrators of the system; and in proportion to the fidelity and intelligence, exercised by them, the system will flourish or decline." He spoke of their responsibility for determining the competency of teachers. Their lack of supervisory visits to the classroom, he hurried to add, was not attributable ". . . to any peculiar deadness or dormancy." No officeholder performed public services " . . . for so little of the common inducements of honor and emolument." Therefore, he urged financial remuneration for their services.[2]

In his third section he dealt with "the apathy of the people themselves toward our common schools." Some persons saw no need

---

[9] Records of the Massachusetts State Board of Education, January 1, 1838, MS in MSDE; Mann Journal, January 1, 1838, MS in MHS.

[1] *First Annual Report of the [Massachusetts] Board of Education together with the First Annual Report of the Secretary of the Board* (Boston, 1838), pp. 22–25.

[2] *First Annual Report*, pp. 27–41; Mann to Elizabeth Peabody, March 10, 1838, Mann MSS: MHS.

for formal education beyond a rudimentary literacy, while others valued it so highly they turned away "from the common schools, in their depressed state," and created their own. He noted ominously that this latter group embraced "a considerable portion, perhaps a majority of the wealthy persons in the state." As noon approached, he hurried on to his fourth section and spoke on the need to improve teaching. Fads and foibles there were in education, but on one question all persons seemed to agree. "There is," Mann announced to no one's surprise, "an intense want of competent teachers in the common schools." Careful not to step on the sensitive toes of a few professionals, he quickly added that this was not to cast "reproach on that most worthy class of persons, engaged in the sacred cause of education. . . ." The fault as he saw it lay not with the teachers, but with an indifferent public. "The teachers," he said, were "as good as public opinion demanded." [3]

In closing, he apologized for the candor of his report. "All the remarks which may seem accusatory of persons connected with it, have caused me more pain to write, than anyone to read." Thus it hurt the one who spanked more than the one who was spanked. Nevertheless, he could not "purchase any temporary gratification for others . . . by sacrificing one particle of the permanent utility of truth." With these words he gathered up his papers, looked up at what he hoped was a genuine satisfaction on the faces of the men around the table, and left the council chamber, having delivered the first of twelve *Annual Reports* which were to become his hallmark in American history.[4]

That afternoon the Board deliberated without him so that, according to Mann, they might "let their minds run whither they would without fear. . . ." With still no word from them by evening, he was "in the deep water of the fidgets" and complained in his Journal "I have not had a Happy New Year. . . ." The next morning the messenger brought him a note from Edward Everett. Breaking the wax seal and opening the folded paper Mann's eyes quickly fixed upon the words, "'You gave us a Noble Report. A New Year begun by you must be a happy New Year to you, let what will betide." With the exception of Edward Newton, the others on the Board concurred, and although not taking the time to send Mann a note, Thomas Robbins acknowledged in his diary that the secretary had "made a

---

[3] *First Annual Report,* pp. 48–66.
[4] *First Annual Report,* p. 70; Mann, Journal, January 1, 1838, MS in MHS.

very good report." Not only did they approve of what they had heard, but they insisted that Mann attend the remainder of their sessions the next day, so that they might more effectively press the legislature into dealing with the problems he had raised.[5]

The next day the General Court would convene and consider some of Mann's proposals for strengthening the common schools. As it did, his "Senatorial life" would come to an end. Now, as he had not known during the previous six months, he could honestly say to himself, "I would not exchange this life, toilsome, anxious, doubtful as it is . . . to be at the head of the 'grave and reverend' Senators tomorrow." Still, even in his moment of satisfaction he had a roaring headache and could do nothing for the rest of the day.[6]

The first week in January, 1838, he tried to begin several projects, but the previous effort to write his *Report* for the Board and his anxiety over its reception had drained the last from his reservoir of strength. Once again he found himself at the breaking point and for a few days could do nothing but go through the motions of work. Finally recouping some of his physical and mental energies, he applied himself to the problem of school construction. In almost every town he had visited, he could not help but notice the stately comfortable homes, dignified meetinghouses, and impressive Greek revival town halls. Most of these buildings could boast of tasteful proportions, a rational floor plan, a careful concern for detail, and an effective orientation to their surroundings. The builders of his day learned much from the past and present and were proud participants in what had become a golden age of New England architecture. Thus the Massachusetts people could hardly plead ignorance when they came to erecting schoolhouses. The Yankee ingenuity which had designed the Windsor and Hitchcock chairs was satisfied to let children bend their spines as they sat for hours like so many birds perched on a backless pine bench. In terms of ventilation, the classroom either had too much or too little, depending on whether it was heated with an undampered fireplace or a wood-burning space heater, yet for some reason the common sense which farmers used in constructing their farm buildings departed when they turned to building a school. In many homes the central entry, with the dining

---

[5] Mann, Journal, January 1, 1838, MS in MHS; Edward Everett to Mann, January 1, 1837 (actually 1838; the Governor, like many others, had forgotten to change his calendar), Mann MSS: MHS; Robbins, *Diary*, II, p. 479; Records of the Board, January 2, 1838, MS in MSDE; Edward Everett, *Diary*, January 1, 1838, MS in MHS.

[6] Mann, Journal, January 2, 1838, MS in MHS.

room on the right and living room on the left, were standard arrangements, but in the classrooms Mann visited, no one floor plan prevailed. Some had benches and desks all at one level; in others there were tiers providing a crude amphitheater arrangement. Some rooms had one scholar to a bench; others had two and three; and in several, Mann remembered as many as ten boys lined up on a seat-worn pine plank. In a few schools, the students were seated on either side of long tables, dining hall fashion. In one place, an ingenious school committeeman had built desks on the sides of the room so that the wall would support the children's backs and in another the opposite was done by attaching desks to the wall so that the students' backs were turned to a centrally located teacher. Clearly, at a time when persons had given considerable thought to their own dwellings and shelters for their farm animals, they exhibited little interest or ingenuity in providing a comfortable environment for their children.[7]

Needing all of the evidence and authority he could bring to bear on the problem, Mann appealed to Dr. Samuel Woodward, Benjamin Silliman, and Dr. Samuel Gridley Howe for information, and each man sent him a detailed reply. Encouraged, he was soon collecting plans for model classrooms which exhibited the best in seating, lighting, and ventilation. As Mann described it to his readers, five-sixths of the children of the Commonwealth would spend "a considerable portion of the most impressionable period of their lives" in these buildings and, for this reason alone, school construction had a high priority on his time.[8]

Much of this he did at night. Daytime hours were for personal persuasion, and Mann shaped himself into one of the most successful lobbyists to walk the halls of the State House. The existing legislation on education consisted of more than seventy fragmentary sections covering everything from teacher licensing to legal requirements that college students pay cash for their purchases at inns and taverns. Even worse, the existing laws were often ambiguous and unenforceable, with the result that what was intended to be mandatory proved to be permissive at best. Thomas Kinnicutt, Speaker of the House and an old friend of Mann's, did his part by appointing men to the Committee on Education, friendly to the cause, including

---

[7] Mann, Journal, January 6, 9, and 14, 1838, MS in MHS; Mann, *Report of the Secretary of the Board of Education on . . . School Houses, Supplementary to His First Annual Report* (Boston, 1838).

[8] Samuel B. Woodward to Mann, March 14, 1838, Woodward MSS: AAS; all three letters are printed in Mann, *Report of the Secretary of the Board of Education . . . on School Houses.*

James Savage and Thomas A. Greene. By February, Mann's lobby was well organized in both chambers and a steady flow of legislative revisions moved from his desk to the State House. He composed drafts to require school committees to keep records and present annual reports to the secretary of the Board of Education on buildings, attendance, and salary expenditures. In addition, he attacked the balkanization of towns into a myriad of anemic school districts and urged the legislature to mandate consolidation. By the end of the session, he had accomplished as much in legislation as had been done in the previous twenty years. What once had been "piecemeal or so many wheels thrown into a heap," he now described as a new framework "with the right adjustment and collocation," and by the end of the session he was convinced, "Every recommendation and suggestion contained in the Reports have been turned into laws." [9]

Cooperative though they were, Mann's friends on Beacon Hill had not changed their habits enough to be generous with public monies. When they finally came to prescribing the duties of his office and fixing his salary, they were lavish in the former category and downright penurious in the latter, expecting him to work miracles but authorizing his pay at $1,500 per annum from which Mann was also to take travel expenses and the cost of maintaining his office. Disappointed he was, but disheartened he was not. Almost welcoming the sacrifice his salary made inevitable, Mann responded with an appropriate rationalization. "One thing is certain," he wrote in his Journal. "If I live and have health, I will be revenged of them. I will do more than $1500 worth of good." For the moment it was more important to the cause that they had followed his advice. "The legislature have made all the modifications of the law which were proposed in our Reports. I drew the main bill, that 'Concerning

---

[9] Mann to J. A. Rockwell, April 30, 1838, Mann MSS: Huntington Library; L. M. Barstow to Thomas Robbins, March 18, 1838, Robbins MSS:CHS; Journal of the House, January 9, 1838, Vol. 60, p. 18, MS in MSA.

The actual legislative accomplishments included Ch. CV, "An Act Concerning Schools"; Ch. LV, "An Act to Defray the Expenses of the Board of Education"; Ch. CV, "An Act Concerning Schools"; and Ch. CLXXXIX, "An Act Concerning the Union of School Districts," *Laws of the Commonwealth of Massachusetts*, 1838. The account of Mann's legislative efforts can be drawn from the following: Boston *Daily Courier*, January 9 and 31; *Independent Chronicle*, January 10; *Columbian Centinel*, January 20 and February 14; *Mercantile Journal*, January 27; Boston *Morning Post*, February 20; and Boston *Weekly Messenger*, February 22, 1838.

Schools' myself," he boasted to Robbins, "and it contains provisions, which will be of immense service to us." [1]

*   *   *

Weekly lectures on education, the preparation of the report on schoolhouses, and the need to lobby for new legislation would have been enough for several men of average ability; but during the first three months of the year Mann took on yet another task which made even greater demands on his time and energy. The previous year he had promised William Dehon of the Society for the Diffusion of Useful Knowledge that he would give a series of lectures the following March. Knowledge was in vogue and a public starved for entertainment seemed ready to patronize almost any local or itinerant lecturer. Weary of a weekly diet of sermons, yet not ready to grant a wholehearted legitimacy to the theater, many found the lecture hall a salutary halfway house, which could be both uplifting and entertaining. Tickets could be had for a talk on "Tribal Customs in Turkey" or a demonstration of John Farrar's steam engine. The cost for a series ranged from 50 cents to $2 and special lecture halls had been designed with a speaker's pit in the center to make demonstrations visible to all. Recently, Jacob Bigelow had lectured on local flora, Henry Ware on life in Palestine, and Edward Everett on Greek antiquities. Not that all the speakers were local men. This year the people of Boston looked forward to a visit by George Combe of Scotland, a barrister turned philosopher and psychologist, who was coming to deliver a series of lectures and demonstrations on self-improvement through phrenology.[2]

From a distance of several months, William Dehon's invitation to speak appeared to be an important opportunity for Mann to bring the cause of education to one of the most prestigious lecture platforms in New England. Personally, he also saw it as the gratifying chance to enter that exclusive circle of celebrated lecturers which included Channing, Emerson, Silliman, and Everett. But now as the

---

[1] *Laws of the Commonwealth of Massachusetts, 1838,* Ch. CLIX, "An Act to Prescribe the Duties and Fix the Compensation of the Secretary of the Board of Education"; Mann to Thomas Robbins, April 27, 1838, Robbins MSS:CHS; Mann, Journal, April 18, 1838, MS in MHS; Mann to J. A. Rockwood, April 30, 1838, Mann MSS: Huntington Library; Thomas Robbins to Henry Barnard, May 4, 1838, Barnard MSS:NYU.
[2] William Dehon to Mann, September 25, and November 2 and 25, 1837, Mann MSS:MHS: Boston *Mercantile Journal,* February 20, 1838.

time grew closer his discomfiture increased, particularly since he could not give the assignment his undivided attention. Previous commitments in the various towns had to be met, even though they were always preceded by his fretting over the reception his ideas would receive and followed by a bone-jarring return trip to Boston. After returning from a speech at Concord to the security of his room at Frances Higginson's boardinghouse, Mann asked himself, "How much holding *forth?*" and dejectedly answered his own query, "So much I'm afraid I shall not hold *out.*" At Newburyport, he was nearly "overcome with fatigue." Still he pushed on to Marblehead, weary and suffering from the chills. Even so he put in an extra appearance at Lynn before returning to Boston "nearly sick," by which he meant "very." [3]

If his health steadily deteriorated, his spirits rose and fell in direct relation to the enthusiasm of his audiences. At Newton, he spoke to a full house despite a driving rainstorm; in Medford, he appeared before "a crammed house"; at West Cambridge, he had "very good listeners." Although his trip to Marblehead taxed him to the breaking point, he considered it "a pretty good mission . . . in which some seed will take root," and after a successful talk in Lexington he recorded "there cannot be a meeting of this kind anywhere which will not distill some particle of dew, at least, upon the thirsting earth." [4] Once accomplished, these assignments quickly became unimportant in the face of his commitment to speak before the élite of Boston. Gradually this impending sense of responsibility displaced any temporary euphoria he had acquired from his lesser speeches. Boston was Athens and to lecture from its most prestigious lecture platform was synonymous with being invited to speak from the Areopagus. Emerson had just completed a series of ten lectures and more than Mary and Elizabeth Peabody had become "Emerson-struck." Channing too had previously inspired an adoring audience with his address on "Self-Culture." Surely anything Mann now said would be measured against these two giants of the lecture platform. Somehow in between his errands on Beacon Hill and his lectures at West Cambridge, Newton, and Marblehead, Mann managed to assemble rough drafts for his first two talks, fully realizing how much

---

[3] Mann, Journal, January 21 and 28, and April 8, 1838, Mann MSS: MHS.

[4] Mann, Journal, January 10, 23, 26, 28, and February 9, 1838, Mann MSS:MHS; for an account of the Lexington Convention, see the Boston *Mercantile Journal,* January 16, 1838.

work remained before they gave evidence of the polish and elegance expected by a Boston audience.[5]

Each night the level in the reservoir of his whale-oil lamp dropped lower than the night before as he tried to wrest more waking and working hours from the daylight and the dark. He had used a gallon of oil in the last three weeks, probably a record for him, and he could see no letup in his schedule. The formal announcement of his talk in the paper the day prior to his first presentation sealed his fate and gave him a thorough case of jitters. "Certainly I never felt so bad about any before," he confided to his Journal, even though he would not admit this even to his closest friends.[6]

Despite all his premonitions, the first talk went well. He had purchased a new black frock coat and pants for the occasion and must have cut a handsome figure as he stood before the eminent Bostonians. Momentarily, he was pained as he sized up his audience. Speaking on "Transcendentalism" the week before, Dr. James Walker had addressed a capacity house. For Mann there was a sprinkling of vacant seats, but he stirred up his spirits, and launched into his topic assuring himself that a lack of public interest was the surest indication of the need for his words. "It is left for someone to excite that interest," he commented after his talk. "That is the work to be done." More sure of himself during the second lecture and speaking in less subdued and polite prose, Mann presented the urgency of his mission and noted "some evident hitchings on the seats now and then." By the end of the third lecture, he felt he had completed his message and left the platform with as much satisfaction as relief. For the moment he cared little about the outcome, "whether it *takes* or *digests*, it is all over." If it was not a signal triumph, neither was it an embarrassing disaster. Now his mind was removed of an "immense pressure." That was the important thing.[7]

---

[5] William Ellery Channing, *Self-Culture: An Introductory Address to the Franklin Lectures* (Boston, 1839), pp. 5–57, Mann, Journal, January 28, and February 19, 1838, MS in MHS.

[6] Mann, Journal, February 25, and March 1, 1838, Mann MSS:MHS; Boston *Evening Transcript*, March 1, 1838; some of Mann's dated whale-oil receipts are in the DHS.

[7] Mann, Journal, March 2, 10, and 16, 1838, MS in MHS. On February 6 and 8, 1838, Mann purchased a "Super French Cloth" coat and pants for $50 and a black frock coat and pants for $45. For his trouble, the Society paid him $90, a respectable sum, but not quite sufficient to pay for his new wardrobe. Mann's signed receipt for the lecture fee is dated April 16, 1838, and is in the Society for the Diffusion of Useful Knowledge, MSS:MHS.

Nathanael Emmons

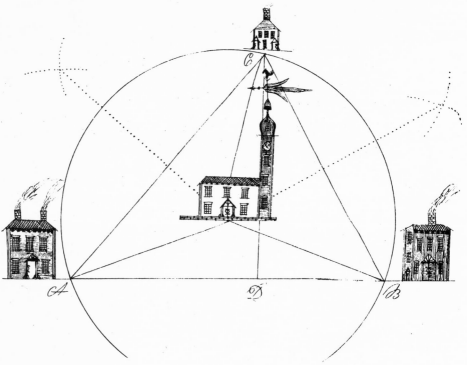

The Homestead on Mann's Plain
A Page from Horace Mann's Geometry Book

FRIENDS AND ASSOCIATES
Samuel Gridley Howe   *Theodore Parker*
Edmund Dwight   *Nicholas Tillinghast*

"Friends of Education"

George B. Emerson   Cyrus Peirce

Samuel J. May   Henry Barnard

STANDING GUARD IN FRONT
OF THE MASSACHUSETTS STATE HOUSE
Horace Mann   Daniel Webster

TWO VIEWS OF ANTIOCH COLLEGE
As Planned
As It Was

Thursday July 8th 1829.

Miss Charlotte Messer.
                                    In obedience to feelings
whose utterance I can no longer refuse, I
take the liberty, of this mode to request per—
mission to visit you hereafter in the char—
acter of an avowed, as I have hitherto done, in
that of a secret, admirer. Although the expression
of this desire requires, in the cold formality, of a
letter, but few words, it springs from feelings,
whose fervor & intensity, cannot be infused
into language; nor can a life of devotion to
your happiness exhaust their energies. — Did
I feel much less, I could say much more, but
the means have no adequacy for the end, for
it is only on the broad canvass of a life, that
the proportions & the coloring, of my esteem for
you can be painted.
      With sentiments of regard for you, which will sur—
vive even the wreck of hope, & flourish in my
heart, though all else should there be desolate, I
shall always remain, as I have been, ever since
I knew the beauties & excellencies of your nature,
your more than friend,
                              Horace Mann,
P.S. An answer will find me at the Hotel
opposite to the market. —

Mann's Proposal to Become an "Avowed"

THE FIRST TWO INSTITUTIONS MANN FOUNDED
State Lunatic Hospital, Worcester, Massachusetts
State Normal School, Lexington, Massachusetts

Two Generations of the New England Conscience
John Quincy Adams
Charles Sumner, ca. 1850

Horace Mann, ca. 1845

Two Schools Where Mann Studied
Brown University
Litchfield Law School

Charlotte Messer Mann

Sophia

Mary

Elizabeth

THE PEABODY SISTERS

TWO INFLUENTIAL FRIENDS
William Ellery Channing
George Combe

Horace, Jr., George Combe, Benjamin Pickman Mann
Mary Peabody Mann

Horace Mann, 1859

This assignment completed, he turned again to his report on school buildings, and by the end of March his copy was ready, complete with statistics, diagrams, and an appendix of letters in support of his arguments. In terms of content it contained little original, but was an eclectic collection from such diverse sources as William Woodbridge on ventilation, John Warren on seating, the 1833 Report of the Essex Teachers Association on the need for playgrounds, and the "Plan of a Village School," originally published by the American Institute of Instruction. By correspondence, conversation, convention, and reading, he had gleaned ideas wherever they were to be found.[8]

Even so, his school building report would carry the same stamp of authorship and the same intensity of argument and vivid illustration found in his other writings. Appealing to Yankee prudence and common sense, he argued for adequate ventilation and proper seating. In Mann's hands, these became urgent issues requiring immediate attention. He offered a simple explanation of the role of oxygen in supporting life and illustrated his points by citing examples of death by asphyxiation, including the number of children dying in a Dublin hospital, the gas seepage in a Naples grotto, and mortalities in the notorious Black Hole of Calcutta. All this he insisted indicated the necessity of more windows, louvres, and ceiling vents, anything to ensure a steady supply of fresh air. Then turning to seating, he quoted John Warren, who claimed that at least half the children in school suffered curvature of the spine, attributable to sitting on backless benches. Therefore Mann also urged the installation of single desks with back supports, and provided a set of drawings for them.[9]

He concluded with a discussion of auxiliary features which he thought essential to a properly functioning school. Although usually overlooked, Mann thought schools should have a playground, a bell and a well, a doormat, a woodshed, a classroom clock (Lowell had installed one which struck at intervals signaling the beginning and ending of recitation periods, but he could hardly expect such a luxury to have wide use in the future). In addition, he published a supple-

---

[8] See, for example, his correspondence with John Pierpont, March 16, 1838, discussing the latter's design of a stove for classroom use, MS in Louisiana State University Archives.

[9] Mann to Nathaniel Davis, March 17, 1838, Miscellaneous Bound: MHS; Mann, *Report . . . School Houses, passim.* For an example of how this report was quoted by school committees, see John White *et al., Annual Report of the School Committee of Dedham for the Year 1839–1840* (Dedham, 1840), pp. 6–7.

ment containing floor plans for three model classrooms. All this he presented to the Executive Committee of the Board. Governor Everett considered it an outstanding document and forwarded it to the House and Senate where the lawmakers recognized the need for a handful of plain unvarnished facts and recommendations rather than a bushelful of theories and quickly authorized the publication and gratis distribution of 6,000 copies to all school committees in the state. If new school construction remained stalled in Massachusetts it was not to be for want of a diffusion of information.[1]

* * *

Mann assumed that most of his endeavors would only bear results at some distant future, and at times he spoke as if it would be the next generation which might first witness a beneficial change. Quite unexpectedly, one of his talks early in 1838, together with one given by Charles Brooks, brought a much more immediate response. On January 18, the House of Representatives had invited Mann to speak to them on some topic dealing with education. Despite inclement weather, Mann had a "pretty full house." Addressing himself to the need for better teachers, he held the attention of his listeners for almost two hours as they became "stiller and stiller to the end." A week later, Brooks spoke on the same topic, devoting his entire lecture to an explanation of the Prussian system of education with its special teachers' seminaries.[2]

Attending both lectures was Edmund Dwight. Too wise in the ways of the world to accept Brooks's thesis that the Prussian system should be accepted *in toto*, Dwight did recognize the need for some new institution to educate teachers and knew the task was far beyond the resources of private individuals and existing institutions. The academies were neither interested in nor equal to this responsibility.

---

[1] Mann, Journal, March 27 and April 1, 1838, MS in MHS; Mann to John Prescott Bigelow, April 16, 1838, Mann MSS:HCL; Edward Everett to Mann, March 1, 1838, Mann MSS:MHS; Records of the Board of Education, March 28, 1838, MS in MSDE.

[2] Mann, Journal, January 18, 1838, MS in MHS. According to Brooks's own account, he "fell in love with the Prussian system; and it seemed to possess me like a missionary angel." Actually, he was blinded to the inherent tyranny in the system and he overlooked sociological factors which made it unsuited to American conditions. Later, he erroneously claimed the credit for starting normal schools in Massachusetts. See his *A History of the Introduction of State Normal Schools in America* (Boston, 1864), pp. 159–179.

A New Shay: The Deacon's Masterpiece

At the Phillips Academy in Andover, Samuel Hall had attempted to incorporate courses in pedagogy into the curriculum, but soon found his classes filled with nothing but the dregs of the student body. New York had designated a dozen or more academies to train teachers, giving each financial grants to carry out the plan, but this also failed. Colleges offered even less prospect for help. Following the myopic Yale Faculty Report of 1828, the faculties at Harvard, Amherst, and Williams found no place in their curriculum for teacher training.[3]

To Dwight, the answer lay in a school especially designed to the single task of training of teachers. True to form, after the House of Representatives lectures, he let several ideas germinate in his mind. Gathering the opinions of others and weighing various alternatives before committing himself to a course of action, he was close to a decision in March as Mann and other friends gathered at his home for a social evening. Gradually the after-dinner conversation focused on the need for teachers' seminaries, with several men present urging an immediate assault on the state legislature. Others counseled caution. For the most part, Dwight let his guests speak their minds while he listened. Then after most of them had left, he drew Mann aside and told him he would provide $10,000 for the improvement of teachers if the legislature would match this amount. Dazzled by the generosity of the offer, Mann thought the plan had a chance. Any morning-after fears he entertained that Dwight might have second thoughts were quickly dispelled the next day with the arrival of an errand boy carrying a message which put Dwight's offer in writing.[4]

Having the needed catalyst, Mann lost no time. The following Monday he dispatched a letter to the president of the Senate and the Speaker of the House with the following intelligence:

Private munificence has placed, conditionally, at my disposal, the sum of TEN THOUSAND DOLLARS to promote the cause of Popular Education in Massachusetts.

The condition is, that the Commonwealth will contribute the same amount from unappropriated funds in aid of the same cause;—both sums to be drawn upon equally as needed, and to be dispersed under the direction of the Board of Education in qualifying teachers for our common schools.

---

[3] For a general description at early attempts at teacher education, see John P. Gordy, *Rise and Growth of the Normal-School Idea in the United States* (Washington, D.C., 1891), pp. 2–55.

[4] Edmund Dwight to Mann, March 10, 1838, Mann MSS:MHS; Mann, Journal, March 10, 1838, MS in MHS.

Confident that the frugal Yankee legislature would find it hard to turn down a proposition which offered an additional dollar for every one it appropriated, Mann concealed his optimism from his associates, sharing his innermost thoughts only with the pages of his Journal. "This appears to be glorious," he exulted. "I think I feel pretty sublime. Let the stars look out for my head." As usual, Dwight wished to remain in the background. His business partner and also a close friend of Mann, James K. Mills, may have contributed part of the $10,000, but Mills's anonymity was even more protected.[5]

As soon as he received the proposal, Thomas Kinnicutt placed it before the members of a Joint Committee on Education for study and recommendations. Not willing to rely on their unaided wisdom, Mann appealed to some of the lawmakers personally and by letter. At the same time, a group in Nantucket sent in a memorial urging acceptance of Dwight's offer. Probably at Mann's instigation, Samuel Gridley Howe also wrote in support of the proposition. Working among the deaf, no one knew the importance of methodical training in teaching better than Howe. "I hesitate not to say," he wrote, "that a school for teachers formed and administered aright, would be [of] as much importance to any State as the Schools for Medicine and Law. . . . A graduate of college, who has never taught a school thinks, when he begins, that all he has got to do is to put into the heads of children part of what is in his own, and . . . pounds, for a long time, before he discovers, that there is more *to be brought out* from the minds of children than there is to be driven *in*." Had Howe actually gone to the legislature and offered his advice, he would have found himself communing with the converted. James Savage reported out the bill and Dwight's offer was soon before the House, where it quickly passed through its three required readings. In the Senate, a friendly reception by Josiah Quincy and his associates was

---

[5] Mann, Journal, March 13, 1838, MS in MHS; House Journal, Vol. 60, March 12, 1838, p. 319; Senate Journal, Vol. 59, March 12, 1838, p. 281, MS in MSA. News of the offer was published in the Boston *Evening Transcript*, March 13, 1838, and the Boston *Daily Advertiser*, March 18, 1838.

That Dwight may have shared expense of the donation with James K. Mills is indicated in Mary Peabody to Elizabeth Peabody, April 18, 1838, Mann MSS:MHS; Miss Peabody wrote that Mills had done something which will "deify" him. Since this is the same expression Mann used in his correspondence with Dwight and Josiah Quincy in discussing the financial needs of the normal schools, Mills may have been an anonymous donor.

followed by an affirmative vote of thirty to one. Governor Everett, no newcomer to teacher education, having observed it firsthand during his university study abroad, signed the bill on the anniversary of the Battle of Lexington, a meaningful coincidence not overlooked by the reformers.[6]

The quick action was both an indication of the changed temper of the legislature and a testimony to Mann's and Dwight's political sagacity. Well aware that more specific proposals had failed previously, Mann kept the exact nature of the future institution intentionally vague, thus offering a poor target for his opponents. Few could claim that Massachusetts teachers were equal to their responsibilities and even less could argue against the need for improvement. The resolve made the money available to the Board, but in no way prescribed a curriculum, student body, tuition, location, or even a name for the schools. Mann did not want to limit his future course of action before he had the money in hand. And it was a successful gambit. Where the legislature on previous occasions had turned down more specific proposals, it was now willing to buy a pig in the poke, if someone else paid half of the bill.

Actually, Mann's strategy was a fine blend of political wisdom and professional ignorance. Once the resolve had been passed, it was evident that the Board was divided on how teachers best could be "qualified." Some members thought the "New York Plan" was the solution, and that they should use the new funds to underwrite pedagogy courses in several academies in the state. Preferring to establish new institutions instead of working through existing ones, however, Mann thought he could carry the majority of the Board with him in time. In their first discussion he predicted "not much will be done" but he nevertheless held the highest hopes for the final outcome. "If we prosper in our Institutions for Teachers," he predicted, "education will suddenly be exalted; if not its progress will be onward still, but imperceptibly slow." [7]

---

[6] The Nantucket memorial was published in the CSJ, I (February, 1839), 33–38. It was this to which Mann referred in his letter to Thomas Robbins, April 27, 1838, Robbins MSS:CHS, when he wrote, "I have known all about Nantucket. They have done nobly, *nobly*, NOBLY."

The quotation from Howe is in Samuel Gridley Howe to Mann, March 19, 1838, Howe MSS:HCL. See also Senate Journal, Vol. 59, April 10 and 12, 1838, pp. 414 and 426, MS in MSA; *Resolves of the Commonwealth of Massachusetts, 1838*, Ch. 70.

[7] Records of the Board, August 31, 1838, MS in MSDE; Mann, Journal, May 27, 1838, MS in MHS.

*   *   *

By the end of June, Mann could observe the first anniversary of his new crusade, but he was much too busy to take an inventory of what had been accomplished. By any measure or standard, it had been a remarkable year of achievement. From every part of the state, he had fired the people's imagination and drawn their support. Even the proposal for teacher education had passed almost unanimously. With the conclusion of each meeting of the Board of Education its members returned to their homes convinced that their efforts were achieving results. Thus Thomas Robbins could write to Henry Barnard that the Board "had succeeded much beyond expectation." [8] Newspaper editors had also rallied behind the cause and it was an especially independent editor who dared write against the growing tide of approval for common schools among his readership. For many people troubled by problems they did not understand, Mann was bringing the long-awaited panacea. Editors described his *Report* as a statesman-like document, pointing equally to educational problems and their effective remedy. They reprinted his *Reports* and lectures in large part, especially in Boston, Salem, Worcester, and Springfield, and from here Mann's words found their way to village presses and even into more distant newspapers in Hartford and Baltimore.[9]

When he issued the call for his second round of county conventions, Mann was no longer advocating an exotic cause nor preparing for an uninformed audience. Upon noting the announcement for the upcoming Worcester meeting, the *Massachusetts Spy* urged those who had missed Mann's speech the year before to ". . . hear one of the ablest and most accomplished men of Massachusetts discuss a subject of deepest interest. . . ." Rocky though the soil of New England was, such seeds of admonition began to take root. Even though

---

[8] L. M. Barstow to Thomas Robbins, March 18, 1838, Robbins MSS:CHS; Thomas Robbins to Henry Barnard, May 4, 1838, typescript copy, Barnard MSS:NYU.

[9] See, for example, the *Connecticut Courant*, January 27, 1838; Boston *Courier*, February 27, 1838; Salem *Gazette*, March 13, 1838; *Massachusetts Spy*, March 14, 1838, for the publication of all or part of Mann's *First Annual Report*.

Examples of favorable accounts of his reforms are found in the Boston *Mercantile Journal* January 16, 1838; Boston *Daily Advertiser*, March 15, 1838; *Independent Chronicle and Boston Patriot*, March 17, 1838; *Massachusetts Spy*, September 19, 1838; Springfield *Republican* October 22, 1838; and Ipswich *Register*, January 26, 1838.

Mann thought his conventions were running a poor third or fourth to religious revivals, anti-slavery meetings, and cattle shows, he was wrong. The cause of the common schools and popular education was on the ascent.[1]

Nor were the accounts of his efforts limited to Massachusetts State borders. To the south, in Connecticut, Henry Barnard and some of his co-workers in the Connecticut legislature kept a close watch on developments in the Old Bay State. "I hope to succeed in establishing a Board of Education, with powers and objects mainly similar to what you now have in Massachusetts," Barnard wrote to Thomas Robbins, and although he had read Mann's *First Report* from cover to cover, he nevertheless urged him to meet with him since Mann had "been over the same ground . . . which I must traverse in Connecticut." At this time Mann's reports found their way across the Atlantic. Through an intermediary, Everett placed them in Lord Brougham's hands, and from Paris, Charles Sumner reported that the celebrated educational reformer Victor Cousin questioned him closely about developments in Massachusetts and "asked particularly about Mr. Mann." [2]

All of these early successes augured well for the reform, but Mann and his co-workers, even in their most sanguine moments, could not accurately assess the magnitude of what they now had under way. Actually, in concrete terms there was little to which they could point. To date, no school buildings had risen from Mann's published diagrams; the normal schools were nothing more than a legislative enactment and a modest bank account. The vast majority of teachers once again starting their tasks the following winter would "keep school" with a birch ferule well in hand, as they had done in the past, and book pedlars would continue to purvey their multifarious wares to gullible parents.

Mann's accomplishment was of a different order. His first campaign was for the minds of men, and by 1838 the tide of battle had begun to turn in his favor in Massachusetts. Not trusting the open democracy of the New England Town Meeting, he believed the first step was to use his carefully staged public meetings, as one friend described it, "to awaken from a lethargic sleep the spirit of the pilgrims

---

[1] *Massachusetts Spy*, September 19 and 26, and October 3, 1838.
[2] Henry Barnard to Thomas Robbins, April 19, 1838, Robbins MSS:CHS; Henry Barnard to Mann, June 7, 1838, Mann MSS:MHS; Edward Everett to B. B. Thatcher, Everett MSS:MHS; Edward L. Pierce, *Memoir and Letters of Charles Sumner* (Boston, 1877), I, 265.

so long slumbering on this important subject." Then, according to Mann as he attempted to instruct a co-worker in his *modus operandi*,

. . . the real work must be done at home, in private conversation, at the fire-side, at the family party, when neighbors meet on the road, & in the common intercourse of life. They may then go to town meeting to express an opinion already formed; but they will not form such an opinion there. Get together, therefore, three, four or half a dozen of your most influential men, agree upon what is best to be done, & then let each one, in the circle where he has influence, explain the reasons for the proposed course.

After that, it was only a matter of recording the public will "in pursuance of a vote of the Town." To those openly opposed to the cause, he advised private persuasion. "I have always found," he counseled an orthodox minister who wanted to help the cause along, ". . . great advantage from seeking a private interview with a man disposed to be troublesome, approaching him under the influence of kind feeling, asking his advice, and then suggesting my own views. Opposition, otherwise insuperable may be overcome in this way." Thus in his first year, through his own efforts and the work of countless others, he had begun to win out over competing ideologies and establish the principle of public education controlled and supported by the public.[3]

In retrospect, the development would seem inevitable because of the apparent absence of alternatives. To his own generation, other options were in serious contention for public support. The quasi-public academy movement was flourishing. Massachusetts alone could boast of more than 300 such institutions. Supporters of academies could rightly point to their superior quality of instruction. Furthermore, once under way, academies required virtually no tax monies in a day when Harvard, Amherst, and Williams still received regular state handouts. "Undemocratic" and "élitist" the academies were, but these epithets by no means meant they were "un-American." Thus at the dedication of a building at the Williston Academy in 1845, Edward Hitchcock would claim it to be "a suicidal policy, to lavish the resources of the state" on common schools (at the time, less than $2 per pupil), since "the system of American Academies" was better "adapted to the character, habits, and wants of this country." Dedi-

---

[3] Ichabod Morton to Mann, April 22 and July 23, 1838, Mann MSS:MHS; Mann to C. Durfee, November 13, 1847, Straker MSS:ACL; Mann to Thomas Davies, Pforzheimer MSS (photostat):BLYU.

cated to a form of excellence not found elsewhere, rendering a public service through the achievements of their graduates, and in some instances even demonstrating an entrepreneurship which could make money, the academies were seen by many to be as American as blueberry pie and the free enterprise system.[4]

Others starting from a different set of premises considered education essentially a philanthropic endeavor. Such organizations as the New York Public School Society operated on the assumption that children from the better homes would be educated according to their parents' wishes. The "public" task of the Society was to provide for the hordes of illiterate children running the streets in the coastal cities and inland mill towns. Appropriately, the Society had organized monitorial schools on plans laid out by Joseph Lancaster. By his methods, a single master assisted by a platoon of older students or "monitors" could teach 500 pupils and more in a single classroom. Since reading and arithmetic lessons were broken down into simple steps and monitors held frequent recitations, much self-teaching took place. These educators may have lacked the necessary expertise and sophisticated programmed learning materials for the task, but their efforts cannot be dismissed by a later generation of educationists as a passing fad or social aberration, educationists who themselves would make a fetish of having no more than twenty-five pupils sealed off in a classroom with one teacher. The redeeming features of the monitorial schools were economy and system. Governor DeWitt Clinton described Lancaster's achievement as one of locating some 40,000 children "as destitute of instruction as the savages of the desert," and then proceeding

by degrees, to form and perfect a system, which is in Education what the most finished machines for abridging labor and expenses are in the mechanic arts . . . it arrives at its object with the least possible trouble and at the least possible expense. Its distinguishing characters are economy, facility, and expedition, and its peculiar improvements are cheapness, activity, order, and emulation.

What the factory system had accomplished in producing blankets, nails, and peppermint sticks, the monitorial approach would now ac-

[4] Edward Hitchcock, *The American Academic System Defended: An Address Delivered at the Dedication of the New Hall of Williston Seminary, in Easthampton, January 28, 1845* (Amherst, 1845). For an introduction to the academy movement, see Theodore Sizer, *Age of the Academies* (New York, 1964), pp. 1–48.

complish in mass producing children with functional literacy and a modicum of Christian morality.

The old scheme of one teacher and thirty children was at least fifty years behind the times and more appropriate to an age of handicraft, so argued the devotees of Lancaster. The new system was efficient; it made minimal demands upon the public treasury; it was open to all and therefore democratic; it provided a new form of Christian charity; and it made a serious attempt to bring thousands of children to a level of literacy never achieved before. With some justification, then, the educational philanthropists could also claim their cause as truly "American." [5]

If the academy was to some degree an undertaking sponsored by the more propertied people of the community and educational philanthropy a new arm of charitable endeavor, then the third option available to Americans at the time, the district school, was clearly an extension of the rural family. Here parents provided textbooks and fuel, made minimal repairs on the schoolhouse, and often boarded the teacher. Through the Town Meeting, New England's indigenous form of participatory democracy, they determined their taxes and set the school calendar so as to mesh with harvest schedules and other more important activities. In such an arrangement, there was little of a bureaucratic buffer to stand between teacher and parent. The responsibility and management of the schools should rest neither with a propertied élite, religious sectarians, nor an educational bureaucracy, but with what Governor Marcus Morton called "those little pure democracies." For good or evil, the district school was of, by, and for the people. It had been around a long time; it was a grass-roots creation which could be responsive to local needs as they were articulated by members of the immediate community; and because or in spite of it, the sons and daughters of the Puritans had learned to read and write.[6]

There were, then, genuine alternatives available. When Americans gradually made their choice, they adopted a form of organization of schooling which permitted them to incorporate ever greater components of what had once been *education* into a more systema-

---

[5] William W. Campbell, *Life and Writings of DeWitt Clinton* (New York, 1849), pp. 309–327. Lancaster's own description of his methods is found in Joseph Lancaster, *Lancasterian System of Education, with Improvements* (Baltimore, 1821), pp. i–xv and 1–34.
[6] *Documents Printed by the Order of the House of Representatives of the Commonwealth of Massachusetts during the Session of the General Court, 1840* (Boston, 1840), House Document, No. 9, *passim*.

tized and formal *schooling*. The future seemed to be filled with great uncertainty and it was no longer safe to depend on less structured and controlled means. Thus, when asked to justify his version of public education before the General Court, Horace Mann would write:

If the spontaneous productions of the earth were sufficient for all, men might be honest in practice, without any principle of rectitude, because of the absence of temptation. But as the population increases, & especially as artificial wants multiply, temptations increase & the guards & securities must increase also, or society will deteriorate.[7]

A great educational burden must be placed upon the schools. But they could only accept this burden if they received far more public financial assistance, became centrally organized, developed a unified curriculum, and assumed a homogeneous clientele. All of these seemed desirable at a time when predictability was at a premium and people still believed they could agree on common political, social, and intellectual goals. For Horace Mann and countless others, the nation was in danger of greater diversity and fragmentation. Patriotism was giving way to unmitigated politics; religion to sectarianism; and Commonwealth to a class society of haves and have-nots. Apparently the rise of the factory and the city only exacerbated those troublesome developments and the older socializing agencies seemed unable to control them. Nor did any of the other educational options available at the time, save the public schools, seem equal to the task. The district schools were far too varied in quality and content. The academies were élitist and ignored the agrarian and urban proletariat which needed education the most. The philanthropic societies, lacking a sufficient financial base, could never raise popular education above its pauper status. And parochial schools would only perpetuate the religious antagonisms which had wracked the European continent for centuries.

At the time when a growing number of persons were no longer satisfied with these older, less comprehensive forms of education, the idea of a public school for all held out the best prospect for the future, even though it might require a much larger portion of a child's time, demand a greater share of the communities' tax revenues, and create an educational establishment. Mann then was fashioning a new vehicle on which to carry the increasing educational burdens of the Commonwealth, and he believed that if enlightened men and

---

[7] Mann to John Shaw, March 7, 1840, Mann MSS: MHS.

women joined in the cause, his efforts could endure for a hundred years.

Inevitably the comprehensiveness of Mann's efforts brought him into conflict with the leaders of some agencies which had had a traditional stake in the education of children. One index of the magnitude of his achievements by 1838 would be the degree to which he had to survive controversies with embattled antagonists, controversies which had been no part of his master battle plan.

CHAPTER XIV

Clubs at the Base
of an Apple Tree

═══════════

TAKE EGOTISM OUT, and you would castrate the
benefactors. Luther, Mirabeau, Napoleon, John
Adams, Andrew Jackson; and our nearer eminent
public servants—Greeley, Theodore Parker, Ward
Beecher, Horace Mann, Garrison—would lose their
vigour.
RALPH WALDO EMERSON

─────────

I T BEGAN WITH a thirty-cent book. While coming down the home-
stretch with his three lectures before the Society for the Diffusion
of Useful Knowledge, Mann received a letter from Reverend Frederick A. Packard, recording secretary of the American Sunday School
Union, enquiring whether John S. Abbott's *Child at Home* would be
suitable for a common school library Mann and the Board were planning to assemble. Too busy at the time to respond, Mann waited a
week before locating a copy of the *Child*, a tenth edition. Scanning its
contents, he discovered the telltale signs of Calvinism he suspected
would be between its covers. Then setting both Packard's letter and
the book aside for several days, he tried unsuccessfully to free his
mind of the matter. The fact that Packard thought such a sectarian
book still had a place in enlightened Massachusetts was almost a personal affront to him and called for a strong letter to bring this Sunday
School man up to date. Furthermore, since *Child at Home* was but
one of a set of 150 titles Packard was promoting, this single book
was only the head of the camel which was surely to follow.[1]

After a lame apology for his delay in answering, Mann bluntly

─────────

[1] Mann, Journal, March 18, 1838, Mann MSS:MHS; Records of the
Massachusetts State Board of Education, January 31 and April 18, 1838,
MS in MSDE. At this same time, Packard began a series of five letters
in the Boston *Recorder* and the New York *Observer*, urging a greater use
of the Sunday School Union's books in New England. See the Boston
Recorder, March 16, 1838, and New York *Observer*, March 10, 1838. A
description of the Union's library is found in the *Thirteenth Annual
Report of the American Sunday School Union* (Philadelphia, 1837), p. 8.

informed Packard that *Child at Home* "would not be tolerated in Massachusetts." Since the book taught that even trivial offenses put the child in danger of "eternal perdition," both the Unitarians and Universalists would rather see the common schools abolished than subject their children to such a doctrine. Dueling with swords and pistols was coming to an inglorious end, but men of Mann's temperament needed a substitute and found the pen a useful weapon in a verbal duel. Yet Mann wrote far beyond his original intent. By citing page and line, he gratuitously lectured Packard on the dangers of sectarianism, his prose becoming more vehement than necessary to make an obvious point. Finally coming to the end of the fourth page, he ended abruptly, adding insult to injury by explaining that he was too busy to take the "time to put these views in better shape." [2]

Packard was not to be put off by a hastily written letter and he was well acquainted with the Massachusetts School Law of 1827 which dealt with the selection of school books and the teaching of religion. In attempting to clarify a troublesome issue and purge the law books of an accretion of conflicting statutes of the past, the legislature had consolidated many confusing laws into two horns of a dilemma. First it ordered that all "Instructors of Youth" in the Commonwealth should "impress on the minds of children, and youth . . . the principles of piety, justice, and sacred regard to truth. . . ." Then it forbade them to use any book "calculated to favor any particular religious sect or tenet." Both Mann and Packard knew the law well and each was ready to advocate only that segment of it in harmony with his own predilections. For Mann, sectarianism was the *bête noire* of the common school and he would give it battle wherever it raised its hoary head. For Packard, "principles of piety" were so necessary that the ban on sectarian teaching was of secondary importance. [3]

Although he could understand how the *Child* might be offensive to Universalists, Packard found it difficult "to conceive how the 'principles of piety' are to be impressed upon the minds of children &

---

[2] Mann to Frederick Packard, March 18, 1838, Mann MSS:MHS; for evidence that the Universalists actually held their own schools, see J. G. A., "Schools," Boston *Trumpet and Universalist Magazine*, XI (November, 1838), 89.

[3] *Laws of Massachusetts*, March 10, 1827, Ch. 143. A more detailed account of the Mann-Packard controversy is presented in Raymond B. Culver, *Horace Mann and Religion in the Massachusetts Public Schools* (New Haven, 1929), pp. 19–110, and William K. Dunn, *What Happened to Religious Education?* (Baltimore, 1948), pp. 117–188.

youth as required by the law of your State, without reference to the character & government of God." Furthermore, he could not understand how these "principles of piety" could be taught "without *'favoring some particular religious tenet.'* " If piety was defined as the fulfillment of one's duty to God, it seemed necessary for children to be taught the nature of God and this raised the possibility of the need for sectarian doctrine.

An ambitious book promoter and a man who expected deference from his inferiors, Packard was disappointed at the prospect of a lucrative market being closed to his line but he was also incensed that such a parvenu to education as Mann would address him in so supercilious a tone. Suppressing his anger for the time being, he responded with a second letter asking Mann if he would examine a series of books, thirty-six in all, from the union's collection and "*specify* such objections as seem . . . insurmountable to their circulation in Common Schools." [4]

The first week in June Mann finished a second reply in which he explained why other books in the series were equally as objectionable as the *Child at Home,* but before he mailed it, Packard paid him an unexpected visit. Keeping their discussion on a polite theoretical plane, each man attempted to take his measure of the other. As Packard prepared to leave, Mann handed him the unmailed letter. Later in the day, when Packard read it, he could hardly believe its author was the same person with whom he had just visited. In it, Mann denounced Packard's belief that piety could only be taught by teaching the existence of a God who meted out punishment to evildoers, large and small. "Is it possible, my dear Sir," Mann asked, "you can mean to say that no person who does not adopt those views can be *pious?* Is no Universalist *pious?*" Clearly, such a teaching was unlawful in Massachusetts schools. Carried away by his own sense of righteousness, Mann neglected to explain that not his alone but the unanimous action of the Board was required to place a book in the common school library and that Packard's books were so sectarian he did not consider them worth the Board's time. [5]

Stunned by what he considered Mann's patent duplicity and convinced the Massachusetts secretary expected to dispense the coveted imprimatur only to those books containing his particular version of

---

[4] Frederick Packard to Mann, March 28, 1838, Mann MSS:MHS.
[5] Mann to Frederick Packard, June 23, 1838, Mann MSS:MHS; Mann to Emerson Davis, June 10, 1838, Straker MSS:ACL; Records of the State Board of Education, April 18, 1838, MS in MSDE.

religious teachings, Packard thought it time to repay private abuse with public exposure. The next day at the meeting of the General Association of Massachusetts at New Bedford, he took to the rostrum and addressed more than 200 prominent Congregational ministers and laymen, charging Mann and the Board with recommending books which were "anti-evangelical." A slashing attack, it was also quick and effective. Apprehensive of the inroads made by Unitarianism after the precedent-setting Dedham Case, the men of the assembly were sensitive to the possibility of yet another Unitarian takeover. Unfortunately, Thomas Robbins who was attending the assembly was ignorant of Mann's exchange with Packard and could only state that the Board "had not yet decided definitely on any book for the use of the schools," and that it had not decided against any book either. Eager to sustain his claim, Packard waved Mann's letter before the convention, offering to read it and prove that the secretary of the Board unilaterally had excluded his books. The attack now becoming personal, several men finally found their feet and insisted that since Mann had no expectation his words might become public, it was improper to read his letter. Stymied, Packard simply reiterated his accusation with added vehemence, insisting it was Mann who was the sectarian and that the ministers of Massachusetts had better be on their guard. During the next three months, Mann and Packard continued to exchange letters but in these Mann was far more circumspect in what he wrote. In one instance he favored his antagonist with a twelve-page dissertation exhibiting religious nitpicking *par excellence,* which Packard repaid in kind, taking twenty-one pages to strain at every gnat.[6]

Rebuffed by the orthodox assembly and unable to draw Mann into public controversy, Packard now made his next move in the public press. In August, he trumpeted his views in the New York *Observer* in an article entitled "Triumph of Infidelity." The fact that he signed the article "Verax" did little to conceal the author's identity from Mann. That the editor of the *Observer* himself was unsympathetic to Packard's claims was evident from an accompanying editorial and the space he gave in a later issue to a "Massachusetts Ex-school Committee Man," possibly Reverend Emerson Davis, to answer the charges. Packard countered with a second article, again repeating

---

[6] Thomas Robbins to Mann, June 6, 1838; Enoch Sanford to Mann, July 13, 1838; Frederick Packard to Mann, July 9, 16, and 22, and September 19, 1838; Mann to Frederick Packard, July 5, 11, and 22, 1838; Mann, Journal, July 23, 1838, all in Mann MSS:MHS.

his charges, this time directed in the form of an open letter to Dr. Heman Humphrey, orthodox president of Amherst College.[7]

At its next meeting, the Board decided not to answer "Verax," hoping that President Humphrey would do the same and that "no further action was necessary." But it was not to be that easy. Newton, an ultra-conservative Episcopalian and a man who made no attempt to conceal his wholehearted admiration for the established Church of England, would not be party to what he thought was a widening gap between Church and State and an opening of the doors of the common schools to a Godless secularism. Written appeals from Governor Edward Everett could not sway him. If other members of the Board would not rescind their decision on the common school library, he would resign. And he did.[8]

Mann thought Newton's resignation good riddance since he had a distinct dislike for this man who had done nothing to help him with his school conventions in the Berkshires. But not only was Newton a wealthy banker and leading Whig from Berkshire County, he also had the ear of Heman Humphrey. For the moment then, it was possible that Humphrey, at Newton's urging, might answer "Verax" and substantially agree with him. To spike such a response, William B. Calhoun and Emerson Davis came to Mann's rescue, advising Humphrey to remain silent. A letter by Calhoun carried additional weight because its author was also on the board of trustees at Amherst, and Humphrey was convinced to steer clear of the controversy. Emerson Davis also appealed to the editor of the *Observer*, who suppressed Packard's series to Humphrey after the first two letters had been published.[9]

---

[7] Mann, Journal, October 27, 1838, MS in MHS; New York *Observer*, August 18, September 8, and October 27, 1838.

[8] Records of the Board, September 1, 1838, MSDE; Edward Everett to Edward A. Newton, July 13 and September 14, 1838, Everett Letterbook, MHS.

Previous studies, unaware of Newton's devout belief in the virtue of an established church, have been unable to explain his behavior on the Board, other than in terms of a general clash between "orthodoxy" and "liberalism." For evidence of Newton's conservatism and admiration of the Anglican Church, see his English travel diaries, Vol. 1, especially an entry dated November 10, 1835, MS in the Berkshire Athenaeum, Pittsfield, Massachusetts. That Newton was recognized as more than a local political power in the Whig-party is clear from Julius Rockwell to Edward A. Newton, January 20, and 28, 1835, Rockwell MSS: Lenox Library, Lenox, Massachusetts. For a brief biographical sketch of Newton, see J. E. A. Smith, *History of Pittsfield, Massachusetts* (Springfield, 1876), pp. 407–408.

[9] Emerson Davis to Mann, October 24 and November 15, 1838; William

Rebuffed a second time, Packard now formed an unholy alliance with the Boston *Recorder*. Anonymously, he published a pamphlet entitled *The Question, Will the Christian Religion Be Recognized as the Basis of the System of Public Instruction in Massachusetts?* Then the *Recorder* promptly had the Reverend Richard S. Storrs, orthodox Trinitarian pastor of Braintree, prepare an approving review in which he claimed the Board had committed itself to "faults and fatal principles that the Common Schools can flourish and accomplish the end they aim at without the aids of Christianity." Mann considered Packard's attacks as "scandalous an outrage amongst men, pretending to decency" as he had ever known. On first impulse, he wanted to answer the charges line by line in some friendly newspaper; but cooler heads on the Board prevailed. Instead, he wrote privately to Storrs explaining his sincere intent to function within the limits of the School Law of 1827.

Storrs responded in a long letter explaining that he wanted neither to oppose Mann nor to add to the burdens of his "highly responsible and thankless office." Nevertheless, he thought Mann was guilty of a "fundamental error" if he believed that "the intellectual and moral improvement of our youth" was possible without being "based upon the religion of the Bible." Storrs also questioned the alleged religious pluralism of a Board where all but three members belonged to "that denomination which has done all in its power to crush orthodoxy throughout the Commonwealth. . . ." Here the matter rested and in the years to come the two men became at least cordial if not warm friends.[1]

If Mann maintained a public silence, his friends did not. Soon the *Recorder*, the *Daily Advertiser and Patriot*, and the *Independent Chronicle*, all Boston newspapers, carried articles in his behalf, one writer even going so far as to claim that what looked like a series of brush fires all over the state was simply the covert attempt of an individual from *"out of state"* who wished to peddle his inferior books in Massachusetts against the better judgment of Mann and his coworkers. Words of support also came from orthodox ministers and at

---

B. Calhoun to Mann, November 11 and 20, 1838; and Heman Humphrey to William B. Calhoun, November 22, 1838, all in Mann MSS:MHS.
[1] Boston *Recorder*, January 11, 1839; Mann to Richard S. Storrs, January 19, 1839; Richard S. Storrs to Mann, February 20, 1839, both in Mann MSS:MHS; Mann, Journal, January 20, 1839, MS in MHS; Mann to Emerson Davis, July 10, 1838, Straker MSS:ACL.

least one Congregational county ministerial association passed a resolution supporting the Board.[2]

Bookselling aside, Packard had honestly believed that men's particular doctrinal beliefs on the Trinity, baptism, and original sin were crucial factors in conditioning their social behavior. Mann thought men's actions were based upon certain general ethical principles shared by all reasonable men. Beliefs in total immersion, the divinity of Christ, or the innate depravity of children had little influence on how one lived as a member of a family or a citizen of a community. Both Packard and Mann conceived of education then as the vehicle for religious indoctrination, but Mann's view was far more broad than that of his antagonist and seemed to be a reasonable response to the dilemma posed by the School Law of 1827. Reactionaries like Newton would never be convinced of this; conservatives like Storrs would be in time; while many others accepted Mann's position with little prompting, their decision being influenced not so much by the logic of the arguments or their intensity as by the necessity of the situation. Children needed to be educated, and if sectarian strife stood in the way, doctrinal specificity could be delegated to the home and the meetinghouse. As Mann described his practical solution to the problem in his Journal, he noted that "the fundamental principles of Christianity may & should be inculcated. This should be done thro' the medium of a proper text-book to prevent abuses. After this, each denomination must be left to its own resources, for inculcating its own faith or creed." Thus the controversy produced more heat than revelation and gave the erroneous impression to later historians that Mann was engaged in a heroic struggle with the outcome in serious doubt. Such simply was not the case. Orthodox Congregationalists, Evangelical Baptists, and liberal Universalists and Unitarians all supported his position. The attacks on the common school reform were in actuality indications that it was beginning to produce good results, or as Mann's friend Emerson Davis described the situation with a picturesque Yankee observation, ". . . you may know a good apple tree by the number of clubs & stones that lay about it. I think our tree will have this sort of evidence to prove that its fruit is good." [3]

---

[2] Boston *Recorder*, January 25, 1839; Boston *Daily Advertiser and Patriot*, January 28, 1839; *Independent Chronicle*, March 23, 1839; *Common School Journal* (hereafter *CSJ*), I (1839), 56–62.

[3] Mann, Journal, January 20, 1839, MS in MHS; Mann to Thomas Robbins, April 27, 1838, Robbins MSS:CHS; Emerson Davis to Mann, October 24, 1838, Mann MSS:MHS.

*   *   *

For all the talk by Alexander Bache, Calvin Stowe, and Victor Cousin about the superiority of the "Prussian system" for training teachers, Prussia seemed a most remote country to the members of the Board who faced the difficult task necessary to start a normal school. Hundreds of pages had been written by Carter, Charles Brooks, and Mann himself on the need for such an institution, but when the members of the Board came to making substantive decisions about the form the school should take, the best guidelines Mann could offer them was to proceed with "Eyes open. . . . It is a difficult subject." And it was. They were not even sure what to call such schools, much less how many they wanted, what they would cost, and who should attend them. But they were certain they must create something for "qualifying teachers for the Common Schools." Having gambled in the legislature and won, Mann was soon at work attempting to parlay his nest egg of $20,000 into something even larger by appealing to local pride. Once the Board had decided to open three or four schools in the state, it was evident that over a three-year period each school must stay within an annual budget of $2,000, just enough to pay the salaries of a principal teacher and an assistant. Not wanting to be like the boy who spent all his money to buy a purse, as he explained to Elizabeth Peabody, Mann let it be known that the location of a school would be influenced by what "strong inducements" communities might offer. If these were in the form of "Academy buildings and a Mansion House or Houses, sufficient for the lodging and boarding of a hundred pupils," then his modest funds could pay for the instructors' salaries, firewood, and chalk.[4]

Driven by a sense of local boosterism, town after town was quick to respond and want whatever it was the Board was contemplating. Several towns in Plymouth County sent their leading citizens to appear before the Board to give assurances of their willingness to do anything necessary. When they asked if the schools were to be co-educational, the Board equivocated, but gave the impression that it preferred them to "be for one sex only." Nor was it prepared with concrete answers to questions about facilities. When a correspondent asked how much money his community should raise in order to attract a school, Mann answered "that it would be impossible for any-

---

[4] Mann to Elizabeth Peabody, July 5, 1838, Mann MSS:MHS; Mann to Thomas Robbins, April 27, 1838, Robbins MSS:CHS.

one," even an architect, to make an estimate of the cost. And he added, "It seems to me the only way is to make a rough estimate, say $10,000, and then to take your pistol and go out into the highway, and see if you can get it," through an "economical-philanthropical-predatory mission." Once the Pandora's box of community involvement was opened, some towns assumed they would also determine who would teach, who would attend, and what would be taught even as they did with their academies. Only gradually and gingerly did the Board assert its authority with the carefully worded resolution, "We suppose it would be advisable that the Board should regulate . . . [the schools]." Two months after the legislation, the Board had decided to call its experiment "normal schools," apparently to protect the endeavor from chauvinistic critics; but three months later Emerson Davis still argued it was best to abandon the whole idea and to appoint professors of pedagogy in some of the academies. Precise statements on control, supervision, auditing, choice of faculty, length of semesters, and the nature of the curriculum were still part of the future. About the only thing of which they were certain was that these schools would remain inferior to the colleges and never grant degrees. To add something of a comic twist to their gropings, at the very time they seemed to be farthest away from resolving their uncertainties, Mann received applications from men who assured him they had exactly the qualifications he was seeking. Understandably, Mann could report to Robbins, ". . . as we have none of the lights of experience, we must throw the light of judgment and common sense forward as far as we can." [5]

And offers of buildings they also received. Hardly had Governor Everett's signature dried on the bill before Seth Sprague urged Thomas Robbins to form a committee to raise funds to bring one of the schools to Plymouth County. Robbins found Ichabod Morton, who soon did the work of three or four. Taking a page from Mann's book, he organized meetings throughout the county. And taking another page from Dwight, he publicly offered to donate $1,000 to the project if the several communities would furnish the rest. All of this activity was to culminate in one grand finale in which the leading men of the

---

[5] Records of the Board, May 31, June 1, August 31, and December 26, 1838, MS in MSDE; Mann to Charles Brooks, June 5, 1838; Mann to Ichabod Morton, August 13, 1839, Straker MSS:ACL; Ichabod Morton to Mann, April 22, 1838; John Parkhurst to Mann, September 10, 1838, all in Mann MSS:MHS; Mann to Thomas Robbins, April 27, 1838, Robbins MSS:CHS.

state joined Mann in convincing the communities in Plymouth County to come forward with the necessary cash.[6]

Governor Everett would be there. Jared Sparks could not come but he was not missed since Morton and his collaborators had convinced both Daniel Webster and John Quincy Adams to lend the support of their presence. From Boston, Mann also lined up George Putnam, orthodox minister on the Board and one of the inner circle of the Harvard Corporation, and Robert Rantoul, Unitarian and a leading Democrat in the state. From Boston, Mann also urged his Plymouth lieutenants to greater efforts with letters to Samuel J. May, Robbins, Morton, and Nathaniel Davis, a recent conscript in the campaign. When Davis agreed to be chairman of the meeting, Mann left nothing to chance and spelled out his specific instructions: "the meeting should be called to order at 10 o'clock . . . a committee should be appointed to determine on some course of proceedings . . . officers should be chosen for the Association . . . my address (if they are willing to hear it) should be delivered. . . . If Mr. Webster is there, reserve him till 5 o'clock in order to keep the people together." Somehow during all this flurry of preparation, Mann also found time to prepare his address to the convention.[7]

Early on September 3, the day of the meeting, Mann hired a saddle horse from David Homer, his livery man, and joined Robert Rantoul for the trip south, the two men traveling together to Hanover. As soon as they arrived, it was evident that Morton and the others had done their work. Every pew of the Episcopal church was filled and people were standing in the aisles. Davis followed his instructions to the letter, and after the preliminaries of organization, it was resolved that Mann should speak. Still avoiding the issue of what final form the normal school should take, Mann said he had not come to "insist upon any particular mode of preparation or of preparation in any particular institutions—whether Normal Schools, special departments in academies, colleges. . . . What I insist upon is, not the form, but the substance." Presenting a crude learning theory assembled from Lockean mental discipline and George Combe's phrenology, and rea-

---

[6] Seth Sprague to Thomas Robbins, April 13, 1838; Mann to Thomas Robbins, April 27, 1838, Robbins MSS:CHS; Ichabod Morton to Mann, April 22 and July 23, 1838; Samuel J. May to Mann, June 16, 1838, all in Mann MSS:MHS.

[7] Mann to Jared Sparks, May 11 and 18, 1838, Sparks MSS:HCL; Mann to Nathaniel Davis, August 31, 1838, Misc. Bound:MHS; Ichabod Morton to Mann, July 23, 1838, Samuel J. May to Mann, June 16, 1838, both in Mann MSS:MHS; Mann, Journal, March 18, 1838, MS in MHS.

soning from analogy, Mann described the original "propensities" of the mind and the power of education to strengthen and alter them. It was as necessary to nurture and exercise these as it was to care for one's muscles. He made other points in his message as well, but this was the heart of it. The general training of the academies, the colleges, or the old-fashioned school of experience were not sufficient to prepare teachers. The demands of the age now required special training. What he said, he said well. It remained for those in the audience to decide for themselves.[8]

After lunch, Charles Brooks presented a carefully worded resolution committing several towns in the area to raise a sum sufficient to provide for a building and fixtures. Morton followed, offering to pay 10 per cent of the amount. Rantoul and Putnam then spoke, the latter admitting that although he had studied all the mathematics offered at Harvard he considered himself incompetent to teach addition and subtraction to young children. With the Brooks resolution still before the group, Davis recognized the former President of the United States, John Quincy Adams. Deprived by his nation of the opportunity to render it the wise leadership his high order of intelligence and ethical character made possible, "Old Man Eloquent" continued to be revered in Massachusetts because of his heroic anti-slavery stand in the House of Representatives and his defense of free speech and the right of petition. From carefully prepared notes he spoke of Sparta and quoted Plutarch. Referring to the advances in Prussia, he held up the specter of European domination if his countrymen permitted monarchies to "steal a march on republics in the patronage of that education on which a republic is based," and he summed up his thoughts with the belief that the resolution "could not but find favor with everyone who will examine and comprehend it."

Still on schedule by late afternoon and with most of the audience willing to stay, it was time for the climax. Davis recognized Daniel Webster and the audience leaned forward to hear the "Mighty Hercules." Webster spoke extemporaneously and said nothing new on the subject. But it was not what he said but how he said it that made the difference. Using a deep resilient voice, which flowed into every corner of the church and filled it with an irresistible rhetoric, he could convince all but the deaf. By the time he had reached his conclusion, no doubt most in the audience agreed with him that the ex-

[8] Mann, Journal, September 4, 1838, MS in MHS. A printed version of Mann's address was published in his *Lectures on Education* (Boston, 1845), under the title "Special Preparation, a Prerequisite to Teaching."

periment of normal schools was truly a "noble one." The question was called, the resolution passed by acclamation, and the spell was broken. All that remained was a benediction by Thomas Robbins. Before the rows of bowed heads, he led the group praying that since the offer to have the first normal school in the state had been made in the "Old Colony [Plymouth County] . . . the mother of us all," he asked that the descendants of the Pilgrims would sustain the high calling of their fathers and "go forward in improvements which are to elevate and bless all coming generations." The audience sang "Old Hundredth" and the meeting was over.[9]

Leaving Hanover for Worcester the next day, Mann believed that ". . . it was indeed a great day for the cause of common schools," and that the corner had been turned in getting a normal school under way in the Old Colony. In this he was wrong. The sweetness of county pride soon turned sour over local jealousy. Scituate refused to raise its portion unless it received the school. The same was true of Plymouth, Hanover, and Bridgewater. The needs of the next generation were cast aside for more immediate concerns. Apparently not a single town in the Old Colony was willing to enhance the prestige of its neighbor. As he moved on his annual circuit through the western part of the state, Mann waited for good news to catch up with him. When he finally received a letter from Seth Sprague he read the disheartening account of how the Scituate Town Meeting had decided to postpone action indefinitely. As the weeks rolled by, only Morton remained undaunted. The first setbacks merely goaded him on. "I have full faith a brighter, more glorious day is at hand," he wrote to Mann in his scrawling hand. But by the end of the year with nothing deposited in the bank and six towns having voted down the normal school proposal, he was left with only one prospect. Bridgewater might come through by itself. Meanwhile, illness pulled Mann's spirits down to another low. Returning from a lecture in Chelsea, he caught a bad cold, took to his bed, and resorted to the unusual medication (for him) of having six leeches applied. Not only was he struggling to regain his health for the mid-December board

<hr>

[9] Robbins, Diary, II, 506–507; John Quincy Adams to Nathaniel Davis, August 19, 1838, Misc. Bound, MHS. For a contemporary account of the meeting, see the Springfield *Republican,* October 6, 1838. The speeches of several of the participants of the meeting are found in Henry Barnard, *Normal Schools and Other Agencies, Institutions and Means Designed for the Professional Educator of Teachers* (Hartford, 1851), pp. 126–130; Jediah Dwelley and John F. Simmons, *History of the Town of Hanover, Massachusetts* (Hanover, 1910), p. 123.

meetings, but fighting off both a despair which stemmed from his failure in the Old Colony and a personal despondency which gripped him every Thanksgiving. Writing from a sickbed he lamented that "our chance of success is small." [1]

From his Plymouth experience, Mann learned that since parochialism was inevitable, it must be exploited. Thus from here on in, he dealt with individual towns. The facilities of the defunct Round Hill School originally started by Joseph Cogswell and George Bancroft were put forward as "ready for use, well adopted to the object and cheap; a beautiful situation; healthful air; unrivaled natural beauties; great facilities of communication in every direction. . . ." The buildings of Governor Dumner Academy were also offered. The town of Lancaster proposed that James Carter's old academy be used rent-free for the next three years, and Josiah Fiske, the man for whom Mann once read law, urged him to consider a site in Wrentham near where Mann had studied geometry with Reverend William Williams.[2]

It was obvious that if it didn't cost very much and would bring the community prestige, almost everyone wanted in. More than a dozen written offers came to Mann before the end of the year. From all of these, the Board finally chose Barre, near the center of the state; Bridgewater, in the southeast; and Lexington, in the vicinity of Boston. Such was the beginning. At least the schools were finally located, but it was with some degree of truth that Mann could speak of the absence of "palpable results." [3]

[1] Mann, Journal, September 4, 1838, MS in MHS; Seth Sprague to Mann, December 3, 1838, Ichabod Morton to Mann, November 19, and December 11, 1838, all in Mann MSS:MHS; Mann to Ichabod Morton, November 22, 1838, Straker MSS:ACL; Mann to T. A. Greene, November 11, 1838, Chicago Historical Society.
[2] Records of the Board, May 3 and 30, and August 31, 1838, MS in MSDE; C. P. Huntington to Mann, May 12, 1838, Josiah Fiske to Mann, April 15, 1838; Josiah Foy to Mann, December 22, 1838, all in Mann MSS:MHS; Mann to Robert Rantoul, June 26, 1838, Mann MSS:Essex Institute; Mann to Jared Sparks, May 18 and August 10, 183[8], Sparks MSS:HCL; Mann, Journal, May 22 and July 23, 1838, MS in MHS.
[3] For other offers of buildings and sites, see C. B. Rising and B. Mills to Mann, May 28, [1838] (Worthington); Minot Thayer to Mann, June 9, 1838 (Braintree); Phineas Allen to Mann, June 14, 1838 (Northfield); Charles H. Holmes to Mann, July 18, 1838 (Topsfield); Thomas Fox to Mann, August 23, 1838 (Newburyport); Sewell Cutting to Mann, September 4, 1838 (Southbridge); John Keyes to Mann, September 18, 1838 (Concord); and Alpheus Harding to Charles Hudson, December 24, 1838 (New Salem), all in Mann MSS:MHS. See also Mann to Samuel B. Woodward, January 24, 1840, Mann MSS:Pennsylvania Historical Society.

His next step was to appoint a faculty. Since no normal schools existed he could not raid another campus. Eventually, he looked to three possible sources, clergymen, high school teachers, and college professors. Emerson Davis and Thomas Robbins were authorized to offer one of the principalships to Reverend Thomas Hopkins Gallaudet, the founder of the American Asylum at Hartford. Among others, enquiries were sent to Reverend Alonzo Potter, later to become the Episcopal Bishop of Pennsylvania, and Reverend Jacob Abbott, author of the popular "Rollo Books" and brother of John Abbott, who had written the troublesome *Child at Home*. All of these drew negative replies.[4]

The first man to accept was Reverend Cyrus Peirce, a former Unitarian minister and principal of the Nantucket High School. Since Peirce was not orthodox, it was mandatory that the principal at Barre should be; and after considerable correspondence, Mann found just the individual he needed in the person of Reverend Samuel Newman, a professor at Bowdoin. The future principal for Bridgewater was found much closer at hand. After again casting about for prospects, Mann selected Colonel Nicholas Tillinghast, a retired army officer and resident of Bridgewater who had taught natural science and moral philosophy at West Point. Around these three men, Mann now hoped to build his plans for "raising the qualifications of teachers."[5]

Of the three, Peirce was certainly the most reluctant to assume the mantle of greatness Mann was about to place upon him. A humble person, unassuming, and troubled by self-doubts, Peirce was also judged one of the finest teachers in the Commonwealth. Well aware of the difficulty of the undertaking, he could ask Mann in all sincerity, "Is it really true that in old enlightened Massachusetts, you can find nothing better?" In all likelihood the answer was No. Not only was Mann convinced of Peirce's pedagogical talents in the classroom,

---

[4] Mann to Thomas Robbins, March 29, 1839, Robbins MSS:CHS; Jacob Abbott to Mann, *et al.*, March 21, 1839 Mann MSS:MHS; Everett Diary, April 17, 1839, MS in MHS; Records of the Board, March 13, 14, 27, and April 12, 1839, MS in MSDE.

[5] Mann to Jared Sparks, June 18, 1839, Sparks MSS:HCL; Samuel Newman to Mann, June 7, 17, and 26, 1839; Cyrus Peirce to Mann, June 4, 1839; Samuel Foy to Mann, June 21, 1839, all in Mann MSS:MHS; Everett Diary, May 28 and June 21, 1839, MS in MHS; Records of the Board, May 29 and 30, and June 21, 1839, MS in MSDE. For biographical sketches of Peirce and Tillinghast, see Henry Barnard, *American Educational Biography, Memoirs of Teachers, Educators, and Promoters of Education, Science and Literature* (New York, 1861), pp. 405–456.

but he was also certain of his ideological soundness. To those who persisted in seeing public schools only as a philanthropic endeavor for the poor, Peirce could write,

When Public Schools were first set up at Nantucket about 12 years ago, their enemies and opposers through odium called them *"Charity Schools"* or *"Charitable Institutions."* I can give no countenance to the opinion that our Public Schools are Public Charities in the ordinary acceptation of the term. I would as soon speak of the County Court or Public Highway or any other public convenience sustained by a tax proportionally assessed on all the citizens as a Public Charity.[6]

If in the future, Peirce was on the brink of despair as he carried his small part of the reform forward, he would have good reason. Starting the normal school at Lexington, he had virtually nothing on which to build. Not a recognized rung in some pre-established educational ladder, his school could not count on a regular flow of applicants graduating from some lower institution. Instead, he would gather in academy dropouts, a few high school graduates, and numerous bright persons who had no more than an elementary education. The curriculum for these prospective teachers was nonexistent and in the area of teaching methods, he had the mixed blessing of less than a dozen books on which to draw his ideas. Nor could he be certain how long his students would be with him. Some members of the Board thought about two years was an appropriate term of study, but no one was certain. Perhaps at no point in his career did Mann let his enthusiasm for reform so completely obscure what little professional knowledge he had about education. Not only did he brush aside the details of getting the normal schools under way, but he expected Peirce to have classes in session at Lexington three weeks after he accepted his new position! Yet so certain was Mann of success, that he saw all attendant problems as picayune. When he ran out of money to equip the school, and found it impossible to borrow money using his law library as collateral, he simply sold his books and used the proceeds to pay Peirce's bills. The day before the opening of the school at Lexington, he would write in his Journal, "Much must come of it, either of good or of ill. I am sanguine in my faith that it will be the former. But the good will not come of itself. That is the reward of

[6] Mann, Journal, June 13, 1839, MS in MHS; Cyrus Peirce to Mann, 1839, Mann MSS:MHS. Throughout the remainder of his life, Mann persisted in misspelling Peirce's name "Pierce," an error which Mary Mann dutifully repeated in her biography of her husband.

effort, of toil, of wisdom." Then the following day, in a building overlooking the triangular Lexington Green where Captain Jonathan
Parker had rallied his men just sixty years before, the doors were
opened on the first state normal school in America.[7]

It rained all day and only three applicants appeared. In what
must have been the understatement of the month, Mann observed
that "in point of numbers, this is not a promising commencement."
But habitually, he only saw this as a temporary setback and the prelude to long-range success. "What remains but more exertion," he
wrote, "more and more, until it *must* succeed." Unfortunately for
Peirce, Mann's exertion remained on a more Olympian level and did
not descend to the day to day problems which kept popping up at Lexington. Thus, three weeks after the school opened, in desperation
Peirce wrote to Mann explaining he had few books and no apparatus.
He did not know who should pay for the pew rents for the students in
the meetinghouse, and whether the students should be given a summer vacation. Since he now had only eight pupils with the "*Stamina*
of good teachers," he also asked if it would not be advisable to "lower
the entrance age to 15." Eventually, Peirce provided his own answers
for most of these questions and literally paid a dear price for poor
planning by the Board. He paid bills from his own pocket and then
hoped Mann would honor his vouchers. When cold weather came he
would stoke the classroom stove at midnight, and then rise again at
four in the morning to keep it going. After every snowfall, the neighbors recognized his familiar form shoveling the walk between the
boardinghouse and the schoolhouse. Somehow despite all of the obstacles, he persevered and Mann could report as early as the beginning of the second semester that he had never been in a school
"where the business of education was advancing so systematically, so
perfectly, so rapidly."[8]

Somewhat wiser by the time he launched the school at Barre,
two months later, Mann attempted to avoid some of the problems he
had created for himself at Lexington. His principal, Samuel Newman, urged the dissemination of more information about the under-

---

[7] Mann to Josiah Quincy, February 10, 1849, Quincy MSS:BPL; Mann
to Jared Sparks, June 18, 1839, Sparks MSS:HCL.
[8] Mann, Journal, July 2 and 3, 1839, MS in MHS; Cyrus Peirce to Mann,
July 30 and December 15, 1839, Mann MSS:MHS; Mann to Jared
Sparks, September 14, 1839, Sparks MSS:HCL. Peirce's own account of
his problems is found in Arthur O. Norton, ed., *The First State Normal
School in America: The Journals of Cyrus Peirce and Mary Swift*
(Cambridge, 1926), *passim.*

taking since, as he reported, "Even the more intelligent part of the community, hardly understands what is meant by a N.S., some are afraid of the Unit. [Unitarian] influences and some of the Orth. [orthodox] influence, and some of the oppression of the rich. . . ." To help spread the word and give the school the publicity it needed, the editor of the Barre *Gazette* printed a number of feature articles on the project and on the opening day Governor Everett, whose promise of a speech was enough to guarantee a large turnout, was on hand. Actually, the Governor was poorly prepared and barely made it in time for the opening. By the end of the day, however, Mann reported that the speech was "excellent" and that the school had "commenced under favorable auspices." Twenty students applied for admission and he expected more within the week.[9]

Newman soon had things well in hand and when the Board appointed Nicholas Tillinghast at Bridgewater, they decided he should complete a six-month apprenticeship at Barre with the Bowdoin professor before opening the next school. By November it was anticipated that as many as sixty students would be enrolling for the next term and that Newman would soon need an assistant. For Mann, the opening at Barre was an important milepost along a road which clearly took its toll. Describing his labors to get the schools under way and writing with typical hyperbole, he claimed that it required "an incredible amount of labour and perplexity." To another he wrote that "the opening of the two normal schools, and finding suitable and acceptable individuals to take charge of them, cost me an incredible amount of anxiety. I believe I counted all the men in N. England over by tale, before I could find any who would take the schools without ruining them. But I trust we have succeeded." [1]

*   *   *

With few people paying any attention to the sporadic outbursts still coming from Packard, Mann was ready to turn upon Orestes Brownson, editor of the Boston *Quarterly Review* and self-appointed gadfly

---

[9] Everett Diary, June 2 and September 5 and 6, 1839, MS in MHS; Mann to George Combe, September 11, 1839, Combe MSS:NLS; Mann to George Briggs, June 21 and September 6, 1839, Briggs MSS:AAS; Samuel Newman to Mann, August 19, 1839, Mann MSS:MHS; Barre *Gazette*, July 5 and 26, August 9 and 30, and September 6, and 13, 1839.
[1] Mann to George Briggs, June 21, 1839, Briggs MSS:AAS; Charles Hudson to Mann, November 26, 1839, Mann MSS:MHS; Mann to George Combe, September 11, 1839, Combe MSS:NLS.

on the rump of the Board of Education. Although in terms of public support at the time, it was probably better for the Board to have this "Proteus of doctrine" as Mann called him, as an enemy rather than a friend, Mann would have considered Brownson a worthy target had the Board not faced the threat of a frontal attack on its efforts. For the moment, then, he was forced to keep out of public print and attempt to curb Brownson's attacks on him through their mutual friend, Elizabeth Peabody.[2]

Judging from the election returns of the early 1830's, the Whig Party seemed invincible in Massachusetts politics and could almost have won any mayoral or gubernatorial race even if it chose its candidates from among the inmates of a local jail. During this period few could have predicted it would founder in the state on a misguided liquor law, and finally disintegrate completely in the 1850's as a national party over the Fugitive Slave Law. Instead, during the summer of 1839, Massachusetts men watched with considerable interest the development of the Amistad Case. Earlier that spring, a schooner, the *Amistad*, was carrying fifty-three slaves from Havana to Guaraja, Cuba. Mutiny broke out and the slaves forced the Spanish crew to sail for Africa. Shrewdly, the captain sailed east during the day and north at night, finally touching Montauk Point on Long Island, where the ship put in for water and the mutineers were arrested and held for trial. The Ambassador from Spain insisted that the slaves were Spanish property and should be returned to their owners; the American prosecution held that they had murdered some of the crew and should be executed; and a number of abolitionists claimed that the slaves were really free persons who had wrongfully been taken from their native country. Lewis Tappan and others raised money for the defense of the mutineers, securing the services of Theodore Sedgwick of New York and Roger Baldwin of New Haven. After two trials, Bald-

---

[2] Basically, Brownson claimed that the Board was un-American, Godless, and Whig. Miss Peabody defended Mann, insisting he was not an *"infidel,"* as Brownson had implied. Brownson continued his attack on the Board with a review of Mann's *Second Annual Report*, in his Boston *Quarterly Review*, II (October, 1839), 393–434, and III (April, 1840), 228–229, claiming the Board's selection of books for the common school library as a "censorship of the press." Then within five years, with all the ardor of a recent convert, he advocated the right of the Roman Catholic Church to use its expurgatory index. See Elizabeth Peabody to Orestes Brownson, July 6, 1839, Brownson MSS: Notre Dame University; Mann to Samuel Gridley Howe, July 21, 1839; Edmund Dwight to Mann, August 9, 1839, Mann MSS: MHS; and *Brownson's Quarterly Review*, II (January, 1845), 1–29.

win, now joined by old John Quincy Adams, successfully defended them before the United States and they were ordered to be returned to Sierra Leone.[3]

But for the time being, the issue of one man's right to own property in the life of another was no direct threat to the triumphant Whigs of Massachusetts. Instead, their immediate stumbling block was the enactment of a most bizarre law requiring consumers of rum, whisky, and gin to buy their ardent spirits in quantities of *at least* 15 gallons. After more than twenty years of failure to reduce the consumption of liquor by voluntary means, and finding drinking habits resistant to more gentle persuasion, the temperance reformers by the late 1830's finally had enlisted the strong arm of the state in their crusade by securing the passage of the "fifteen gallon law," the predecessor to legal prohibition. Believing the grog shop, forerunner of the saloon, to be their main nemesis, they forced a bill through the General Court outlawing all sales of liquor in quantities of *less* than 15 gallons![4]

Although dismissed by most social historians as "special class legislation" aimed at the workingman, this was not the intent of the reformers. They believed the grog shop was undermining the family and destroying the laboring man's will to work. By limiting all sales of ardent spirits to a substantial amount they would put drinking back in the home where it could be controlled. A majority of both parties supported the measure in 1838, but as soon as enforced, it became one of the most unpopular laws ever enacted in Massachusetts. Since Governor Everett had signed the measure

---

[3] John Quincy Adams, *Arguments of John Quincy Adams before the Supreme Court of the United States, in the Case of the U.S., Appellants vs. Cinque, and other Africans, Captured in the Schooner Amistad* (New York, 1841), *passim; Africans Taken in the Amistad,* U.S. 26th Congress, 1st Session, House Executive Document 185 (New York, 1840), *passim.*

[4] The best detailed account of this controversy leading up to the legislation is found in Krout, *Origins of Prohibition,* pp. 262–273; for examples of literature published by the several factions, see Jonathan Phillips, *et al., An Address to the People of Massachusetts by the Friends of Temperance and of the Statute of 1838,* "For the Regulation of the Sale of Spiritous Liquors" (Boston, 1838); n.a., *An Appeal to the Country People of Massachusetts, by a Committee Opposed to the Law* (Boston, 1838); Jonathan Phillips, *et al., The Boston Opposition to the New Law for the Suppression of Rum Shops and Grog Shops, Fully Detached and Plainly Exposed; Being an Appeal to the Country People of Massachusetts to Protect Themselves* (Boston, 1838); n.a., *A Reply to the Report of a Committee of Those Opposed to the License Law* (Boston, 1838); n.a., *Letters to the Hon. Harrison Gray Otis by a Citizen of Massachusetts* (Boston, 1839).

into law, Marcus Morton, a Democrat who had tried unsuccessfully twelve times for the governorship since 1828, made the Democratic Party the standard-bearer for its repeal. In the November elections one Whig after another went down to defeat. When the General Court convened at the beginning of the year, Morton squeezed into the gubernatorial chair by the majority of a single vote. Thus not only did Massachusetts finally have a Democratic Governor, but the Board of Education had a new chairman *ex officio*.[5]

Since the resolutions adopted by the Democratic State Convention the previous October had made no mention of the Board, Mann did not know what to expect of Morton. Once assuming office, however, the Governor did not remain silent for long. In his inaugural address, after reaffirming the appropriate folklore and pieties about the importance of the "Education of the people," he proceeded to claim that the responsibility and management of the common schools "should rest upon the inhabitants of the towns." Speaking like a latter-day Taft Republican, he argued that "in the town and district meetings, those little pure democracies," were to be found the best means of controlling the schools without any adventitious supervision from the state. Such sentiments, when set alongside his general policy that retrenchment should be a substitute for taxation and his determination to abolish all "supernumerary officers, or agencies, or commissions not immediately necessary for the public good," made it evident that Morton was out to abolish the Board and its Secretary.[6]

Amazingly, Mann was not alert to the threat even after Morton's speech. Clearly the recommendation to retrench and return all responsibility for the common schools to those "little pure democracies" would wipe out any gains he had made towards centralization and homogeneity in the schools. Apparently he was too busy awaiting the next broadside from Bronson or Packard to see where the real threat lay. Curiously, he stopped the February issue of the *Common School Journal* just before it went to press, inserted a portion of Morton's address, and added editorially that the new

---

[5] For a general discussion of Massachusetts politics during this period, see Arthur B. Darling, *Political Changes in Massachusetts, 1824–1848* (New Haven, 1925), pp. 157–250.

[6] *House Documents* No. 9 (January, 1840), "Address of His Excellency Marcus Morton, to the Two Branches of the Legislature, on the organization of the Government for the Political Year Commencing January 1, 1840," *passim*. Boston *Evening Transcript*, January 22, 1840; *Bay State Democrat*, January 22, 1840.

Governor had "fully endorsed" the past efforts of the Board. Privately he explained Morton's silence on the Board by saying "*Probably he did not know of its existence.*" [7]

Others in the General Court read their cues from Morton more quickly. They ordered the Board to give an accounting of its expenditures "from the time of its establishment to the present time, including the salary of the Secretary and all incidental expenses related to that department," and they directed the House Committee on Education "to consider the expediency of abolishing the Board of Education and the Normal Schools and to report by bill or otherwise." Moving with shameless haste four days after their assignment, the majority of the committee reported out a bill to kill the Board, discontinue the normal school experiment, and give back Edmund Dwight his $10,000.[8]

Reasoning by a "damned if the Board did and damned if it did not" logic, the majority report argued, "If, then, the Board has any actual power, it is a dangerous power, touching directly upon the rights and duties of the Legislature; if it has no power why continue its existence, at an annual expense to the Commonwealth?" To this it added the red herring of foreign influence, warning that the Board really wanted to saddle Massachusetts with the Prussian system of education and place "a monopoly of power in a few hands, contrary, in every respect, to the true spirit of our democratical institutions." Furthermore, it condemned the normal schools as an unnecessary waste. High schools and academies "cost the Commonwealth nothing and they are fully adequate . . . to furnish a competent supply of teachers," it concluded. Considering the short time the common schools were open in the course of a year, it seemed foolish to assume that teaching in them would ever become a distinct profession. If there were districts which desired more competent teachers than they now had, they should simply pay better salaries.[9]

Mann was stunned the day he learned of the majority report, and that night he must have slept with clenched fists. Early in January, he referred to "political madmen . . . raising voice and arm against the Board"; again in February, he spoke of "partisan men

[7] Mann, Journal, January 19 and 26, 1840, MS in MHS; *CSJ*, II (February, 1840), 47.
[8] House Journal, Vol. 62, January 30, March 3, 7, 10, 11, and 13, 1840, pp. 117–118, 269, 303, 306–307, 317, 328, and 344, MS in MSA.
[9] *House Documents*, No. 49 (March, 1840), pp. 2–14; Boston *Daily Advertiser*, March 12, 1840.

. . . making efforts to demolish the Board"; but not until the General Court had been in session for two months did he single out Marcus Morton as the arch villain and favor him with a brand of rhetoric reserved heretofore for Packard and Brownson. Privately he attacked the Governor for having "committed that high treason to truth which consists in perverting great principles to selfish ends," but only when the Committee on Education began considering ways of abolishing the Board did he really acknowledge that the fat was in the fire. Even then it was not until the majority report was made public that he finally fought back.[1]

Responding to the challenge, Mann wrote John Shaw, a member of the committee, a long letter explaining why the Board and its normal schools were absolutely necessary in Massachusetts. There was now a greater diversity of institutions and in some cases a "contrariety of their interests." Compounding the problem was ". . . the new exposure to error, and the new temptations to dishonesty, which grow out of the more dense population." All of this intensified the need for a "change in public sentiment." From Mann's letter and information from Samuel Gridley Howe, Shaw, and Thomas Greene, the two minority members of the committee, prepared a report and had it before the House in four days. In an effort to be fair, the House ordered the printing of 2,000 copies of each document.[2]

Using Mann's letter as a general outline, Shaw answered each accusation against the Board. To the charge of religious and political conspiracy he answered that the members of the Board differed in religion and politics and were a "mutual watch and check upon each other's sectarian or party preferences." That the Board could disseminate information without encroaching on the rights of citizens was demonstrated by Mann's report on *School Houses*. To the charge of foreign influence, Shaw answered that in Mann's *Second* and *Third Annual Reports*, he had shown the Prussian system far too coercive to be suited to the Commonwealth, since Massachusetts' institutions seemed to spring up from a seedbed of voluntarism. Defending the normal school experiment, Shaw claimed that it would be wrong to break the contracts with Peirce and Newman, the

---

[1] Mann, Journal, January 5 and February 2, 1840, MS in MHS; Mann to George Combe, February 22, 1840, Combe MSS:NLS; Mann to Henry Barnard, March 2 and 7, 1840, Barnard MSS:NYU; House Journal, Vol. 62, March 7, 1840, pp. 306–307, MS in MSA.
[2] Mann to John Shaw, March 7, 1840, Mann MSS:MHS; House Journal, Vol. 62, March 7, 10, and 11, 1840, pp. 306–307, 317, and 328, MS in MSA.

students, the citizens of Barre, Bridgewater, and Lexington who had raised money, and particularly with Edmund Dwight. Surely if the legislature abolished the normal schools it would not be because they had failed, but because they had "fallen prematurely, by the hand that should have sustained them." [3]

Since he had commitments to speak before the Lyceum and the Mercantile Library Association of New York City, Mann had to leave Boston just as the actual floor debate began. It took the entire day of Wednesday, March 18, to air the arguments of Allan Dodge, author of the majority report, and Frederick Emerson, author of a spelling book Mann had refused to endorse for the common schools. Shaw then led the counterattack on Dodge and Emerson and soon supporters of the Board came to their feet from both sides of the aisle. The next morning was to be the showdown. [4]

In New York City it rained very heavily and so few people appeared for Mann's Thursday night Lyceum lecture that it was necessary to postpone the program. He returned to his room as the rain continued and paced nervously about in "ignorance & suspense" with no way of knowing what the outcome had been in Boston until the arrival of the mail packet the next day. Friday morning brought a clear sky and a letter from Samuel Gridley Howe. Almost jumping from the top of the page was the exclamation "Hurrah for old Massachusetts!" And Howe continued,

Throw up your cap, my dear man, and shout, though you should be in Broadway, when you hear the news of this day—the infamous Report of the bigots and bookmakers is rejected by a vote of 245 to 182. . . . ! Many of the vandals shall disappear from the list of the next year's representatives.
. . . I have not for a long time experienced such a triumph, nor witnessed so much honest exaltation in others, as I have this last hour. . . . The *cause* has triumphed.

Considering the Democratic Governor's declared opposition and the fact that the pro-Board delegations from Boston and New Bedford could not make the session, it was a resounding reaffirmation for Mann's efforts. The vote was also a stunning setback for the advocates of democratic localism and Morton had about as much

---

[3] *House Document*, No. 53 (March, 1840), pp. 2–22.
[4] Boston *Daily Advertiser*, March 19 and 20, 1840, *CSJ*, II (1840), 239 ff; Mann to Henry Barnard, March 2, 1840, Barnard MSS:NYU; Mann, Journal, March 19, 1840, MS in MHS.

chance of being re-elected the following January as he had of becoming the king of England. Never again would Mann have to face such concerted opposition in the legislature.[5]

* * *

A careful study of the documents shows that Mann first underestimated the intensity of the religious and political attacks upon him and the Board. Then when he finally responded, he overreacted and later exaggerated the significance of these episodes, giving them a melodramatic quality in which the virtuous unsullied cause of public education was saved from the hands of arch villains like Packard, Brownson, and Morton by selfless, enlightened men such as himself. To recognize this is to gain important insights into his character and *modus operandi* as a reformer frequently missed by social and educational historians.

Although the intensity of opposition coming from such partisans as Morton, Dodge, and Frederick Emerson was real, they did not have anything approaching the political support they needed to abolish the Board. With the overt support of the Governor, Dodge still fell more than sixty votes short on the crucial vote. Even if by some magic he had been able to obtain these, his efforts faced a stone wall of opposition in the Senate. During the same session, while the attacks continued in the House, the upper chamber did not make a single move to place the question of the Board on its agenda. Furthermore, an attack by Brownson, who was soon to show the dimensions of his radicalism by urging the destruction of virtually every institution in society, was an indirect vote of confidence to the Board for many public and religious leaders at the time.[6]

Both Mann and his biographers have also perpetuated the myth of melodrama in recounting the religious controversies. Here they have cast the orthodox clergy as villains and liberal Unitarians as the saviors of the cause. There were, obviously, men of orthodox and conservative views who opposed Mann, some of them disagreeing with him to the point where they resorted to the press, leaving a

[5] House Journal, Vol. 62, March 19, 1840, p. 386, MS in MSA; Mann, Journal, March 21, 1840, MS in MHS; Samuel Howe to Mann, [March 19, 1840], Howe MSS:HCL; Boston *Daily Atlas*, March 20, 1840.

[6] Senate Journal, Vol. 61, 1840, *passim*, MS in MSA. With the publication of "The Laboring Classes," Boston *Quarterly Review* (July, 1840), 358 ff., Brownson eliminated himself as a serious threat to Mann and the Board of Education.

trail of pamphlets, sermons, and published letters later to be found and cited by students of the common school movement. Yet this soft polemical evidence is not supported by concrete facts. From the outset (although his anti-orthodox complex never let him recognize their contributions), orthodox leaders were among Mann's staunchest allies and rendered him invaluable service in explaining the nature of his efforts to the brethren of the cloth. His support from within the Board from such eminent clergymen as George Putnam, Thomas Robbins, and Emerson Davis, all orthodox Congregationalists, is evident from their correspondence with him. Other men who were leaders in local and county Congregational ministerial associations also gave Mann's efforts an unqualified endorsement and individual ministers stood by him from the very beginning. As a response to his speech before a county convention in Worcester, the assembly resolved to organize a speaker's bureau to carry Mann's message to every hamlet in the county. Sixteen men volunteered, eight of whom were ministers and the majority orthodox. Near the end of the Packard controversy, Reverend Jacob Abbott, brother of the author of *Child at Home,* advised Mann to ignore the Sunday School editor's barbs.

Even Richard Storrs and Heman Humphrey, two of the most religiously orthodox men in the state, joined the cause after initial misgivings, the latter becoming a member of the Board. And perhaps the most telling evidence of general support from Congregational, Presbyterian, and Baptist clergymen came from one of their official journals, the *American Quarterly Register.* Reviewing Mann's latest *Report,* its editors endorsed "the annual document of the Board of Education, proceeding from the eloquent pens of the Governor, and of Mr. Mann the Secretary." [7]

At times, Mann made every effort to keep up the false appearance that he and a small handful of the enlightened were the last line of defense against an active orthodox bent on repealing the Law of 1827 which prohibited the use of sectarian texts in public class-

---

[7] For examples of orthodox support for Mann within the Board, see Thomas Robbins to Henry Barnard, May 4, 1838, Barnard MSS:NYU; Thomas Robbins to Mann, November 14, 1837; Emerson Davis to Mann, October 24 and November 15, 1838, and March 6, 1839; for support from the leader of a ministerial association, see Enoch Sanford, January 1 and July 13, 1838; also see Jacob Abbott to Mann, December 7, 1839, and Heman Humphrey to William B. Calhoun, November 22, 1838, all in Mann MSS:MHS. The account of the Worcester conventions is found in the *Massachusetts Spy,* October 3, 1838; *American Quarterly Register,* XIII (August, 1839), 80.

rooms. Actually, the law always had strong support from all religious denominations. When it was first proposed, the legislative committee promoting it was predominantly orthodox. Furthermore, it was viewed at the time as a measure to legalize a de facto prohibition, then in existence. Later, in 1835, it was re-enacted almost unanimously by a General Court which included many orthodox members. When pressed on the issue, Mann himself conceded that already when he came to the secretaryship in 1837, sectarian religious instruction "had been, not entirely, but mainly discontinued, long before the existence of the Board." Since that time, it was only necessary to examine the school committee reports to see that all but two disclaimed "the desire to introduce sectarianism into the schools." Furthermore, he also acknowledged that whenever the subject of moral and religious instruction came up at a common school convention, sectarianism had virtually no support.

Yet as late as 1844 he still maintained that "the orthodox have hunted me this winter as though they were bloodhounds and I a poor rabbit." Privately he admitted that they were "losing strength" and that the chance of regaining it was "fast passing out of their hands." But he insisted nevertheless, about the same time, that "an extensive conspiracy is now formed to break down the Board of Education as a preliminary measure to teaching sectarianism in the schools." And he maintained his conspiracy complex even though Thomas Kinnicutt, as trusted friend of more than two decades and one of the most experienced politicians in the state, assured him the same year that "if an attempt were made in the legislature, to procure the passage of a law authorizing sectarian teaching on religious subjects in our schools, even with the express assent of the districts, it would meet with signal defeat." If, then, the political dimensions of Mann's controversies have been blown up out of proportion by educational historians, they have not been more so than the religious.[8]

Considering that Mann was attempting a uniform system of educational reporting, increased taxation, town supervision, and the establishment of normal schools, all departures from the past and prone to controversy, it is surprising just how much of a community of consensus supported the common school reform movement. Most

---

[8] Worcester *National Aegis,* February 21 and 28, 1827, and June 4, 1844; Mann, *Common School Controversy . . .* (Boston, 1844), p. 26; Mann to George Combe, July 30 and December 1, 1844, Combe MSS:NLS; Thomas Kinnicutt to Mann, December 3, 1844, Mann, MSS:MHS.

newspapers endorsed the Board, and whenever a writer raised his pen to attack Mann two or three rushed to his defense. Similarly, the annual reports of the town school committees offer little evidence of disagreement and a considerable common desire to cooperate. In short, there was far more consensus than controversy even though Mann intentionally gave the opposite impression.[9]

Why then did Mann and his associates brush all contrary evidence aside and want to believe that their cause was ever in imminent danger? Part of the explanation for this can be found in the way Mann perceived his role as a reformer. Believing he had an uphill battle all the way and needed local support in every part of the state, he not only organized an informal corps of "Friends of Education" as he called them, but welded them into a cohesive unit by emphasizing the seriousness of the problems they faced. If within every person there is a mother-lode of fear and uncertainty, Mann was able to mine this and mint it into the pure coinage of reform endeavors. Through controversy he cast himself as the militant and heroic leader by minimizing the commonality his movement had with other educational endeavors and emphasizing differences between the "Friends of Education" and those favoring academies, local district schools, and philanthropic endeavors among the dispossessed. Rarely was he willing to tolerate a neutrality or open-endedness on educational issues and he exhibited not the slightest trace of a more generous charity towards those who disagreed with him. Instead, he polarized those within education and stereotyped his opposition as benighted men who stood in the path of progress. Brownson was the "Proteus of doctrine," Morton the "secret enemy of the Board," and those representatives in the House who questioned the merits of the Board "political madmen." Working for him then was a hero-traitor dynamic which Mann used on his opponents with telling effect.

That Mann's role as the hero in the movement was securely fixed in the minds of his followers can be seen from numerous letters written at this time. In none of them, however, was it more romantically expressed than in a letter from Samuel Gridley Howe to George Combe, in which Howe offered his own version of Mann's apotheosis:

---

[9] For an analysis of the town reports, see Jonathan Messerli, "Consensus and Controversy in the Common School Reform," *Teachers College Record*, 66 (May, 1965), 749–759.

. . . the divine may direct my attention to the pages of the Bible, the naturalist to the wonders of creation, the astronomer to the glories of the firmament, in order to make me learn the power and love the goodness of God; but I learn more of this power and I love more His goodness, when I contemplate such a character as Horace Mann. . . . I would that the world would know him better; I would that he were made transparent, & conspicuous to all men, that they might see the beauty, and know the capacity of human nature.[1]

It is not surprising, then, despite claims that Mann laid the basis for a philosophy of public education, that there is a relative dearth of philosophical content in his writings. Aside from his common-sense and moralistic discussions on the need for educated citizens, a nonsectarian curriculum, taxation of private property for the education of all children, and several excursions into theories of teaching and learning which he might better have left unexplored, Mann's *Annual Reports* and published lectures are most sparse of philosophical issues. Theoretical discussions made him impatient. Such things he thought unnecessary. Thus when Elizabeth Peabody attempted to be the conduit between Emerson and Mann and raised some theoretical questions concerning the common school reform movement, Mann replied with a not too carefully concealed irritation,

Oh my dear lady! If a tough question were before a District Sch. Meeting about doing something for the school;—or before a Town Meeting about helping any side or limb of humanity forward, how think you, your oracle [Emerson] would lead or manage the minds of his people, which we call great by country! Oh these Reformers and Spiritualizers who can do everything well on paper! They can tell exactly how a road ought to be laid between here and New Orleans, but can they lay it? [2]

Philosophical discussions only impeded results and besides, they carried the troublesome implication that he just might be wrong. Those who opposed him did so because they lacked moral rectitude and honest motives. Marcus Morton, then, was merely an ambitious

---

[1] Samuel Gridley Howe to George Combe, August 17, 1839, Combe MSS:NLS.
[2] Mann to Elizabeth Peabody, Mann MSS:MHS. An attempt to glean an anthology of educational thought from Mann's twelve *Annual Reports* produced a very slim volume, the anthologist skipping entire reports for lack of substantive discussions. See Lawrence Cremin, ed. *The Republic and the School* (New York, 1957).

political hack sacrificing principle for selfish gains; Frederick Packard and Frederick Emerson were unscrupulous book hustlers threatening the minds of innocent children. Desperately, Mann struggled for the opportunity to demonstrate his sincerity to himself so that he might know that he was right and his opponents therefore wrong. Developing a bigotry of purpose, he worked toward his self-conceived goal. In studying this reform, one cannot escape the monomania at work in Mann, and its corollary, the total absence of self-doubt among the reformers. In fact, among them one finds the same hyper-certainty, narrowness of purpose, and adamancy which Mann utterly detested in his opponents. To be sure, doubts and uncertainties abounded on the pages of his private Journal, but these were, in fact, a carefully constructed façade to conceal his real character and gain the reader's sympathy. His uncertainty over the reception of a speech he was about to give at a county convention brought him to a cold sweat, and he nurtured genuine doubts about the collective wisdom of the General Court on educational questions. He also honestly questioned his physical resources and the adequacy of time he had available to carry the work forward; but never within the several hundred pages of his Journal did he once admit to self-doubt or acknowledge a weakness of conscience or a lapse of will. There was then little humility in the man. After meeting a wealthy merchant in Baltimore who gave him numerous accolades for his educational achievements, Mann took satisfaction from the fact that he had "got thru' the day, without much pain to the love of approbation." Here then was a paradox to which he would not admit: the more humility he claimed, the more his self-conceit was in the ascendancy.[3]

He knew he was right and, like a Grand Inquisitor, he would not grant his opponents the same indulgence. One searches in vain for any admission either that his ideology was in error or his efforts ill-conceived. He knew what society needed and how to accomplish it. Writing to a correspondent he would say, "Now, where social institutions are not widely established, or where the manners and customs, and the tone of feeling that pervade society, among a people whose law is public opinion, are wrong, then the machinery is out of order, and those who can both perceive how it is, and how it should be, are commissioned to set it right." Thoughts of his own

---

[3] Mann, Journal, March 31, 1840, MS in MHS; Mann to Elizabeth Peabody, March 10 and December 12, 1838, Mann MSS:MHS.

fallibility were anathema to him.[4] Many other New England reformers thought of themselves as the "Lord's chore boys," but Mann found it necessary to fashion himself into something more active and aggressive. In him was an eagerness to suffer, a desire for glory, and a will to power over the minds of men. He would be the true apostle in a country of unbelievers. "The orthodox have quite outgrown their obsolete notions, & have got a religion, which can at once gratify their self-esteem & destructiveness," he would say, and then add for self-assurance, "they shall not unclench me from my labours for mankind." To help others to a heavenly city he willingly spent his time in an earthly purgatory. Persecution had its delights and masochism the deepest of inner satisfactions. This required that he drown all natural love and personal longing, and put on a new man with an indomitable will to succeed. "I should be sorry to die, & see my part of the work undone; I should be infinitely more sorry to see it undone, & live," he wrote to Mary Dwight. Driving and crowding himself on remorselessly, he forged his will into a steel battering-ram capable of breaking the cast-iron mold of the past and the social inequalities which it formed. In Mann, there was what Herman Melville described in Ahab," an infirmity of the firmest fortitude." [5]

But this did not mean that he was naked to his enemies. Through his troubled childhood and the tragic years following Charlotte's death, Mann had slowly devised for himself a twofold subjective security which came to fruition during the years of his common school reform. First, he was willing to pay the sacrifice necessary to be subsumed within a great cause. And since he wished all to understand this, he publicized it wherever possible. Believing that only through martyrdom did one gain a lasting recognition, he told Henry Barnard, his Connecticut counterpart, that

You and I and others have to work on it, with embarrassment and obstruction, but when I look afar into the future and see the beautiful and glorious development it shall have in other hands, I find not satisfaction in my toils, merely, but I feel a pride in being stationed at this more honorable post of labour. Let us go on and buffet these waves of opposition with a stout arm and a confiding heart.

---

[4] Mann to George Combe, November 8, 1840, Combe MSS:NLS.
[5] Mann Journal, October 27, 1838, MS in MHS; Mann to Mary Eliot [nee Dwight] Parkman, 184[0]?, Mann MSS:HCL.

To Samuel Gridley Howe, he paraphrased the same thoughts, presenting them in an even stronger millennial tone.[6]

Beyond the security which came from residing within the bosom of the cause, Mann fashioned a second line of security which permitted him to relate any failures he encountered to causes external to himself. On his forty-third birthday he lapsed into a morose reverie,

The father & mother who brought me into life, and both left it. The whole circle of relatives has been thinned—parts of it, wholly broken & swept away. Of three sons, I alone survive, & my life has been more death than life, save that in the grave there are no such pains as mine. . . . Existence is no boon to me. One thing, however, remains. If I cannot live for myself, I can live for others. If I have nothing for which to thank heaven on my account, let me at least have the pleasure of doing some good to my kind. This is the only impulse, which, now, for some wearisome years has sustained me. . . . I will not repine. Repining supposes hope, & hope with me is nearly or quite extinct.[7]

A maudlin self-pity, yes, but Mann was far too sophisticated to leave it at this. For every setback he had a reason, and his ego remained intact. If he failed it was because of his health, his demoralized spirit after Charlotte's death, and the scores of benighted men obstructing progress. For none of these was he personally responsible. If unsuccessful, he was like a Greek tragic hero who could not overcome his fate. On the other hand if Mann succeeded, it was a personal accomplishment. Most of the people with whom he dealt were either for him, such as Howe, or unalterably opposed to him, as Packard or Morton. Only a rare person like Ralph Waldo Emerson could avoid the love-hate axis and observe his character more accurately: "Take egotism out, and you would castrate the benefactors, Luther, Mirabeau, Napoleon, John Adams, Andrew Jackson." And coming closer to home, Emerson added, "and our newer servants— Greeley, Theodore Parker, Ward Beecher, Horace Mann, Garrison —would lose their vigor."[8]

---

[6] Mann, Journal, September 8 and 29, 1839, and February 2, 1840, MS in MHS; Mann to Henry Barnard, May 4, 1839, and March 21, 1840, Barnard MSS:NYU; Mann to Samuel Gridley Howe, March 21, 1840, Mann MSS:MHS.

[7] Mann, Journal, May 3, 1839, MS in MHS.

[8] Bliss Perry, ed., *The Heart of Emerson's Journals* (New York, 1958), p. 298.

*   *   *

Paradoxically, the more inflexible Mann became in his "immutable principles" and his belief in the commonality of mankind, the more he faced an emergent society of growing sectarian, ethnic, and partisan diversity and the unveiling of more distant cultures radically different from his own. The time had not come in his own country for a revolt of the masses and participatory democracy, but he was witnessing a pluralistic evolution which followed in the wake of a shift of native Americans from the farm to the factory and the beginnings of a major wave of European immigration. The possibility of greater diversity now made public schools mandatory. In his explanation to John Shaw on why the Commonwealth needed the Board of Education and a centralized system of common schools, Mann predicted that "as population increases, & especially as artificial wants multiply, & temptations increase, the guards and securities must increase also, or society will deteriorate." The task called for a great effort by the moral and intellectual élites of the nation, who must utilize public authority to fashion and shape the common schools in their own image.[9]

One key in this endeavor was to change general public sentiment, and Mann succeeded in this as few other humanitarian reformers did. Another was what he referred to as "raising the qualifications of teachers." His job was to create a new *aristoi* of motives and morals from the rank and file, train them in the normal schools, and place them in public school classrooms. At first the only credentials they would need would be a dedication to the cause. The early converts would mainly undergo a short indoctrination course that theirs was the holiest of all callings. But subsequent novitiates, attending schools more generously supported by the state and enjoying the beginnings of a body of knowledge about teaching and learning, would gradually develop a sense of professionalism.

Somehow Mann hoped to steer between the Scylla of local anarchy and the Charybdis of Prussian coercion and centralization. Although he did not understand it at the time, the teacher élites he hoped would come forth to staff the schools never appeared, but in their stead came an educational bureaucracy of the *hoi polloi*, a corps of sub-élites which would determine norms, pass on the curriculum, and gain for itself that hallmark of all professions, the au-

---

[9] Mann to John Shaw, March 7, 1840, Mann MSS:MHS.

thority to decide on those who could join its privileged ranks. Now a more unified and efficient organization was possible, and through his efforts Mann was laying the basis—especially in cities like Boston, New York, and Chicago—for a centralized and rationalized educational system, complete with prescribed curricula, licensed teachers, a hierarchical administration, and all of this predicated upon the assumption that public schools could accomplish mass behavioral changes.

For all their subsequent cant and educationese about professionalism, it is safe to say that most teachers in nineteenth-century America were equipped at best with a false sense of importance, a "bag of tricks," and a faulty memory of how they themselves had once been taught. Supplanting older pedagogical artisans and entrepreneurs, they were little more than dedicated and upwardly mobile taskmasters, technicians, and civil servants. For such persons to teach unprecedented numbers of children, it was necessary for knowledge to be divided into subjects within the curriculum, and subjects subdivided into lessons of bits and pieces of information, then reorganized, classified, labeled, and given some hierarchy of values. In this way, the chasm between ignorance and learning would not be negotiated only by the insightful leaps of a talented few. It would be filled in with hundreds of textbooks, thousands of assignments, and an infinitude of words, numbers, and facts, so that the multitudes could cross over in lockstep fashion with less intellectual effort, albeit with far more drudgery and boredom.

Although the early devotees of the public schools pushed forward the idea of graded instruction whenever given the opportunity, they never quite achieved this goal. But where their rhetoric and persuasion failed, the textbook triumphed. Function followed form when William Holmes McGuffey devised an incredibly popular series of reading books of graduated difficulty. At least teachers finally had the means for arranging their pupils according to a Procrustean classification of grades, based upon the narrow skills of oral and silent literary reading, regardless of the pupils' other talents and accomplishments. Theoretically at least, a rationally managed system made possible predictable outcomes and a closer control over input and output. Chance, spontaneity, creativity, and individual differences were sacrificed. The result was an educational superstructure supposedly capable of producing moral individuals, responsible parents, loyal citizens, and productive laborers. Thus, as in the production of material goods, so in the education of children, the entire nation would experience a shift from *Gemeinschaft* to *Gesellschaft.*

Although too politically astute to advocate immediate centralized control, Mann repeatedly referred to the necessity of an educational *system*. He was hypersensitive to any criticism of Prussianism, but tighter supervision and centralization were implied in much of what he attempted. Furthermore, he thought of children not as individuals but as masses of pupils or an entire generation needing to be trained. There was in this man's mind both the power and compulsion towards an invincible abstractness. Children were not children, but a generalized mass of statistics needing training. Not individual learners with idiosyncratic interests, talents, and aspirations, they were to him young humanity—a humanity almost always understood in the abstract. One of the first to notice that the education of a single child held no interest for him was Samuel Gridley Howe. After receiving nationwide attention by teaching Laura Bridgman, Howe attempted to explain why Mann responded to her progress differently from others. Reasoning that for Mann, Laura symbolized the potential of education which staggered the imagination, he went on to observe with an insight remarkable for a close friend that "such minds as his seem to have an intensive tendency to . . . buy and sell and manage . . . ton weights, but cannot or will not handle a single pound." In this, Howe's judgment was later confirmed when Mann could not let an article on Laura in the *Common School Journal* speak for itself, but felt compelled to add editorially that here was an

. . . account of one of the most remarkable cases, on record, of what the human mind can accomplish, when bereft of its principle organs of sense. Here is a girl without power of sight, of speech, of hearing, and with only a dim and obtuse perception of smell and taste,—a soul literally entombed in a body,—yet making acquaintance with the external world, and awakening her own inward power of thought and feeling, through the sense of touch alone. . . .

If a child, who is deprived of the senses, learns so much, and behaves so well, what ought those children to learn and to do, whom God has blessed with the means of knowledge and of doing good? [1]

The thought that their endeavor might prove to be an imperfect panacea at best was to think the unthinkable for Mann and other "Friends of Education." At the same time, they did not realize how

---

[1] Samuel Gridley Howe to George Combe, March 3, 1840, Combe MSS:NLS; *CSJ*, II (March, 1840), 91.

far they had actually gone in shifting the educational prerogatives of the family and the church to the public school. Fretting about the Packards and the Mortons, they could not recognize the significance of what they had begun. They were laying the three sides of a triangular base for a system of comprehensive schooling. First they had fused the concept of public control with that of public support, two concepts which were never joined in the academies and the charity schools. Then to complete this base, it was only necessary to add a third, the concept of compulsory attendance. Once these three were secured, a foundation would be created for the public school.

But an educational system staffed by trained teachers and administrators was only one means to an end. Mann was attempting to create an institution capable of providing all children with a common experience. Sectarianism, partisan politics, and ethnic loyalties were a threat to the good society as he envisioned it, and his response was a system of schools which could teach republicanism and a non-denominational version of Christianity.

Mann was deeply disturbed when Governor William Seward proposed public monies for Irish-Catholic schools in New York City. Characteristically, he interpreted this as a partisan attempt to get "the Catholic votes in New York," but the source of his real concern was his fear that parochial schools would fragment the community. Here was no revolt of the masses such as the twentieth century would later witness, but a beleaguered effort to maintain diversity in the face of spreading alienation in the city and attrition of both ethnic and religious subcultures. But Mann did not understand this. For him, both the Irish-Catholics and the orthodox Congregationalists were a threat to enlightened republicanism. His motto was *E pluribus unum* and his means to achieve it was the public school.[2]

Not that Mann embraced industrial progress and the growth of cities without serious reservations. Nor did he simply fashion his schools to keep the propertied people in power as the neo-Marxist would like to believe. The problems which accompanied the growth of factories and cities seemed to cause acute hardships among certain sectors of the community and therefore placed new burdens on some of its institutions. With remarkable insight, Mann could analyze the limitations of the Warren Street Chapel Association and its record of having helped more than 1,500 children.

---

[2] Mann to George Combe, October 1, 1840, Combe MSS: NLS.

This institution seeks out those children who seem to be outside of all the favorable influences of civilization. As shadows are always deepest where the light is brightest, those who are in the shadow of the bright light of civilization, are in the deepest darkness. Our institutions for moral, social, & religious improvement seem to have, in most instances, answered their end or fulfilled their promise, where the community has been bro't within the circle of their action; but a portion of the community are outside that circle, & therefore are even worse situated relatively, than they would be in a less advanced state of society.

Noble though it was, the Chapel Association was much too solitary an endeavor to deal with the problems at hand. Through its heroic efforts, it pointed to the need of a far more comprehensive system for helping the young.[3]

For Mann this meant a departure from the older informal and less structured forms of training. Previously, education was the result of parental care, the indoctrination of the church, and the thousand and one more or less incidental lessons which came from growing up in a cohesive community. To this were added the minimal offerings of the district school, with its recitations drawn from a few venerated and usually dog-eared textbooks. Bemoaning this "meagerness of fare" and fearing that a divisive pluralism was developing, Mann could no longer trust these less deliberate processes.

What was needed was a system of intellectual and moral education for all the people. Since Mann believed in the fundamental uniformity among men in all nations and in all ages, he concluded that human nature was everywhere and always the same. The key to human behavior was motives, and the same motives produced the same action. Therefore, he advocated an educational program based upon correct principles and motives which would prompt the learner to transcend his selfish desires and parochial interests. Mann never tired of telling his audiences that "*motives are everything,* MOTIVES ARE EVERYTHING." And when an individual took an opposite view, his almost reflexive response was to ignore the possible merits of the argument but impute his opponent's motives. Not that he was unaware of this weakness. To Samuel Gridley Howe he wrote, "I tell you upon my honor, that for years I have felt bound to guard against suspecting motives, merely because I found a difference of opinion." Yet when challenged publicly or privately, he

---

[3] Mann, Journal, March 28, 1839, MS in MHS.

quickly mounted his charger ready to do battle with an enemy whose motives he knew to be base and self-seeking.[4]

In his time there was an ever greater need for training which would guarantee the right conduct regardless of the contextual circumstances. It was to Mann's credit that he sought out the most distinguished authors of the day for his district school library series, including Washington Irving, George Bancroft, Nathaniel Hawthorne, and Richard Henry Dana, Jr. However, he considered fiction dangerous unless it was carefully edited and its prose studded with moral teachings. Mann conceded to Elizabeth Peabody that her young friend, Nathaniel Hawthorne, had written *Twice-Told Tales* "beautifully," but for the schools, he needed "something nearer home to duty & business." Incredible though it seems, he found no moral significance in the "Wedding Knell" and he asked Miss Peabody if she really thought Hawthorne capable of writing "something graver & sterner." Viewing most "popular literature" as "a popular curse," he would not conceive of giving his authors a free rein. Instead, Mann reserved the right to insist upon a highly didactic content in whatever they prepared.[5]

Mann called on Richard Henry Dana, Jr., and urged him to doctor up his *Two Years Before the Mast,* so that it could be included in the common school library. According to his prescription, which he thought would only amount to "some slight modifications," this meant the addition of

. . . as much of exact information, as possible, in regard to the geography, natural features of the countries visited, the customs, manners, etc. etc. of the people seen, together with some of the natural productions,—botanical and zoological,—of different places, etc. Many of the scenes and events, which the work describes would also admit the introduction of moral sentiments, suited to the class of readers for which it is intended.

---

[4] See Mann's *Lectures on Education* (Boston, 1845), especially "Special Preparation, a Pre-requisite to Teaching," pp. 63–116; Mann to Samuel Gridley Howe, February 22, 1850, Mann MSS:MHS.

[5] Elizabeth Peabody to Mann, March 3, [1838], and Mann to Elizabeth Peabody, March 10, 1838, Mann MSS:MHS; Mann to George Bancroft, July 11, 1839, Bancroft MSS:MHS; Edward Everett to Washington Irving, November 7, 1839, Everett MSS:MHS. In 1837, for the sum of $100, Hawthorne and his sister Elizabeth had written *Peter Parley's Universal History* anonymously. See Alexander C. Kern, "A Note on Hawthorne's Juveniles," *Philological Quarterly,* XXXIX (April, 1960), 242–246.

Astounded by Mann's presumption, Dana politely explained that "there was such a thing as unity in a book," and that to take his narrative and burden it with statistics and didactics "would destroy its character, almost as it would that of a drama." Mann responded by insisting that "a narrative, a description, had no value except as it conveyed some moral lesson or some useful fact." Since Dana's book was an interesting narrative, Mann thought it "should be made use of for valuable purposes." Then compounding the insult, Mann pointed out that the Board planned a small series for children and a larger series "of works of a more standard character," and that *Two Years* could only be part of the former. Only gradually realizing what had taken place in his office after Mann had left, Dana concluded that he had never seen "such an exhibition of gaucheness and want of tact" in his life. "If some enemy," he later wrote, "had employed him to come to try my patience to the utmost, he could not have executed his task better." Before him had been nothing less than the manifestation of "a school-master gone crazy." [6]

Surely there was an irony to be found in Mann's efforts to housebreak the masses. Under the guise of providing a common moral and intellectual experience for the children of both rich and poor, he exposed his almost chronic fear of a divisiveness which would destroy the domestic peace of the nation. In particular, he feared an unprincipled partisanship and a spreading sectarianism and ethnicity. In actuality, however, the "masses" whose behavior troubled his composure rarely reacted *en masse,* but demonstrated a pluralism of motives, and were unwilling to adopt uncritically his set of WASP values as promulgated through the schools. Within their loyalties to their families, churches, neighborhoods, laboring associations, and ethnic enclaves, they acted according to a rich variety of motives and exhibited a degree of independence and idiosyncrasy not always present in the older nativist groups. But if there was an irony in Mann's fear of the masses, especially those who were still hyphenated Americans, when indeed these very people were the most resistant to mass appeals, there was a second and perhaps greater irony here. In attempting to broaden and systematize the function of schooling, and create a uniformity of what took place in the classrooms of the Commonwealth, he was inadvertently narrowing the concept of education. To create an educational ecology

[6] Mann to Richard Henry Dana, Jr., March 29 and September 17, 1847, Dana MSS:MHS; Charles F. Adams, *Richard Henry Dana* (Boston, 1890–91), I, 117–120.

of formalism was to risk sacrificing many of the imaginative, spontaneous, poetic, and aesthetic indigenous lessons to be experienced in the emerging American culture.

Mann never envisioned that graded instruction could also mean a mind-numbing regimentation as repressive as anything accomplished by the Boston masters, nor did he expect that children someday would spend one-sixth of their lives, and some of their most formative years, in an environment of cells and bells. Although he would laud the new Hancock and Quincy schools in Boston with their monotonous individual classrooms and long corridors as his "idea of a perfect school edifice," he did not recognize that these secure, prison-like structures would become prototypes for a thousand others. Neither did he understand that such buildings could isolate children and wall them off from a direct and vital relationship with their physical and cultural environment, surrounding them instead with two-dimensional symbols and abstractions carefully and tastefully packaged to ensure a growing consumership, even if this meant a competence of mediocrity.[7]

Few understood the momentous social movement then under way, and even fewer understood that within it the very nature of education and the society which it shaped would change, with the implementation of a comprehensive public system based on textbooks, lesson plans, graded instruction, and certified teachers. One man who did was Emerson. After attending one of Mann's educational conventions in Concord, he returned to the Old Manse and gave words to his sense of misgiving:

Sad as it was to see the death-cold convention yesterday morning, as they sat shivering, a handful of pale men and women in a large church, for it seems the Law has touched the business of education with the point of its pen and instantly it has frozen stiff in the universal congelation of society. An education in things is not. We are all involved in the condemnation of words, an age of words. We are shut up in schools and college recitation rooms for ten or fifteen years and come out at last with a belly full of words and do not know a thing. We cannot use our hands, or our legs, or our eyes, or our arms. We do not know an eatable root in the woods. We cannot tell our course by the stars, nor the hour of the day by the sun. It is well if we can swim and skate. We are afraid of a horse, of a cow, of a dog, of a cat, of a spider. Far better was

---

[7] Mann to T. M. Brewer, June 21, 1848, Straker MSS: ACL.

the Roman rule to teach a boy nothing that he could not learn standing. . . .

As in other opinions, Emerson preferred to meditate and write rather than act. Many of his contemporaries, on the other hand, preferred to follow an idea or movement rather than listen to a critique. Hence, they were ready to march behind the new organizational banners which Mann had unfurled.[8]

[8] Ralph Waldo Emerson, *Journals*, V (Cambridge, 1911), 250–251.

CHAPTER XV

New Vistas

WHAT IN THE DARK I had taken to be a stump of
a little tree appearing above the snow, to which I
had tied my horse, proved to have been the
weathercock of the church steeple.
RUDOLPH ERICH RASPE

B Y THE SPRING of 1840, his body was worn to the point where he
had to stop and take a complete rest. The previous autumn, he
had traveled the length and breadth of the state several times over
by horseback, stage, and train and had spoken almost daily. During
those weeks when he was at his office in Boston, he attempted to
prepare his abstract on the schools, write his *Fourth Annual Report,*
and keep up a correspondence of more than twenty letters a day. And
then there were the "innumerable question askers," as he called the
curious and the concerned coming to his office, who ranged all the
way "from the mother whose first child is only four weeks old,
up to the father who is sending his son to college." All this was part
of Mann's "regular" schedule for 1839, but in addition this year,
he had launched the *Common School Journal* and now knew what
it meant to have a printing press rumbling in the back of his mind.
And finally, after hundreds of letters and interminable meetings, he
had the normal schools at Lexington and Barre under way. Only half
jesting, he described himself as "a white slave without any abolitionist to comfort me." [1]

Of necessity, he turned down social invitations whenever possible and drove himself at his desk until the early hours of the morning. His chair at an oyster dinner at Quincy's would be vacant, as it
would be at a reception at the Lorings'. And on those occasions where
it was mandatory that he at least attend bodily, his mind still remained back at his desk ruminating through a stack of school reports. With each "regret" he sent to a disappointed host, his friends
became increasingly concerned about his welfare. In turn Mann

---

[1] Mann to George Combe, February 11, 1839, Combe MSS: NLS.

characteristically enjoyed their pity, because it cast him more clearly in their minds as a martyr, ready to sacrifice his pleasure and health for the good of others. The effort to open the doors of the normal schools came close to making his martyrdom permanent. A week after the opening at Lexington, he complained that he was "suffering—under an entire incapacity for labor. My brain," he continued, "utterly refused to accomplish any work *in its line.*" Until this time, the mind had continued to drive an unwilling accomplice; but by the middle of summer, both mind and body required more than the concession of a few days' rustication in Wrentham.[2]

After another agonizing "anniversary week" of Charlotte's death, even Mann was convinced that he must rest. He left Boston by stage, heading "down east" to Portland, Maine, where he stayed at the Cape Cottage resort on Casco Bay with Mr. and Mrs. George Combe. Combe was a Scottish barrister turned philosopher and phrenologist. Mann first learned of Combe's ideas from his book, the *Constitution of Man,* which attempted to fuse Scottish common-sense philosophy with the phrenological teachings of Johann Spurzheim and lay a philosophical groundwork for the doctrine of human perfectibility. Combe contended that the mind was composed of more than thirty faculties or "propensities," including "combativeness," "benevolence," "self-esteem," and "veneration," and that the relative strength of each could be determined by measuring that specific part of the cranium which housed it. Thus a high and large forehead where "benevolence" reputedly resided indicated the strong development of that desirable personality trait, while a large occipital development where the more animal propensities were located suggested inclinations toward more base and selfish behavior. Once a person's individual faculties were assessed, it was then possible through education to repress the more negative propensities and nurture those such as "veneration" which had a positive social value. Moreover, Combe ruled out the supernatural and claimed only the existence of natural laws, which controlled human mental development as rigorously as they governed the physical world. A primitive attempt at behavioral psychology, phrenology gained numerous adherents on this side of the Atlantic, particularly among the old

---

[2] Mann, Journal, July 28, 1839, MS in MHS; Mann to Josiah Quincy, April 4, 1838, and Mann to Mrs. Josiah Quincy, n.d., July 4, 1839, and December 18, 1841, all in Quincy MSS:BPL; Mann to R. C. Waterston, June 15, [1839], Mann MSS:BUA; Mann to Jared Sparks, June 18, 1839, Sparks MSS:HCL; and Samuel Gridley Howe to George Combe, March 5, 1839, Combe MSS:NLS.

devotees of mental discipline, who saw this as a refinement of their doctrines of "strengthening the mind" and "exercising the mind as a muscle."[3]

For Mann, Combe's book was both revelation and reassurance, reaffirming his older beliefs and raising his sights to even greater possibilities for human perfectibility. He sent his sister a copy of the *Constitution of Man,* together with a plaster-of-Paris head with all the phrenological propensities carefully mapped out. "I know of no book written for hundreds of years which does so much to 'vindicate the ways of God to man,'" he assured her. "Its philosophy is the only practical basis for education." So complete a convert did he become that he claimed the doctrines advanced in the *Constitution* would "work the same change in metaphysical science that Lord Bacon wrought in natural." When Combe came to Boston for a series of lectures, Mann was on hand for all of them and was particularly impressed with the lecture on morality. Reporting to James K. Mills, who could not attend because of illness, he wrote:

We had a divine lecture from Mr. C. tonight. It was on moral responsibility. Heads badly organized, dragged down into vice by the force of evil passions, he considered as *moral patients;* those which were balanced and hung poised between good and evil, he held liable to triumph or to fall according to circumstances; but on those, nobly

---

[3] Mann, Journal, May 25, 1837, MS in MHS; George Combe, *Constitution of Man Considered in Relation to External Objects* (Boston, 1841), pp. 1–26 and 42–87. Combe's book enjoyed a phenomenal reception both in the United States and abroad. By 1838, more than 70,000 copies had been printed in English. It was translated into German, French, and Swedish, and also adapted for use as a classroom textbook. Also see William Jolly, ed., *Education, Its Principles and Practices as Developed by George Combe* (London, 1879), *passim.* A historian of this movement warns the contemporary student not to confuse the later charlatanism with the early attempts to make this a constructive scientific psychology. He writes:

In its own time phrenology, like Freudianism, was a serious, inductive discipline, accepted as such by many eminent scientists, doctors, and educations; its aberrations were results not so much of charlatanism or credulity as of the limitations of early 19th century scientific method and medical techniques. However mistaken some of its anatomical deductions may have been, scientific it was in its determination to study the mind objectively, without metaphysical preconceptions. Its priority in this field is recognized in the histories of medicine and psychology, and many of its fundamentals are as commonplace today as they were radical a century ago.

See John D. Davies, *Phrenology: Fad and Science, a 19th Century American Crusade* (New Haven, 1955), pp. x–xi.

endowed, to whom heaven had imparted the clear sighedness [sic] of intellect and the vehement urgency of moral power, he imposed the everlasting obligation of succoring and sustaining the first in their weakness and temptation and of so arranging the institutions of society as to withhold the excitements of passion and supply the incentives to virtue to the second class. It was like the voice of God. . . .

Combe had summarized Mann's *raison d'être* and succinctly sketched "those nobly endowed" with whom Mann easily identified himself. With good reason, at the conclusion of the lecture series, Mann could write to Combe with effusive gratitude, "We see that there will be a new earth, at least, if not a new heaven, when your philosophical and moral doctrines prevail." The two men became the closest of friends and it was a testimony to Combe's influence over Mann that where others had failed, Combe was able to convince him to take a vacation.[4]

Combe was a dignified person with unconventionally long hair, each sedate and well-brushed lock speaking of duty and moral responsibility. Even-tempered and rarely given to indulging in the pleasure of the moment, he had cultivated his penchant for seeking basic moral premises underlying human events to the point where he all too gladly dispensed a wholesome, albeit often gratuitous, advice to those with whom he spoke. Mann found the company of this philosopher and the setting of the Cape Cottage an ideal retreat. Located on a knoll near the bay, the cottage provided a land- and seascape, half earth and half ocean and sky. From its porch, Mann watched the sloops and schooners glide between the islands,

---

[4] Mann to Lydia Mann, November 9, 1838; Mann to James K. Mills, November 7, 13, and 14, 1838, all in Mann MSS:MHS; Mann, Journal, October 8, 10, 12, and 29, 1838, MS in MHS; Mann to George Combe, February 11, 1839, Combe MSS:NLS. For a biography of Combe, see Charles Gibbon, *Life of George Combe, the Author of the Constitution of Man* (London, 1878).

Although phrenological terms are found in his writings prior to 1837, Mann was not an active participant in the movement as were such leading Bostonians as Reverend Henry Ware, Dr. Samuel Gridley Howe, Reverend Joseph Tuckerman, Abbott Lawrence, and John Pickering. These men were active in the Boston Phrenological Society, founded in 1832, but one searches in vain for any mention of Mann in its transactions prior to 1837. See Nahum Capen, *Reminiscences of Dr. Spurzheim and George Combe* (Boston, 1881), pp. 119–225, and *Annual of Phrenology*, I (1834), 339, and II (1835), 501–506 and 511.

Combe's Boston lectures created something of a minor sensation. For divergent reactions, see the Boston *Daily Courier*, October 2, 3, 8, 12, 13, and 15, 1838, and the Boston *Evening Transcript*, September 29, October 9, 10, and 18, 1838.

moving in and out of the harbor, their white sails unsullied by smoke and filled with a southern breeze. Now and then the antics of a school of porpoises entertained them. The two men often took long afternoon walks, picking their way around tidal pools along the rocky shoreline, Combe stopping now and then to fashion a crude ship from pieces of driftwood and set it out to sea. And when the fog gave little promise of "burning off" in the morning, they would hire a gig and visit the inland. But the pleasure of the setting was only secondary to the stimulation of their discussions. In the course of a day, their topics would range far afield. Invariably by evening, however, they retreated inside their cottage from the swarms of mosquitoes and talked about their favorite theme, the power of formal and systematic education to remake the world. Upon his return from Casco Bay, Mann wrote to Combe with appropriate phrenologese, "Never have I passed a week in a way more congenial to my coronal region." [5]

*   *   *

Back in Boston, Mann was again in perpetual motion, organizing and holding six major conventions and dozens of smaller meetings; but the experience of Cape Cottage would not easily wear off. Thus, although he had previously declined an invitation to join the Combes on a trip west, during the spring of 1840, he now reconsidered and consented to go along. There was also a monetary reason for his decision. Recognizing that retrenchment was the order of the day under Governor Morton, and that Mann's friends in the legislature would be fortunate if they could prevent his salary from being cut as Morton's was, Edmund Dwight wrote to Mann that he was adding $500 to that which Mann received from the state and that he was committing himself to this for ten years, going so far as to rewrite his will accordingly.[6]

Mann began his tour with a speaking engagement in New York City, and a visit to Philadelphia and Washington, D.C. In New York a snowstorm kept down the size of his audience at the Mercantile Library Association, but as he continued south, the weather im-

[5] George Combe to Mann, July 19, 1839, Mann MSS:MHS; Mann, Journal, August 6, 11, and 13, 1838, MS in MHS; Mann to George Combe, September 11, 1839, Combe MSS:NLS; George Combe, *Notes on the United States of North America* (Philadelphia, 1841), II, 124–132.
[6] Mann to George Combe, May 6 and 12, 1839, Combe MSS:NLS; Edmund Dwight to Mann, March 2, 1840, Mann MSS:MHS.

proved. In Philadelphia the Combes introduced him to Alexander Bache, whom they had met aboard the *Great Western* on their voyage to the United States. Bache was president of Girard College and author of the *Report on Education in Europe*. The following evening Mann was also introduced to some of "the leading men of the city" at a reception. The next day he visited several schools, looked in at Independence Hall, and spent the evening discussing reform movements with Lucretia Mott, Quakeress, feminist, and anti-slavery advocate, who had heard of Mann's work and wanted to meet him.[7]

Then he and the Combes left for Washington by train, traveling a distance of 140 miles in eleven hours. As he approached the capital for the first time, Mann could not repress a sense of high expectation, but no sooner had he arrived than he felt terribly depressed by his first sight of slaves. "This is the first day I ever set my foot upon soil polluted by slavery," he recorded in his Journal, and the experience cast a pall over him for the rest of his stay. From Massachusetts, several hundred miles north from the Mason-Dixon Line, he could read accounts of the anti-slavery agitation of John Quincy Adams, and his efforts in the House to defend free speech and the right of petition with a sense of secure detachment. But now the experience of seeing Adams's "clients" in the flesh forced him to think of the problem in a more human and personal dimension. On Sunday, he went to church and forced himself to sit through a "roaration." Still unable to shake the first impressions of slavery from his mind, he wrote his own doxology for the worship service. "Oh, when," he asked, "will the world be free from the drag-chain of most of the clergy!"[8]

Monday found him sightseeing with the Combes on Capitol Hill. Mann was properly impressed with the intended magnificence of the yet unfinished structure, but was predictably disappointed with the "magnates" of the House and Senate inside. For these men, politics and the art of compromise was a way of life. From Mann's point of view, this made them inferior beings. Later the same day, he climbed to the top of the unfinished Washington Monument, still less than a third of its final height but already dwarfing the Bunker Hill Monument back in Charlestown. If Mann could not view the House

---

[7] Alexander D. Bache, *Report on Education in Europe, to the Trustees of the Girard College for Orphans* (Philadelphia, 1839); Gibbon, *Combe*, II, 28–29; Mann, Journal, March 19 and 28, 1840, MS in MHS; George Combe to Mann, April 25, 1839, Mann MSS: MHS.

[8] Mann, Journal, March 28 and 30, 1840, MS in MHS.

and Senate without mixed emotions, the same was true as he stood atop the monument and looked at the city below. Considering that the nation had already spent $200,000 on the obelisk, enough money to start 100 normal schools, he could not but consider this "a great sum." Then with a second thought, he conceded it was "for a great man," who "left his monument, however, in the improved condition of his country,—that is the only noble monument." [9]

From Washington, they moved north to Baltimore and then west to the great expanse of the Ohio River Valley. They traveled the first sixty miles by train to the end of the tracks, and then boarded a stagecoach, moving on to Hagerstown. Finally, after three days, averaging seven or eight miles an hour depending on traveling conditions, they arrived at Cumberland and the beginning of the National Road. If the dust of the dry gravel post road was an improvement over the smoke and cinders of the train, the discomfiture of their travels was increased by the bone-jarring washboard ruts and holes which no set of sheaf springs seemed able to neutralize. Each night they lodged or "laid over," as Mann noted the local expression, at inns along the way. As there was usually only one accommodation at each stop, the travelers were at the mercy of their itinerary. The end of one day might find them at a Pennsylvania Dutch tavern with cleanly swept unfinished pine floors, sparkling earthenware, delicious food including the traditional "seven sweets and seven sours," and fresh linen bedding. Again, their lot might be a dirty inn, run by a slovenly innkeeper, with tobacco cuds on the floor, greasy food on the table, and bedding which smelled from the perspiration of one's nameless predecessors, especially after they crossed over into Virginia.

From Cumberland the road made its onslaught on the Alleghenies and the next two days were as memorable for Mann as any on the tour. As the coach began to climb the grades, it was difficult to see any distance because of the closeness of the hills and vegetation. As a result, the mountains seemed no larger than the Berkshires back home. What was different and did impress him was their wild, rugged character. Everywhere he looked, he saw jagged outcroppings of granite or layer upon layer of dark green slate, which had successfully resisted the intrusion of trees and ferns. Where the roadway cut through the side of a hill, he noted thick jet-black seams of coal and thin layers of mica glistening in the sun. Earlier

[9] Mann, Journal, March 31, 1840, MS in MHS.

in the year, he had attended a series of lectures on geology by Benjamin Silliman. At its conclusion, Mann thought that the Yale scientist had "demolished the *six days* account of creation" and "reduced the Deluge to a mere puddle." Now with every turn of the road he found evidence that millions of years and mighty cataclysmic upheavals were the real processes of creation.[1]

The closeness and almost oppressiveness of such ponderous geological masses made his next experience all the more dramatic. At Laurel Hill, the summit, the coach stopped and Mann and the Combes alighted. Walking to a clearing in the trees they came upon a sight for which there was no counterpart back in Massachusetts, not even from the top of Mount Greylock. "All at once, as tho' a curtain has been withdrawn, the great valley of the West burst upon us," was the way Mann later recorded his first impressions. "Away in the horizon, far as the eye could reach, and as far to the South and to the North, as in a direct line before us, we saw all that the convexity of the earth's surface would allow." Although less immediately striking, even more powerful was the travelers' slow awareness that even this vast visible stretch was but a small fraction of the land beyond. Until now Mann's domain had been that narrow coastal ribbon along the Atlantic, with Boston the hub of his world. For the moment, it was simply impossible to enlarge one's perspective sufficiently to encompass such an expanse. Only later would Mann admit, "territorially how insignificant Massachusetts appears to me. It is not large enough for a dooryard for the West." Before him lay untapped power, fertile farm land, broad navigable rivers, and undiscovered mineral wealth, all waiting to be developed by the young nation. Surely, here was enough room for the restless spirit of man. The thought of it all was overpowering and somewhat fearful. For certain, the area would soon fill up with farms and factories. Mann wondered if there would be schools and colleges as well. With such openness and opportunity, would the moral and intellectual keep pace with the material development? [2]

He could understand why the sons of old-line New England families such as George Prentice, James Freeman Clarke, Edward Jarvis, and Lyman Beecher had sought their future to the west. Little wonder also, that thousands of Vermont and New Hampshire

---

[1] Mann, Journal, April 5, 1840, MS in MHS; Mann to George Combe, February 22, 1840, Combe MSS:NLS.

[2] Mann, Journal, April 5, 1840, MS in MHS; Mann to George Combe, May 9, 1840, Combe MSS:NLS.

men had left their boulder-strewn hillside farms for this. Others such as George Ripley and Bronson Alcott might believe the future of the nation depended on the results of their Utopian experiments at Brook Farm and Fruitlands, but how puny and insignificant these were when compared with the challenge of this great heartland. The sight from this western battlement outside of Laurel Hill was merely a view, but it was an ample prelude for what still lay ahead.

Once again en route, the coach plunged down the western side of the slope. Mann thought they were moving along a precipitous descent, his notions all the more confirmed as he looked out the window to see the driver pulling the long brake lever with the brake shoes almost on fire from the friction against the iron rims of the wheels. The road ended at Wheeling, Virginia, where with no small relief, the party, dirty and bruised, gratefully boarded the relative comforts of a river steamer for the two-day trip to Cincinnati. By comparison to the washboard road, the pounding of the steam pistons was almost melodious. On the foredeck there were neither cinders nor dust to irritate the eye. One only sat and watched the open country glide by. Anxious to learn about this territory, Mann engaged his fellow travelers in conversation, and asked the pilot about specific distances. As best as one could reckon, it was almost 500 miles from Cincinnati to Pittsburgh, and the Ohio was not only navigable for this entire distance, but shallow draft steamboats could go up the Monongahela for another 90 miles. Again, what a trickle was the Charles River and how miniscule the Blackstone Canal by comparison. There were hundreds of bends in the Ohio, and each brought with it a new vista of green rolling countryside with virgin woodlands and the beginnings of prosperous farms and occasional river settlements. Although the extent of the land easily impressed Mann, who had become a city dweller, he still retained enough memory of the farm in Franklin to appreciate these fields and meadows of rich black loam whose fertility would outproduce anything back home. As each day followed another the collective experience became strong enough to convince him that "the only way to get at all an adequate idea of this country is to travel through it." [3]

Finally, after rounding a last bend in the river, the city of Cincinnati appeared in the distance. As the boat eased closer, Mann could make out dozens of busy wharfs jutting into the river, piled high with pork barrels, grain sacks, and farm tools. Still closer he

---

[3] Mann, Journal, April 5 and 8, 1840, MS in MHS.

could smell the odor of the slaughteringhouses and anticipate that his party would be soon greeted by reception committees of house-flies. Here was the largest inland metropolis in the United States, still troubled by muddy streets and ramshackle frame firetraps; but its boosters with little modesty had appropriated for it the title of the "Queen City of the West," and aimed to make it live up to it in the near future. At the moment, its economy was based on the hog industry, and its leading citizens, who shipped sausage, bacon, hams, and salt pork via New Orleans to every port along the eastern sea-board, were dubbed the "hog aristocracy." [4]

Once ashore, Mann soon was in touch with a number of former New Englanders, most of them now enjoying the prosperity his ill-fated brother Stanley had failed to find. He also spent an evening with Nathan Guilford, referred to by some as the "author of the school system of Ohio." In 1825, as a member of the state Senate, Guilford had written and championed a bill to establish a system of public schools. Before they left the town, Mann and Combe spent the entire day riding to North Bend in order to meet General William Henry Harrison who, Mann judged with considerable political in-sight, might be "a probable candidate for the next Presidency, as any in the country." The hero of Tippecanoe had been sick and ap-peared pale and thin to Mann. His face was gaunt, his skin heavily wrinkled over his forehead and cheekbones, and his general manner rather lackluster.

Mann was also struck by the humbleness of his surroundings —a simple house with the original logs in some of the walls still ex-posed, others covered with a rough-sawn wainscoting. The furni-ture was unpretentious and eclectic, giving the appearance of having been collected from various branches of the family. "I should think," Mann observed, "that half the farmers and merchants in Norfolk County had a room quite as well *set off* as the best room of General Wm. H. Harrison, the leading Whig candidate for the Presidency of the United States." What he did not know at the time was that within a few months, this very humble house, with its unfurnished log walls, would provide Harrison with a political hallmark strong enough to project him into the White House. Naturally, Mann and Combe could not pass up the opportunity to make a phrenological analysis of the General. From the shape of his head, Mann judged him to have little love of self-esteem and that he was neither acquisi-

---

[4] Mann, Journal April 8, 11, and 12, 1840, MS in MHS.

tive nor combative. Most likely, he was a tolerably moral man since he was blessed with the "absence of the great mischief-working propensities." Although the candidate said nothing profound, Mann acknowledged that he exhibited a good deal of common sense. Thus before them was a military hero, neither imaginative nor philosophical, but a sensible and good-natured man from humble origins, and in the age of Webster, Clay, Calhoun, and John Quincy Adams, these were exactly the qualifications Americans sought in filling the highest office in the land.[5]

The following day the party moved farther down the river to Louisville. If this Kentucky town was more rough-hewn and short of the genteel culture being nursed by its north bank rival, it was just as thriving and optimistic. Here were almost 3,300 slaves, and a northerner like Mann could not help but think that the difference between bondage and freedom was just the width of the Ohio River. Mann also probably noted that more bourbon than milk was consumed in the town. Here a veritable covey of former New Englanders had taken up their abode. Mann met James Freeman Clarke, whose appearance must have reminded him of those painful days following Charlotte's death when he stayed in Mrs. Clarke's boardinghouse. Here also was Dr. Edward Jarvis, who was attempting to get a system of public schools under way. Earlier Jarvis had written to Mann asking for his *Annual Reports* and complaining, "We are a century behind you in the education of the People. A slaveholding state cannot appreciate an educated labourer as you do. . . . By the aid of your counsel and your examples we may follow in the footsteps of Massachusetts." Interestingly enough, when Mann sent Jarvis his *Reports,* they were packed together with a shipment of Boston-made footwear, the Hub supplying the West with both shoes and ideas. Somewhere also in Louisville was the unmarked grave of Stanley Mann. Whether the younger brother inquired among those who might have known about his last days and the location of his final resting place is not known. If he did, he never mentioned it in his Journal.[6]

The farthest west Mann and the Combes traveled was Frankfort, the capital of the state. They found it a small town of 2,000

---

[5] Edward Jarvis to Mann, February 25, 1840, Mann MSS:MHS; Mann, Journal, April 20, 1840, MS in MHS.
[6] Mann, Journal, April 20, 1840, MS in MHS; Edward Jarvis to Mann, February 25, 1840, Mann MSS:MHS; Ben Casseday, *History of Louisville* (Louisville, 1852), *passim.*

people, quiet and sequestered, giving the impression of an aspiring gentility and stateliness with its capitol building surrounded by sweeping lawns and graced with a large water fountain. While Mann and Combe breakfasted in a tavern one morning, they suddenly fell silent and listened unobtrusively to the conversation between a local judge and a revivalist minister at the next table. Both Mann and Combe could not tell if they were more interested in the subject under consideration, namely, the merits of the present Governor, who was known as a "praying man," or the pronunciation and frontier figures of speech used by these two men from "Kaintuck." [7]

From Frankfort it was north and east for the long trip back home. At Maysville, Mann left the Combes, expecting to meet them again in Cincinnati. Somehow, he missed them and went on alone to Pittsburgh. Once again, traveling on the Ohio, he attempted to put his feelings into words.

What a noble river this Ohio is, extending more than one thousand miles to its entrance into the Mississippi, and from the point of junction, helping to swell the waters of the "Father of Rivers" more than twelve hundred miles more to its mouth, in the Gulf.—thus making 2200 miles of steamboat navigation, entirely inland, towards the East.—about the same distance north, and still more West, on the Missouri and its branches. Dry up their rivers and what would this vast country be;—continue them, and the question may be put with still greater significance, what will this country be. It has been created on a splendid scale of physical magnificence.

And then concluding this entry in his Journal with a typical moral speculation,

Are its intellectual and moral proportions to be of a corresponding greatness? We trust in God, they are, for if such an energy of physical nature predominates, it well had to be extremes of licentiousness, of brutal indulgence of all kinds, such as the world has never yet exhibited.[8]

Even as early as 1840, when one walked the streets of Pittsburgh, the deposits of soot were everywhere and Mann quickly labeled it the "town of iron, coal and smoke." Because of a lack of

---

[7] Mann to George Combe, February 28, 1842, Combe MSS:NLS; Mann, Journal, April 20, 1840, MS in MHS.
[8] Mann, Journal, April 24, 1840, MS in MHS.

water power, others had predicted that Pittsburgh and the area to the west would never be a major center of manufacturing, but Mann, on the other hand, could see that the absence of water power was no hindrance as long as there was an abundance of coal. To visit Pittsburgh was to see that "steam is the great agent. The city," he reported, "is darkened with smoke, the air is full of it, the sun is obscured by it," and it was all that his weak lungs could take.[9]

When the Combes finally rejoined him, their party boarded a small canal boat for the trip to Philadelphia. As a fresh-air advocate, Mann found the interior "state room" almost intolerable, later quipping that the "risks were not those enumerated in a marine policy, nor in an Episcopal prayer book, but equal to either." By the third day they arrived at Johnstown, the western terminus of the Portage Rail Road. Thirty-six miles long, the road consisted of eleven levels of track, each, with the exception of the last, connected to the one above by rails laid on an inclined plane. Thus, an engine and cars by moving back and forth from one "switch back" to another could move up the face of the mountain until the summit was reached at an elevation of almost 2,500 feet. This, together with four bridges and a 900-foot tunnel, was heralded as one of the great engineering feats of the day.[1]

On the other side of the Alleghenies, the passengers boarded a second low-ceilinged canal boat and once again Mann worried about suffocating. Two days later they were at Harrisburg on the banks of the Susquehanna where they boarded a train for Philadelphia. On their way, the engine jumped the tracks, jolting the passengers out of any false sense of security they might have had riding on this most modern transportation. Then with the engine back on the track, there was further delay while the crew tried in vain to get the boiler fire started. Apparently the fireman had stoked the fire box with green wood and the dense smoke clogged the cinder screen at the top of the smoke stack. Later the same night, it was a weary and grateful threesome that finally arrived in Philadelphia.[2]

In the city of "Brotherly Love," Mann had the painful experience of parting with the Combes who were now about to embark on their

---

[9] R. W. Haskins, *New England and the West* (Buffalo, 1843), pp. 19–20; Mann, Journal, April 24, 1840, MS in MHS.
[1] Mann, Journal, May 2, 1840, MS in MHS. A detailed description of the Portage Rail Road is found in Harriet Martineau, *Society in America* (3rd ed., London, 1837), II, 15–21.
[2] Mann, Journal, May 2, 1840, MS in MHS.

return to England. As he watched the *British Queen* edge away from the quay, his admiration for George Combe almost knew no bounds. Before the trip began he had considered him "the completest philosopher" he had ever known. Now after this trip he had come to believe that Combe also had no moral peers. "I have never been acquainted with a mind which handled such great subjects with such ease & as it appears to me with such justness. My journeying with him has been to me a source of great advantage and delight. He has constantly gratified my strongest facilities. The world knows him not. In the next century I have no doubt he will be looked upon as the greatest man of the present." His sense of loneliness gradually returning to him, Mann took a train to New York, a boat along Long Island Sound to Stonington, Connecticut, and a second train to Boston, thus ending a journey of fifty days and nearly 3,000 miles.[3]

*   *   *

Back in Boston, both the expanse of the West and the long philosophical discussions with Combe soon seemed to have taken place in the distant past and on some other planet. Mann was inundated with tasks needing immediate attention and none seemed so large as the stack of mail which had accumulated during his absence. Anxious textbook authors asked for his endorsement; a school committee needed a teacher who would work for $6 a week and "boarding round"; an attorney enquired if Irish children whose fathers were working on railroad construction were entitled to a free education while the tracks were being laid through their town; and there were dozens of admiring persons from near and as far away as Mississippi, Canada, and Great Britain who were asking for copies of his *Annual Reports.* Once the most pressing letters were answered, he sent out announcements of dates and places for his next round of conventions, worked on his major address, struggled to organize a morass of school statistics into a readable abstract, and made last-minute arrangements for the opening of his third normal school at Bridgewater. Soon he was again on the road, beginning with meetings at Tisbury, Nantucket, Fall River, Westport, and Plymouth, covering the southeastern part of the state in three weeks.

By the fall of 1840, one sensed a shift within the reform. Not

---

[3] Mann, Journal, August 11, 1839, and May 10, 1840, MS in MHS; George Combe to Mann, July 12, 1840, Mann MSS:MHS; Mann to George Combe, May 9, 1840, Combe MSS:NLS.

only did Mann exhibit less interest in these local meetings, but the people seemed less eager to attend. Of course Pittsfield provided his annual nadir. Making an impression on the Berkshires was like pounding on Gibraltar with one's bare fists. But now elsewhere there was a slackening of enthusiasm and a declining attendance at his meetings. Increasingly in his Journal he made such entries as "Wellfleet, a miserable, contemptible, deplorable convention," "meagre convention last week at Barre," and for the general meeting for all of Franklin County, "a convention most miserable in point of numbers." Admittedly, 1840 was a difficult year since Mann was in competition with political rallies and it seemed that nothing he could say from the rostrum was as contagious as the chant of "Tippecanoe and Tyler too!" And for a teetotaler such as Mann, it was mortifying to witness the emergence of an abominable jug of hard cider as the symbol of republicanism and the Whig Party. During the fall of 1840, more convinced than ever, Mann would write that "Politics are the idol which the people have gone after," especially when Emerson Davis and several other "Friends of Education" from Westfield left his convention at midpoint to attend a Whig rally in the next town.[4]

This loss of fervor was due to more enduring reasons than a passing presidential campaign. For one thing, it was simply impossible for Mann to maintain the intensity of his revivalistic approach. Physically his frame and his vocal chords just could not continue their output. This fall during a tour of eleven weeks, his voice all but left him on several occasions. Emotionally, too, it was impossible for him to speak year after year in imminent apocalyptic warnings, and then, like a Millerite, be forced to postpone the date of Judgment Day. By other indices the reform was making significant gains without such a body-destroying effort. Each abstract revealed a general increase in attendance and financial support across the state. Since the Board had proven to be an engine for neither Unitarianism nor Whiggery, it enjoyed the confidence of the legislature and the public; thus the reform of the common schools was evolving from an emotional and moral phase to one of codification and organization.[5]

---

[4] Mann, Journal, September 15 and 30, and October 2, 1840, MS in MHS.
[5] Mann to Rebecca Pennell, October 12, 1840; Mann to Samuel Gridley Howe, March 17, 1842, both in Mann MSS:MHS; Mann to George Combe, February 28, 1842; Samuel Gridley Howe to George Combe, September 29, 1840, both in Combe MSS:NLS.

Not that there was any less for Mann to do. In fact, he was more busy in 1840 than any year before. Even with his annual circuit still ahead of him, he was already so weary from his work that he promised himself, "I now resolve never to undertake so much work in so short time again. It is a violation of the natural and organic laws." Then later, he would tell Henry Barnard that once again after taking the pledge, he had broken it, confessing "like a froward child who breaks the parental orders, gets punished, repents, and when tempted breaks them again." Actually, his behavior was more similar to a drunkard who took the pledge repeatedly only to return to his intemperate ways.[6]

Certainly his most dramatic achievements in 1840 and the two years following took place in the legislature. The year 1842 was a crucial one for the normal schools. In order for them to continue, new funds had to be voted and their fate could not have come up before a more friendly jury. Josiah Quincy, Jr., one of Mann's oldest friends was president of the Senate; Thomas Kinnicutt, an old political ally dating back to the days when the two men had worked to get the Worcester Hospital approved, was Speaker of the House; and John G. Palfrey, former minister and editor of the *North American Review*, was chairman of the House Committee on Education. Mann worked closely with Palfrey, meeting several times each week as the two men prepared a report for the House recommending far greater authority for the town school committees at the expense of local district boards, including the power to dismiss incompetent teachers, to prohibit children under four years and adults over twenty-one from attending common schools, and to maintain standards on school construction.[7]

The real test of sentiment in the General Court was tied to money and with Dwight's $10,000 near an end, Mann needed a full $6,000 annually to keep the normal school experiment alive. Although he expected no major opposition, he wrote to Barnard, "We hope in fear." The actual bill met some opposition in the House, as the friends of Harvard, Amherst, and Williams saw the normal schools infringing on their prerogative for an annual state grant to bail them out of their chronic financial difficulties, but once again,

---

[6] Mann, Journal, August 9, 1840, MS in MHS; Mann to Henry Barnard, September 13, 1842, Barnard MSS:NYU.
[7] John G. Palfrey, Journal, January 15, 27, 1842, MS in HCL; Mann to Thomas Robbins, March 8, 1842, Robbins MSS:CHS; Mann to Calvin Stowe, March 15, 1842, Mann MSS:MHS.

Palfrey came to Mann's support. By a political maneuver, astute for one so new to the game, and a spirited speech in behalf of the normal schools, Palfrey carried the day with a three to one margin. In the Senate, under Josiah Quincy's disciplinary gavel, a mere four votes were cast in opposition. The following evening "Honest John" Davis, who had been a stickler for approving normal school vouchers, signed the bill into law and the experiment had a new lease on life for another three years, "virtually amounting, as I think," Palfrey reported to Barnard, "to a perpetuating of them. . . ." As in other political creations, once they had been in existence for a few years, it would be most difficult to kill them. To his niece Rebecca Pennell, Mann crowed, "Our triumph in the Legislature was magnificent. I am keeping perpetual jubilee. . . . Eighteen thousand dollars for the normal schools. . . . No change in parties or politics can get this out of our hands." In his Journal he was no less bullish.

Language cannot express the joy that pervades my soul at this vast accession of power to that machinery which is to carry the cause of education forward, not only more rapidly than it has ever moved, but to places where it has never reached. This will cause an ever-widening circle to spread amongst contemporaries and will project influences into the future to distances which no calculation can follow . . . *the great work is done!* We are now to use the power wisely with which we have been intrusted.

For Mann, the enactments were barely second in importance to the origins of the common schools. For good reason, these were halcyon days for Mann and the cause.[8]

*　　　*　　　*

Ironically, at the very time that Mann had won a state endorsement of the normal school idea, the actual experiment had

---

[8] Mann to George Combe, February 28, 1842, Combe MSS:NLS; Mann to Henry Barnard, February 19, 1842; John G. Palfrey to Henry Barnard, March 4, 1842, both in Barnard MSS:NYU; John Davis to Mann, May 26, 1841, Mann to Rebecca Pennell, March 14, 1842, both in Mann MSS:MHS; Mann, Journal, March 3, 1842, MS in MHS. The record of the legislation as it moved through the General Court is found in the Boston *Daily Atlas*, February 19, 21, 24, 25, and March 1 and 3, 1842, and the Boston *Morning Post*, February 7, 9, 10, 14, and 18, and March 3 and 4, 1842.

never been in more trouble. In fact, nothing could have been more symbolic of their sad state of affairs than that at the very time when Palfrey was shaping the strategy in the House on their behalf, Samuel P. Newman, the first principal at Barre, was lying on his deathbed, and on the day that the General Court extended the life of the normal schools for another three years, Cyrus Peirce resigned his principalship at Lexington. Problems came from several sources, including the fact that once having gotten the schools established in Barre and Lexington, the residents of both towns remained cool to them to say the least. Lexington welched on its financial agreement to house the first school, and at Barre, where there was not apathy and duplicity, there was outright opposition. For a time, it looked as if Mann would have several town and gown fights on his hands. Perhaps other college towns had learned to overlook the youthful pranks and eccentricities of students as part of the rites of passage, but with students who planned to become teachers, no such indulgence was allowed. One anonymous resident of Barre, who had no misgivings about instituting a double set of standards, claimed that the behavior of a prospective teacher should be beyond reproach. However, he continued,

Profane swearing has been generally practiced among the male members of the school. Four of them are real intemperate swearers and have proved a great annoyance to *the few* who hold this practice in abhorrence . . . the requirement to attend public worship on Lord's Day has not been carried into effect, but instead thereof it may be said, that, as a general thing, the scholars stay at home and study as on other days.

He also complained of "that *Bedlam* of a boarding-house" and finally concluded that if youth were to be entrusted to "*such teachers*" from "*such schools*," he for one would pray " 'God save the Commonwealth of Massachusetts!' " [9]
More serious, however, were the heavy burdens placed upon Peirce and Newman and the rapid turnover of students. After a year of teaching, serving as admissions officer, stoking fires at four in the morning, shoveling snow in the winter, and doubling as father confessor to twenty-five girls more intent on marriage than the classroom, Peirce could not face up to another semester. "I have done for the school what I could; and beyond the wholesome taxing

---

[9] "A member of a School Committee" to Mann, August 25, 1840; Cyrus Peirce to Mann, April 4, 1842; Samuel Newman to Mann, May 25, 1841, all in Mann MSS:MHS.

of my energies," he complained to Mann, "exhausted nature calls for repose, and she must have it." About the same time, Newman wrote to Mann that he found "the work of arranging studies and classifying the school exceedingly laborious and perplexing." For Mann, resignations at this time were out of the question and he responded with letters of encouragement and the promise to hire an assistant for each man.[1]

Peirce had the additional burden of a lazy steward in charge of his boardinghouse. A person of unusual mildness and patience, Peirce became so angry with him that he hoped for the opportunity to give him a good kick on "the nether part of his corporality" and send him traveling. What was needed was a matron to oversee this part of the school and double as a counselor to the girls. Unfortunately, the remedy almost killed the patients. Mann hired Dorothea Lynde Dix for the job, but no sooner was she in charge of the boardinghouse than she made it clear that all those within her domain were to conduct themselves according to her particular version of propriety. Peirce agreed that the young ladies should not go walking or riding alone with the local boys, but he saw no reason why they could not walk in twos and threes to the post office, nor why young men could not call on them at the house when they were properly chaperoned. Believing his girls were on the verge of mutiny as Miss Dix moved to implement further her version of a Puritan convent, he complained to Mann that "her nice notions and strait-laced prudery may render her somewhat disagreeable to the young folks, who must sometimes *laugh loud,* and run and jump, as well as study and sit up *prim.*" Forced to support one or the other of the antagonists, Mann reluctantly backed his principal, and while the normalites lost a matron and mother superior, the mentally ill soon gained their most eloquent advocate of the nineteenth century.[2]

At Bridgewater it was decided that the principal should have an assistant from the very outset, but when the Board proposed a female for the position, Nicholas Tillinghast, Colonel, United States Army, Retired, probably for the first time in his life challenged a superior officer. A confirmed bachelor, upon accepting his new responsibilities he had finally taken on "a permanent assistant," as

---

[1] Cyrus Peirce to Mann, November 26, 1840; Samuel Newman to Mann, January 11, 1841, both in Mann MSS:MHS; Mann to George Putnam, January 18, 1840, Washburn MSS:MHS.
[2] Cyrus Peirce to Mann, August 7, and September 13 and 14, 1841, Mann MSS:MHS.

Samuel Newman described it, because "every schoolkeeper ought to have a wife, and a good one too." Beyond this, he would not go. Limiting his arguments entirely to "professional" considerations he wrote to Mann, ". . . it would be almost preposterous to give any woman that I have ever seen the duty of instructing some of the young gentlemen of this school in some of the branches that I wish an assistant for—they have been accustomed to think, and to demand at every step the reasons of the process pursued, and the mathematical branches . . . requires [sic] one who has made them a real study to meet the demands which could be made for information." Women could neither think logically nor teach men and there the matter rested.[3]

Aside from overwork and poor pay, a normal school principalship would not have been so bad had it not been for the students. While Mann assumed most normalites would complete a two-year course of study, he grossly overestimated their previous education and their thirst for additional learning. For most of them, a thorough review of elementary arithmetic and English grammar was necessary and the handwriting of one class was so illegible that a special remedial teacher was considered. To make matters worse, after spending a semester with Peirce or Newman and obtaining their "bag of tricks," the normalites deserted their masters, lured away by the opportunity to earn a dollar or two more each week than their "untrained" competitors. With memories of Bowdoin College still fresh in his mind, Newman found this intolerable. "The plan of receiving *some* 25 or 30 new scholars every term, most of whom are to remain three months only, has been, as it must be, ruinous to the whole concern," he warned Mann. And he followed with a second letter, stating, "We must, that the school may have the confidence of the public, make some good teachers. This cannot be done unless young men can be induced to come and stay long enough to derive essential benefits from the school." A month later, not seeing any way to hold his students on campus, he complained of "unqualified despondency," but with a new semester in the offing and the prospect of a large enrollment which would permit him to turn down most "three month enlistments," his spirits took an upward turn. Unfortunately, just as he seemed to have his problems worked out, he took sick unexpectedly and died. Unable to fill the

---

[3] Samuel Newman to Mann, January 11, 1841; Nicholas Tillinghast to Mann, May 7, 1841, both in Mann MSS:MHS.

shoes of this ill-fated man immediately, Mann was forced to suspend the school for two years.[4]

Although Mann achieved a delaying action by granting him a furlough, Peirce ultimately made good on his threat to resign. In such poor health that even a semester's rest would not help him, he finally achieved his intent by writing to Mann, "And now my dear Sir, let me go. I have done my work for the Normalty." Probably Mann was piqued by Peirce's persistence. Peirce had asked him to speak to his class before he retired, but Mann chose not to come. Thus when Peirce took leave of his pupils with farewell remarks which an observer described as "simple and touchingly beautiful," Mann was prominent by his absence.[5]

Undaunted, Mann hoped to convince Henry Barnard to fill one of the vacancies. "Connecticut is not the place for you now. Let Cincinnatus leave Rome," Mann pleaded, sensing the possibility of a major coup, "and in her distress, she will send for and implore his return. I look upon a change in public opinion in Connecticut, as certain, within a period not distant. With New York on on [sic] side and Massachusetts on the other, her frozen heart will be warmed into life." Barnard, whose office had just been abolished by the state legislature, gave the idea serious thought, going as far as to suggest not one but two assistants. Then, having some second thoughts about taking charge of something not much more advanced than an academy, "as either of your schools now are," he candidly told Mann, Barnard chose against the principalship in favor of reform work in Rhode Island.[6]

Meanwhile, Mann convinced Reverend Samuel J. May, former pastoral assistant of William Ellery Channing and now Unitarian minister at Hanover, to replace Peirce. May, a member of the Peace Society, a temperance advocate, a champion of equal rights for women, and an ardent abolitionist, accepted humbly, believing that in the training of teachers he could embrace still one more reform. But if good intentions brought him to this decision, conscience

---

[4] Samuel Newman to Mann, May 25, June 25, and September 11, 1841; Cyrus Peirce to Mann, August 7, 1841, all in Mann MSS:MHS.

[5] Records of the State Board of Education, May 25, 1842, MS in MSBE; Cyrus Peirce to Mann, April 4, June 5, and August 25, 1842; R. C. Waterston to Mann, September 6, 1842, all in Mann MSS:MHS.

[6] Mann to Henry Barnard, June 25, July 27, August 8, and September 13, 1842; William G. Bates to Mann, August 24 and November 28, 1842, all in Mann MSS:MHS; Mann, Journal, April 28, September 4 and October 20, 1842, MS in MHS; Henry Barnard to Mann, June 11, August 9 and 19, and September 3, 1842, Barnard MSS:NYU.

scruples soon gave him second thoughts. If a black girl applied for admission, he would feel compelled to let her in, yet all the time knowing that this would raise enough public outcry against the normal school experiment to kill it. Better someone else should turn down the Negro applicant. Mann convinced May to wait until that bridge had to be crossed, and May agreed, but he soon found another bridge whose crossing Mann could not delay.[7]

May was one who believed that a teacher, like every other citizen, had a right to participate in public causes, both those popular and those less so. Accordingly, the next year he spoke at an abolitionist meeting in nearby Waltham and took several students with him who were also converts to the cause. As soon as Mann got wind of this, he wrote May a long lecture on the subject of duty. Claiming that such an activity inevitably required May to spend less time in the classroom, he reminded his principal that "we want good teachers of our common schools, and that is what the State and its patrons of the Normal Schools have respectively given their money to prepare; and any diversion of it to any other object is obviously a violation of the trust." May defended himself by return mail, stating that his responsibilities to the school came first, but that he had no intention of withdrawing from the abolitionist society nor resigning his office in it. Furthermore, since he was speaking extemporaneously at its meetings, one could hardly claim that his classroom preparation suffered as a consequence. And finally he stated prophetically that the "heresy" of abolitionism was ". . . rapidly becoming orthodoxy in our Commonwealth. It is embraced by a much larger portion than you are aware of, of that class of the people which furnishes most of our school teachers." May added that if Mann was to get upset every time he made an anti-slavery statement, he would resign.

Uncomfortably on the defensive, Mann countered with a long list of expediencies. Opponents of the school still would say May was neglecting his duties; the Democrats might use the issue of abolitionism to cut funds from the schools in the next session, although the lawmakers by Mann's own words had voted to continue support for the district school libraries by a *"crushing majority"*; and Mann

---

[7] Samuel J. May to Mann, July 29, 1842, in Samuel J. May, *Memoir of S. J. May* (Boston, 1882), p. 173; Samuel J. May to Mann, September 29, 1842, Mann MSS:MHS; Mann, Journal, April 28, 1842, MS in MHS; Mann to Samuel J. May, July 27, 1842, in Mann, *Life*, I, 164.

expected to tap rich men for more money, but he claimed, the "moment it is known or supposed that the cause is to be perverted to, or connected with any of the exciting party questions of the day, I shall never get another cent." What the cause needed was "discreet and energetic management," not contamination with "collateral subjects" and "fanaticisms or hobbies." For a man of principle, these were shoddy arguments. The two cases being stated, each backed away from his extreme position and May continued both as principal and abolitionist.[8]

Thus from such unlikely human resources—an ill-fated professor, a prudish spinster, a retired army officer with an incurably anti-feminist bias, a man who attempted to resign with the coming of each spring, an abolitionist who refused to be gagged, and a motley group of three-month enlistments—did Mann push forward his normal school campaign.

*   *   *

With the exception of May's extracurricular activities, most of Mann's problems in 1841 and 1842 were the well-concealed growing pains of rapidly developing organs within the greater common school movement. What the public actually saw was a robust organism, growing at a swift rate, and promising to achieve even more beneficent ends in the future. No event during this period demonstrated this fact so well as the reception Mann received when invited to attend a New York State convention of school superintendents held in Utica.

Three years before, he had been invited to Albany by Governor Seward and others to present a series of lectures on education. Believing he might be entering into hostile country, Mann first sought out Edward Everett who urged him to go. Mann returned from his foray unimpressed and gave New York little additional thought other than recalling that he was smoked and spit upon in a tavern, cheated in a store, and damned in church. In the meantime, some of the leaven from the ferment for reform at work in Massachusetts had begun to work in the Empire state, and Mann's willingness to

[8] Mann to Samuel J. May, February 6 and 22, 1843, in Mann, *Life*, I, 169–171; Samuel J. May to Mann, February 8, 1843, May MSS:BPL; Samuel J. May, *Some Recollections of Our Antislavery Conflict* (Boston, 1869), p. 313.

attend the Utica convention augured well for the New York reformers.[9]

Mann was assured by his friend Francis Dwight that his audience would consist of "plain, common sense men, sincerely devoted
to their duties and anxious faithfully and successfully to discharge
them." To prepare the soil for the seed of Mann's message, Dwight,
who was the editor of the *District School Journal for the State of
New York,* devoted an issue prior to the convention to Mann's *Fifth
Annual Report.* Then, he and other "Friends of Education" distributed some 18,000 copies of the document throughout the state,
part of them a German translation so that they would also reach
"thousands of immigrants who are equally with ourselves interested
in the only means of preserving the institutions of our common
country," as he explained his activities in the *Journal.*[1]

Mann took the train to Worcester and boarded a stage from
there to Albany, stopping at Springfield and Pittsfield. Outside Pittsfield the coach followed the old Boston to Albany post road, past the
Shaker village at Hancock with its celebrated round barn which
housed forty-six cows. Supposedly because it lacked corners, it had
no place for the Devil to hide. Out in the fields on both sides of the
road, the celibate brothers and sisters, helped along by a scattering
of adopted children, were setting out the crops they would later
harvest and package as garden seeds and medicinals to be shipped
to markets all over the country. As he passed by, they did not look
up at the fast-moving coach but remained intent upon their ritual of
work as if to emphasize their separation from the rest of the world.
Mann knew they had resisted all attempts by local school committees to supervise the education of the children in the community,
and for the moment, he was at a loss how to make this communal
group, known for the quality and integrity of its products, conform
to the educational standards he was advocating.

Once having climbed the last ridge of the Berkshires, the coach
hurtled down a winding road towards the Hudson River, jostling its
passengers and making it difficult for them to spot the old limestone

---

[9] Mann, Journal, February 27 and March 2, 1839, MS in MHS; William H.
Seward to Mann, January 8, 1839; Edward Everett to Mann, Feb-
ruary 6, 1839, all in Mann MSS:MHS; Mann to George Combe, February
22, 1840, Combe MSS:NLS; Albany *Journal,* February 19 and 22, 1839.
[1] Francis Dwight to Mann, March 30, 1842, Mann MSS:MHS; Samuel
Gridley Howe to George Combe, May 30, 1842, Combe MSS:NLS;
[Francis Dwight], "Fifth Annual Report," *District School Journal for the
State of New York,* II (May, 1842), 81.

marker which announced the end of Massachusetts and the beginning of New York. He stopped at a second Shaker village at Lebanon
Springs, with its large white frame dormitories and simple wrought-
iron fence held by rough-hewn stone posts. As he left the town, his
last impression of this industrious sect was the sight out of the left
side of his coach of a massive four-story stone and frame barn, one
of the largest ever built in the country. By evening he had crossed
the Hudson and was in Albany. Here he laid over for the Sabbath
before moving on still farther west.[2]

At Utica, once past the booksellers in the lobby of the First
Presbyterian Church, he met such notables as Joseph Henry, Alonzo
Potter, John Griscom, Thomas Hopkins Gallaudet, and George B.
Emerson. The convention under way, Potter soon had the following
resolution before the group:

Resolved, That the best police for our cities, the lowest insurance of our
houses, the firmest security for our banks, the most effective means of
preventing pauperism, vice and crime, and the only sure defense of our
country, are our common schools; and woe to us, if their means of
education be not commensurate with the wants and the powers of the
people.

After a few other remarks, he called on Mann to speak to the question as if to take a measure of his Massachusetts guest at the very
outset of the convention. Quickly Mann found his thoughts, agreeing to the bald claim that the common schools were a vital social
panacea, and giving it his own moralistic imprint. The resolution
was true, he said, because the schools could ameliorate the ills of
society better than any other institution. Whereas the church only
reached half the people, and then mainly influenced them when
they were adults and set in their habits, the common schools could
reach all in their youth and form "the very motives of human action." Expanding on his subject, he finally concluded that those
working for common schools were "devoted to the most sacred of
causes."[3]

Mann sat down to a sustained applause. His listeners knew an
eloquent spokesman for the schools was in their midst and that

---

[2] Mann, Journal, May 3, 1842, MS in MHS.
[3] Mann, Journal, May 10, MS in MHS; a detailed account of the convention can be followed in the Utica *Daily Gazette,* April 21, and May 3,
4, 5, 6, and 7, 1842, and the *District School Journal for the State of New
York,* II (June, 1842), 98–103.

evening he reaffirmed their first impressions with the delivery of one of his prepared lectures. According to Griscom, one of the first Americans to publish a description of European schools, Mann "furnished the most decisive evidences of a mind fluent in bright and just conceptions, eloquent, racy, and commanding, yet modest and restrained in manner." Mann had nailed his thesis on the wall before a community of believers and in the next two days was asked repeatedly to place his imprimatur seal on ideas which were voiced in the discussions. At one point he had to make peace between Potter and Emerson. Although the two men had just collaborated in writing *The School and the Schoolmaster,* they were at odds on the value of normal schools, Emerson insisting they were absolutely essential to the common school cause and Potter claiming them only beneficial along with academies and colleges. Mann managed to side with Emerson without really challenging Potter and the convention moved on to less controversial topics. At its conclusion, he was given a vote of thanks by acclamation and jubilantly reported back to Boston that New York had seen the light. "We have had a grand time," he wrote to Howe, "we found a fine spirit prevailing amongst the deputies . . . there is not only a readiness, but an anxiety to learn." With such progress, there was even hope for benighted Connecticut. And Mann felt so good about the convention that he took off another five days to visit Niagara Falls and call on temperance reformers along the way.[4]

*   *   *

Shortly after he returned from the Utica convention, Boston made it patently clear to Mann that he was finally a prophet in his own country as well as abroad. In history, the accolade of a city has taken the form of various prizes from laurels to vestal virgins, but characteristically, Boston determined it could give no greater honor to its favored sons than an invitation to deliver its annual Fourth of July oration commemorating the "martyrs" of the Boston "massacre" of 1770. In the past Edward Everett, Harrison Otis Gray, and

---

[4] Mann, Journal, May 10, 15, and 17, MS in MHS; Mann to Samuel Gridley Howe, May 5, 1842, Mann MSS:MHS; Charles Sumner to William E. Channing, May 26, 1842 in Edward L. Peirce, *Memoir and Letters of Charles Sumner* (Boston, 1877), II, 209–210; John Griscom, *Memoir of John Griscom, LL.D.* (New York, 1859), pp. 292–296; John Griscom, *A Year in Europe* (New York, 1823); George B. Emerson and Alonzo Potter, *The School and the Schoolmaster* (New York, 1842).

Josiah Quincy had been so honored as the city signified its approval of their political and mercantile achievements. Now after the crusade had had its out of town performances for several years, the city fathers had determined to place their own seal of approval on Mann's work for the common schools. With such recognition, he could almost turn his back on the Berkshires as relatively inconsequential. After all, to be summoned to Boston was equal to having scaled Mount Olympus itself.[5]

He responded to the invitation to speak by retreating to Wrentham and giving his speech as intensive preparation as any in his career. A reformer would search in vain for more severe critics to his cause than in Boston. Yet, paradoxically, a Boston audience was a challenge and nowhere in the nation was there a better opportunity for success; for the reformer who came here to purvey his ideas knew they would be unmercifully winnowed of all their impracticality before being accepted as new grist in its active humanitarian machinery. Thus when the Boston Harbor cannon boomed, signaling the sunrise on the sixty-sixth anniversary of American Independence, Mann was ready to speak before the most prestigious and influential audience he had ever faced. The city was decked with colors and the air was galvanized with patriot enthusiasm. Out in the bay and along the wharfs, ship captains had run up a full complement of flags and pennants. Buntings hung from windows and above the doors of stores and houses on every main street. Around the Boston Common marched hundreds of children from the Warren Street Chapel, carrying bouquets and wreaths in memory of the sons of the Revolution, and on its grounds, hucksters sold spruce and birch beer from gaily painted wheelbarrows. As the morning hours passed, Mann watched and gradually entered into this pomp and ceremony which his fellow Republicans had mustered. At half past ten, he took his place in the procession led by the Washington Light Guard, left the City Hall, and proceeded past the throngs of people along to the place where he was to speak. On the dais, officials and clergymen took their seats and after the introductory invocations and a reading of the Declaration of Independence, Mann rose and stepped to the rostrum.[6]

He appeared tall and erect, and remarkably slender in his black

---

[5] Mann, Journal, June 9 and 30, and July 3, 1842, MS in MHS; James Spear Loring, *One Hundred Boston Orators* (Boston, 1853), p. 603.
[6] Boston *Daily Atlas,* June 29 and 30, July 1 and 4, 1842; Boston *Evening Transcript,* July 5, 1842.

waistcoat, satin vest, and gray doeskin trousers. His heavy head of silver-gray hair and pale complexion gave him an authority of age beyond his actual years. With a confidence which could only come from the thousand and more speeches he had made in the last six years, he began with a smooth, controlled, flowing style which permitted him to speak in a commanding cadence and gave his voice an engaging musical quality, bringing the vitality of emphasis and contrast to the eloquence he had committed to paper. A graceful movement of his outstretched arm or a bending forward towards the audience increased his listeners' sense of the powerful conviction of his ideas so evident in his eyes and the facial lines about his mouth and forehead. After the appropriate rhetorical liturgy honoring the revolutionary fathers, Mann moved to the challenges faced by his contemporaries. His remarks then would be ". . . a demonstration that our existing means for the promotion of intelligence and virtue are wholly inadequate to the support of a Republican government." Gone were the old dependable relationships, the divine rights of kings, the interlocking feudal privileges, the prerogatives of the clergy, and the ancestral allegiances of the commoners. What then did his listeners expect in their place? For Mann, the answer was a virtuous citizenry, perhaps not as free as Jefferson's yeomen but well trained in the "unchangeable principles of rectitude" and equal to their new responsibilities as republicans. Drawing from Biblical, classical, and patriotic mythology, he reinforced his contention that since men were not born with the ability to govern themselves, they must be educated in the common schools for this. Sodom and Gomorrah were constant reminders of what happened to societies where vice reigned unchecked; it was as foolish to assume his generation could reach the zenith of prosperity and happiness without a thorough training of the young as it was for Phaeton to mount his chariot and attempt to drive the horses of the sun; and he noted that every churchyard in New England sheltered "the graves of heroic dead, whose simple inscriptions . . . proclaim that they sought toil as a pleasure and rejoiced in self-sacrifice, that they might do good to us, whom they only saw with their eyes of faith." [7]

Surely now their eye of faith must have dimmed. Across the nation ran an invidious line of shame, ". . . on one side of which

---

[7] Mann spoke from an undated MS now in Mann MSS:MHS. The first edition of his remarks was published as Mann, *An Oration Delivered before the Authorities of the City of Boston, July 4, 1842* (Boston, 1842).

all labor is voluntary; while, on the opposite side, the system of involuntary labor, or servitude prevails." More immediately ominous was the terror unleashed both North and South. Risking offending the genteel sensitivities of his audience by resorting to images one commentator described as "strongly effective . . . not uniformly elegant," Mann catalogued "the lynching of five men at one time at Vicksburg; the valley of the Mississippi from St. Louis to New Orleans, lighted almost as with watch fires, by burning of human beings; the riots and demolitions, at New York, at Philadelphia, at Baltimore, at Alton, at Cincinnati. . . ." and lest any in his audience delude themselves with some false security of distance, he reminded them that right across the Charles River in Charlestown, vicious men had burned down a convent and school. All too easily, men passed from judgment to passion and from passion to violence.

Then challenging the wealthy and well-fed establishment before him to move forward rather than retreat towards some elusive Augustan age of élitism, Mann asked:

Are there any here who would counsel us to save the people from themselves by wresting from their hands this formidable right of ballot? . . . And, answer me this question; you! Who would conquer for the few, the power which has been won by the many; you! Who would disfranchise the common mass of mankind, and recondemn them to become helots, and bond-men, and feudal-serfs;—tell me, were they again in power of your castles, would you not again neglect them, again oppress them, again make them the slaves of your voluptuousness, and the paupers or the victims of your vices? Tell me, you royalists and hierarchs, or advocates of royalty and hierarchy. . . .

To any reactionaries before him, the Franklin Dexters and the Edward Newtons, Mann demanded they change their public philosophy and recognize that "the whole people must be instructed in the knowledge of their duties," and that "they must be elevated to a contemplation and comprehension of those great truths on which alone a government like ours can be successfully conducted. . . ." Reaching an impassioned climax he hoped none would dare to forget, Mann pleaded with his audience to

Pour out light and truth, as God pours sunshine and rain. No longer seek knowledge as the luxury of a few, but dispense it amongst all as the bread of life. Learn only how the ignorant may learn; how the innocent may be preserved; the vicious reclaimed. Call down the

377

astronomer from the skies; call up the geologist from his subterranean exploration; summon, if need be, the mightiest intellects from the Council Chamber of the Nation; enter the cloistered halls, where the scholiast muses over superfluous annotations; dissolve conclave and synod, where subtle polemics are vainly discussing their barren dogmas; —collect whatever of talent, or erudition or eloquence, or authority, the broad land can supply, *and go forth,* and TEACH THIS PEOPLE.

Only when he had finished did he notice the sweat streaming down his face. For a moment, as he stepped to his seat there was a fearful stillness with only the sound of his last few words still ringing in his ears. Then as he sat down, every other possible sense was driven from his mind by the sound of a thunderous applause. Each time he rose to acknowledge his listeners' acclaim, he grew faint, realizing how much he had given of himself to his message. Gratefully, he sought the support of his chair. He had triumphed in Boston, and as he walked from the dais to the main floor of the temple, he knew he was doing for his own generation what his ancestors had done at Lexington, Concord, and Breed's Hill.

CHAPTER XVI

Another World

═══════

WHO UPON ENTERING an American schoolroom, and witnessing the continual exercises in reading and speaking, or listening to the subject of their discourse, and watching the behavior of the pupils towards each other and their teacher, could, for a moment, doubt his being amongst a congregation of young republicans? And who, on entering a German academy, would not be struck with the principle of authority and silence, which reflects the history of Germany for the last half a dozen centuries? What difficulties has not an American teacher to maintain order amongst a dozen unruly little urchins; while a German rules over two hundred pupils in a class with all the ease and tranquility of an Eastern monarch.

FRANCIS GRUND

─────────

HORACE MANN recorded the passing of 1843 in his Journal with a most uncharacteristic, if momentary satisfaction. "Sunday. A New Year!" he announced. "The past year is now beyond mortal or immortal control. To me, to the cause I have at heart, it has been a most auspicious year." Even so, he could not refrain in the same entry from envisaging the future as doom ever ready to descend, only kept suspended by "human exertion" and his willingness to "die in the cause." His Fourth of July oration had been the most important event for him in the past year, but within a few months he was to bungle his way into a far more significant affair with an ungainliness unexpected in one so adroit.[1]

Unlike Mann, most of Boston's honored orators either had raised storms of controversy with their remarks or failed to stir even a ripple of reaction. Seeking some constructive middle ground between these extremes, Mann had delivered a manifesto which not only stirred his élite listeners, but had gained additional converts to his cause. While the smell of fireworks still hung about the Common, a delegation from City Hall completed the final act of their

─────────

[1] Mann, Journal, January 1, 1843, MS in MHS.

civic ritual, calling on him at his office and requesting a copy of his oration for publication. As soon as the type was locked in place, the presses rolled and did not stop until 20,000 copies were ready for free distribution. To be sure, there were a few dilettantes to complain that his speech lacked the literary elegance expected of a speaker so honored by Boston. While Charles Sumner acknowledged that it was "powerful and in pictures," he criticized it for its "vicious style." Far more typical, however, was the response of the general public. "If I do not greatly err," wrote a correspondent from Washington, D.C., "it is the best discourse on the subject in the English language . . . he shows the American Patrician[s] that while they are trifling with toys and toying with trifles, the great and controlling interest—the cornerstone of their own safety—scarcely receives a thought." And William Ware, writing in the *Christian Examiner,* no doubt spoke the sentiments of many when he pronounced Mann's oration "the most valuable discourse ever delivered on a fourth of July." [2]

To obtain such accolades, Mann had paced himself on a course which carried him to the brink of success but short of the self-destruction just beyond. Believing he could not continue with such a ruinous singlemindedness, Edmund Dwight argued with Mann that since his critical work with the Board was now behind, he should re-enter political life. Others thought he could not continue his self-imposed celibacy, but lacked the temerity to suggest to his face that he remarry. Almost in despair, Howe complained of Mann's "morbid sensitivity" and the "tenacity with which he clings to the memory of [his] wife and his extreme sensitiveness on the subject. . . ." Unwittingly, they exaggerated. What Howe and Mann's other confidantes did not know was that as early as 1840, he had begun to relax his intense devotion to his dead wife to the extent that he took some interest in other women. He accepted token gifts from Mary Eliot Dwight, later to marry Dr. Samuel Parkman, and responded with affectionate notes implying more than a casual relationship with her. At times too, he wrote regularly to Mary Peabody, including a note penned late one evening after something unexpected had prevented him from paying a call on her. Apologizing for not appearing, he complained, "I was obliged to send my heart to bed

[2] Mann, Journal, July 12 and August 21, 1842, MS in MHS; Charles Sumner to George S. Sumner, August 15, 1842, Sumner MSS:HCL; James Wadsworth to Mann, October 7, 1842, Mann MSS:MHS; *Christian Examiner,* XXXIII (November, 1842), 258–262.

supperless." He closed his note with a request and promise: "When you have time transcribe your heart and send it to me, and I will do the same to you." All of this he kept discreetly concealed from the genteel gossipmongers among his cultured acquaintances, as he slowly began to contemplate what had been so long unthinkable. But each time he started to build an escape from the past, it collapsed like a house of cards with the return of another "agonizing anniversary" of Charlotte's death.[3]

Then to the surprise of everyone, including himself, he decided upon a second marriage. From someone as fastidious and organized as Mann, one might have expected a proper and restrained courtship. In fact, the months preceding his marriage witnessed an almost semi-public comic sequence of indecisions, which only a long-suffering spinster with an unshakable will to matrimony could have endured. With the Combes back in Britain, Mann had entertained thoughts of a tour of European educational institutions. Once having convinced himself of the virtues of a trip, he persuaded Howe, another Combe devotee, to come along. At the same time, Howe had begun to court Julia Ward of New York City and according to one of his bachelor friends, the young lady had "cast the glamour of her witchery over him." For a time, Howe attempted to keep his emotions reined in by his reason, according to the best of phrenological practices, but he soon was completely captivated by the strong-willed and vivacious Julia. With wedding bells in the offing, Howe planned a European honeymoon and suggested that Mann come along as additional company; and he agreed! Then, with the trip less than a month away, Mann enlarged the ungainly trio to a happy foursome by proposing marriage to Miss Mary Peabody.[4]

Mann's actions must have caught everybody by surprise, including an amazed Miss Peabody. From the first day she had seen

---

[3] Edmund Dwight to Mann, September 6, 1841; Mann to Mary Peabody, June 1, 1840; Mann to Mary Mann, May 19, 1848, all in Mann MSS: MHS; Samuel Gridley Howe to George Combe, January 31, 1841, Combe MSS:NLS; Mann to Mary Eliot Dwight Parkman, March 19, [1840], and November 11, 1840, Mann MSS:HCL. Although his friendship with her had been one of long standing, Mann made no attempt to introduce Mary Peabody to other members of his family. See Mary Peabody to Rebecca and Eliza Pennell, April 23, 1843, Mann:MHS.

[4] George Hillard to Henry Wadsworth Longfellow, July 2, 1842, Hillard MSS:HCL; Charles Sumner to Henry Cleveland, February 15, 1843, Berg MSS:NYPL; Charles Sumner to Sarah P. Cleveland, February 23, 1843, Berg MSS:NYPL; Harold Schwartz, *Samuel Gridley Howe* (Cambridge, 1956), pp. 109–113.

this broken man with a gaunt spectral countenance at Mrs. Clarke's boardinghouse, she had dared hope that she might become the second Mrs. Mann, even though this meant ever to dwell with him within the shadow of brighter times. From those first days, Mary had lived the waiting game and endured disappointments and frustrations which would have demoralized all but the most iron-willed of women. Patiently biding her time, hoping for the day when this man would extricate himself from his self-imposed melancholy, and living for nothing more than to become second in his affections, she desperately sought what she knew could only be a consolation prize. Fate had decreed that she would only know weak men within her immediate family. Her father was a sometime dentist and an incurable tinkerer with unworkable improvements for false teeth; her two brothers survived a sickly childhood only to die upon reaching maturity. Thus Mary Peabody was forced to play a more masculine role about the home simply to give the family stability. Upon receiving news of the wedding, one Boston wag observed that "whoever marries a Peabody must look after the *housekeeping*," but another commentator was probably more accurate in noting that Mann was the first strong male in her life, "well-filled in all respects to be the protector and *more* than father or brother to Mary."

Her younger sister Sophia had married Nathaniel Hawthorne in 1842. Elizabeth was busy editing the *Dial,* just barely keeping her creditors satisfied with the meager earnings of her bookstore, which specialized in Transcendental literature and served as a watering place for its devotees. Mary continued to do her share, keeping school, tutoring the Quincy children for a time, and briefly attempting the role of impresario for several luckless textbook authors. Nevertheless, she never relinquished her hope that someday Mann would overcome his veneration for Charlotte's memory and give a portion of his troubled heart to her. As she wrote to Sophia after the Hawthornes had moved into the Old Manse in Concord, "I think nothing is more favorable than happiness. A holy marriage and a cheerful life are the best guarantees of happy motherhood, according to my creed." But not even in her most intimate conversations with her sisters did she reveal that the only marriage which would bring her a full measure of happiness was to live at the side of Horace Mann. Such was the incredible will of this quiet and seemingly gentle woman, that for all her yearning and heartbreak, she kept her feeling for him the most closely guarded of her secret treasures. "I could only bear it," she confessed, "because it was my own secret and never infected anyone that loved me." [5]

As late as six weeks before his planned departure for Europe on May 1, Mann still gave no open indication of the step he was about to take. What goaded him finally to propose to Mary is a mystery, but on March 26 he asked for the hand of what must have been the most surprised and relieved woman in Boston. Now believing that her hopes were about to be realized, Mary trembled whenever her beloved Horace left her, fearing it might all be just a cruel dream. Soon after news of the forthcoming wedding reached their circle of friends, wedding gifts began to arrive at the Peabody home. A flower painting, two inlaid card cases, an agate-handled paper knife, a feathered penholder, and a Sheffield-plated cake basket, all of these might have had little practical value, but for Mary each served the most important function of signifying that her wedding was about to happen. "Tell Mr. H. if the thing will not stand omens," she wrote to Sophia Hawthorne, "he may come and shoot me at ½ before eleven tomorrow for May day is to be the day." [6]

During the weeks of April, Mann busied himself with changes in his travel plans. From Daniel Webster, he received an official assignment to carry diplomatic pouches, thus giving him certain privileges abroad. He also wrote to a large number of persons ranging from those for whom he had little respect such as Marcus Morton to those he almost venerated like Amos Lawrence and Joseph Story, asking each for general or specific letters of introduction. And he made promises to deliver parcels for friends, including a copy of the *Dial* that Ralph Waldo Emerson wanted Thomas Carlyle to read. With $2,000 deposited with Baring Brothers in London, Josiah Quincy, Jr., agreeing to fill several speaking engagements for him, and George B. Emerson promising to edit the copy for the intervening issues of the *Common School Journal*, everything was apparently ready and Mann set the wedding date for April 25. Then

---

[5] Mary Peabody Mann to Horace Mann, Jr., [1865?], Straker MSS:ACL; Mary Peabody to Sophia Hawthorne, [late 1842], and [April 1843], Berg MSS:NYPL; Caroline Healy [Dall] to Theodore Parker, April 10, 1843; Theodore Parker to Caroline Healy [Dall], April 4, 1843, Dall MSS:MHS.

[6] Mann, Journal, March 26, 1843, MS in MHS; Mann to George Combe, February 28, 1843, Combe MSS:NLS; George Combe to Horace Mann, March 16, 1843, Mann MSS:MHS; Mary Peabody to Sophia Hawthorne, March 28, April 30, [1843], and several letters written between Sophia's and Mary's weddings, Berg MSS:NYPL; Mann to Mrs. Josiah Quincy, Jr., March 30, 1843, Quincy MSS:BPL.

at the last minute, Sam Ward, Julia's brother and guardian, considered it too dangerous for his sister to sail for Europe on the packet ship leaving from New York, and insisted she take a steamship from Boston a week later. Howe changed his sailing plans and Mann postponed his marriage until May 1, the day the two couples were to leave from Boston on the *Britannia*. On the night of April 30, Horace Mann wrote in his Journal:

Tomorrow is the day appointed for my marriage and departure for Europe. It cannot be otherwise, now, nor would I have it otherwise if I could. Yet how much of weal or woe may spring from these events,—perhaps involving life or death. . . . I believe, I have a true and generous heart, to sympathize with, to work with, to rest upon; and surely on earth, there is no treasure to be compared with this. Oh Mary I think you will bless me. I trust I shall bless you.

Mann blotted the wet ink and set his quill aside. He looked again at the sentences he had written, illuminated in the soft warm light from his whale-oil lamp. Apparently satisfied, he closed the book. With these words linking the past to the future, he brought his Journal of the last seven years to an end. He would never make another entry.[7]

And it poured all morning on May Day. Out in Concord, Sophia was marooned by the muddy roads and abandoned her plans to come into Boston. In Providence, Lydia held security more dear than sentiment and stayed at home. So did every one of the small circle of friends who had been invited. As the morning moved on towards noon and still no friends arrived, Mann no doubt anxiously checked the passage of time on the new gold watch he had purchased two weeks before. Then at half past eleven, with just two and a half hours to sailing time, he could wait no longer. Mann joined Elizabeth, Dr. and Mrs. Peabody, and Reverend James Freeman Clarke in the parlor of the Peabody house at 13 West Street. Mary entered the room wearing a simple white grasscloth dress, trimmed with a small band of lace about the neck, the gift of one of

---

[7] Receipt from Baring Brothers and Company, London, April 25, 1843, Mann MSS:DHS; Daniel Webster to Mann, April 14, 1843, Mann MSS: MHS; Mann to Joseph Story, April 25, 1843, Story MSS:LOC; Mary Peabody to Sophia Hawthorne, [April, 1843], Berg MSS:NYPL; *Correspondence of Thomas Carlyle and Ralph Waldo Emerson* (Boston, 1883), II, 33. Mann to George Combe, April 19, 1843, Combe MSS:NLS; Mann, Journal, April 30, 1843, MS in MHS; Mann to H. Hale, April 29, 1843, Franklin MSS: Sterling Library, Yale.

her former students. She wore no jewelry, save a small gold chain around her head which Mann had given her for a wedding present. Just as they were about to begin, a messenger brought word that Sophia was not on the way. Mary and Horace then joined hands before Reverend Clarke and made their vows. Elizabeth reported she had never seen Mann more radiant, and that for the moment at least, the enormous burden of the past had been purged from his mind. By noon the rain had stopped and the wedding party moved down to the Cunard Wharf, Mary's mother still insisting it would be more safe to travel by sail. The newlyweds went on board to join the Howes and claim their stateroom. At seven minutes past two with the gangplank raised, the last hawser was loosed. Massive belches of black smoke rolled upward from the stacks between the three masts, and the deck began to vibrate as the giant paddle wheels on the starboard and port sides churned up the murky dock-side water. As the *Britannia* eased away and pointed her prow to-wards the Atlantic, the crowd of spectators on the wharf raised three cheers and the passengers standing along the railing returned the salute. As he stood by his new wife, Mann joined in the first two but the third became caught in his throat.[8]

*   *   *

Almost as soon as the *Britannia* had navigated past the islands in the bay and the Boston skyline settled below the horizon, there was a visible change. With the sharp bite and sparkle of the ocean air, Mann seemed to forget some of the moral imperatives towards duty which were so much of the very atmosphere he breathed in Massachusetts. Once beyond the three-mile limit and "out of the jurisdiction of the American Temperance Society," as he wrote back home, he and Mary jettisoned a few of their inhibitions and actually joined their shipmates in a round of brandy, no doubt feeling a bit guilty and giddy all in one. On board there were no meetings, no speeches and no plans to organize conventions. That which Mann had come to accept as his normal habitat was gone for the moment, and in its place were seemingly endless daylight hours.

---

[8] Elizabeth Peabody to Rebecca Pennell, May 1, 1843; Elizabeth Peabody to Rawlins Pickman, May 1, 1843; Mann to Rebecca Pennell, May 5, 1843; Mary Mann to Elizabeth Peabody, May 5, 1843, all in Mann MSS: MHS; a description of the *Britannia,* an early steamship of the Cunard White Star Company, is found in Warren Card to Robert L. Straker, March 31, 1839. Straker MSS: ACL.

Relaxing next to Mary on the deck with little seasickness to trouble him, time was only marked by the ringing of the ship's bell and the arc of the sun's path across the sky. With each new day, it required more effort to think about the unfinished tasks he had left behind and remember the thousands of illiterate children he still considered his charges. Perhaps this floating microcosm populated by seventy well-mannered and congenial inhabitants and buffered from the cares of the world by a seemingly limitless saltwater moat was the real world and that which he had left behind was only a labored dream, a frenetic fantasy of the past, now imperfectly remembered. Almost he let the hypnotic sway of the ship convince him this was so, and then on the thirteenth day, as Cape Clear, the southernmost tip of Ireland, rose from the depths of the ocean, the shouts of "Land Ho!" broke into his reverie. Quickly Mann's mood changed from leisure to expectancy. And the relaxation of the past fortnight could be seen for what it was, only a brief interlude, an opaque shell, temporarily containing and concealing Mann's pent-up impatience and his irresistible compulsion to wring every opportunity for good works from the precious moments of his tour abroad.[9]

Once he set foot on the Liverpool dock, he paced about, anxious to make up for the "lost time" on board and any other moments he might have wasted in the last several years. With Mary in tow and the Howes in dutiful pursuit, Mann plunged into his European itinerary. Honeymoon notwithstanding, this was to be no peregrination but travel with a purpose. Barely ashore, they were on their way to morning worship at James Martineau's church. Then in the afternoon and evening, Mann visited the famous Blue Coat School in Liverpool, a showplace of the Anglican Church, attending vespers and then falling in step with the troops of young lads, on their way to their commons and a meal of dry bread, cheese, and water. The next morning he was back, inspecting classes and watching recitations. Anxious that he not forget a single fact, he began a copious journal of his observations, only to learn that the accumulation of a dozen pages of notes each day was a burden to which even he was not equal.[1]

He had justified his tour on the basis of learning all he could

---

[9] Mary Mann to Mrs. Nathaniel Peabody, May [2?], 1843, Mary Mann to [Elizabeth Peabody], May 3, [1843], May 15, [1843], and July 9–10, 1843; and Mann to Rebecca Pennell, May 15, 1843, all in Mann MSS: MHS; Mann to George Combe, May 15, 1843, Combe MSS:NLS.
[1] Mary Mann to Elizabeth Peabody, May 15, 1843, and Mann to Rebecca Pennell, May 15, 1843, Mann MSS:MHS.

about schools, prisons, and asylums. To this end, as soon as he reached London, he sought out the leading moralists and reformers of the day, James Simpson, Sir James Kay-Shuttleworth, Richard Cobden, and Lord Brougham. With these men, he would discuss reform topics well into the night, only to be up early the next day for a round of inspections, perhaps to see the ventilating system in the House of Commons or to observe the discipline of silence used in Newgate Prison. All this became personally important to him far beyond the need to gain educational information.

Mann was all too poorly prepared for the force of the new experiences he was about to receive. Not really certain of himself, and coming from a nation which lacked a realistic sense of its own destiny by holding to the myth of its innocence and virtue, he found it difficult to come to terms with what he saw. Ostensibly, he had gone to Europe to learn whatever he could, particularly in the area of education; but he was not capable of recording objectively what he observed and later make selections for adoption back in Massachusetts. Needing to reassure himself that the destiny of the world rested with the United States and not with Europe, he increasingly found it necessary to pass ungenerous judgments on European social institutions and practices. At first he gauged the Old World mainly by norms familiar to him. A palace hall was "as long as West Street," and a school occupied a "space as large as our State house." St. James Cemetery was not nearly as impressive as Mount Auburn. Only something as incomparable as St. Paul's forced him to capitulate, if but momentarily, in his biased game of comparison. This he conceded to be "extremely beautiful" and "as large as 64 of our largest churches." As he and Mary climbed to the dome, they were totally unprepared for the dazzling vista of the sprawling city below them, "an expanse surpassing five New Yorks." [2]

For a time, such a referential system sufficed; but the more he penetrated into English society, the more he found his own culture wanting. He began to sense this as he came to Eaton Hall, one of the castles of the Duke of Westminster, outside the old walled town of Chester. The grounds surrounding the castle extended for several miles and as his party approached it, they passed a solitary stag here and there before coming on a herd of deer grazing nonchalantly on the well-kept lawns. The garden next to the castle was a

---

[2] Mary Mann to Elizabeth Peabody, May 21, 1843, Mann MSS:MHS.

fine arboretum of botanical specimens transported from distant lands wherever the proud British flag now waved. By comparison, thoughts of the Boston Common with its rows of mottled sycamore trees, graveled walks, and plebeian frogpond were embarrassing. Once inside the building, he found it impossible to conceal his amazement and wonder. Mann walked on polished marble floors more beautiful than people could afford for table tops back home. Proceeding from one hall to another, each with its giant, exquisitely carved golden-framed mirrors giving the rooms the impression of even greater size, he saw walls covered with hunting trophies, handsome portraits, and magnificent richly colored tapestries, the accumulation of many generations. Again, he was embarrassed to think that the ballroom in a Bulfinch house would be a mere butler's pantry when compared to such luxury.[3]

But this was only the beginning. Within a few days, he and Mary were visiting Windsor Castle, admiring paintings by Rubens and Vandyke and strolling through some of its 2,300 acres of parks. Even more overwhelming was their visit to Stafford House, belonging to the Duke of Sutherland, so elegant it was said that even Queen Victoria was envious of it. And perhaps for good reason, thought the Manns. At the door they were met by a doorman in white breeches, scarlet coat, and a "powdered head." Once inside, they walked along a corridor filled with beautiful inlaid cabinets, paintings, and statuary. In the main vestibule, their eyes followed the graceful path of a most handsome circular staircase of polished stone and imported hand-carved woods. On the wall were paintings of an immense size, some of English landscapes, others of battle scenes. From here they stepped into the family sitting room with its own version of richness and beauty. Chairs, sofas, and ottomans were covered in satin damask and flanked by tables, cabinets, and silver candelabra. And finally, there was the ballroom, one hundred feet long, walled by mirrors and topped with dazzling crystal chandeliers.[4]

If the Manns were taken aback by the riches with which the

---

[3] Mann to Josiah Quincy, June 1, 1843, Quincy MSS:BPL; Mann, *Life*, I, 175–176; Mary Mann to Elizabeth Peabody, May 21, 1843, Mann MSS: MHS.

[4] Mary Mann, *Mann*, I, 183–184; Mary Mann to Elizabeth Peabody, May 30 and 31, 1843, Mann MSS:MHS. While in London, the Manns and the Howes took an apartment at 31, Upper Baker Street, across from Regency Park. For a time, they were handicapped in their sightseeing, since Howe suffered from lameness and was forced to remain in his quarters. See Mann to George Combe, May 29, 1843, Combe MSS:NLS.

English aristocracy had furnished their houses, they were also chagrined by the extravagance with which individuals adorned themselves. Attending a dress ball for Polish relief at Almacks, they found it hard to believe that so much gold and silver satin brocade, ermine, embroidery, and jewelry could be brought together in one place. Although Mary thought the jeweled hairpieces of the women false and pretentious, she could not help becoming excited at the sight of a ballroom floor with several hundred elegant men and women stepping through a Polish quadrille. Mann was far less charitable, conceiving the entire event as a "caricature of humanity." He was especially disturbed by the women's low-cut dresses. "About twenty ladies were beautifully and tastefully dressed," he conceded, but "the money of the others apparently did not hold out; for their dresses rose just above the waist." Equally upsetting to him was the fact that among the men, he did not see a single head which gave phrenological evidence of "strength and benevolence." Thus with a confused ambivalence about their own republican simplicity, he and Mary "sauntered round the room," among the 700 guests, " 'unknowing and unknown.' " [5]

Recognizing that America in no way approached Europe in luxury and refinement, Mann was forced to contend with a cultural shock he had not anticipated. To survive and maintain some degree of self-certainty, he forced a dialectical law upon his confusion which he hoped would help buttress his own values. Such wealth could only exist by exploiting the poor and keeping them enslaved in ignorance. Where there was elegance, there would also be poverty. Thus in America, the absence of luxury and sophistication was a sign of health. Sights of the sordid, the pathetic, and the squalid in England reassured him of the superiority of his own country. The necessary antidote to seeing the dazzling beauty of Queen Victoria's jewels was to visit the London rag market or the Jews' quarter, walking through its narrow twisting lanes with a policeman, careful not to step on the animal and human excrement along the way. As he passed by the buildings, on both right and left from openings which masqueraded as doorways came the stench of urine and garbage, together with the aroma of exotic cooking even more strange to his nostrils. After such an experience, he was then prepared for a Polish ball or a tour of Windsor Castle.

---

[5] Mary Mann to Elizabeth Peabody, June 15, 1843, Mann MSS:MHS; Mann, *Life,* I, 190.

One morning he went with Charles Dickens to visit West-minster Bridewell, a prison for younger criminals. Outside in the prison yard, he saw several inmates walking on a treadmill, un-knowingly pumping water for fountains in the warden's garden. Inside they passed through dark corridors, lined on each side with rows of cells. Peering through the small grates in the iron doors they could see the vacant stares of one victim after another, each in solitary confinement and forced into the most rigid discipline of silence. Dickens observed that a woman whose child was born to such a fate was justified to commit infanticide, and Mann was almost ready to agree as he watched the guards empty a van of a new contingent of inmates, one a lad no more than twelve years old, sobbing at the prospect ahead of him. There, and not the crown jewels in the Tower of London, were the real adornments of British culture. For every art museum and castle there were several prisons and a dozen workhouses. And for every aristocrat living in luxury, there were a hundred convicts and a thousand illiterate children. To Josiah Quincy Mann reported, "I have seen equipages, palaces, and the regalia of royalty, side by side with beggary, squalidness, and a degradation in which the very features of humanity were almost lost in those of the brute." For this, Mann held the nobility, the rich, and the Anglican Church to blame. With Mary, he agreed completely, as she wrote home, "Give me America with all its raw-ness and want of polish. We have aristocracy enough at home and here I trace it to its founydations [sic]." [6]

Although he did not admit it publicly, a new fear began to warp his perception of Europe. If England had surrendered to this prostitution of its resources, was there not some iron law of social degeneration predestining the United States towards the same ends? This he would not admit. Such a cynical view undermined every-thing he believed, but he did concede the possibility of unprincipled men leading his country on a downward course. Thus with each additional day in England, his tour took on a new sense of urgency. Architectural masterpieces and the scenic beauty of the countryside only were helpful to him for their moral promptings. Visiting the famous York Cathedral, his experience was far more moral than aesthetic. "To me," he wrote in his travel journal, "the sight of one child educated to understand something of his Maker, and of that

---

[6] Mann to James K. Mills, June 1, 1843; Mary Mann to Elizabeth Pea-body, May 21 and June 15, 1843, Mann MSS:MHS; Mann, *Life*, I, 179–183; Mann to Josiah Quincy, June 1, 1843, Quincy MSS:BPL.

Maker's works, is a far more glorious spectacle than all the cathedrals which the art of man has ever reached. . . ." Recalling his impressions of the beauty of Loch Lomond, he could only respond, "Amidst all this, however, I confess my heart often turned to the fortunes of the rising generation at home; and were it not that I hoped here to replenish my strength, to enter with renewed vigor into their service, I would have preferred to be closeted in narrow apartments, working for them, to all the joy of beholding this magnificent display." Early one morning, climbing alone on a narrow path bordered on each side by the fragrant heather covering the Scottish highlands, he reached a vista point overlooking Loch Katrine. Since from below the ascent to this spot seemed impossible, he now moralized:

"It is in this way," thought I, "that great and difficult enterprises are accomplished. . . . If he looks around and about him, and sees . . . what is now within his reach and at his command, and addresses himself with all zeal and industry to do what can be done, to take the step next to the one just taken, he will gradually yet assuredly advance, and at last will find himself at the point of elevation which from below seemed unattainable."

With each step came another moral, and each stone a sermon.[7]

His English experience then convinced Mann that if the United States was truly to transform history and not to succumb to violent social revolution, its salvation lay in greater efforts to educate the young. After describing Eaton Hall to Josiah Quincy, he added, "Every particle in all that structure is the representation of human tears and groans. . . . Does this look as if God had made one flesh upon the earth? Does this look as though a new commandment had been given that ye love one another. . . ? Look! look at that camel just as he [is] dying, trying to escape from hell by darting through the eye of the needle!" And he promised Quincy, "Oh! if I ever return, how I shall work to save our people from the miseries which are here so abounding." England had provided him with a new mandate and he must get to the German provinces immediately. After a short stay in Scotland, he was so anxious to get to the mainland that he was ready to risk missing George Combe, who was then convalescing in southern Europe. Paris held few attractions

[7] Mary Mann to [Elizabeth Peabody], June 18 and 21, 1843, Mann MSS:MHS; Mann, *Life,* I, 191–194.

for him. "I want to find out," he wrote to Combe, "what are the results, as well as the workings of the celebrated Prussian system." It was now up to this country to provide him with the means by which he was to carry out his mission at home.[8]

* * *

Reeling from his English experience, as he and Mary boarded the *Leeds* at Hull for Hamburg, Mann virtually willed that the Prussian schools would provide him with the answers. And those still missing, he would have to supply with some of his own making. He was familiar with the writings of John Griscom, Alexander Bache, Calvin Stowe, and Victor Cousin. All had lauded the Prussian achievement of wiping out illiteracy and creating a sense of national unity. Further reinforcing Mann's certainty that the answers to his problems in Massachusetts were to be found in the country of Friedrich Wilhelm IV was the prodding of his friend George Combe. For Combe, Prussia had not only completely recovered from her humiliation at the hands of Napoleon, but was now "*the* Kingdom of Germany on whose development, political, educational and industrial all the rest hang" and its schools were "the grand objects of interest in Europe and America." In fact, so convinced was he of this that he urged Mann to forego the aesthetic delights of a trip to Munich and even by-pass Emanuel von Fellenberg's celebrated school at Hofwyl in order to concentrate on the schools of Prussia.[9]

That the destiny of Germany should hang on Prussia was remarkable. Compared with other parts of Europe, it had few of the obvious resources from which national eminence was constructed. Lacking cities bustling with manufacturing and mercantile activities, it had based its rise on an agrarian economy rooted in its sandy soil, bereft both of fertility and mineral wealth. By diligence, sacrifice, and a Spartan commitment to national goals, Prussia had arrived on the scene as the leading power in the European heartland. Ruled by an absolute monarch whose will was carried out by a ruthlessly disciplined army and a narrow-minded and highly efficient bureaucracy, in an age of incipient nationalism, Prussia was admired as a model by other aspiring nation-states. Its citizens were well fed and clothed, literate and absolutely loyal, even if this meant

---

[8] Mann to Josiah Quincy, June 1, 1843, Quincy MSS:BPL; Mann to George Combe, May 21, 1843, Combe MSS:NLS.
[9] George Combe to Horace Mann, July 16, 1843, Combe MSS:NLS.

they were also cogs in a national machine whose lives took on meaning largely in terms of some manifestation of national purpose. Work, sacrifice, and patriotism were Prussian ideals, all synthesized into an unquestioning obedience to the state. Such was the envied and admired achievement of the Prussian rulers, and the credit for their accomplishment rested with the most organized system of education on the continent. No creation of some fickle village or town board, the schools were an instrument of the state and their curricula were first and foremost a matter of national political policy. Through them, schoolmasters carried out a program of instruction which systematically, efficiently, and unswervingly aimed at achieving national rather than individual, familial, or local goals.

Unfortunately, Mann's trip by steamboat up the Elbe to Magdeburg and then east on land by rail consumed several extra days on his itinerary. On the very day he arrived in Berlin, he found its teachers' seminaries, *Bürgerschulen*, and the best of its elementary schools all closed for vacation. To compound his disappointment, he learned that Howe could not join him. Having been expelled from Prussia in 1832 for his efforts to help Polish refugees, Howe's expulsion order was still on the books and the King showed no inclination to revoke it. Therefore, as Mann described it, his travel companion remained "hovering on the coasts, I know not where, awaiting not the breath of heaven, but that of a Monarch." So desirous was Mann to find the answers he sought in this country that closed school doors and Howe's absence proved to be only minor setbacks in achieving his purposes. Although the live children were elsewhere, he was satisfied to tour empty classrooms, speak with administrators and vacationing schoolmasters, and mine the mountains of official reports for nuggets of practical information.[1]

A few of the schools for the poor (*Armenschulen*) were still

---

[1] Mann to George Combe, July 11, 1843, Combe MSS:NLS; Mary Mann to Elizabeth Peabody, July 9, 1843, Mann MSS:MHS. In January, 1832, Howe had gone to Prussia with funds for Polish relief. Suspicious of his activities, the Berlin chief of police ordered his arrest. Expecting the *Polizei* the next morning, and not knowing how he might be charged, Howe spent the night feverishly sorting out the papers he carried, deciding which ones might prove incriminating, and hiding them in the hollow head of the bust of the Prussian King which stood in his room. At dawn he was escorted to the Ministry of Police and put in solitary confinement. No charges were ever filed, but he was held incommunicado for four weeks and then released. According to Howe's daughter, the "incriminating papers" remained in the bust until retrieved by Mann on this trip. Harold Schwartz, *Samuel Gridley Howe* (Cambridge, 1956), pp. 43–47.

open, and Mann visited these as well as several orphanages and asylums. Since Friedrich Diesterweg's teachers' seminary was closed and he out of town, Mann made three unsuccessful calls on Frau Diesterweg and then gave up. The rest of their time he and Mary used for another round of museums and a tour of the palace of Frederick the Great at Potsdam. From those schools they did visit, they came away with a strong sense of the professional competence of Prussian teachers. "The teachers are admirably qualified and full of animation," Mary wrote home and although she knew few in Massachusetts would believe her, she reported that "we have not seen a teacher with a book in his hand in all Prussia, no not one!" Equally impressive was the obediency of the children. She had seen something of this in Cyrus Peirce's normal school in Lexington, but this he accomplished with a personal "iron rule." Here obedience was part of the warp and woof of the educational fabric. It seemed as if German children were instilled with an "innate respect for superior years . . . here the teachers have respect because they command it." Not that Mary was insensitive to the patent oppression in Prussian society, but so convinced was she of the redemptive power of education that she believed it would do "its legitimate work here and then all will be well, even politically." [2]

Nor was the quality of the German *Lehrer* lost on her husband. Mann believed they constituted "the finest collection of men I have ever seen,—full of intelligence, dignity, benevolence, kindness and bearing. . . ." In the United States he and others had advocated greater employment of women teachers because they were more kind and forbearing. Such an argument, he concluded, would not be understood in Germany. Never had he witnessed "an instance of harshness and severity; all is kind, encouraging, animating, sympathizing." Whether it was really so is a moot question. What was important was that Mann perceived it so and interpreted what he saw as a quality of order, discipline, and pedagogy far superior to anything back in Massachusetts.[3]

Probably the high point of his trip on the continent was a reunion with George Combe in Leipzig and a tour of the few schools open there. Then after the two men had exhausted their possibilities, they and their wives took to the countryside of Saxon Switzerland, a beautiful Alpine region twenty-five miles west of Dresden. By day

---

[2] Mary Mann to Elizabeth Peabody, July 9, 10, and 21, 1843, Mann MSS:MHS.
[3] Mann, *Life*, I, 201–202.

they visited hospitals, asylums, and schools. At night, after dinner, they always returned to their favorite topic, the changing of modern man's behavior through a reform of his political and educational institutions. The week with George Combe only heightened Mann's sense of loss when the two parted. Although at the time neither man had the courage to express what was foremost in his mind, each understood, as Mary later described it, "that it is not likely we may meet again in our mortal pilgrimage." And she was right.[4]

Returning to Leipzig after a visit to Wartburg Castle, Mann was escorted by the director of the city schools, Dr. Charles Vogel. Not only did he again notice the exceptional quality of the teachers, but he paid great attention to the specific methods they employed. Instead of the children being expected to learn individual letters by rote memory, then syllables, and finally words, they were given books with pictures of common objects. Underneath each picture was its simple name. When questioning the pupils about what they read, their teachers expected a *Vollständig* or complete answer. Often children used the blackboard, an exotic practice in Boston, and it was with no small amount of incredulity and admiration that Mann reported that "children of six years old often write extremely well, and draw with a free hand and in the upper classes we have seen boys of twelve go to the blackboard and draw from memory a map of Russia or Saxony with all the mountains and rivers and many of the towns." No doubt under a strong Pestalozzian influence, the teachers made the continual attempt to relate words to pictures and concrete objects. In one school, Mann even observed an arithmetic lesson using a prototype of Cuisenière rods. Carefully, the teacher posed questions which only could be answered by resorting to the rods and plotted in a way which anticipated programmed learning and modern reinforcement theory. Each new set of questions, Mann observed, "being based on learnings from the last. Each progressing just a little farther than the previous exercise." When Mann suggested that these city teachers were all university graduates and superior to those in rural classrooms, Dr. Vogel insisted that the training of country schoolmasters was "probably more thorough and complete in regard to all the approved modes and processes of teaching" than those of his own staff. Unable to visit the rural areas, Mann accepted him at his word.[5]

---

[4] Mary Mann to Rebecca Pennell, August 7, 1843, Mann MSS:MHS; Mann, *Life*, I, 204–208.

[5] The account of Mann's experiences in the Leipzig schools is taken from

From Leipzig, the Manns moved on to Frankfurt. By a remarkable coincidence, while leaving a church they had just visited, they met none other than Samuel Gridley Howe coming up the steps. That he and Mann should find each other accidentally in all of Germany was a chance in a million, but for the two to meet in front of a church of all places lowered the probability by several factors. In Frankfurt they decided to tour Heidelberg together and found it the most beautiful city on their trip. Then they moved on to Baden-Baden, where Howe and Mary browbeat Mann until he agreed to taking the "water cure" for his various ailments. Each new day brought a larger dosage of water until poor Mann feared he would burst by "mere hydrostatic pressure." After a week, he abandoned it, consoling himself that it would take no more than an equal time to recover from the therapy. For a glutton or toper, a diet of the best Marienbad vintage might have been helpful, but for Mann, who ate little and drank less, the results of continued treatment might have been disastrous.[6]

After Baden-Baden, the Howes parted for Italy, not to see the Manns again for another year. Mann and Mary then traveled down the Rhine by steamboat, passing well-manicured terraced hills and storybook castles perched on magnificent vistas along the way. From here they crossed over into Holland, with its networks of canals, checkerboard fields, and herds of sleek "happy cows" as Mary described them. At Utrecht they inspected several schools and a hospital for the insane. Since Mann's guide spoke no English, the two made the best of their limited conversational Latin. It was no better for Mann at Leyden, where a certain Mr. Bodel who showed him around was both very short and hard of hearing. Try as she would, Mary could not conceal her irreverent laughter as she watched Bodel and Mann attempt to communicate. "Poor little Bodel," she reported, "was putting up his hearingest ear which was very deaf to my dear tall husband who was pouring into it very bad German." But classrooms must be visited and books and apparatus studied, so the tour went on. Before leaving this small country, Mann also looked in at

---

a MS dated July, 1843, in the Mann MSS:MHS. Although the record is in Mary Mann's handwriting, the content seems to have been that of her husband. Also see Mann to George Combe, August 25, 1843, Combe MSS:NLS.

[6] Mann to George Combe, August 25, 1843, Combe MSS:NLS; Mary Mann to Elizabeth Peabody, August 21, 1843, Mann MSS:MHS; Samuel Gridley Howe, *Journals and Letters*, ed. Laura E. Richards (Boston, 1906), I, 136–139.

schools in Haarlem and Amsterdam, happily noting that the Dutch had outlawed corporal punishment and developed superior ventilation systems, while Mary commended their *Hausfrauen* for not using featherbeds.[7]

Moving south to Brussels, the Manns had their closest brush with royalty on the entire trip. Strolling in the park in front of King Leopold's palace, they noted people gathering in expectation of the arrival of Queen Victoria and behaving, as Mary described them sarcastically, as "other *republicans* do on like occasions." Troops stood at attention and there were flags, flowers, and garlands in profusion, "cannon ready to be fired, musicators ready to musicate, and thousands of people on tip toe, or chairs toes, on fences, in trees, on houses, at windows." When the Queen finally appeared, the crowd became a mob and moved forward in a frenzy to get a closer view. Mann and Mary, caught up in a sea of moving bodies, were pushed as if by some distant pervasive inhuman force. More than a little frightened, Mary found refuge behind a tree, preferring, as she reported, "the soundness of my limbs to being squeezed to death for nothing, for I was too little to see over the heads in front of me. Even my tall husband did not catch a glimpse though he stood his ground. Then there was a hurrahing and a flourish of trumpets," she continued, "and Victoria was in the palace. They brought forth a purple carpet and an armchair which signified she was to come out on the balcony and thousands would wait for another hour and then they took in both carpet and chair. . . ."[8]

In Paris it was another whirling tour of prisons, asylums, and schools. Since Mann had letters of introduction from the Prefect of Police, almost all doors opened to him, including one jail with over 500 *"filles publiques."* In the time remaining he took in the conventional attractions, Notre Dame, the Arc de Triomphe, the Louvre, and the Jardin des Plantes. Finally he visited Versailles, clearly the most elegant place on his entire five-month itinerary. Again he was depressed by the number of military mementos and paintings which now adorned its tremendous halls. "The spirit of the whole breathes of war," he wrote, "the canvas glows with martial fire. The whole scene is red with the blood of battle. It seems to be rather a temple dedicated to Mars than the work of a civilized nation in the eight-

---

[7] Mary Mann to Elizabeth Peabody, August 21, 1843, and Mary Mann to [Elizabeth Peabody], September 10, [1843], Mann MSS:MHS.
[8] Mary Mann to [Elizabeth Peabody], September 10, [1843], Mann MSS: MHS.

eenth century. . . ." He also noted as he passed by several portraits that, phrenologically, Louis XVI had the "head of an idiot" while that of Napoleon was "magnificent." Luckily, he and Mary visited on one of the days of the *Grandes Eaux,* when the fountains were flowing in all their splendor. Walking through the gardens and seeing this gallery of mythical heroes in stone, surrounded by tritons, dolphins, and sea monsters, almost brought to life by the play of water, was an experience not quickly forgotten. The image of France that lodged in their memory the longest, however, was a foundling home in Paris. Here, mothers wishing to abandon their babies simply placed them in a crèche set into the street side of a brick wall, there to be taken in from the inside by one of the Sisters of Charity. An attendant told Mann that about 100 infants had been abandoned the previous week. The appalling thought that as many as 5,000 ill-fated children would pass through the wall in the next year agitated the humanitarian side of Mann. It was more than enough to heighten his anxiety about the future and intensify his desire to hurry back to the unfinished task in Massachusetts.[9]

A short stay in England and a tour of Ireland, in which Mann reinforced his hatred of the Church of England by noting how it was plundering this troubled land, and he was more than ready to return. As the *Britannia* left Liverpool and headed west, an intense Horace Mann stood on her decks. From what he had seen during the last months, his mission had become far more urgent than he realized. Even more disconcerting was the fact that he no longer possessed the luxury of certainty about the manifest destiny of his own country. He had met Europeans who hoped for its future but entertained grave doubts, which he now also shared. Thus William B. Hodgson, an English reformer, urged greater educational effort in the United States. Speaking of Mann's report on his European tour Hodgson would write,

God grant it may help stay the downward course of events which threatens, or as some would say *promises* to render the United States (liberty's great experiment) a warning light to all other nations! Outrages in your country fill one's heart with much deeper dismay than those committed in one's [sic] own. Here we expect these things, they are part of the old leaven of evil which we are struggling to centralize; but on the other side of the Atlantic, every breach of law or honour

---

[9] Mann, *Life,* I, 219.

tends to make British liberals lose heart and hope; while the friends of exclusive privileges, of things as they are, are proportionally emboldened.

Hodgson like others held a double standard. Given the centuries of evil from which it had grown, injustice in Europe was understandable. The United States, however, had the advantage of beginning as Eden and could maintain its innocence and liberalism. It was the hope of a better world to come. If, with such an advantage, starting without the impediments of the past, it too fell victim to militarism, exploitation, and violence, what hope was there for others? [1]

But the loss of innocence for the returning native was only one part of Mann's consternation as he thought about the events of the past five months. On a much more practical level, he struggled with himself over the issue of republican government. Was it safe to place political power in the hands of all the people? In Europe the answer was an emphatic No. While most in his own country held the opposite view, Mann himself wavered. Frequently returning to his mind were the concerns of George Combe. Using the Germans as a point of comparison, Combe had once written,

The enlightened Germans who know your country have again and again made this remark to me. "You," said they, "teach that national happiness can be reached only thro' national education, intelligence, and *morality*. The United States are trying to experiment whether this condition can be reached by placing power in the hands of the *ignorant* masses. In Germany, especially in Prussia, we are trying the experiment whether we cannot reach it sooner and with less intermediate evil by placing power in the hands of the moral and enlightened, and employing it for the enlightenment and civilization of the masses, with the view of giving them political power in proportion to their attainments in knowledge and morality! "Time," they say, "will show which plan will succeed best; but in the interim, so far as America has gone, we prefer the steady peaceful morality of our own system, to the turmoil, dishonesty and mobbish tyranny of the Americans."

Here then was the key issue. In moments of rising confidence, Mann insisted that the future was being written in America and not in Europe. Yet there were always recurring doubts, intermittently exacerbated by "the turmoil, dishonesty and mobbish tyranny" of his own countrymen. His hope, then, resided in his own version of a far more

---

[1] William B. Hodgson to Mann, December 4, 1844, Mann MSS:MHS.

organized and comprehensive system of education for the entire nation. And this meant that the future of republicanism was tied irrevocably to public education and therefore rested on him and those of like mind.[2]

[2] George Combe to Mann, July 16, 1843, Mann MSS : MHS.

CHAPTER XVII

Running a Tilt like a Mad Bull

========

CAN YOU DO anything for a brain that has not
slept for three weeks?
                                    HORACE MANN

LIFE'D NOT BE worth livin' if we didn't keep our
inimies.
                                    MR. DOOLEY

T HE VOYAGE HOME was a nightmare four times over. "We suffered four of the worst passages that have been experienced
since St. Paul's shipwreck . . ." was the way Mann described it.
The night he and Mary came across the Channel from Dieppe to
Brighton, the water was so rough that several ships were lost. It was
no better crossing the Irish Sea from Milford Haven to Waterford,
or on the return trip from Dublin to Liverpool. These three, however, were just a prelude to the final ordeal awaiting them. From
Liverpool to Halifax and Boston, the *Britannia* weathered some of
the heaviest seas in her service. Pitching and rolling, she struggled
to make headway through the mountainous waves directly in her
path while vainly attempting to hold an even keel against the mur-
derous swells crossing her course. They endured sixteen days without letup, and to Mann it seemed as if the ship was always headed
into a gale, bravely defending herself against "a heavy sea which
struck day after day like a pugilist directly into the nose of the vessel." [1]

It was almost impossible to remember that the same decks, now
nearly always awash, had been the place several months before
where he and Mary had basked in the sun and looked out across a
peaceful sea. No passengers dared go above, and for the most part
Mann stayed in his bunk, there to suffer fatigue, fight down nausea,
and endure the terrible desire just to stand once again on firm

----

[1] Mann to George Combe, April 28, 1844, Combe MSS: NLS; Mary Mann
to Elizabeth Peabody, October 31, [1843].

ground. Neither Columbus nor the Pilgrims could have viewed land more gratefully than he and Mary, as the pilot on the *Britannia* steered the ship past the outer islands and into Boston Harbor the first week in November. Always thin in comparison to most men, Mary thought Mann now looked "like a shadow even to himself" as they walked down the gangplank, but she knew the two of them faced a most sanguine future and she had no doubt but that she would soon "fatten him up." [2]

*　　*　　*

Given the burdens of the past he still carried with him, Mann could not have faced more promising domestic and public prospects. In Boston, he and Mary rented two sunny rooms in a genteel board-inghouse, and as the end of November approached, for the first time in a decade he looked forward to Thanksgiving Day. Writing to James K. Mills and thanking him for the numerous times he had spent the holiday with Mills and his wife, Mann added, "I am taking my happiness now in another way, but I shall think of you both *gratefully and affectionately.*" [3]

The normal schools were thriving. Thomas Robbins no doubt expressed the view of many who visited the institution at Lexington when he observed, "I think it is the best school I have ever been in." Although Samuel J. May was about to leave, Mann understood that Cyrus Peirce, having successfully integrated the schools on Nan-tucket, was ready to return and "do some good for the cause." Equally cheering was the news that Henry Barnard was dissatisfied with his work in Rhode Island and had reopened the question of moving to Massachusetts and taking over one of the normal schools. Realizing he had missed a golden opportunity in not getting Barnard to come two years before, Mann wrote to James K. Mills asking for enough money to get a normal school under way in Springfield. "Could Mr. B. have been supplied with the means of conducting the school on a large as scale as he desired," Mann reminded Mills, "he would have undertaken it, and before this time, instead of an addled egg, we should have had a good chicken, herself to lay eggs soon." And he continued, "I wish our wealthy men could realize what condi-tion they and their's will be in, with the power in the hands of the

---

[2] Mary Mann to Sophia Hawthorne, November 6, 1843, Berg MSS:NYPL.
[3] Mary Mann to Rebecca Pennell, January 31, 1844; Mann to James K. Mills, November 29, 1843, both in Mann MSS:MHS.

people, and that people partly ignorant and partly wicked,—which will be worse than if they were all ignorant or all wicked. . . . Now I say the real insurance offices are the School Houses, provided you have a good *actuary* in each and not a jackass." [4]

Above and beyond this, Mann was now the possessor of sheaves of notes on every kind of European educational institution. From these he believed he could fashion a blueprint for the schools of tomorrow. In his mind, it was not only possible, but necessary, to graft the best of what he had seen especially in Scotland and Germany onto his own robust native republican institutions. Upon his return, he was struck by the frequency with which he heard his countrymen speak of their nation's destiny. For Mann, this perception of the future was too passive and fatalistic. How much better if, instead of thinking of their destiny, men should think of their mission. For Mann, the chief means to his own self-conceived goals were the common schools and the chief ends were educated men and women who understood the laws of nature and acted wisely according to them. "It is thro' a knowledge of these laws," he wrote to Combe, "that the individual can be brought into harmony with the universe; and that the progress of the race can be placed upon a secure basis." To help mankind live according to the laws of nature was his purpose, and few men have believed they could achieve so much with so little and in so little time. Considering what was possible with a single normal school, Mann wrote to Mills, "If I had a few thousand dollars I know I could, very perceptively hasten the millennium. God having time enough on his own hands lets these things drag along strangely; but I confess I am so constituted that I feel in a hurry." Progress and human perfectibility were undeniably part of a providential plan. He had simply arrogated to himself the task of accelerating the agenda of the Almighty. [5]

And finally, there was one other positive factor in his future whose development would move along at its own pace, regardless of how impatient Mann became of its slow, steady progress. Mary was "in a family way" and expecting the "blessed event" about the end of February. [6]

---

[4] Robbins, *Diary*, II, 714–715; Cyrus Peirce to Mann, November 12, 1843; Mann to James K. Mills, November 29, 1843, both in Mann MSS:MHS. The account of the integration of the schools on Nantucket is found in the *Liberator*, June 9, 1843.

[5] Mann to George Combe, April 28, 1844, Combe MSS:NLS; Mann to James K. Mills, November 21, 1843, Mann MSS:MHS.

[6] Sophia Hawthorne to Mary Mann, December 10, 1843, and Mary Mann

*   *   *

Once the six months' accumulation of mail was cleared from his desk, Mann and Mary retreated to Wrentham where he quickly immersed himself in the writing of his *Seventh Annual Report*. Mary meanwhile busied herself, sewing pieces for the new baby's layette. In the past, his *Reports* had presented statistics, outlined priorities among educational needs, and offered a common sense and moralistic rationale for public education. Each *Report* in turn had been followed by new piecemeal legislation and a tightening up of school committee procedures affecting textbook purchases, schoolhouse repairs, the consolidation of districts, and the exercise of a little more discrimination in the hiring of next year's teachers. He intended the *Seventh Report* to be different. "I desire to make it impulsive," he wrote to Combe, "in regard to the educational movement in my own country." Mann's European experience had given a new urgency to his tasks and forced him to think of his work in more long-range, even apocalyptic terms.[7]

Many another proud American traveler returning from the grand tour at the time would have agreed with Mary Mann when she wrote, "Right glad we are that America with all its youthful faults is our native land—without being blind to these we see its advantages over those time burdened nations whose evils so much time will be necessary to cure that by the eye of faith is that cure discernable." It was not so easy for her husband. Begrudgingly, he conceded the institution of liberty to England, but he insisted the remainder of its trinity was aristocracy and poverty. In Prussia he found autocracy, educational *égalité*, and a nationalistic form of fraternity. Both countries, then, as they worked towards a better future, carried with them a burden bequeathed by the dead hand of the past. Was it possible, however, with all their impediments, that by increased attention to education they actually could surpass the United States; or could his own country, with its rawness, vulgarity, and lack of sophistication, achieve the millennium first, without passing through the monarchical and ecclesiastical purgatories so evident in European history? Of this he was anything but certain. And George Combe, who wrote to him just as he was wrestling with the problem, shared his doubts.

to Sophia Hawthorne, February 22, 1844, both in Berg MSS:NYPL; Sophia Hawthorne to Mary Mann, January 30, 1844, Mann MSS:MHS.
[7] Mann to George Combe, August 25, 1843, Combe MSS:NLS.

"The Prussian and Saxon Governments by means of their schools, and their just laws, and rational public administration . . . are doing a good deal to bring their people into a rational and moral condition," said Combe, and continued,

. . . it is pretty obvious to thinking men that a few years more of this cultivation will lead to the development of free Institutions in Germany and that if it should then turn out that a people educated into freedom by despotisms, surpasses in all the higher elements of wisdom and virtue and consequently in happiness a people who have been the architects of their own freedom and fortunes, the cause of democracy will be disgraced and that of humanity degraded, because the principle will be evolved and strengthened, that nations, like children, must be governed and nurtured into maturity by powerful and enlightened orders, and cannot be trusted, safely, to themselves, to find their own way to general enjoyment.

Perhaps it was Prussia and not the United States which held the scepter for the future. Such a fearful prospect Mann refused to contemplate. Instead, he held to the belief that with a system of public education in many ways similar to that in Prussia, the triumph of republicanism was still possible. Without public education, he believed his nation ever teetered on the edge of political anarchy.[8]

Having seen European schools superior to those in Massachusetts, Mann believed it necessary to tell the truth, even if the truth hurt. That he only saw a few in operation was only a minor hindrance. He would interpolate where hard facts were missing and go on to extrapolate an educational prescription for Massachusetts and the rest of the nation. There were some items in short supply on both sides of the Atlantic. In Europe as in Massachusetts, one all too rarely found a single desk for each pupil. Instead, most children were forced to perch on long backless benches, so high from the floor that the smaller pupils' legs and feet dangled. Mann did report a few exceptional schools, large enough to be "uniformly divided into classrooms" with an entire room "appropriated to each class so that there is no interruption of one class with another." He also noted the exemplary practice in Prussia of providing each child with a slate and pencil.[9]

---

[8] Mary Mann to Elizabeth Peabody, October 31, 1843, Mann MSS:MHS; George Combe to Mann, November 14, 1843, Combe MSS:NLS.
[9] Mann, *Seventh Annual Report of the Secretary of the Board* (Boston, 1844), pp. 48 and 86.

On the basis of what he had seen, Mann made a special case for changes in the teaching of reading. Criticizing the standard American practice of beginning by memorizing the names of the alphabet and then learning to read two- and three-letter combinations, he urged his readers to consider the merits of beginning reading by teaching entire words. "I am satisfied," he wrote, "that our greatest error in teaching children to read, lies in beginning with the alphabet;—in giving them what are called the 'Names of the Letters,' *a, b, c, & d*. How can a child to whom nature offers such a profusion of beautiful objects,—of sights and sounds and colors . . . how can such a child be expected to turn with delight from all these to the stiff and lifeless column of the alphabet?" Instead, children should be taught entire words and only gradually concern themselves with the sounds of small combinations of letters, "so that the sound of a regular word of four letters is divided into four parts; and a recombination of sounds of letters makes the sound of the word." Thus Mann urged the word method with a growing dependency on what he called *"phonics,"* a concept he intended to popularize, and he despaired of improving the teaching of reading until the teachers had mastered the techniques.[1]

It was evident that most of the positive descriptions in his *Report* came from the Prussian schools. Marvelous and harmonious as this ordered and systematic creation was, the *deus ex machina* was the well-trained teacher. Intelligent, efficient, and loyal, he was the product of the *Lehrerseminarien*, where he studied subject matter and pedagogy for three years and became convinced of the nobility of his calling. Not every teacher candidate succeeded. In the process, misfits were culled from each annual crop, for the Prussians were as efficient in training teachers as they were in training military officers, both being deemed essential for achieving political supremacy in Europe. The fact that seminary students had been recruited from the lower classes, were considered inferior to those who studied at the university, and were forever barred from teaching in the *Gymnasia* or preparatory schools for the Prussian upper-middle class and aristocracy did not seem to bother Mann. What impressed him was that they became far more competent and committed to their profession than all but the most select of American teachers.[2]

Once in the classroom, they taught without a textbook in hand.

---

[1] *Seventh Annual Report,* pp. 91–99.
[2] *Seventh Annual Report,* pp. 129–136.

Their lessons were well prepared and they made good use of blackboards, maps, globes, and other learning devices. By their exemplary conduct, they injected an enthusiasm into teaching which was obviously contagious. Mann was amazed at the absence of emulation as a crutch for motivating study, but what impressed him the most was the fact that the Prussian teachers were so well trained in managing their classrooms that corporal punishment, that mainstay of the American teacher, was virtually nonexistent. Apparently, a respect for the authority of the teacher, drilled into German children from early childhood on, and the satisfaction they gained from knowing that their learning would someday be put to serve the nation, were ample motivation.

This is not to say that all was meritorious across the Rhine. Mann acknowledged that students indoctrinated with an unquestioning loyalty to the Prussian Kaiser were hardly free-thinking individuals. But this was a minor ill, endemic in a despotic nation, and easily remedied in a republican society. "If the Prussian schoolmaster," Mann argued,

has better methods of teaching reading, writing, grammar, geography, arithmetic, &c., so that in half the time, he produces greater and better results, surely, we may copy his modes of teaching these elements without adopting his notions of passive obedience to government, or of blind adherence to the articles of a church.

Since by "the ordinance of nature," he continued, "the human faculties are substantially the same all over the world . . . the best means for their development and growth in one place, must be substantially the best for their development and growth everywhere." The heart of his *Seventh Annual Report* contained the message that the United States had fallen behind the Prussians in education, and in order to catch up and move ahead, it was now mandatory to create a truly professional corps of teachers, produce a systematic curriculum, and develop a more centralized and efficient supervision of the schools. The Prussians offered a model in practicality and efficiency which his own countrymen would be well advised to follow. This was his prescription and he desperately hoped it would be accepted while there was still time.[3]

---

[3] *Seventh Annual Report*, p. 22 and *passim*.

*　　*　　*

The copy of his *Report* sent to the printer, Mann attempted to fulfill a number of lecture engagements before the baby was due. He stopped at Concord where his sister-in-law, Sophia Hawthorne, received him as if he were a combination of dignitary and invalid. She and Hawthorne dispatched a sleigh from the Old Manse to the station so that Mann would "not be chilled by the long walk." When he arrived, she served him a supper of cooked apples, milk, "syrup boiled to put in his hot watter [sic]," and currant jelly. Unfortunately, there was no "dyspepsia bread" available in Concord, so Mann had to settle for graham crackers and "simple gingerbread." Worrying that he could not keep warm in a bedroom heated only by an open fireplace, Sophia set up a cot in Hawthorne's study and transformed it into "a sweet little bedroom." For all of this, neither she nor Hawthorne attended the lecture, the pregnant Sophia explaining later to Mary that "I never have been out in the evening, and Mr. Hawthorne would not leave me to hear Paul preach at this time. . . ." From Concord, Mann carried the common school gospel to New Hampshire, or what he preferred to call "Missionary ground . . . coming next after the Fiji Islands." Then hurrying back south, he returned to Boston, resolving not to leave Mary's side until the baby arrived.[4]

Horace Mann, Junior, was born February 24, and like many another mortal father, Horace Mann, Senior, rejoiced "that the child is perfect." It was not an easy birth. Mary was bedridden for more than a month and Mann later described her suffering as "fearful." As news of the event moved from friend to friend, Mann accepted congratulations, but refused himself the twin indulgences of satisfaction and happiness. Instead, he nursed a morbid worry that Horace, Junior, might be a failure. Deciding to keep a journal of his son's development, he catalogued all the moral mishaps which might lie in his way. Only when he had put such a list of grim imponderables to paper did the new father consider himself justified in experiencing nothing "but a dubious and trembling joy."[5]

---

[4] Sophia Hawthorne to Mary Mann, January 30, 1844; Mann to James K. Mills, November 29, 1843, both in Mann MSS:MHS; Sophia Hawthorne to Mary Mann, [February 7, 1844]; Mary Mann to Sophia Hawthorne, February 22, 1844, both in Berg MSS:NYPL.

[5] Horace Mann, MS journal of the first four years of Horace Mann, Jr., HCL (hereafter, Mann, Journal of Horace Mann, Jr.). Mann also fretted

So intent was Mann on the baby's future that some time elapsed before he noticed that, once again, he and the Board had been attacked in the press. In an unsigned article in the *Christian Witness,* the official organ of the Massachusetts Episcopal diocese, an anonymous author had asked wherein Mann's advocacy of non-sectarian religious instruction in the public schools differed in any way from Stephen Girard's bequest to establish an orphanage and school in Philadelphia. Deriving his plan from Tom Paine's *Age of Reason* and Constantin, Comte de Volney's *Views of Religion,* Girard expressly had prohibited the teaching of religion in his school and even forbade the presence of clergymen within its buildings. Implying that Mann had the same malice aforethought, the attacker also criticized the Board for establishing its own brand of godless sectarianism. To Mann's query about the identity of the author, Mark de Wolfe Howe, *Witness* editor, replied that he was a "highly respectable" man who "would not misrepresent the facts." For the moment, Mann might have ignored the matter, had he not learned that the writer was none other than his old enemy, Edward A. Newton, who had again surfaced. Then to heap fuel on the conflict, Howe himself actively became involved, publishing three editorials in support of Newton.[6]

When one examines the exact nature of the controversy, it is evident that Newton and Howe had several axes to grind. First, they claimed that Mann and the Board, under the guise of carrying out the mandates of the School Law of 1827 which forbade the use of sectarian textbooks, had promulgated a system of instruction almost identical to that outlined in Stephen Girard's will. Although the law had been passed ten years before, it was not until Mann came to his post that there was a de facto prohibition of church doctrine and organization in the classroom. Secondly, Newton maintained that instruction in anything less than evangelical doctrines in a predominantly orthodox community was a form of sectarianism. Going beyond this and accurately anticipating the future, he predicted that

---

about the shape of his son's head. From a phrenological interpretation there were indications of "great firmness & self esteem," but Mann hoped "his head will alter."

[6] Mark DeWolfe Howe to Mann, February 27, 1844, Mann MSS:MHS; [Edward A. Newton], "Christian Education," February 23, 1844; [Mark DeWolfe Howe], "The System of Public Education in Massachusetts," March 8, 1844; "Christian Education," March 15, 1844; "The Bible in the Schools," March 29, 1844; all in the *Christian Witness and Church Advocate.*

the day would come when the "Papists" would press their position and insist that the Protestant translation of the Bible was sectarian and could not be used in the schools. And thirdly, Newton attempted to breathe new life into the moribund contention of the majority report of the 1840 legislative Committee on Education that the Board was "wholly useless and burdensome as a State institution." [7]

Now itching to give these two devils their due, Mann demanded that Howe publish his three rebuttals of Newton's charges. Howe published the first, but refused to do the same with the second and third, while continuing to open his columns to Newton. Mann then went to the Boston *Daily Courier*.[8] In his responses, Mann pointed out that unlike Girard College, five of the eight members of the Board were clergymen, and of these, three were orthodox. He also noted the hundreds of ministers of every denomination serving on school committees. To the accusation that he and the Board were infiltrating the schools with their own version of religious instruction, Mann presented some significant facts about the state of religious instruction prior to his coming to office:

In nine eastern counties of the State, containing more than five eighths of its population, the teaching of the Assembly's Catechism and of Orthodox doctrines, had been, not entirely, but mainly discontinued, long before the existence of the Board. The Catechism had been objected to by the Orthodox Baptists themselves. In many places, the discontinuance dates back, at least, to the beginning of the present century. I have met with many persons, educated in our schools, who never saw the Assembly's Catechism. So convinced was public sentiment of the equity and justice of the law of 1827, against sectarian teaching in the schools, that in all the common school conventions I have ever attended, in almost all of which the subject of moral and religious instruction has been introduced, there has been but one instance where such teaching was advocated; and there it was resisted on the spot by an Orthodox clergyman.

---

[7] For a more complete analysis of the religious issues in the controversy, see Raymond B. Culver, *Horace Mann and Religion in the Massachusetts Public Schools* (New Haven, 1929), pp. 181–188.

[8] Horace Mann, "To the Editor of the *Christian Witness* . . . ," *Christian Witness and Church Advocate*, March 29, 1844; Mann, "Common Schools and the *Christian Witness*," and "Our Common Schools," Boston *Daily Courier*, April 9 and May 29, 1844; Mann to Nahum Capen, n.d., [ca. March, 1844], Mann MSS:BUA.

And he added that in the thousand or more school committee reports filed in his office, all but two supported his position.[9]

Not willing to let the matter rest here, Mann's friends also raised their pens in his support. One of them roundly castigated Newton and Howe in three installments in the *Courier* entitled "No Schools Without a Bishop." "T.P.," probably Theodore Parker, lent his virile quill to the cause in the Boston *Daily Advertiser*, and other articles appeared in the *Bay State Democrat*, Worcester *National Aegis*, Westfield *Newsletter*, Salem *Observer*, and *New England Puritan*. Equally significant was the unsolicited support from S. M. Burnside, who was considered the "father of the bill" which became the School Law of 1827. Writing in the *National Aegis*, Burnside explained that at the time his committee met some seventeen years before, already then they had assumed that no "doctrines of dogmatic theology had been taught in our schools for many years," thus putting the lie to Newton's contention that Mann had forced his own interpretation of the law onto the schools. By the end of the summer, the *Common School Controversy*—a compendium of newspaper articles by Newton, Howe, Mann, and others—was published with the net effect of underscoring the strength of Mann's position. At worst, Newton and Howe were reactionary ecclesiastical troublemakers; at best, they were gadflies on the rump of an incipient educational establishment. In either case, Mann and his lieutenants had thought it necessary to bring their heaviest artillery to bear on them.[1]

Why did Mann expend so much of his limited time and energy on such small fry? Somehow, he could never emancipate his mind from a conspiracy and persecution complex when even the slightest opposition to him appeared in print. Besides the almost unanimous

---

[9] Horace Mann, *et al.*, *The Common School Controversy; Consisting of Three Letters of the Secretary of the Board of Education, of the State of Massachusetts, in reply to Charges Preferred against the Board, by the Editor of the Christian Witness and by Edward A. Newton, Esq., of Pittsfield, Once a Member of the Board; to which are added Extracts from the Daily Press, in Regard to the Controversy* (Boston, 1844), p. 26.
[1] Mann to Nahum Capen, n.d., [March, 1844], Mann MSS:BUA; Watchman, [pseud., William B. Fowle], "No Schools Without a Bishop," Boston *Daily Courier*, March 12 and 30, and April 16, 1844; T.P. [Theodore Parker?], "Mr. Mann's Letter to the *Christian Witness*," Boston *Daily Advertiser*, April 8, 1844; Worcester *National Aegis*, February 21, 1827, April 3, and May 29, 1844; Salem *Observer*, April 13, 1844; Westfield *Newsletter*, April 12, 1844; *Bay State Democrat*, May 24, 1844; *New England Puritan*, June 5, 1844; Mann, *et al.*, *Common School Controversy* . . . (Boston, 1844), *passim*.

support he had from the press, he himself admitted that "the best portion of the orthodox" were with him, as were "almost all the other denominations," and "even the great mass of Episcopalians themselves." Yet despite all this evidence to the contrary, he was convinced "that an extensive conspiracy" had been formed "to break down the Board of Education as a preliminary measure to teaching sectarianism in the schools." Moreover, he took these attacks personally as well, and could complain to George Combe that "the orthodox have hunted me this winter as though they were bloodhounds and I a poor rabbit."

Six months before, he had worked on his *Seventh Annual Report,* believing he was preparing the guidelines for the Massachusetts school system of the future. Now he was embroiled in a battle over picayune questions he thought had been answered at the end of his controversy with Frederick Packard. Sometime early in the summer, he slipped into a state of depression, probably the first since his marriage. Believing himself alone and the singular object of attack, at the very moment when men from all over the state were rallying to his side, he confided to James Mills that he was ready to quit.

Can you, without saying a word for me—not a word—talk with Ned [Edward Loring], and [George] Hillard and G. B. Emerson, and see whether they don't think it is best for me to retire,—not to give up the ship, but take away the target. As it is, I am worked and worried to death. Many nights I hardly get any sleep, and the absence of sleep is not far from insanity.

Weary, disappointed, and embittered, he had come to the painful conclusion that he might be a liability to the cause.[2]

*   *   *

Had this been the only controversy during 1844, Mann might have relinquished his secular mitre to someone such as George B. Emerson. But the dispute with Newton was to be merely a rough channel crossing compared with the tempest he was next to weather. Soon to be buffeted by the accusations of thirty-one Boston schoolmasters, a self-anointed élite among the teachers of Massachusetts, Mann found it necessary to remain at his post and vindicate himself

---

[2] Mann to George Combe, April 28, July 30, and December 1, 1844, Combe MSS:NLS; Mann to James Mills, May 22, 1844, Mann MSS:MHS.

and his *Seventh Report*. Ironically, by attacking the man they considered their persecutor, the masters closed off a retreat that Mann was seeking and forced him to remain as their embattled antagonist.

During the late spring and early summer, there was little to foretell the gathering storm. His *Report* was well received and the list of persons from Massachusetts sending him accolades read like a Who's Who in government and education. Mann also received approving letters from other states and from as far away as England, Scotland, and Italy.[3] During the summer, Mann got wind of some local rumblings against his *Report*, but it was not until September that a committee of the Association of Masters of the Boston Public Schools made their bitter disagreement with him manifest with the publication of *Remarks on the Seventh Annual Report of the Hon. Horace Mann*. For the last six years, these respected masters had detached themselves from Mann's annual critique of Massachusetts education, wanting to believe that each of his strictures carried an implicit "excepting the schools and teachers of Boston." But Mann had never made this explicit, and each year they felt themselves pressed closer on target. With the *Seventh Annual Report*, they could not but believe that his shafts were now directed at them. Finally moved to defend themselves, they fought back with a vehemence more typical of a blood feud, marshaling every verbal weapon of invective and scorn available, heretofore employed only upon their hapless pupils. Taking the paranoid posture that Mann intended the *Report* to be a covert slur on their professional reputations, the masters felt compelled to refute not a few but every one of his observations and common-sense recommendations for better

---

[3] For examples of individual responses to Mann's *Report*, see Robert Winthrop to Mann, March 28, 1844; Abbott Lawrence to Mann, March 28, 1844; Josiah Holbrook to Mann, July 11, 1844; William C. Woodbridge to Mann, June 2, 1844; and Edward Everett to Mann, July 10, 1844, all in Mann MSS:MHS. The only substantive critical correspondence seems to have come from Reverend Thomas Hopkins Gallaudet. In his report, Mann reported as superior the teaching of the deaf by lip reading rather than by sign language. The method was largely untried in the United States, and was viewed by Gallaudet and others as unworkable, but Mann persisted in his views, getting additional information from Germany and Holland. See Thomas H. Gallaudet to Mann, May 13, 1844; George Varrentrappe [Frankfort] to Mann, September 13, 1844; Charles Vogel [Leipzig] to Mann, September 13, 1844; and K. Sybrandi [Haarlem, Holland] to Mann, September 22, 1844, all in Mann MSS:MHS; Mann to Henry Barnard, May 15, 1844, Barnard MSS:NYU; William Willard to Thomas H. Gallaudet, July 1, 1844, Gallaudet MSS:LOC.

teacher training, increased motivation for learning, and the abolition of corporal punishment. That their detractor was an outsider
who had never earned his stripes in the classroom only heightened
their need to castigate him in the public press.[4]

It was high time, they said, to "correct erroneous impressions."
What these were, they spelled out in a document of some 150 pages.
In the first of the four sections, they belittled the normal schools as
propaganda agencies for Mann's "hot bed theories, in which the pro-
jectors have disregarded experience and observation." *Inter alia*, the
masters denounced Mann's desire to remove "all fear, emulation,
and punishments" from the classroom, sniggered at his espousal of
phrenology, and insisted that through his glaring misrepresenta-
tions, he had attempted to excite the prejudices of the ignorant with
a denigration of the Boston schools as abusive and unfounded as the
acerbic judgments on American society of Mrs. Trollope.

In a second section, they challenged Mann's observations on
the Prussian schools. Defending their own textbook recitation
method of teaching, they conceded that while the "oral method" in
which the teacher actively taught excited the interest of the learner,
they insisted that the net result of this was to vitiate the pupil's potential for "forming the habit of independent and individual effort."
Their third section contained a critique of Mann's advocacy of the
"word method" in teaching reading and their own defense of the
"abcderian" approach. And finally they dismissed Mann's belief that
interest was a better motivation to learning than fear as dangerous
sentimental nonsense. "Duty," the masters insisted, "should come
first, and pleasure should grow out of the discharge of it." Thus they
defended corporal punishment. To abolish it was to invite the destruction of authority in the classroom and, with it, the corruption of
the morals of the young. Such were the four main attacks contained
in the *Remarks*, but reading between the lines, it was evident that
Mann's real sin was to have had the temerity to challenge an educational establishment of long standing. While the last two decades
had witnessed a growing chorus of disenchantment with schoolteachers in Massachusetts, the Boston masters had remained beyond
the reach of criticism. Now that he had broken their taboo, they

---

[4] William B. Fowle to Mann, July 11, 1844, and George B. Emerson to
Mann, July 16, 1844, both in Mann MSS:MHS; *Remarks on the Seventh
Annual Report of the Hon. Horace Mann, Secretary of the Massachusetts
Board of Education* (Boston, 1844).

would see that Mann paid the penalty of public exposure for his indiscretion.[5]

No doubt the motivations of several of the masters were honest, but for the most, they were base and self-seeking. Even a man as moderate as George B. Emerson conceded that "there was some talent, a vast deal of ignorance, and an infinity of self-sufficiency among them." Mann characteristically lumped them all together in one villainous conspiracy. Writing to Theodore Parker with typical volatile rhetoric, he described the *Remarks* as ". . . begotten, conceived, gestated, born, nurtured in disappointed self-esteem." For him, the only question remaining was what modes he should use for their total annihilation.[6]

Some among Mann's associates advised him to turn the other cheek, believing the reactionary *Remarks* contained their own refutation. Even as mercurial a person as Charles Sumner advised "Moderation!"[7] As late as the middle of September, Mann reported to Parker that he was "not yet determined what to do, but shall be governed by my friends. . . ." But he made his decision inevitable by seeking advice only from a small circle of associates he knew were bruising for a fight. One also should not overlook the strong influence of Mary Mann, who easily assumed the righteous indignation of an Old Testament prophet when she believed an attack upon one of her family was unjust. Thus, predisposed to return an eye for an eye, the only question before Mann was the intensity of his response. "Would you keep all destructiveness out," he asked Howe, "or would you let in a sardonic touch of it now and then, just to keep folks from yawning over my reply?" In any case, he added, he would make certain "who shall be Mordecai and who Haman." Actually, in terms of public opinion, it would have been better for Mann, now considered something of an educational giant, to remain aloof from the entire affair, and let Howe, Parker, and George B. Emerson deal

---

[5] For a discussion of Mann's position on the teaching of reading, see Nila Banton Smith, *American Reading Instruction* (Newark, Del., 1965), pp. 74–82.
[6] George B. Emerson to Mann, July 16, 1844, Mann MSS:MHS; Mann to Theodore Parker, September 18, 1844, Parker Letterbook, 11, MHS.
[7] A year later, when Sumner himself had become embroiled in controversy, Mann wrote to him, "When aggression is not violent, and immediate danger does not demand immediate resistance, propose mediation. I agree to all that. Take every step possible to avert so great a calamity; but if all proves unavailing, then I cannot refrain from saying FIGHT!" Mann to Charles Sumner, September 8, 1845, Sumner MSS:HCL.

with these pygmies. Henry Barnard and Francis Bowen (editor of the *North American Review*) both thought so. Bowen believed that

the cause will do well enough, and Mr. Mann will long enjoy his triumph, if his more ardent and uncompromising friends will not insist on his stooping his head, shutting his eyes, and running a tilt like a mad bull, against the Boston schools and prejudices of two thirds of the population of the city. He has too many enemies already. . . .

And there were others. But Mann thought both he and the cause had been unjustly attacked. Impatient at how slowly the mills of God ground out justice, he believed it necessary to facilitate the process so that his accusers be answered and punished immediately after their crimes.[8]

He received some support in the newspapers and a good deal more from George B. Emerson's *Observations,* a scathing attack on the masters, setting them off as the educational antediluvians they were. He also received unexpected support of a kind from within a separate wing of the Boston schools. The Primary School Board, upset by the masters' claims that the products of their schools had not been taught to read properly, bluntly stated that the masters were in error. In the previous six years, not one of their graduates had been refused admission to the grammar schools because of reading deficiencies.[9]

By the middle of November, the *Reply* was out, and even a superficial perusal of its 176 pages gave the reader to understand that

[8] Charles Sumner to Samuel Gridley Howe, September 11, 1844, in Pierce, *Memoir and Letters of Charles Sumner,* II, 319; Mann to Theodore Parker, September 18, 1844, Parker Letterbook, 11, MHS; Mann to Samuel Gridley Howe, September 25, 1844; Henry Barnard to Mann, December 7, 1844, both in Mann MSS:MHS; Francis Bowen to Charles Sumner, December 19, 1844, Sumner MSS:HCL.

Some indication of the degree of wrath possible from Mary Mann can be found in her response to the treatment of northern prisoners in Confederate prisons: "I have hoped that our government would cull out from our prisoners of war the most valuable officers, man for man if necessary, a lesser number of that would answer the purpose, and shoot or hang them." Mary Mann to Ethan Allen Hitchcock, November 18, 1863, Hitchcock MSS:LOC.

[9] Luther [pseud.], "The Schoolmaster's Review of Mr. Mann's Report," Boston *Daily Courier,* September 24, 1844; George B. Emerson, *Observations on a Pamphlet, entitled "Remarks on the Seventh Annual Report of the Hon. Horace Mann, Secretary of the Massachusetts Board of Education"* (n.p., n.d.); *Report of the Special Committee of the Primary School Board on a Portion of the Remarks of the Grammar Masters* (Boston, 1844).

Mann was here the polemicist, caustic, scornful, and severe. Although decrying the masters' use of corporal punishment on their pupils, Mann poured out a verbal punishment upon them, believing this was certainly a time when it was better to give than to receive. That in the process he might build a large reservoir of bitterness against him, not easily dissipated in the future, was a risk he willingly took.[1]

The masters, he insisted, had imposed the most reactionary practices upon children out of a selfish defense of their own vested interests. They based discipline upon unquestioned authority, physical force, and the creation of a perpetual fear of pain. In place of this he proposed the promptings of duty, affection, and a love of knowledge. In short, he was urging more teaching and less flogging. After defending each of his observations and insisting his conclusions were the only possible ones valid, he closed his *Reply* with a catalogue of achievements he and the Board had to their credit. Pontifical and adamant as he was, Mann believed this stance was his prerogative as the bearer of righteousness and the defender of justice.

At this point, two of the masters considered the heat too intense and withdrew. The twenty-nine remaining worked day and night, scrutinizing each of Mann's statements for even the most petty inaccuracies. In less than two months, they produced a document of over 200 pages entitled *Rejoinder to the "Reply" of the Hon. Horace Mann; Secretary of the Massachusetts Board of Education, to the "Remarks" of the Association of Boston Masters, upon His Seventh Annual Report*.[2] Along with a good deal of nitpicking, they restated their previous arguments, although this time recasting them in a generally more subdued tone. On the subject of corporal punishment, however, they refused to give any ground. Since children were innately evil, they must be taught to obey. "All authority is of God and must be obeyed." When this authority, delegated to the teacher, was resisted by pupils, as was often the case, physical compulsion was necessary—so reasoned Joseph Hale, the author of the last section.

Mann did not have his *Answer* to the *"Rejoinder"* to the *Reply* to

---

[1] Nahum Capen to Henry Barnard, October 24, 1844, Barnard MSS:NYU; Horace Mann, *Reply to the "Remarks" of the thirty-one Boston Schoolmasters on the Seventh Annual Report of the Secretary of the Massachusetts Board of Education* (Boston, 1844).
[2] (Boston, 1845).

the *Remarks* ready until the summer of 1845. Finally off the press, it was an attempt to refute their arguments while defending his own. Once again, he also questioned their motives, while exhibiting his own growing impatience, exasperation, and weariness as the battle of words dragged on. By this time, he was finding less gratification in imposing his terrible verbal severity and merciless punishment on his opponents. Words and arguments became increasingly hollow, and each succeeding pamphlet seemed an unsatisfying echo of the one before it.[3]

In part, this was due to the protracted length of the debate; in part it was also due to the fact that he had come upon more effective means than mere words for wreaking revenge upon the masters. While continuing his public ridicule of them, he pushed forward his plans to purge them from the schools. If some of his lieutenants could be elected to the Boston School Committee and gain a majority there, a thorough housecleaning was possible. Having recently returned from his European tour, Samuel Gridley Howe was anxious to enter one of the races, and replied to Mann that "Now is the time for your friends to come to your aid, and I for one will do what little I can. . . . Now if you will show me how to work I will do it." At a stormy Whig convention, both Howe and Sumner were nominated. And in the subsequent election, Sumner was defeated but Howe won, as did other men favorable to reform, including Theophilus Parsons, later to become a prominent Harvard law professor; Reverend Rollin H. Neale, a Baptist; William Brigham, an attorney; Reverend Harris C. Graves, editor of the *Christian Reflector;* and Reverend James I. T. Collidge, a Unitarian. Although not constituting a majority on the committee of twenty-four, their numbers together with Howe's uninhibited penchant for confrontation served notice on the masters that they were in for no small amount of trouble in the coming year.[4]

The reformers' chance came the following May, when Howe, Parsons, and Neale were appointed to conduct the annual examination of the grammar schools. Previously more ceremonial than evaluative, this year the procedure was in for revisions from top to bottom, the most notable of these being an insistence by Howe that in

[3] *Answer to the "Rejoinder" of Twenty-nine Schoolmasters, Part of the "Thirty-one" Who Published "Remarks" on the Seventh Annual Report of the Secretary of Massachusetts Board of Education* (Boston, 1845).
[4] Mann to Samuel Gridley Howe, October 8 and 19, 1844, Mann MSS: MHS; Samuel Gridley Howe to Mann, October 9, 1844, Howe MSS:HCL; Boston *Advertiser,* December 12, 1844.

place of oral questioning the students would be required to take standardized written tests. Now aware of the nature of the attack from the reformers, the masters petitioned the mayor that Howe be removed from the committee, but he refused to interfere. All summer, the three men conducted what amounted to a whirlwind investigation whose outcome was surely foreordained. Beginning early in the morning, as if armed with a search warrant, each man swooped down unexpectedly on a school and administered examinations the committee had written and privately printed. To be sure that the master in one school did not disclose the contents of the test to another, all schools were tested on the same subject on the same day. Since there were nineteen schools to cover, each man raced from school to school. In order to establish some comparative validity for their instrument, Rollin Neale also traveled to Roxbury, Hartford, and New York, where he administered the same examinations.[5]

The result of all this was a sweeping indictment of the entire grammar school system and especially its teachers. Howe claimed the masters were helpless without their textbooks. The mental faculty they cultivated the most was the pupil's memory. The main learning activity was the drill. To make things worse, children memorized wrong answers and made repeated mistakes in grammar, punctuation, and spelling. They had been trained to mouth answers to questions from texts, but they had not been taught to think, they could not organize material other than as it appeared in their books, they could not deduce original conclusions, and they had learned few of the cognitive skills important to higher levels of intellectual activity. Composition had become an ossified grammar, poetry the parsing of phrases, and arithmetic the transposition of different numbers into set formulas or recipes for "doing problems." Howe's report also urged the appointment of a full-time salaried superintendent over the schools and the abolition of the dual master system where one teacher taught writing and another English and other subjects. But most important was his plea for abandoning corporal punishment. In school after school, he had found evidence of whippings and floggings, in one case, a master admitting to more than fifty instances of corporal punishment in a single week! It was time to place the birch rod in a museum of Americana and resort to more

---

[5] Mann to Samuel Gridley Howe, May 7 and June 20, 1845, Mann MSS: MHS; Samuel Gridley Howe to Mann, May 8 and September, 1845, Howe MSS:HCL; Mann to Samuel J. May, July 4, 1845, in Mann, *Life*, 238–239.

humane measures for the motivation of learning. For Mann, the report was a "pile of thunderbolts" exceeding in size that available to Jupiter. Reading it, one could not escape the conclusion that "children could learn, if the teachers had taught." [6]

The Boston *Atlas* called the report "masterly," while the Boston *Times,* defending the masters, labeled it a "libel on our schools by its errors and mis-statements." But its real impact could only be measured with the redesignation of the masters. Largely automatic heretofore, and based on seniority, this year there was to be an upheaval if Howe had his way. In this he was only partially successful. Of the thirty-one, four were removed and a larger number transferred. Less than what he had hoped for, Mann nevertheless thought it was "a work, which, twelve months ago, would have been deemed as impossible as to turn four Peers out of the British House of Lords." In addition, the use of corporal punishment, while still legal, was drastically reduced. A superintendent was appointed five years later and each school had a "principal" teacher with a number of assistants. And finally, written tests were adopted as the standard procedure for examination. Thus, writing to Combe before these decisions had been made, Mann accurately predicted that "the old notion of perfection, in the Boston grammar and writing schools is destroyed; the prescription by which the masters held their office and appointed, indirectly, their successors, is at an end." [7]

The masters also tried to retaliate with a flanking movement of their own, by establishing a state teachers association which they hoped would repudiate the Board and its secretary. Calling meetings at Marblehead and Worcester, they made it clear that only practicing schoolteachers were welcome. But this meant that men like Cyrus Peirce and Samuel J. May could attend, and when it came to the election of officers, those supporting Mann also gained places on the executive committee. Within a few years Mann's henchmen went on to dominate the organization, his own nephew, Calvin Pennell,

---

[6] Mann to Samuel Gridley Howe, August 18, 1845, Mann MSS:MHS; "Reports of the Annual Visiting Committees of the Public Schools of the City of Boston," *City Document,* 26 (Boston, 1845); Mann to Cyrus Peirce, October 7, 1845 in Mann, *Life,* 241–242; Mann to George Combe, September 25, 1845, Combe MSS:NLS.

[7] Boston *Atlas,* August 11, 1845; Boston *Times,* September 1, 1845; Mann to Samuel Gridley Howe, June 21, 1846, Mann MSS:MHS; "First Semi-Annual Report of the Superintendent of Public Schools of the City of Boston," *City Document,* 73 (Boston, 1851); Mann to George Combe, September 25, 1845, Combe MSS:NLS; Mann to T. M. Brewer, September 21, 1845, Agnes C. Storer MSS:MHS.

playing a leading role in this shift of power. The masters were no more successful in their attempt to have other state teachers conventions adopt resolutions critical of Mann's ideas. At Syracuse, New York, Frederick Emerson, another enemy of long standing, was supported by a clique of Albany masters, but he was challenged by an opposition led by Samuel J. May and his mission remained unaccomplished.[8]

Besides the opportunity to bring his ideas on education to a much wider audience, the controversy prompted a second group of thirty-one—this time, some of the most respected names in Boston and Cambridge society—to come forth with a proposal to raise $5,000 to build another normal school. The list included Henry W. Longfellow, and was headed by Charles Sumner. As soon as the legislature agreed to match the funds, the project was under way. Once again, many complications arose over the location of the school and what amounts the competing towns were willing to raise, but the Board finally agreed upon Westfield. Even after Sumner had the greatest difficulties raising the money and ended up by making a larger contribution than he had planned, Mann feared all might be lost at the last minute when the planned program for the dedication ceremony included speeches by Ralph Waldo Emerson and Theodore Parker. Clearly gun shy by this time, Mann wrote to Cyrus Peirce that "it WILL NOT DO. I respect and esteem both those gentlemen, as much as any one, but the school *must be preserved.*" He urged that at least one staunch orthodox speaker be included in the program and then, "one of those men *may* do, but not both—better neither." Mann had his way. Reverend Heman Humphrey, orthodox president of Amherst, did the honors, and the Westfield Normal School was under way.[9]

---

[8] Samuel J. May to Mann, April 26 and September 7, 1845; William B. Fowle to Mann, April 29 and May 3, 1845; James Ritchie to Mann, November 24, 1845; W. H. Wells to Mann, December 18 and 19, 1845, all in Mann MSS:MHS; Samuel J. May to William B. Fowle, May 9, 1845, Fowle MSS:MHS; Charles Northend to Henry Barnard, December 17, 1845; W. H. Wells to Henry Barnard, December 18, 1845; Mann to Henry Barnard, December 26, 1845, Barnard MSS:NYU; "State Convention of County and Town Superintendents," *District School Journal of New York,* IV (June, 1845), 41–59.

[9] Mary Mann to Sophia Hawthorne, [January, 1845], Berg MSS:NYPL; Records of the Massachusetts State Board of Education, March 25, 1845, MS in MSDE; Mary Mann to Charles Sumner, [ca. January, 1845], Sumner MSS:HCL; Mann to Henry Barnard, July 19, 1845, Barnard MSS:NYPL; Charles Sumner to Mann, June 5 and 13, 1845; Mann to Cyrus Peirce, July 19 and 26, 1845; Heman Humphrey to Mann, July 10,

*   *   *

In his controversies with Newton and the Boston thirty-one, Mann had triumphed in the eyes of the public. Furthermore, he had achieved reforms in pedagogy and school administration which expedited the advance of public support and control of education. To accomplish this he paid a greater institutional and personal price than he recognized.

In bringing a sense of righteousness and imperativeness to the cause, Mann had developed an aura of charisma easily recognized and admired by others. At the same time, with each successive campaign through the state, his ideas also became institutionalized. Gradually the spontaneity and enthusiasm of his message became routine as more formal associations formed in his wake to take up the work. His insights and nascent conclusions were translated into systematic procedures by teachers, administrators, textbook publishers, and school committees, all to the satisfaction of a growing number of Victorian parents. For those who held out for the status quo, or proposed a different blueprint for the future of education, the incipient public school bureaucracy he was forming was still too amorphous and diffuse a target for their attacks. Instead, they focused their disapproval on Mann, the visible and acknowledged leader of the movement.

But by 1845, the crucial battles were over, even though the Marcus Mortons, Packards, and Newtons did not know it; nor did Mann, who still believed that he must defend each inch of ground won, never realizing that every advance he made was secured by new quasi-professionals with their licensing, rules, administrative procedures, and hierarchical structure. This new priesthood, complete with academic rituals and educational jargon, would never give ground to a counter-insurgency of sectarians, politicians, the very wealthy, and the very poor. Thus while Mann drew the fire of the opposition to himself, the educationists steadily moved in behind him, consolidating their gains. Only later, after he had left the movement, did he realize this. "The Common School cause in Massachusetts," he later wrote, "was so consolidated—as the French say about their republicanism,—that I felt sure nothing could overturn it. It was only annoyances and obstructions, that we had to

---

1846, all in Mann MSS:MHS; Mann to P. W. Chandler, February 5, 1845, Horace Mann Mutual Insurance Co.

look after, and these had dwindled away until they had fallen into the hands of some of the meanest spirits with which God suffers the earth to be afflicted." Such was the shift which had taken place in the common school movement in the 1840's.[1]

During this period, Mann paid a greater personal price than he realized. To Combe, he admitted that because of the controversy, "I have suffered considerably in my reputation." Other letters also bore the telltale signs of fatigue and weariness, and he again considered the possibility of stepping aside to let a less controversial figure take his place. The disputes with Newton and the thirty-one had destroyed some of the zest he had brought to the cause.[2]

Nevertheless, on separate occasions, he still managed to evoke some of his old fire and captivate his audience. Once, speaking in New York, his presentation received wide circulation, appearing in newspapers as far west as Ohio. Calling Mann "one of the greatest and best men of the age," the Toledo *Blade* reprinted large sections of his address in order to give its readers a better sense of Mann's claims about the power of schooling. Both great orators and great criminals, maintained Mann, had recently been babes in arms. The great power of Laplace and Newton was once so infantile that they "could not trundle a hoop," and but a few years ago, the ends of the fingers of Sir John Hershel, the British astronomer, "were to him the outside of the universe (applause)." Mann also could be more earthy, at least by Victorian standards:

I think that those sons and daughters whose faces and bodies are covered with blotches and scabs and scars by inheritance, should be released from the injunction of that holy ordinance that commands us to honor our father and mother. The farmers, it is known, will take the greatest possible pains to give a cow a straight back in order to improve the breed; and I think fathers should take at least the same amount of pains with their daughters—for I cannot deem a straight back in a cow more important than a straight spine in a woman! (laughter, blushing and applause). Pardon me, my friends, but these truths must be told— more important than life itself, and fastidious ears must not stifle an important appeal to the human heart. (very great applause).[3]

There were other times when speaking was simply a chore. On one occasion, at the end of a particularly disappointing day, he wrote:

---

[1] Mann to William B. Fowle, April 17, 1848, Mann MSS:MHS.
[2] Mann to George Combe, September 25, 1845, Combe MSS:NLS.
[3] Toledo *Blade*, November 7, 1845.

Nantucket. Aug. 28. Saturday. After a miserable day, at a miserable tavern, in the miserable town of Edgartown, & a miserable failure in attempting to get up a Convention, I left that place, at 10 oc'lk today, in miserable humor for this. Tired, jaded, exhausted, devitalized, extinct, the first news on my arrival here, is that I am advertized to Lecture, tomorrow evening. . . . But it cannot be helped, & I must steam up the old machinery once more, & make it go.

Having drained so much of his energies with controversies, it was just impossible to breathe new life into attendance statistics and school-house construction. Coming back from one of Mann's speeches in Stoughton, a listener could not escape a sense of disappointment as he reported that Mann's remarks had been "good enough but rather dry[,] he did not have a single eloquent sentence in the lot[.]" [4]

---

[4] Mann, Journal, August 28, 1841, MS in MHS; Edward L. Pierce to Henry L. Pierce, April 20, 1845, Pierce MSS:MHS.

CHAPTER XVIII

Family and Nation

In love of home, the love of country has its
rise.
    Charles Dickens

Save for the brief interlude of his marriage to Charlotte, Horace Mann had moved about like a Bedouin since first leaving Franklin some thirty years before. An "Arab life," he called his existence in Dedham and Boston, staying at hotels and boarding-houses more because of necessity than convenience. For four years his office was his home, and a horsehair couch in a corner across from his cluttered desk doubled as his bed. Holidays he spent with his sisters, Lydia and Rebecca, if there was time for the coach trip to Wrentham. Otherwise, he frequently accepted the standing invitations of James K. Mills, Josiah Quincy, or Edward Loring. Although his hosts made every effort to make him feel a part of their family circle, their very solicitousness made him sense all the more that he was always the outsider. And each time he returned to his empty quarters, he endured a period of masochistic brooding over his loneliness. That it was necessary and must continue, he never doubted.[1]

One reason for his austere existence was monetary, and since Mary Peabody had had virtually no dowry, it was now necessary for the two of them to live almost as cheaply as one. Thus they began their married life in a boardinghouse, a custom quite respectable at the time, but in the eyes of Sophia Hawthorne, a family disgrace. From the bucolic security of the Old Manse in Concord she scolded Mary, insisting that marriage belonged in a home, not in one or two rented rooms. For the time being, Mann could not afford to be convinced. Instead, he and Mary took two comfortable sunny rooms in Boston. Then, in 1845, they spent their summer in Concord, boarding for $10 a week in quarters which overlooked the

---

[1] Mann to George Combe, February 25, 1847, Combe MSS: NLS; Mann to Samuel Gridley Howe, [July, 1846], Mann MSS: MHS.

river and afforded them a fine view of the sunset. Learning of their plans the previous spring, Sophia predicted that it would be "the summer of summers" for Mary. And she was right. After several months of witnessing the comforts the Hawthornes had found at least temporarily, it was evident to Mann that his boardinghouse days were numbered. Returning to Boston in the fall, he rented a house at 77 Carver Street, and it was only a matter of time until he would decide to own his own home.[2]

The decision was forthcoming even without Sophia's gratuitous goading. Once young Horace Mann, Jr., began to toddle about, a boardinghouse room became a prison. Possessing a "keenness of . . . emotions" and "an intensely high nervous temperament," as his father described him, Horace was easily spoiled by his parents. "When left alone," Mann observed, "he shows signs of uneasiness and discontent and raises his clamour louder and louder until he can command attention." If the Manns indulged in too much affection and permissiveness for their firstborn, it was not without reason. Clearly, they were uncertain and anxious about his future. Mann's own parents could not have been more wrong as they once looked at him sleeping in his cradle at the Franklin homestead and confidently envisioned a life for their offspring much as they themselves had known. No one realized their mistake better than Mann and the knowledge of this haunted him, threatening to unravel what remnants of certainty still remained about his son's future. So few things now were predictable since an inscrutable and amoral fate, neither providential nor benign, seemed to be governing men's lives. Mann's emotions moved back and forth between hope and fear as if impelled by a pendulum, expressing themselves in both extremes and in all degrees of uncertainty in between.[3]

Besides the young Horace's "paroxysms of passion," his phrenologically minded father fretted about the shape of his head. The back of his skull, where the more primitive faculties allegedly were housed, seemed to be developing more rapidly than his forehead, where the "higher propensities" resided. As a result, Mann monitored Horace's mental and physical growth with an anxious eye, certain his son had a "combative nature," and was therefore in need of "conscience and reason, so that he will be disposed to contest

[2] Sophia Hawthorne to Mary Mann, April 6, [1845], Berg MSS:NYPL; Mary Mann to Mrs. Rebecca Pennell, October 18, 1845, Mann MSS:MHS.
[3] Mann, Journal of Horace Mann, Jr., July 13, 1844, and July 27, 1845, MS in HCL.

what is wrong." Again he wrote, "I think he has conscientiousness, and this, if strong, will effect wonders on the whole character. He must cultivate veneration & benevolence. What can be done shall be done." Just how this was to be accomplished was another matter. For both novice parents, corporal punishment was as anathema as giving the baby rum. Mann hoped that suppressing displays of parental love when Horace misbehaved would be punishment enough. Mary agreed in theory, but found the practice hard to follow. To keep her child insecure and uncertain about the affection of others seemed cruel and a little hypocritical. Thus as the volume of Horace's wailing increased, Mann steadfastly turned away from the child; but once his back was turned, he learned that "the intensity of maternal love" interfered with his own strategy and it was obvious to him that "one deviation from the rule" nullified the "effects of a hundred observances." [4]

It was from more than his own personal experiences that Mann sensed an uncertainty about the future of his firstborn. He had become the guardian of two of his nephews, Calvin Pennell and Thomas Stanley Mann, Jr., both fatherless from their childhood. Although both had grown up in Franklin under similar social circumstances, they must have been born under different stars. Calvin had been a conscientious student at the local academy, and was now teaching school. In moral rectitude and social commitment, he followed the model of his uncle all too closely. By painful comparison, Thomas, Jr., was a thorn in the flesh. Mann's added sense of responsibility for him no doubt stemmed from feelings of guilt for having abandoned the boy's father in the Midwest some years before. By late adolescence, the younger Thomas had progressed but a little when measured against his uncle's demanding standards. Since he had done poorly at school in Attleboro, Mann had sent his nephew to study with Calvin, but Thomas quickly found his cousin "the same person that he used to be only much worse." The correspondence which followed not only gave an untiring account of his mounting unhappiness, but also provided impressive evidence that Thomas was making little headway in penmanship, spelling, or grammar. A life of letters obviously not for him, Mann apprenticed Thomas to a carpenter, agreeing to terms which included room and board, $25 wages for the first year, and ten weeks off each winter to attend school.

---

[4] Mann, Journal of Horace Mann, Jr., April 27, 1845, MS in HCL.

Disgruntled with this arrangement as well, Thomas stuck it out for a while, reasoning that anything was an improvement on life with the overbearing Calvin. Mann, however, soon began receiving disconcerting accounts that his nephew was neglecting the work-bench in favor of the local tavern. Even more serious were the reports that he was using profane language. In his letters Thomas denied the accusations, insisted upon his innocence, and then returned to that perennial theme of all students, the need for money.

I am now in want of a pair of pants, which I suppose will be between $4.00 and $5.00. If you can let me have $5.00, I should like it very much. I think this will be sufficient to purchase all that I shall need till next spring. My teeth trouble me some and perhaps I shall have to get some filled. The academy closed a few days ago. When it commenced there were but about 15. We had a much better school at the close than at the commencement, for most of the scholars that left were the ones that made the disturbance.

At his wits' end, Mann nevertheless sent the money. Somehow and with no small amount of pushing and pulling, Thomas, who seems to have successfully resisted the Protestant ethic, finally eked out an existence as a semi-skilled jewelry maker. A niche far less pretentious and virtuous than desired for him by his ambitious uncle, it was satisfactory to him and sufficiently obscure to permit him to disappear into the anonymity of the past.[5]

For Mann, the trials with Thomas amounted to a sequence of sermons, all pointing to the pre-eminent importance of moral training for his own son. He believed that once Horace, Jr., had internalized a repertoire of moral directives, he could steer a straight

---

[5] *Massachusetts Teacher*, I (January, 1848); Thomas S. Mann to Mann, January 14, 1845, June 13, 1846, September 8, 1846, and November 9, 1846; A. F. Peabody to Mann, May 29, 1846, all in Mann MSS:MHS. Poor Thomas finally found satisfaction in making jewelry, but Lydia, his aunt, took a dim view of this, and Mann no doubt did too.

In this connexion, I would inform you that Thomas has at last got work in jewelry, if trinkets made of copper deserve that appellation. He is at the Falls here, in A.[ttleboro] and it is said with a very good man, but I cannot concieve [sic] of a man of sound moral principles, and an enlightened understanding, making articles of copper, with the supposition that they will eventually pass into poor silly girls' hands, as gold; and I am as much opposed to Thomas' employment, as I have been to his being with his mother all winter without any work. [Lydia Mann to Mann, March 15, 1849, Mann MSS: MHS.]

course in a world of unpredictable opportunities and temptations. Speaking of this ethical development, Mann observed,

If as Pope says [sic], "to enjoy is to obey he obeys; so far, he is fulfilling the purposes of his existence. But this is plainly the result of obedience to the physical laws,—the only laws which as yet, apply to him. Should he, under the proper guidance, first of others, afterwards of himself, obey the intellectual & moral laws, I have not the slightest doubt that new worlds of enjoyment, ten thousand times more exquisite than he has ever yet felt or can feel at the present, will reward his fidelity to them.

A wise and responsible father hedged his bets against an indeterminant future, and for Mann, this meant that he must give the most scrupulous attention to the rearing of his son. On every hand, children were growing up either trapped in the narrow Calvinistic beliefs of their parents or simply abandoned to a complete agnosticism. It was then more than a passing fancy which prompted Mary to spend long hours with Horace, introducing him to her own transcendental idea of God. From a hundred platforms, Mann had lectured that the need for better schools was predicated upon the assumption that parents could no longer be entrusted to perform their traditional roles in moral training and that a more systematic approach within the public school was necessary. Now as a father, he fell back on the educational responsibilities of the family, hoping to make the fireside achieve for his own son what he wanted the schools to accomplish for others.[6]

Thus as he considered his own rootlessness over the past two decades, and sensed the need for a stable and secure environment in which to bring up his son to be a moral man, Mann decided that a change was in order. "I have been a wanderer for twenty years," he reported later to a correspondent, "and when anyone asked me where I lived, I would say in the language of another, 'I do not live anywhere; I Board.' This Arab life, I could bear while I was alone, but when I had 'wife and means' to carry from place to place, it became intolerable." Then with the arrival on December 27, 1845, of his second son, George Combe Mann, who, to the great relief of his father, was born with "a head *planned* and *executed* on the principles of Phrenology," there could be no further delay. "If either you

---

[6] Mann, Journal of Horace Mann, Jr., March 2 and June 25, 1844, and July 25, 1847, MS in HCL.

or I are ever to own any house besides the narrow one with only one room in it," he wrote to Cyrus Peirce, "it is time we were thinking of it." For the first time in his life, at the age of fifty, Mann prepared to establish a home.[7]

The decision once made, there was still the problem of money. Since his return from Europe, Mann had augmented his meager salary by twisting the lion's tail and lecturing on "Great Britain" at Lyceums. For $20 he would hold forth at a local rostrum, and for more distant places such as Brooklyn and Philadelphia he received up to four times as much; but this still was not enough additional income to permit him to buy in Boston. Looking in villages on its periphery, where building lots were less expensive, Mann chose West Newton, a hamlet of forty families. Located on the Boston and Worcester Railroad and just one and a half hours from the city, the village was particularly attractive to Mary since the normal school at Lexington had been relocated here. Horace and George could later attend its model classroom under the watchful eye of "Father" Peirce.[8]

Since land prices here had begun to appreciate, it seemed safe to borrow against the future. Peirce found a two-acre wooded site on a hill overlooking the railroad station which he divided with Mann. Mann paid 25 per cent down, borrowed $4,000 from James K. Mills, who preferred to remain anonymous and was never referred to more specifically in the family correspondence than as a "dear friend," and engaged L. B. Bartlett, a local builder, to erect his house. Of necessity, the structure which Mann facetiously referred to as a "shanty" was a modest affair and boasted of "but one luxury . . . a room for a friend, and a plate at the table." Surrounded by wooded rolling hills, yet untouched by industrial blight, the setting was idyllic. Mann instructed the builder to remove just the minimum number of trees, and the foliage which remained helped to conceal the garish gothic trimmings under the eaves of the house. Mann also insisted that a ventilating duct connect each room to the attic, and Mary's one requirement was a "bathing room" between the master bedroom and the nursery. Describing to Sophia what she considered surely one of the marvels

---

[7] Mann to George Combe, February 13 and 25, 1847, Combe MSS:NLS; Mann, Journal of Horace Mann, Jr., January 27, 1847, MS in HCL; Mann to Cyrus Peirce, May 16, 1846, all in Mann MSS:MHS.
[8] Mann to Samuel Gridley Howe, [July, 1846]; Mann to Cyrus Peirce, May 7, 1846, both in Mann MSS:MHS.

of modern plumbing, she wrote that she would have "a pump, with a cock into the boiler which is set beneath it—another to draw it from the boiler into the great bathing tub—also a cock into the tub from the pump (for cold water) and all conveyed away through a tube without a *lift* in any direction." [9]

Like many another couple building their home, the Manns found their costs mounting while their contractor steadily fell behind his schedule. More than once, Mann paced the floor during a sleepless night worrying about money and once in a moment of weakness, Mary proposed that they abandon the entire project. But Mann would have his house. Boarding in West Newton the last month, they finally moved in on Christmas Eve. That night, the kerosene lamps filled the rooms of the structure with a sense of life and sent soft warm light out through the windows and across the white snowdrifts lying at the foot of the old oaks and hemlocks which stood about the building. Three weeks later the varnish was still soft, Mann's books remained unpacked, and the bare floors still awaited carpets, but the Manns knew that secure feeling which stemmed from ownership. As Mary described it, they were finally "settled" and she found this "inexpressibly satisfactory." With all the new space, she seemed "less hurried and less worried." She hoped that the move would usher in a new and more peaceful period in their lives. In this, she was only partially satisfied. New it would be, but because the Manns had moved from Boston and just across the line into Norfolk County and the Eighth Congressional District, this small geographical fact, totally unnoticed at the time, would set the stage for a series of compelling events which would draw Mann into greater controversies and demand even greater sacrifices from him.[1]

---

[9] Cyrus Peirce to Mann, May 16 and 20, and July 8, 1846; Mann to Cyrus Peirce, May 24 and July 13, 1846; Mann to Samuel Gridley Howe, July, 1846; Mann to E. Clap, November 11, 1846, all in Mann MSS:MHS; Mary Mann to Sophia Hawthorne, January 16, 1847, Berg MSS:NYPL; records of Mann's payments to Bartlett between September 16, 1846, and January 13, 1847, are in the Mann MSS:DHS; a list of Mann's lecture dates and fees for this period is in the Mann MSS:MHS.
[1] Mary Mann to Sophia Hawthorne, January 11, 1847, Berg MSS:NYPL; Mann to Henry Barnard, December 20, 1846, Barnard MSS:NYU. Adding to Mann's worries was the fact that his foot became lame during 1846. An open sore developed on it which only slowly healed; at one point Mann was confined to his house for seven weeks. Mann to George Combe, April 25, 1847, Combe MSS:NLS; Mann to Mary Mann, August 26, 1846, Mann MSS:MHS.

* * *

Weary from his bout with the Boston schoolmasters, and suspecting that he might have won nothing more than a war of words, Mann was glad to retreat to West Newton and escape further battle. With the normal schools established in the public mind and his other schemes well on their way, he could now draw back from the firing line as much as he wished, and let his lieutenants push the movement forward. But after traveling through the educational wastelands of the state, controversies seemed to cling to his coattails like cockleburs.

By an a priori reasoning, only his opponents were fallible, and therefore, the more they pressed their case, the more he felt justified in dismissing the substance of their arguments and imputing their motives. To compromise with such enemies was to concede to evil. He lived in a world of primary and simple moral verities, with causes and effects as clearly operative and identifiable as he thought they were in a Newtonian physical universe. Having drawn a sharp and adamant line between right and wrong, he found it virtually impossible to turn aside when someone challenged his educational posture. Rarely did Mann exhibit a humility in the face of complex or irreconcilable social controversies. His was a rigid and occasionally arrogant security, built upon a set of simplistic moral laws, but all the more brittle and tenuous because it could not tolerate ambiguities, imponderables, or the plurality of contradictory "truths." There was then in Mann an Achillean vulnerability. Were he to face opponents, especially in the political realm, who espoused opposite positions with a legitimacy equal to his own, his moral righteousness and stiff-neckedness would make him prone to disaster.

Late in 1846, with little remaining of his conflict with the Boston masters save a few undistributed copies of his *Reply* and a residue of unresolved bitterness, Mann received word that a certain Reverend Matthew Hale Smith had preached and published a sermon, "The Ark of God on a New Cart." Through a labored exegesis of II Samuel 6: "And they set the ark of God on a new cart," Smith claimed that Mann and the Board had fashioned the common schools into a new vehicle which did not carry out religious instruction as commanded by God. For Smith, the moral was clear. As the Children of Israel were punished for moving the ark on a conveyance instead of carrying it on the shoulders of ordained priests, so the people of Massachusetts would be punished if they did not stop using the common schools as a vehicle for nonsectarian religious instruction in the schools. With less than felicitous phrases, Smith accused Mann of attempting "1. To get out of them the Bible and all religious instruction. 2. To abolish the use of the rod, and all correction, but a little talk. 3. To make common schools a counterpoise to religious instruction at home and in the Sabbath schools." Mann could have ignored Smith. Weeks after the sermon, and after considerable enquiry, George B. Emerson reported that "scarcely anybody knows" him; but by this time, Mann was already back on his charger ready for another verbal joust. When he heard of this, Emerson could only add regretfully, "I am sorry to hear that you have even taken any notice of him." [2]

Mann answered Smith in a public letter, attempting to show that the Board had encouraged the use of the Scriptures in the common schools. In the normal schools, where the Board had direct jurisdiction, it required "the daily use of the Bible." Continuing in a tone of unconcealed exasperation, Mann added,

Everyone who has availed himself of the means of arriving at the truth, on this point, knows that I am in favor of religious instruction in our schools, to the extremest verge to which it can be carried without invading those rights of conscience which are established by the laws of God, and guaranteed to us by the Constitution of the State.[3]

Smith answered by a public letter which Mann considered a "compact tissue of evasion, misstatement and unwarranted inferences," and before the controversy had run its downhill course, Smith published his original sermon together with some of the correspondence between Mann and himself, to which Mann replied with a *Sequel to the so-called Correspondence between the Rev. M. H. Smith and Horace Mann. Surreptitiously published by Mr. Smith, containing*

[2] Matthew Hale Smith, *The Bible, the Rod, and Religion in the Common Schools* (Boston, 1847), p. 11. The sermon was reprinted in the Boston *Recorder*, October 15, 1846; George B. Emerson to Mann, January 19, 1847, Mann MSS:MHS. From 1829 to 1840, Smith had been a Universalist minister. Then, converted to Calvinism, he joined the First Church in New Haven. On October 10, 1846, he had preached his sermon attacking Mann in the Church of the Pilgrims in Boston. See his autobiographical account in his book, *Universalism . . . An Examination of the System of the Universalists . . . with the Experience of the Author* (New York, 1847), pp. 12–55.
[3] *The Bible, The Rod, and Religion in the Common Schools*, pp. 24–33.

a letter from Mr. Mann, suppressed by Mr. Smith, with the Reply therein Promised.[4]

In the latter, Mann reaffirmed his commitment to a common denominator of religious teaching in the schools and stated his position with characteristic hyperbole.

. . . you accuse me before the world, of being opposed to religion in our schools. I regard hostility to religion in our schools, as the greatest crime which I could commit against man or against God. Had I the power, I would sooner repeat the massacre of Herod, than I would keep back religion from the young. My own conscience acquits me of your accusation. I call the All-searching Eye to witness that it is as false as anything ever engendered in the heart of man or friend.

Then moving from principle to pragmatism, Mann, who bore an intense hatred of religious externals, heaped his sharpest sarcasm on his detractor and raised the specter of what would happen if doctrinal instruction should be decided by an annual plebiscite in each community as Smith had advocated. As the religious majorities shifted, one could expect the following theological chaos:

This year there will be three Persons in the Godhead; next year, but One. . . . This year, the everlasting fires of hell will burn, to terrify the impenitent; next year, and without any repentance, the eternal flames will be extinguished. . . . This year, the ordinance of baptism is inefficacious without immersion; next year one drop of water will be as good as forty fathoms.[5]

And as could be expected, Smith countered with a *Reply to the Sequel,* restating his previous arguments as if Mann had never dealt with them and, in due course, indulging himself with gratuitous attacks on Mann's personal religious beliefs.[6]

With good reason, Mann believed that Smith was "a child of sin and Satan" and "one of the wild beasts of Ephesus." When forced to produce something concrete to substantiate his claims, Smith pushed his personal witchhunt forward and leveled two accusations at the students at the normal school at West Newton. First, he charged them with infidelity since they went walking on the Sabbath

---

[4] (Boston, 1847); Mann to Matthew Hale Smith, December 24, 1846, Mann MSS:MHS.
[5] *Sequel to the So-Called Correspondence,* pp. 40–41.
[6] Matthew Hale Smith, *Reply to the Sequel of the Hon. Horace Mann, being a Supplement to the Bible, the Rod, and Religion in the Common Schools* (Boston, 1847).

other than to worship. He also claimed that Cyrus Peirce was aiding and abetting their infidelity by encouraging the normalites to go into Boston to hear the preaching of that arch-heretic, Theodore Parker. Peirce could have anticipated the attack because he had been warned by Mann. The fact that the only minister in West Newton was orthodox and an insufferable preacher, from whom Peirce and some of the students prayed daily for deliverance, was of small account to Mann when the future of the school was at stake. Actually, Smith was raising a hollow issue, even though citizens and taxpayers still expected more circumspect conduct from their teachers than they did from their doctors, lawyers, or merchants. And only someone as crotchety and conservative as old Heman Humphrey thought there was mortal danger in Peirce's "compound of Quakerism, Transcendentalism, and Parkerism." [7]

Continuing his inquisition, Smith leveled a second charge at the normalites by accusing them of immorality. According to him, at one of their parties the students presented several tableaux, including a scene from colonial Virginia. In it, one of Peirce's teaching assistants allegedly took the part of Pocahontas and appeared "with her legs bare up to the knee, her arms bare above the elbows, and her bosom bare also." For a few days, when the sensational charges reached the newspapers, a few no doubt were titillated by the risqué account, but to most of these incipient Victorians whose modesty would soon compel them even to cover piano legs with ruffles, Smith's charges simply were not credible. Most of the Boston newspapers sided with Mann and Peirce, and before the end of the year, the *New Englander,* influential spokesman for orthodox Congregationalism, reviewed all the attacks on Mann from Packard to Smith and found them without merit. [8]

[7] Mann to George Combe, February 25 and April 25, 1847, Combe MSS: NLS; Mann to Cyrus Peirce, July 13 and August 1, 1846; Cyrus Peirce to Mann, April 17, 1847; Heman Humphrey to Mann, July 2, 1846, January 14 and 26, and May 12, 1847, all in Mann MSS:MHS.
[8] William B. Fowle to Mann, February 6 and March 5, 1847; Cyrus Peirce to Mann, April 17, 1847, all in Mann MSS:MHS; M.H.S. [Matthew Hale Smith], "State Normal School at West Newton," Boston *Recorder,* June 3, 1847; Cyrus Peirce, "Mr. Smith and the State Normal School at West Newton," Boston *Recorder,* June 17, 1847. For newspaper support of Mann and Peirce, see the Boston *Recorder,* January 14 and June 10, 1847; *Christian Register,* March 6, 1847; Boston *Daily Chronotype,* March 10, 1847; Boston *Daily Courier,* March 18, 1847. The final *coup de grâce* for Smith came in [Emerson Davis], "The Common School Controversy in Massachusetts," *New Englander,* V (October, 1847), 513–522.

* * *

That Smith took special aim at the normal schools was one sign that they now were sufficiently established to present a solid target to their critics. At Bridgewater, a new building had been erected, much to the satisfaction of old Ichabod Morton. Nicholas Tillinghast, its principal, was now assisted by Christopher Greene, direct descendant of General Nathanael Greene and, like Tillinghast, a graduate of West Point. Under David Roe, Westfield, the youngest of the normal schools, was flourishing, and at West Newton so many students were applying that Mann and the Board finally could require a promise from each applicant that she would remain for at least three terms (one year) and three weeks of practice teaching. Equally encouraging was the fact that the school had begun to draw daughters from other than lower-class families.[9]

Not that such encouraging developments had come about without further sacrifice from Mann. New facilities at Bridgewater, Westfield, and West Newton had been provided by the $5,000 subscription raised by Charles Sumner and a matching appropriation by the General Court. Since Josiah Quincy had secretly bought the old Fuller Academy building in West Newton and deeded it to Mann, both men assumed that little additional was needed to have it ready for classes. Even so, Mann ran out of funds before the school was finished. The Board authorized $500, but with the need for a new furnace, Peirce reported expenses of almost twice the figure and before the end of the year the bill had again doubled. Still Mann refused to back away from his objective of a set of exemplary teaching rooms in the normal school. By this time it was not enough to "hold normal school classes in an *ab*normal house." For a week he made the

---

[9] Mann to Henry Barnard, August 5, 1846, Barnard MSS:NYU; David S. Roe to Mann, August 8, 1846, and Nicholas Tillinghast to Mann, June 7 and August 7, 1846, both in Mann MSS:MHS; Mary A. Greene, *Nathaniel T. Allen, Teacher Reformer, Philanthropist* (privately printed, 1906), pp. 30–31.

A description of the school at West Newton is found in Per Adam Siljeström, *Educational Institutions of the United States, Their Character and Organization*, trans. Frederica Rowan (London, 1853), pp. 191–196. Among other things, Siljeström noted that the student body was composed of twenty-three daughters of laborers, four of ship captains, three of clerks, sixteen of farmers, two of newspaper editors, twenty-nine of widows, and three orphans.

rounds of the wealthy of Boston. "Three Lawrences and one or two of the Appletons were applied to," he wrote to Peirce and dejectedly reported, "not one of them would give me a cent."[1]

Two months later, as the speaker at the dedication of the new building at Bridgewater, Mann put into words just how important he considered the normal schools.

I believe Normal Schools to be a new instrumentality in the advancement of the race. I believe that, without them, Free Schools themselves would be shorn of their strength and healing power, and would at length become mere charity schools, and thus die out in fact and form. Neither the art of printing, nor trial by jury, nor a free press, nor free suffrage, can long exist to any beneficial and salutary purpose without schools for the training of teachers. . . . Coiled up in this institution, as in a spring, there is a vigor whose uncoiling may wheel the spheres.

And as the due dates on the bills for West Newton drew near, Mann was ready to put his personal money where his ideas were. With all sources of private philanthropy exhausted, he borrowed $2,000 from Josiah Quincy, using his twenty-one shares of the Boston and Worcester Railroad as security, even though he had planned to use these as partial payment for his new house. To be sure, it was no exaggeration when he claimed that the normal schools would succeed even if this meant "by tapping my own veins."[2]

With these schools, Mann had constructed an educational bridgehead which could be exploited by the next generation of educators after the Civil War. For the immediate task of improving the performance of the thousands of teachers already keeping school, he needed a more mobile and less intellectually demanding mechanism. Reasoning that some normal school training was better than none at all, he decided to bring the schools to the teachers in the form of two-week institutes. Once again, Edmund Dwight came forth with seed money and the General Court matched his gener-

---

[1] Mann to Cyrus Peirce, June 6, August 12, and December 14, 1844; Cyrus Peirce to Mann, December 12, 1844, both in Mann MSS:MHS; Mann to Josiah Quincy, August 7, 1844, Quincy MSS:BPL.

[2] Mann to Josiah Quincy, September 25, 1846, Quincy MSS:BPL; Mann to Cyrus Peirce, June 6, 1846, Mann MSS:MHS; *Mercantile Journal*, August 27, 1846; Mann, "Remarks at the Dedication of the State Normal School-House at Bridgewater," in Henry Barnard, *Normal Schools and Other Institutions, and means Designed for the Professional Education of Teachers* (Hartford, 1851), pp. 161–165.

osity. With this in hand, Mann organized four institutes, limiting their enrollments to 100 applicants each. For those who could not afford the cost of room and board away from home, a total of about $4, he also paid for these expenses.[3]

As in the case of the inauguration of the Lexington Normal School, an inauspicious and confused beginning ultimately augured well for the undertaking. Opening his campaign where he thought it was most needed, Mann started in the Berkshires, or the "Arctic regions" of the state, as he called them. To be sure that these westernmost residents would have "a good deliverance out of the bondage of ignorance," Mann took Governor George Briggs in tow to be on hand for the opening. Through a mistake, the two men arrived early and found the classroom they expected to use in disorder. As neither was one to stand on his dignity when the future of the common schools was at stake, each borrowed a broom, rolled up his sleeves, and started to work. To their no small amazement, the first teachers to arrive later found none other than the Governor of the Commonwealth and the former president of the Massachusetts Senate sweeping up the last dust and cobwebs and arranging the benches and tables.[4]

There were other problems as well. Coordinating an institute in Taunton with "berrying time" when schools were closed and the pupils were out picking huckleberries was not an insurmountable task. More difficult was that of keeping a tight rein on book agents, who descended upon the institutes like hungry locusts, and the academy masters who attempted to enroll their graduating students so that they could support themselves temporarily until they found more promising careers. But the major problems centered upon the staff. Since the institutes required as many as a dozen instructors and guest speakers, Mann found himself all the more dependent upon local ministers. Much to his surprise, many of them came forward to help, orthodox as well as liberal, often contributing more in hortatory rhetoric than pedagogical substance, but their very

---

[3] Mann first officially proposed these in his *Eighth Annual Report of the Board of Education* (Boston, 1845), pp. 69–74; a general description of the first institutes is found in Mann, *Ninth Annual Report of the Board of Education* (Boston, 1846), pp. 43–55; Mann to Cyrus Peirce, October 22, [1845], and November 3, 1845, Mann MSS:MHS; Mann to Alvan Lamson, March 30, 1846, Mann MSS:BUA; Mann to William Wells, March 30, 1846, Mann MSS:PHS.

[4] Mann to Cyrus Peirce, October 7, 1845; Cyrus Peirce to Mann, October 5, 1845, both in Mann MSS:MHS; Mann, *Life*, p. 242.

presence and cooperation gave the institutes a necessary imprimatur and community sanction.[5]

When Mann brought in specialists from out of town he achieved mixed results. Miss Tilden, Peirce's assistant, could be counted upon to do a good job in drilling the teachers in the rudiments of arithmetic. David Page, author of a popular book on teaching methods, knew how to condense a good deal of common sense about teaching and maintaining discipline into a few lectures. And Lowell Mason, the hymnologist, taught the groups how to conduct singing in the classroom. But when William B. Fowle took the opportunity to promote his own textbooks and advocate the monitorial system, Mann had to keep him in line. Always attempting a moderate course in matters of pedagogy, Mann could tolerate Fowle's behavior, but he considered Bronson Alcott's ideas on teaching far too subversive to be safely presented to teachers. According to Alcott, whose pilgrimage currently was taking him through a period of benign transcendental anarchy,

The Secretary of Education deemed it unsafe to introduce me to the teachers, and, on pressing my desire to give them the benefit of my experience as an educator, I was informed that my political opinions were esteemed hostile to the existence of the State, and that I could not aid the cause of popular culture. . . . Yet many of the teachers expressed a wish to know something of the principles and methods upon which my enterprises in education had been conducted, and of which they had but vague notions.

Mann had neither the taste nor the time for Alcott's pedagogy.[6]

Instead, he believed that what common-school teachers needed

---

[5] Cyrus Benson to Mann, June 16, 1846; Mann to Cyrus Peirce, October 22, [1845]; William B. Fowle to Mann, August 12, 1846; all in Mann MSS:MHS. Some idea of the importance of ministers in the undertaking can be drawn from the following exerpt from one of Mann's co-workers in the field:

I invited in your name the gentlemen, whom you mentioned, to lecture, and have received returns, the Rev. Mr. Harding will give a lecture—Rev. Mr. Strong declines in consequence of the state of his health—Rev. Mr. Everett will be present on the 20th of August and lecture in the evening—Rev. Mr. Packard Jr. will endeavor to be present and lecture the evening of the 25th—Rev. Mr. Nash, the teacher of Mount Pleasant School, Amherst will be present and lecture on Sabboth evening. . . ."

John Stacy to Mann, August 10, 1846, Mann MSS:MHS.

[6] David Page to Mann, November 9, 1846; William Wells to Mann, November 5, 1846; William B. Fowle to Mann, November 29, 1846, all in Mann MSS:MHS; Bronson Alcott, *Journals of Bronson Alcott*, ed. Odell Shepard (Boston, 1938), p. 195.

was the most elementary instruction in methods. In arithmetic he had his instructors review "the fundamental rules and their methods of proof." They also drilled their classes in grammar and name and place geography. One period was spent teaching teachers how to write a simple letter. And so that his staff did not commit the pedagogical contradiction of subsequent professors of education who have lectured on the merits of teaching by the discussion method, Mann kept reminding his staff that they should always *"exhibit* as well as *explain,* the style of teaching recommended." For "commencement" both staff and students went to a nearby scenic spot for a picnic, but even here, Mann did not let recreation interfere with duty. When the members of the North Adams Institute gathered in a park for their outing, Mann went along, and as they closed their picnic baskets after finishing their lunch, he mounted a moss-covered marble boulder and gave them a valedictory on their high calling as teachers.[7]

By the time the first four institutes were completed and all the teachers had returned to their classrooms, ready to give battle with their new armory of techniques, Mann was satisfied that his scheme was "eminently successful." In this, the General Court concurred and promptly appropriated funds for another round of institutes the coming year. As in other attempts at reform, the institutes were at best a partial solution to the very large problem of training teachers. In his pedagogical world, unlike his moral universe, Mann could work pragmatically, settling for half a loaf rather than none at all.

*   *   *

Until recently, most historians who have taken note of Mann have placed his ideas and efforts within the great American liberal tradition. Identifying his unqualified belief in the perfectibility of man and society, which he based upon some cosmic law of progressive enlightenment and rationality, as this was facilitated by an emerging public school system, they have interpreted his accomplishment as one more victory in a triumphant liberalism. Few other achievements in the nineteenth century were its equal in mar-

[7] Mann, *Ninth Annual Report,* pp. 43–45; *Berkshire Hills,* October 1, 1900. A detailed eyewitness account of one of these institutes is found in John W. Porter to [?], March, [1846], Bangor, Maine Historical Society; see also Mann, *Tenth Annual Report* (Boston, 1847), pp. 98–99, and Mann to Mary Mann, August 26, 1846, Mann MSS:MHS.

shaling different levels of government to take an active and positive social role in improving the quality of the lives of its citizens. "The money and the talent," Mann once claimed, "employed to barbarize mankind in war, if expended for education and the promotion of the arts and peace, would bring on the millennium at once." Public education, adequately financed, then provided the best means for achieving a golden age of humanitarianism, affluence, justice, and peace, heretofore existing only in the unfulfilled hopes and dreams of men and women. As he wrote to Samuel J. May, Mann was absolutely certain "that schools will be found to be the way that God has chosen for the reformation of the world." And few others were so anxious to accelerate the timetable of the Almighty. This positive and optimistic social commitment, together with his eloquent humanitarian appeals on behalf of the common man, prompted several generations of historians to canonize him among the great liberal heroes and make him a sort of secular saint for schoolchildren in the American pantheon.[8]

Not so, however, for a later group of scholars and educationists who have concluded that for all his insistence upon a greater public involvement in the educational sector, Mann was really a crypto-conservative. Fearing radical democracy and Jacksonian egalitarianism, he took refuge in the institutions of law and property. That he labored to guarantee the opportunity for all to become literate is conceded. However, it is argued that this was but the necessary means to train the masses more effectively in a secular morality which would domesticate them and make them respect the property rights of others. This then was a limited and restricting vision, with Mann essentially supporting the status quo and allowing governmental action only to the extent that it upheld a propertied and social élite. As a corollary to this, Mann's latter-day critics have noted that he promoted an obsolete and misleading Protestant ethic of self-help and individualism at the very time when the avenues for individual social and economic ascent were being constricted by the emergence of corporate giants. To preach that all who worked hard, saved, and invested their earnings could share in a boundless American affluence was to participate in a cruel hoax in an age of emerging factory towns, sweatshops, child labor, tenement housing, and yellow-dog contracts.

Here and there, in his private writings, Mann has given some

---

[8] Mann to George Combe, February 25, 1847, Combe MSS:NLS; Mann to Samuel J. May, September 22, 1848, Mann MSS:MHS.

HORACE MANN·*Chapter XVIII*

plausibility to the claims of his more recent critics. To Theodore Parker, he once wrote that his was a work of "conservative reform." He meant by this, "the removal of vile and rotten parts from the structure of society, just as fast as salutary and sound ones can be prepared to take their places." And to George Combe he described the common schools as "many buttresses to hold our fabric firm." Noting that political upheavals in Europe were often followed by even more authoritarian and reactionary governments, he assured Combe that he was working "to make this a revolution that will not go backward." [9]

To force Mann's efforts into either a conservative or a liberal mode according to some later ideological interpretation, however, is to end up with too many unused pieces, some of them far too important to ignore. The most significant of these was his recognition of the unlimited power of a *system* of education, staffed by a professional bureaucracy, to bring about mass behavioral changes and therefore eradicate every evil which had ever troubled society. More specifically, he recognized as few others of his day, that ideals, norms, attitudes, behaviors, and skills all could be achieved through carefully controlled pedagogical procedures, rather than trusting to the more haphazard process of acculturation. If men as late as a century before his time believed that earthquakes and storms were the result of divine intervention, and only later recognized these as the phenomena of a physical world in which many of the forces of nature could be explained and manipulated through an understanding of scientific laws, Mann believed that the moral and intellectual development of children was not a capricious dispensation from God nor some metaphysical mystique, but proceeded according to scientific laws, and that once learned these could be applied through a systematic approach to public education for all. By carefully identifying the input and rigorously controlling the process, the desired output was as clearly ordained as any scientific experiment or well-engineered industrial process.

True, the ideal had been stated before on both sides of the Atlantic. Thomas Jefferson and Benjamin Rush had advanced proposals for a comprehensive public school system, as had numerous European intellectuals, including the French *philosophes*. But while these men had speculated on the possibilities of a more ordered educational system, their efforts remained largely stillborn. A gen-

---

[9] Mann to Theodore Parker, May 22, 1847, Mann MSS:MHS; Mann to George Combe, November 14, 1847, Combe MSS:NLS.

eration later, Mann added a new dimension to the domain of educational endeavors. More than anyone before his time, he recognized the dazzling potential of popularized education and convinced innumerable persons of the validity of his cause. If all children everywhere were essentially the same, then all could be taught, once the correct techniques and goals were determined. All could learn, regardless of the accident of birth or socio-economic status. Public education more than any other human endeavor meant an equality of opportunity. Clearly, Mann was able to harness pedagogical science in the service of nineteenth-century republicanism.

By 1847, Mann had become so convinced of the power of education that he sent out a circular and questionnaire to a group of experienced teachers, including Catharine Beecher, David Page, John Griscom, and Jacob Abbott, which implied the most grandiose claims for the schools. In it, he solicited their opinions on "how much of improvement, in the upright conduct and good morals of the community, might we reasonably hope and expect, if all our Common Schools were what they should be. . . ." To make his meaning absolutely clear, Mann urged his respondents to abandon the "European fallacy," which defined education as the mere attainment of literacy, insisting that "the naked capacity to read and write is no more education than a tool is to a workman, or a telescope is to a Laplace. . . ." For him the word "education" deserved a "far ampler and loftier significance." Explaining in some detail, he continued,

> . . . its domain extends over the threefold nature of man;—over his body, training it by systematic and intelligent observance of those benign laws which secure health, impart strength and prolong life; over his intellect, invigorating the mind, replenishing it with knowledge, and cultivating all those tastes which are allied to virtue; and over his moral and religious susceptibilities also, dethroning selfishness, enthroning conscience, leading the affections outward in good-will towards men, and upward in reverence to God.

In other words, Mann proposed to expand the scope of training and schooling, with its potential for control, orderliness, and predictability, so that it would encompass almost all the ends achieved by the far broader processes of formal and informal socialization. That in enlarging the European concept of *schooling*, he might narrow the real parameters of *education* by enclosing it within the four

443

walls of the public school classroom was a risk he felt his generation must take.[1]

With this more comprehensive definition at least established on paper, Mann then asked, "Under the soundest and most vigorous system of education which we can now command, what proportion or percentage of all children who are born, can be made useful and exemplary men,—honest dealers, conscientious jurors, true witnesses, incorruptible voters and magistrates, good parents, good neighbors, good members of society?" In short, he was asking if the school with a carefully constructed curriculum and scientific methods of instruction could succeed where government, religion, and the family had previously failed.

The answers he received were striking on at least three counts. First, his respondents all spoke hypothetically. Rarely, if ever, had they seen in action the modest conditions set out by Mann, that is, ten months of schooling, trained teachers, and an organized curriculum. But if such were possible, and this was their second point, then they were certain that virtually all children could be trained to become good and useful citizens. If Mann's conditions were achieved, John Griscom predicted a failure rate of "less than *one half of one per cent.*" David Page thought there would not be "*a single case,*" and Catharine Beecher wrote that she had "no hesitation in saying, I do not believe that *one,* no, *not a single one,* would fail of proving a respectable and prosperous member of society. . . ." A third point grew out of the previous two. A system of instruction which would work for some, would work for all. In making this claim, Solomon Adams stated it most explicitly. "If a well-conducted education produces benevolence, justice, truth, patriotism, love to God, and love to man, in one case, the same education, in the same circumstances, will produce the same results in all cases." There was here, Adams claimed, "the great law of uniformity." [2] And in this could be found the justification for a social and political policy which was almost unthinkable at least a generation and perhaps as little as a decade before, namely, enforced compulsory schooling for all children in institutions supported and controlled by the state. Thus by his *Eleventh Annual Report,* Mann

---

[1] A copy of Mann's circular and the responses he received were included in his *Eighth Annual Report* (Boston, 1848), pp. 49–85.

[2] John Griscom to Mann, August 27, 1847; David Page to Mann, November 20, 1847; Catharine E. Beecher to Mann, August 20, 1847; and Solomon Adams to Mann, November 24, 1847, all in Mann MSS:MHS.

felt secure in demanding "the gathering into the schools, during their entire term, of all children in the community, between the ages of 4 and 16 years." [3]

After reviewing the school abstracts for 1847, Mann could also report to Governor George Briggs that "Our progress now is steady, and I think we have got some headway." It even seemed as if Mann's relations with the teachers had improved considerably. At least one correspondent claimed that "there has never been a time within the last ten years when the great body of teachers of the state and the Board of Education were so near acting in *concert* and harmony as at the *present time.*" For good reason then, near the end of 1847, Mann wrote to George Combe,

Our cause is flourishing. Other states are coming into the ranks of improvement. Public sentiment in Rhode Island, under the administration of Mr. Barnard as School Commissioner is revolutionized. New Hampshire has appointed a School Commissioner. Vermont has established a Board of Education, and even the democratic State of Maine has within the last twelve months organized a board nearly on the same principles, and with the same objects, as that of Massachusetts. All these are as many buttresses to hold our fabric firm. . . . [4]

What this amounted to was the vision of an entire nation going to school; and in the process, the country would gain the means of delivering itself from the poverty, crime, anarchy, disease, and ignorance which had plagued mankind since the beginning of recorded history.

*   *   *

But a new group of detractors was soon to the fore. The abolitionists, mainly in the persons of William Lloyd Garrison and Wendell Phillips, seemed intent on at least embarrassing, if not actually harassing Mann. With the law prohibiting black-white marriages rescinded in 1843 and separate schools for Negroes in Lowell, Nan-

---

[3] Mann developed a long discussion on this topic, pp. 107–125. The only exceptions he made to this all-inclusive rule were sickness and "when any parent or guardian prefers to educate his children at home, or in a private school," but only with the proviso that while "the *means* of education . . . be left wholly optional with every one . . . assurance is given to the State that the *end* is attained."

[4] Mann to George N. Briggs, October 4, 1847, Briggs MSS:AAS; Mann to George Combe, November 14, 1847, Combe MSS:NLS.

tucket, and Salem abolished by this time, the segregated schools of Boston remained one of Jim Crow's last citadels in the state. Failing to enroll black children in other than the Smith Grammar School, a Boston building so rundown and neglected that it defied renovation, Garrison and Phillips next tried to crack the normal school at Bridgewater with its lily-white faculty and student body.[5]

When he heard that they were sending four black applicants, Nicholas Tillinghast asked Mann and the Board for a policy, but much to the relief of many, the Negro applicants did not materialize. Phillips also attacked Mann's *Eleventh Annual Report* for not dealing with racial discrimination, but Mann chose not to respond.[6]

In a more personal way, Mann had made his stand against segregation. The year before, after agreeing to speak at the New Bedford Lyceum, he learned that the organization had refused to open up its membership to Negroes. He then canceled his agreement with them. Subsequently, when a new Society of Lectures was formed, "in order," as one of its founders described it, "that all who wish to procure tickets without any distinction of color can attend," Mann gave them a lecture, even though the majority sentiment in the community was against him for doing so.[7] When the opportunity came for an even more personal commitment, Mann also acted quickly and unequivocally. Late in 1847, Miss Chloe Lee, a Negro from Roxbury, applied for admission at West Newton. Since she seemed at least as mentally alert and academically prepared as all but his best students, Cyrus Peirce, who had led the battle in Nantucket for integrated schools, readily accepted her. For Miss Lee, however, a more formidable obstacle remained in her way. Try as she would, no one in West Newton would offer her board and

---

[5] Garrison's newspaper attack on Boston school segregation included the following articles in the *Liberator:* "No Caste in Public Schools," March 7, 1845; "Public Schools," March 7, 1845; "Meeting of the Primary School Committee," June 27, 1845; "Intolerance of the Primary School Committee," June 27, 1845; "Separate Schools for Colored Children and Others," July 17, 1846; "Extracts from the Majority Report on the Caste School," August 21, 1846. Also see *Report of the Minority of the Committee of the Primary School Board, on the Caste Schools of the City of Boston with Some Remarks* [by Wendell Phillips] *on the City Solicitor's Opinion* (Boston, 1846), and *City Document No. 28, Reports of the Annual Visiting Committees of the Public Schools of the City of Boston* (Boston, 1846).

[6] Nicholas Tillinghast to Mann, August 4 and 7, 1846; Christopher Greene to Mann, August 3, 1846, all in Mann MSS:MHS; *Liberator*, "Horace Mann and the Colored Schools," December 24, 1847.

[7] Joseph Ricketson to Mann, October 23 and 26, 1846, Mann MSS:MHS.

room. Upon learning of her predicament, Mann and Mary opened their spare room to her, and for all intents she became a member of their family. Little did Mann expect, when earlier he had predicted that the only luxury in his new house would be a "room for a friend, and a plate at the table," that this would be used by a black girl who had been turned away from every other home in the village.[8]

Again, not all agreed with this action. Sophia Hawthorne was scandalized by her sister's lack of good sense. It was one thing for Mary to conduct her life according to liberal Christian motives, but taking in Miss Lee was going far beyond the Sermon on the Mount. "All that I question," wrote Sophia, "is your right to *oblige* your *guests* to tolerate her presence if it be distasteful or disagreeable to them." Sophia had heard that Miss Lee had a strange odor and that the Lorings, upon a recent visit, intentionally left early in the afternoon so that they would not have to take tea with her. Edmund Dwight, putting his sense of *noblesse oblige* to what he considered an ultimate test, squirmed and felt extremely uncomfortable, but made it through a meal sitting across from Miss Lee. All this Mary and Mann took in their stride and looked upon with some degree of amusement. But this was essentially an individual problem, resolved by Mann's principled action and the remarkable fortitude of Chloe Lee, who learned to tolerate indignities from her classmates and the residents of West Newton.[9]

---

[8] Mary Mann to Mann, [1848], Mann MSS:MHS; Eben S. Stearns *et al.*, *Historical Sketches of the Framingham State Normal School* (n.p., 1914), pp. 7–25. According to Mary Mann, with the Mann family as her support, she was more than equal to all the slights, innuendoes, and insidious discriminations which were the cultural products of centuries of racism. Describing her, Mary wrote,

She said to Lydia yesterday that she should never have come to this school for the good she could get, but because she knew some one must begin and suffer the indignities to make way for others who might fare better. There seems to be no taint of jealousy in her, but she feels many slights at school. She says she could not stay if she was not so happy here. . . . She presents the uncommon spectacle of a person able to look upon the whole thing and judge of it as a third person.

[9] Sophia Hawthorne to Mary Mann, January 16, 1848, Berg MSS:NYPL; Mary Mann to Sophia Hawthorne, June, 1848, Straker MSS:ACL; Mary Mann to Mann, June 22 and July 1, [1848], Mann MSS:MHS. Within the greater community, Mary Mann must have been considered so far left to the general public consensus that she was close to the lunatic fringe in her attitudes toward the Negro. Even so, with all her liberality toward Miss Lee, one finds in her writings a deeply seated racism, as evidenced by her assumption that black is evil and white is virtuous. Thus she wrote,

Meanwhile, others among Mann's circle of friends, especially Howe, Sumner, and Parker, were planning a more direct collective assault on human servitude and the white racism which it reinforced. To them, slavery was a national malignancy requiring more than the placebo of opening an occasional school door to ambitious blacks who wanted in. Up to this time, many northerners had considered the Missouri Compromise of 1820 an adequate brake on the extension of slavery and a hedge against the further growth of southern political power in Congress. While they delighted in the prospect of a northern tier of free states extending clear to the Pacific Ocean, they were equally pleased that southern "manifest destiny" came to a plebeian halt at the Sabine River, the present boundary between Louisiana and Texas. On the other hand, by 1840, many southerners bitterly resented the fact that the Compromise had dealt them the short end of the political bargain.

In 1844, with the prospect of annexing the Lone Star Republic, which had successfully "rebelled" against Mexico, both southerners and northerners alike saw the necessity of a new series of political adjustments over the extension of slavery. To men like Howe and Sumner, the concept of "Southern Slavocracy" was more than a piece of Garrisonian propaganda. It was galling enough that President John Tyler, with the adept machinations of John C. Calhoun, had pushed the annexation of Texas through Congress by constitutionally questionable means early in 1845; but things looked more conspiratorial when, later the same year, an even more hawkish President, James K. Polk, entered the White House with the avowed intent of expropriating California at the expense of a hapless Mexican government. Still preoccupied with some of the Boston schoolmasters and reactionary clergy, Mann nevertheless had the time to worry that the annexation of Texas could be the prelude to a decade of bitter sectional strife.[1]

Although he felt Polk was maneuvering the nation into an unconscionable war with Mexico, Mann limited his criticisms to his private correspondence. Surely there was something wrong when a

---

The more I know of Miss Lee's beautiful soul, which is snowy white, before God, that sort of white that they say Angels' robes are made of, the more I mourn for her that it is clothed in such an integument, and the more glad I am, that I have had an opportunity of seating her at my table with the magnates of the land, and showing the respect I bear irrespective of colour.

To Mary, Miss Lee was white on the inside. It was such a misfortune that she was black on the outside.
[1] Mann to George Combe, February 28, 1845, Combe MSS: NLS.

republican nation which claimed itself to be the champion of freedom and peace could appropriate $10 million, call up 50,000 men
to carry out an open act of aggression, and lay the basis for the
spread of slavery, all this while refusing to help the Irish who were
suffering through a protracted and disastrous potato famine.[2] So divisive did the annexation of Texas and the Mexican War become
that they accomplished what Massachusetts Democrats had all but
despaired of achieving, namely, a split in the state Whig Party. Besides Howe and Sumner, other young radicals including Henry
Wilson, John G. Palfrey, and Charles Francis Adams challenged
party stalwarts like Daniel Webster and Robert C. Winthrop, and
the financial gray eminences behind them, including Abbott Lawrence, Nathan Appleton, and Mann's patron, Edmund Dwight.
Massachusetts Whigs of a conservative persuasion considered the
annexation of Texas and the Mexican War as a *fait accompli*. To
dissent was not only to kick against the goad but to endanger their
tenuous coalition with southern Whigs, who were reluctantly supporting a high protective tariff against European textiles. For the
moment, however, Mann avoided any public statement, not because
he was neutral, but because he believed that partisanship on his
part would jeopardize the common school cause. It was even with
some misgiving that he sent a private note to George Briggs, con-
gratulating him on his re-election as Governor. "I do not allow
myself to mingle at all," Mann wrote, explaining his reticence, "in
the political contests of the day,—at least no further than to give
a silent vote, 'without note or comment,'[3] as the phrase is,—but
still, as one bound to feel the deepest interest in the cause of education, [I] cannot forbear to express my great pleasure, that you are
to be *officially* at the head of the Board of Education for another
year."[4]

Piously labeling themselves "Conscience Whigs," the radicals
pejoratively dubbed their opposition as "Cotton Whigs," whose mills
along the Merrimack and countinghouses in Boston had bound them

---

[2] Mann to George Combe, February 25, and April 25, 1847, Combe MSS:
NLS.
[3] Mann no doubt referred here to the conditions to be met in the common schools when the students were required to read the Bible.
[4] Mann to George Briggs, October 4, 1847, Briggs, MSS:AAS. For a
background on the political issues disrupting the Whig Party in Massachusetts, I have benefited especially from Harold Schwartz, *Samuel
Gridley Howe* (Cambridge, 1956), pp. 150–176, and David Donald,
Charles Sumner (New York, 1960), pp. 130–159.

with a thousand threads of their own spinning to King Cotton and his new form of southern imperialism. Among the Cotton Whigs, none seemed more vulnerable to their verbal shafts than Robert C. Winthrop. A direct descendant of the first Governor of the Massachusetts Bay Colony, Winthrop was that *rara avis* of the day, a true aristocrat in politics. By a shrewd fusion of principle and pragmatism, he had fashioned for himself a sound political base and was seen by some as the heir apparent to Daniel Webster. To the radicals, however, he was a malefactor who had supported the army appropriations bill for the Mexican War and thus, like his father (who had openly opposed the seditious Hartford Convention during the War of 1812), had withstood local and regional political pressures and voted for what he considered the national interest. Such an action was applauded by his patrons, who hoped to curry favor in the South for a higher tariff. It also kept his own political fortunes alive by keeping him in reach of southern votes, which were necessary for any national office he might seek. In typical hyperbole, Sumner used the columns of the Boston *Whig*, lately the official mouthpiece for the radicals, to lacerate Winthrop as an imperious patron of sin, more interested in cotton than men, who had voted for *"an unjust war, and natural falsehood, in the cause of slavery."* Pushing dissent to the verge of libel, if not treason, Sumner thought it would only be justice if the American army met disaster south of the border "like the legions of Varus. Their bleached bones, in distant valleys when they were waging an unjust war, would not tell such a tale of ignominy to posterity, as this lying act of Congress." [5]

That the slaveholder could force his white cavalier hand into the very "cradle of American liberty" in New England was made patently clear in 1846, when a Negro slave named "Joe" jumped ship and made it to shore before he was recaptured and transported back to New Orleans. Considering this a blatant act of kidnapping, an outraged populace gathered at Faneuil Hall. Old John Quincy Adams, wracked with pain, nevertheless stirred himself about for one last public appearance in Boston. In a voice feeble and barely audible, he warned a hushed audience straining to hear his every word, "We have tried the 'let alone system' long enough. . . . Slavery which has long been brooding over this country like an incubus, has at last spread abroad her murky wings, and has covered us with

---

[5] Boston *Whig*, July 27, and October 27, 1846.

her benumbing shadow. It has silenced the pulpit; it has muffled the press; its influence is everywhere." [6]

Aside from sharing in a collective anger, the assemblage organized the "Boston Committee of Vigilance," with an executive committee including Theodore Parker, Wendell Phillips, Richard Henry Dana, and Louis Hayden, a Negro attorney. Howe was elected its chairman, and in its meetings, which Mann sometimes attended, the group pledged that other fugitive slaves who made it to Boston would not meet the same tragic fate as "Joe." Still Mann persisted in avoiding any public stand, and when Howe ran a poor third against Winthrop on an anti-slavery, anti-war ticket, Mann considered his friend to have made "a great mistake." He had won nothing and lost some of his well-earned popularity, thus vitiating some of his effectiveness in other humanitarian reforms, a consequence Mann wished to avoid for himself.[7]

For the moment, it was just as well. Sumner, Howe, and Adams were political neophytes grappling with complex political issues they feared more than they comprehended. For all of their high-minded intentions, at this stage of their apprenticeship they did as much mischief as good for the cause of human freedom. At the Massachusetts Whig Convention, their rigid moral dogmatism put the trump cards in the hands of their opponents. By insisting that Webster take a strong anti-slavery stand before the convention endorsed him for the presidency, Sumner and Howe weakened his chances in the South, and in turn strengthened the candidacy of General Zachary Taylor, the covert candidate of wealthy Cotton Whigs like Nathan Appleton and Abbott Lawrence. Thus, in their quest for moral purity in politics they diminished the chances of a northern man genuinely opposed to slavery and made the nomination of a southern slaveholder and hero of the Mexican War almost certain. In addition, their vitriolic attacks on Winthrop assured him of strong Whig support elsewhere, particularly in the South; and when he returned to Congress in 1847, after defeating Howe, he was elected to the powerful office of Speaker of the House. That their high-minded efforts could miscarry, Howe and Sumner could not comprehend. So emotionally involved had they become in their

---

[6] *Address of the Committee Appointed by a Public Meeting Held at Faneuil Hall, September 24, 1846* (Boston, 1846); Laura E. Richards, *Samuel Gridley Howe* (New York, 1935), pp. 192–193; Thomas Wentworth Higginson, *Cheerful Yesterdays* (Boston, 1898), pp. 124 ff.; Schwartz, *Howe,* p. 160.

[7] Mann to George Combe, April 25, 1847, Combe MSS:NLS.

cause that to tell them to stop agitating over slavery was like urging a man with fever and the ague to stop shaking.

Although the battle reports from Mexico were equal to a chauvinist's fondest hopes, the war remained immensely unpopular in many sections of the country. Henry Clay, now aged seventy, considered this military escapade below the Rio Grande so dangerous to the future of the nation that he emerged from retirement and spoke out against it in the Senate. In the House, John Quincy Adams, aged eighty-one, denounced the war as one more part of a damnable cabal to extend slavery and establish a permanent southern hegemony in Congress. Clay no longer dominated the actions of the chamber, but his eloquence still commanded its imagination. Adams, odiously moral, troubled by a moody introspection, and ever wrestling with an anxiety over his own soul and that of his country, stood in the House like an ancient and adamantine Elijah among a body of degenerate Israelites bent upon their own destruction. On February 21, 1848, he collapsed in the House and was carried by some of his colleagues to the rotunda and then to the Speaker's room. The House adjourned immediately, as did the Senate, upon hearing of his illness. Both chambers met the following day, and quickly adjourned. The next evening he was dead.[8]

Massachusetts mourned one of her noblest sons and Mann attended a memorial service in Boston in his honor. Gratified with the ceremony, he was then upset at the drinking party which followed in the Revere House, an "Irish wake" he called it, recouping some small satisfaction from the fact that his closest friends were prominent by their absence. As a special tribute to Adams's memory, the House voted that his seat remain vacant thirty days. This gave the Whigs in Massachusetts additional time to find a replacement to represent the Eighth Congressional District. In the meantime, as the debate over territorial expansion and slavery increased in intensity and bitterness, so also grew the need for Massachusetts to send more than a lackluster political faithful on its behalf. Both the sentimentalists and the anti-slavery agitators outside Massachusetts backed the candidacy of Charles Francis Adams, son of the former President. From as far away as Washington, D.C., a correspondent wrote to Sumner, "All our friends here with one accord, desire to see Charles Francis Adams occupy the seat. . . . It would be a noble spectacle. . . . He is needed here; and never was there so

[8] *Congressional Globe*, February 21, 22, 23, and 24, 1848, *passim*.

favorable a time to advance the Anti-Slavery cause in Congress and the nation, as now." But Sumner knew only too well that Boston Whiggery and not Washington would call this shot, and that because of his intemperate attacks on the actions and character of Robert Winthrop and other party stalwarts, Charles Francis Adams was *persona non grata* among the Cotton Whigs. Far wiser would it be for the local anti-slavery men to find an anti-slavery man *sotto voce*, whose previous silence on the Texas question and the Mexican War would make him acceptable to both wings of the party. And from Sumner's appraisal of possible candidates, no one fit that description so well as Horace Mann.[9]

By the middle of March, Sumner was uncertain of the outcome of the Whig search for Adams's replacement. "It is impossible to say *at this moment*," he wrote to Joshua Giddings, a Congressman from Ohio and a vehement anti-slavery man, "who will be the candidate in the 8th District. . . . But be assured," he continued, "no person can be elected who does not *cordially join with us*. There is talk today of Horace Mann—who is thoroughly with us." To a query as to whether Mann would be a "Palfrey man," John G. Palfrey, one of the inner circle of the Boston Conscience Whigs, replied that it was enough that he be a "Mann man." In the meantime, several leading Whigs in Norfolk County had been in touch with Mann to determine if he would accept the nomination if given to him at the party caucus on March 15. Mann's answers contained just the precise ambiguity to give them hope. "How can I with propriety say '*no*,' till some responsible body has made me the offer," Mann wrote to E. W. Clap, the postmaster and local Whig spokesman in West Newton; but so as to keep the door to a new office ajar, he continued, "and how can I say '*yes*,' before I am asked?" And he added that overworked but nevertheless effective cliché in the repertoire of every candidate seeking office, "were such a proposition made to me by any body of gentlemen acting in behalf of the voters in the district, I should give the subject the consideration which its importance deserves." Obviously, in such a political situation, it took two to make a seduction.[1]

---

[9] Mann to Josiah Quincy, March, [1848], Quincy MSS:BPL; H. B. Stanton to Charles Sumner, February 25, 1848, Sumner MSS:HCL; Charles Sumner to Joshua R. Giddings, March 16, 1848, Giddings MSS:OHS; Martin D. Duberman, *Charles Francis Adams, 1807–1886* (Boston, 1961), p. 135, and Charles Francis Adams, Diary, March 4 and 7, 1848, MS in MHS.
[1] Charles Sumner to Joshua Giddings, March 16, 1848, Giddings MSS:

Mann's letter was all that Clap needed. "It was just what I wished and was used as I thought proper *without your leave. . . .*" he wrote to Mann. When the party met at the Phoenix House in Dedham, the West Newton postmaster placed his friend's name in nomination. Out of a total of eighty-seven votes cast the first time, Mann led a list of four by a small margin. He gradually picked up strength on the second and third rounds, and received a clear majority on the fourth. The next day, along with reporting Mann's nomination, the Boston *Journal* commented editorially that "the good people of the Eighth District will require no pledges from Mr. Mann . . . on any of the great political questions of the day. They have a guarantee in his past life that if elected to Congress he will always be found on the side of reason, justice and patriotism." Before actually choosing Mann, the convention had resolved to nominate a candidate "whose principles shall be in consonance with those of his predecessor, whose fidelity to the great principles of human freedom shall be unwavering—whose Voice and Vote shall on all occasions be exercised in extending and securing liberty to the human race." Little wonder that Mann, with a mixture of honesty and false humility, believed that to ask him "to '*fill*' Mr. Adams' place," would be a good deal like "asking a mouse to fill the skin of an elephant." [2]

With the nomination in hand, Mann's election was all but a foregone conclusion. The Boston Whigs were happy that so illustrious a standard-bearer had returned to their fold after a self-imposed exile of twelve years. Much of the press supported him. The Boston *Atlas,* spokesman for the "Cottonocracy" as Garrison called it, claimed Mann's nomination as "the very best that could have been made by the Whigs of his district, if they could have had the whole State from which to elect." Its arch opponent, the Boston *Whig,* was equally enthusiastic. Even some of the doctrinaire anti-slavery people in the Liberty Party, such as Stephen Higginson, supported him, and to make his candidacy completely unassailable, his Demo-

---

OHS; John G. Palfrey to Charles Sumner, February 28 and March 11, 1848, Palfrey MSS:HCL; William B. Fowle to Mann, March 1, 1848, and Mann to E. W. Clap, March 11, 1848, Mann MSS:MHS. Also see Frank Otto Gatell, *John Gorham Palfrey and the New England Conscience* (Cambridge, 1963), pp. 154 ff.

[2] Mary Mann to George Combe, July 16, 1848, Combe MSS:NLS; Mann to E. W. Clap, March 11, 1848; E. W. Clap to Mann, March 16, 1848; George Alden to Mann, March 16, 1848; Thomas French, *et al.*, to Mann, March 15, 1848, all in Mann MSS:MHS.

cratic opponent privately conceded the election to him. "It seems to me to be clear enough," E. K. Whitaker wrote to Mann, "that the mantle of Mr. Adams is destined to be yours." Still, Mann refused to indulge in any premature enthusiasm. On the eve of the election, he wrote to Howe, "I have become quite stoical,—not from philosophy, so much as from callosity." [3]

The first week in April, the voters of the Eighth District did what everyone expected of them. They elected Horace Mann by a landslide and dramatically altered the course of his life. For Mann, who was weary of constantly jousting with petty self-seeking men such as the Boston masters and Matthew Hale Smith, the victory at the polls held out the prospect of a felicitous bridge to a less strife-torn life. A leader more than a manager, and never a system builder in the bureaucratic sense, Mann had led the reform through his power of persuasion. Now where he had taken giant strides for the last decade, it was the task of lesser men to inch along and institutionalize his vision of educating an entire nation. Considering the consequences of his decision, a fortnight after the election, he wrote to a friend:

The Common School cause in Massachusetts, was so consolidated—as the French say about their republicanism,—that I felt sure nothing could overturn it. It was only annoyances and obstructions, that we had to look after, and these had dwindled away until they had fallen into the hands of some of the meanest spirits with which God suffers the earth to be afflicted. But here all is new; and I risked my fortunes on an untried and hazardous voyage. But the die is cast, and I must bide the result, let its face come up which ever way it may be.[4]

There were a few persons who considered his re-entry into politics a blow to the common schools; but most of his closest associates, such as Henry Barnard, Josiah Quincy, and Thomas Kinnicutt, all of whom understood Mann's strengths and limitations, believed it

---

[3] Josiah Quincy to Mann, March 16, 1848; Stephen Higginson to Mann, March 16, 1848; Henry Wilson to Mann, March 17, 1848; E. K. Whitaker to Mann, March 25, 1848; and Mann to Samuel Gridley Howe, March 29, 1848, all in the Mann MSS:MHS. Support for Mann can be found in the Boston *Atlas*, March 25, 1848; Boston *Recorder*, March 17, 1848; Salem *Gazette*, March 17, 1848; Hingham *Patriot*, March 17, 1848; and Roxbury *Gazette*, March 18, 1848. Among the handful of newspapers opposing Mann were the *Liberator*, April 7, 1848; Norfolk *Democrat*, March 31, 1848; and the Boston *Chronotype*, March 29, 1848.
[4] Mann to William B. Fowle, April 17, 1848, Mann MSS:MHS; Mary Mann to George Combe, July 16, 1848, Combe MSS:NLS.

to be a wise move. In addition to becoming a major voice in the defense of human liberty, they expected him to promote the cause of public education on a more national scale.[5]

Officially, Mann played down his continued educational role. In his letter of acceptance to the nominating convention, he promised to dedicate himself, if he were elected, to *"Unwavering fidelity to the great principles of human freedom"* and the *"exercise on all occasions, of voice and vote, in extending and securing liberty to the human race."* Then, concluding with a more personal note, he added that he had preferred to remain as secretary to the Board, but the real possibility of slavery in the new territories forced him to alter his own more immediate priorities. "The enactment of laws which shall cover vast territory, to be applied to myriads of human beings who are hereafter to occupy that territory, is a work which seems to precede and outrank even education itself," he told his supporters. Most agreed, although Josiah Quincy thought that freedom without education was an impossibility. As Mann readied himself for the trip to Washington, Quincy urged him to remember that he was going on behalf "of every child that now is, or that for centuries will be, between here and Oregon. Your knowledge and reputation will at once make you the rallying point for the friends of education. . . ." He would be carrying with him the impressive credentials of an untiring and selfless humanitarian. The future then looked promising for Horace Mann, moralist and educator now turned politician.[6]

But appearances could be deceiving. Supported by both Cotton and Conscience Whigs, as well as by members of the Liberty Party, Mann was a coalition candidate. Privately, he was unalterably opposed to the Mexican War, but under certain circumstances, his conscience would permit him to vote for a slaveholder such as Zachary Taylor, a position Sumner would soon find reprehensible. Thus he would leave Massachusetts representing a divided constituency, and after his initial period of grace, each faction could attack him for not adhering to its own doctrinaire position. The temper of the times did not include a charity which would permit him to occupy

[5] Josiah Quincy to Mann, March 16, 1848; Eben Avery to Mann, March 27, 1848; Henry Barnard to Mann, April 4, 1848; and Thomas Kinnicutt to Mann, April 4, 1848, all in Mann MSS:MHS.
[6] Josiah Quincy to Mann, March 16, 1848, Mann MSS:MHS. Mann's letter of acceptance was published in the Boston *Daily Advertiser*, March 23, 1848. It was later included in his *Slavery: Letters and Speeches* (Boston, 1851), pp. 1–9.

some high moral ground. Instead, he would be forced to descend into the valley and there experience the wicked political crossfire which could destroy all but the most adept and resilient of men.[7]

To be sure, he journeyed to the Capitol unimpeded by explicit campaign pledges or party instructions. But he did carry with him the greater burdens of contradictory expectations within the Whig Party and the impossible hopes of his would-be supporters. As a northern Whig, it was contradictory to expect him to support measures which would strengthen a coalition with the party in the South, while still maintaining an implacable opposition to the extension of slavery. And those Massachusetts well-wishers who expected a performance of him in the House equal to that of John Quincy Adams, while he maintained a lofty, political neutrality from which he could promote common schools on a national level, surely expected the impossible. Such was the challenge awaiting this man from Massachusetts who had agreed to carry Elijah's mantle.

---

[7] Mann to E. W. Clap, March 24, 1848, Mann MSS:MHS.

CHAPTER XIX

Sisyphus

===

GREAT BOONS, such as can only be won by great
labor, are to be secured; great evils are to be van-
quished . . . the disabilities of poverty; the pains
of disease; the enervations and folly of fashionable
life; the brutishness of appetite, and the demon-
isms of passion; the crowded vices of cities, thicker
than their inhabitants; the retinue of calamities
that come through ignorance; the physical and
moral havoc of war; . . . these are the hosts
against which a war of extermination is to be
waged . . .

HORACE MANN

As HE BOARDED THE TRAIN in Boston and found his place on the
coach, thoughts of West Newton and his unfinished work for
the Board seemed to occupy the seat beside Mann. Mary was again
pregnant. Her father and Elizabeth had moved to West Newton to
be with her and this knowledge gave him some small comfort. He
was also relieved with the knowledge that this time, during labor,
the doctor planned to administer an anesthetic, a relatively untried
practice in and about Boston but worth the risk, given Mary's terrible suffering during the last two childbirths. "You have had me
with you before," he would write, clumsily attempting to assure her,
"but now a divine power is to be with you in the shape of chloro-
form." Although a United States Representative, he wished to write
his twelfth, and probably final *Report*. Uncertain of his re-election
to a full term in the fall, he had still retained his secretaryship. He
also hoped to fulfill the expectations of Sumner, Parker, and Howe.
Few official campaign pledges he had made, but he knew nevertheless that they expected him to speak out against the extension of
slavery into the new territories. Thus as he was jostled about in the
swaying railroad car rolling on during the night, and occasionally
falling into snatches of sleep, only to be jarred awake when the
train hit a curve, he understood that in the months to come he must
wear the old hat of educational reformer and the new one of anti-

slavery legislator. What he did not have was even the slightest premonition that he soon must wear still a third.[1]

Alighting from his car and walking through the train shed which was Washington's excuse for a depot, he quickly found a hotel room. After dispatching notes to some of the Massachusetts delegation, he then took to the outdoors for a walking tour of the capital. To those he passed, Mann must have presented a striking figure. He dressed meticulously in public, frequently wearing a black frock coat, gray cravat, and starched high collar. He was tall and thin, with a bushy head of snow-white hair, carefully combed straight back. By now he stood with just a trace of a stoop. The years too had deepened the lines in his face, giving his countenance either a concerned or severe appearance, depending upon the predilection of the observer. Now more frequently he found it necessary to wear his gold-rimmed spectacles, always when he read, but even at other tasks.

Wherever he looked, Mann could see the twin conditions of great aspirations and painful incompleteness. If cobblestones were ubiquitous, so was mud. The Washington Monument was largely a clay pit from which had emerged a square foundation of massive rough-hewn granite blocks, while along its side moved a sluggish flow of water, part creek, part open sewer, bounded by weed-choked banks.[2] Mann hurried past the west side of the Capitol building, taking his path along the wide semicircular arc of a paved walk. He found the flowers and flowering shrubs and trees particularly pleasing. "How beautiful this is," he reported to Mary, "the lawns and cultivated trees and flowers below . . . make one of the most beautiful scenes I ever beheld." The peach trees were in full bloom and the lawns already as green as the Boston Common would be in June. Jonquils and crocuses were out and there was a warm sensuous emerald sheen on all the trees from the millions of leaf buds about to open. To be sure, this was a place much closer to spring and summer than the wooded hills around West Newton.

Mann, however, unconsciously pushed aside the unfinished state of Washington and the reassuring signs of an early spring

---

[1] Mary Mann to Mann, April 14, 1848, and Mann to Mary Mann, April 19, 1848, Mann MSS: MHS; Boston *Daily Advertiser*, April 17, 1848.

[2] Mann's description is drawn from George W. Bungay, *Crayon Sketches and Off Hand Takings* (Boston, 1852), p. 181. The description of Washington, D.C., is based upon Mann's letters and Constance McLaughlin Green, *Washington Village and Capital, 1800–1878* (Princeton, 1962), pp. 152–229.

from the forefront of his mind. What impressed him far more than these was the human condition he witnessed at every hand. Try as he would to concentrate on the distant buildings slowly giving form to L'Enfant's dream of a city of true republican grandeur, he found himself staring with troubled eyes at the presence of black slaves wherever he looked. Whether they were smartly uniformed hackmen or domestics, buxom mammies with full-length skirts carrying baskets of laundry, or simply drifters looking for a comfortable place in the sun, he found his gaze fastening on these persons condemned to servitude, and the more he looked, the more disconcerting it seemed. The sight of black children with their ebony hair and ever-ready big ivory smiles troubled him the most, since they constituted a direct challenge to his pet formulas of human progress and perfectibility. They stared up at this tall white-haired man in a well-tailored frock coat and seemed to be telling him that the best their future could hold for them was the bitter-sweet mixture of an unquenchable joy for life accompanied by an inescapable suffering and servitude. In Massachusetts it seemed sufficient just to open classrooms to black children and place books and slates in their hands. There the Chloe Lees had a chance. But in the nation's very capital, where the architecture of each new public building tried to outdo its rivals in symbolizing republican ideals, through the accident of birth these children were the victims of a vicious system, reinforced by the iron hand of history which sentenced them to a lifetime of human misery and exploitation.

Impulsive questions surged through his mind and he could not keep from translating their self-evident answers into admonitions to himself and others. Was it possible that slavery was a fatal flaw in his nation's noble republican experiment? Mann asked himself if a black man fleeing to northern soil became free, even if his flight stopped short of the Canadian border. He knew that the menacing outstretched hand of the slave catcher had recently reached as far as Boston to grasp a poor helpless "Joe," and there was little reassurance that it would not happen again, no matter how many times Samuel Gridley Howe and his Committee of Vigilance held mass meetings at Faneuil Hall. As long as men wanted to be free, they would flee from their oppressors and seek sanctuary; but even the soil of Massachusetts, once made sacred to the cause of liberty by the sacrifices of her patriots, was no longer the ground of freedom. More troubling was the thought that he was now to enter a chamber where a group of southern men with a few northern sympathizers were using every argument and political maneuver at their disposal to extend this cursed institution clear to the Pacific Ocean. Standing on a knoll within the shadow of the Capitol and looking out beyond the great bend in the Potomac into Virginia, Mann attempted to generate a positive set of feelings about this new scene of action. "But the thought," he later recorded, "what kind of people live between me, and the western and southern horizon, saddens the emotions excited by the beautiful scene. As well may it be said here as in Greece, that 'All save the spirit of man is divine.' " [3]

*　　*　　*

On April 13, 1848, Mann was ushered into the House chamber by several of the Massachusetts delegation, including his old friend, Julius Rockwell, who had also left a wife back home expecting a baby. Speaker Winthrop then administered the oath of office and Mann's membership was official. He sat for a short time at his seat and then was escorted about in the corridors and introduced as the great educational reformer from New England. Throughout the day it was an unending pageant of new faces, bearded and shaven, middle-aged and elderly, friendly and taciturn. Some were polished gentlemen; others seemed closer to the "half horse–half alligator" species. All were given names, most of which he would forget by the next morning, and the ritual of introduction was always sealed with a hand clasp.[4] By the end of the week, he had taken two rooms at Mr. Gordon's, away from the noise of Pennsylvania Avenue and just a three-minute walk to the Capitol. With each new session in the House, his astonishment grew at the intensity of feelings over the territorial question and the issue of slavery. Sitting at his place, he took advantage of a short lull in the debate to pen a quick note to Mary. "The subject which was under discussion yesterday, occupies the House again today. The South is on fire. The most fierce and fiery speeches are made. . . . Where it will end, there is no fore-

---

[3] Mann to Mary Mann, June 20, 1848, Mann MSS:MHS.

[4] According to a later account, among the Congressmen Mann met was Abraham Lincoln, who saw Mann as a sophisticated and articulate easterner. Elizabeth Peabody, who claimed Lincoln told her of the meeting, also mentioned that the young Illinois Congressman was moving through a period of despondency and that the older Mann encouraged him to continue in his political career. See Jane C. Hoge, "Go to a Fair to Rest?," in *Noble Women of the North*, ed., Sylvia G. L. Dannett (New York, 1959), pp. 334–338.

seeing." And the next day, back at his room at Gordon's, he dispatched Samuel Gridley Howe a more complete account of the emerging confrontation.

For two days past, we have had a Southern tornado,—not a meteorological affair, but a psychological one. Slavery, of course, has been the theme. I can give you no description of its fury,—nor will reports,—for it is strange, how cool and tame everything looks, when reported in the next mornings' papers. But we have had threats, insults, the invocation of mob-rule and lynch law; and, indeed, all the whole Southern armory has been exhausted upon us. Their orators, Venable, Haskell, Bayly, etc. begin as though they were calling up a herd of slaves from a distant cotton field. You would hardly think that the doomed wretches had time to make their appearance when the speakers begin to gesticulate, as though they had the task in hand, and were cutting in to the flesh before and behind. If this represents the manner and the wrath with which they put it on to the poor slaves, with scourge in hand,—and I presume it does,—then you must conceive how the skin is chopped and the blood spilled. The debate has lasted four days, and southern men, almost exclusively, have had the floor. Just at the close, yesterday, however, Root of Ohio, obtained it and made a well conceived and most opportune speech,—Root is a block of granite,—and as strong. He was conciliatory, facetious, earnest, and gave some mortal thrusts. But you must see the debates themselves, and imagine the rest; for I like the minister who could not print the thunderstorm, and so would not the sermon.[5]

As if there was not enough excitement in the chamber, Mann found even more on the outside two days after he had taken his oath of office. On April 15, official Washington took time out to celebrate the expulsion of the reactionary Louis Philippe and the establishment of the Second French Republic. Bands led torchlight processions down Pennsylvania Avenue and a crowd gathered in front of the White House to hear Senator Henry Foote of Mississippi take the occasion to offer a panegyric on man's undying quest for liberty. Ironically, while the Senator spoke, a small number of Negroes seemed to be taking inspiration from his words and slipped away from the crowd. A few others left the houses of their masters

---

[5] Julius Rockwell to Lucy Rockwell, July 5, 1848, Rockwell MSS: Lenox Library; Mann to Mary Mann, April 21, 1848, and Mann to Samuel Gridley Howe, April 22, 1848, both in Mann MSS: MHS.

and by twos and threes they hurried down the back alleys and side streets of the city, keeping within the shadows as best they could. One of them was Daniel Bell, a freeman who had earned his own manumission. Bell was the father of eight children, all of whom recently had been given freedom by their late master. The white heirs, not wishing to be deprived of some $3,000 worth of property, were contesting the will, and Bell, not trusting the courts, had decided on a bold move to save his family. By late evening, he had them together down on the riverfront at the White-house Wharf, where a small schooner, the *Pearl*, was ready to cast off down the Potomac. Others had joined him as news of his plan moved by word of mouth from one slave to another. Uncertain that this was the right thing to do, they hurried up the gangplank, each carrying a small bag or bundle of belongings, the miserable mementos of a lifetime of bondage. Frightened and not knowing what would happen next, they peered into the dark and caught sight of the face of a friendly white man with a ship lantern who helped them climb down into the hold, where he told them to lie down on a floor littered with chips and bark from the previous cargo of cordwood. Mothers held their small children to them, several half-moaning, half-singing prayers. Finally they were all in. Packed together side by side as their ancestors had once been stowed coming to the New World on a slaver, they now hoped to escape to freedom.

At midnight, with a total of seventy-six "passengers," Captain Daniel Drayton and his assistant Edward Sayres cast off their lines, ran up the mainsail, and headed down the river. What they did not know was that two slaves had become lost in their search for the wharf and needed directions from a colored hackman. By dawn, the *Pearl* was past Alexandria, but the hackman had second thoughts about what he had done and told his master. A certain Mr. Dodge offered the use of his small steamboat and more than thirty angry owners, armed to the teeth, climbed on board to pursue the fugitives. With a six-hour lead and favorable winds, Drayton still had a good chance of escaping, but at the mouth of the Potomac, he ran into adverse winds. Rather than remain "in irons," he steered his craft into Cornfield Harbor. Unfortunately, he was spotted by his pursuers at two in the morning. They boarded his schooner, overpowered him, ripped away the canvas covers, and lowered a lantern into the dark hold, there to recognize the frightened faces of their prey. Drayton, Sayres, and a cook named English were bound and taken aboard the steamboat, and the *Pearl* with its pitiful cargo was towed back up the river.[6]

A mob of more than 4,000 had gathered at the wharf to meet them. One enraged owner lunged at Drayton with a bowie knife, only to have his arm deflected by a constable at the last second. The prisoners were dragged through a sea of angry faces, which seemed to scream at them like so many ferocious animals suddenly given the power of speech. Several men moved towards them with coils of rope and the police just managed to prevent a lynching party by getting the prisoners into a hack and rushing them to the District Jail, a three-story brick building which they quickly surrounded with a heavy guard. Thwarted, the mob roamed the streets, beating up hapless blacks who happened to be in their way, and then on to the office of Gamaliel Bailey, editor of the anti-slavery *National Era.* After breaking its windows and threatening the courageous Bailey, whom they considered the instigator of the plot, they were finally driven off by the police. "A great commotion in the city," was the simple understatement Mann sent to the pregnant Mary.[7]

Joshua Giddings, outspoken anti-slavery Congressman from Ohio, risked the wrath of the mob to enter the building to be sure that Drayton, Sayres, and English had decent treatment and legal counsel. He also prevailed on David A. Hall, a Washington attorney, to represent the prisoners before the justices who held court in the jail. For his services, Hall was denounced by John C. Calhoun as a "maniac" and Senator Henry Foote promised he would be hung if he ever set foot in the "sovereign" state of Mississippi. As for the fugitive blacks, with the exception of several of Daniel Bell's children, who were ransomed, "justice" was cruelly swift. A Baltimore slave broker had them chained into coffles and the entire lot was shipped to a dealer in Georgia. Such sordid details Mann kept from Mary. Instead, he sent her the briefest description and concluded with the comment, "All parties this morning are committed to jail. So *might*

---

[6] Information on the flight of the *Pearl* and its capture has been taken from [Richard Hildreth], *Personal Memoir of Daniel Drayton* (Boston, 1853), *passim*, and Mann, *Slavery: Letters and Speeches*, "Sketch of the Opening Argument in the Case of the United States *vs.* Daniel Drayton . . ." (Boston, 1851), pp. 84–118; Boston *Evening Transcript*, April 20, 25 and 26, and May 1, 1848.

[7] Mann to Mary Mann, April 18, 1848, Mann MSS:MHS. In the future it would be Bailey who had sweet revenge on his pro-slavery enemies. Two years after the case of the *Pearl*, he would use his columns to publish the book-length novel of an obscure woman writer. The author was Harriet Beecher Stowe and the novel was *Uncle Tom's Cabin.*

prevails over *right.*" And he added wishfully and perhaps prophetically "It will not always be so." [8]

News of the affair spread north, and anti-slavery advocates
thought they might have a *cause célèbre* with which to topple slavery
in the nation's capital. In Boston, Samuel Sewall, Sumner, and
Howe began to raise a legal defense fund, as did C. D. Cleveland in
Philadelphia. For the moment, they seemed almost embarrassed by
a wealth of talent. Governor William Fessenden of Maine and Governor William Seward of New York both offered their services for
the defense, as did Salmon P. Chase of Ohio. They even considered
retaining the great Daniel Webster, but the abolitionists on the
committee for defense distrusted him.[9]

Amidst all this excitement, Benjamin Pickman Mann arrived
in the house at West Newton on April 30. Lydia notified Mann by
the new marvel of telegraphy of the birth of his third son. Hoping
for a girl and worried about Mary's ability to undergo childbirth for
a third time, Mann was both disappointed and relieved upon receiving the news. "Oh dearest," he wrote to her, "It is not what we hoped,
but it is like a gleam from heaven to be relieved from the anxiety I
have felt for two or three days past." As soon as she was able, Mary
described their new son to him, taking special pains to assure the
concerned father that Benjamin had a well-shaped head.[1]

As if Mann then did not have enough to occupy his mind at the
time, Sumner and Howe, aided and abetted in Washington by John
G. Palfrey, kept up a steady pressure on him, urging that he bolt the
party as a protest against the Cotton Whigs, and if not this, at least
take a public stand against the extension of slavery. As soon as
Mann had arrived, Joshua Giddings confidently predicted he would
join the ranks of anti-slavery men; but a fortnight later, with still no
public statement from Mann, Sumner had begun to consider his
silence a sign of cowardice. "I am anxious that your name and your
words should commence their career of influence from the Capitol,"
he admonished, and added, "It is by such efforts that Public opinion

[8] David Hall to Charles F. Adams, May 3, 1848, Adams MSS:MHS; Mann
to Mary Mann, April 18, 1848, Mann MSS:MHS; Joshua Giddings, *History of the Rebellion: Its Authors and Causes* (New York, 1864), pp.
272–280.
[9] Salmon P. Chase to Mann, May 27, 1848, Mann MSS:MHS; John
Blanchard to C. D. Cleveland, May 17, 1848, Slave Papers: LOC; Samuel
Gridley Howe to Mann, July 18, 1848, Straker MSS:ACL.
[1] Lydia Mann to Mann, May 1, 1848; Mann to Mary Mann, May 1, 1848;
Mary Mann to Mann, May 5 and 6, 1848, all in Mann MSS:MHS; Lydia
Mann to Mann, May 2, 1848, Straker MSS:ACL.

is formed. You can contribute mightily to that opinion." Although John C. Palfrey and Joshua Giddings continued to draw unto themselves the most vitriolic denunciations for their outspoken anti-slavery stand, Mann remained mute, much to the consternation of Howe and Sumner.[2]

"I would pay great deference to your judgment,—" Mann wrote to Sumner, "but I can hardly think that . . . any discreet person could expect that a private soldier, not yet two days in the camp would rush forward and assume a post among the leaders." The consequences of such arrogance even Sumner should understand. "Such a presumptuous act,—as everybody here would have deemed it,—would have neutralized the effect of the best speech that any man could make, and, of course, of an infinitely better speech than Horace Mann will ever make." And he added, so that Sumner should understand that as a new Washingtonian he was entitled to political intelligence not available to those who stayed close to home, "[General Zachary] Taylor has been sinking and sinking to a very low depth. His last letter revived the courage of his friends considerably, but I think it gives them no solid ground of hope. As for Mr. Clay, he was afraid of being murdered and so he committed suicide." [3]

But Sumner was not to be mollified by such excuses when he considered that the future of the nation, and even of mankind, was at stake. Two weeks later, with still no report of a maiden speech by Mann in the Boston newspapers, he gave the screw one more turn. "A speech from you on the Slavery question and the morality of politics," he wrote to Mann, "would have an important influence on public sentiment. I wish it had been made a fortnight ago. . . . *Yours* is a voice of power. What you say must produce an echo. I desire that it should commence its work of influence soon." [4]

Failing with his plea of newness in the job, Mann fell back upon a second line of defense. Sumner and Howe should appreciate that, unlike Adams, Giddings, and Palfrey, he was wearing a second hat. Until the Board had found his successor and he had time to publish his *Twelfth Annual Report*, he must remain as politically

---

[2] Joshua Giddings to [?], April 15, [1848], and Charles Sumner to Joshua Giddings, May 6, 1848, Giddings MSS:OHS; Charles Sumner to Mann, May 4, 1848; M. M. Fisher to Mann, May 17, 1848, both in Mann MSS:MHS; by this time Howe no longer considered himself a Whig. See Samuel Gridley Howe to Mann, June 23, [1848], Straker MSS:ACL.
[3] Mann to Charles Sumner, May 7, 1848, Mann MSS:MHS.
[4] Charles Sumner to Mann, May 24, June 21 and 25, 1848, Mann MSS:MHS.

neutral as possible. To Mary, who had done little to conceal the pressure from Mann's local constituency that he speak out against slavery, he justified his stance with the explanation that,

. . . situated as I now am,—that is filling the office of Secretary of the Board, if I come out at first and take any leading or prominent part in politics, I shall be accused of political interference, through the influence of my office,—a thing, which as you know, for so many years, I have tried to keep clear of. I feel therefore, unpleasantly hampered, at the present time. Were it not for the necessity thus laid upon me, I should be inclined to heroic measures.

Thus Mann had contrived a period of grace for himself which he thought entitled him to stay clear of the debate over the extension of slavery in the House and absent himself from the forthcoming Whig presidential convention in Philadelphia.[5]

In the meantime, Sumner and Howe had come up with a less political, albeit just as public means by which Mann could take a stand against slavery. Who, they asked, was better qualified to be chief defense counsel for Daniel Drayton and Edward Sayres? Anxious to see that the defendants would not be sacrificed by the Garrisonians on their committee to their own purposes, Howe thought Mann was an ideal choice. Extending Mann something of a left-handed compliment, he wrote, ". . . if worst comes to worst no man in the country will make more out of a bad case than you can." Samuel Sewall agreed, assuring Mann that "ample funds will be raised for the defense of these men." Mann made a brief enquiry into the merits of the case and wrote Sumner for advice. Given the hostility against these men, there was every likelihood of speedy injustice. Mann learned that they were to be tried under Maryland laws, some more than a century old. An act passed in 1796 merely imposed a fine for helping slaves escape, but an earlier act of 1737

[5] Mann to Charles Sumner, June 28, 1848; Mann to Mary Mann, June 9 and 14, 1848, both in Mann MSS:MHS. Mann officially resigned from the Board on May 31, 1848, but he hoped they would ask him to stay on until he completed some unfinished tasks. "I have written a letter to the Board declining a re-election *for another year,* but I suppose the Board understands that I am willing to fill the office for a time . . . *inter nos,* I hope they will give me a chance to make one more report." The Board agreed that he could stay on until December. Mann to Mary Mann, May 29, 1848, Mann MSS:MHS. See also Records of the Massachusetts Board of Education, May 31 and June 1, 1848, MS in MSDE; J. W. I. [Ingraham] to Mann, June 1, 1848, Mann MSS:MHS; Mann to George N. Briggs, May 20, 1848, Briggs MSS:AAS.

provided the death penalty for slave stealing. The punishment was later changed to twenty years' imprisonment and a heavy fine. Knowing that the prosecuting attorney, Phillip S. Key, son of the author of the national anthem, was out for blood and a maximum of notoriety, it was almost a certainty that they would be accused of slave stealing. Mann learned that Key was also out for blood money by going for "an awful batch of indictments." Because of the severity of the punishment upon conviction, several indictments against Drayton and Sayres should have been sufficient. But not for Key. Entitled to collect a fee of $10 for each indictment, he planned to draw up seventy-six against each of the defendants.[6]

Mann also saw the possibility of testing the constitutionality of slavery in the District of Columbia. Although not optimistic of the outcome in the courts, he believed that an adverse ruling would help build up national sentiment for legislation to accomplish the same end. Howe came to Washington to help Mann make up his mind, his mission all the more urgent since Seward and Fessenden had both backed out, leaving a great void in the defense, and even Hall, no doubt fearing local retaliation, withdrew. Howe promised Mann a "distinguished lawyer" from the North, and with hope that Salmon P. Chase would come to his aid, Mann stepped into the breach. Informing Chase of what he considered the main issues in the case, he wrote: "I think we can make this an occasion for helping on the cause, so that slavery shall at least be declared *illegal,* if not *unconstitutional.*" Thus to his secretaryship and his Congressional mission, he added a third office, the defense of two luckless men who had failed in their attempt to help more than seventy slaves to freedom.[7]

*   *   *

Still Mann held off speaking out publicly against slavery. As May moved into June, two things held him to his silent "neutrality." The first was a trip through Virginia, his first travel south of the

[6] Mann to Mary Mann, June 24, 1848; Mann to Samuel Gridley Howe, June 30, 1848; Mann to Charles Sumner, May 30, 1848; Samuel Sewall to Mann, April 26, 1848, all in Mann MSS:MHS; Samuel Gridley Howe to Mann [July] 18, [1848], Straker MSS:ACL.
[7] Mann to Samuel Gridley Howe, April 27 and May 1, 1848; Charles Sumner to Mann, May 5, 1848; Mann to Mary Mann, May 9 and 12, 1848, all in Mann MSS:MHS; Mann to Salmon P. Chase, June 17, 1848, Chase MSS:PHS.

Potomac. The second was the results of the presidential nominating conventions. Having agreed to take the Drayton-Sayres Case, Mann joined several of his Congressional colleagues for a short journey down the Potomac and then across land to Richmond. At Mount Vernon he was troubled to find everything about the premises "in the last stages of dilapidation and decay." "Ruin threatens all. It is God's retribution for man's wickedness," he wrote, and then asked, "What, thought I, would the former occupant say, either of his home or his country, could he return?" [8]

In Richmond Mann was impressed by the classic beauty of some of its residences and public buildings, but he did not fail to note the squalid slums within their shadows which approached those of the worst mill towns in the North. A few plantations he visited he found well managed, but the majority were run down and badly neglected by New England standards. To him it looked as if the southern farmer was locked into an unproductive system he could neither escape nor reform. Aside from several manicured gardens he visited, for the most part he found crumbling fences, razorbacked hogs, gullied fields, and little pedigreed livestock other than riding horses. Labor was not for the virtuous yeoman but for the slave, who tried to avoid it unless forced to perform by fear of the lash. Try as he would, Mann could find here no place for the gospel of hard work and thrift, and the satisfaction and self-esteem he thought came from these.[9]

From Richmond he took the railroad to the Appomattox River, where he boarded a steamboat for Fort Monroe. Mann was impressed by this military base, but not for reasons put forth by his hosts. Although mounting 500 guns, which cost more than $3 million, and claiming to be "one of the greatest fortifications in the world," the fortress for Mann was "a horrible sight." As the proud commanding officer guided the Congressional delegation about, Mann could only think,

When mankind shall have labored for eighteen hundred years, to improve and elevate the race as they have to demoralize it, and no favorable effect is produced, then, perhaps, the friends of improvement may begin to despond, if not despair; but until this experiment is tried and has failed, no advocate of reform should abandon his hopes or remit his exertions.

---

[8] Mann to [Mary Mann, May, 1848], letter fragment in Mann MSS:MHS.
[9] Mann to Mary Mann, May 21 and 23, 1848, Mann MSS:MHS.

On his return to Washington, he reported to Mary, "I have seen as much, or more of slavery than I ever saw before. The whole face of the country is stamped with the curse. The riches of the nation are turned into poverty, its fertility into barrenness; and man degrades himself as he degrades his fellows." From his tour he had received a powerful conviction that anti-slavery was the cause of the decade. "If I were sure," he wrote after he had returned to Washington, "that we would exclude slavery from the new territories, I should think little of anything else." [1]

While he was gone, the Democrats had gathered in Baltimore and nominated Lewis Cass of Michigan for their presidential candidate. An avowed expansionist and dilatory on the slavery question, Cass was the type of compromise candidate who could slip into the first office of a divided nation. The Whigs followed with a convention in Philadelphia. Once more passing over their ancient standard-bearer, Henry Clay, they repeated the precedent of 1840 and Tippecanoe by nominating "Old Rough and Ready," General Zachary Taylor, on the fourth ballot. Mann thought the Whig Party was "either broken and destroyed, or else . . . stultified and disgraced . . ." by putting forth Taylor, a slaveholder and military man. Moreover, he knew this action would further split the party in Massachusetts and make his official neutrality even more tenuous. Those Cotton Whigs back home who pushed for the election of Taylor had at least plausibility, if not an impeccable morality, on their side. Their immediate task was to capture the White House, and as Mann admitted to himself, "if Taylor be not supported, Cass will be elected, which will be, at any rate, the *worst* of very bad evils." But there was a disturbing dialectic at work. He believed that "the North has yielded to the South on every hand—now they are called to yield once more . . . this conflict of opinion will distract my Congressional District, probably more than any other in the State; and there is no State which will suffer so much as Massachusetts." [2]

Meanwhile, Sumner reported that the anti-Taylor movement was sweeping Massachusetts "like a hurricane," and as the turbulence in the House over the extension of slavery to new territories

---

[1] Mann to Mary Mann, May 25 and 26, and June 2, 1848, Mann MSS:MHS.

[2] Mann to Mary Mann, June 10, 13, and 14, 1848, Mann MSS:MHS. Not all agreed with Mann's concern about the likelihood of his re-election. Charles Francis Adams thought all Massachusetts Whigs were in trouble, save Palfrey and Mann. See Charles Francis Adams to John G. Palfrey, July 2, 1848, Adams MSS:MHS.

rose to a new intensity, Mann vainly sought to avoid this political maelstrom by clinging to some rock of immutable principle. "The principles," he wrote to Mary,

on which all the best men of the North profess to act,—the great principles for the advancement of civilization have been sacrificed to sustain the War-Fever and the Slavery-grip. I do not feel as tho' I could sustain this at any rate. I trust there will be a movement at the North, which shall look to the other objects, which shall be led on by men, who inscribe Peace and Liberty on their banners.

But while men cried peace, there was no peace. And liberty was a hollow abstraction at best, more likely a cruel mockery, as long as men and women were enslaved and the Congress failed to devise the political means to emancipate them.

Sumner could play the game of principle as well as Mann. Pursuing his quarry like a slavehunter's bloodhound, he solicited Mann, "We hope that you will join the movement—I am tempted to say unreservedly. I mean surrender to the *Principles*, which we advocate. . . . Let us stick to our principles and to the men who will sustain them." Still Mann pleaded for time. Sumner should understand that he "came into class" after the other Congressmen "had read the book half through," so that he had all the back lessons to make up. Running out of what was admittedly a most limited patience, Sumner fired back, ". . . I would have you back at the head of our Schools, unless you feel able and willing to be the champion of freedom as you have already been the champion of Education." [3]

Equally dogged in his attempt to maintain some principled position above immediate partisan issues, even at the expense of his alleged neutrality, Mann came to an agonizing decision. "I must begin these three days," he wrote to Mary,

to lay out the foundations of a speech, on the grounds of admitting a new territory into the Union. This is the great question. All Oregon is now to be provided with a territorial government, and if we obtain New Mexico and Upper California, provision also must be made for them. Shall they be permitted to hold slaves in those territories, or shall they not? This is the greatest question of the age . . . and I need a month to study it. I do not intend to speak *very soon*. . . .

---

[3] Mann to Mary Mann, June 9, 1848: Charles Sumner to Mann, June 21 and 25, and July 2, 1848; Mann to Charles Sumner, June 24, 1848, all in Mann MSS:MHS.

A month of preparation was a luxury not allowed many men in the House at that time. Mann had little more than two weeks to prepare for "the greatest question of the age." [4]

At 2:15 P.M., the last day of June, he gained the floor and began his maiden speech. According to Palfrey, the hall suddenly became quiet. Every member present hurried to his seat and waited "with greedy ear." They had come to listen for several reasons.[5] Most of them knew of Mann's reputation as an eloquent and indefatigable spokesman for common school education. And as the selfless friend of children, he came relatively unblemished to an arena where many men had known sin. As Mann rose, pulling his slender form up to a full six foot one, they could hope to hear a sample of the oratory which had moved men and women back in Massachusetts to renewed efforts for their sons and daughters. They were also politicians to their very sinews. Knowing that the Massachusetts delegation was split down the middle, they would weigh Mann's statements to see if he leaned towards Webster and Winthrop or stood ready to join Palfrey, Sumner, and Charles Francis Adams. The few who knew he would oppose the extension of slavery listened with no less interest since they wanted to know if Mann would remain a Whig, or join those who planned to organize a third-party movement at Buffalo.

The first group did not have long to wait. Almost with his very first sentence Mann asserted that notwithstanding recent southern arguments to the contrary, Congress not only had power to legislate for the territories, but it had the duty to exclude slavery from them. Beginning with a legal argument, he claimed that since Congress had the power to acquire territory, ". . . the power *to govern what is acquired* must be implied also." What followed was a full explication of his point, replete with legal citations, beginning with John Marshall and *McCullough* v. *Maryland.* To support his contention, he went on to argue that since the three branches of government were coordinate, the alleged inability of Congress to legislate on territorial matters meant that the judicial branch had no authority "to *adjudicate* for the territories," and if this were so, the executive

---

[4] Mann to Mary Mann, June 10, 13, and 14, 1848, Mann MSS:MHS; Mary Mann to George Combe, June 16, 1848, Combe MSS:NLS.
[5] John G. Palfrey to Charles Francis Adams, June 30, 1848, Adams MSS:MHS.

branch had not right to administer them. "These rights," he insisted, "must stand or fall together." [6]

Satisfied with his legal case, Mann then offered economic reasons why slavery should forever be excluded from the territories. Presenting a line of reasoning which must have sounded like so much Yankee nonsense to his listeners from Dixie, Mann observed that slavery had been a suffocating depressant on southern life. "Though slaves are said to be property," they were in actuality "the preventers, the wasters, the antagonists of property." The reason for this was clear to all who wished to see. Enslave a man and you destroy his ambition, his industry, and his ingenuity. "When he moves his tardy limbs," Mann continued, "it is because of the suffering that goads him from behind, and not the bright prospects that beckon him forward in the race." To pit slave labor against free was to pit an ox against a locomotive.[7]

The argument according to the gospel of hard work completed, Mann then turned to the doctrine of self-help and education. By nature, the institution of slavery required the slave to be kept in ignorance. But if slavery had caused the blight of ignorance and superstition on the Negro, it had also created a malignancy which undermined the potential of the whites by making their education all but impossible. "Common schools cannot exist where the population is sparse. Where slaves till the soil, or do the principle part of whatever work is done, the free population must be sparse. Slavery, then, by an inexorable law, denies general education to the whites." [8]

Having put his southern audience on the rack, Mann was unwilling to let matters rest here. Instead he followed up with a devastating comparison of southern and northern accomplishments. As he proceeded to belittle southern culture, his colleagues squirmed uncomfortably in their seats until Congressman Thomas Henry Bayly rose to his feet and broke the tension, challenging Mann's claim that "With New England habits of industry . . . the State of Virginia, which skirts us here on the south, would support all the population of the New England states, and fill them with abundance."

---

[6] Mann, "Speech Delivered in the House of Representatives of the United States, June 30, 1848, on the Right of Congress to Legislate for the Territories of the United States, and Its Duty to Exclude Slavery Therefrom," *Slavery: Letters and Speeches* (Boston, 1851), pp. 13–23.

[7] *Ibid.*, pp. 32–35.

[8] *Ibid.*, pp. 39–43.

MR. BAYLY. We have as great a population as New England now.

MR. MANN. As great a population as New England!!

MR. BAYLY. We send fifteen representatives. [A voice. And how many of them represent slaves?]

MR. MANN. Massachusetts alone sends ten representatives. [A voice. And the rest of New England twenty-one more.]

Encouraged by this unexpected support, Mann went on to compare school enrollments, libraries, authors, patents issued, and other indices, all to the detriment of the South. But still he was not finished.[9]

To those who thought that only abolitionist rabblerousers in the North were against the extension of slavery, Mann wanted it understood that the crusade against human servitude was the cause of men of reason and good will everywhere.

Sir, how often, on this floor, have indignant remonstrances been addressed to the north, for agitating the subject of slavery? How often have we at the north been told that we are inciting insurrection, fomenting a servile war, putting the black man's knife to the white man's throat. The air of this hall has been filled, its walls have been, as it were, sculptured, by southern eloquence, with images of devastated towns, of murdered men and ravished women; and, as a defense against the iniquities of the institution, they have universally put in the plea that the calamity was entailed upon them by the mother country, that it made a part of the world they were born into, and therefore, they could not help it. I have always been disposed to allow its full weight to this palliation. But if they now insist upon perpetrating against the whole western world, which happens at present to be under our control, the same wrongs which, in darker days, Great Britain perpetrated against them, they will forfeit every claim to sympathy. Sir, here is a test. Let not southern men, who would now force slavery upon new regions, ever deny that their slavery at home is a chosen, voluntary, beloved crime.

Finally, fusing passion and reason into powerful hammer blows, Mann came down with a peroration he hoped would shatter the hardest of men's hearts,

Sir, on the continent of Europe, and in the Tower of London, I have seen the axes, the chains, and other horrid implements of death, by

[9] *Ibid.*, pp. 44–45. To make things even more galling, Mann drew his data from a respected southern author, William Gregg, *Essays on Domestic Industry, or an Inquiry into the Expediency of Establishing Cotton Manufacturers in South Carolina* (Charlestown, 1845), which candidly admitted to the intellectual and productive inferiority of the South, its indolence, and lack of industry.

which the great defenders of freedom for the soul were brought to their final doom,—by which political and religious liberty was cloven down; and all the ghastly implements of death ever invented by religious bigotry or civil despotism to wring and torture freedom out of the soul of man;—fairer and lovelier were they all than the parchment roll of this House on which shall be inscribed a law profaning one additional foot of American soil with the curse of slavery.[1]

He had spoken for almost an hour. Some men were stunned by the intensity of his moral fervor. Men like Abraham W. Venable of North Carolina and Richard K. Meade of Virginia controlled their anger, secure in the knowledge that when given the floor, they would administer this parvenu schoolteacher a lesson in political debate. And still others took comfort in the knowledge that they had found a new ally and powerful voice, one possibly the equal to John Quincy Adams. The speech finished, Palfrey sat back in his seat and quickly penned a note to Charles Francis Adams, confirming his prediction that Mann was sound on the slavery question. "Mann has made a capital speech, and commanded perfect attention and strong interest." And as Palfrey completed the sentence, someone passed up the aisle, placed a hand on his shoulder, and said, "Well, Massachusetts has reason to be proud of her sons." The voters of the Eighth Congressional District of Massachusetts had chosen a man who was willing to carry Elijah's mantle.[2]

Mann's own assessment of his performance was less positive. "Well, dearest," he wrote to Mary with the sense of relief and emptiness which follows a major effort, "I have made my speech. All first speeches are listened to, and so mine was." To Howe he reported that he had "devirginated" himself, but the product was more of an "abortion." However he viewed the merits of its substance, he did admit that it could possibly accomplish more than any of his other writings and speeches. The reason for this, he wrote to Samuel J. May, was "that it was said in *Congress*, and by *a member of Congress*. . . ."[3]

That a national platform was a decided asset he quickly learned from the public response to his speech. Almost every Massa-

---

[1] *Ibid.*, pp. 58 and 72.
[2] John G. Palfrey to Charles Francis Adams, June 30, 1848, Adams MSS:MHS.
[3] Mann to Mary Mann, [June 30, 1848], Mann MSS:MHS; Mann to Samuel Gridley Howe, June 30, 1848, Personal Miscellaneous MSS:LOC; Mann to Samuel J. May August 5, 1848, in Mann, *Life*, pp. 268–269.

chusetts newspaper carried excerpts of it together with favorable editorial comments. Even Garrison opened his columns in the *Liberator* to it and Edmund Quincy added editorially that it was "lucid, forcible, and eloquent," and "the best Anti-slavery lecture, properly so-called, that has been delivered before the National Lyceum."[4] And the letters poured in. From New England, New York, and Pennsylvania came little less than impassioned support. "I cannot forbear thanking you for the noble speech which you made a little while ago in the House," wrote Theodore Parker. "It is nobler than anything your predecessor ever said in the House." Similar sentiments came from George B. Emerson, Heman Humphrey, William A. Alcott, and Dorothea L. Dix. Even a few independent souls from the South took courage from Mann's stand. Most correspondents asked for a printed copy of the speech; some requested a half dozen, and one enthusiast in Maine enclosed a mailing list of forty men whom he wanted to receive copies.[5]

Conversely, Mann could take an equal measure of assurance from the attacks he drew upon himself. If his speech had not demolished the southern outer defense of slavery, it must have at least pricked the inner conscience and wounded the pride of some of its defenders. Smarting from the attack, a southern caucus decided that they could not let Mann's remarks go unanswered. The assignment fell to Abraham Venable of North Carolina, who sarcastically announced in the House that he would respond to the "very learned gentleman from Massachusetts." Venable's rebuttal ignored Mann's

---

[4] For sample newspaper responses in Boston to Mann's speech, see the Boston *Daily Courier*, July 3, 1848; Boston *Evening Transcript*, July 5, 1848; Boston *Daily Advertiser*, August 1 and 2, 1848; *Christian Register*, August 5 and 12, 1848; *Liberator*, August 4, 1848.

[5] Theodore Parker to Mann, August 6, 1848; George B. Emerson to Mann, July 28, 1848; Heman Humphrey to Mann, July 28, 1848; William A. Alcott to Mann, July 31, 1848; Dorothea L. Dix to Mann, August 19, 1848; and Jonas Foster to Mann, August 2, 1848, all in Mann MSS:MHS. A typical response to Mann's speech was written by John Westall of Fall River, August 8, 1848, and included the following sentiments:

Will you please send me some copies of your Speech in the House of Representatives on the 30th of June last? There is a great desire to read it here, and I shall be glad to assist in giving it the widest circulation.

I thank you for your noble defense of Freedom, and the Right of all to the most complete Education. It is exceedingly cheering to us, to hear the successor of him who fought so nobly for the Right of Petition, defending in "Thoughts that breathe and words that burn," the greater right of Soul-Liberty.

Mann MSS:MHS.

legal arguments and concentrated on his misunderstanding of southern culture. With an affected sense of moral indignation and wounded pride, he claimed that Mann had "described manners which he never saw, institutions with which he is unacquainted, and domestic relations which he does not understand." Even worse, by comparison, he had conveniently ignored the "wild and wicked schemes" of Garrison, the "rantings" of Abby Folsom, and the excesses of Millerism, Mormonism, and Quakerism. Free soil and not the slave states had nurtured fanaticism. If the North would just try for once to understand the southern position, it would admit to the beam in its own eye and forget about the motes of which it now made such inflammatory accusations.

Venable could not leave the field, however, without a personal attack on this Yankee educator who had the temerity to expose the seamy side of southern life.

His heart, as well as his intellect, is so absorbed in his chivalrous attempt to revolutionize the framework of our social institutions, that nothing else can engage his attention. The kidnapper and the felon—the whole African race, whether happy, contented, or the reverse, are subjects of his sympathizing efforts; but his own race and countrymen are either forgotten or libelled. . . . Sir, this is a deplorable picture—that a gentleman and a scholar, a man of irreproachable life and character should give the sanction of his name to the broad denunciation of his Southern fellow-citizens, from their external to the most internal relations of life! I would say that this is a bowie-knife civilization with all its savage accompaniments and its nurseries the schools of vulgarity and impurity!

A weak and yet fantastic rebuttal of sweet talk, mock innocence, and personal invective, all wrapped up in the form of southern stump oratory. If Yankees such as Mann would just look at the facts, they would understand that slavery was a blessing to white and black alike.[6]

But much to Mann's amazement, he found that Sumner was still not satisfied. Although New England newspapers had supported Mann *"una voce,"* Sumner complained, "but I wish (Oh! how I wish!) you had said that you would not vote for Taylor or Cass. That would have been a snapper in your Whip." Mann should understand that the two-party system in New England was in a shambles, collapsing before the slavery issue which was moving across the

---

[6] *Congressional Globe,* July 29, 1848, pp. 1006–1010.

political scene like an irresistible juggernaut. The two Democratic newspapers in Norfolk County had "hauled down their Cass flags" and more than one editor had written the obituary for "Whiggery" in Mann's district. In Massachusetts, Conscience Whigs, Locofoco (radical) Democrats, and Liberty Party men were organizing a coalition meeting in Worcester as a prelude to a national anti-slavery third-party convention in Buffalo. "The good men are rallying," Sumner reported, giving Mann a day-by-day account by letter and urging him to become a leader of the movement rather than be swept under by its political tidal wave which had begun to form. "The tide is rising so fast," he warned, "that like that of the Bay of Fundy, it promises to drown the swine politicians. I pray that you may not be caught by it." In short, Mann's self-appointed political consciences in New England would not be satisfied until he publicly denounced the official Whig presidential nominee, the slaveholding Zachary Taylor, and formally severed his ties with the Whig Party.[7]

Now pushed to the wall by his friends, Mann went to Palfrey for aid and wrote to Governor George Briggs for comfort. Palfrey assured him that as a member of Congress he was under no obligation, the pressure from the Conscience Whigs notwithstanding, to endorse one of the presidential candidates, and that as secretary to the Board he should avoid any "excited party controversy" until he had completed his final *Report*. Briggs simply replied that no person or party had the right to demand that Mann take a public stand on the presidential election. For Mann, this was advice gladly followed, particularly since in giving birth to the Free Soil Party, the Buffalo convention had found it necessary to resuscitate Martin Van Buren for its presidential standard-bearer, a politician Mann considered irredeemably corrupt.[8]

His stance on the presidential issue now clarified to the degree

---

[7] John Shorey to Mann, July 15, 1848; Charles Sumner to Mann, July 2, 3, 4, and 5, 1848; Mary Mann to Mann, June [really July] 6, and July 7, 1848; Samuel Downer to Mann, July 1, 1848, all in Mann MSS:MHS; Charles Sumner to Joshua Giddings, July 5, 1848, Giddings MSS:OHS; Samuel Gridley Howe to Mann, July 7, 1848, Straker MSS:ACL.

[8] John G. Palfrey to Mann, July 8, 1848; George N. Briggs to Mann, July 20, 1848; William Jackson to Mann, July 17, 1848; C. D. Cleveland to Mann, June 19, 1848, all in Mann MSS:MHS; Mann to Samuel J. May, August 5, 1848, in Mann *Life*, pp. 268–269. Apparently many politicians in Massachusetts did not know what Mann planned to do. Thus Garrison, while supporting Mann for his anti-slavery speech, would also write, "I have very little doubt that Horace Mann will go for the Louisiana bloodhound. If he should ———!" William Lloyd Garrison to Edmund Quincy, August 10, 1848, Garrison MSS:SC.

that he thought he could at least defend it, and his position on the extension of slavery to the territories clearly defined, Mann found himself much more at home in the House through July and early August. The vehemence and pseudo-heroics of Congressmen attempting to rationalize the new military appropriations bill led him to believe that the small nonpartisan anti-slavery block was gaining momentum. The more he listened to the war hawks, the more it became, as he reported, "a perpetual ringing in my ears of the 'glorious war,' 'undying laurels,' 'gratitude of the country,'" and a hypocritical and sanctimonious camouflage for the fact that American lives had been intentionally sacrificed in the Mexican War to enable the South to transplant its "peculiar institution" into new territories. But whether it was money for the military or the establishment of territorial governments in Oregon, California, and New Mexico, he was convinced that the root issue was slavery.[9]

A showdown test of anti-slavery sentiment in the House was inevitable, and it came with the vote on a compromise bill which would have allowed the question of slavery to be decided by the residents in each of the new territories. For Mann, the stakes were unbelievably high. "The future welfare and greatness of the territories has very little to do with the question," he wrote back home. "The fate of millions and millions is to be voted upon. . . ." And on such an issue, it was time for men to stand up and be counted. Although he considered the typical tone of the House to be more like that of "bedlam" than a deliberative body, as the roll call on the compromise bill began, to his amazement, "it became still as a church. Everyman wanted to know how every other man voted." As the clerk moved down the list, the ayes and nays were neck and neck. Only near the end was the outcome clear. By a count of 112 to 98 the House voted to table the measure.[1] With this done, it then moved on to send the Oregon Bill to the Senate, which established a territorial government for this part of the country, but specifically excluded slavery from it. After a bitter clash between Webster and Calhoun, the Senate agreed, but attached an amendment to the bill which amounted to a reaffirmation of the Missouri Compromise. Thus the price of free soil in Oregon was to be an uncertain future for those territories below 36° 30'. Aroused to the danger, the anti-slavery coalition of northern Democrats and Whigs, and incipient

---

[9] Mann to Mary Mann, July 14 and 18, 1848, Mann MSS:MHS.
[1] Mann to Mary Mann, July 18 and 29, 1848, Mann MSS:MHS.

Free Soilers, rallied a majority of thirty-nine votes in the House and sent their original version back to the Senate. Unexpectedly, the Senate was equally adamant and once more returned the measure with the Missouri Compromise rider. Only after another round of open debate and behind closed-door negotiations did the Senate grudgingly agree to the original House proposal. "It is one of the most glorious things that has happened this century," Mann jubilantly reported to Mary. "All our discussions on the subject of slavery this session have tended to it." And later he wrote, still feeling the sweet sense of vindication, "Is not this worth coming to Washington to see? It is a great triumph, and the first upon which we can really rely." After the reprehensible conduct of Congress in promoting the Mexican War, Mann thought that he had had some part in bringing it once again a little closer to the side of justice.[2]

Still Mann resisted all attempts to make him identify himself with any party and sought the higher ground of a principled position above partisanship. Even so, in achieving this, he was more involved in political expediency than he willingly admitted. On principle, he could not support Cass, Taylor, or Van Buren for the presidency, yet he refused to state this publicly for fear of losing his Congressional seat in the next election. Instead, by defending Drayton and Sayres, he was doing his part for the abolition of slavery in the District of Columbia, also one of the objectives of the new Free Soil Party. By speaking out against the extension of slavery to the new territories, he was in agreement with most northern anti-slavery men among the Whigs and Democrats, thus enjoying a broadly based political support. This, together with his excuse of the secretaryship, allowed him to be above partisan loyalty while remaining a nominal Whig, and enjoying whatever political benefits came his way.

Increasingly, the moral and economic issues with which men were forced to grapple did not respond to simplistic principled action. In his own case, and much to his mounting discomfort, Mann found it necessary to compromise behind a façade of intended integrity. As one section of the nation closed ranks for the defense of an inhuman institution, in the face of a relentless campaign of remonstrances from the North, moral differences began to harden in the depths of men's hearts and became far too intransigent to be palliated by unessential concessions or camouflaged by some verbal

---

[2] Mann to Mary Mann, August 11 and 13, 1848, Mann MSS:MHS.

sleight of hand. Nor could one any longer trust, as Mann still believed, that the evil of slavery, like other social problems, would be solved as part of the "invincible march of progress." Only gradually and reluctantly was he learning of the fallibility of his romantic liberal belief in the power of reason and the inevitable perfectibility of men and institutions. Unlike the high ground of selfless enlightenment from which he wished to act, the nightmare of slavery was drawing him into a slough of greed, moral self-righteousness, passion, prejudice, and deeply rooted honest misunderstandings. From such imponderabilia, rational deliberations, much less rationalizations, could not extricate him.

As the events were eroding away the truths which the men of the nineteenth century held self-evident, perhaps it was both merciful and misleading that changes came upon them in such miniscule day-to-day installments, so that they noted a brick tumbling down here and a piece of cornice falling there, but did not recognize the disintegration of their entire edifice of reason and enlightenment. Little of this Mann recognized at the time. For him it was enough that by late July, and with great effort, he had fashioned a precarious political base for himself from an immiscible amalgam of principle and expediency. Although dissatisfied with it, he had little time to meditate on its shortcomings and contradictions. Unwilling to postpone their cases any further, Judge Thomas H. Crawford of the Criminal Court of the District of Columbia had ruled that it was time for Drayton and Sayres to stand trial.

*   *   *

Mann was ill-prepared on several counts. For one thing, he had not argued anything significant in court for the last twelve years. Then, too, although Howe's committee in Boston had promised him assistance from some eminent lawyer, none was forthcoming. The abolitionists on the committee would not agree to anyone they did not like *abolitionally,* Mann learned from Howe. He also learned that only piddling contributions were coming in and this meant that Daniel Webster, whose fee was $1,000, could not be retained. Then after Seward and Fessenden had informed the committee of their inability to serve, Salmon P. Chase backed out as well. Almost desperate, Mann took it upon himself to engage the services of James M. Carlisle, a respected Washington attorney, and the Boston committee dispatched the young Richard Hildreth to give what help he could. "This has crowded me excessively," Mann complained to Mary; "I am not prepared to go on trial Monday. I shall avail myself of the slightest legitimate excuse to procure a continuance. . . ." [3]

With the adjournment of Congress, Palfrey, Rockwell, and Winthrop could return to Massachusetts and avoid any further punishment from the oppressive Washington summer. The heat on the streets was blistering, the high humidity made it a burden to breathe, and it was like an oven in the courtroom where the spectators, including most of the forty-one owners, were packed in almost as tightly as the inhabitants of a slave ship. Mann found himself in a perpetual sweatbath, the starch in his collar going limp and soggy by the time Judge Crawford had mounted the bench. From the outset, it was evident that a travesty on justice was about to be played out and Mann thought he would have to work miracles if he was to get Drayton off with just a conviction for transporting rather than stealing slaves. Mann's request for a continuance was summarily dismissed by Crawford, who made little pretense of concealing his hostility towards the defendants. Crawford also ruled that Phillip Barton Key, the district attorney, did not have to specify which prisoner was to be tried until after the jury was impaneled. To make matters worse, the jury was drawn from a motley pool of drifters and idlers combed from the streets and local grog shops. Key also must have been out for some record in crime and punishment. He not only intended to win a conviction on each and every one of the 345 indictments against the defendants, but was not above exploiting the prejudices and emotions of the moment and asking for nothing less than 800 years' imprisonment for poor Drayton! Little wonder that some considered the trial "one of the most ferocious attacks upon the rights and liberties of the citizen ever made." [4]

The jury chosen, Key then announced that he was trying Daniel Drayton for *stealing* two slaves belonging to Andrew Hoover, valued at $2,000. He denounced Drayton as a liar, felon, thief, and rogue,

---

[3] Mann to Mary Mann July 22, 23, and 25, 1848; Salmon P. Chase to Mann, July 16, 1848; Mann to Samuel Gridley Howe, July 3, 1848, all in Mann MSS:MHS; Mann to Salmon P. Chase, July 3, 1848, Chase MSS:PHS; Samuel Gridley Howe to Mann, [July] 18, [1848], Straker MSS:ACL; Samuel J. May to John Blanchard, July 1, 1848, Slave Papers: LOC.

[4] Mann to Mary Mann, July 23, 24, and 26, 1848; *National Era*, August 10, 1848; *Liberator*, August 11, 1848; Mann to A[riel] Parish, August 24, 1848, Misc. Papers:LOC.

warning the jury that if Drayton went unpunished, Washingtonians might as well abandon all their slave property. By comparison, Mann's opening remarks were more tempered as he struggled to rephrase his ideas to make them understandable to his audience. He pleaded for sympathy for the defendant, who had been "torn from his family and immured in a loathsome cell . . . pursued by a mob, from near the river's side . . . to the very doors of the jail," and now was forced to remain imprisoned by an excessive bail of $76,000.

Carefully, Mann reconstructed the events of the evening of April 15, including the torchlight procession, the blazing bonfires, and the illumination of the speakers platform on the steps of the White House. He then began to read from a newspaper clipping which he held out prominently for all to see.

. . . the age of TYRANTS AND SLAVERY is rapidly drawing to a close; and that happy period to be signalized by the universal emancipation of man from the *fetters of civil oppression*, and the recognition *in all countries* of the great principles of *popular sovereignty, equality and* BROTHERHOOD, is at this moment, visibly commencing.

Visibly angry at the sentiments expressed, Judge Crawford broke in on Mann and cautioned him. "Such inflammatory language," he warned, "cannot be allowed in this court. We have institutions that may be endangered by it. The court thinks it its duty to interfere. The counsel cannot be allowed to proceed with such inflammatory language." Sensing that Mann may have been quoting Garrison in the *Liberator*, Key jumped to his feet and demanded to know the name of the newspaper from which Mann was reading and the author of the remarks. With the knowing smile of a man who had just trapped his adversary, Mann gladly obliged, identifying the clipping from the *Washington Union* and the "incendiary" author as none other than Senator Henry Foote of Mississippi, who had spoken these very words from the speakers' platform at the French independence celebration on April 15. Now furious, Judge Crawford looked straight at the defense counsel and snapped, "Mr. Mann knows Mr. Foote did not mean his language for our slaves." Mann had made a telling point, even though he had further antagonized the judge. Because of the presence of human bondage in the capital, any man who spoke of liberty might be encouraging slaves to seek their own freedom and therefore become guilty of incendiary and treasonable conduct.[5]

Then began the presentation of testimony, and again it was clear that justice was a fugitive if not a complete stranger in the courtroom. Judge Crawford allowed spectators to talk and joke with the jury, and Mann was appalled when one member of the jury told a joke about a bottle of rum while Crawford was ruling on a question the counsel for the defense had raised. A government witness claimed he overheard Drayton say that if he had gotten away, he would have made a fortune selling the slaves. Unfortunately, he did not change his mind until the next trial and so the damage was done. Key claimed that a brig stood by at the mouth of the Potomac, ready to carry the slaves to Cuba, but no evidence was given as to the name of the ship, or proof of its existence.

Near the end of the testimony, Mann presented fifteen points in a bill of exception. Knowing a verdict of guilty was a foregone conclusion, he was laying the basis for an appeal in the Circuit Court. This put Crawford in a bind. Wanting to rule as much in favor of the prosecution as possible, he knew that an excessive bias might invite a reversal of Drayton's conviction. Choosing his words carefully, he ruled on each point, including the opinion that color was *prima facie* evidence of slave status in the District of Columbia. With such a ruling, Mann felt Crawford had played into his hand once more. "We have presented some points for the court to decide upon, which they could not decide against us, without exposing themselves to have the whole set aside for false direction. We feel better," he reported to Mary. Now clearly fighting on the side of justice and free of the irritating ambiguities ever present in the House, for the first time since coming to Washington, he could return to his quarters at Gordon's and sleep the sleep of the just.[6]

In his closing remarks, Key offered only a brief summation, including the preposterous *non sequitur*, "Gentlemen of the jury, you see he transported the slaves; he had them on board his vessel, he *must* have stolen them. It is the plainest case of larceny I ever had." Mann's summation took two hours. In it he continued to lay the groundwork for his next move to win freedom for Drayton.

---

[5] Mann, "Sketch of the Opening Argument in the Case of the United States *vs.* Daniel Drayton . . . ," *Slavery: Letters and Speeches* (Boston, 1851), pp. 88–108; *National Era,* August 10, 1848; *Liberator,* August 11, 1848; New York *Herald,* July 31, and August 2 and 4, 1848.
[6] Mann to [Mary Mann], August 2, 1848, Mann MSS:MHS.

Judge Crawford then instructed the jury that if they believed Drayton had made the seventy-six slaves discontented and persuaded them to go with him on the *Pearl,* he feloniously carried them away, regardless of his ultimate intent, and was therefore guilty of larceny. Even with such biased instructions, it was necessary for the jury to deliberate through the night and following morning. Originally eight voted for guilty and four for acquittal. By early afternoon, the minority gradually gave way and by 2:30 P.M. they reported they had found Daniel Drayton guilty of stealing two slaves. With immodest haste, Judge Crawford sentenced him to prison for forty years.[7]

While awaiting the verdict, a new jury was impaneled for the second indictment against the defendant. The next day much of the same evidence was presented and on August 9, a second verdict of guilty was brought in against Drayton. From all of this Mann was anything but discouraged. ". . . I think the law is on our side," he wrote to Mary, "and we mean so far to get the principles on record, that if we fail here, we can get the decision reversed in a higher court. Don't feel at all uneasy about me. I am in a *good* work—Maybe, it will turn out to be a *great* one." And again he wrote, "I feel in this case as though I were not working for Drayton and Sayres only but for the whole colored race." Once more, for at least the time being, he had found the certitude of a man who believes he is fighting for a principle.[8]

Most men struggling for principles believe that time is on their side, and Mann was no exception. By August 9 he sensed that "the fury of the fight has very much burnt itself out," and in this he was right. With two convictions against Drayton to his belt, Key then moved to try Sayres. When Mann objected, calling Crawford's attention to the fact that Drayton's bail was so high that he must remain in jail and therefore was entitled to a speedy trial, he was overruled and Sayres's first trial proceeded. Attempting an optimistic prediction, Mann observed, "it looks better than the others, and I do not see how it is possible, even with the most prejudiced jury; and a fore determined judge, to convict him." On August 13, the jury required just fifteen minutes to return a verdict of not guilty of stealing slaves. Three days later, at the conclusion of a second trial,

[7] Mann to Mary Mann, August 5 and 7, 1848, Mann MSS:MHS; *National Era,* August 10 and 24, 1848; *Liberator,* August 11, 1848.
[8] Mann to Mary Mann, August 7, 14, and 16, 1848, Mann MSS:MHS; Mann to George N. Briggs, August 16, 1848, Briggs MSS:AAS.

despite an angry diatribe from Key, a new jury required even less time to come in with a similar decision. Sayres then pleaded guilty to transporting slaves illegally and was fined $7,400. Apparently one scapegoat was to be sufficient to soothe the slaveholders' wrath and Drayton was to be their man.[9]

* * *

And so the first round was finished. Action on the remaining thirty-nine indictments against Drayton was postponed indefinitely and Mann must next look to preparing an appeal of the two convictions, probably to be heard in December. In West Newton, from the middle of August on, Mary, young Horace, and Georgie would look down the hill at almost every westbound train coming down the track in the hope that "Papa" would be on it. With each disappointing day, Mary would buoy up the spirits of her sons, and knowing that Mann was equally as unhappy with this forced separation, she assured him, "We know you are working in a holy cause, and we can wait." The same day she wrote this, she could also read in the *Liberator,* "The Hon. Horace Mann appears to have done himself great credit as counsel for the accused, and managed his case with much skill and energy." Meanwhile in Washington, Mann discussed the next legal steps to be taken with Carlisle. He then visited Drayton in his cell and found him "firm and collected, resolved to bide his fate." [1]

His bags packed, it was a bone-weary but more contented Horace Mann who headed to the train depot and boarded his car for the long trip home. He would travel two successive nights to reach Boston. With him he carried the honest satisfaction of having defended Drayton and Sayres, and having spoken out against slavery from the floor of the House, while still remaining nonpartisan. But the effort had taken its toll. He felt "Utterly prostrated, exhausted, extincted and defunct," as he put it, perhaps this time with only minor exaggeration, and added, "A sand-bag is elastic and *springy* compared with my body." And two days later, a westbound train unlike any other that summer stopped at the West Newton station. "Papa" had arrived! Mann's tired frame and measured steps revealed some-

---

[9] Mann to Mary Mann, August 6, 7, 11, 13, and 16, 1848, Mann MSS:MHS.
[1] Mann to Mary Mann, August 14, 1848; Mary Mann to Mann, August 18, [1848], both in Mann MSS:MHS; *Liberator,* August 18, 1848.

thing of the ordeal of mind, body, and conscience he had just been through, but with the sight of Horace, Georgie, and Mary with the new baby in her arms rushing down the road to meet him, all this and the last months of separation were instantly forgotten.[2]

Forgotten also were the new appeals to be made for Drayton, the writing of his twelfth and final *Annual Report,* and the more immediate task of getting re-elected to Congress at a time of political uncertainty. As he dropped his bag, picked up Horace and Georgie in his arms, and looked at Mary proudly holding the four-month-old Benjamin, all the troubling political and educational issues of the day were suddenly transported to another planetary system. It was simply enough to be home.

---

[2] Mann to A[riel] Parish, August 24, 1848, Misc. Papers:LOC.

CHAPTER XX

The Ordeal of Compromise

<hr>

IT MAY BE WELL for the statesman to know that
statesmanship easily degenerates into opportunism
and that opportunism cannot be sharply distinguished from dishonesty. But the prophet ought to
realize that his higher perspective and uncompromising nature of his judgements always has a note
of irresponsibility in it. . . . The moral achievement of statesmen must be judged in terms which
take account of the limitations of human society
which the statesman must, and the prophet need
not, consider.

REINHOLD NIEBUHR

<hr>

IF THERE WERE immutable laws governing the Newtonian universe of the nineteenth century, so were there more immediate
political imperatives. The first task of any politician was still to get
elected. Too exhausted to speak at cornerstone layings and schoolhouse dedications, Mann nevertheless drew on a last residue of energy upon his return to West Newton to prepare a letter to the electors
of the Eighth Congressional District. In it he pledged himself to oppose the expansion of slavery to the new territories, but conveniently
skirted the issue of whom he would support for the presidency. Actually, he was attempting what Sumner had warned was impossible.
Claiming to be a Whig and appealing for party support, he still did
not want to be considered a party candidate, insisting that to be so
would impair his concluding efforts on behalf of the common
schools.[1]

Contradictory and self-defeating though his letter may have
been in the long run, for the moment it brought the results he
wanted. In separate conventions, both the Whigs and the Free Soilers nominated him as their candidate for Congress. Actually, the

<hr>

[1] Mann, "Letter from Horace Mann," Boston *Daily Courier,* September 1, 1848; Mann "Address . . . to the Electors of the Eighth Congressional District," Boston *Daily Advertiser,* September 2, 1848; see also the
Boston *Daily Republican,* September 1, 1848, and the Boston *Evening
Transcript,* September 1, 1848.

Whigs had little other choice, but some of the more radical Free Soilers swallowed hard before they endorsed Mann. If he were a member of the party of Winthrop, Webster, and Amos Lawrence, they questioned how he really could be against the extension of slavery. Yet to nominate anyone else was to throw away their vote, and so they reluctantly conceded to him the benefit of the doubt. Prodded along by Edmund W. Clap and E. L. Keyes, the Free Soilers finally resolved unanimously,

. . . that this Convention entertain the fullest confidence in the integrity and ability of the present Representative of this District in Congress; and as we believe him to be sound and true on the now paramount question of the extension of Slavery and have faith in his eloquence to illustrate the enormous moral evils of that institution and the intolerable political encroachments of the Slave Power—therefore we *unanimously nominate* the Hon. Horace Mann. . . .

A second resolution put on record that their endorsement was not because of the "support awarded him by the Whig Party, *but in spite of it*. . . ." Given Mann's speech in the House and his voting record, the convention concluded, "We are left no room to doubt that he is 'with us, and of us, and for us,' on the right side of that broad line of principle which separates at a like distance the supporters of Cass and Taylor, from those of Van Buren and Adams." [2]

The Whigs met the following day, and in their morning session nominated Mann by acclamation, asserting that ". . . his position in regard to free principles, free soil, free men, and free speech . . . was but a satisfactory fulfillment of the expectations of the Whigs, when they nominated him to succeed the illustrious Adams. . . ." In his pre-election maneuvers, luck seemed to be in Mann's corner. An early movement to nominate Henry Wilson as the Free Soil candidate collapsed before the opening gavel at the convention. And good fortune would have it that an ambitious young Whig Congressman from Illinois, Abraham Lincoln, who was stumping Massachusetts for the party and roundly lambasting the local Free Soilers as political spoilers, came to Dedham only after Mann had both nominations sewed up. In arguing that anyone opposed to the extension of slavery should vote for Zachary Taylor, Lincoln, ardently Whig

---

[2] E. L. Keyes to Mann, September 3, 1848; E. W. Clap to Mann, September 14 and 20, 1848; Mellatiah Everett to Mann, September 19, 1848, all in Mann MSS:MHS; Boston *Daily Republican*, September 20, 1848.

and inordinately abusive of the Free Soilers, was ripping open old political wounds in the Eighth District which Mann had hoped to heal over.[3]

Minimizing the differences in party endorsements, Mann sent virtually the same letter of acceptance to both groups. He promised to carry on the defense of Drayton and Sayres and pledged to build upon his anti-slavery stand, assuring his constituents, ". . . had I the tongue of an angel, or the pen of inspiration, I believe I could use them in no holier theme than in kindling abhorrence at the wrongs suffered by the slave, and in melting the universal heart of humanity into pity for his lot. . . ." The twin endorsement was enough to get Mann elected. The first week in November, along with Zachary Taylor and many other Whigs, Mann won at the polls, receiving 11,000 out of 13,000 votes cast, a landslide equal to any ever given by the voters to his predecessor.[4]

Yet in Mann's case, the one-sided victory was more apparent than real, a fact quickly picked up and publicized by the Garrisonians. Analyzing the options both parties had in the district, Edmund Quincy made it painfully clear that Mann had pulled off a clever political maneuver by his nonpartisan stance and placed the leaders of both parties in a quandary. "Each party wanted the credit of choosing him," Quincy argued, "and wished for the weight that his name and influence would throw into their scale. Both claimed him as belonging to them, and dared the other to presume to set up anybody else." Mann's lopsided victory then was the result of a temporary marriage of convenience between two bitterly hostile parties. With a showdown on slavery imminent in the next Congress, Quincy predicted that one of the two parties would surely find themselves betrayed by Mann's future actions; in a colorful phrase he added

---

[3] H. C. Foster to Mann, August 2, 1848; B. F. Copeland, *et al.*, to Mann, September 21, 1848, both in Mann MSS:MHS; Boston *Daily Advertiser*, September 23, 1848; Boston *Evening Transcript*, September 21, 1848; Albert Beveridge, *Abraham Lincoln*, I (Boston, 1928), 469–476. "I can sympathize with your joy," Sophia Hawthorne wrote to Mary Mann, "that your husband will not defile himself with party fury. Mine also is high and dry out of the slough of political warfare. . . ." But little did she realize that a landslide for Zachary Taylor would even reach into the "high and dry" of the Salem Customs House. Sophia Hawthorne to Mary Mann, October 15, 1848, Berg MSS:NYPL.
[4] Mann, "To the Whig Convention (and also to the Free Soil Convention, *mutatis mutandis,*) Accepting Their Respective Nominations for the Thirty-First Congress," *Slavery: Letters and Speeches* (Boston, 1851), pp. 119–120; *Christian Register*, October 7, 1848; Boston *Daily Republican*, November 15, 1848; Boston *Daily Advertiser*, November 16, 1848.

that they would have nobody to thank but themselves when "the pig came out of his poke and went whole hog against them." And in Washington, the editor of the *National Era,* Gamaliel Bailey, offered the same sentiments, if in a less earthy form. Mann's political neutrality had served him well to date, but had there been the necessity of a run-off election in the House for the presidency, Mann's neutrality would have been at an end, and he would become anathema to one of the two parties which supported him. What Bailey did not foresee was that the same situation, albeit with less intensity, could emerge with the choice of the Speaker of the House.[5]

*   *   *

But this could wait until December when the new House convened. Before that time, Mann had promised to prepare his twelfth and valedictory *Report.* There were some who thought this was adding too much to his present burden, but like his Puritan ancestors, Mann needed to give an accounting of his last twelve years of stewardship for the Board. He also expected to convince the Board to select Henry Barnard as his successor. So involved had he become in politics and in defending Drayton and Sayres, that he had lost touch with George Briggs and George B. Emerson. In the meantime, the conservative majority on the Board wanted a cooling-off period in which Mann's gains could be solidified and institutionalized, and had decided on Reverend Barnas Sears, a Baptist minister, who believed it was "now more necessary to *guide* than to *arouse* the legislature in its actions." [6]

With some embarrassment, Mann reported this development to Henry Barnard. When he learned of Sears's silence upon receiving the appointment and realizing an antagonism on the Board towards Barnard, Mann wrote confidentially to Briggs urging him to consider George B. Emerson. "Not a man in Massachusetts stands more prominently, than he. Not one would be more acceptable," were Mann's

---

[5] Q. [Edmund Quincy], "Honorable Horace Mann," *Liberator,* October 6, 1848; *National Era,* September 28, 1848.

[6] Barnas Sears to Mann, February 11, 1850, Mann MSS:MHS; Samuel Gridley Howe to Mann, July 4, 1848, Straker MSS:ACL; Sears subsequently followed Francis Wayland as president at Brown before becoming general agent of the Peabody Education Fund, a philanthropy which attempted to establish public schools in the South after the Civil War. See J. L. M. Curry, *A Brief Sketch of George Peabody, and a History of the Peabody Education Fund Through Thirty Years* (Cambridge, 1898), pp. 35–69.

words, but he was also saying that almost anyone was better than an orthodox clergyman. Sears finally accepted, and Mann had nothing remaining but to gather his ideas and write his *Twelfth Annual Report*. This was to be finished before the end of November since he was due back then in Washington for the resumption of the Drayton and Sayres trial.[7]

He labored on the *Report* for a month and when finished, he had written his most eloquent and compelling testament to justify the existence of public education. In part he dwelled on past accomplishments. "Under the Providence of God," he wrote, "our means of education are the grand machinery by which the 'raw material' of human nature can be worked up into inventors and discoverers, into skilled artisans and scientific farmers, into scholars and jurists. . . ." Mann went on to enumerate the powerful ways in which public schooling could make a revolutionary difference in the lives of people.[8] Although the laws of health and safety were ordained by God, knowledge and obedience of them was up to man's free will. Therefore, there was an ". . . uncompromising necessity that all children should be instructed in these laws; and not only instructed, but that they should receive such a training . . . as to enlist the mighty forces of habit on the side of obedience."[9] Schooling could also eliminate poverty and guarantee an abundance for all who wished to participate. Massachusetts was in danger of succumbing to the "domination of capital and the servility of labor." This meant it would follow the European pattern in which men were divided into classes. According to Mann, "some toil and earn, others to seize and enjoy," with an end result of the "grossest inequalities." Far better that all had an equal chance to learn and earn. And he concluded, "Education, then, beyond all other devices of human origin, is the great equalizer of the conditions of men—the balance wheel of the social machinery."[1]

---

[7] Barnas Sears to Mann, November 27, 1848; Henry Barnard to Mann, October 1, 1848; Emerson Davis to Mann, September 21, 1848; George B. Emerson to Mann, September 25, 1848, all in Mann MSS:MHS. Mann to Henry Barnard, September 13 and October 4, 1848, Barnard MSS:NYU; Mann to George N. Briggs, October 3, 1848, Briggs MSS:AAS; Records of the Massachusetts State Board of Education, September 12, 1848, MS in MSDE.
[8] Mann, *Twelfth Annual Report of the Board of Education Together with the Twelfth Annual Report of the Secretary of the Board* (Boston, 1849), p. 42.
[9] *Report*, pp. 43–53.
[1] *Ibid.*, pp. 53–75.

That schooling had tremendous social and economic resources was not to overlook its political potential. Representative government based on a broad electorate was an impossibility without a comprehensive system of public schooling. "A republican form of government," said Mann, "without intelligence in the people, must be, on a vast scale, what a mad-house, without superintendent or keepers, would be, on a small one;—the despotism of a few succeeded by universal anarchy, and anarchy by despotism, with no change but from bad to worse." A far more positive approach would be for the schools to teach and indoctrinate ". . . those articles in the creed of republicanism, which are accepted by all, believed in by all, and which form the common basis of our political faith. . . ." [2] In turn, the "creed of republicanism" was based upon a sound morality, and it was here that public schooling could play its most important role. Lashing out like an old Puritan divine, Mann painted a picture of doom and gloom descending. "For every lock that is made, a false key is made to pick it . . . the great ocean of vice and crime overleaps every embankment, pours down upon our heads, saps the foundations under our feet, and sweeps away the securities of the social order of property, liberty and life." Everything had been tried by past civilizations but one simple formula: " *'Train up a child in the way he should go, and when he is old he will not depart from it.'* " So simple and so predictable was this admonition that there was "no more reason to doubt the result, than there would be in an optical or chemical experiment." Admittedly, the vehicle of the public schools was "limited and imperfect," but he insisted that it was "far beyond any other instrumentality," because it was "comprehensive and decisive." [3] And in a ringing conclusion, he proclaimed that the "Massachusetts system" he had labored to establish was in every way,

. . . a *Free* school system. It knows no distinction of rich and poor, of bond and free, or between those who, in the imperfect light of this world, are seeking through different avenues, to reach the gate of heaven. Without money and without price, it throws open its doors, and spreads the table of its bounty, for all the children of the State. Like the sun, it shines, not only upon the good, but upon the evil, that they may become good; and, like the rain, its blessings descend, not only upon the just, but upon the unjust, that their injustices may depart from them and be known no more. [4]

---

[2] *Ibid.*, pp. 76–90.
[3] *Ibid.*, pp. 90–98.
[4] *Ibid.*, p. 140.

Mann had written more than an accounting of his stewardship. Janus-faced, he was looking as much to the future as to the past. In place of an old Puritanism, established and sanctioned by the state, he was promoting a new secular establishment with teachers as a quasi-clergy and a new ethical morality in place of an outmoded sectarianism. Public education would usher in a new popularization of knowledge and a golden age of well-being. Therefore, as certainly as the sun would rise the next morning, he could predict that the common school, "energized as it can easily be, may become the most effective and benignant of all forces of civilization." [5]

*   *   *

Mann read the major portions of his *Report* to the Board and then hurriedly packed his bags for Washington. A cold rain struck his face as he walked down from the house on the hill to the train station at West Newton. Again, Mary fretted about his safety, especially since he was taking a steamer along Long Island Sound for part of the trip. Upon his arrival in the capital, he put her mind at ease and even boasted that he had slept part of the time between Philadelphia and Baltimore. Drayton's appeal was now before the Circuit Court. Again the testimony was presented, along with the bills of exception which had been denied by Judge Crawford. When all the evidence was in, the tribunal ordered a new trial. As Mann said, the judges demolished "one after another, the abominable decisions, by which the Judge in our trials last summer, decided against us. . . . I struggled against his nefarious conduct, like a man struggling for his life, but it was in vain *then;* but not in vain now." And to Howe, Mann exulted, "*Laus Deo, Gloria in excelsis, Magnifique, pretty good.* The decision is in our favor." For Drayton it was then back to the District Court as his purgatory must continue before he could win freedom. For Mann it was a personal victory and a blow against slavery in the District of Columbia.[6]

For Mary, it was the beginning of new hope. There soon would be an end to the trial and with the *Report* completed, she assured her

---

[5] *Ibid.*, p. 42.

[6] Mann to Mary Mann, November 26, 1848, and February 19 and 20, 1849; Mary Mann to Mann, November 28, 1848; Mann to Samuel Gridley Howe, February 19, 1849; Samuel Sewall to Mann, February 16, 1849, all in Mann MSS:MHS; Mann's appeal and an account of the proceedings are in *Drayton* v. *United States*, 7F. Cas. 1063 (no. 4074) (D.C. Cir. 1849).

husband that she looked forward "with a perfect longing" to his comparative leisure next year; but, she added, "it would be 'just like fate' —would it not? if something should transpire to spoil it." And again she wrote, "Whenever you go away it seems as if the time was only *sham* time as it were—a short link to keep time together . . . these extended links in the chain of time are hard to fill up. . . ." Mann shared this sense of loneliness and was particularly despondent on Christmas Day, which he spent alone in his rooms at Gordon's. He fell upon a second low the day he completed the galley proofs of his last *Report*. With his ideas in print, there was such a finality about his resignation from the secretaryship, twelve years of effort now at an end. As his last corrections were made, the walls of the room seemed to close in on him and he found himself struggling for breath. "There was not air enough in the room to inflate my lungs," he reported to Mary, "so I had to rush forth where I could breathe in all outdoors." And there was such a little prospect for anything but continued separation from his family and another two-year struggle in the House. "You don't know how lonely I am here," he wrote to Samuel Gridley Howe, and to Mary he complained, "It is not a life congenial to me. The great question of freedom or slavery is the only one worthy to keep me here." At the moment his all-absorbing desire was "to get the territories free, and then to emancipate myself." [7]

Mann also began to brood more over the future of his sons. Then when Mary wrote that George B. Emerson's son had committed suicide, literally blowing off his head, he was without words to describe his shock. To make things worse, one of the Senators boarding at Gordon's received word that his twenty-three-year-old son had died unexpectedly. With increasing frequency, Mann filled pages of his letters to Mary with directions on how to raise their three boys. Little seemed permanent in his universe and he feared that unless every precaution and preparation were made, they would face an even more unpredictable world of change than the one through which he had maintained his course. [8]

As a Congressman from Massachusetts, his morning's mail brought more than the daily letter from a lonely wife. Nor was his

---

[7] Mann to Mary Mann, December 25 and 28, 1848, and January 25, 1849; Mary Mann to Mann, November 26, and December 17 and 25, 1848; Mann to Samuel Gridley Howe, December 27, 1848, all in Mann MSS:MHS.

[8] Mann to Mary Mann, December 30, 1848, and January 28, 1849, both in Mann MSS:MHS; Samuel Gridley Howe to Mann, December 29 [1848], Straker MSS:ACL.

time totally consumed in planning high strategy in the cause of anti-slavery. With each day came requests for autographs, enquiries about appointments to West Point, and calls for free government publications. One group in Boston aimed a letter-writing campaign at him for the erection of a lighthouse and from all over the country came petitions for cheaper postage rates. Widows enquired about their pensions, and the appeals of unhappy officeseekers, especially those in quest of postmasterships, seemed endless.

For members of the House facing the grim task of seeing their way through the slavery controversy, the idealistic antics of Horace Greeley, editor of the New York *Tribune* and newly elected Representative, must have provided something of a black comedy during the session. Failing to convince the Congress to change the name of the country to "Columbia," he set himself about other tasks of reform, including an attempt to expose the padded travel accounts of his new colleagues. Outraged at the unmitigated effrontery of this *nouveau venu*, the House membership ran roughshod over his demand for an investigation. Even Mann, for all his moral rectitude, was guilty of an overcharge on his rail travel, but it was a niggardly amount. When compared to a midwestern Congressman who charged an additional $1,000, Mann was convinced that he was far from getting his share of the "pickings and stealings." [9]

From more honest sources, Mann did realize several unexpected windfalls. His railroad bonds, which he had used as collateral for the loan on the West Newton Normal School, had just received a dividend and he was $200 the richer. Then his friends instigated a movement to have the state reimburse him for his out-of-pocket money, amounting to as much as $500 a year during his secretaryship. With mixed emotions of amazement and pleasure, he reported, "I do not think it ever happened to me, in my life, not in a single instance, to have my dish right side up, when it rained porridge." If he must be away from home, there was at least enough money now for Mary to pay the bills.[1]

Once again, with the session under way, Sumner and Giddings were troubled by Mann's silence in the House. For Sumner, it

---

[9] James Parton, *Life of Horace Greeley* (Boston, 1869), pp. 293–304; Mann to Mary Mann, January 2, 1848 [really 1849], Mann MSS:MHS; Mann to George Boyd, January 20, 1849, Straker MSS:ACL.
[1] Mann to George B. Emerson, December 9, 1848, and February 6, 1849; Mann to Mary Mann, January 2, 1848 [really 1849], Mann MSS:MHS; Mann to Josiah Quincy, February 10, 1849, Quincy MSS:BPL.

seemed but a simple matter for Mann to "treat the House to his argument, recently made in the Court-House against the Constitutionality of Slavery in the District." But Mann bided his time. From the South, there were threats of dissolution of the Union which Mann considered as treasonable as the old Hartford Convention. He also thought this was more talk than substance and that the pro-slavery sentiment in Congress had crested and begun to subside. If the anti-slavery men could just hold out until Zachary Taylor's inauguration, he felt assured the new territories would come in to the Union as free. Then they would see "whether the Union is a rope of sand or a band of steel." [2]

As the tension again mounted in the House, Mann began to shed some of his melancholy and decided to respond to Sumner's proddings. Many anti-slavery men who were not out-and-out abolitionists held up the abolition of slavery in the District of Columbia as one of their immediate objectives. This too had been one of Mann's goals when he agreed to defend Drayton and Sayres. Thus it was appropriate for him to address himself to this question by translating his courtroom arguments into a full-blown speech in the House. The result was a vehement attack, as scathing as anything he had leveled at the Boston masters. In it, Mann decried the presence in the capital of "slave pens . . . the horrid and black receptacles where human beings are penned like cattle, and kept like cattle, that they may be sold like cattle. . . ." [3]

Then presenting his subject in a broader perspective, he continued,

By the law of nature and of God, the slave, like every other man, is entitled "to life, liberty, and the pursuit of happiness;" he is entitled to his earnings,—to the enjoyment of his social affections,—to the development of his intellectual and moral faculties,—to that cultivation of his religious nature which shall fit him, not merely to feel, but by reason of righteousness, temperance, and a judgement to come, he is entitled to all these rights, of which he has been cruelly despoiled; and when he

[2] Charles Sumner to Joshua Giddings, December 27, 1848, and January 4, 1849, Giddings MSS:OHS; Mann to Mary Mann, December 28, 1848, and January 9, 15, and 16, 1849, Mann MSS:MHS; Julius Rockwell to Lucy Rockwell, January 16, 1849, Rockwell MSS:Lenox Library.
[3] Mann, "Speech Delivered in the House of Representatives of the United States, February 23, 1849," *Slavery: Letters and Speeches* (Boston, 1851), p. 122.

catches some feeble glimmering of some of them, we withhold the rest, and defend ourselves and pride ourselves that he is better off than he would have been in some other country or in some other condition.[4]

Such a sweeping declaration could not go unchallenged. Hoping to bait Mann and get him to respond with an ill-conceived endorsement of miscegenation, a pro-slavery Congressman from Pennsylvania interrupted him and asked Mann if he would give slaves equal political *and social rights*. Recognizing the intended trap, Mann faced his antagonist and gave him an extemporaneous lecture on equality:

I would give to every human being the best opportunity I could to develop and cultivate the faculties which God has bestowed upon him, and which, therefore, he holds under a divine charter. I would take from his neck the heel that has trodden him down, I would dispel from his mind the cloud that has shrouded him in moral night; I would remove the obstructions that have forbidden his soul to aspire; and having done this, I would leave him, as I would leave every other man, to find his level,—to occupy the position to which he should be entitled by his intelligence and his virtues. I entertain no fears on the much dreaded subject of amalgamation. Legal amalgamation between the races will never take place, unless, in the changed condition of society, reasons shall exist to warrant and sanction it; and, in that case, it will carry its own justification with it.

Once having raised the red herring of interracial marriage, Mann's pro-slavery southern colleagues and their dough-faced compatriots were not to get off this easily. Returning in kind with double measure, Mann heaped upon them the sharpest sarcasm and rebuke.

But one thing I could never understand,—why those who are so horror-stricken at the idea of *theoretic* amalgamation, should exhibit to the world, in all their cities, on all their plantations and in all their households, such numberless proofs of *practical* amalgamation. I could never see why those who arraign and condemn us at the north so vehemently, because, as they say, we obtrude our prying eyes into what they call a "domestic" or "fireside" institution, should have no hesitation in exhibiting to the world, through all their borders, ten thousand, and ten times ten thousand, living witnesses, that they make it a bedside institution. . . . In the complexion of the slave, we read the horrid history of the guilt of the enslavers. They demonstrated that the one

---

[4] Mann, *Slavery*, p. 131.

race has been to the other, not the object of benevolence, but the victim of licentiousness.[5]

Reaching a climax, Mann prophetically warned that they were not just approaching a crisis of dissolving the Union, they were moving on to the far more profound issue of whether Negroes, both free and slave, were to share in their birthrights as Americans. The present injustice, he insisted, "will not last forever. If the rights of the black race are thus withheld from them, it is just as certain as the progress of time that they too, will have their Runnymede, their Declaration of Independence, their Bunker Hill, and their Yorktown."

To have stated his position so bluntly required not only what Theodore Parker called a "magnificent morality," but a total effort of mind, soul, and body. New enemies he surely made with this speech, but at least he had placated his impossible taskmaster in Boston for the time being. To Sumner he wrote, "You are a Pharaoh. You spurred and goaded me to speak. . . . We are a strange contradiction, for our desires are infinite, with only finite powers of performance." Nevertheless, he had been moved by a sufficient sense of urgency and power to tell his own generation that it was time to recognize the black as a fellow American, brother, and even brother-in-law.[6]

With both chambers working feverishly towards an adjournment and the territorial question still unresolved, tempers flared more frequently. Resorting to every parliamentary trick in the book, the anti-slavery forces fought a delaying action until the next Congress and a new Whig President. As Mann simplified the situation for Mary, "the slave party and those democrats who act with them, has [sic] sought from the beginning of the session to provide the way for bringing in the new territories as states, without any restrictions as to slavery." Finally the last session, which began on Saturday, March 3, and continued until five o'clock Sunday morning, deteriorated into a night of turmoil and violence. At least two fist fights broke out, with blood spurting freely in one of them, but no territorial bills were passed and Mann could report "the victory is ours." Anxious to leave the city, he remained only an additional day to sit through the almost inaudible inaugural address by Zachary Taylor

---

[5] Mann, *Slavery,* pp. 143–144.
[6] Mann, *Slavery,* p. 145; Mann to Charles Sumner, February 27 and [March 1, 1849], Mann MSS:MHS; Theodore Parker to Mann, November 14, 1849, Parker MSS:LOC.

and survive the disgusting press of officeseekers and other latter-day Whigs who filled the ballrooms at the White House levee. Then it was onto his train and to the North and West Newton.[7]

* * *

By previous standards, the next nine months were relatively peaceful for Mann. He was recalled to Washington the first week in May to take up Drayton's defense once more since the Boston and Philadelphia committees could persuade neither William Seward nor Salmon P. Chase to step in. Once again both men found more important matters to occupy their time and at the last minute, Mann answered the urgent plea from Samuel E. Sewall and Samuel Gridley Howe. But not first without several sleepless nights. Finally, he came to the conclusion, as he later described it, "I could not think of Drayton, and of his cause, afterwards, without self-reproach, if I were not with him in his hour of trial." [8]

By the time of the retrial, Mann must have known most of the testimony from memory. As there was now less legal maneuvering and a reasonably impartial judge, the first case moved along quickly and the jury found Drayton not guilty of grand larceny. Mann then assumed that the prosecution would not press the remaining seventy-three indictments, but he was caught by surprise when Key, in a move of petulance and desperation, brought in General Walter Jones, one of the most distinguished members of the Washington Bar, and announced he would proceed with the remaining indictments. Once again, the selection of the jury honored justice in the breach, with the federal marshal doing his best to round up candidates with pro-slavery sentiments, including the son-in-law of one of the plaintiffs. Mann soon found Jones "an antagonist vastly superior" to Key, and even though he felt he had a strong case, which he summarized in a three-hour speech to the jury, he also was uneasy about the outcome. "The party spirit of the people here is fierce and fanatical, beyond expression," he complained to Mary. It was simply

---

[7] Mann to Mary Mann, March 4, 1849; Josiah Quincy to Mann, March 5, 1849, both in Mann MSS:MHS; Robert C. Winthrop, Jr., *Memoir of Robert Winthrop* (Boston, 1897), pp. 91–93.
[8] Mann to Salmon P. Chase, March 29, 1849, Chase MSS:PHS; J. Mandeville Carlisle to Mann, April 30, 1849; Samuel E. Sewall to Mann, April 6, 1849; Mann to Samuel Gridley Howe, May 9, 1849, all in Mann MSS:MHS.

impossible, he feared, for someone with strong anti-slavery convictions to get a fair trial in the capital. In this, his fears were unfounded. The jury came in with a second not guilty verdict. At last conceding defeat after more than two years of litigation, Key let the seventy-two remaining indictments be lumped together, and in the final trial, it took the jury just fifteen minutes for a third not guilty verdict. Drayton then pleaded guilty to the lesser offense of helping slaves to escape and the judge fined him $140 for each slave, making a total of $10,360. Unable to pay the fine, he went back to his cell, while Mann began plans to obtain a pardon from President Taylor.[9]

While still in Washington, Mann was appointed one of the official visitors of West Point. The assignment took up most of June and provided Mary and the boys with the chance to join their father at the Point for an impromptu vacation. Mann traveled directly from the capital, taking the last part of his trip up the Hudson by way of a river steamer. Slightly jaundiced about new scenery, considering the traveling he had done the last few years, the journey up the river came as an unexpected pleasure. Moving away from the city, his craft soon was passing along the base of the Palisades on the west bank, a long series of perpendicularly fluted cliffs and spires. Beyond them in the distance for a time, making the scene all the more indelible in his mind, was a black thunderstorm with lightning chains snaking their way through the clouds. Farther up the river, the storm gave way to a lofty rainbow arching across as much of the horizon as the eye could see. As the vessel pushed against the current, homes and mansions became more scattered while nature began to predominate, with gentle rolling tree-covered hills framed by the river below and the gray-purple profile of the distant Catskills beyond. The only disconcerting sight on the entire passage was the view of Sing Sing Rock, crowned by an ominous vaultlike ornament, the largest prison in the world.[1]

At West Point, Mann visited classes, interviewed some of the

---

[9] J. Mandeville Carlisle to Reverdy Johnson, March 3, 1849, Attorney General's MSS, Letters Received:NA; Mann to Mary Mann, May 6, 7, 8, 9, 11, and 13, 1849; Mann to Samuel Gridley Howe, May 9, 1849; Mann to Charles Sumner, May 12, 1849, all in Mann MSS:MHS; Mary Mann to Mary Messer, May 28, 1849, Mann-Messer MSS:BUA; *National Intelligencer*, May 11, 1849; *National Era*, May 17 and 31, 1849; Boston *Daily Advertiser*, May 17, 1849.
[1] Mann to Mary Mann, June 5, 6, and 7, 1849, Mann MSS:MHS; Elizabeth Peabody to Mrs. Elizabeth Peabody, June 18, 1849, Straker MSS:ACL; Boston *Emancipator* May 3, 1849.

instructors and cadets, and reviewed a dress parade. Although impressed with the order and system established at the academy, he found that his entire nature rebelled at its military atmosphere. He succeeded in concealing his feelings for the most part, but when the commanding officer insisted that he address the graduating class, after some misgivings, Mann agreed and spoke on the need for military education to shift its goal from warfare to working for peace. Although a welcome interlude, the visit to the Point in no way changed his mind about the futility of military expenditures. As the result of his inspection, Mann deviously resorted to a negative merit system in making his appointments to the academy. Reviewing each candidate "*physically, intellectually,* and *morally,*" as he explained the process to Sumner, he then selected "the poorest and lowest specimen of the whole, as good enough for food for powder." [2]

Back in Massachusetts, Mann was gratified by word that the General Court had ordered the reprinting of 10,000 copies of his *Tenth Annual Report* for free distribution. In July, he was invited to Harvard Yard, where President Jared Sparks conferred the honorary degree of "*utriusque Legis tum Naturae et Centium tum Civilis Doctorem*" (Doctor of Both Natural and Civil Laws) upon him. In August and September he sat still long enough on several occasions for the popular sculptor Thomas Carew to do a marble bust of him, and throughout the fall, he replenished his depleted coffers by speaking at lyceums, often four and five nights in a row. For each performance he received $15 or $20, depending upon the distance. Early next year his financial prospects would look even better as the firm of Ticknor and Fields came out with his *Thoughts for a Young Man,* printing five editions totaling more than 10,000 copies in the first six months. During this time, he also found the opportunity to travel to Philadelphia to give the presidential address to delegates from fifteen states gathered at the Convention of Teachers and Superintendents of Public Schools, an address so admired by Longfellow that he read it to his class at Harvard. While in Philadelphia, Mann received an enquiry about his possible interest in the presidency of Girard College. He would have been inclined to take the position, particularly since it paid $3,000 a year and required far less exertion than his present work. The formal offer, however, was not forth-

---

[2] Mann to Charles Sumner, August 31, 1850, Mann MSS:MHS; the undated MS [June 15, 1849], of Mann's remarks is in the Mann MSS:MHS; Boston *Evening Transcript,* June 25, 1849.

coming, no doubt scuttled by his old enemy Frederick Packard, who was influential among Girard's board of directors.[3]

Almost by an inverse ratio, as Mann's fortunes improved, those of his brother-in-law, Nathaniel Hawthorne, declined. On June 8, Hawthorne learned that his position at the Salem Customs House was not beyond political tampering. Back in power as the result of the Taylor victory, the Whigs of Essex County cast about for Democratic officeholders who could be replaced by the party faithful. One of their earliest finds was Hawthorne. Earlier, Sophia had urged her husband to ask Mann to speak to the President to secure the Customs House position, but Hawthorne thought this demeaning. Compounding Hawthorne's troubles was the death of his mother and the new necessity of caring for his two sisters. Now that the blow had fallen, Sophia kept a stiff upper lip, assuring her sister that "we are suddenly in a condition of unexpected freedom from official duties, and my Pegasus never liked to be chained to the desk of the Customs House." [4]

Now faced with the immediate responsibility of supporting his family and two sisters, Hawthorne was more realistic about his situation. As soon as Mann offered to help, he accepted, even stating that he would go back to the Customs House, if he could be vindicated of the trumped-up charges against him. Meanwhile some of his friends also offered assistance. "Could there be any permanent literary avocation found for him?" George Hillard wrote to Longfellow, thinking a position as proof reader for a publisher might be possible. In the meantime, Hawthorne concentrated on his writing, planning a children's book and working long hours to complete his first novel, a "romance" as Sophia called it, containing "a moral as terrific and stunning as a thunderbolt." She referred to *The Scarlet Letter*. Unable to help his brother-in-law through political channels, Mann did offer him the use of his house at West Newton. Finding

---

[3] Charles Upham to Mann, March 21, 1849; Sophia Hawthorne to Mary Mann, October 21, 1849; Charles Sumner to Mann, November 13, 1849; Gideon Thayer to Mann, October 19, 1849, all in Mann MSS:MHS; Mann to James B. Nicholas, October 15, 1849, Horace Mann Mutual Insurance Company, Springfield, Illinois; Lucretia Mott to Elizabeth Cady Stanton, October 25, 1849, Garrison, MSS:SC; Mann to Henry Barnard, November 27, 1849, Barnard MSS:NYU; *American Journal of Education*, XXIV (1873), 330–333; Boston *Daily Advertiser*, July 19, 1849; William S. Tryon and William Charvat, eds., *Cost Books of Ticknor and Fields and their Predecessors, 1832–1858* (New York, 1949), pp. 153–159.
[4] Sophia Hawthorne to Mary Mann, June 9, August 12, and November 4, 1849, Mann MSS:MHS.

nothing "very cheap" and permanent for the moment, the Hawthornes moved in with the Manns for a time while Hawthorne completed his manuscript for *The Blithedale Romance.* Later, critics would expend an inordinate amount of energy arguing whether the character of Zena was drawn from Margaret Fuller, so much so that they missed the striking psychological and ideological similarities between Hollingswood, the compulsive and egocentric prison reformer, and the personality and career of Horace Mann.[5]

It had been a relatively relaxed summer for Mann, once Drayton's case was out of the way, but the winter was soon to set in, and with it came the next session of Congress. Like the honking of geese flying south as the harbinger of the season to come, letters from Sumner began to appear in the mail with the same old refrain: Mann's latest public statements were too Whiggish in tone and had ignored the cause of Free Soil. Sumner had even heard rumors that the Whigs would nominate Mann for Governor so as to replace him in Congress with a Cotton Whig. While the Free Soilers as yet had few doubts of his integrity, Sumner thought more than a few had begun to question Mann's courage. Fortunately for his own composure, Howe stood by Mann, with his taint of Whiggism and all. In return, Mann sent Howe a long letter explaining his recent political course. "My Free Soil principles," he wrote, summing up his present position, "are as firm as ever. I shall make the freedom of the territories . . . the question paramount to all this. But when I can aid others which I deem to be very important to the welfare of the country, without compromising that, I shall do so." And from such a position he was ready to work as he could in the thirty-first Congress.[6]

*   *   *

Gathering in the Senate the first week in December was as colorful and impressive a group of statesmen and politicians as ever came into the upper chamber. The great triumvirate, Webster, Clay,

---

[5] Nathaniel Hawthorne to Mann, June 26, 1849, Pforzheimer MSS (photostat): BLYU; Nathaniel Hawthorne to Mann, August 8, 1849, Berg MSS:NYPL; George Hillard to Henry W. Longfellow, June 9 [1849] and January 4 [1850], Hillard MSS:HCL; Sophia Hawthorne to Mary Mann, February 12, 1850, Mann MSS:MHS.
[6] Charles Sumner to Mann, October 19, 1849; Mann to Samuel Gridley Howe, November 11, 1849, both in Mann MSS:MHS; Charles Sumner to Joshua Giddings, October 19 and November 3, 1849, Giddings MSS:OHS.

and Calhoun, was back together for the last time; from the South had come Sam Houston, Jefferson Davis, and "Hangman" Foote; William Seward represented New York; out of the Midwest had journeyed "Old Bullion" Benton, Salmon P. Chase, and the "Little Giant," Stephen A. Douglas; and from the far West had come the "pathfinder," John C. Frémont. But Sumner was more worried about the collection of men gathered in the House and whom they would elect as their new Speaker. While Mann assured him that he would not support Howell Cobb, a pro-slavery Democrat from Georgia, he was not necessarily opposed to Robert C. Winthrop, who usually voted as a faithful Cotton Whig. With the Democratic and Whig numbers in the House almost equal, the thirteen Free Soilers were in a strong bargaining position. Unfortunately, they refused to support any candidate who was not simon pure and unalterably opposed to the extension of slavery to the territories. They finally threw away their votes, supporting David Wilmot, who had no chance to win the Speakership. On December 3, after a long deliberation, Mann cast his first vote for Winthrop, only his second or third preference. With no candidate receiving a majority, and the majority rule re-affirmed by the membership, the balloting continued on to the next day. By December 7, thirty-eight ballots had been cast, all with inconclusive results as the two parties officially held with their stand-ard-bearers, while casting about for possible compromise candidates.[7]

On the fortieth ballot, Mann even received five votes. From the forty-first to the fifty-first ballot, Mann switched to Thaddeus Stevens, who now had Free Soil support and a few Whig votes. From here to the sixtieth ballot, Mann moved back and forth between Winthrop and Stevens as the party regulars worked to extricate themselves from the deadlock by "going round and round, like a squirrel in a cage," as Mann described the frenetic maneuvering. Tempers became frayed and it was likely the walls of the House had never heard such violent language. To expedite these actions, it was decided to end debate between each round of ballots. Then on December 22, after sixty-two roll calls, the rule for the majority to elect the Speaker was suspended, thus depriving the Free Soilers of their last chance to cast the saving vote. On the next ballot, Howell Cobb was elected by a plurality of 102 votes to 100 for Robert Winthrop.

---

[7] Charles Sumner to Joshua Giddings, November 29, 1849, Giddings, MSS:OHS; Mann to Mary Mann, December 2, 3, 5, and 22, 1849, Mann MSS:MHS.

As far as Mann was concerned, the Free Soilers had become spoilers by blocking the election of Winthrop who was against the extension of slavery to the territories and allowing the Democrats to elect the pro-slavery Cobb. By refusing even to entertain thoughts of compromise and coalition, they had allowed, according to Robert Winthrop, "one of the fiercest, sternest, strongest pro-slavery men in all the South" to become Speaker.[8]

Bitterly, Mann complained of an advantage wasted just as the territorial issue was reaching a critical showdown. And who had let this happen?, he asked rhetorically. The blame rested squarely on the Free Soilers, "who at any time during the last three weeks might have prevented it. . . ." For his voting record, Mann expected to be excoriated in the columns of the *Liberator*, and he was. Perhaps, too, he could have predicted the outraged reactions of Sumner. True to form, with the first mail possible after the final ballot, Sumner's letter was there, upbraiding Mann for not voting in a more uncompromising manner against the "Slave Power." How strange, Mann mused, "is that hate of an evil thing, which adopts the very means that secure its triumph. How strange that love of a good thing, which destroys it." It was almost as if the Free Soilers had had a death wish for themselves and their cause.[9]

In the weeks which followed, Mann found himself being ground into political oblivion between the nether stone of the Whig Party and the upper stone of the Free Soilers. The Free Soil press rebuked him for ballots he had cast for Winthrop, conveniently ignoring his support of Thaddeus Stevens. At the same time, the Boston Whigs carped about his party apostasy in not supporting the official Whig candidate for the lesser office of clerkship of the House. Mann's Free Soil friends claimed he had fallen from grace and become irredeemably Whig, although Sumner wrote to Giddings that there was still a remote chance that Mann would join them "unequivocally." Lucretia Mott, the Quakeress and humanitarian reformer who had taken of late to reading all of Mann's anti-slavery

---

[8] Mann to Mary Mann, December 16, 17, and 23, 1849, Mann MSS:MHS; an account of the voting in the House can be found in the issues of the *National Era*, including December 6, 13, 20, and 27, 1849; Robert C. Winthrop, Jr., *Memoir of Robert C. Winthrop* (Boston, 1897), pp. 96–101.

[9] Mann to Mary Mann, December 23, 1849; Charles Sumner to Mann, December 29, 1849, Mann MSS:MHS; *Liberator*, December 28, 1849; for a similar response to Mann's from another Massachusetts Whig, see Julius Rockwell to Lucy Rockwell, December 6 and 12, 1849, Rockwell MSS:Lenox Library.

speeches, held out the same hope. But George Julian, an intense anti-slavery man from Ohio who once held Mann "about number one" in his estimation, had concluded by this time that "In politics he is a great coward. . . ." Mann's old friend, Samuel J. May, thought that his recent actions had "greatly alienated the regards of many former friends and supporters. . . ." And if this were not enough totally to unsettle a person, the mail brought an abundance of gratuitous and crackpot advice on how to solve the "negro problem," including a proposal that a system of reservations be set up for blacks as they already had been established for Indians. "You may rest assured of what I tell you," one correspondent advised him. "Emancipation would have carried in Kentucky and would carry at this time in N.C. if there were a territory of that kind to which to remove them, but unless [this is done], another century, yea five of them will not Emancipate South Carolina or North Carolina." Once again Mann's certainty of himself and his position was undergoing a steady attrition. His letters to Mary at times indicated an all-consuming desire to retire from these wars and seek the security and peace of West Newton. Forced to stay in Washington, however, the only relaxation and retreat he could find from the conflicting ideas which whirled about inside his brain was to go into the yard in back of Gordon's and chop wood, much as he had done as a boy in Franklin.[1]

It is not the easiest thing to comprehend the reasons for the sound and fury which was mounting in the Congress. During the struggle in the House over the election of a Speaker, a movement was under way for the establishment of a southern convention to lay the groundwork for secession and a new confederacy, already dubbed by the Richmond *Enquirer* as the "United States South." At first glance, one wonders what the South wanted. Of the thirty states in the Union, fifteen were southern. A southern slaveholding President was in the White House. Its cotton culture was facilitated by free trade, and only the most anti-slavery agitators, the abolitionists, challenged its right to have slavery within its state borders. Yet

[1] Mann to Mary Mann, January 8 and 29, 1850; Ephraim Wilson to Mann, January 24, 1850; Edmund Clap to Mann, January 16 and 21, 1850, all in Mann MSS:MHS; Charles Sumner to Julian Giddings, February 12, 1850, Giddings, MSS:OHS; Lucretia Mott to George Julian, January 31, 1850; George Julian to Isaac Julian, January 25, 1850, both in Julian-Giddings, MSS:LOC; Samuel J. May to Richard Davis Webb, February 19, 1850, May MSS:BPL; Boston *Emancipator*, December 27, 1849.

psychologically and morally it was under a relentless and penetrating moral attack from which existing political bulwarks were of little use. Attempting to extricate themselves from a siege mentality, young southern Hotspurs began to dream of more radical alternatives, including a great slaveholding republic incorporating Cuba and parts of Mexico and governed by a planter aristocracy of breeding and wealth, blissfully free of northern industrialism and the fanaticism it bred.

Older men such as Zachary Taylor discounted secession as a serious threat. Dining at the White House and sitting next to the President "with only a lady in between," Mann was amazed at the simplicity with which this former military officer thought the impending crisis could be resolved. Judging from the level of the discussion of political affairs, Mann was convinced that he was a "simple-minded old man," who "talks as artlessly as a child about the affairs of state." Mann was even more amazed that Taylor found little to criticize when a guest from across the table pronounced that disunion could be nipped in the bud, "without shedding a drop of blood." All that was necessary was for the President to dispatch the navy to blockade southern ports at the first sign of rebellion. For Mann it was almost inevitable that a military man could produce nothing else than a military solution.[2]

Fortunately, more sensitive and sophisticated politicians did sense the gravity of the situation and cast about for possible compromises. "There are dark clouds over hanging the future," Mann reported to Mary, "and worse, they are full of lightning." And many in the Congress agreed, including the ancient Henry Clay. Beginning with an unassailable article of faith that, regardless of the validity of the immediate moral and economic arguments against slavery, the interests of liberty would be served best through the preservation of the Union, Clay fashioned his last great compromise and presented it to the Senate on January 27, 1850, in the form of a series of resolutions touching the main aspects of the sectional controversy. Essentially, they were four in number: (1) the prompt admission of California with its constitution prohibiting slavery; (2) the establishment of territorial governments in Utah and New Mexico, the matter of slavery to be decided at a later date; (3) a new fugitive slave law which the North must agree to enforce; and (4) the abolition of the slave trade in the District of Columbia. The initial reac-

---

[2] Mann to Mary Mann, March 1, 1850, Mann MSS:MHS.

tion from many parts was opposition, and from what he could learn at the dining table at Gordon's and glean from the conversations in Capitol corridors, Mann was certain it had little chance of passage since southerners were "taking strong ground against it." He thought there would be equal opposition from the North.[3]

Clay, however, was not about to retreat from an initial rebuff when he thought the future of the nation was at stake. In a speech which lasted the better part of two days, he earnestly appealed for concessions from both the North and the South. Still a graceful figure, although only a shadow of "Young Harry of the West," he appeared to spectators in the galleries and to the Senators on the main floor as a man of matchless patriotism and with an almost hypnotic power of appeal. Occasionally his voice faltered, his lungs wracked with pain, but this only made the audience thrill more to this courageous statesman as he struggled for one last triumph of volition over the ravages of time. Pleading his cause before an assembly where there were more than a few moist eyes, Clay concluded with the warning that no state had the right to secede from this great nation and that if the South made the attempt to do so, it would be the prelude to a bloody war. Mann too was moved by Clay's selfless effort to perpetuate the Union. "There is hardly another slaveholder in all the South who could have perilled his popularity to such an extent," he wrote. "I think, regarded *as a compromise*, Mr. Clay has done pretty well." But if he was moved, he could not let himself be convinced. He had decided not to support the resolutions, "rebellion or not." The admission of New Mexico and Utah without the prohibition of slavery would have been the bitterest of medicines to swallow, but he would positively gag on a fugitive slave law which gave the slave-hunter free rein in the North. "I consider no evil so great as that of the extension of slavery," he wrote to Mary at the conclusion of Clay's appeal, and a week later he added for emphasis, "I do not concede their right to carry slavery into the territories *at all*. . . . I should prefer dissolution even, terrible as it would be, to slavery extension." [4]

Although Mann thought there was sufficient opposition from the South to defeat the compromise, he also wanted to put his position on public record as part of an attempt to rally northern Whigs who were still undecided. A week after Clay's speech, he gained the

---

[3] Mann to Mary Mann, January 30, 1850, Mann MSS:MHS.
[4] Mann to Mary Mann, February 6, 7, and 14, 1850, Mann MSS:MHS; Carl Schurz, *Henry Clay* (Boston, 1887), II, 330–341.

floor of the House for what was to be his most intransigent and scathing denunciation of slavery to date. And there was more. Convinced of the wickedness of slavery, he succumbed to the temptation to attack the South as well, for its defense of the institution, thus driving some of the southern opposition to the compromise into Clay's coalition of conciliation.[5]

Mann claimed that those really deserving the epithet "abolitionist" were southerners intent on abolishing "freedom, justice, equity, and a sense of brotherhood." After reviewing his previous arguments supporting the right of Congress to legislate for the territories, he insisted, "The conclusion, then, is irresistible, that when you come to the boundary line between a slave state and a free state, you come to the boundary line of slavery itself. On the one side of the line, down to the nadir and up to the zenith, the blackness of the slave code pervades all things; but on the other side, as high above and deep below, is the purity of freedom." Admittedly, if the South seceded the result would be "*war*." And this would not be a romantic adventure. "If the two sections of this country," he warned, "ever marshall themselves against each other, and their squadrons rush to conflict, it will be war carried on by such powers of intellect, animated by such vehemence of passion, and sustained by such an abundance of resources, as the world has never before witnessed." [6]

Like a bitter acid, Mann's sarcasm cut its way into areas previously given sanctuary by his Congressional colleagues. He accused the South of rewriting the Declaration of Independence. By a grotesque inversion of Jefferson, they were now proclaiming,

We hold these truths to be self-evident that men are not created equal; that they are not endowed by their Creator with inalienable rights; that white men of the Anglo-Saxon race, were born to rob, and tyrannize, and enjoy, and black men, of the African race, to labor, and suffer, and obey. . . .

For the new constitution of the "United States South" Mann proposed the following:

We, the people of the "United States South," in order to form a more perfect conspiracy against the rights of the African race, establish

[5] Mann, "Speech Delivered in the United States House of Representatives, February 15, 1850, on the Subject of Slavery in the Territories, and the Consequences of a Dissolution of the Union," *Slavery: Letters and Speeches* (Boston, 1851), pp. 180–227.
[6] Mann, *Slavery*, pp. 183–184, 198, 204–205.

injustice, insure domestic slavery, provide for holding three million of
our fellow beings, with all the countless of their posterity, in bondage,
and to secure to ourselves and our posterity the enjoyment of power,
and luxury, and sloth, do ordain and establish this constitution for the
"United States South."

And he concluded with the uncompromising imperative, "better disunion,—better a civil or a servile war,—better anything that God in
his providence shall send, than an extension of the bonds of slavery." [7]

    It was a slashing attack and for his efforts, Mann was both vili-
fied and lauded. "No sane man can believe such declarations," one
southerner responded from the floor, but if this was a fair sample of
northern opinion, "then the dissolution of the Union is as certain to
take place as it is that night succeeds the day. . . ." Ever attempting
to curry southern favor, Robert Winthrop thought it "produced nothing but offence. . . . Some of its sentiments are food for nothing
but to inflame the South. . . ." Back home the response was different. The Boston *Transcript,* often a defender of Whiggism, pronounced Mann's speech "one of the noblest as well as the ablest
speech of the session. . . . We need, at this crisis," it continued,
"men like Mr. Mann in the councils of the nation. Would that we had
more from the North like him." As secretary to the Board, he had
worked from within, renewing and reforming the common schools,
attempting to save the system at all costs, regardless of travesties the
common schools promoted in the name of education. Now facing
the evil of slavery, he was unwilling to work in the same way for the
preservation of the Union. By this time Mann had burned his bridges
against any retreat. Goading him on at this point was the rumor
spread by the Free Soilers that the northern Whigs were about to
sell out on the compromise in exchange for a protective tariff. This,
he assured Howe, was "superlatively false." And to make doubly sure
it did not happen, he reported that "with all my might" he was preparing the copy of his speech for the printers.[8]

    Mann based part of his prediction that the compromise was
doomed on the sharp dissent of many southerners, none more promi-

---

[7] Mann, *Slavery,* pp. 216–217 and 225; Mann to Mary Mann, January 28, 1850, Mann MSS:MHS.
[8] *Congressional Globe,* March 6, 1850, Appendix, p. 258; Robert Winthrop
to Edward Everett, March 17, 1850, Everett MSS:MHS; Boston *Daily
Evening Transcript,* March 12 and 25, 1850; Mann to Samuel Gridley
Howe, February 22, 1850, Mann MSS:MHS.

nent than that from the failing voice of John C. Calhoun. On March 4, with the debate over the resolutions reaching a crescendo of epithets, claims, and counterclaims, Calhoun sat in the Senate, grim and emaciated, too weak to deliver his own remarks. Senator James Mason of Virginia came forward to read it for him. "The cords that bind the States together," he began his ominous warning, were snapping one by one. If the Union were to be saved, the North must stop oppressing the South and "do justice by conceding to the South an equal right in the acquired territory," meaning that both California and New Mexico should be admitted as slave states. Furthermore, it must once and for all muzzle its anti-slavery agitators.[9]

Mann's prediction was also based on his belief that the northern Whigs would rally to defeat it, once the last of the triumvirate, Daniel Webster, had spoken against it. Although Webster was under great pressure to support the compromise, Mann was confident that he would stand foursquare against it, given his solid defense of the Wilmot Proviso and his oft-stated antipathy towards slavery. "I do not believe he will compromise the great question," Mann reported to Mary on March 4. "He will have too much regard for his *historic* character and for his consistency to do any such thing. At least I hope so."[1]

On March 7, expecting him finally to break his silence on "the great question," spectators filled the galleries of the Senate two hours before it convened. Daniel Webster was to give his last great oration as a Senator from Massachusetts. He began at noon. Confident and calm, he opened with words which became classic for a century and more: "I wish to speak today, not as a Massachusetts man nor as a Northern man, but as an American." For the next three hours and eleven minutes, he spoke with only an occasional glance at his notes. On several counts, the speech was uncharacteristic of Webster. Unrhetorical and containing a minimum of imagery, its restraint seemed to render its message all the more compelling. And that message was that the time had come as it came to few generations of Americans to rise above party and sectional interests and preserve the Union through this Compromise. He criticized the moral "absolutists," who thought "that what is right may be distinguished from what is wrong with the precision of an algebraic equation." California and New Mexico could safely come into the Union without a

[9] Mann to Mary Mann, March 4, 1850, Mann MSS:MHS; Margaret L. Coit, *John C. Calhoun, American Patriot* (Boston, 1950), pp. 490–494.
[1] Mann to Mary Mann, March 4 and 6, 1850, Mann MSS:MHS.

proviso against slavery since their geography made human bondage an unprofitable endeavor. From here he went on to recapitulate the grievances of the North and the South. Both had their legitimacy, but he added, turning to Calhoun who was slumped in his chair, wrapped in a long black coat and glaring at his ancient opponent, "Peaceable secession is an utter impossibility." In closing, he appealed to his colleagues' sense of patriotism and urged them to abandon their thoughts of dissolution in the South and agitation in the North and join together to enjoy "the fresh air of Liberty and Union," and "the harmony and peace of all those who are destined to live under it." For a moment, deathly silence. Then a deafening applause as friends nearest him rushed up to clasp his hand and praise him for his words. Daniel Webster had finished what he considered the single most important act of his long political career.[2]

Opposing slavery, he had decided that only through the preservation of the Union could it be kept from spreading. A seceded South would perpetuate its "peculiar institution" and help it spread elsewhere. Always abhorring radicalism and extremism, he had sided with Clay rather than Calhoun. Slavery could be tolerated for the present until some solution was worked out. The Union must be preserved at all costs. On it depended all the freedoms so heroically achieved by selfless men in the past. To destroy it would carry the nation back into the Middle Ages. It was a courageous speech and it would have killed any northern man of lesser stature.

Mann was stunned. "He is a fallen star! Lucifer descending from heaven! He has disappointed us all," was his anguished report to Mary. "His intellectual life," he wrote again, "has been one great epic, and now he had given a vile catastrophe to its closing pages. . . . I am overwhelmed." The ideological battle lines had been drawn more sharply, but the Whig ranks were in a shambles. "There is a very strong feeling here, among the Whigs of the New England delegation, and we shall do what we can to uphold our cause. It is a terrible battle," Mann reported. How could he have done it? All too quickly Mann was convinced that his hero was making a play for southern support in one last futile bid for the White House. Later, when Mann had the chance to study Webster's speech, he was no less adamant in denouncing it. "It has all the marks of his

---

[2] Claude M. Fuess, *Daniel Webster*, II (Boston, 1930), 212–217; Herbert D. Foster, "Webster's Seventh of March Speech and the Secession Movement of 1850," *American Historical Review*, 27 (January, 1922), 245–270.

mind," he conceded, "clearness of style, weight of statement, power of language; but nothing in my mind can atone for the abandonment of the territories to what he calls the law of nature, for the exclusions of slavery. . . . The existence of slavery depends more on *conscience* than *climate.*" Slaves could work in the gold mines of California and New Mexico as well as the cotton fields of Mississippi. Either the Massachusetts Whigs must disown Webster's stand, or "Massachusetts Whiggery not only will be dead, but it ought to go down." [3]

And for the next weeks, the Massachusetts Whigs were in a turmoil. Party loyalties disintegrated, friendships of long standing were ripped asunder, and even families split down the middle over the Compromise. No newcomer to controversy, Mann was not prepared for James K. Mills's refusal to speak with him, and it became necessary to pay back his loan on the West Newton house through Samuel Gridley Howe, who served as an intermediary. Even Robert Winthrop wished that Webster had made a different speech; to Edward Everett he confided that the arguments about climate precluding slavery at best were "pretty loose," and after cataloguing his other objections he instructed Everett, "Pray destroy this letter." Governor George Briggs wrote to Mann, "How the Whig Party can retreat or faulter [sic] in maintaining the position they have taken, with honor or honesty, I cannot see. . . . They have in a thousand different forms and on as many occasions, by their orators, and presses declared their intention of doing all in their power to extend the Wilmot Proviso over all the territories. . . ." Although Mann also heard that his denunciation of slavery had upset many home state Whigs, Briggs, Thomas Kinnicut, Edmund Clap, Theodore Parker, and Charles Francis Adams, all urged him to stand his ground. Therefore, he concluded, "They must hear my free soil doctrines whenever they hear me." [4]

After the initial shock waves following Webster's speech, Mann became aware of the gradual shift of sentiment in favor of the

---

[3] Mann to Mary Mann, March 8, 10, and 15, 1850; Mann to Samuel Downer, March 21, 1850; Mann to Edmund Clap, March 11, 1850, all in the Mann MSS:MHS.
[4] Robert Winthrop to Edward Everett, March 17, 1850, Everett MSS: MHS; George Briggs to Mann, March 22, 1850, Rockwell MSS:Lenox Library; Edmund Clap to Mann, June 10, 1850; Theodore Parker to Mann, May 6, 1850; Charles Francis Adams to Mann, July 29, 1850; Mann to Edmund Clap, March 11, 1850; Mann to Samuel Gridley Howe, February 9, 1853, all in Mann MSS:MHS.

Compromise, despite his best efforts and those of Seward, Giddings, and Chase. A majority of persons were weary of agitation. With Webster's formula, peace in their time was a possibility. By April 1, southern opposition was leaderless. Calhoun was dead, and Webster and Clay served as his pallbearers. To Mann, Calhoun's private life may have been "unimpeachable," but his public career had been "one of the greatest disasters that has ever befallen the country." Also expediting a change in northern opinion were two economic considerations. When he returned to Boston for a public rally attended by more than 1,000 leading citizens, Webster let it be known that New England manufacturers would not get their protective tariff as long as slavery agitation and the territorial question remained a thorn in the side of the South. Augmenting the change in feeling was an auxiliary agreement to pay Texas bondholders, mainly northern bankers, 77 per cent of par value for securities that they had purchased at bargain basement prices of 5 to 15 per cent. With this Mann could only report that "the current has set in the wrong direction." And again, "Public affairs are looking worse here, more dangerous for the cause of liberty." [5]

At the height of the debate, Mann was forced to return to West Newton as young Horace was seriously ill with a high fever of unknown origins, and Mary was bedridden with a case of boils. While at home, the Whig leaders in his district asked him to present his *"views and opinions upon the question of the immediate admission of California, and other questions now before Congress, arising out of the acquisition of territory by the treaty with Mexico."* Mann responded with a long public letter which reviewed the Missouri Compromise, the Mexican War, and the more recent controversy over Clay's Compromise resolutions. He then discussed Webster's speech, underscoring his thesis that climate prohibits slavery and his legal justification that alleged fugitive slaves were not entitled to a trial by jury. To Mann it was inconceivable that "A man may not lose a horse without a right to this trial; but he may his freedom." From this he could only conclude that "Mr. Webster speaks for the South and slavery not for the North and for freedom. . . ." [6]

As part of his efforts to carry his message to the people, Web-

---

[5] Mann to Mary Mann, March 1, 6, and 9, 1850, Mann MSS:MHS.
[6] Mann, "Two Letters on the Extension of Slavery, and on the Right of an Alleged Fugitive to a trial by Jury," *Slavery: Letters and Speeches*, pp. 236–314; Boston *Daily Evening Transcript*, May 4, 1850; Boston *Daily Atlas*, May 6, 1850.

ster published a response to an enquiry from the citizens of New-buryport, Massachusetts. In his defense of the Compromise, he took special aim at the dissident Whig Congressman from the Eighth District. Lowering the level of the debate one notch, Webster insinuated that Mann was poorly schooled in the law. "This personal vituperation does not annoy me," he wrote with mock aloofness, "but I lament to see a man of Massachusetts, so crude and confused in his legal apprehensions, and so little acquainted with the Constitution of his country, as these opinions evince Mr. Mann to be." Having returned to Washington, Mann fought back as Sumner and others delightedly egged him on. He had 20,000 copies of his speech published for distribution in the South and as many more for the North. In addition, in a second letter to his constituents, he defended his "stray horse" analogy, quoting one of Webster's associates, Joseph Story, to establish its accuracy.[7]

Newspapers, individuals, and even institutions of higher learning began to take sides as the conflict between Mann and Webster came out into the open. The mercurial *Liberator* was back again in Mann's corner, as was the strongly anti-slavery Boston *Atlas*. The *Courier, Advertiser,* and *Post,* all influential Boston papers, pilloried Mann and lauded Webster. The *Courier* was especially vindictive, deploring Mann's "bitterness and wrath," and claiming him to be his own worst enemy. From the floor of the Senate, Lewis Cass of Michigan made a scurrilous personal attack on Mann. Meanwhile at Brown, Mann's alma mater, the trustees withdrew their plans to award him an honorary doctorate, with the smug satisfaction that "Harvard would be glad to take back what they gave last year." The Reverend Dr. Moses Stuart of the Andover Theological Seminary published a pamphlet defending Webster, and going one better, offered proofs that slavery was justified by God according to the Old Testament, a publication in which Webster took much satisfaction. Some of the leading Boston brahmins now found courage and collected signatures on a petition endorsing Webster's stand. In turn, they were disdainfully dismissed by Emerson as "aged and

---

[7] Daniel Webster, *Letter from the Citizens of Newburyport, Massachusetts, to Mr. Webster in Relation to His Speech Delivered in the Senate of the United States on the 7th of March, 1850 and Mr. Webster's Reply* (Washington, D.C., 1850); Mann, "To the Editors . . . ," Boston *Daily Atlas*, June 10, 1850; Mann to Mary Mann, June 7, 1850; Mann to Charles Sumner, June 6, 1850; Charles Sumner to Mann, May 30, 1850, all in Mann MSS:MHS; Mann to George Manchester, May 20, 1850, Mann MSS:EI.

infirm people, who have outlived everything but their night cap and tea and toast." [8]

Webster considered Mann's rebuttal "weak, though malignant." Needing to carry his battle for the Compromise to a national audience, he could not afford to become too entangled with Mann. Thus he instructed his Boston followers "to dispose of him." But before he left the New England scene, he addressed one more letter to the citizens of Kennebeck River. In it he noted that "In classical times there was a set of small but rapacious critics, denominated *captatores verborum,* who snatched and caught on particular expressions . . . birds of rapine which preyed on words and syllables, and gorged themselves with feeding on the garbage of phrases, chopped, dislocated and torn asunder by themselves. . . ." With Mann particularly in mind, he added, "Such critics are rarely more distinguished for ability and discussion than for that manly, moral feeling which disdains to state an adversary's argument otherwise than fairly and truly as he meant to be understood." And true to form, Mann pounced on this. Picayune though it seems, it was more important to prove Webster's Latin wrong than his knowledge of trial by jury. To err in legal matters was permissible, but to be wrong in a classical reference was unforgivable to a New England constituency. Dashing in where even Sumner warned him not to tread, Mann challenged Webster's Latin, claiming no such expression existed in the classics and that the nearest thing to it was a term denoting toadies or sycophants who hung on each word from their idol to praise and flatter him, a perfectly apt expression for the wealthy Bostonians backing Webster. Before the controversy had run its course through more than a hundred columns of newspaper print, even the Harvard faculty became involved, with Cornelius Felton, professor of Greek, taking up the cudgels for Webster before doing his homework, only to be put down by Charles Beck, professor of Latin, who came to Mann's rescue.[9]

---

[8] Mann to Mary Mann, June 9 and August 18, 1850; William Schouler to Mann, May 6, 1850, both in Mann MSS:MHS; T. M. Brewer to William Schouler, May 10, 1850, Schouler MSS:MHS; Mann to Josiah Quincy, September 10, 1850, Quincy MSS:BPL; T[heron] Metcalf to Francis Wayland, August 30, 1850, Wayland MSS:BUA; Fuess, *Webster,* II, 226–230; Moses Stuart, *Conscience and the Constitution, with Remarks on the Speech of Webster on Slavery* (Boston, 1850).
[9] Daniel Webster to Fletcher Webster, June [?], 1850, Everett MSS:MHS; Mann to Charles Sumner, June 23 and August 30, 1850; Charles Sumner to Mann, June 21 and 23, 1850, and September 15 [1850], all in Mann MSS:MHS; William Seward to Mann, January [?], 1851, Seward MSS:

By the end of June, Mann was not only reconciled to the presence of a slaveholder in the White House but was convinced that President Taylor, for all his lack of sophistication, was a "godsend" since he had become a major force in preventing the extension of slavery. On Independence Day, the aging President sat in the brutal sun during ceremonies at the Washington Monument, enduring one of Senator "Hangman" Foote's interminable orations. Later, attempting to cool off, he drank an excessive amount of iced milk, possibly contaminated. Then, what the rigors of the Mexican campaign could not accomplish, the unhealthy conditions of the capital and a clutch of doctors and quacks could. Stricken with gastroenteritis, he was bled, blistered, and doped. With the aid of quinine, calomel, and opium, and a large mustard plaster on his abdomen, the medical profession finally killed him. Mann considered his death little short of a "calamity." Ironically, he now could think of no northerner strong enough to stand against the South as this southern slaveholder had done. "I fear there will not be firmness and force enough in all the North to resist him [them]. The future is indeed appalling." One reason for this was the growing political influence of Webster over Millard Fillmore, who took Taylor's place. While Taylor had leaned heavily on the advice of William Seward, it was expected that Webster would have an almost Faustian power over the new President. And this alone was enough to make Mann gloomily predict that "A dark hour is before us." [1]

Meanwhile, what Clay and Webster had set in motion, all the Free Soilers and abolitionists in the nation could not stop. By the end of August, they had gained approval on the critical bills in the Senate and it was now up to the House, where Mann reported, "We are at last, at the hand to hand encounter." And here too, the combined forces in the North and the South wanting compromise and peace did their work. Congressmen who had steadfastly stood by the Wilmot Proviso moved over with immodest haste to the coalition. Describing their defection, Mann wrote, "what makes it all so

University of Rochester; Webster, "Letter to the Citizens on the Kennebec River," Boston *Advertiser*, June 22, 1850; Codex Alexandrinus [pseud. Cornelius Felton], "Mr. Mann and Mr. Webster," Boston *Daily Advertiser*, August 24, 1850; Q.E.D. [pseud. Charles Beck], "The Boston Codex Alexandrinus and the 'captatores verborem' of Daniel Webster," Boston *Daily Atlas*, November 12, 1850; George F. Hoar, *Autobiography of Seventy Years* (New York, 1903) I, 98–99.
[1] Mann to Samuel Downer, June 28, 1850; Mann to Mary Mann, July 9, 10, and 12, 1850, all in Mann MSS:MHS.

terrible is, that these bills passed by treachery,—the grossest treachery by those who were chosen to do directly the opposite thing." On
September 6, Mann dejectedly reported, "the infernal Texas boundary bill has just passed. Dough if not infinite in quantity, is infinitely soft." The next day the California bill was approved and five
days later it was all over. The opposition although still adamant
was overwhelmed by a vote of 105 to 73, as the House of Representatives passed the infamous Fugitive Slave Bill.[2]

*   *   *

Back home, the Webster forces were jubilant, but in their elation they did not forget the directive from their master to "dispose"
of Mann. From what Mann could learn, they were making every
move to purge him from the Whig Party. Actually, he would have
preferred either to retire from politics or run for the governorship,
but now he had no chance for the gubernatorial chair, and his ego
and sense of personal justice forced him to seek re-election. In
Washington, he knew not whom to believe. Downer reported that
the "Websterites are active and will have a definite plan of action.
They will actively but secretly get all their friends possible nominated to the convention. . . ." And another correspondent predicted "an effort will be made to throw you overboard. . . ." Yet
Downer also assured Mann that there were at least 7,000 Whigs
in all of Norfolk that had not bowed down before the "Cottoncracy."
Things looked even more gloomy when a Webster Whig swamped
Charles Sumner in a contest for the Congressional seat vacated by
Robert Winthrop.[3]

Preparing their groundwork carefully in Mann's district, the
Webster Whigs planned to pack the nominating convention. Assisting them inadvertently were the Free Soilers, who met prior to the
Whig Convention and nominated Mann with a series of resolutions
which were as anti-Whig as they were anti-slavery. In his letter of

---

[2] Mann to Mary Mann, September 6, 9, 12, and 17, 1850; Mann to
Samuel Downer, September 13, 1850; Mann to Samuel J. May, Septem-
ber 21, 1850, all in Mann MSS:MHS.
[3] Mann to Samuel Downer, August 15, 1850; Samuel Downer to Mann,
August 22, 1850; Charles Sumner to Mann, August 27, 1850; Mann to
Samuel J. May, September 21, 1850; Mann to Charles Sumner, August 26
and 30, 1850; G. R. Russell to Mann, September 3, 1850, all in Mann
MSS:MHS.

acceptance, Mann defended his course of action in such a way as to make himself sound more like a Free Soiler than he was. Then in a long speech before the Whig Convention, instead of challenging his defamers to put their finger on his first vote or speech in Congress which was not true to Whig principles, Mann launched into a long attack on the Compromise, thus playing into the hands of his opponents. Perhaps a different speech might have produced different results, but the pummeling Mann had endured during the last few months had destroyed some of his resilience and political acuity. During the morning session, an informal ballot was held. Out of 117 votes, Mann received 56, just 3 short of a majority. The remaining 47 ballots cast were split about evenly between two opponents. After lunch and some intensive bargaining, the third candidate withdrew. Then in the first official balloting, Mann's supporters had their first real proof of the efficiency of the Webster machine. Samuel Walley, a political unknown but a loyal Webster man, received 63 votes to 54 for their candidate. Horace Mann would not be the Whig candidate for Congress. He would now go it alone as a Free Soiler.[4]

*   *   *

After another exhausting campaign, his future was in the hands of the voters of the Eighth District. On election day, more than 13,000 of them went to the polls to exercise what John Greenleaf Whittier that year called the "recuperative principle of democracy." The next day, the young Walter Gale, who was staying with the Manns and gave music lessons to Horace, Jr., and George, walked down to the railroad station to obtain the election news. Upon hearing the results when the train pulled in from Boston, he took to his heels and ran all the way up the hill at full speed. Still at some distance from the house, with what little breath remained,

---

[4] Charles Sumner to Joshua Giddings, September 7, 1850, Giddings MSS: OHS; Charles Sumner to Mann, October 30, 1850; T. M. Brewer to Mann, November 4, 1850, and November 6, 1850, all in Mann MSS:MHS; Boston *Daily Advertiser*, October 31, 1850; *Norfolk County Journal,* October 26, 1850; Boston *Daily Courier,* October 31, 1850; Mann, "Letter Accepting the Nomination of the Free Soil Convention for Representative to the Thirty-second Congress," and "Speech Delivered at Dedham, November 6, 1850, by Special Request of a Convention of Whig Voters of the Eighth Congressional District," both in *Slavery: Letters and Speeches,* pp. 340–389.

he shouted the results to Mann. The people of the Eighth District had sent Horace Mann back to Congress by a margin of forty-one votes! [5]

---

[5] J.G.W. [John Greenleaf Whittier], "The Election in Massachusetts," *National Era*, November 21, 1850; Boston *Daily Advertiser*, November 26, 1850; Reminiscences of Walter Gale, MS in the possession of Loriman S. Brigham, Montpelier, Vermont.

CHAPTER XXI

The Statesman and
the Prophet

================

. . . my zeal grows and glows to continue the
contest with evil. I love the good causes more than
ever; more than ever I want to fight for them; and
the most painful idea connected with death is that
I must be at most a looker on and not a participant.
HORACE MANN

————————

T HAT HE HAD WON and many Webster Whigs across the country
had gone down to defeat was one of many events which fore-
shadowed the final dissolution of the Whig Party. Taking his family
with him for the next session of Congress, which convened on December 2, Mann was amazed en route to learn that his victory had
gained him nationwide publicity. With every stop he made along
the way, he was congratulated, lionized, and pressed for still another speech. Strangers surged forward to grasp his hand and speak
to him as if he were an old friend, and women and children
stretched on tiptoe just to get a glimpse of this white-haired
man who had become a new hero of the anti-slavery movement
and an irreconcilable foe against the Compromise of 1850. Mann
even learned that a Maine shipbuilder had planned to name a ship
after him, until a financial backer in Boston vetoed the idea, fearing
injury to the vessel if it put in at a southern port. "My whole journey
was a sort of oration," was the way he described it. "I was greeted
by Whigs and Democrats, indiscriminately, and free soilers looked
upon me as something to be sworn by. . . . Sometimes I was the
David that killed Goliath, and sometimes the man who killed Cock
Robin." [1]

---

[1] Mann to Samuel Gridley Howe, December 8, 1850, Personal Misc. MSS:
LOC; Mann to Cyrus Peirce, December 14, 1850; Samuel Downer to
Mann, December 15, 1850; Mary Mann to Rebecca Pennell, December 10,
1850, all in Mann MSS:MHS.

Back in Massachusetts, the Free Soil vote had drawn so many votes away from the Whigs and the Democrats that no party received a clear majority in the contest for the governorship and other state offices, thus throwing the election into the General Court. In order to have a state government, some sort of coalition was necessary, and the Free Soilers, led by the shrewd and sophisticated Henry Wilson, set about to make a deal with the Democrats. Although it was now time for the Whigs to cry foul as compromise was in the wind, there was more here than the immediate greed to hold office to justify a coalition. Believing Massachusetts was long overdue for a general reform of its government, the Democrats' most important objective was to capture the State House. The Free Soilers wanted to fight for anti-slavery principles and were seeking a national platform. Thus, with more than a greed to divide the political spoils to motivate them, leaders of the two parties reached an agreement after innumerable negotiations on Beacon Hill. With Free Soil votes, the Democrats elected George Boutwell as Governor, a man whom Samuel Downer described as "a cautious, prudent, sagacious country merchant or trader." In addition, it was agreed that the Free Soilers would support the Democratic candidates for Lieutenant Governor, the Speaker of the House, a majority of seats on the Governor's Council, and the unexpired months of Webster's senatorship.

In return, the Democrats promised to support Free Soilers for the presidency of the Senate, the rest of the Governor's Council, and the six-year senatorship which was to begin March 4. Barely were the election returns in when Mann recognized the possibility of such an arrangement. More important, he saw in it the chance for Sumner to go to Washington as a Free Soil Senator. "A six years course will give him a *status* that nothing can shake," Mann predicted. And again he wrote, "His presence here would be beyond value. The fact that Massachusetts should choose such a man at such a time would have great moral force. . . ." Unfortunately for Sumner's cause, he was not the most popular candidate. A splinter group of dissident Democrats balked at the prospect of sending "a red-hot abolitionist" to Washington for a six-year stay even if George Boutwell were Governor. Recognizing he was likely to be defeated by a Free Soiler, Robert Winthrop, the Whig candidate for the Senate, wrote, "If I had the privilege [of] naming a Free Soil successor, it would be Samuel Hoar. . . . Even S. C. Phillips, or

Mann, would not nauseate me. But, I confess, my stomach revolts from Sumner." [2]

The balloting for the senatorship began in the House on January 14, 1851, and much to the amazement and then indignation of his floor generals, five defecting Democrats prevented Sumner's majority. By January 22 the Senate had elected him, but on the two following sessions in the House, five rounds of balloting showed he was as far away from a majority as at the start. Meanwhile, the Whigs stubbornly held with Winthrop, their fervor heightened by nightmarish thoughts that their failure meant Sumner's election. So animated were Amos Lawrence and other wealthy Whigs that they raised a fund ostensibly to help Whig Representatives forced to stay in Boston for the prolonged session while their business affairs suffered, but really intended to purchase whatever means necessary to defeat this "red-hot abolitionist."

During this time, Sumner struggled to know his own desires. Before the first ballot, he had confided to Mann, "I have searched my heart, and have its answer. I do not desire to be a Senator; nor have I ever, directly or indirectly suggested even a willingness to take the place." Then after the first month of inconclusive votes, Sumner realized that once his foot was in the door, to back out would give too much aid and comfort to the enemy and devastate his ego to boot. "If I could retire at this moment, without seeming to retreat, and without injuriously affecting our cause," he confided to Mann, "it would give me pleasure to do so. I should like to be dropt gently into quiet life." Mann, however, would not countenance any such withdrawal. Attempting to bolster Sumner's spirits he wrote, "Remember, it is the darkest time just before the day. . . . *You* must now take the field, and vindicate your cause, before the people,—not *yourself;* that I do not say, but the *cause.*" If this had a familiar ring to Sumner it would be understandable, since he had given Mann virtually the identical advice the previous autumn when the Whigs had attempted to purge him from the party for his attacks on Webster.[3]

Deadlocked, the senatorial contest ground on in the House

[2] Mann to Samuel Gridley Howe, January 13, 1851, Personal Misc. MSS: LOC; Mann to Samuel Gridley Howe, November 27, 1850, and January 19 and 28, 1851; Samuel Downer to Mann, December 15, 1850, and January 20, 1851; T. M. Brewer to Mann, January 13, 1851, all in Mann MSS:MHS; Winthrop, *Memoir of Robert Charles Winthrop*, p. 145.
[3] Charles Sumner to Mann, January 11 and 30, 1851; Mann to Charles Sumner, February 14, 1851, all in Mann MSS:MHS.

through February and March and well into April, with the peripatetic Sumner still no nearer a majority. The adjournment less than a month away, on April 23, the voting gave the first evidence of a crack developing in his opposition. Webster had sent new directives from Washington that the party should switch its support from Winthrop to a more unequivocal defender of the Compromise of 1850, and a few Whigs, rather than expedite the *coup de grâce* to the state party by voting for a candidate foursquare for the Fugitive Slave Law, switched to Sumner. On April 23, the House stayed in session eleven hours, but a careful recount showed still one vote lacking for a majority. Then on April 24, the next ballot found Sumner two votes short. A second ballot was ordered and this time out of 384 votes cast, Sumner had 193, exactly the number needed. Suddenly Boston was polarized into enthusiasts and Cassandras. In Washington, Mann was elated for the sake of the *"cause"* and his own sake. Help was now on the way. *"Laus Deo!* Good, better, best, better yet!"* were his congratulations to Sumner, and he added, "By the necessity of the case, you are now to be a politician,—an honest one." But for the moment, his delight grew out of his own better sense of justice. The state which had sent Daniel Webster to the Senate, the man who had attempted to ride him out of the party for his anti-slavery heresy, was now dispatching Charles Sumner, ardent Free Soiler and an irreconcilable foe of the Compromise of 1850.[4]

*   *   *

In the House, Mann's testing of the political winds made him convinced that little could be done about the Fugitive Slave Law for the time being. "There is no more chance of repealing or modifying the Fugitive Slave Law," he reported to Downer at the beginning of the new session, "than there is of making a free state of South Carolina." Nevertheless, he felt compelled to conduct what he called "a Demonstration upon it" since "we cannot lose anything now, *because we have lost all.* Our dangers are prospective. Cuba, Mexico, Nicaragua are the game now afoot." For the moment, making a "Demonstration" for Mann consisted of laying the legal basis

---

[4] Mann to Sumner, April [?], 1851, Mann MSS:MHS. For the history of the coalition and the election of Sumner, I have benefited from Donald, *Charles Sumner*, pp. 189–203, and Schwartz, *Samuel Gridley Howe*, pp. 170–176.

for establishing the unconstitutionality of the law. On February 28, he gained the floor to read a carefully prepared manuscript studded with more than 100 case citations. Unwilling to be submitted to an hour-long denunciation of the law and a biting comparison of it to the infamous Alien and Sedition Acts, the Speaker imposed the five-minute "gag rule" on Mann, but not before he had the chance to declare in the best libertarian tradition, "Sir, I hold treason against this government to be an enormous crime; but great as it is, I hold treason against free speech and free thought to be a crime incomparably greater." Stymied, Mann then announced that he would avail himself of "the common opportunity of submitting these remarks to the House and country through the ordinary medium of the press." The result was the combination of a comprehensive legal brief arguing that the law violated the spirit and the letter of the Constitution, and an eloquent plea earnestly urging its repeal. Filling eighty-two printed pages, it contained the results of countless hours of work on the Drayton and Sayres cases, the many exchanges with Sumner and Carlisle, and his own assimilation of Locke, Blackstone, Coke, Hooker, and Montesquieu. In a moving conclusion, rhetorically as forceful as that of Patrick Henry, he wrote, "In the name of my constituents, and by the memory of that 'old man eloquent,' in whose place it is my fortune to stand, I demand its repeal. I demand it," he continued, "because it is a law which wars against the fundamental principles of human liberty," and "because it is a law which conflicts with the constitution of the country, and with all the judicial interpretations of that constitution, wherever they have been applied to the white race." The overall product was Mann at his best, with all of his compelling power of persuasion when committed to a cause.[5]

Returning to Massachusetts at the close of the session, Mann had the opportunity to witness the real handiwork of the Fugitive Slave Law. After a black named "Shadrach" had been "emancipated" from the courtroom in Boston by a vigilante group during a hearing, the United States commissioner was determined not to have a second successful challenge to federal authority. When Thomas Sims, a seventeen-year-old black, was arrested on the streets of Boston on

---

[5] Mann to Samuel Downer, December 22, 1850, Mann MSS:MHS; Mann, "Speech Delivered in the House of Representatives of the United States . . . February 28, 1851, on the Fugitive Slave Law," *Slavery: Letters and Speeches*, pp. 390–472; *Congressional Globe*, February 28, 1851, Appendix, p. 237; *Liberator*, March 21, 1851.

a complaint from a Georgia slaveowner, 400 police ringed the Court House during the trial. To offer double security, George Curtis, the U.S. commissioner, ordered chains wrapped around the building, beneath which the justices of the Massachusetts Supreme Court were forced to bow as they entered and left. Curtis then ruled that Sims must be returned to his alleged owner and the luckless victim was manacled and marched under heavy guard between two rows of militia down to the Long Wharf, where he was put on board the brig *Acorn* and shipped to Savannah.[6]

While the court was deliberating, the Boston Vigilance Committee called a mass protest meeting. Being refused the use of Faneuil Hall, Mann remarked, "when the courthouse is in chains, Faneuil Hall will be dumb." Moving to the Tremont Temple, the committee was late in getting its program of speeches, letters, and resolutions under way, and for the moment saw the rostrum usurped by Abby Folsom, known as the "flea of conventions," who jumped to the stage and began cataloguing the evils plaguing society, each of her indictments followed by the shrill refrain, "It's the capitalists!" When he had order restored, Samuel Gridley Howe turned the meeting over to Horace Mann, who had agreed to serve as president and give the opening speech. Mann set the tone, denouncing the Fugitive Slave Law and defending a fugitive's right to trial by jury, while at the same time deprecating the use of extralegal means to re-establish justice. Other speeches by Thomas Wentworth Higginson, Wendell Phillips, and John G. Palfrey followed, as the meeting which had started at ten in the morning took on marathon proportions and lasted almost until midnight. Before it dispersed, by a thundering affirmation the assembled group approved resolutions reaffirming the right of habeas corpus and a jury trial to alleged fugitives and declared that no one could aid in returning a fugitive slave without violating the laws of humanity and God. Wisely, Curtis postponed his decision until four days later,

---

[6] Mary T. Higginson, *Thomas Wentworth Higginson* (Boston, 1914), p. 112; Ralph Korngold, *Two Friends of Man* (New York, 1950), pp. 219–222. During the first eighteen months after the Fugitive Slave Law, only twenty-six slaves were returned from Pennsylvania, a dozen from New York, and one, Thomas Sims, from Boston. Surely the passage of the law had its own form of tokenism, since it was estimated that as many as 20,000 fugitive slaves resided in the North and as many as 500 in Boston alone. No doubt financial considerations reinforced human decency. The rendition of Sims cost the United States $6,000 and his alleged owner $3,000. In 1854, the return of Anthony Burns cost $65,000.

and the Tremont Temple rally served the constructive purpose of letting angry citizens give vent to their frustrations without resorting to violence.[7]

Mann was astounded to see how an unmitigated rationalization masqueraded as sound legal reasoning in Curtis's ruling in the Sims Case. "If it is not a scandal to the profession, as well as an abhorrence to humanity, then there is no law or gospel left upon the earth," he wrote to Sumner, and added, "I *burn* to *roast* him, and trust I shall ere long have a chance to do it." The chance came at the Free Soil Convention at Lancaster the following month. Continuing his campaign of dissent on the Fugitive Slave Law, Mann claimed that by this enactment, "the liberty of a resident of Massachusetts,—a man every way entitled to a jury trial, as much as you or I,—has been sacrificed by a United States Commissioner in the city of Boston." Then finding each part of Curtis's decision riddled with legal errors, Mann rebuked the hard-pressed official by claiming that one would search history in vain to find a "judge whoever sat upon a bench where the common law was recognized and administered, however corrupt he may have been, [who] ever advanced a more atrocious doctrine." Once the government deprived one class of citizens of its rights, Mann warned his all-white audience, no one was safe, and every man, woman, and child should recognize the law for what it was, "a living monster, uncaged and turned loose amongst us, to rob us and devour us at its will." Smarting under Mann's scathing attack, Curtis defended himself in the columns of the *Advertiser* and not satisfied with this, filed a libel suit against Benjamin B. Mussey, the publisher who had brought out a one-volume collection of Mann's anti-slavery letters and speeches which included this attack on the commissioner. Curtis later dropped the case and it was a private joke between Mann and Mussey whether the suit was for injuries done him in his judicial character or to "vindicate his wounded vanity." [8]

[7] Mann, "Speech Delivered, on Taking the Chair, as President of the Great Mass Convention . . . Held at the Tremont Temple in Boston, April 8, 1851," *Slavery: Letters and Speeches*, pp. 523–535; Boston *Daily Advertiser*, April 9, 1851; Boston *Evening Transcript*, April 8, 1850; Mann to Samuel Gridley Howe, [April, 1851], Mann MSS:MHS.
[8] Mann, "Speech on the Fugitive Slave Law, Delivered at Lancaster, Massachusetts, May 19, 1851 . . . ," *Slavery: Letters and Speeches*, pp. 473–522; Mann to Charles Sumner, April 29, 1851; Benjamin B. Mussey to Mann, December 6, 1851; Mann to Edmund Clap, January 5, 1851, all in Mann MSS:MHS; Boston *Daily Advertiser*, May 29, 1851; *Liberator*, May 30, 1851; *Commonwealth*, May 22, 1851.

Mann spoke to an enthusiastic audience in Lancaster, but traveling about the state, he found feelings so polarized about the Compromise that he never knew whether he would face a body of hecklers or a gathering of the faithful. Having had the chance to practice on Ralph Waldo Emerson, who had also taken the stump to denounce the law, a group of 100 Harvard students, most of them from the South, hissed and hooted at Mann when he spoke at Cambridge several nights later. Cheering for Webster, they pounced on any statement in which Mann alluded to freedom. Finally, with the chant "Webster and Union, three cheers for Webster!", they broke up the meeting before marching out of the hall and down Massachusetts Avenue to taunt Edward Everett at his residence. Apparently, they felt Everett was entitled to their special abuse since he had previously resigned from the presidency at Harvard in protest against the Harvard Corporation, which had refused to admit a qualified black applicant.[9]

Yet for all the tidal wave of words uttered by courageous angry men bent on destroying the Fugitive Slave Law in 1851, none of their efforts created anything like the powerful groundswell of moral indignation accomplished by a book from the pen of the obscure wife of a Bowdoin College professor, Harriet Beecher Stowe. After paying her $300 for the first three or four installments, Gamaliel Bailey, editor of the *National Era*, announced he was publishing *Uncle Tom's Cabin, or the Man That Was a Thing* in serial form, beginning June 5, 1851. Before it had run its course and Mrs. Stowe wearily brought it to a close, she had written some forty installments. Since the *Era* had a small circulation, the real impact of *Uncle Tom's Cabin* came with its publication as a book in 1852, which moved one caustic commentator to claim that it was an epistle from Hell, debauched "with murder, lust, illicit love, suicide, sadistic torture, profanity, drunkenness, and barroom brawls." More accurately, it was a pathetic tale of both whites and blacks, barbarized by the institution of slavery and suffering the tragedy of broken families, the infamous horrors of the auction block, the sadistic cruelty of plantation overseers, and the terror of being hunted by the slavehound.

Outraged but never speechless, southern readers denounced the book as a fabrication of lies and the product of a perverted abolitionist mind. Believing she must defend her veracity, Mrs.

---

[9] *Commonwealth,* May 15 and 24, 1851.

Stowe prepared a second volume, *Key to Uncle Tom's Cabin,* a documentation drawn mainly from southern accounts of atrocities and sufferings described in her first work. Gathering information, she consulted with Mann, and was particularly grateful for the information he gave her on the subsequent events surrounding the captives of the ill-fated *Pearl.* In one case, Mann informed her a girl had been auctioned six times during the seven weeks following her capture. Delighted that he could help, Mann was anxious to "put her on the track of some enormities" which would help "deepen the damnation of her accusers." About this same time, Sumner had obtained a presidential pardon for Drayton and Sayres, both of whom had languished in their wretched Washington jail cells for more than four years. Just before their release, Mann and Sumner learned of a covert move to extradite them to Virginia in order to try them for aiding several slaves on the *Pearl* who had come from Alexandria. By quick action, Sumner forced their release, and hurried them into a coach which sped the two men out of Washington and north to free territory in a flight which was as anxious as Eliza's fictional crossing of the Ohio River with her son. If Mrs. Stowe received only a fraction of the royalties due her from her book and its adaptations, Mann neither asked nor received a cent for the weeks and months of work he put in defending Drayton and Sayres. For him, it was enough to know that because of the unflagging zeal and sacrifice of Mrs. Stowe, himself, and thousands of other fellow laborers, in the courtroom, the legislative forum, the rostrum, and the press, on every available front, the cause of human freedom would still triumph.[1]

*   *   *

The Mann family could not live on causes alone, even if their income was augmented by a Congressman's modest salary. With what free time he could find in the spring and fall between political speeches and the sessions in the House, Mann went on the Lyceum circuit, describing the process as "selling some of my own wind." After using his speech on Great Britain as his main stock in trade

---

[1] Leonard Bacon to Mann, January 10, 1851; Mann to Mary Mann, August 12 and December 10, 1852, all in Mann MSS:MHS; Mary Mann to Mrs. Elizabeth Peabody, January 25, 1852, Berg MSS:NYPL; Mann to Francis Jackson, May 11, 1851, Anti-Slavery MSS:BPL; *National Era,* June 5, 1851; Catherine P. Gilbertson, *Harriet Beecher Stowe* (New York, 1937), pp. 173–180.

for a number of years, he found that his "Thoughts for a Young Man" had become an even more popular offering, and subsequently he prepared a companion piece on womanhood. For a man given to various ailments, a lecture tour was hardly a therapeutic diversion. Far from it. There was the endless problem of matching dates and places. One had to consult the calendar, maps, railroad time tables, and even the almanac, since some Lyceum committees required a specific date, while others, especially those in rural communities where farmers must return over dark roads at the end of the program, specified "sometime between the First Quarter and the Full of every moon during the cold season." The fare at local inns was always a chancy thing and Mann, troubled by dyspepsia, lived in constant fear of alimentary problems. Always on the verge of a severe cold, he worried about drafts, and rarely found a room away from home which was both warm enough and well ventilated. He abhorred rooms heated with fireplaces and considered pot-bellied stoves a menace to his lungs, but once beyond the city limits of Boston or New York, he rarely found inns or homes with furnace heat. Often rising before dawn in order to travel and be in time for his next lecture, he must break the ice on the water in the pitcher on his wash stand. Maintaining the schedule once established and getting from one place to another was a constant challenge. Not all towns could be reached by train, and more than a few times Mann was forced to resort to "a miserable stage with a miserable team" to meet an obligation. Sometimes a spring thaw would draw the frost out of the ground early and he would travel all day through a sea of mud; a March freshet could wash out a bridge, necessitating an unplanned delay; and he was ever in anticipation of a "hard-hearted old-fashioned Puritanical snow-storm." In the spring of 1851, immediately after the Tremont Temple meeting, he took to the road for a circuit through upper New York, lecturing at Buffalo, Lockport, Syracuse, Oswego, Auburn, Rome, and Utica. The following fall he traveled through Maine, New Hampshire, and Vermont. Each was a grueling itinerary for a fortnight, but at $20 to $50 a night plus expenses, or at 10 cents per head, he could return to West Newton with several hundred dollars in his purse. More important was the knowledge that in most places he continued to draw large crowds and could look forward to a larger number of applications for the coming season.[2]

---

[2] Mann to Mary Mann, April 13 and 17, 1851, and March 2, 1852; Mann to Samuel J. May, July 4, 1851; Austin Craig to Mann, Novem-

Now completely ousted from the Whig Party, Mann was welcomed with open arms by the Free Soiler wing of the coalition. At its state meeting in Worcester in September, he was elected president of the convention and upon assuming the chair, gave the major address. Afterwards dozens of requests for appearances from both within and without the state came to him, and during the fall campaign of 1851 he took to the stump, speaking every night for three weeks before the election. The Dedham *Gazette* lauded him for his efforts in comparison with the "vaunted promises" and "wretched performances" of the Whig Party, while the Springfield *Republican*, in political rhetoric typical of the bitterness which followed the Compromise, claimed he had "the heart of the demagogue, the tricks of a demagogue, the saintly pretenses of a demagogue, the personal ambition of a demagogue, the shifting policy of a demagogue, the dastardly spirit of detraction of a demagogue . . ." Once again the election for Governor was thrown into the General Court, and once again the coalition chose George Boutwell. More important was the stronger showing of the Democrats at the expense of the Free Soilers. Apparently the memory of the Compromise was already beginning to fade in the minds of some Massachusetts voters.[3]

The following spring, Mann slipped away from Washington to New York to attend a "Great Temperance Banquet," where he shared honors with Sam Houston. Mann spoke on four successive evenings, once to an audience of 5,000. The assignment proved a new challenge to him. Two weeks before, he had had all his teeth extracted, the dentist finding small saclike accumulations of pus at the base of their roots. "Mumbling and munching and making lip sounds" and fearing he might not produce anything more than some sort of "Irish gibberish," he nevertheless kept his date with the temperance workers. Things turned out reasonably well, considering his false teeth did not catch up to him until later on his tour, and a New York newspaper correspondent only commented

ber 14, 1851, all in Mann MSS:MHS; Mann to A. P. Wiggin, November 13, 1851, Colby College Library; Mann to Elizabeth Montfort, March 26 and April 3, 1851, Anti-slavery MSS: Maine Historical Society.
[3] Mann to George Combe, December 5, 1851, Combe MSS:NLS; Mann, "Speech Delivered at Worcester, September 16, 1851, on Taking the Chair as President of the Free Soil Convention," *Slavery: Letters and Speeches*, pp. 536–564; Boston *Daily Advertiser*, September 22 and 23, 1851; *Liberator*, October 10, 1851.

that he had a slight speech impediment due to what he considered the loss of several front teeth.[4]

From New York City, he moved on to Syracuse where he spoke two nights and then traveled to Rochester, Auburn, Danville, Geneseo, and Lima, giving twenty-five lectures before returning. In most places, Mann's reputation preceded him and the crowds were large. Even in a small town of less than 1,000, he would have an audience of over 700, some persons traveling as far as fifteen miles by buggy to hear him. Since he had made arrangements with some groups to receive a percentage of the receipts, the trip was financially successful and he accumulated enough money on this to pay off several hundred dollars owed to James K. Mills. Money problems always weighed heavily on Mann's mind, and he considered long-term debts nothing less than a "nightmare." That fall, despite the fact that the political campaign prevented a full schedule of appearances, he still managed to travel 1,000 miles in a week, lecturing four times and sleeping on the railroad three nights in a row. And the one day he took to an open buggy, it turned out to be a "world of mud." He described himself on his arrival at Mount Morris as "regularly plastered, encrusted, veneered, Mac mud ized,—hat, face, coat, cloak, and wherever the mud-hail could strike me." But all this, he assured one correspondent, was a "Mahomedan [sic] paradise compared to the gnawings of debt," and when he sent Howe enough money to pay off one of his obligations exceeding $1,000, he spoke with a sense of unconcealed relief that at least *one* of the flock of vampires is plucked from my breast." [5]

While on the road, Howe had written to Mann urging him to consider campaigning as a Free Soiler for the gubernatorial chair in the coming election. Mann answered facetiously that after this bone-jarring circuit was concluded, he would be a candidate for nothing else than a rocking chair. Then in a more serious vein, he reported to Howe that while in Lima, New York, he had spoken to

---

[4] Mann to Mary Mann, [February 18, 1852], [February 20, 1852], and March 2, 1852; Mann to Cyrus Peirce, February 13, 1852, all in Mann MSS:MHS; Mary Mann to Mann, [February, 1852], Straker MSS:ACL; Mary Mann to Mrs. Elizabeth Peabody, January 29, 1852, Berg MSS: NYPL; Mann to William Seward, February 13, 1852, Seward MSS: University of Rochester.

[5] Mann to Mary Mann, February 22 and 26, and March 16, 1852; Mann to Cyrus Peirce, March 27, 1852; Mann to Samuel Gridley Howe, March 11 and December 14, 1852, all in Mann MSS:MHS.

the Reverend Eli Fay, chairman of a committee appointed by the Christian Connexion—a Protestant denomination which hoped to establish a college. Mann was drawn into the conversation for several reasons. First he picked up the signal of nonsectarianism: while other church-founded colleges often were conceived of as proselyting instruments, the Christian Connexion wanted to provide a liberal curriculum which included religion but was free of even the taint of sectarianism. The second signal he responded to was their desire that it be co-educational, a radical departure from conventional practices at the time. And finally, he was flattered to learn that they were looking for a man to be president who was an educational leader of national stature, such as himself, and were willing to pay him $3,000 per annum if he would assume the leadership of their venture. All this Mann also related to Mary and then asked, "How would you like to go and be the wife of its President?" [6]

Taking the informal overtures from Fay seriously, upon his return to Washington, Mann wrote to his friends and associates looking for advice, but phrasing his questions in such a way as to imply that he had already decided to accept the offer if it actually materialized. Six months before, he had confided to Barnard, "If I were not fighting for *vital*, sacred principles, I would abandon the whole cause. . . . But the magnitude of the interests at stake make all personal considerations, ease, time, money, social position etc. etc. insignificant. *Freedom* must precede *education*." Still, thoughts of returning to education gave him a welcome psychological diversion from lecturing and serving his time in the House where, having weathered the fierce storms of 1849 and 1850, he now found the affairs before the chamber stuck in the doldrums. A pro-Webster administration was systematically carrying out the conditions of the Compromise to strengthen its own position, appointing officers in the new territorial governments in New Mexico and Utah, who were silent, if not openly pro-southern, on the matter of slavery. Otherwise, Congress did little more than furnish the backdrop for what Mann called an "intrigue for the respective candidates," meaning Webster, Pierce, Scott, Cass, Douglas, and Houston. He took some satisfaction in learning of Webster's defeat in the Whig presidential convention in Baltimore, at the hands of Winfield Scott, but no candidate of either party had his enthusiastic endorsement. The only Democrat he favored was Sam Houston, a man he considered

---

[6] Mann to Samuel Gridley Howe, March 11, 1852; Mann to Mary Mann, March 9, 1852, both in Mann MSS:MHS.

"of some conscience and honor," largely on the basis of his advocacy of temperance. And in the fall election, he apathetically cast his vote for Winfield Scott simply because Scott was against slavery and a "very honorable and high-minded man." [7]

Then, too, after the Thomas Sims affair, there was no new rallying catalyst from which to launch the next attack on the Fugitive Slave Law. In Massachusetts, politics more than principles prevailed as Democrats and Free Soilers maneuvered and negotiated to continue their marriage of convenience, an arrangement bound together more by a fear of the resurgence of Cotton Whiggism than shared political goals. In all of this, aside from the issue of antislavery, the one chance Mann saw to get the parties moving back towards a more constructive program was to make the cause of temperance a political objective, much as Neal Dow had done in Maine the year before by forcing through a law prohibiting the manufacture and sale of ardent spirits, the first of its kind in the nation. When Howe pressed him on the issue of the governorship, Mann replied that he would not run, other than on "the temperance platform,—I mean the Maine law." But he doubted if the coalition would agree to this. And he was right. More prudent politicians in the Bay State, remembering the fiasco of the "fifteen gallon law," would have no part of it. [8]

Yet when he considered the consequences, not only of leaving politics but of leaving Massachusetts for a college in the Midwest, there were so many imponderables along that path that he ended up in a quandary. He could not decide to accept the presidency, Mann wrote to Howe,

and cannot do so without calling your wisdom and friendship into counsel. Of course, you will see that it will cause the breaking of many ligaments that will never be healed in no case any stronger ones than those which bind me to you. On the other hand, there are some attractions,—an anti-sectarian college, etc.

And what that et cetera included but remained unsaid was that Mann was seeking some retreat from the destructive and debilitat-

---

[7] Mann to Henry Barnard, August 8, 1851, Barnard MSS:NYU; Mann to Samuel Gridley Howe, April 18, 1852; Mann to Cyrus Peirce, February 13, 1852; Mann to Edmund Clap, June 24, 1852; Mann to Samuel Downer, July 27, 1852; Mann to Theodore Parker, August 10, 1852, all in Mann MSS:MHS; Mann to George Combe, July 1, 1852, Combe MSS:NLS.

[8] Mann to Samuel Gridley Howe, March 11, 1852; Mann MSS:MHS.

ing arena of political controversy which he had endured for the last five years. Samuel Downer, who thought New England was well past its zenith as a political and cultural leader of the nation, urged Mann to go west. "Our active talent is seeking new fields," he wrote, ". . . it seems to me the opinions of [the] valley of the Mississippi, whatever it [they] may be, must give tone to the destinies of this country and we shall soon look to see what and how they think and what they will do and not to New England. . . ." Catharine Beecher —whose father, Lyman, had gone to Cincinnati as president of the Lane Theological Seminary in order to establish a bridgehead for Protestantism in the Ohio River Valley some twenty years before— knew the cultural and geographical topography of the area well. To Mann's enquiry about founding a college there, she gave a candidly pessimistic reply. Mann should anticipate students who would be a "strange medley of raw, ignorant boys—not one tenth of whom will stay over a year and will go off unlamented." Any founder of a college west of the Alleghenies, she warned, was asking for a "legion of cares, perplexities, charges, and disappointments." Letters from other friends supported either the Downer or the Beecher positions, and from such conflicting advice, Mann was to chart his future course, whether to continue in politics or to return to education.[9]

Clearly he needed more information. Writing to Eli Fay, Mann went to some lengths to explain his interest and then raised several questions. From what he had learned, the college would offer an opportunity for "redressing the long-inflicted wrongs of woman by giving her equal advantages of education—with men." Then, too, the prospect of developing a college purged of sectarianism, which could "enlighten the human mind with all the true knowledge and with science," and help every student prepare for "that most important of all duties, the determining of his religious belief for himself," he found almost irresistible. Mann also raised certain questions about the governance of the school: what powers the president would have, whether his niece and nephew, Rebecca and Calvin Pennell, could join the faculty, and whether the salary would actually be $3,000. With all of this, he reassured Fay of his interest. All his life he had worked to reform and improve established institutions. Here was the chance to begin with a *tabula rasa*, "to organize

---

[9] Mann to Samuel Gridley Howe, March 11 and May 4, 1852; Samuel Downer to Mann, April 20, 1852; Catharine Beecher to Mann, June 14, 1852, all in Mann MSS:MHS; Mann to Henry Barnard, July 7, 1852, Barnard MSS:NYU.

the institution, to stamp certain great features upon it, and to give it its direction and momentum." [1]

To an anxious man, Fay's reply was less than satisfactory. The responsibility for running the college would be shared by the president and A. M. Merrifield, who was to serve as the business manager of the school. All actions, of course, were presently subject to the approval of Fay's temporary committee, which was authorized to get the school under way, and subsequently subject to the actions of a board of trustees to be selected from the Christian Connexion. Thus, Fay could say nothing definite about the possibility of Rebecca and Calvin Pennell joining the faculty at this time. Now having second thoughts about salary, his committee feared it would be no more than $2,000 since the Christians were themselves mainly poor people and could not understand the need for such an excessive figure. With such information, Mann's enthusiasm began to wane. In the meantime, other intelligence from the Midwest proved equally discouraging. When Calvin Stowe heard of the project, he held up his hands in despair at the thought. Mary also had had second thoughts. Catharine Beecher's warning she first discounted because of Miss Beecher's unmitigated sectarianism, but it continued to "haunt" her. Ever fretting over the health of her family, she began to worry whether "fever and ague attacks strangers in that region." Considering it necessary to drive a hard bargain, Mann held out for his conditions on salary and the appointment of his niece and nephew, while gradually cooling to the project and believing that by his adamancy, there was "little chance of 'closing hands.'" And by the middle of August, he wrote to Howe, "on the whole, I think the chances of my going are diminishing." [2]

For all his interest in furthering education, Howe was glad to receive this news. While the Christian Connexion laid plans to save the great heartland from godlessness and barbarism, other more worldly groups in Massachusetts were laboring to rescue their state from the politically corrupting influences of slavery, cotton, and intemperance. As part of this, Howe and Theodore Parker pumped the gubernatorial candidacy of Mann. Parker, no doubt intrigued

---

[1] Mann to Eli Fay, May 13 and 31, 1852, in Mann, *Life*, pp. 365–370; Mann to Mary Mann, August 11, 1852, Mann MSS:MHS; Mann to Gerrit Smith, May 23, 1853, Gerrit Smith MSS:Syracuse University.
[2] Eli Fay to Mann, July 12, 1852; Mann to Mary Mann, July 17 and August 5, 1852; Mary Mann to Mann, July 19 and August 8, 1852; Mann to Samuel Gridley Howe, August 18, 1852, all in Mann MSS:MHS; Mann to Henry Barnard, July 7, 1852, Barnard MSS:NYU.

with thoughts of a modern version of Plato's philosopher king lead- ing the Old Bay State, predicted "we may elect Mann for Governor and such a governor no State ever had." Meanwhile, Howe put for- ward Mann's name before various party committees. At the Free Soil Convention at Lowell in September, it was evident that a caucus of temperance men within the party would demand a candi- date committed to their own narrow cause. The Palfrey backers, realizing their candidate could not win endorsement, and fearing the nomination of Henry Wilson whom the more genteel Free Soil- ers still considered an unregenerate hunker, reluctantly switched to Mann. In a series of rousing speeches, Mann's case was put before the convention and, on September 15, he was nominated by accla- mation as the Free Soil candidate for Governor. On the same day, the special committee of the Christian Connexion appointed him president of their new school at Yellow Springs, Ohio.

Although in the previous gubernatorial election, Palfrey had made a poor showing, Mann decided he had a chance to win if he could pull together the votes of the old anti-slavery Whigs, the Free Soilers, and the temperance men among the Democrats. Moreover, he expected that if a coalition of Democrats and Free Soilers con- trolled the General Court and no gubernatorial candidate received a majority, the position would go to him. In the three weeks before the election he was on the road campaigning with more vigor than any Free Soiler to date. For seven successive evenings, he held the attention of his audience at two and three hours a clip. One day he crossed over into New Hampshire to lend a hand to the Free Soilers there. In addition, he found time for the endless receptions and conferences with local party bigwigs in the towns where he spoke, and also managed to compose several position papers which were published in the newspapers. Ultimately it was for the voters to de- cide, and when the returns were in the first week in November, it was evident that Mann had made an excellent campaign, polling 27 per cent of the ballots, an increase of six points over Palfrey's record the previous year; but he had failed in his attempt to split the Whig vote. Not only did their candidate receive 45 per cent of

---

[3] Mann to Samuel Gridley Howe, August 16, 1852, Mann MSS:MHS; Theodore Parker to Charles Sumner, September 6, 1852, Parker Letter- book, MHS; John G. Palfrey to Charles Francis Adams, September 14, 1852, and John G. Palfrey to the Free Soil Convention, September 14, 1852, both in Adams MSS:MHS; Samuel Gridley Howe to Charles Sumner [?], 1852, Howe MSS:HCL; *Commonwealth,* September 16, 1852.

the vote, but more important, they had gained a slim majority in the General Court, and therefore had the means to fill the governorship with their own standard-bearer. Thus not only had the Massachusetts voters returned the State House to the Whigs after a brief control by the coalition; they inadvertently had found Antioch College its first president.[4]

*   *   *

Mann blamed his political defeat on the twin demons of rum and pro-slavery. "We must . . . rely on the future," he consoled Mary, "since we have so little encouragement in the present." And once again for Mann, the future hinged on education. The first thing President Mann did was call a faculty meeting at West Newton of those chosen by the committee, including Rebecca and Calvin Pennell. In intellectual accomplishments it was not a distinguished group, but in its first two days of meetings the faculty exhibited a sense of dedication and consecration which augured well for the undertaking. Mann was particularly delighted to learn of the considerable unanimity of his staff in several areas, and reported, "We were all teetotalers; all anti-tobacco men; all anti-slavery men . . . all anti-emulation men,—that is, all against any system of rewards and prizes designed to withdraw the mind from a comparison of itself with a standard of excellence, and to substitute a rival for that standard." The meeting began at 9 a.m. in Mann's home, and within the next two days the group had drawn up a tentative curriculum for a high school or preparatory department at the college and an undergraduate course of studies. Eli Fay sat in on all the sessions, and A. M. Merrifield of Worcester, a man of boundless energy and enthusiasm if somewhat lacking in system, order, and a sense of reality, who was presently overseeing the construction of the college buildings, paid a call and stayed through dinner. At its conclusion, one of the idealistic young members of the group, Ira Allen, wrote in his diary, "a glorious meeting it was" and "harmonious in all respects." [5]

---

[4] Mann to Mary Mann, October 31, 1852; Josiah Knight to Mann, September 20, 1852, both in Mann MSS:MHS; Norfolk *Democrat*, October 22, 1852; *Commonwealth*, November 4, 1852; Boston *Daily Advertiser*, November 9, 1852; Martin Duberman, *Charles Francis Adams*, pp. 182–184.
[5] Mann to Mary Mann, November 23, 1852; Mann to Austin Craig, November 8, 1852, both in Mann MSS:MHS; Ira Allen, Diary, November 4, 1852, MS in ACL.

This completed, Mann took to the road, traveling west with a dual purpose. This season, he had scheduled by far his most ambitious lecture tour, including stops in Pennsylvania, Ohio, Illinois, and Michigan. He also planned to visit the campus at Yellow Springs and meet some of the local people promoting the project. Now enjoying a transmontane reputation, he could limit himself to the larger cities. This time his itinerary included Pittsburgh, Cleveland, Cincinnati, Toledo, and Chicago, and he was particularly pleased, although he quickly disdained the pleasure, to see large placards on fences and posts in Scranton announcing "Horace Mann, President of Antioch College . . . the distinguished orator of the West." He gained further publicity on his tour when several days before his appearance in one town Andrew Jackson Davis, the "seer of Poughkeepsie," billed as having telepathic and prophetic powers, went into a trance during his performance. In this state, Davis began to mumble and finally was understood to be asking if Horace Mann was soon to lecture on "womanhood" in the same hall. When answered in the affirmative, Davis proceeded to astound his audience by giving verbatim, paragraph upon paragraph, portions of what Mann would say. Hearing of the episode upon his arrival, Mann suspected that Davis had simply memorized parts of his womanhood speech which had been published in the New York *Tribune* the week before. Therefore, when he took to the rostrum that evening, he omitted those sections Davis had memorized and improvised others. All this gave Mann added notoriety. With audiences as large or larger than he expected, including "a tremendous house" in Cincinnati, he could report with a sense of small triumph to Howe, "I hope soon to get off another of the vampires," even if it meant that once again he would be separated from his family at Christmas.[6]

In Cincinnati Mann met Judge William Mills, who had given the land at Yellow Springs for the college. Mills, an incurable optimist and entrepreneur, was hard at work amassing his first million dollars, most of which he expected would come from the spiraling values of his real estate in Yellow Springs if only the population of the town would grow to 20,000 inhabitants. Mann liked Mills's ebullience, finding him a man who had "his head cleared of all the old

---

[6] Mann to Mary Mann, December 19, 23, and 28, 1852; Mann to Samuel Gridley Howe, December 14, 1852, all in Mann MSS:MHS; Mann to Dr. [?] McBean, January 24, 1853, Charles Roberts MSS:Haverford College.

cobwebs," and the following day, the two men traveled north on the Little Miami Railroad. Originally the route for this new line was to by-pass the town on its way to Xenia, but through Mills's one-man campaign, which included a successful fund-raising tour in the East, he had won the route for Yellow Springs. Fortuitously, the train ran right in front of the campus, the proper modern ornament, he thought, for an institution which would be the leading college in the Midwest.[7]

It was raining when the two men stepped off the train at Yellow Springs. Looking westward up a gentle slope, Mann could see the walls of what would be an immense red brick building starting to take shape. Where once had been a handsome hardwood forest, nothing but a field of stumps remained as lifeless monuments to the insatiable midwestern drive for the wealth produced by record wheat and corn crops garnered from the rich Ohio soil. But Mills's enthusiasm for the undertaking was irrepressible and Mann found himself believing the vision of a grassy landscaped setting, adorned by a collection of Victorian academic buildings connected by colonnaded walkways and topped with towers and turrets which would command the countryside for thirty miles around. And this despite the fact that in front of him at the moment was nothing but a sea of black sticky Ohio mud, supporting stacks of lumber, piles of red bricks, heaps of sand and gravel, and the beginnings of walls and scaffolding.

On the positive side, Mann was more impressed with what nature had accomplished than with what men had done in the area. To the east, the campus overlooked a beautiful ravine or glen, at places 100 feet deep, and touted by the local boosters as "alpine" in dimensions. Along its sides were small cliffs and cascades, and through it ran the Yellow Spring, so named because the water, rich in iron, deposited its red and yellow mineral content on the rocks where it came from the ground. Here in the glen, the vegetation had remained unmolested, save for an area once occupied by a resort hotel and the remains of an Owenite group's futile attempt to achieve a communal utopia several decades before. Besides a tour of the area, Mills took Mann to his home, where he invited virtually every resident of Yellow Springs to pass through his parlor and meet the famous Mr. Mann who was to be the new president. Then weary of the hand-shaking (it seemed westerners grasped

---

[7] Mann to Mary Mann, December 21, 1852, Mann MSS: MHS.

more firmly than easterners) and with Mills's assurance that both dormitories and the administration and classroom building would be finished well before the first students arrived next fall, Mann boarded the train again to make a connection for Toledo. From there he would go to Chicago and Michigan, before returning to the capital and his last session as a member of the United States House of Representatives.[8]

Back in Washington, the work of the House moved along vote upon vote, but Mann's heart and mind were agitated by thoughts of the challenge awaiting him in Ohio. Some of his concerns were of the most elevated and philosophic nature, others centered on the myriad of details needing attention before the school could begin. Rebecca Pennell wanted him to be certain that the classrooms would have blackboards on all of the walls. The professors at Antioch would teach rather than hear recitations if she had her way, and her uncle agreed. Mary suggested that the college should organize a common kitchen and laundry facilities for the students and professors' families, and even a communal sewing machine, such as were maintained at the North American Phalanx, a utopian community in New Jersey originally patterning its organization and operation after the ideas of the French philosopher, Charles Fourier. "Where is this North American Phalanx,—or whatever it is,—which has cooking and washing apparatus, and how can I direct Mr. Merrifield so that he can visit it . . . ?" Mann asked, not wanting to overlook any idea or arrangement from which his school might benefit. Equally present in his mind were many thoughts of the irrational things done in colleges and society at large and how he could avoid them at Antioch. He felt that women were often too vainglorious about externals, especially their dress, and as a consequence, had become slaves to clothes designers and manufacturers. "When will mankind, especially womankind, have a declaration of independence against fashion?" he asked. Therefore at Antioch, young women would be trained to shun externals and develop an inner strength of character. And they would have every opportunity to share in a full course of studies, not just the more abbreviated form as at Oberlin. Mann was stunned when he asked permission for two normal school girls to attend a series of lectures by Louis Agassiz at Harvard and was refused. Informed in language that

---

[8] Mann to Mary Mann, December 23 and 28, 1852; Mann to Samuel Downer, February 13, 1853, all in Mann MSS:MHS; Mann to George Combe, June 15, 1853, Combe MSS:NLS.

contained a classic nonreason, he was told that his request had been presented to the Corporation, and they were "of the opinion that it is not expedient to depart from the long established usage of the University by opening the public lectures at Cambridge to ladies." At Antioch, reason and morality would prevail over tradition and prejudice. By this time he felt so strongly about instilling a sense of duty and an adherence to rules based upon moral principles that he forgot some of his initial distaste when first visiting West Point, and promised, "If I have my way, and be supported in carrying it out, I will have some West Point at Antioch. . . . It will be good for some of the professors, as well as for some of the students." In the meantime, Howe made one last effort to dissuade him from the Antioch project, but Mann had turned his face west. "I find my mind, within the last few months, has taken an entirely new tack," he assured the doubting Howe, "the rudder has been put hard up on the opposite side. My associations are all clustering round a new nucleus;—new prospects, new labors, new hopes, new dangers, and new devices to avoid them." [9]

Much of Mann's time went into the preparation of Antioch's first catalogue. Prospective students should expect a curriculum which would include Latin, Greek, mathematics, English, history, philosophy, and natural science, all required subjects. In English there would be less emphasis on literature and more on composition skills and public speaking. In natural science there would be considerable physiology. But this was not to be the lock-step sequence of courses found in most colleges at the time. Antioch would begin with an elective system, enabling students to choose from courses in history, art, and methods of teaching. In addition, modern languages could be substituted for advanced Greek. And finally, students would find a faculty at Antioch which would lecture and teach rather than hold recitations. All of this was in keeping with achieving the aims of the new college, which were four in number, according to the catalogue. First, by fostering co-education, the school would attempt to elevate the entire human race rather than just half of it. As far as possible, it also would teach and require good health habits. A third objective would be the achievement of excellence as measured by intrinsic merits rather than by competition and emulation. And lastly, the school would stress sound ethical

[9] Mann to Mary Mann, January 20 [January (?)], February 6, and February 25, 1853; James Walker to Mann, March 5, 1853; Mann to Samuel Gridley Howe, February 9, 1853, all in Mann MSS:MHS.

and moral principles rather than attempt an indoctrination in religious dogma. A diploma from Antioch then would not only attest to a graduate's intellectual accomplishments, but was to be a certificate of character and a pledge by the holder that he or she would devote himself or herself to humane and benevolent ends.[1]

In February Mann paid a last visit to the White House, attending an affair to which he had been invited; but he was still so bitter over the Compromise that he avoided President Fillmore's reception line, unwilling to "touch the hand that signed the Fugitive-slave Law." After the inauguration of Franklin Pierce, he left Washington with few regrets. On his way back to West Newton, he wrote to Mary, "I am a free man again. What a Congressional life I have had, but I have fought a good fight, and I come out with a clear conscience." The remainder of the summer, he wrote to friends and publishers asking for book donations to the Antioch library, and used the last days of his franking privileges to mail a substantial collection of government publications to the college. Then too there were dishes, clothes, and books to be packed, furniture to be crated, and the countless decisions to be made on what should be taken, what should be left or given away, and what could be purchased in Ohio. Mann hoped to sell his house, but was only able to rent it. Finally, there were the painful good-byes. Perhaps the most touching among the many was Mann's farewell to a gathering of Free Soilers. Grown men sat listening to him with tear-filled eyes as he reminisced about their struggles for human freedom and the need to remain faithful to their high calling. As Mann spoke to them, they began to realize that this tall, thin, white-haired man with the clear pale complexion and steadfast gaze had come to be their elder statesman, in the short history of their political movement. And now he was about to leave them.[2]

*   *   *

The Manns arrived at Yellow Springs by mid-September. A relative, probably the faithful Calvin Pennell, met them at the station

---

[1] Robert L. Straker, "Brief Sketch of Antioch College" (Yellow Springs, 1954), pp. 5–7 (mimeographed).

[2] Mann to Mary Mann, February 23 and March 5, 1853; Henry Wadsworth Longfellow to Mann, September 8, 1853; Edward L. Peirce to Mann, September 17, 1853, all in Mann MSS:MHS; Mann to [?] Jenks, *et al.*, August 6, 1853, Horace Mann Mutual Insurance Company; *Commonwealth*, September 1, 13, 16, and 17, 1853.

in a wagon. As the party moved up the slope to their temporary quarters in the village, they could see the rising towers of Antioch protruding outrageously high from the surrounding flat farmland. Garish, presumptuous, and utterly nonutilitarian, A. M. Merrifield's version of Smithsonian Gothic would appear irredeemably ugly to the tastes of a later generation. But to the Manns, Judge Mills, and thousands of midwesterners, it was the harbinger of the shift in political and cultural leadership from the Atlantic coast to the great heartland of America soon to come. The scepter was yet to be attained, but surely here was one of its gems.

And for many Ohioans, another proof of the validity of their visionary geopolitics was the fact that a famous educator and statesman had left a brilliant career in the East to cast his lot with them. On Inauguration Day, October 5, they traveled to Yellow Springs to see this man and hear him speak. By carriage and train they came, as well as by horseback and farm wagon, more than 3,000 in all. Knowing local overnight accommodations would be inadequate, and most unable to afford the cost of an inn anyway, they arrived prepared to sleep in their wagons and carriages or in bedrolls on the ground. A half an hour before the ceremonies began, they crowded around a temporary speakers' platform erected in front of the main building. On it sat Mann, lean, erect, and elegant in his long black coat. Next to him was Elder John Phillips, swarthy, broad-shouldered, and muscular, whose booming voice compensated in volume for what he lacked in articulation. A self-made man, Phillips was a leader in the Christian Connexion and had been dubbed "Antioch John" because he had barnstormed in New York and the Midwest, raising more money and twisting more arms of the brethren to bring the college to Ohio than anyone else. On the platform also was the Governor of the state and other dignitaries whom Judge Mills had herded together. And the remaining seats were occupied by Mary Mann, the new faculty members, and their wives, an arrangement which made it difficult for the audience to identify Rebecca Pennell, the new "professoress," and probably the first full-fledged woman college professor in the country. In a fervent appeal for funds which would have done James G. Finney justice, Elder Phillips managed to raise a collection of more than $600. The Governor spoke, as did other officials, and a band which Mills had brought by train from Springfield provided musical interludes between the speeches.

After lunch the ceremonies moved into the chapel, which was

quickly filled, with the overflow clustering outside its windows and doors. Up to this time, for the vast majority of persons gathered for the inauguration, the affair had the familiar tones of a religious revival meeting and a political rally. But when Mann finally stepped into the pulpit and began an address which lasted two hours, its printed version exceeding 27,000 words, they understood by his charisma and his opening words that this was neither a mere politician nor a revivalist, but a true statesman, educator, and orator.

He began by dedicating Antioch to the honor of God and the service of humanity. Then, reviewing the history of the western world, and cataloguing the great achievements of scientists, inventors, and philosophers, he concluded that each advance was accompanied by an increase in greed, injustice, and violence. The result of this was a painfully slow, almost glacial rate of progress for civilized man. But now, by the middle of the nineteenth century, with an understanding of the laws of the universe, rational man was harnessing the forces of nature and accelerating the rate of progress. More important, by following the dictates of reason and living a life ordered according to principles ordained by an omniscient and benevolent creator, Mann predicted nothing less for the future than ultimate human perfectibility. God had set the rules. It was now up to enlightened men and women, fully exercising their reason and their free will, to turn away from selfish ends and construct a world free from war, poverty, disease, and religious and political persecution. To achieve such a millennium, modern men would require educational institutions of the highest order, and at this moment in time, Mann was offering his personal pledge to labor to the limits of his mind and body to make Antioch the prototype for other institutions. It would rise above denominational rivalries, partisan interests, and class prejudices, and usher in a new golden age of peace, justice, and well-being.

As he spoke, Mann could not help but notice the devout attention of his audience. Before him was a sea of earnest upturned faces. Many of the men had sunburned, leathery complexions, the telltale pale white band high across their forehead indicating the boundary of their straw hat brim and signifying a life of labor in the open field under the bright Ohio sun. Here and there a baby cried, and in the distance, a dog occasionally barked, but Mann had spoken under far more difficult circumstances than this. How much better were these honest, humble, rustic people at Antioch than the arrogant, spoiled, perverse eastern sophisticates who had broken up some of his speeches against the Fugitive Slave Law.

Finally, summarizing what he thought youth needed to be equal to the challenge of the second half of the nineteenth century, Mann concluded with a glowing description of a new trinity composed of a healthy body, a rational mind, and a virtuous soul or "moral nature":

I have now, my friends, sketched the great necessities of a race like ours, in a world like ours. A body grown from its elemental beginnings in health; compacted with strength and vital with activity in every part; impassive to heat and cold, and victorious over the vicissitudes of seasons and zones; not crippled by disease nor stricken down by early death; not shrinking from bravest effort, but panting, like the fleetest runner, less for the prize than for the joy of the race; and rejuvenant amid the frosts of age. A mind as strong for the immortal as is the body for the mortal life; alike enlightened by the wisdom and beaconed by the errors of the past; through intelligence of the laws of Nature, guiding her elemental forces, as it directs the limbs of its own body through the nerves of motion, thus making alliance with the exhaustless forces of Nature for its strength and clothing itself with her endless charms for its beauty, and, wherever it goes, carrying a sun in its head with which to explore the realms of Nature and reveal yet hidden truths. And then a more moral nature, presiding like a divinity over the whole, banishing sorrow and pain, gathering in earthly joys and immortal hopes, and transfigured and rapt by the sovereign and sublime aspiration to know and do the will of God.

And he closed with a promise. It would be Antioch's task, and that of those who followed her standards, "to restore the beauties of paradise to earth, and to usher in the era of millennial holiness and peace."

Stunning, elevated, and optimistic sentiments they were, and even visionary. Yet in a cruder, more parochial, and less eloquent form, they had all been said before from a thousand platforms and pulpits during the recent decades, often producing a sense of pious achievement by their spokesmen and a temporary rosy glow of hope in their audiences. But the message at the Antioch dedication was different for all its similarity to these. Unwilling to forget on Monday what he had preached on Sunday, Antioch's new president intended to forge a truly enlightened institution, and hold himself, his faculty, and his students to his own high aspirations. And there were more than a few who believed that he could do it. With such intellectual talents and spiritual dedication, Mann had convinced his new clients that he could make a college thrive in the Sahara.[3]

---

[3] Mann, *Dedication of Antioch College, and Inaugural Address of Its President, Hon. Horace Mann; with Other Proceedings* (Boston, 1854); *Christian Inquirer,* October 15 and 22, 1853; *National Era,* November 10, 1853.

CHAPTER XXII

The Impossible Dream

AND I BESEECH YOU to treasure up in your hearts
these my parting words: *Be ashamed to die until
you have won some victory for humanity.*
HORACE MANN

. . . and the wages is just same? I was stuck.
I couldn't answer that.
MARK TWAIN

H E HAD DELIVERED HIS *Weltanschauung,* but before he could export this optimistic doctrine of educational progress elsewhere, he must first make it take root and flourish at Yellow Springs. Many back East thought this was just what Mann would do and that it was only a matter of time until Antioch would have a bountiful harvest. Located in the great American heartland, its college towers overlooked seemingly endless vistas of black soil, which offered the foundation for a restless nascent democracy and the happy prospect of record crops of wheat and corn. As new states came into the Union, immigrants from New England, New York, and Pennsylvania were amazed how easy it was to facilitate the inauguration of public school systems. To them, the eastern seaboard was tired and aging, filled with entrenched institutions, and showing the telltale signs of a social and economic rigor mortis. Not all agreed in their diagnosis of what was wrong, but Samuel Downer, writing to Mann, thought the East was "filling up with a great mass of Foreign Ignorance and Foreign Poverty and Foreign instincts." Far better to leave this behind for a fresh start in the Ohio River Valley, there to build a new society unfettered by the decrepit hand of the past and as yet uncorrupted by hordes of immigrants. After two centuries, the settlement along the Atlantic coastline had been but the beginning, the prelude to a great epic still to be played out between the Appalachians and the Rockies. Midwest optimism knew few bounds and it was not just the wide-eyed real estate speculator who suffered from a virulent form of land fever and expected the national capital to be moved into the great Mississippi Valley within his lifetime.[1]

It took more than a sectional chauvinism, however, to make colleges spring forth from prairie grass and hardwood forests. In countless communities, this chauvinism was given the added twin compulsion of a robust local boosterism and an aggressive denominationalism. And whenever these two forces converged in a community, a college or an academy was sure to emerge. Even the smallest of towns expected to have their institution of higher learning. Local boosters knew no railroad builder would be foolhardy enough to by-pass them, no entrepreneur blind enough to miss the golden opportunities in their midst, and no church group so backward as to forego the chance to grace their setting with a Princeton of the West. Land speculation was rampant and in community after community, wherever men gathered, there was more talk on how to acquire easy mortgage money and subdivide large tracts into building lots, than discussions about the organization of democratic town government. The few skeptics who refused to be swept along with the high tide of enthusiasm were told to look at the wealth which had come to the early promoters of Cincinnati and to the fortunes now being reaped by the adventuresome and daring in St. Louis, Cleveland, and Chicago, and to a lesser extent in Indianapolis, Columbus, Fort Wayne, and, hopefully, Yellow Springs.

A few towns did grow to a size in keeping with their promoters' hopes. Some even were adorned with prestigious institutions of higher learning. But in most cases, the relationship between speculation and college founding proved to be one of precarious and usually ill-fated symbiosis. The majority of entrepreneurs and would-be benefactors who also pledged money for colleges could not survive the ride on a boom-or-bust pendulum and found themselves more often gathering in bankruptcy court than at board of trustees meetings.[2] Failing to become major commercial centers, most towns did manage to expand slowly, beginning from a nucleus of several general stores, a grain elevator and grist mill, a tavern, a livery stable, and a few other shops. All too often, however, colleges founded on the most grandiose expectations had no such resiliency. Launched with some of the most harebrained financial schemes imaginable, their response as the economic atmosphere soured was

---

[1] Samuel Downer to Mann, April 20, 1852, Mann MSS:MHS.
[2] Out of eleven major backers of Antioch all but two, including Judge Mills, were brought to insolvency or near it.

as quick as litmus. As business went, so went the colleges, only more so. Between 1820 and 1860, only seventeen out of forty-three survived the panics of 1837 and 1857 in Ohio. Less than 10 per cent hung on in Missouri, and in Texas, forty were launched only to have all but two fail by the Civil War.

Equal to local boosterism as a force in college founding was a fervent denominationalism filling up the great religious void of the Ohio River Valley. Fanned by the emotional preaching of Bible-pounding evangelists, revivals swept across the central plains like wind-driven grass fires, catching up all in their path. Unwilling to let this second great awakening dissipate into apathy and backsliding, more systematic and ecclesiastically minded churchmen such as Lyman Beecher worked tirelessly to garner the new harvest into regular church membership. Beecher made a career of presenting gloomy predictions of political anarchy and the rise of Papism, if the faithful failed to form congregations and found colleges as new outposts for republicanism and Protestantism. Heeding the call, Presbyterians and Congregationalists became enthusiastic college builders, as did the more anti-intellectual Baptists and Methodists. Believing themselves creating effective instruments for proselyting, they considered colleges the best means to keep the second and third generations of settlers secure in the faith. The fate of millions of souls, perhaps the very fate of the nation itself, hung on the outcome, and the prospect of winning such a victory for Protestantism through conversion, baptism, and higher education was a dazzling challenge that dedicated men could not resist.

By comparison with most established church groups of long standing, the Christian Connexion which founded Antioch was a small body with a relatively simple creed. Its origins had grown out of a spontaneous revolt against extreme religious formalism near the end of the eighteenth century in New England, New York, and Pennsylvania. Once free of the theological baggage carried along by other orthodox bodies, and wishing to remain unencumbered by it, the Connexion took anyone into its communion who accepted its platform of: "The Bible, our only creed; Christian character, our only test of fellowship and communion; private judgement, the right and duty of all men; our aim, the union of all Christians and the conversion of sinners." In order to be a minister among them, no theological training was necessary, it being sufficient to have "the gift of the spirit." By mid-century this sect, no doubt wishing to emulate the educational achievements of other Protestants, formally decided to found a college at its general convention on October 2, 1850, in Marion, New York. That the college would be nonsectarian was an afterthought and largely due to the work by Reverend Eli Fay, who headed the committee which was to get the school under way. More important to its early promoters, and the thousands of Christians who saved their pennies and quarters for it, was that it be a dramatic symbol that their denomination had now come of age. Furthermore, they expected their school to "rank with the best of our American colleges" within two years.[3]

At first, it was assumed that Antioch, so named because "the disciples were called Christians first in Antioch" according to Acts 11:26, would be built "somewhere on the thoroughfare between Albany and Buffalo." Then as the contributions from Ohio proved to be several times larger than New York and Pennsylvania combined, Elder John Phillips and other Ohioans claimed the school for the Buckeye state, clinching their case with the very worldly argument that coal, wood, and lumber all were cheaper there, flour was less costly, as was pork, and it was possible each spring to buy enough eggs for 4 cents a dozen "to sink a steamboat." And Phillips added, with something less than Christian love, that those easterners who opposed the move to Ohio could go over to the Baptists.[4]

At this point, still other worldly considerations prompted the Christians to give Ohio the prize. After having convinced the Little Miami Railroad to build one of its trunk lines through Yellow Springs, Judge William Mills and other leading citizens who had invested heavily in its real estate believed that the only thing now lacking before their town would be the equal of Athens, Ohio (if not Greece), was the establishment of a college. While the leaders of the Connexion were still debating over the location of their school, Judge Mills offered them the donation of twenty acres for a campus. The proposal, particularly because it came from a man whose salesmanship was irresistible, was readily accepted. Thus, in its beginnings, Antioch appeared to be the fortuitous coincidence of a nonsectarian dedication to furthering education and the selfless philanthropy of Judge Mills; but behind this façade of piety and

---

[3] J. R. Freese, *History and Advocacy of the Christian Church* (Philadelphia, n.d.), pp. 137–150; Robert L. Straker, *Brief Sketch of Antioch College* (Yellow Springs, 1954), pp. 1–5; *Christian Palladium,* June 1, 1850, and August 29, 1851.

[4] *Christian Palladium,* August 23, 1851; Robert L. Straker, "The Master-Builder from Massachusetts: Merrifield and the Founding of Antioch College," *Antioch Alumni Bulletin,* VI (November, 1934), 6–11.

generosity was the real intent of an ambitious religious body to gain its share of the national limelight, and the ambitious desire of local entrepreneurs to garner real estate profits. Rarely has the history of American higher education witnessed such a convenient marriage of aggressive denominationalism and boosterism as in the founding of Antioch College at Yellow Springs, Ohio.

*   *   *

Such a setting was now to be the proving ground for Horace Mann's belief that he could raise up the moral and intellectual leaders for the coming decades. Since the classrooms were still unfinished, as soon as the breakfast dishes could be cleared from the dining hall tables, the day after his inauguration, numbers of hopeful candidates for Antioch sat down to take written admission examinations. Here for the next several days, according to Mann, "the cook and the professor held individual empire." It was a motley group which peopled this empire. In age they ranged from fourteen to forty. A few unlettered ministers who had recently left their pulpits were on hand, hoping for at least the patina of a college education. A goodly number of farmers' and mechanics' sons and daughters also came to apply, as did a sprinkling of young persons from prominent families in the East, lured to Yellow Springs by the reputation of its illustrious president. But it was only as Rebecca and Calvin Pennell went over the results of the examination that they began to comprehend the magnitude of the task which they faced. Boomers for the college such as John Phillips may have claimed that it would be equal to Harvard before its first graduating class, but the plain truth which emerged from the admissions examination was that out of several hundred applicants, only two women and six men were qualified to start in the freshman class. The rest were barely able to do remedial work in the high school or preparatory division at Antioch. As Mary Mann dejectedly reported to a friend back in Massachusetts who had claimed that all Ohioans were dullards, "I do not think you ever imagined the profundity of their ignorance. Many of these great *women* cannot read intelligibly. . . . Our college is in fact a school." [5]

---

[5] Mann, "Demands of the Age of Colleges," in Joy Elmer Morgan, *Horace Mann at Antioch* (Washington, D.C., 1938), p. 270; Mary Mann to Mrs. Cyrus Peirce, October 28 to November 11, 1853, Mann MSS: MHS; Harvard Forrest Vallance, "A History of Antioch College" (unpublished Ph.D. dissertation, Ohio State University, 1936), p. 480.

But in time a college it would be. And for Mann, the beginning
was now and he plunged into his task with a zeal and devotion
surpassing even his earlier efforts for the common schools. From
the outset there was no chance to meditate on the nature of the
undertaking. In fact, so staggering was the challenge before him
that at times he wanted to forget what he had promised in his
inauguration address. "I have not had time to balance pros and
cons," he wrote to Howe, "I just submit my back to the winds of
destiny with but one care,—which is to keep the ship's crew in
order." By "order," Mann meant nothing less than a Spartan regimen. Faculty and students arose at the six o'clock morning bell. By
7:45 Mann expected them to have dressed, washed, and breakfasted and be in their seats for chapel. The remainder of the day
until bedtime was a rigorous routine of instruction and study, relieved only by two meals and two periods of exercise, thirty minutes
before lunch and two hours in the afternoon.[6]

The difficulty of maintaining such a schedule with a collection
of students, most of them totally unprepared to meet the demands
of academic discipline, was compounded by the half-finished state
of the college buildings. With no exaggeration, Mann would explain
to an audience, "If Adam and Eve had been brought into this world
as prematurely as we were brought on the premises of Antioch
College, they must have been created about Wednesday night." The
weather turned cold early that fall and the students and faculty
shivered and sneezed while A. M. Merrifield made up his mind on
which stoves to order. Classes were held in rooms where the plaster
was still wet. Attempting to bolster his own spirits and those of his
new co-workers, Mann remarked that they had only their "love of
the cause" to keep them warm; but this, though very good in morals,
was "very bad in physiology." There was a library room but no books,
not even a shelf to store them if a fugitive freight shipment found
its way to the campus. There were no blackboards, no desks, and
no chairs for the classrooms. To make things worse, the hydraulic
system installed to pump water up from a spring in the glen to a
cistern near the dormitory broke down and it was necessary for
the students to carry their pitchers and pails in midwinter to a
hastily constructed water tower a quarter of a mile from their

[6] Mann to O. C. Marsh, July 7, 1854; Pforzheimer MSS (photostat);
BLYU; Mann to Samuel Gridley Howe, December 5, 1853, Mann MSS:
MHS; Morgan, *Mann at Antioch*, pp. 70–76.

dormitory. And until the ground froze and the first solid snow came, everywhere there was mud, inside the buildings as well as out. Here and there the workmen had put down pieces of scrap lumber for temporary walkways between Antioch Hall and the dormitory, but these floated on a semi-liquid base, only to sink in ooze when stepped upon. For the students, along with books, pens, ink, and paper, another essential implement for a college education was a small wooden scraper which they used to keep the mud from balling up too thickly on the bottoms of their shoes.[7]

Mann's little band of family and faculty laughed at such tribulations because they could not bear to weep. All paid a heavy price in making the necessary physical and emotional adjustments to the new surroundings, but none quite so much as Mary. For this woman who was ever ready to follow her husband to purgatory and back, Antioch was the supreme test of her devotion. Mud was only a matter of endless sweeping, scraping, and scrubbing; with other problems it was not to be so easy. Twice cattle and pigs leveled the garden and orchard which she had set out with cuttings from the East. After several weeks without any news about her furniture and other belongings, she was informed that they were not delayed but lost, probably having gone down in a boat which had sunk in a storm on Lake Erie. Fortunately the report was false, but after forty days of waiting while her family lived out of a few suitcases, she had the heart-sickening experience of opening one crate after another only to find many of her worldly possessions broken or water-soaked. The furniture could be re-upholstered and her stained linens could be bleached, but there was no way to replace the broken crystal and china which had been in the Peabody and Palmer families for several generations.

After she had furnished the temporary quarters in the dormitory for her family while waiting for workmen, who seemed to take three times as long as any Yankee carpenter to finish the president's manse, she turned her efforts to giving the students some training in the social amenities. By New England standards, their raw rural manners were abominable. At afternoon levees, she instructed the girls in the etiquette of wearing white gloves and the art of serving tea, while encouraging the young men to attend, dressed in waistcoat, starched shirt, and cravat if they owned these. Her stomach

---

[7] Mann, "Demands of the Age of Colleges," in Morgan, *Mann at Antioch,* pp. 270–271; Mann, *Life,* pp. 405–413.

turned when she saw the lack of any sanitary conditions in the college kitchen, but her plea for more soap and hot water fell on deaf ears. When she asked the steward to have the dining hall tables set with napkins donated to the college, he refused, as he did to her request to have dessert served from a clean dish instead of on the plate from which the main course had been eaten. Apparently the rough-hewn democracy of the frontier was also thin-skinned and easily took offense at what it thought was any intended criticism of its folkways. Adding to Mary's discontent was the fact that Mann became bedridden for several weeks the first spring and even after getting back on his feet, he seemed to lack some of his previous vitality. All this she learned to tolerate and endure with the spirit of a reluctant Stoic, but when a pig ran into the dining hall during a meal, much to the delight of the students who were finding college long on study and short on entertainment, she was close to the breaking point.[8]

With the president's manse finally finished a year after they had arrived, Mary gratefully moved out of the dormitories. The new house was heated by handsomely carved marble fireplaces, each fitted with a cast-iron firebox. The parlor was more spacious than its counterpart in West Newton, as was her new sitting room. One bedroom she furnished in heavy black walnut, another in dark oak, and in her own, she put in furniture "white with flowers and gilt edges" which Mann had bought for her in Cleveland. Happily she reported that this made the room "as pretty a chamber as I ever looked into." Fortunately, none of the crystal pendants from her favorite candelabra were lost en route and the portraits of Channing and Laura Bridgman survived the trip unscathed. With Channing's likeness hung in Mann's study, the presence of this secular icon gave her a sense of security and order which helped her face the ordeal of another school year. "There are a great many new students and many have left owing to the discomfort suffered during the last term. It is only surprising that they staid as long as they did," she reported to her father, and then added more hopefully, "But the cistern and the pump from the spring are both in operation now, and the cooking is clean . . . the cockroaches *not* cooked in the dried apple sauce." And finally when the calla lily from her mother

[8] Mann, *Life*, pp. 405–413; Mary Mann to Mrs. Cyrus Peirce, October 28–November 11, 1853; Samuel Downer to Mann, January 4 and March 16, 1854; Mann to Theodore Parker, May 30, 1854, all in Mann MSS:MHS.

bloomed a second time, Yellow Springs began to look a little more like New England.[9]

*   *   *

Against such a background, Mann now attempted to implement his ideas on higher education. From a limited faculty he hoped to present as broad and liberal a curriculum as any college in the country. Basic would be Latin, Greek, English, mathematics, history, and the natural sciences. He also insisted that physiology and hygiene be required of every student and that astronomy, geology, civil engineering, and political science at least be available as electives. Since many expected to become teachers, he offered the theory and practice of teaching in the junior year. And for the seniors, he himself planned to teach the course in moral philosophy which was to be the capstone of their college experience, uniting the disciplinary arches of the humanities, social sciences, and natural sciences into a strong vault of humanitarianism.[1]

All this could be gathered from the small print in the college bulletin. Education at Antioch was to be much more, however, and its real essence could only be discovered by actual observation. Mann expected to achieve that age-old concept of a sound mind in a sound body, and to go the Greeks one better and insist on the development of a sound moral conscience as well. Thus it could be said that the college was an amalgam of the best intellectual endeavors of Harvard and Yale, the athletic drill of West Point, and the social conscience of a normal school. Then, too, the teaching was to be different. Rarely would students memorize for recitation, still a basic procedure in most colleges at the time. Instead, the emphasis was on teaching and lecturing. For the rest of the faculty, Mann set a model of more individualized instruction, first introducing a subject in general terms, then soliciting specific interests from students, and finally launching them on their own study projects, the results of which they reported back to the class at a later time. He also expanded the walls of the classroom, urging his biology instructor to use the glen below the campus as an outdoor laboratory

---

[9] Mary Mann to Dr. Nathaniel Peabody, September 17, 1854, Berg MSS: NYPL; Mary Mann to Rebecca Pennell, [1854], Mann MSS:MHS.
[1] Antioch College Catalogue, 1853–54, *passim*, copy in the Teachers College Library, Columbia University.

and taking pride in Austin Craig's efforts to visit jails and hospitals as part of the course in political science.

The high point of each day, Mann hoped, would be the chapel exercises and he gave great care to his sermons, considering the other demands on his time. Powerful and compelling, his words seemed to find a far more receptive audience than he had had in the House of Representatives. Regularly, he dealt with the topics of sin, freedom, retribution, and temptation, but all these were but variations on the more general theme of duty to God and man. "Happiness," as he told his students in the first of a series of sermons which were later to be published, "can alone come from the performance of Duty." Save for his greater emphasis on chapel, all of Mann's innovations became the harbingers of reforms on other campuses. Yet more important than the individual reforms was the total *Gestalt* of the Antioch experience. At Yellow Springs, Mann was determined that his students would gain a sense of community while developing their lifelong commitment to honor God and serve mankind. And this would be its hallmark for the next century. "We are trying a great experiment," Mann wrote to Henry Barnard, "and it shall not fail through any deficiency or lukewarmedness on my part." [2]

Unfortunately, others had not fulfilled their responsibilities as well as Mann in getting Antioch off to a good start. Troubling reports came to his desk that Merrifield was mishandling the college finances, and that each month the list of its unpaid creditors grew larger. Mann investigated and after a hasty and very uncomfortable accounting from Merrifield and Mills, he was stunned to learn that there was insufficient money to cover the faculty salaries, let alone the payments due on the college mortgage. The chief problem was an ingenious and disastrous scholarship system instituted by the Connexion. In an effort to raise money for an endowment, John Phillips and others had fanned out across the countryside like patent

---

[2] Morgan, *Mann at Antioch*, pp. 70–76; Mann, *Twelve Sermons Delivered at Antioch College* (Boston, 1861), *passim;* Mann to Henry Barnard, July 12, 1855, Barnard MSS:NYU; Mann, *Life*, pp. 452–453; for an excellent eyewitness account of the school, see Ezra Gannett, "Antioch College," *Quarterly Journal of the American Unitarian Association*, V (November, 1857), 92–110. According to Mann, Gannett had gone to Antioch a disbelieving "Saul" and returned a completely converted "Paul." One student later claimed Mann's teachings were of "the exalted type such as made a permanent imprint upon the young mind, lifting it into the realm of lofty ideals . . ." L. W. Tulleys, "Recollections of Student Days under Horace Mann," *Antiochian*, II (November, 1920), 1.

medicine hucksters, selling Antioch scholarships. At first glance it seemed like a foolproof method of raising money for an endowment. In actuality, it proved to be the work of fools. For $100 an individual purchased a tuition-free scholarship to the college, not for four years, but in *perpetuity*. In addition, he held the right to designate its successive recipients. At other schools, when five or six scholarships were sold for every one claimed, the interest on $600 was just adequate to cover the cost of instruction and since the annual tuition at Antioch was approximately $25, five scholarships invested at 6 per cent would have produced enough income for one student, but hardly five. Two factors, however, made the system totally unworkable. First, after deducting his travel expenses for selling scholarships, Phillips had only $80 left for the college. Then, because of Mann's reputation, far more students came to Antioch claiming scholarships than anyone anticipated. Little wonder that when all the facts were in, he ruefully admitted that "the college was founded upon a rotten basis." [3]

The Christians also assumed that outright gifts would be sufficient to pay for the total cost of Antioch's impractical but expensive buildings. Here too, they produced more dreams than cash. Thus when the bills for bricks and mortar came due, Mills and Merrifield appropriated the scholarship money which was the college's dubious endowment. The result was full classrooms and almost certain bankruptcy. As Mann attempted to explain the paradox of numbers and income to an incredulous Howe, he wrote, "There is every prospect of our having a large gathering here next fall; if our creditors do not in the meantime swamp us. But numbers bring us no *pecuniary* strength; they rather abstract it from us; because as all pay their tuition by scholarships, the more we have of them to teach, the poorer we are . . . the money available is in inverse proportion to the number of pupils." Then to make the debacle almost total, Phillips sold some scholarships simply by letting an individual sign a note promising to pay the school 6 per cent interest each year. To many, this looked like the opportunity for an investment as good as railroad stock. Since they expected tuition costs to increase, they believed their scholarships could soon be sold for twice the original cost. Unfortunately, as the economic situation worsened after 1855, many of them defaulted on their payments, leaving scholarship holders halfway to their degree but stranded

---

[3] Mann to E. Conant, September 17, 1857, Mann MSS:MHS.

without any support, thus adding further financial burden on the school.[4]

The school had been open barely a year when Mann was forced to admit to Samuel J. May, "Our college is now on its last probation. The Trustees, at their last meeting, agreed to make one energetic effort between this and next April, and if, by that time, they cannot redeem it, then to abandon it." But the situation was even worse than this. Antioch had never been on financial probation at all, as Mann thought, but was hopelessly bankrupt on the day it opened. Besides Mann's efforts and the willingness of some of his faculty to miss paydays, the only thing which kept it alive was the complete chaos of its financial records. Merrifield had considered the expenditure of $400 for a bookkeeper an unnecessary expense and managed the college accounts in his own freewheeling way. With his undisciplined enthusiasm he had sown an economic wind, only to leave Mann and the faculty to reap the whirlwind when the bills came due. Perhaps he believed that if the Christians failed to support the school, the Lord would provide.[5]

But the Lord refused the route of direct divine dispensation and chose to work, if at all, through the fumbling efforts of fallible men. After a showdown meeting in March, 1854, the "energetic effort" and money Mann had hoped for did not materialize. Judge Mills resigned as treasurer of the college and an auditing committee was appointed to find out once and for all just what their total indebtedness was. They knew that Merrifield had spent $70,000 more than what remained of the endowment, but a careful review of his records and unpaid bills shocked even the most pessimistic among the trustees. For a moment, upon hearing the report, Mann was so despondent that he could not bring himself to explain to Howe just how desperate things really were, but to another, more distant friend he candidly reported the grim facts.

Effort after effort has been made to pay off the debts; but they have all failed. We have thought from time to time that they would succeed; but we have been deplorably disappointed. At last it became apparent that

---

[4] Mann to Austin Craig, October 26, 1854; Mann to Samuel Gridley Howe, July 24, 1855, both in Mann MSS:MHS; Mann, *Life*, pp. 405–413; Straker, "Merrifield and the Founding of Antioch College," *Antioch Alumni Bulletin*, pp. 6–11.

[5] Mann to Samuel J. May, October 22, 1855, Mann MSS:MHS; Mann to Theodore Parker, December 24, 1855, Parker Letterbook, MS in MHS; Amos S. Dean, "Antioch College," *Christian Inquirer*, January 7, 1854.

the indebtedness of the college would not only require all the scholarship-fund for its payment, but would render every scholarship-holder liable for an additional amount beyond his scholarship, and equal to it; that is, every owner of a scholarship would lose his scholarship, but be liable for one hundred dollars besides.

Apparently, according to Ohio laws, the scholarship holders now were liable for the unpaid debts of the school. Only after it was too late did Mann realize the magnitude of Antioch's financial problems, so consumed had he become in its educational mission. Others more detached from the undertaking recognized its will-o'-the-wisp economic foundation very quickly. Howe thought the undertaking foolhardy from the beginning, and it took Samuel Downer only a short visit to Yellow Springs to recognize what was happening. "The Christian Sect," he wrote to Mann,

however glorious may be their platform, are rather small potatoes . . . the college was built without any definite idea how it was to be carried on, or through, and . . . many agents lived in better clover from its resources than they ever did before . . . my dear friend Horace Mann, was selected looking to his reputation, to furnish capital, to help the matter through, and I fear to some extent [will be] its victim.[6]

Perhaps for the first time in his life, with the educational future of hundreds of students on his conscience, Mann forgot about motives, especially those of William Mills, A. M. Merrifield, and John Phillips, and simply labored to save his college. Well aware that he could not return to New England, and believing he had no alternative but to stick it out, come triumph or failure, he wrote to Theodore Parker: "When I think of what was once my home and sphere, a feeling which I suppose must be like Turkish fatalism comes over me, and I say to myself 'Here sir, you are, and here you must remain. Fate has you in its grip and resistance is impossible. No secondary cause releases you, at least for a time.' . . . I am working in faith." To Boston and New York he dispatched Amos Dean and Austin Craig, both on his faculty, hoping they might tap the purses of wealthy Unitarians. His emissaries pointed out that, to date, the Unitarians had but one society in the Midwest and had done nothing to influence the future of higher education there. In

---

[6] Ira Allen, Diary, March 14, 1855, MS in ACL; Mann to E. Conant, September 17, 1857; Samuel Downer to Mann, August 20, 1855, both in Mann MSS:MHS.

New York City, several ministers agreed to raise collections and after a visit to Yellow Springs, Reverend Ezra Gannett offered his good offices in Boston. But many potential donors in the Old Bay State held back. They had not forgotten Mann's political apostasy, memories which had now been resuscitated by the rendition from Boston of Anthony Burns and the beginnings of agitation on the Kansas and Nebraska territories. For the moment, even Mann's friends, including Quincy, Howe, and Downer, were unwilling to move until they understood just what the true financial situation at the school was and could be certain that any funds they raised would really save Antioch for Mann and not just perpetuate the financial blunders of the Christian Connexion.[7]

*   *   *

At the time, many of the men in Massachusetts who might have come to Mann's rescue were again preoccupied with political questions. In Congress, Senator Stephen A. Douglas, a heavy speculator in Chicago real estate and extensive land tracts farther west, was pulling every wire he could in Washington to win a central rather than a southern route for the proposed transcontinental railroad. To gain the handful of southern votes he needed, Douglas agreed to push forward a version of the Kansas-Nebraska Bill which would allow the question of slavery for this territory to be decided by what was euphemistically called "popular sovereignty," meaning that the question was to be decided by a plebiscite of the settlers there. This meant the final dismantling of the old Missouri Compromise of 1820, which had held the line against slavery at 36° 30'. News of this new effort rekindled in Mann some of the old anger which had fired his struggle with Daniel Webster over the Fugitive Slave Law. "The North, in 1850," he wrote to Theodore Parker, evidently with financial as well as humanitarian problems on his mind, "invested its capital in Slavery; the Kansas-Nebraska bill is the first payment of interest." Although he now believed subsequent events had vindicated his political course of action in those years

---

[7] Mann to Theodore Parker, January 1, 1854, Parker Letterbook, MS in MHS; Mann to E. W. Clap, February 28, 1854; Mann to Samuel Downer, May 8, 1854; Josiah Quincy to Mann, March 17 and June 6, 1854; Ezra Gannett to A. S. Dean, November 14, 1854; Mann to Mary Mann, November 27, 1855, all in Mann MSS:MHS; *Christian Inquirer,* October 14, 21, and 28, 1854.

of uninterrupted controversy, he confessed to Sumner that he became more pessimistic each day and now thought that the nation was well on its way to 500 years of the hell of slavery, from which only "the power and wisdom of God" could save it.[8]

After the devastating struggle over the Compromise of 1850, what little remained of the old Massachusetts political structure of John Quincy Adams, Daniel Webster, and Robert Rantoul, Jr., seemed certain to be blown away by the new political storm to come out of Kansas and Nebraska. "So entirely are people unsettled, sick, and disgusted with things as they are, and with those that are trying to better them," Samuel Downer reported, that they had become irrational and were seeking simplistic negative solutions to problems of imponderable dimensions. For many bewildered and frustrated persons, the answers were to be found in the xenophobic and anti-Catholic panaceas promoted by the Know-Nothing Party. "Know Nothingness is rampant in Mass. . . ." a correspondent bitterly conceded to Mann. "Its objects are every way bad . . . it imperils freedom in our land. It directs the attention of the people from the grand issue. It keeps up the spirit of caste, the bone and sinew of pro-slavery. 'D——d nigger' and 'cussed furriner' express the same feeling. How hostile to the noble doctrine that a man is a man and entitled to the rights and regards of a man. . ." Samuel Downer was even more discouraged, vividly describing for Mann in far-off Ohio just how chaotic the situation was.

Politics is in a perfect *mess*. Some kind of fusion will come out of it. Whig Party nowhere, Demo. very small. Free Soil small. Republic small. Anti pope and anti slavery large (and active). Temperance pretty large and doubtful. Pure native American small and active. Catholic perfectly quiet. There is material to work upon. Nobody knows what will come of it.[9]

Surely with such intelligence, Mann must have experienced some ambiguous second thoughts about his decision to leave the Old Bay State. Yet as he stared at the impossible task of saving Antioch, he could not also suppress the recurring thought that had

[8] Mann to Theodore Parker, May 30, 1854, Parker Letterbook, MS in MHS; Mann to Charles Sumner, March 13, 1854; Mann to Samuel Gridley Howe, July 3, 1854; both in Mann MSS:MHS.
[9] Josiah Quincy to Mann, March 7, 1854; Samuel Downer to Mann, November 13, 1854, and August 25, 1855; Edward Pierce to Mann, January 18, 1855, all in Mann MSS:MHS.

he stayed in Massachusetts, he might have been Governor. Although not the most accurate of political weather vanes, Downer had no doubts on this. "If you were here," he wrote to Mann, "we could this year have put you in [as] Governor by almost acclimation [sic] I think . . . so entirely are people unsettled, sick and disgusted with things as they are, and with those that are trying to better them." In this particular political augury, Downer may have been right. When the votes were tallied later, the Know-Nothing Party had swept the election.[1]

*   *   *

Mann could not have returned across a bridge he so deliberately had burned, had he wanted to. For him the political battle against slavery was lost. It was now necessary to start again by training a new generation of moral leaders and this was a task for the educator and not the politician. First, though, he must fend off the financial disaster which threatened both the school and his family. Obviously there was little money for his salary and that of the other faculty. Those professors who were also ministers preached for their bread during school recesses and vacations, hoping to hold on until better times came to the campus. Others waited in vain for the back salary for a short time and then gave up and left.

Thus Mann took to the road, now more than ever making extended circuits whenever he could. Fortunately, his popularity as a lecturer was never greater and this enabled him to command a minimum of $50 for each appearance. In 1854 and 1855 he made six swings through the Midwest, traveling as far west as Beloit, Wisconsin, and as far north as Ann Arbor, Michigan. Each of these trips filled him again with a divided sense of the tremendous potential and small accomplishments of the country. As his train moved along towards Chicago in what he described to Mary as "a wonderful country . . . almost perfect dead level," it seemed to him as if he were traveling through an unending sea of prairie grass as high as a horse's breast and hiding the wheels of a passing wagon so that it appeared to be floating along on its way. He saw, too, and felt the frenetic spirit of land speculation which animated the atmosphere in every hotel lobby where he stayed. One could ride

---

[1] Samuel Downer to Mann, November 13, 1854, Mann MSS: MHS.

for miles at a time over vast stretches of soil, black with a richness three feet deep in places, and yet recognize that speculation prevented countless immigrant and native Americans, trapped along the eastern seaboard, from settling on this good land at a fair price. For them the entrance fee to such a bounty was far too dear.[2]

On the road most of the day and speaking at night, he was ever at the mercy of bad cooks and drafty rooms. Loneliness was almost always his constant companion. On one trip after riding five hours in a freight train, he was stranded by a snowstorm in Syracuse on Thanksgiving. Alone in the depot and waiting for his delayed connection, he ate a bowl of oyster stew and a piece of pumpkin pie in the "refreshment room." "I could have deserved better things, and though I am ready to say the Lord's will be done," he wrote to Mary, "I cannot believe he would have objected to my having a better time." God willing or not, there seemed no other way. So weary did he become at one point on his itinerary in Illinois, he wrote home that this would be his last circuit so far from Yellow Springs. Still he also found more compensations than money for all his tribulations. His western audiences were "docile" and seemed uncorrupted by the influences of the East. He was also surprised and pleased how often strangers recognized him and greeted him *"as the Mann."* But if his reputation raised the expectations of those who bought tickets to hear him, not everyone left the lecture hall completely satisfied. A listener at the University of Michigan thought Mann presented "some passages of great strength and beauty" but along with these was also "no little pedantry." Recording his disenchantment with Mann, he later wrote in his Journal,

Pres[iden]t Mann is full 6 feet I should judge uncommonly slender, with very narrow shoulders, long neck & high head. There is a good deal of stiffness in his manner, and a good deal of inflation in his enunciation of his best passages. His countenance is rather noble. His head is not large in circumference but uncommonly high. His head is tolerably well covered with long grey hair. I should take him to be at least sixty years of age.

On the whole I was disappointed not that the lecture was inferior, it would have done a man of fair abilities great credit, but it was not in keeping with the higher order of talent which I had imagined Mr. Mann

---

[2] Mann to Mary Mann, [August, 1854], August 6 and 10, 1854; Samuel Downer to Mann, January 15, 1854, all in Mann MSS:MHS; *Milwaukee Sentinel*, March 27, 1855; *National Intelligencer*, November 19, 1855; *National Era*, November 29, 1855.

possessed. I feel at a loss to imagine how he could have written the Webster letters, and his speeches in Congress.

Others still thrilled to his words, and after every lecture, wherever he spoke, faddists moved up to the platform, swarming around him and urging him publicly to endorse their dietary, cold-water, abolitionist, anti-war, or temperance causes. Many others, especially young persons, were captivated by his perception of a better world and Mann knew that with the completion of each tour, he could expect a new rush of applicants to the Antioch campus.[3]

The following winter and spring, he was again on the road in Ohio, Pennsylvania, and New York, and for three days he was snowbound in Rochester. Then at the end of 1854 he made a long tour through the East, lecturing and calling upon potential donors to the college. At Syracuse he spoke with Samuel J. May and Gerritt Smith. In Albany he suffered through an interminable interview with a woman suffragette whom he could only label as "one of the Women's Rights Macedonian phalanx." From New York State it was on to Burlington, Vermont, and then finally into Massachusetts, where there were countless friendships to renew and several long visits with Howe, Downer, and Elizabeth Peabody. But his itinerary was a relentless taskmaster which would not let him remain in any one place and forced him on to Providence, Hartford, and New Haven before turning him again to the West. For many months he had anxiously awaited this trip, but in spite of all the warm handclasps and friendly faces, New England no longer had the spell it once held over him. Regardless of how precarious his future at Antioch was, in Massachusetts he only found vestiges of the past, perhaps no better symbolized than in the statue of Daniel Webster in front of the State House overlooking the Common, hastily erected by the Cotton Whigs upon the death of their hero. Mann wrote to Parker that "Many of the houses in Boston appeared to me like living tombs containing the dishonored dead," but nothing so much as his own house in West Newton so clearly spoke of his inability to return. Brambles and weeds had taken over the garden. The apple trees looked as if they could not survive another summer of neglect. The roof of the house had leaked and the ceilings were badly

---

[3] Mann to Mary Mann, August 6 and 10, 1854, and November 26, 1857, all in Mann MSS:MHS; Frederick Bissell Porter, Journal of Frederick Bissell Porter, April 20, [1854], MS in Michigan Historical Collection, University of Michigan.

stained. Paper and paint were peeling from the walls and the floor-boards had begun to curl. The house was his last physical anchor in Massachusetts, and after a brief heart-sickening inspection, Mann was ready to rid himself of it with few regrets. He instructed Downer to sell it for whatever he could realize, even if this meant putting it on the auction block. At the same time, he wrote to Mary back in Yellow Springs, telling her to have the wood ashes from the cellar spread on their garden plot and then have it plowed for seeding next spring.[4]

Back in Antioch, the greater the financial obstacles, the greater Mann conceived his mission to his students. "I can endure anything for these young people," he would say. He hoped to broaden their intellectual and religious horizons by bringing the outstanding lec-turers of the day to the campus, often underwriting their fees out of his own pocket. Several times he failed to get Emerson to stop at Yellow Springs, but he was successful in attracting Horace Greeley, Salmon P. Chase, Theodore Parker, and Bayard Taylor. While visit-ing the Manns, Sumner, Howe, and Josiah Quincy also met with the students on a more informal basis. Less welcome on the campus was the steady visitation of faddists and fellow travelers ever seek-ing an audience and the chance for new converts.[5]

If Mann stood ready to endure anything for his students, he also expected of them the high price of moral and intellectual con-formity for his sacrifice. Essentially, he saw his task as "the mould-

---

[4] Mann to Joseph C. Devin, January 27, 1855; Mann to F. A. Jones, June 26, 1855, both MSS at Horace Mann Mutual Insurance Company; Mann to Mary Mann, November 18 [1855], 21, 24, and 27, 1855; Mann to Samuel Gridley Howe, December 5, 1854 and June 14, 1855; Samuel Downer to Mann, November 11, 1854, all in Mann MSS:MHS; Mann to Theodore Parker, December 24, 1855, Parker Letterbook, MS in MHS. Downer finally sold the house for $6,700, but with the transaction he sadly acknowledged that here was the final proof that Mann was really gone from Massachusetts; Samuel Downer to Mann, June 11, 1856, Mann MSS:MHS. Equally disturbing on this trip and subsequent ones was Mann's recognition that even many of his old friends in Boston were too busy with their own affairs to have a genuine interest in his life and death struggle for Antioch. Thus Mann complained to Howe, "I spent one hour with Parker who talked on high themes, but asked me not one word about the College,—not one word!" Mann to Samuel Gridley Howe, December 26, 1857, Mann MSS:MHS.
[5] Mann to Ralph W. Emerson, August 3, 1854, Emerson MSS:HCL; Mann to Theodore Parker, July 1, 1854, Parker Letterbook, MS in MHS; Mary Mann to Mrs. Nathaniel Peabody, [1854?], Berg MSS:NYPL; Mann to Bayard Taylor, January 5 and 15, 1855, Taylor MSS:Cornell University; T. Starr King to Mann, July 13, 1854; Josiah Quincy to Mann, November 20, 1854, both in Mann MSS:MHS.

ing of youthful mind and manners," and he considered this "the noblest work that man or angels could do." Mere intellectual learning without a moral underpinning was worse, he feared, than no learning at all. Therefore, he set out to create a constricting paternal environment which would not tolerate misconduct in any form. From the outset, he made it his goal to persuade every student to sign a pledge against the use of tobacco and alcohol. Horseplay and practical jokes were outlawed; he also forbade card playing; and he frowned sufficiently on dancing that most students discontinued it "voluntarily" rather than invite the devastating look of admonition from the president's stern countenance.[6]

For several months after the college program was under way, he spent every available evening with his students, urging them to renounce some of their former habits. Usually beginning in a deceptively gentle manner, his appeals to students came, as Mary described them, "in silvery, flute-like tones of rebuke such as would make flints melt," but the hardened and intransigent, he admonished with words more fearful than "flute-like." With a premature sense of triumph, he wrote that "With the exception of . . . *three* others, whom I have not yet conquered, I have got every young man's name to a pledge against the use of tobacco in all forms. There are about 150 of them, and I have spent at least a hundred hours upon them, exhorting, explaining, arguing and ridiculing, until they surrendered. It is now fairly abolished. Profanity is my next devil in order." By the end of the year, he thought the victory over the sins of sloth, tobacco, alcohol, and profanity all but complete. "We have not one fourth part of the cases of discipline," he reported to Howe. All this he had accomplished without any physical coercion, relying instead on the means of a sort of secular confessional.

Obedience without punishment, order without *espionage*, great diligence without any trace of an artificial system of emulation, are our characteristics. Still there is a laxity belonging to a very imperfect state of home education, and the impulses of unrestrained appetites, in strong organizations. I . . . spend a great deal of time in private, intimate, and often confidential conversations with the students. I never grant an excuse for illness without inquiring into its causes and giving an admonition and caveat.

---

[6] Mann to Samuel Downer, November 9, 1853, Mann MSS:MHS; Mann, *Life*, pp. 410–414.

And to George Combe he reported,

When I have an interview with a reckless or perverse student, and pass into his consciousness, and try to make him see mine, I always shed tears, I cannot help it; and there is a force in honest tears not to be found in logic. This labor is diminishing as the spirit of the school, its *animus* improves. And we really have the most orderly, sober, diligent, and exemplary institution in the country.

It was then with a genuine sense of achievement that Mann could report that orchards and gardens in Yellow Springs went unmolested by Antioch students. For this the townsfolk were grateful. They also claimed the president could hear the drop of a whist card on campus from any place in the village. Of course, there were still a few incorrigibles who refused to heel in, and these Mann simply expelled from the school.[7]

Of himself Mann expected even more severe and demanding standards. Along with his personal campaign against the use of tobacco, alcohol, and profanity, he also was determined to purge himself of any carnal desire for emulation, even if this meant an almost ludicrous conduct in the eyes of his associates. While on a short summer vacation in Michigan, his family and that of another college president, George L. Cary, shared the expense of renting a bowling alley near their cottages. Mann agreed to the arrangement, but only on the condition that the facility would be used solely for individual exercise and recreation. No games were to be played in which there were contestants whose scores could be compared. Rather than be exposed to the temptation of competition and emulation, Mann insisted that each person in either family be allowed to exercise his or her muscles without any reference to what the muscles of another had accomplished.[8]

Yet some of the probity and piety at Antioch was superficial and once the president's back was turned, the old Adam manifested itself among the students. More vehemently did Mann denounce

---

[7] Mary Mann to Mrs. Cyrus Peirce, October 28 to November 11, 1853; Mann to Samuel Gridley Howe, March 11 and November 2, 1854, and December 26, 1857, all in Mann MSS:MHS; Mann to George Combe, May 18, 1858, Combe MSS:NLS; Mann, *Life*, pp. 410–414 and 438–439.
[8] George L. Cary, "Antioch at the Time of Horace Mann," *Horace Mann Centenary* (Yellow Springs, 1896); for examples of Mann's demanding educational advice to young persons, see Mann to George Manchester, December 4, 1852, Mann MSS:EI; Mann to S. C. Williamson, January 14, 1854, Western Reserve Historical Society.

their misconduct, sometimes singling out and rebuking an individual student in front of his peers at chapel. In time, he prepared a report attacking the informal students' "code of honor" by which they refused to bear tales on their classmates. Then when he tried to impose such a system of "voluntary" informants on the campus, his charges effectively, albeit surreptitiously, sabotaged his program. Rebuffed, but only temporarily, Mann threatened to refuse a degree to anyone who, while having met all instructional requirements, still remained an "immoral character." By the time a student donned his "Collegiate toga," according to Mann,

his day of probation is about to close. Then if he be guilty of any of the vices that torment society,—intemperance, lasciviousness, gaming, or blasphemy, profanity, obscenity—he should be cut off; that the power of knowledge should not be added to the power of vice;—in fine that for colleges to bestow education and the honors of a degree upon vicious youth is an offence against public morals. . . . If God spares my life, and the bigots will let me work, I will yet have this doctrine the common law of colleges.

And still later he wrote,

One thing we must do, which has never yet been done, we must have a public demand for a reform in the *Morals* of our Colleges. For God's sake and man's sake, let this most important of all reforms be neglected no longer.

Such coercive sentiments from one who had risked his career in the cause of anti-slavery, Howe found hard to believe. Mann, he feared, was seeking the liberal goals of co-education and nonsectarianism by increasingly illiberal means. Henry Barnard agreed, and when Mann pressed him to reprint his "Report on the 'Code of Honor,' Falsely So Called," in the *American Journal of Education,* Barnard did so only with the greatest reluctance.[9]

Dissent from students and friends was far less serious, however, than the dissension which emerged within the Antioch faculty.

---

[9] Mann to Samuel Gridley Howe, July 4, 1857, Mann MSS:MHS; Samuel Gridley Howe to George Combe, August 29, 1857, Combe, MSS:NLS; Mann to Henry Barnard, November 3, 1856, Barnard MSS:NYU; Mann to Lyman C. Draper, April 2, 1859, Draper MSS: Wisconsin State Historical Society; Mann, *et al.,* "Report on the 'Code of Honor,' Falsely So Called," in Mann, *Life,* 585–596; Mann, "College Code of Honor," *American Journal of Education,* III (March, 1857), 66–70.

If the love of money was not the root of all evil, surely the plain lack of regular salaries was a major source of disaffection among the professors and leading members of the Connexion. With college finances ever worsening, those who "preached for their bread" returned to the campus at the end of each summer all the more prone to eat a bread of bitterness. Irregular and insufficient wages ate into their early sense of mission, leaving the dry bones of a narrow sectarian jealousy which finally took the form of personal attacks on Mann for allegedly mishandling the affairs of the college.

After two disappointing years which had been long on idealism and short on funds, the young Ira Allen, so dedicated and hopeful at the first faculty meeting at West Newton, turned against Mann. Allen soon found a fellow malcontent in the Reverend William Doherty, professor of logic and rhetoric, and a cell of dissent soon grew to include A. M. Merrifield, Judge Mills, and Elder Ladley, the minister of the local Christian Church. Added to the problem of finances was an ugly jealousy between Allen and Rebecca Pennell, fed by Mann's patent support of his niece. Increasingly, the faculty and trustees' meetings contained hidden agendas, but the opposition did not risk an open confrontation until the need for a new principal of the preparatory school arose. After a good deal of un-Christian wrangling, the trustees chose Allen's candidate. Mann bided his time and finally got rid of Doherty and Allen by refusing to reappoint them. In retaliation, Allen went to the press with a biased version of the ills troubling the institution. Under the premature title, *History of the Rise, Difficulties, and Suspension of Antioch College,* he went to great lengths in picturing himself as a martyr to Mann's soulless attempt to steal the school from the Christians and make it an outpost of Unitarianism. Fortunately, Mann did not stoop to answer Allen's charges but left this assignment to Reverend Eli Fay, who published the short *Rejoinder to Ira W. Allen's Pseudo "History" of Antioch College.* When the school did not collapse as the result of his exposé, Allen returned to the campus and unsuccessfully tried to turn the students against their president. The controversy almost proved the death blow to the school, since it dried up most sources of funds which still remained among the Christians. Yet from a more long-range perspective, it was a painful blessing in disguise, only slowly realized. The piddling sums Mann might still have received from the Connexion would only have prolonged Antioch's agony. Attempting to pull the remainder of his faculty back together after the controversy, Mann ruefully conceded that he had good "reason to fear that the last sands of Antioch are running out . . . unless we can have some *wholesale* instead of *retail* donations, our institution sinks." [1]

*   *   *

With each passing day, Mann understood more bitterly what it meant to be a prophet save among his own constituents. At the very moment when a growing number of disaffected Christians in the Connexion were hounding his heels at every step he took to rescue the college, the Gentile world sought out his counsel on the widest range of questions. The daily mail to the campus always included enquiries, many of them trivial and a few of major import. Could Mann recommend an Ohio woman to become the vice regent of the Mount Vernon Association? A doctor from Troy, New York, began: "Although I have not been personally introduced to you, yet I have frequently heard you lecture. My object in writing you, sir, is to obtain your opinion . . ." and a Quaker in Virginia wrote that he "should be glad if thou would give me thy views of the best method of conducting the education of children from the earliest at which any distinct efforts are required to adult age." A young man in Iowa asked how he might study law in order to help in the struggle against slavery, and a large landowner in Bloomington, Illinois, wanted help to start a normal school. [2]

There were more substantial requests as well. Legislators from Kansas and Iowa asked him to prepare reports for them which would facilitate the establishment of public school systems. Mann found time to accept the Iowa invitation and with two other commissioners composed a document during the autumn of 1856 which became the basis for the state school law of 1858. A visit to Saint Louis was followed by a commitment from its educational leaders

---

[1] Mary Mann to Mann, November [25?] and 27, 1855, Mann MSS:MHS; Mann to S. R. Wells, June 10, 1856, Regional History MSS:Cornell University Archives; Mann to Gerritt Smith, January 1, 1856, in Mann, *Life*, 477–478; Ira W. Allen, Diary, *passim*, MS in ACL; Straker, "Merrifield and the Founding of Antioch College," *Antioch Alumni Bulletin*, VI (November, 1934), 10; Ira W. Allen, *History of the Rise, Difficulties and Suspension of Antioch College* (Columbus, 1858); Eli Fay, *Rejoinder to Ira W. Allen's Pseudo "History" of Antioch College* (Yellow Springs, 1851).

[2] See, for example, Pamela Cunningham to Mann, September 3, 1858; Marcus Mendenhall to Mann, June 30, 1856; Dr. Isaac Mitchell to Mann, April 27, 1856, all in Mann MSS:MHS.

to build the first public normal school west of the Mississippi River. In Saint Louis, also, men attempting to get the new Washington University on a strong intellectual foundation sought out his advice. Then influential individuals in Iowa and Wisconsin enquired if he would accept the presidencies of their respective state universities, while the trustees of Northwest Christian, later to become Butler University, formally offered him the presidency of their institution in Indianapolis. There were times when Mann gladly would have exchanged places with Job, but to each of these enquiries he responded with an unambiguous finality which made it clear that his own future was bound irrevocably to the fortunes of Antioch.[3]

Sectarian opposition and the dunning of creditors barely dented Mann's own conviction in the rightness of his mission, but when the faithful began to leave the campus, believing Antioch was a lost cause, he could not avoid the sense of isolation which must come to a captain standing alone on the quarter-deck of a sinking vessel. From the very beginning there had been a steady turnover as paydays were missed with increased frequency, but by 1856, the small dedicated band he had brought together was falling apart. Lured by promises of more secure opportunities elsewhere, practicality triumphed over idealism. A great loss was Calvin Pennell, one of the most dependable co-workers Mann ever had. Unwittingly, on a trip to Saint Louis, Mann himself had set the stage for an offer to his nephew to come there and accept a new principalship at twice his Antioch salary. Mann understood the necessity for Calvin to go, but it was a severe personal blow to him all the same, and he conceded that "one of the cornerstones is pulled out from under Antioch." Equally painful to him but even more personal was the marriage of his niece Rebecca to Amos Dean, also on the Antioch staff. For Mann, nothing had been too good for his favorite niece since she had been Cyrus Peirce's prize pupil at the Lexington Normal School. Surely, Mann now thought, she deserved a more exemplary man, perhaps made in his own mold, but in any case not the pedestrian Dean. On this important issue, Rebecca for once

---

[3] John Krum to Mann, February 25 [1856?]; Mann to Mary Mann, May 20, 1856; Mann to Cyrus Peirce, December 10, 1856; J. D. Low to Mann, June 8, 1856; James Grimes to Mann, July 28, 1856; Lyman Allen to Mann, April 5, 1856; Frederick Humphrey to Mann, January 8, 1858; John Young to Mann, June 9, 1858, all in Mann MSS:MHS; Mann to Amos Dean, September 12, 1856, Pforzheimer MSS (photostat): BLYU; Clarence Ray Aurner, *History of Education in Iowa* (Iowa City, 1914), I, 30–54.

defied her uncle. Strong-willed and aggressive enough to overcome many of the anti-feminine prejudices of her time, she probably found in Dean a man she could at least manage, if not entirely dominate. Mann grudgingly consented, but during the wedding in the president's manse, he was visibly upset. Not so Mary, who viewed this development with a sense of relief and vindication, having believed for a long time that the ambitious Rebecca had received more of her uncle's attention and confidence than she deserved.[4]

The most severe blow to Mann during this period came with the defection of Austin Craig. Gentle, sensitive, and espousing a religious liberalism almost identical to that of Mann's, Craig had become a sort of youthful Channing in Mann's eyes and hopefully the one who would be his successor as president. After a barrage of appeals, the young minister had left his congregation in Blooming Grove, New York, to join the Antioch faculty. Once there, in a short time he became in a small degree for Mann what Melancthon had been to the more impulsive and charismatic Luther. But then Craig soon wearied of the constant controversy on campus, became terribly homesick, and finally retreated once again to the security of his Blooming Grove parish. No sooner was he gone when Mann realized the awful void his absence created and drew on every appeal in his repertoire to coax Craig back to Yellow Springs. Since Elder Ladley was ill and could not continue, there was opportunity for the young man to become the next minister in the village church, while doubling as college chaplain. For a short time, Craig came back and gave Antioch a second try but found that neither he nor his prospects had changed. Now even Mann recognized the finality of what his reluctant protégé had been saying all along, but the recognition was not accompanied by an understanding of his decision. In desperate straits, under constant attack from the Christians, harassed by creditors, and now losing the very persons he had counted upon to save the school, Mann judged Craig's refusal little short of apostasy, and he lashed out at the young man with the severity of language of one who believed himself betrayed:

I have just received yours of the 16th instant. It wrings my heart. Amid the enthusiasm of past efforts and the frightful labors that now

---

[4] Mary Mann to Ada Badger, December 1, 1859; Mann to Mary Mann, August 20, 1856; Mann to Austin Craig, September 5, 1856; Mann to Cyrus Peirce, December 10, 1856, all in Mann MSS:MHS.

stare me in the face—made necessary by your refusal to touch them with the end of your finger—a few words are forced from me.

Please never speak to me again of the *Practice* of *Duty*, but only of its *Theory*. Please never speak to me again of Jesus Christ as a being whose life and sacrifices are *to be imitated* but only to be talked about.

. . . Were I to wait until tomorrow, perhaps were I to wait but an hour, my old love for you (and what man did I ever love so well) might come back again, and I could not then utter them. *Farewell.*

But a desperate man could not even wait one hour.[5]

With expenses exceeding tuition income and donations from the Christians declining rapidly, the only way the trustees made up their immediate deficit was by paying Mann and the rest of the faculty a fraction of their salaries. Even this proved to be a misleading placebo and, by 1856, Mann knew that a showdown was imminent. The difference between victory and defeat was a simple matter of hard cash. Only money for the college, as he described it, could "pluck it from the abyss into which it threatens to fall." And should he fail, so also would "the cause of Liberal Christianity and a free-thoughted education" in the great valley of the West.[6]

In January, 1856, he hurried to New York City "with no little apprehension" for a long-overdue emergency meeting. Here during the day he worked to save Antioch, meeting with a small group of devoted men, a few from the Connexion, but the majority of them Unitarians. At night he worked to maintain his family finances, lecturing to capacity crowds. After a review of the accounts of the college, it was evident that nothing less than $100,000 would save Antioch from the hands of its creditors. One man promised to raise $25,000. A group from New York, Pennsylvania, and New Jersey set their goal at $30,000, and Mann's friends from New England became accountable for another $25,000. If there was still enough interest in Ohio to raise a final $30,000 they might yet be out of trouble. On paper, it was a successful meeting and Mann left with a sense of genuine accomplishment, writing to Mary at first chance that "Antioch is safe."[7]

<hr>

[5] Mann to Austin Craig, September 5, 1856, July 3 and August 7, 1857, and July 20, 1858, all in Mann MSS:MHS; for a more complete account of Mann's lengthy correspondence with Craig, see, Mann, *Life*, pp. 461–512, and *passim*.

[6] Mann to Gerritt Smith, January 1, 1856, in Mann, *Life*, pp. 477–478.

[7] Mann to Theodore Parker, February 5, 1856, Parker Letterbook, MS in MHS; Mann to Mary Mann, January 31, 1856, Mann MSS:MHS; New

The trip back was an ordeal in nineteenth-century winter travel that no Currier and Ives lithographer could sentimentalize. Mann was snowbound three days in Buffalo and when the weather cleared, the temperature dropped to 30 degrees "on the wrong side of zero," as he gave the account. Nevertheless, he took to the road, anxious to meet with a group of Christians in Pennsylvania. Even with his frail lungs he somehow survived the journey, but so intense was the cold that his driver froze his ears, hands, and feet. Still the trip ended in hope. With money from the pledges scheduled to begin the following January, Mann believed Antioch's immediate debts could be paid and the salaries of its beleaguered faculty guaranteed for the next five years. Thus after a series of pessimistic reports and false starts, by May he could write that the school finally would be rescued "out of the slough of insolvency." [8]

For Mann, Antioch became the symbol of all he had ever worked for. Within the microcosm of its campus he found both the hope and despair that was so much a condition of life for the nation. By 1856, as Mann looked backwards and forwards, he could only report "a strangely mingled feeling made up of pain and joy, to say nothing of a readiness or unreadiness to die." To George Combe he wrote on his sixtieth birthday,

I am too intensely interested in the great questions of human progress, of humanity itself, to be willing to quit the field in this stage of the conflict. The vital questions of pauperism, temperance, slavery, peace and education, covering as they do many digits of the orb of human happiness, I cannot relinquish, I cannot leave, without a feeling of the disruption of breaking heart-strings from objects which they have intwined. You may tell me the work will go on, and perhaps it will; but I want it should go on in my day. I long to see it. I want to help it, to expend myself upon it; and life seems bereaved of its noblest functions and faculties if it fails in this.

If something as moral and enlightened as Antioch could fail, in what else was there hope to achieve the victory over superstition, bigotry, greed, and the irrational? Mann was particularly incensed

York *Times,* January 28, 29, 30, and 31, 1856; New York *Tribune,* January 28 and 29, 1856.
[8] Mann to Theodore Parker, February 5, 1856, Parker Letterbook, MS in MHS; Mann to Mary Mann, January 31, 1856; Mann to Austin Craig, February 21 and September 5, 1856, all in Mann MSS:MHS; Mann to George Combe, May 4, 1856, Combe MSS:NLS; *Christian Inquirer,* March 29, 1856; *Christian Palladium,* January 19, 1856.

at the French, who seemed to have forgotten all the sacrifices their fathers had made for them to secure liberty and equality and who were now bent on marching back to the dark ages with their inordinate celebration over the birth of a new ruling prince. "What a ridiculous ado they made in France," Mann wrote to Combe, "about six pounds of baby; our births are human liberty." But neither could he be sure of his own country. As he read accounts of the violence in Kansas and feared a pro-slavery takeover there, aided and abetted by President Franklin Pierce, he also saw the real prospect of an unchecked spread of human bondage. At Yellow Springs, incredible though it seemed, the only thing which prevented his college from bestowing its benefits on the next generation was a mere $100,000, a pittance when compared with what the nation squandered every day on military expenditures, or what he thought rich men like John Jacob Astor wasted on useless luxuries. Attempting to fathom this perversion of priorities, he could only record: "When I feel our wants, it makes me desire wealth, and it gives me feelings of intense condemnation for the manner in which so much wealth is spent." Such contradictions between what should have been and what was, he struggled to resolve in his own mind. And as long as they remained unresolved, they ever threatened to crack his adamantine belief in progress and human perfectibility.[9]

As with crises in the past, the effort to save Antioch took a heavy toll on Mann. His insomnia had returned and his physical frame was further weakened by recurring hemorrhoid attacks. Finally his suffering became so unbearable that he agreed to a painful operation, but this proved only partially successful and his days continued to be haunted by the constant fear of their return. "I am removed but a very small distance from such suffering," he wrote to a correspondent, and when an attack came, his only source of relief was the use of ice suppositories. The problems of maintaining the debt-ridden college while fending off his sectarian adversaries had begun to deplete his mental strength as well. Worry, frustration, and the fear that it all might be in vain brought him to the first stages of a nervous breakdown. For a short time, he suffered a partial paralysis of speech, and when he did speak, he uttered nonsensical words so irrelevant they even sounded strange to his own ears. And he could do nothing to control himself. Then the attack passed over as quickly as it came and those who had witnessed it never raised the

---

[9] Mann to George Combe, May 4, 1856, Combe MSS:NLS.

subject with him. He never referred to it either. Each of these ill-nesses was to Mann the dreaded sign of "that terrible fellow 'Old Age.'" More frequently now, he confessed to Samuel J. May, he heard "the sound of his footsteps," and he added, "I dread him greatly, not so much however for what he does, as for what he will prevent me from doing."[1]

Thus late in the summer of 1856, with the unbearable Ohio heat adding to his misery, he simply had to retreat from Yellow Springs for a short vacation. Since Mary and his three sons were on an extended visit back East at the time, he left with Rebecca and Amos Dean for Mackinaw Island in Michigan. The thought of Rebecca rather than herself combing Mann's hair each night rankled Mary, but she was tied down in the East. On the trip across Lake Erie, Mann slept well, not even waking when the boat docked in Detroit. The next day he arrived at the island and found it "a most delightful summer retreat" in which to take long walks along the rock-strewn shoreline and through groves of dwarfed evergreens, stunted and skewed away from the prevailing offshore winds. Unfortunately, Rebecca became ill for three days and this prevented his complete relaxation. Almost with a sense of justice, Mary later wrote that the vacation for Mann did not have the desired effect because of his "depression of spirits while absent from his family" and also because of the presence of an "invalid relative instead of cheerful companions." On the way back, Mann spoke at several institutes, but soon after he returned, he again fell ill and needed several weeks to recover. It was evident that his vacation had fallen far short of his needs.[2]

*   *   *

During the autumn of 1856, he still felt assured that Antioch would weather its financial storms. Then in the following January when the first pledges were to come in, in place of money came

---

[1] Mann, *Life,* p. 415; Mann to George Combe, May 4, 1856, Combe MSS: NLS; Mann to Samuel J. May, February 27, 1858, in Mann, *Life,* pp. 514–516.

[2] Mann to Theodore Parker, June 16, 1856, Parker Letterbook, MS in MHS; Mann to Mary Mann, July 20, 25, and 30, and August 3, 1856, all in Mann MSS:MHS; Mann to Samuel J. May, July 18, 1856, Personal Misc. MSS:LOC; Mann, *Life,* p. 492.

heartbreaking reports. What had been promised in good times was now not forthcoming as the country edged closer to a depression. By the summer, a financial panic was abroad in the land and particularly disastrous to the area surrounding Yellow Springs were the declining fortunes and final bankruptcy of the Ohio Life Insurance Company. Stockholders found their assets worthless, depositors lost their life savings, and numerous friends of Antioch defaulted on their pledges. Now with a shortage of liquid assets everywhere, the Connecticut insurance company which held a mortgage on the college pressed for its payments, long overdue. And to make matters worse, some students who feared the school would soon be shut down went elsewhere where they could be more certain of graduating.

Ironically, as the trustees gathered at Yellow Springs early in July, 1857, they took on the contradictory tasks of graduating the first class of Antiochians to leave for the outside world and then determining the steps necessary to declare bankruptcy. For a brief moment, only commencement was in Mann's mind. Fifteen students had completed their course of studies and he wanted them to be presented to the public as the living proof of Antioch's mission. Governor Salmon P. Chase came down from Columbus for the ceremonies. Reverend Henry Bellows, one of the fund raisers from New York, was there, as was Reverend Ezra Gannett, a leading Unitarian of New England. Mann intended it to be "a wonderful week" and he took special pains with his baccalaureate address, giving a full-blown justification for his belief that only an individual of proven moral character should be given the imprimatur of a college diploma. Although Howe again found much in Mann's speech to question, Whitelaw Reid, editor of the Xenia *News* and later to succeed Horace Greeley as head of the New York *Tribune*, judged Mann's remarks as "characteristically beautiful and powerful—just what the public had been led to expect." When it came to awarding the degrees, Mann began with the conventional statement used by many college presidents: "By virtue of the authority confided in me by the charter of Antioch College, and in consideration of the proficiency you have made in the liberal arts and sciences," but then he interjected a statement of his own making, *"in further consideration also of the reputable character you have maintained and the exemplary life you have led,"* before returning to the regular version and concluding, "I hereby admit you to all the honors and prerogatives of the First Academical Degree." Antioch had graduated its first class.[3]

And yet Antioch had also "failed." Once more the trustees reviewed their meager assets; once more they attempted to separate worthless promises from bona fide pledges; once more they worked to untangle the hopeless mesh of A. M. Merrifield's accounts; and once more they were unwilling to cut the Gordian knot and declare bankruptcy. Still there remained the hope that the money could be raised and when they finally broke off their meetings and left the campus, they once again left with the renewed sense that the school still could be saved. Mann too succumbed to the same wishful thinking. So hopeful was he, in fact, that he thought he was soon to receive a regular salary, even though he had not received a cent from the trustees for an entire year. "With a fair chance to work out our destiny," he wrote, "we think we should find some 'nuggets' at least in dead men's graves, if not live men's pockets." As there was nothing more he could do immediately, he gathered up his family for another vacation on Mackinaw Island. This time, Rebecca was not along and Mary made certain that she alone would help him relax each evening by running a comb through his hair.[4]

Back in Boston, there was far less optimism. With the financial squeeze as tight as ever, Samuel Downer warned Mann that "there is not, nor will be, for the present, much revival in business, our manufacturing interest is very prostrate of collections." And Josiah Quincy reported that after consulting with a number of his associates he considered it "impracticable to raise $25,000 at the time." Instead of letting Antioch be auctioned off to the highest bidder, he was negotiating with the Connecticut Life Insurance Company at Hartford, hoping to convince them that it was better to sell the mortgage at a discount to him and his associates than proceed with foreclosure. For the moment, Quincy failed in his mission and Antioch was officially scheduled to be auctioned on June 6, 1858. Weary and

---

[3] Ezra Gannett to Mann, June 20, 1857; Mann to Austin Craig, July 3, 1857; Mann to Samuel Gridley Howe, July 4, 1857, all in Mann MSS: MHS; Mann, *Life*, pp. 502–503, and V, 499; Mann, "Baccalaureate Address of 1857," in Morgan, *Mann at Antioch*, pp. 319–360; *Christian Inquirer*, July 11, 1857; *Gospel Herald*, August 13, 1857.

[4] Mann to Samuel Gridley Howe, July 4, November 9, and December 26, 1857, and February 3, 1858; Mann to Austin Craig, July 3, 1857; Mann to Samuel Downer, August 6 and October 16, 1857, all in Mann MSS: MHS; Mann, *Life*, pp. 506–507; *Christian Inquirer*, June 20, 1857; *Gospel Herald*, August 13, September 24, and November 19, 1857; New York *Tribune*, August 28, 1857.

at a loss where next to turn, Mann reported to George Combe that "now unless help comes from some quarter, we shall disband." Then with the advertised sale less than a month away, Quincy and his associates gained a nine-month postponement of the foreclosure and Mann breathed a special sigh of relief. Perhaps what he had dreaded most was not the prospect that Antioch might fail, but that in failing, it would also fall into the hands of a Calvinist group. Just recently he had received word that Presbyterians were gathering funds in order to bid against the Unitarians if the property came to the auction block.[5]

Again that autumn, another large group of freshmen appeared at Yellow Springs. After welcoming them and getting them organized into a class, Mann turned his thoughts to the series of meetings in the East which must be held to raise money. Competing with these thoughts with increased frequency was Mann's concern about death. Two years before, George Combe had written to him describing his loneliness and a particular experience of his in which he believed himself to be dying. Mann assured the aging Combe of his undying friendship. "I do not only think of you, but in a very and important and extensive sense, *I am you,*" he wrote. Then when a letter came in 1858, closed with black sealing wax and postmarked Edinburgh, August 30, Mann sadly read the inevitable, realizing that in the death of this dear friend, some part of his own life had also moved on into the hereafter. Closer at hand were other signs of the ravages of time. With each trip back East he was troubled by the appearance of his former associates. Cyrus Peirce he found "weak, paralytic, and almost coming within Shakespeare's description of old age, with each of the *sans*." Samuel J. May was also seriously ill, and when Downer complained of his own sickness, Mann replied: "My brain is, I fear worse than yours. The last year's work, with last vacation's work on the back side of it, was too much; and I am suffering severely." Especially during the winter of 1858, his brain knew no rest. Increasingly nervous, he found that even the presence of his sons no longer relaxed him. Momentarily at least, he still gained respite on solitary walks down in the glen, but always he must return and as he climbed the last few steps on the path and came up to the edge of the ravine, there stood Antioch Hall, its pre-

[5] Josiah Quincy to Mann, March 27, May 6, and June 30, 1858; Samuel Downer to Mann, February 6, 1858, all in Mann MSS:MHS; Mann to Samuel J. May, February 27, 1858, in Mann, *Life,* pp. 514–516; Mann to George Combe, May 18, 1858, Combe MSS:NLS.

sumptuous towers the physical embodiment of all the financial and mental burdens he continued to bear.[6]

There was no place to turn. As Mary described the situation, if her husband could have retired "from the field without wrecking the whole cause, he would do so, but he is entangled in a mesh, the knots of which can only be untied by *success*." Therefore he stubbornly labored on from week to week, always looking for some way in which his efforts could triumph. With reports from Quincy that money was finally beginning to come in to his committee, perhaps enough to buy it at auction, Mann again turned his thoughts to improving the school. Somehow in the course of two decades, he had forgotten all the troubles Dorothea Dix had caused in Cyrus Peirce's Lexington Normal School with her straitlaced morality. Now ever worried about the conduct of his female students, he wrote to her, enquiring if she would come to Antioch as dean of women. "I have tried to make our girls believe their charms and attractions were given them, not for self aggrandisement, not to gratify the love of approbation, but for the highest moral ends. So beautiful & divine an instrument should only perform the noblest and most exalted functions. . . . Who can inculcate, who can daguerreotype ideas like these, like the one I am addressing,—my blessed friend," he wrote to her. For all the flattery, Miss Dix declined the offer, and he continued to seek elsewhere for an individual who could "daguerreotype ideas" in his students.[7]

On April 20, 1859, the auctioneer's hammer, so long postponed by the best of unfulfilled intentions, finally fell on the bankrupt Antioch. For a price of $40,200 a group of Mann's friends organized by Josiah Quincy made the purchase. They insisted upon an ironclad guarantee that they were obtaining an absolutely unencumbered title and they were equally adamant about the need to establish a new and fiscally responsible board of trustees to whom they would deed over the property; but not before they had assurances that the school

---

[6] Mann to Mary Mann, October 7 and 10, 1858; Mann to Samuel Gridley Howe, December 26, 1857; Robert Cox to Mann, August 30, 1858; Mann to Samuel Downer, November 8, 1858; all in Mann MSS:MHS; Mann to George Combe, May 4, 1856, Combe MSS:NLS; Mann to Samuel J. May, February 27, 1858, in Mann, *Life*, pp. 514–516; see also *Life*, pp. 543–545.

[7] Josiah Quincy to Mann, April 13, 1859, Mann MSS:MHS; Mary Mann to Dorothea L. Dix, March 5, 1859; Mann to Dorothea L. Dix, March 7, 1859, both in Dix MSS:HCL.

in the future would be free of the sectarianism which had so bedeviled Mann's efforts in the past.[8]

Now freed of its disastrous financial schemes and of the petty denominationalism which ran so counter to its high ideals, Antioch had been redeemed. This made the forthcoming commencement by far the happiest in its brief history. Again Mann invited Governor Chase, along with Governor Bengham of Michigan, assuring the anti-slavery Chase of an especially warm reception since "with scarcely an exception," as Mann described it, "we are all 'Black' Republicans." Unfortunately, many of the faculty had left prior to the auction and this meant that Mann tended to all the details of the ceremony, making the arrangements and listening to and criticizing all the formal presentations which the students would make. The week before graduation he worked day and night, somehow finding enough time to write out a first draft of his baccalaureate address. Actually, so inspired was he with the prospect that Antioch would now fulfill its mission that he could have extemporized for two hours, continually holding the rapt attention of his audience. On June 29, 1859, after the graduates had received their diplomas, Horace Mann mounted the pulpit in the Antioch chapel and under its vaulted ceiling gave his last baccalaureate address and one of the most eloquent speeches of his entire career.[9]

Perhaps he sensed a deep premonition that he would never deliver another, and this private knowledge gave an urgency to his words such as they had never had before. Once past his simple introduction, he spoke of the "Phoenix spirit" which welled up inside him, a metaphor absent in his previous writings. "I yearn, for another warfare in behalf of right, in hostility to wrong," he told the group of adoring young faces before him,

where, without furlough, and without going into winter quarters, I would enlist for another fifty-years campaign and fight it out for the glory of God and the welfare of men. . . . But alas! that cannot be; for while the Phoenix spirit burns within, the body becomes ashes. Not only would

[8] Josiah Quincy to Mann, April 13 and 27, 1859, both in Mann MSS: MHS; "Order for the Sale of Antioch College," *Christian Inquirer*, March 26, 1859; see also April 2, 9, and 16, 1859; New York *Post*, April 23 and 25, 1859.
[9] Mann to Salmon P. Chase, June 10, 1859, Chase MSS:PHS; Mann to Samuel Gridley Howe, June 27, 1859, Mann MSS:MHS; *Daily Cincinnati Gazette*, June 30, 1859; New York *Post*, July 6, 1859.

the sword fall from my hands; my hand would fall from the sword, I
cannot go with you. You must pursue your conquering march alone.

He then dealt with the inevitability of evil. Did this then mean that
it was absurd to call men wicked? On the contrary, *"Though evil be
inevitable,"* he insisted, *"it is remediable also; it is removable, ex-
pugnable."* But beyond this, because men had the power to destroy
evil, they also had the obligation to destroy it. He then elaborated on
the necessity of self-improvement and the imperative to serve others, building his case with vivid historical illustrations as he moved
upward to sentiments which more than any others he wished to
burn indelibly in the minds of his graduates. Perhaps all the sacrifice and suffering, all the worry and frustration, and all the sleepless
nights and sectarian controversy were but a small price to pay for
this one last chance to pass the torch of humanitarianism on to
these young idealists before him. Finally, after describing Lord Nel-
son's fortitude at the Battle of Trafalgar, Mann brought his ideas to
a ringing climax that summed up the vision which had inspired
much of his life:

So, in the infinitely nobler battle in which you are engaged against
error and wrong, if ever repulsed or stricken down, may you always be
solaced & cheered by the exulting cry of triumph over some abuse in
church or state, some vice or folly in society, some false opinion or
cruelty or guilt which you have overcome! And I beseech you to treasure
up in your hearts these my parting words: *Be ashamed to die until you
have won some victory for humanity.*[1]

*   *   *

---

[1] Mann, "Baccalaureate Address Delivered at Antioch College, 1859,"
MS in Mann MSS:MHS; Mann, *Life*, pp. 554–575; apparently Mann
snatched enough time from his schedule to make some last-minute
changes in his address, broadening its scope and changing his last exhortation from its more passive tone to something intensely active.
Mann's first version read, ". . . may you always be solaced & cheered
by the exulting cry of triumph over some false opinion, or cruelty or
guilt, &, I beseech you to treasure up in your hearts, these, my parting
words: *Be ashamed to die until some victory for Humanity has been
won.*" One of his students was so moved by Mann's appeal that he wrote
a letter to his friend describing Mann in words which might have been
a fitting epitaph: ". . . one of nature's noblemen & withal, a most
exemplary person in all the phases of a statesman, scholar & philanthropist"—George W. Boyd to H. A. Fletcher, July 9, 1859, Straker MSS:ACL.

The following day, Mann was nearly speechless with fatigue, but instead of resting, he drove himself to attend one more round of college meetings, which dragged on for another two days. He also busied himself with plans for an extended trip to Boston and an appearance at a national meeting of normal schools at Trenton, New Jersey. Gradually, however, fatigue gave way to a recurring fever which robbed him of his sleep and appetite. Worsening each day, it finally flared up like a virulent fire in his veins so that rest was impossible. Perhaps Mary would have noticed the first danger signals, had not all three of their sons been ill at the same time, Benjie being down with a serious case of typhoid fever. Mann reluctantly abandoned his projected trip to the East, but sent Horace, Jr., to stay with the Howes as soon as he recovered.[2]

By mid-July, the weather turned brutally hot and the super-heated atmosphere assaulted his nostrils when he breathed. The grass withered and yellowed as the once cool moist soil beneath it turned to a burning dust. Hardly a breath of air stirred across the treeless campus and the naked red brick buildings baked under the merciless summer sun. Those slight evening breezes which did come brought no relief but only mocked him, being the harbinger of the heat which was as certain the next day as the morning sun which preceded it. Farmers' wells were running dry and each day Mann scanned the western horizon hoping for some sign that the terrible drouth would be broken and rain would bring relief to the parched earth. One evening an all too brief thundershower passed over, and he remarked what a beautiful gentle staccato it made on the tin roof of his back porch, but with the return of the sun in the morning, so also came the heat and the dust.

The last week in July his weakened frame became the battle-ground between a raging fever and chills accompanied by an uncontrollable shaking. Each day his throat became more swollen until even liquids were an ordeal for him to swallow. Finally, on July 31, he could not rise from his bed. His will power no longer adequate to drive his failing body, he became a captive in his own bedroom. The local doctor sent an urgent message to Cincinnati for help, while the students now came to the manse taking shifts at his bedside, bathing his forehead as his temperature rose and then covering him with quilts when the chills returned. Recognizing signs of the end, Rev-

---

[2] Mann to Samuel Gridley Howe, June 27, 1859, Mann MSS:MHS; Mann to Henry Barnard, July 4, 1859, Barnard MSS:NYU; New York *Post,* July 8, 1859.

erend Eli Fay began to sense the inconsolable grief he must soon endure, while Mary moved from sickroom to sickroom in the house, almost like an automaton, supervising the care of her two convalescent sons, while grimly suppressing thoughts of the staggering tragedy and terrible burden she must now bear. At times she was so weary that her defenses were about to collapse. Then somehow she regrouped her sagging spirits, believing she "could bear to see him die glorious," but "could not have borne to see him live dishonored." [3]

On the evening of August 1, a specialist from Cincinnati arrived and examined Mann. Although believing the case hopeless, he prescribed carbonated liquids, thinking that additional carbon dioxide in Mann's stomach might somehow help him improve. Later that night Mann suffered his worst, his pulse running as high as 135, and although he rallied in the morning, now even Mary abandoned all hope. Struggling to speak through his swollen lips, Mann asked how he was. When the doctor hesitated, he added, "If I am going to die, I would like to know it. I have many things to say, and it will take some time to say them." He was then told that he had but a few hours to live.

More than anything else, his had been a life of the word and this was the way he wished it to end. Sensing death and the final loneliness and isolation he had held at bay all his life now closing in upon him, he would make still one last effort to exhort those around him to work on tirelessly for the humane society he had sought for the last three decades. During the next hour, while all others were removed, he spoke to Benjie and George, urging them to be honest and dutiful. Looking up into Mary's tear-stained face, he spoke of his love for her and his plans for their sons' education, assuring her there was enough money saved for this purpose. For a while he talked to her of Sumner, Howe, and Downer, and wanted to be sure that she would also tell Elizabeth of his enduring love for her. Mary promised to bury him next to Charlotte in Providence and he agreed, but only if she consented to be buried there as well. Then, as the boys left, a severe chill throbbed through his frame as if to wrench the last essence of life from him. No added coverlet equal to this, Mary quickly moved back to the bed, wrapped her arms around her

---

[3] Mary Mann to Sophia Hawthorne, [August?], 1859, Berg MSS:NYPL; the events surrounding Mann's death, I have drawn from a variety of sources including Mary Mann to Ada Badger, December 1, 1859; Mary Mann to Sophia Hawthorne, August 4, 1859, both in Mann MSS:MHS; Boston *Daily Transcript*, August 3, 1859; Dedham *Gazette*, August 6, 1859.

shaking husband, and lay beside him until the warmth of her body drove away the cold clammy shroud which held him in its clasp.

As word that the president was dying spread across the campus, students and friends hurried to the manse and quietly filed into his room. Standing silent around his bed, the only sign of life they could recognize was his gasping as he struggled for air. Then opening his eyes, he began to speak. Hoping to record his last words, Rebecca Dean snatched up several sheets of paper from his desk and began to take notes, perhaps not realizing until later that on the back side of them, Mann had previously recorded his students' last grades. To Amos Dean he said, "God bless you, take care of your wife—take care of her for my sake." To Rebecca, "You have been to me the loveliest, dearest, gentlest, faithfulest daughter, sister, friend, almost wife. Good bye." At times, he suffered short spells of delirium, as the fever triumphed momentarily over his mind, but even during these periods, the words "Man," "Duty," and "God" broke their way through his incoherent speech for all to hear. One by one the students moved to the side of the bed. To the first he said, "be as I have known you, faithful to every duty." Another he cautioned against overwork and pleaded with him to care for his health. And to a third whom Mann had loaned money, he said, "Mrs. Mann will return your note. You need never pay it." Each he closed with a cold and unsteady hand clasp, but to the end, his eyes were full of life, still the vital windows for the powerful mind within. Then tiring for a moment, he asked the group to sing a hymn. With words often choking in their throats they sang softly and then Eli Fay prayed, struggling for an expression of gratitude at a time when his heart and soul were torn by a terrible anguish. During the prayer, Mann seemed to gain strength and as he looked toward Fay, now too grief-stricken to hear his words, Mann gasped, "Preach God's laws, Mr. Fay, *preach them* & not doctrine!" Rebecca asked if he did not wish to rest. Slowly he moved his head from side to side and then said, "Mr. Birch—Good old Mr. Birch. You have been faithful to me— Stick by the College." [4]

At about noon another chill wracked his body and for a short time he again was in a delirium fighting for words which would not

---

[4] Several deathbed accounts have survived. I have depended particularly upon W. G. Sherwin, "Death-Bed of Horace Mann," *Christian Inquirer*, October 1, 1859, and the MS notes dated August 2, 1859, in Rebecca Pennell Dean's handwriting, Mann MSS:MHS. Also see the Boston *Daily Transcript* February 15, 1887.

come. Then quite quickly he recovered and said, "Now I feel as though I could sleep if all is quiet," and Mary motioned for all of them to leave. As they filed out, Calvin Pennell entered the house, having just arrived from Saint Louis, but Mary thought it now better for him to wait. And with this, his mind's work completed, Mann remained tranquil, perhaps now once more recalling from his memory those few things to be remembered to the end. He opened his eyes at times as traces of a peaceful serene smile began to form on his lips and an utter peace and simplicity rested upon his pale countenance. By late afternoon, the shadows of the few trees about the manse began to lengthen and fall across the window of his room. As Mary and several others watched for any sign of change, they noticed his lips move and heard him say faintly in a tone of complete reconciliation, "Now I will bid you all goodnight." It was now five o'clock as the last sun was declining in the west and the dark flood moved in. Horace Mann was ready to die. His breath became almost imperceptible and finally his heart stood still.

*　　　*　　　*

On August 4, a student climbed up into the room beneath the bell tower at the college and slowly and rhythmically pulled on the rope. The mourners fell into step as the tolling of the bell set a solemn cadence for the procession of students and friends who accompanied Mann's body from the manse to a temporary burial place on the campus. At the graveside, Reverend Eli Fay struggled again for the words of a brief eulogy and prayer, the students sang a hymn, and the coffin was lowered into the ground. High above, the dark clouds which had formed in the west that morning were now finally bringing relief to the dry earth, the large raindrops all the more noticeable as they fell on top of the coffin resting on the bottom of the pit. Others would carry on at Antioch. It was now time for Horace Mann to storm heaven.[5]

In Boston, Samuel Gridley Howe was too grief-stricken to write to Mary immediately, but he soon called together Josiah Quincy, Ezra Gannett, Gideon Thayer, Samuel Downer, and a few others. Having failed once to make good on his threat to pull down the

---

[5] Eli Fay, "Remarks Made at the Funeral of Honorable Horace Mann," *Christian Palladium*, September 3, 1859.

statue of Daniel Webster in front of the State House, Howe and his friends now vowed that there would be a statue of Mann there of equal prominence. In Europe, Sumner was completing a convalescent tour of the continent in preparation for his return home to join others in a massive effort to destroy the evil of slavery. And the following month, across the country countless numbers of children, more than ever before, would be hurrying on to their classrooms, fulfilling in part Mann's vision of an entire nation going to school.[6]

---

[6] Samuel Gridley Howe to Mary Mann, August 10, 1859, Mann MSS:MHS.

Biographical Sources

A List of Manuscript Collections, Records, and Letterbooks Cited

THE FOLLOWING IS A LIST OF THE MAJOR PRIMARY SOURCES UPON WHICH THIS LIFE OF HORACE MANN HAS BEEN BASED. IT DOES NOT INCLUDE INDIVIDUAL SCATTERED ITEMS WHOSE LOCATIONS ARE IDENTIFIED IN THE FOOTNOTES.

Adams Family MSS., Diaries and papers of John Quincy Adams and of Charles Francis Adams, *Massachusetts Historical Society.*

Allen, Ira, Diary, *Antioch College Library.*

Anti-Slavery MSS., *Boston Public Library.*

Bancroft, George, MSS., *Massachusetts Historical Society.*

Barnard, Henry, MSS., *New York University Library.*

Briggs, George, MSS., *American Antiquarian Society.*

Brown University—President Letterbooks, 1811–1836, *Brown University Archives.*

Brown University, Records of the United Brothers Society, *Brown University Archives.*

Brownson, Orestes, MSS., *Notre Dame University Archives.*

Chase, Salmon P., MSS., *Pennsylvania Historical Society.*

Combe, George, MSS., *National Library of Scotland.*

Cuba Journal, Berg Collection, *New York Public Library.*

Dall, Caroline, MSS., *Massachusetts Historical Society.*

Dix, Dorothea L., MSS., *Houghton Library, Harvard College.*

Emerson, Ralph Waldo, MSS., *Houghton Library, Harvard College.*

Everett, Edward, Letterbook, *Massachusetts Historical Society.*

Everett, Edward, MSS., *Massachusetts Historical Society.*

Fowle, William B., MSS., *Massachusetts Historical Society.*

Franklin, Benjamin, MSS., *Sterling Library, Yale University.*

Gallaudet, Thomas H., MSS., *Library of Congress.*

Garrison, William Lloyd, MSS., Sophia Smith Collection, *Smith College Library.*

Giddings, Joshua, MSS., *Ohio Archaeological and Historical Society.*

Hillard, George, MSS., *Houghton Library, Harvard College.*

Howe, Samuel Gridley, MSS., *Houghton Library, Harvard College.*

Julian, George—Giddings, Joshua, MSS., *Library of Congress*.

Mann, Herman, Journals, *Dedham Historical Society*.

Mann, Horace, Journal of Horace Mann, Jr., *Houghton Library, Harvard College*.

Mann, Horace, MSS., *Brown University Archives*.

Mann, Horace, MSS., *Dedham Historical Society*.

Mann, Horace, MSS., *Massachusetts Historical Society*.

Mann, Horace, MSS., smaller collections are found in the *Case Western Reserve University Library; Chicago Historical Society; Colby College Library; Cornell University Library; Essex Institute; Haverford College Library; Henry E. Huntington Library, Horace Mann Mutual Insurance Company, Springfield, Illinois; Horace Mann School, New York City; Library of Congress; Louisiana State University Archives; Maine Historical Society; Pennsylvania Historical Society*.

Mann, Horace—Messer, Charlotte, MSS: *Brown University Archives*.

Massachusetts, Commonwealth of, General Court, Journals of the House and Senate, *Massachusetts State Archives*.

Massachusetts, Commonwealth of, Records of Courts Martial, etc., *Adjutant General's Office, Military Archives*.

Massachusetts, Commonwealth of, School Returns, 1835–1839, *Massachusetts State Archives*.

Massachusetts State Board of Education, Records of the Board, *Massachusetts State Department of Education*.

May, Samuel J., MSS., *Boston Public Library*.

Messer, Asa, MSS., *Brown University Archives*.

Miscellaneous Bound, *Massachusetts Historical Society*.

Norfolk County, Court Dockets, 1824–1830, *Court of Common Pleas, Dedham, Massachusetts*.

Palfrey, John G., MSS., *Houghton Library, Harvard College*.

Parker, Theodore, Letterbooks, *Massachusetts Historical Society*.

Parker, Theodore, MSS., *Library of Congress*.

Peabody, Elizabeth, Mary, and Sophia, MSS., Berg Collection, *New York Public Library*.

Personal Miscellaneous, *Library of Congress*.

Pforzheimer, Walter, MSS., *Beinecke Library, Yale University*.

Porter, Frederick Bissell, Journal, Michigan Historical Collection, *University of Michigan*.

Quincy, Josiah, MSS., *Boston Public Library*.

Robbins, Thomas, MSS., *Connecticut Historical Society*.

Rockwell, Julius, MSS., *Lenox Library, Lenox, Massachusetts*.

Biographical Sources

Schouler, William, MSS., *Massachusetts Historical Society.*

Seward, William H., MSS., *Rhees Library, University of Rochester.*

Slave Papers, *Library of Congress.*

Smith, Gerrit, MSS., *Syracuse University Library.*

Sparks, Jared, MSS., *Houghton Library, Harvard College.*

Story, Joseph, MSS., *Library of Congress.*

Straker, Robert L., MSS., *Antioch College Library.*

Sumner, Charles, MSS., *Houghton Library, Harvard College.*

Washburn Autograph Collection, *Massachusetts Historical Society.*

Woodard, Samuel B., MSS., *American Antiquarian Society.*

Wrentham, Massachusetts, Town Records, *Second Precinct, Town Hall, Franklin, Massachusetts.*

Permissions and Illustrations Sources

A List of Permissions
and Sources for Illustrations

Rev. Nathanael Emmons, D.D.:
> in Nathanael Emmons, *The Works of Nathanael Emmons, D.D., Late Pastor of the Church in Franklin, Massachusetts*, ed. Jacob Ide (Boston, 1842), I, frontispiece.

Mann homestead:
> in Mortimer Blake, *A History of the Town of Franklin, Massachusetts* . . . (Franklin, 1879), facing p. 258.

Page from Horace Mann's geometry copy book (1816):
> in Antiochiana Collection, Olive Kettering Library, Antioch College.

Early engraving of Brown University:
> Courtesy of Special Collections: The John Hay Library of Brown University.

Sketch of Tapping Reeve's Law School at Litchfield, Connecticut:
> reproduction in possession of author, source unknown.

Silhouette of Charlotte Messer Mann:
> Courtesy of Special Collections: The John Hay Library of Brown University.

Horace Mann's proposal of marriage to Charlotte Messer:
> Mann-Messer MSS: Special Collections, John Hay Library of Brown University.

State Lunatic Hospital at Worcester, Massachusetts (1837):
> in *Massachusetts Insane Hospital, Worcester. Reports and Other Documents Relating to the State Hospital, Worcester* (Boston, 1837), frontispiece. (Courtesy of the Boston Medical Library in the Francis A. Countway Library of Medicine.)

Lexington (Massachusetts) Normal School (ca. 1842):
> in Arthur O. Norton, ed., *The First State Normal School in America: The Journals of Cyrus Peirce and Mary Swift* (Cambridge, Mass., 1926), p. xlix.

Silhouettes of the Peabody sisters, Sophia, Mary, and Elizabeth:
> from a group silhouette of the Nathaniel Peabody family, Courtesy of the Essex Institute, Salem, Massachusetts.

William Ellery Channing:
> in *Memoir of William Ellery Channing* (Boston, 1848), II, frontispiece.

George Combe:
> in *Life of George Combe* (London, 1878), I, frontispiece.

Samuel Gridley Howe:
> in *American Journal of Education* (1862), XI, 320.

Theodore Parker:
> in John Weiss, *Life and Correspondence of Theodore Parker* (New York, 1864), I, frontispiece.

599

Edmund Dwight:
> in *American Journal of Education* (1857), IV, frontispiece.

Nicholas Tillinghast:
> in *American Journal of Education* (1856), II, 369.

George B. Emerson:
> in *American Journal of Education* (1858), V, 418.

Cyrus Peirce:
> in *American Journal of Education* (1857), IV, 273.

Samuel J. May:
> in Samuel J. May, Jr., *Memoir of Samuel Joseph May* (Boston, 1873), frontispiece.

Henry Barnard:
> in *American Journal of Education* (1855–56), I, frontispiece.

Two generations of the New England conscience:

John Quincy Adams:
> United States Signal Corps Photo, Brady Collection (Courtesy of the National Archives).

Charles Sumner (ca. 1850):
> The Metropolitan Museum of Art, Gift of I. N. Phelps Stokes, Edward S. Hawes, Alice Mary Hawes, Marion Augusta Hawes, 1937.

Horace Mann (ca. 1845):
> copy of engraving in possession of the author.

Mann Statue, State House, Boston, by Emma Stebbins:
> Courtesy Richard Hale, Jr., Archivist of the Commonwealth of Massachusetts.

Webster Statue, State House, Boston, by Hiram Powers:
> in Walter Muir Whitehill, *Boston Statues* (Barre, Mass., 1970), p. 26 (Courtesy Barre Publishers and Katharine Knowles, photographer).

Antioch as it was planned *and* as it was when opened:
> both in Antiochiana Collection, Olive Kettering Library, Antioch College.

Horace, Jr., George Combe, and Benjamin Pickman Mann *and* Mary Peabody Mann:
> both in Antiochiana Collection, Olive Kettering Library, Antioch College.

Horace, Mann, 1859:
> The Metropolitan Museum of Art, Gift of I. N. Phelps Stokes, Edward S. Hawes, Alice Mary Hawes, Marion Augusta Hawes, 1937.

Quotations Sources

A List of Sources for
Chapter Opening Quotations

Quotation page   Albert Camus, *The Myth of Sisyphus and Other Essays* (New York, 1955), p. 91.

Chapter I   Horace Bushnell, "The Age of Homespun," *Work and Play* (New York, 1881), pp. 395–396.

II   James Holmes to Horace Mann, April 7, 1821, Mann MSS: MHS.

III   Alexis de Tocqueville, *Democracy in America*, ed. J. P. Mayer and Max Lerner (New York, 1966), p. 247.

IV   "Principal Events of the Year 1828," *Boston Recorder*, January 15, 1829.

V   John Hayward, *The Massachusetts Directory; Being the First Part of the New England Directory* (Boston, 1835), p. 149.

VI   Ralph Waldo Emerson, "Man the Reformer," *The Complete Works of Ralph Waldo Emerson*, with biographical introduction and notes by Edward Waldo Emerson (Boston, 1903), 1, pp. 248–249. (Centenary Edition).

Henry David Thoreau, *Walden, or Life in the Woods* (New York, 1939), p. 81.

VII   Ecclesiastes 3:1–2.

VIII   Job 9:20 and 28.

IX   Thomas Babbington Macauley, "Parliamentary Reform, I," a speech delivered to the House of Commons, March 2, 1831, in Thomas Babbington Macauley, *Prose and Poetry* (Cambridge, Mass., 1967), p. 675.

X   William Ellery Channing to George Combe, March 19, 1840, Combe MSS:NLS.

XI   Nathaniel Hawthorne, *The Blithedale Romance* (Boston, 1871), pp. 15–16.

XII   *Horace Mann, Seventh Annual Report of the Board of Education together with the Seventh Annual Report of the Secretary of the Board* (Boston, 1844), p. 198.

XIII   Henry David Thoreau, "Civil Disobedience," *Miscellanies* (Boston, 1893), p. 132.

Nathaniel Hawthorne, "The Celestial Railroad," *Hawthorne's Short Stories*, edited with an introduction by Newton Arvin (New York, 1946), p. 236.

XIV   Ralph Waldo Emerson, *Journals* (June 1863), (Cambridge, Mass., 1913), IX, p. 519.

XV   (Rudolph E. Raspe *et al.*), *The Adventures of Baron Munchausen* (London, 1948), p. 8.

Quotations Sources

Chapter XVI	Francis Grund, *The Americans in Their Moral, Social, and Political Relations* (Boston, 1837), pp. 133–134.
XVII	Horace Mann to Dr. Edward Jarvis, February 10, 1844, Mann MSS:MHS.
	Finley Peter Dunne, *Mr. Dooley in Peace and in War* (Boston, 1899), p. 99.
XVIII	Charles Dickens, *The Old Curiosity Shop and Pictures from Italy* (Boston, 1907), I, p. 315.
XIX	Joy Elmer Morgan, ed., *Horace Mann at Antioch* (Washington, D.C., 1938), p. 361.
XX	Reinhold Niebuhr, *Leaves from the Notebook of a Tamed Cynic* (Hamden, Conn., 1956), pp. xi–xii.
XXI	Horace Mann to Cyrus Peirce, December 10, 1856, Mann MSS:MHS.
XXII	Horace Mann, "Baccalaureate Address of 1859 (at Antioch College)," *Life* (Boston, 1891), p. 575.
	Mark Twain, *Adventures of Huckleberry Finn* (New York, 1917), p. 128.

Index

Emmons, Nathanael (*continued*)
indoctrinates Franklin youth,
13; influence of his preaching, 9–11; model for Harriet
Beecher Stowe character, 68;
refuses to forgive Stephen
Mann, 22–3; retires, 91;
teachings rejected by Mann,
20

Erie Canal, 102, 108

Everett, Edward, 241, 246–7, 257,
317, 327, 371, 374, 514; appeals to Newton, 313; ap-
points Mann, 242; approves
Mann's first *Annual Report*,
289–90; approves Mann's
school plans, 298; attends
education convention, 318;
as a popular lecturer,
294; speaks at dedication,
325; supports common school
fund, 223; supports normal
schools, 301; taunted by
Harvard students, 529; urges
State Board of Education, 239

Faneuil Hall, 92, 197, 282–4, 450,
460, 527

Fay, Eli: attends first Antioch
faculty meeting, 539; author
of *Rejoinder to Ira Allen*,
571; eulogizes Mann, 588; at
Mann's death bed, 586–7;
proposes Antioch College to
Mann, 534; replies to Mann,
536–7; supports nonsectarian
higher education, 534, 536

Federalist, The, quoted by Mann,
155

Fellenberg, Emanuel von, 392

Fessenden, William, 465

"Fifteen Gallon Law," 327, 535

Fillmore, Millard, 518, 544

Fisher, Alexander Metcalf, 27, 60,
65, 68

Fisher, George, 38, 51

Fiske, Josiah J., 55, 57, 76; ac-
cepts Mann as law appren-
tice, 50; holds Stanley Mann's
assets, 175; law office a disappointment to Mann, 61; offers academy at Wrentham,
321

Folsom, Abby, 477; gadfly of conventions, 527

Foote, Henry, 505; quoted by
Mann, 483; speaks at Washington Monument, 518;
speaks at White House, 462–
3; threatens to hang D. A.
Hall, 464

Fowle, William B., 439

Frankfort (Ky.), 359–60, 396

Free Soil Party (Mass.): attacked
by Lincoln, 490; compromises
with Democrats, 523–5;
Mann bids members fare-
well, 544; Mann's sole party
allegiance, 520; nominates
Mann for Congress, 488–9,
519; nominates Mann for
governor, 538; power wan-
ing, 563; questions Mann's
courage, 504; urges Mann to
seek governorship, 533; wel-
comes Mann's membership,
532

Free Soil Party (national), 511,
518; becomes a political
spoiler, 506; as a reaction to
the extension of slavery, 478–
80; supports Thaddeus Stevens for Speaker, 505

Frémont, John C., 505

Friedrich Wilhelm IV (King of
Prussia), 392, 393

"Friends of Education," 342

Fruitlands, 357

Fugitive Slave Law, 326, 519,
525–9, 527 *n.*, 535, 544, 547,
562

Fuller, Margaret, 504

Index

Index

Index

MANN, HORACE (*continued*)
Charlotte's grave, 218–19;
sense of loss, 163–4;
struggle to understand
the will of God, 171–4,
176–9, 181
RETURN TO POLITICS—burn-
ing of the Charlestown
convent, 191–2; elec-
tion of 1834, 194–9;
Elizabeth Peabody's efforts
to bring Mann back
into politics, 188–99
passim; Mann heads Ur-
suline investigation, 192–
3; Mann's disillusionment
with political celebra-
tions, 189–90; political
attacks on Mann, 196–
7; reform of debtor laws,
200–2; revision of
Mass. laws, 203–6;
Whig support, 195–8
AS SENATE PRESIDENT—be-
lief in the need for strong
state action, 215–16;
comparison of cynical
politicians with Taylor
and Howe, 232–6; defini-
tion of private and public
interest, 208–9; first
election to Senate
presidency, 206–7; obe-
dience to "stern mandate
of duty," 237–9; reaction
to the Broad Street
riot, 237; re-election as
President of the Senate,
221; support of railroad
legislation, 207; as a Whig
partisan, 207
MANN, HORACE, (8) *early humanitarian reforms:*
ADVOCACY OF PUBLIC ROLE
IN HUMANITARIANISM—
110, 122, 134, 137
ANTI-SLAVERY ATTITUDES—
advocates course of mod-

MANN, HORACE (*continued*)
eration, 211; blames Pru-
dence Crandall's persecu-
tion of abolitionists, 210–
11; criticizes abolitionists,
214; early racism, 150;
supports American
Colonization Society, 183–
4, 210; urges Howe to
accept black pupil, 184;
willing to hire "black
lady" housekeeper, 150
TEMPERANCE—attacks
petition of American
Society for the Promotion
of Temperance, 118–19;
belief in moral suasion,
185; belief that in-
temperance is the unitary
cause of crime and
poverty, 122; elected
vice-president of Mass.
Temperance Society,
230; embraces total
abstinence, 212–13;
eschews legal prohibition,
185–8 *passim;* first
legislative efforts for
temperance reform, 117,
119–22, 148, 155; lauded
as a "friend of temper-
ance," 197; lauds a
temperate Independence
Day celebration, 230;
"Mann's License Bill,"
120–1; organizes Boston
temperance rally, 227–9;
President of Dedham
Temperance Society, 118;
publishes *Comparative
Profits,* 186–7, 197;
resigns presidency of
Suffolk Temperance
Society, 258; ridiculed for
views on temperance, 196;
speaks at temperance
convention, 185–6; works
on liquor legislation,

xix

Index

INDEX

Index

Index

Index

A NOTE ABOUT THE AUTHOR

JONATHAN MESSERLI was born in Albany, Oregon, in 1926. He was graduated from Concordia Teachers College, River Forest, Illinois, in 1947, and received his M.A. (1952) from Washington University and Ph.D. (1963) from Harvard University. From 1947 to 1957 he taught, first, at the Lutheran High School in St. Louis; later, at the St. Louis Country Day School. In 1960–1, he was Coordinator of the International Teacher Development Program at Harvard; 1963–4, Assistant Professor of History and Education at the University of Washington; 1964–8, Assistant Professor and then Associate Professor of History and Education at Teachers College, Columbia University. Since 1968 he has been Dean of the School of Education at Hofstra University.

A NOTE ON THE TYPE

This book was set on the Linotype in a face called Primer, designed by Rudolph Ruzicka, who was earlier responsible for the design of Fairfield and Fairfield Medium, Linotype faces whose virtues have for some time been accorded wide recognition.

The complete range of sizes of Primer was first made available in 1954, although the pilot size of 12-point was ready as early as 1951. The design of the face makes general reference to Linotype Century—long a serviceable type, totally lacking in manner or frills of any kind—but brilliantly corrects the characterless quality.

In the designs for Primer, Mr. Ruzicka has once again brilliantly exemplified the truth of a statement made about him by the late W. A. Dwiggins: "His outstanding quality, as artist and person, is *sanity*. Complete esthetic equipment, all managed by good, sound judgment about ways and means, aims and purposes, utilities and 'functions'—and all this level-headed balance-mechanism added to the lively mental state that makes an artist an artist. Fortunate equipment in a disordered world . . ."

Composed, printed, and bound by
Kingsport Press, Kingsport, Tennessee.
Typography and binding design by

WARREN 🔶 CHAPPELL